computer science
illuminated

NELL DALE | JOHN LEWIS

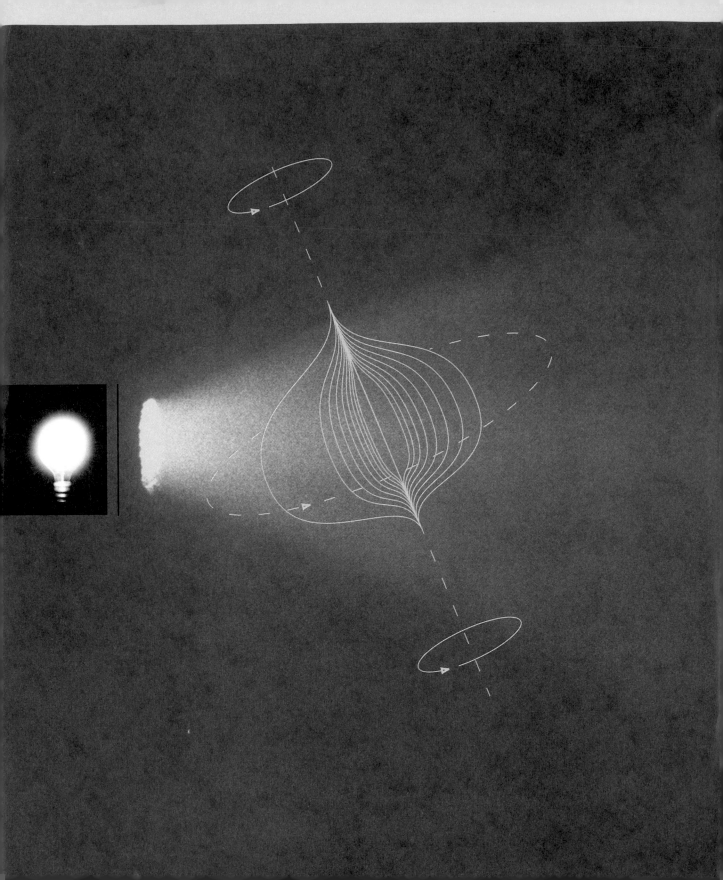

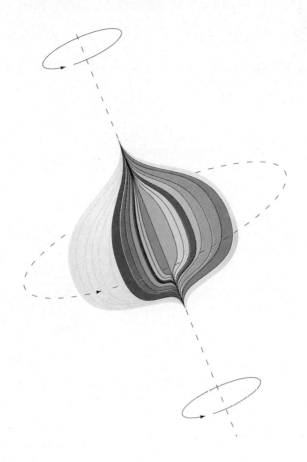

computer science
illuminated

NELL DALE | JOHN LEWIS
University of Texas, Austin **Villanova University**

JONES AND BARTLETT PUBLISHERS
Sudbury, Massachusetts
BOSTON   TORONTO   LONDON   SINGAPORE

Jones and Bartlett Publishers is pleased to provide **Computer Science Illuminated's** book-specific website. This site offers a variety of resources designed to address multiple learning styles and enhance the learning experience.

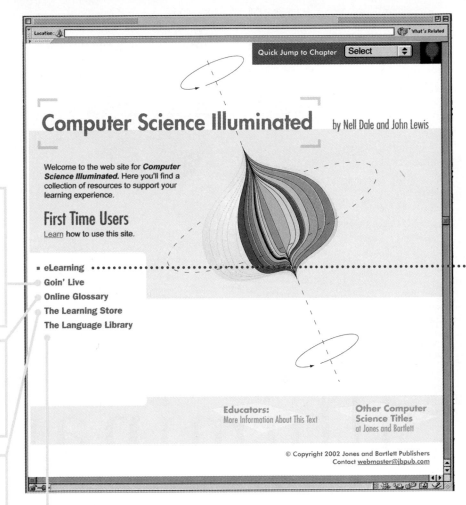

Goin' Live
This step-by-step HTML Tutorial will guide you from start to finish as you create your own website. With each lesson, you'll gain experience and confidence working in the HTML language.

Online Glossary
We've made all the key terms used in the text easily accessible to you in this searchable online glossary.

The Learning Store
Jones and Bartlett Publishers has a wealth of material available to supplement the learning and teaching experience. Students and instructors will find additional resources here or at http://computerscience.jbpub.com

The Language Library
Here you will find two complete chapters that supplement the book's language-neutral approach to programming concepts. A JAVA language chapter and C++ language chapter are included and follow the same pedagogical approach as the textbook.

http://csilluminated.jbpub.com

eLearning

Our eLearning center provides chapter-specific activities that will actively engage you in the learning process. Each activity directly correlates to material presented in the text to help you gain command over chapter content.

Interactive Review
You can check your general understanding of key concepts with this dynamic chapter review.

Animated Flashcards
Computer science is rich with vocabulary, and these virtual flashcards will help you quickly master new terms and definitions.

Live Wire
Explore the Web through these links that will send you to a plethora of relevant sites that expand upon the concepts you've discovered in the text.

Cryptic Crossword Puzzles
For a fun review of chapter material, challenge yourself with these interactive crossword puzzles.

Ethical Issues
Learn more about the new social challenges that come with the development of computer and Internet technology through these discussions and links.

Did You Know?
Find out more about the fun facts and stories included as callouts in the text. Here you'll find an extensive collection of material ranging from historical information to the latest technological developments.

Biographical Sketches
Be introduced to some of the many people who have made substantial contributions to the computer science field.

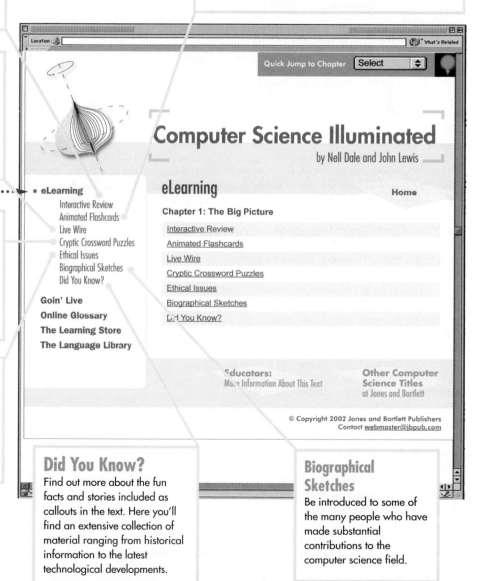

Computer Science Illuminated
by Nell Dale and John Lewis

eLearning

Quick Jump to Chapter Select

- eLearning
  Interactive Review
  Animated Flashcards
  Live Wire
  Cryptic Crossword Puzzles
  Ethical Issues
  Biographical Sketches
  Did You Know?

Goin' Live
Online Glossary
The Learning Store
The Language Library

eLearning   Home

Chapter 1: The Big Picture

Interactive Review

Animated Flashcards

Live Wire

Cryptic Crossword Puzzles

Ethical Issues

Biographical Sketches

Did You Know?

Educators: Other Computer
More Information About This Text   Science Titles
                              at Jones and Bartlett

© Copyright 2002 Jones and Bartlett Publishers
Contact webmaster@jbpub.com

World Headquarters

Jones and Bartlett Publishers
40 Tall Pine Drive
Sudbury, MA 01776
978-443-5000
info@jbpub.com
www.jbpub.com

Jones and Bartlett Publishers Canada
2406 Nikanna Road
Mississauga, ON L5C 2W6
CANADA

Jones and Bartlett Publishers
International
Barb House, Barb Mews
London W6 7PA
UK

Library of Congress Cataloging-in-Publication Data
Dale, Nell B.
    Computer science illuminated / Nell Dale, John Lewis.
       p. cm.
    ISBN 0-7637-1760-6
    1. Computer science. I. Lewis, John (John Allan), 1963- II. Title.

QA76 . D285 2002
004—dc21   2001050774

Chief Executive Officer: Clayton Jones
Chief Operating Officer: Don W. Jones, Jr.
Executive V.P. and Publisher: Robert W. Holland, Jr.
V.P., Design and Production: Anne Spencer
V.P., Manufacturing and Inventory Control: Therese Bräuer
Editor-in-Chief: J. Michael Stranz
Production Manager: Amy Rose
Senior Marketing Manager: Nathan Schultz
Web Product Manager: Adam Alboyadjian
Senior Development Editor: Dean DeChambeau
Associate Production Editor: Tara McCormick
Editorial Assistant: Theresa DiDonato
Production Assistant: Karen Ferreira
Cover Design: Night & Day Design
Composition: Northeast Compositors
Copyediting: Roberta Lewis
Proofreading: Diane Freed Publishing Services
Illustrations and Technical Art: Smolinski Studios
Printing and Binding: Quebecor World Taunton
Cover Printing: John Pow Company, Inc.

This book was typeset in Quark 4.1 on a Macintosh G4. The font families used were Sabon, Franklin Gothic, Futura, and Prestige Elite. The first printing was printed on 45# New Era Matte.

Printed in the United States of America
06 05 04 03 02   10 9 8 7 6 5 4 3 2 1

To my wife Sharon and my son Justin—why I do what I do.
John Lewis

To Al, my husband and best friend, and to Bamsi Bear, one of man's best friends, who took care of us faithfully for 12 years.
Nell Dale

John Lewis, Villanova University

John Lewis is a leading educator and author in the field of computer science. He has written a market-leading textbook on Java software and program design. After earning his undergraduate degree, M.S., and Ph.D. in computer science at Virginia Tech, John joined the faculty of the Department of Computing Sciences at Villanova University. He has received numerous teaching awards, including the University Award for Teaching Excellence and the Goff Award for Outstanding Teaching. His professional interests include object-oriented technologies, multimedia, and software engineering. In addition to his teaching and writing, John actively participates in the Special Interest Group on Computer Science Education (SIGCSE), and finds time to spend with his family or in his workshop.

Nell Dale, University of Texas, Austin

Well respected in the field of Computer Science Education, Nell Dale has served on the faculty of the University of Texas at Austin for more than 25 years and has authored over 20 undergraduate Computer Science textbooks. After receiving her B.S. in Mathematics and Psychology from the University of Houston, Nell entered the University of Texas at Austin where she earned her M.A. in Mathematics and her Ph.D. in Computer Science. Nell has made significant contributions to her discipline through her writing, research, and service. Nell's contributions were recognized in 1996 with the ACM SIGCSE Award for Outstanding Contributions in Computer Science Education. In the summer of 1994, Nell retired from full-time teaching, giving her more time to write, travel, and play tennis. She currently resides in Austin, Texas with her husband Al and their dog Maggie.

brief contents

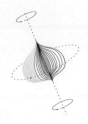

Laying the Groundwork

The Information Layer

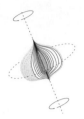

The Hardware Layer

The Programming Layer

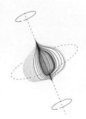

The Operating Systems Layer

The Applications Layer

The Communications Layer

In Conclusion

Preface

Welcome to **Computer Science Illuminated!** This book provides a broad and thorough exploration of computer systems within a computer science context. Although this is classified as a CS-0 book, we realize that the term CS-0 means different things to different people.

Independently, both of us have written successful textbooks on various topics, but this book represents our first opportunity for such a comprehensive exploration of computing. We're thrilled to join forces to offer this book.

We take pedagogy seriously—and we know you do, too.

This book is designed as a breadth-first introduction to the field of computer science, providing a comprehensive and rigorous exploration of a variety of topics. It provides a general understanding of computers in all their aspects, and it lays a solid foundation to support further study. Therefore, this book is appropriate both for computer science majors beginning their studies and for non-majors seeking a broad but complete overview.

Choice of Topics

We used many sources in putting together the outline of topics for this text. We looked at course catalogue descriptions and book outlines, and administered a questionnaire designed to find out what you, our colleagues, thought should be included in such a course. We answered the following three questions and asked you to do the same.

- What topics should students master in a CS-0 course if it is the only computer science course they will take during their college experience?
- What topics should students have mastered before entering your CS-1 course?

- What additional topics should your CS-1 students be familiar with?

The strong consensus that emerged from the intersections of these sources formed the working outline for this book. Students who master this material before taking CS-1 have a strong foundation upon which to continue in computer science. Although our intention was to write a CS-0 text, our reviewers have pointed out that the material also forms a strong breadth-first background that can serve as a companion to a programming-language introduction to computer science.

Organization

In Chapter 1, we set the stage with the analogy that a computing system is like an onion that has evolved layer by layer over time. The history of hardware and software is presented beginning with the computer and machine language, the heart of the onion. Higher level languages such as FORTRAN, Lisp, Pascal, C, C++, and Java followed, along with the ever-increasing understanding of the programming process using such tools as top-down design and object-oriented design. The operating system with its resource-management techniques developed to surround and manage these languages and the programs written in them.

Sophisticated general-purpose and special-purpose software systems that allowed non-computer people to solve problems were developed to form another layer. These powerful programs were stimulated by parallel theoretical work in computer science, which made such programs possible. The final layer is made up of networks and software—all the tools needed for computers to communicate with one another. The Internet and the World Wide Web put the finishing touches on this layer.

Through our teaching experience we have discovered that complex concepts are easier to understand if handled one layer at a time rather than in one big bite. Thus, the book is organized into the following sections:

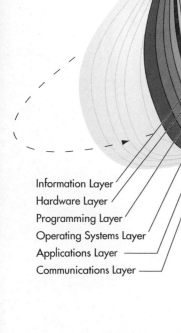

- Information Layer
- Hardware Layer
- Programming Layer
- Operating Systems Layer
- Applications Layer
- Communications Layer

- Information Layer
- Hardware Layer
- **Programming Layer**
- Operating Systems Layer
- Applications Layer
- Communications Layer

These layers, taken in this order, examine a computer system from the inside out. Research has shown that students understand concrete examples more easily than abstract ones even when the students themselves are abstract thinkers. Thus, we begin with the concrete machine, and add one layer at a time, each abstracting the details of the previous level, so that other aspects of computing can be explored. We believe that a thorough understanding of one layer makes the transition to the next abstraction easier for students.

Individual chapters within each layer focus on particular aspects of that layer. The next section provides a synopsis of each chapter.

The design of this book is extremely modular. The layered view of a computing system provides flexibility to instructors who may choose to emphasize topics differently or place them in a different order. We revisit the onion analogy at the opening of each chapter, showing how the current discussion fits into the big picture.

Synopsis

The first and last chapters of the book form bookends: Chapter 1 describes what a computing system is and Chapter 17 explores what computing systems cannot do. The chapters in between look in depth at the layers that make up a computing system and explain, one step at a time, how a computer does what it does.

Chapter 1 lays the groundwork for the rest of the book, establishing terminology and explaining the history of computing. The evolution of the hardware and software levels that make up the history of computing systems form much of the underlying structure of the layers explored throughout the book.

Chapters 2 and 3 examine a layer that is largely conceptual, yet permeates all other aspects of computer processing. We call this layer the information layer, and it reflects how information is represented in the computer. Chapter 2 covers the binary number system and its relationship to other number systems (such as decimal, the one we humans use on a daily basis). Chapter 3 investigates how we take the myriad types of information we manage—numbers, text, images, audio, and video—and represent them in a binary format.

Chapters 4 and 5 explore the hardware layer. Chapter 4 describes gates and circuits, which control the flow of electricity in fundamental ways. This core electronic circuitry gives rise to the discussion in Chapter 5 of specialized hardware components such as the Central Processing Unit (CPU) and memory, including how they interact within a von Neumann architecture.

Chapters 6 through 9 cover aspects of the **programming layer**. Chapter 6 examines the problem-solving process, both human and computer related. George Polya's human problem-solving strategies guide the discussion.

Examples of both top-down design and object-oriented design are presented. Chapter 7 covers the concepts of both machine language and assembly language using Pep/7, a simulated computer. Chapter 8 covers the concepts of high-level programming languages. The concepts are illustrated in brief examples from four programming languages: Ada, Visual Basic .NET, C++, and Java. Chapter 9 emphasizes the role of abstract data types and data structures in the programming process.

Chapters 10 and 11 cover the operating systems layer. Chapter 10 discusses the resource-management responsibilities of the operating system and presents some of the basic algorithms used to implement those tasks. Chapter 11 deals with file systems, including what they are and how they are managed by the operating system.

Chapters 12 through 14 cover the applications layer. This layer is made up of the general-purpose and specialized application programs that are available for public use to solve problems. We divide this layer into the sub-disciplines of computer science upon which these programs are based. Chapter 12 examines information systems, Chapter 13 examines artificial intelligence, and Chapter 14 examines simulation, computer-aided design, and embedded systems.

Chapters 15 and 16 cover the communications layer. Chapter 15 discusses various aspects of computer networks, including how they evolved and how they manage the transmission of data. Chapter 16 explores the World Wide Web and some of the technologies that give it the impact it has today.

Chapter 17 concludes with a discussion of the inherent limitations of computer hardware, software, and the problems that can and cannot be solved using a computer. Big-O notation is presented as a way to talk about the efficiency of algorithms so that the categories of algorithms can be discussed. The Halting problem is presented to show that some problems are unsolvable.

Language Issues

Note that the programming layer of this book deals with various aspects of programming without going into detail on any one language. In fact, we deliberately present high-level programming constructs in several languages for students to see a variety of syntax, and to reinforce that the underlying conceptual ideas are far more important than the particular language used to implement them.

A more detailed introduction to two high-level programming languages, Java and C++, are provided on this book's web site. Any instructor wanting to expose their students to the details of a language may use these chapters to supplement the book.

Special Features

We have included three special features in this text in order to emphasize the history and breadth of computing as well as the moral obligations that come with new technology. Each chapter includes a *Short Biography* of someone who has made a significant contribution to computing. The people honored in these sections range from those who have contributed to the information layer, such as George Boole and Ada Lovelace, to those who have contributed to the communications layer, such as Doug Engelbart and Tim Berners-Lee. These biographies are designed to give the reader some historical perspective and awareness of the men and women who contributed and are contributing today to the world of computing.

Our second feature, *Callouts*, are sidebar sections that include interesting tidbits of information about the past, present, and future. They are garnered from history, from today's newspapers, and from the authors' experiences. These little vignettes are designed to amuse, to inspire, and to intrigue.

Our third feature is the *Ethical Issues* section included in each chapter. These sections are designed to illustrate that along with the advantages of computing comes responsibility. Privacy, hacking, viruses, and free speech are among the topics discussed. At the end of each chapter's exercises we include a selection of Thought Questions. Among the questions presented here are questions relating to the ethical issue presented in the chapter.

Grace Murray Hopper

From 1943 until her death on New Year's Day in 1992, Admiral Grace Murray Hopper was intimately involved with computing. In 1991, she was awarded the National Medal of Technology "for her pioneering accomplishments in the development of computer programming languages that simplified computer technology and opened the door to a significantly larger universe of users."

Admiral Hopper was born Grace Brewster Murray in New York City on December 9, 1906. She attended Vassar and received a Ph.D. in mathematics from Yale. For the next 10 years, she taught mathematics at Vassar.

In 1943, Admiral Hopper joined the U.S. Navy and was assigned to the Bureau of Ordnance Computation Project at Harvard University as a programmer on the Mark I. After the war, she remained at Harvard as a faculty member and continued work on the Navy's Mark II and Mark III computers. In 1949, she joined Eckert-Mauchly Computer Corporation and worked on the UNIVAC I. It was there that she made a legendary contribution to computing: She discovered the first

only to be recalled within a year to full-time active duty. Her mission was to oversee the Navy's efforts to maintain uniformity in programming languages. It has been said that just as Admiral Hyman Rickover was the father of the nuclear navy, Rear Admiral Hopper was the mother of computerized data automation in the Navy. She served with the Naval Data Automation Command until she retired again in 1986 with the rank of Rear Admiral. At the time of her death, she was a senior consultant at Digital Equipment Corporation.

During her lifetime, Admiral Hopper received honorary degrees from more than 40 colleges and universities. She was honored by her peers on several occasions, including the first Computer Sciences Man of the Year award given by the Data Processing Management Association, and the Contributors to Computer Science Education Award given by the Special Interest Group for Computer Science Education, which is part of the ACM (Association for Computing Machinery).

Admiral Hopper loved young people and talks on colle...

From a garage to the Fortune 500

Boyhood friends Steve Jobs and Steve Wozniak sold their respective Volkswagen van and programmable calculator to raise the money to finance their new computer company. Their first sale was 50 Apple Is, the computer that they had designed and built in a garage. In six short years Apple was listed in the Fortune 500, the youngest firm on this prestigious list.

ETHICAL ISSUES

Napster

In 1999, Shawn Fanning launched a file-sharing program that took the music industry by storm, rapidly gaining the praise of millions and the criticism of many. Nineteen-year-old Shawn had only recently dropped out of his first year at Northeastern University to pursue a solution to the difficulty of downloading and exchanging music over the Net. With the support of his uncle, Shawn tackled this problem with dedication and ingenuity and, in a few months, developed an answer. Shawn wrote source code that wove together a search engine, file sharing, and Internet Relay Chat, making it possible for anyone to easily access and trade music files. Napster was born, and with it a fresh controversy over intellectual property rights and privileges.

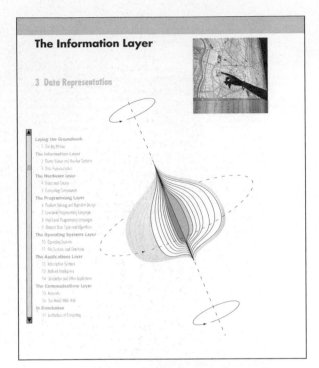

Color and Typography are Signposts

The layers into which the book is divided are color coded within the text. The color of the outside layer of the onion pictured on each chapter opener corresponds to the layer of that chapter. The same color is repeated in bars across the top of the pages of the layer. For each chapter, the slide on the side of the chapter opener shows where the chapter is within the layer. We have said that the first and last chapters form bookends. Although they are not part of the layers of the computing onion, we have given each a color that shows up in the onion, the slide, and the color bar. Open the book anywhere and you can immediately tell where you are within the layers of computing.

We use different fonts for algorithms, including identifiers in running text, and program code, to visually separate the abstract from the concrete in the programming layer. You know at a glance whether the discussion is at the logical (algorithmic) level or at the programming language level. We color addresses in red in order to clarify visually the distinction between an address and the contents of an address.

Color is especially useful in Chapter 7, Low-Level Programming Languages. Instructions are color coded to differentiate the parts of an instruction. The operation code is green, the register designation is clear, and the addressing mode specifier is blue. Operands are shaded gray. As in other chapters, addresses are in red.

Web site

A web site, **http://csilluminated.jbpub.com**, includes a wealth of additional information. Additional biographies, more information about some of the callouts, and updates that relate to ethical issues are all available on the text's web site.

Available for download are introductory chapters on Java and C++ and the Pep/7 virtual machine.

A number of interactive exercises have been developed to enhance the reader's learning experience. Please refer to the two-page web site walk through for a complete description of these activities.

Acknowledgments

We would like to acknowledge the hard work of our colleagues who reviewed the manuscript and helped shape the development of this book:

C. Michael Allen, University of North Carolina, Charlotte

Lofton Bullard, Florida Atlantic University

Cerian Jones, University of Alberta

Calvin Ribbens, Virginia Tech

Susan Sells, Wichita State University

Tom Wiggen, University of North Dakota

In addition, several individuals reviewed special sections of the manuscript for us: Mary Dee Harris, Chris Edmondson-Yurkanan, and Ben Kuipers of the University of Texas, Austin Department of Computer Science; Dave Stauffer at Penn State; John McCormick at the University of Northern Iowa; Mike McMillan at Pulaski Technical College; Steve Maleno at Reuters, Inc., and Dan Joyce of Villanova University. Thanks, friends and colleagues. Your comments and suggestions were invaluable. Thanks also to Sandy Bauman who took an old snapshot and turned it into a portrait.

Mere words can't possibly express what we owe to all the publishing professionals who worked so hard to make this book a reality. To Michael Stranz, Amy Rose, Anne Spencer, Dean DeChambeau, Theresa DiDonato, Tara McCormick, Adam Alboyadjian, Karen Ferreira, and Nathan Schultz at Jones and Bartlett and Mike and Sigrid Wile at Northeast Compositors— we thank you.

I must also thank my tennis buddies for keeping me fit, my bridge buddies for keeping my mind alert, and my family for keeping me grounded. ND

I thank my family for understanding the long hours it takes to put together a project like this, and I thank my friends and colleagues in the Department of Computing Sciences at Villanova University for their support. JL

Laying the Groundwork

1 The Big Picture

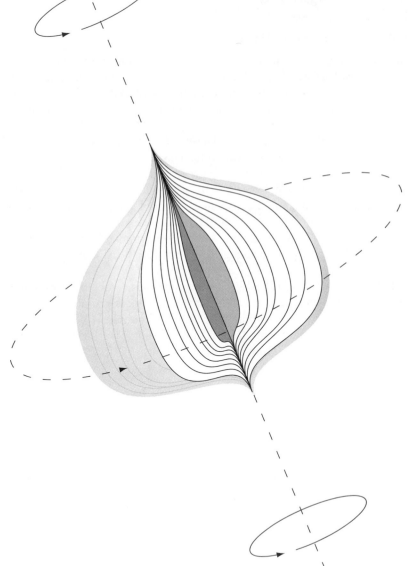

Chapter 1

The Big Picture

This book is a tour through the world of computing. We explore how computers work—what they do and how they do it, from bottom to top, inside and out. Like an orchestra, a computer system is a collection of many different elements, combined to form a whole that is far more than the sum of its parts. This chapter provides the big picture, giving an overview of the pieces that we slowly dissect throughout the book and putting those pieces into historical perspective.

Most of you have grown up during the age of the personal computer. *Hardware*, *software*, *programming*, *web surfing*, and *e-mail* are probably familiar terms to you. Some of you can define these and many more computer-related terms explicitly, whereas others may have only a vague, intuitive understanding of them. This chapter gets everyone on relatively equal footing by establishing common terminology and forming the platform from which we will dive into our exploration of computing.

Goals

After studying this chapter, you should be able to:

- describe the layers of a computer system.
- describe the concept of abstraction and its relationship to computing.
- describe the history of computer hardware and software.
- describe the changing role of the computer user.
- distinguish between systems programmers and applications programmers.
- distinguish between computing as a tool and computing as a discipline.

1.1   Computing Systems

Computing system
Computer hardware, software, and data, which interact to solve problems

Computer hardware
The physical elements of a computing system

Computer software
The programs that provide the instructions that a computer executes

In this book we explore various aspects of computing systems. Note that we use the term computing system, not just computer. A computer is a device. A **computing system**, on the other hand, is a dynamic entity, used to solve problems and interact with its environment. A computing system is composed of hardware, software, and the data that they manage. **Computer hardware** is the collection of physical elements that make up the machine and its related pieces: boxes, circuit boards, chips, wires, disk drives, keyboards, monitors, printers, and so on. **Computer software** is the collection of programs that provide the instructions that a computer carries out. And at the very heart of a computer system is the information that it manages. Without data, the hardware and software are essentially useless.

The general goals of this book are threefold:

- To give you a solid, broad understanding of how a computing system works
- To develop an appreciation for and understanding of the evolution of modern computing systems
- To give you enough information about computing for you to decide whether you wish to pursue the subject further

The rest of this section explains how computer systems can be divided into abstract layers and how each layer plays a role. The next section puts the development of computing hardware and software into historical context. This chapter concludes with a discussion about computing as both a tool and as a discipline of study.

Layers of a Computing System

A computing system is like an onion, made up of many layers. Each layer plays a specific role in the overall design of the system. These layers are

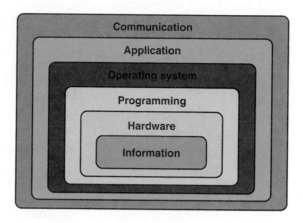

Figure 1.1 The layers of a computing system

pictured in Figure 1.1 and form the general organization of this book. This is the "big picture" that we continually come back to as we explore different aspects of computing systems.

You rarely, if ever, take a bite out of an onion as you would an apple. Rather, you separate the onion into concentric rings. Likewise, in this book we explore aspects of computing one layer at a time. We peel each layer separately and explore it by itself. Each layer, in itself, is not that complicated. In fact, we point out that a computer actually only does very simple tasks. It just does them so blindingly fast that many simple tasks can be combined to do larger, more complicated tasks. When the various computer layers are all brought together, each playing its own role, amazing things result from the combination of these basic ideas.

Let's discuss each of these layers briefly, and identify where in this book these ideas are explored in more detail. We essentially work our way from the inside out, which is sometimes referred to as a bottom-up approach.

The innermost layer, information, reflects the way we represent information on a computer. In many ways this is a purely conceptual level. Information on a computer is managed using binary digits, 1 and 0. So to understand computer processing we must first understand the binary number system and its relationship to other number systems (such as decimal, the one we humans use on a daily basis). Then we can turn our attention to how we take the myriad types of information we manage—numbers, text, images, audio, and video—and represent them in a binary format. Chapters 2 and 3 explore these issues.

The next layer, hardware, consists of the physical hardware of a computer system. Computer hardware includes devices such as gates and circuits, which control the flow of electricity in fundamental ways. This core electronic circuitry gives rise to specialized hardware components such as the computer's Central Processing Unit (CPU) and memory. Chapters 4 and 5 of the book discuss these topics in detail.

The programming layer deals with software, the instructions used to accomplish computations and manage data. Programs can take many forms, be performed at many levels, and be implemented in many languages. Yet despite the variety of programming issues, the goal remains the same: to solve problems. Chapters 6 through 9 explore many issues related to programming and the management of data.

Every computer has an Operating System (OS) to help manage the computer's resources. Operating systems, such as Windows 2000, Linux, or the Mac OS, help us interact with the computer system and manage the way hardware devices, programs, and data interact. Knowing what an operating system does for us is key to understanding the computer in general. These issues are discussed in Chapters 10 and 11.

These previous (inner) layers focus on making a computer system work. The application layer, on the other hand, focuses on using the computer to solve specific real-world problems. We run application programs to make use of the computer's abilities in other domains, such as helping us design a building or play a game. The spectrum of domain-specific computer software tools is far-reaching, and involves specific subdisciplines of computing such as information systems, artificial intelligence, and simulation. Application systems are discussed in Chapters 12, 13, and 14.

Computers no longer exist in isolation on someone's desktop. We use computer technology to communicate, and that communication is a fundamental layer at which computing systems operate. Computers are connected into networks to share information and resources. The Internet evolved into a global network so that there is almost no place on Earth that you cannot communicate with via computing technology. The World Wide Web makes that communication relatively easy. It has revolutionized computer use and made it accessible to the general public. Chapters 15 and 16 discuss these important issues of computing communication.

Most of this book is about what a computer can do, and how it does it. We conclude with a discussion of what a computer cannot do, or at least cannot do well. Computers have inherent limitations on their ability to represent information, and they are only as good as their programming makes them. Furthermore, it turns out that some problems cannot be solved at all. Chapter 17 examines these limitations of computers.

Sometimes it is easy to get so caught up in the details that we lose perspective on the big picture. Try to keep that in mind as you progress through the information in this book. Each chapter's opening page reminds you of where we are in the various layers of a computing system. The details all contribute a specific part to a larger whole. Take each step in turn and you will be amazed at how well it all falls into place.

Abstraction

The levels of a computing system that we just examined are examples of abstraction. An **abstraction** is a mental model, a way to think about something, which removes or hides complex details. An abstraction leaves only the information necessary to accomplish our goal. When we are dealing with a computer on one layer, we don't need to be thinking about the details of the other layers. For example, when we are writing a program, we don't have to concern ourselves with how the hardware carries out the instructions. Likewise, when we are running an application program, we don't have to be concerned with how that program was written.

Numerous experiments have shown that a human being can actively manage about seven (plus or minus two, depending on the person) pieces of information in short-term memory at one time. This is called Miller's law, based on the psychologist who first investigated it.[1] Other pieces of information are available to us when we need it, but when we focus on a new piece, something else falls back into secondary status.

This concept is similar to the number of balls a juggler can keep in the air at one time. Human beings can mentally juggle about seven balls at once, and when we pick up a new one, we have to drop another. Seven may seem like a small number, but the key is that each ball can represent an abstraction, or a chunk of information. That is, each ball we are juggling can represent a complex topic as long as we can think about it as one idea.

We rely on abstractions every day of our lives. For example, we don't need to know how a car works in order to drive to the store. That is, we don't really need to know how the engine works in detail. You need to know only some basics about how to interact with the car: how the pedals and knobs and steering wheel work. And we don't even have to be thinking about all of those at the same time. See Figure 1.2.

Even if we do know how an engine works, we don't have to think about it while driving. Imagine if, while driving, we had to constantly think about how the spark plugs ignite the fuel that drives the pistons that turn the crankshaft. We'd never get anywhere! A car is much too complicated for us to deal with all at once. All the technical details would be too many balls to juggle at the same time. But once we've abstracted the car down to the way we interact with it, we can deal with it as one entity. The irrelevant details are ignored, at least for the moment.

Abstract art, as the name implies, is another example of abstraction. An abstract painting represents something, but doesn't get bogged down in the details of reality. Consider the painting shown in Figure 1.3, entitled *Nude Descending a Staircase*. You can see only the basic hint of the woman or

Abstraction A mental model that removes complex details

Air cleaner

Oil dip stick

Alternator

Power steering reservoir

Radiator

Brake fluid reservoir

Windshield washer tank

Fuse box

Battery

Oil filler cap

Figure 1.2   A car engine and the abstraction that allows us to use it

Figure 1.3   The abstract painting *Nude Descending a Staircase, No. 2, Copyright © 2002 Artists Rights Society (ARS), New York/ADAGP, Paris/Estate of Marcel Duchamp*

the staircase, because the artist is not interested in the details of exactly how the woman or the staircase look. Those details are irrelevant to the impact the artist is trying to create. In fact, the realistic details would get in the way of the issues that the artist thinks are important.

Abstraction is the key to computing. The layers of a computing system embody the idea of abstraction. And abstractions keep appearing within individual layers in various ways as well. In fact, abstraction can be seen throughout the entire evolution of computing systems, as we explore in the next section.

1.2   The History of Computing

The historical foundation of computing goes a long way toward explaining why computing systems today are designed as they are. Think of this section as a story whose characters and events have led to the place we are now and form the foundation of the exciting future to come. We examine the history of computing hardware and software separately because they each have their own impact on how computing systems evolved into the layered model we use as the outline for this book.

This history is written as a narrative, with no intent to formally define the concepts discussed. In subsequent chapters, we return to these concepts and explore them in more detail.

A Brief History of Computing Hardware

The devices that assist humans in various forms of computation have their roots in the ancient past and have continued to evolve throughout the present day. Let's take a brief tour through the history of computing hardware.

Early History

Many people believe that Stonehenge, the famous collection of rock monoliths in Great Britain, is an early form of calendar or astrological calculator. The *abacus*, which appeared in the sixteenth century, was developed as an instrument to record numeric values and on which a human can perform basic arithmetic.

In the middle of the seventeenth century, Blaise Pascal, a French mathematician, built and sold gear-driven mechanical machines, which performed whole-number addition and subtraction. Later in the seventeenth century, a German mathematician, Gottfried Wilhelm von Leibniz, built the first mechanical device designed to do all four whole-number

Stonehenge Is Still a Mystery

Stonehenge, a Neolithic stone structure that rises majestically out of the Salisbury Plain in England, has fascinated man for centuries. It is believed that Stonehenge was erected over several centuries beginning in about 2180 B.C.. Its purpose is still a mystery, although theories abound. At the summer solstice, the rising sun appears behind one of the main stones, giving the illusion that the sun is balancing on the stone. This

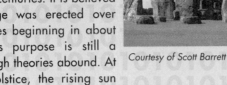
Courtesy of Scott Barrett

has led to the early theory that Stonehenge was a temple. Another theory, first suggested in the middle of the 20th century, is that Stonehenge could have been used as an astronomical calendar, marking lunar and solar alignments. And yet a third theory is that Stonehenge was used to predict eclipses. Regardless of why it was built, there is a mystical quality about the place that defies explanation.

operations: addition, subtraction, multiplication, and division. Unfortunately, the state of mechanical gears and levers at that time was such that the Leibniz machine was not very reliable.

In the late eighteenth century, Joseph Jacquard developed what became known as *Jacquard's Loom*, used for weaving cloth. The loom used a series of cards with holes punched in them to specify the use of specific colored thread and therefore dictate the design that was woven into the cloth. Though not a computing device, Jacquard's Loom was the first to make use of an important form of input: the punched card.

It wasn't until the nineteenth century that the next major step was taken, this time by a British mathematician. Charles Babbage designed what he called his *analytical engine*. His design was too complex for him to build with the technology of his day, so it was never implemented. His vision, however, included many of the important components of today's computers. His design was the first to include a memory so that intermediate values did not have to be re-entered. His design also included the input of both numbers and mechanical steps, making use of punched cards similar to those used in Jacquard's Loom.

Ada Augusta, Countess of Lovelace, was a most romantic figure in the history of computing. Ada, the daughter of Lord Byron (the English poet), was a skilled mathematician. She became interested in Babbage's work on the analytical engine and extended his ideas (as well as correcting some of his errors). Ada is credited with being the first programmer. The concept of the loop—a series of instructions that repeat—is attributed to her. The programming language Ada, used largely by the United States Department of Defense, is named for her.

During the later part of the nineteenth century and the beginning of the twentieth century computing advances were made rapidly. William Burroughs produced and sold a mechanical adding machine. Dr. Herman

Ada Augusta, the First Programmer[2]

On December 10, 1815 (the same year that George Boole was born), a daughter—Augusta Ada Byron—was born to Anna Isabella (Annabella) Byron and George Gordon, Lord Byron. At that time in England Byron's fame derived not only from his poetry but also from his wild and scandalous behavior. The marriage was strained from the beginning, and Annabella left Byron shortly after Ada's birth. By April of 1816, the two had signed separation papers. Byron left England, never to return. Throughout the rest of his life he regretted that he was unable to see his daughter. At one point he wrote of her,

> I see thee not. I hear thee not.
> But none can be so wrapt in thee.

Before he died in Greece, at age 36, he exclaimed,

> Oh my poor dear child! My dear Ada!
> My God, could I but have seen her!

Meanwhile, Annabella, who eventually was to become a baroness in her own right, and who was educated as both a mathematician and a poet, carried on with Ada's upbringing and education. Annabella gave Ada her first instruction in mathematics, but it soon became clear that Ada was gifted in the subject and should receive more extensive tutoring. Ada received further training from Augustus DeMorgan, today famous for one of the basic theorems of Boolean algebra. By age eight, Ada had demonstrated an interest in mechanical devices and was building detailed model boats.

When she was 18, Ada visited the Mechanics Institute to hear Dr. Dionysius Lardner's lectures on the "Difference Engine," a mechanical calculating machine being built by Charles Babbage. She became so interested in the device that she arranged to be introduced to Babbage. It was said that, upon seeing Babbage's machine, Ada was the only person in the room to understand immediately how it worked and to recognize its significance. Ada and Charles Babbage became lifelong friends. She worked with him, helping to document his designs, translating writings about his work, and developing programs for his machines. In fact, Ada today is recognized as the first computer programmer in history.

When Babbage designed his Analytical Engine, Ada foresaw that it could go beyond arithmetic computations and become a general manipulator of symbols, and thus would have far-reaching capabilities. She even suggested that such a device eventually could be programmed with rules of harmony and composition so that it could be produce "scientific" music. In effect, Ada foresaw the field of artificial intelligence more than 150 years ago.

In 1842, Babbage gave a series of lectures in Turin, Italy, on his Analytical Engine. One of the attendees was Luigi Menabrea, who was so impressed that he wrote an account of Babbage's lectures. At age 27, Ada decided to translate the account into English, with the intent to add a few of her own notes about the machine. In the end, her notes were twice as long as the original material, and the document, "The Sketch of the Analytical Engine," became the definitive work on the subject.

It is obvious from Ada's letters that her "notes" were entirely her own and that Babbage was acting as a sometimes unappreciated editor. At one point, Ada wrote to him,

> I am much annoyed at your having altered my Note. You know I am always willing to make any required alterations myself, but that I cannot endure another person to meddle with my sentences.

Ada gained the title Countess of Lovelace when she married Lord William Lovelace. The couple had three children, whose upbringing was left to Ada's mother while Ada pursued her work in mathematics. Her husband was supportive of her work, but for a woman of that day such behavior was considered almost as scandalous as some of her father's exploits.

Ada died in 1852, just one year before a working Difference Engine was built in Sweden from one of Babbage's designs. Like her father, Ada lived only to age 36, and even though they led very different lives, she undoubtedly admired him and took inspiration from his unconventional and rebellious nature. In the end, Ada asked to be buried beside him at the family's estate.

Hollerith developed the first electro-mechanical tabulator, which read information from a punched card. His device revolutionized the census taken every ten years in the United States. Dr. Hollerith later formed a company that is known today as IBM.

In 1936 a theoretical development took place that had nothing to do with hardware per se but profoundly influenced the field of Computer Science. Alan M. Turing, another British mathematician, invented an abstract mathematical model called a *Turing machine*, laying the foundation for a major area of computing theory. The most prestigious award given in Computer Science (equivalent to the Fielding Medal in Mathematics or a Nobel Prize in other sciences) is the Turing Award, named for Alan Turing. A recent Broadway play deals with his life. Analysis of the capabilities of Turing machines is a part of the theoretical studies of all Computer Science students.

By the outbreak of World War II, several computers were under design and construction. The Harvard Mark I and the ENIAC are two of the more famous machines of the era. The ENIAC is pictured in Figure 1.4. John von Neumann, who had been a consultant on the ENIAC project,

Figure 1.4 The ENIAC, a World War II-era computer
U.S. Army Photo

started work on another machine known as EDVAC, which was completed in 1950. In 1951 the first commercial computer, UNIVAC I, was delivered to the Bureau of the Census. The UNIVAC I was the first computer used to predict the outcome of a presidential election.

The early history that began with the abacus ended with the delivery of the UNIVAC I. With the delivery of that machine, the dream of a device that could rapidly manipulate numbers was realized; the search was ended. Or was it? Some experts predicted at that time that a small number of computers would be able to handle the computational needs of mankind. What they didn't realize was that the ability to perform fast calculations on large amounts of data would radically change the very nature of fields such as mathematics, physics, engineering, and economics. That is, computers made those experts' assessment of *what needed to be calculated* entirely invalid.[3]

After 1951 the story becomes one of the ever-expanding use of computers to solve problems in all areas. From that point, the search has focused not only on building faster, bigger devices, but also on the development of tools to allow us to use these devices more productively. The history of computing hardware from this point on is categorized into several "generations" based on the technology they employed.

First Generation (1951–1959)

Commercial computers in the first generation (from approximately 1951–1959) were built using *vacuum tubes* to store information. A vacuum tube, shown in Figure 1.5, generated a great deal of heat and was not very reliable. The machines that used them required heavy-duty air-conditioning and frequent maintenance. They also required very large, specially built rooms.

The primary memory device of this first generation of computers was a *magnetic drum* that rotated under a read/write head. When the memory cell that was being accessed rotated under the read/write head, the data was written to or read from that place.

The input device was a card reader that read the holes punched in an IBM card (a descendant of the Hollerith card). The output device was either a punched card or a line printer. By the end of this generation, *magnetic tape drives* had been developed that were much faster than card readers. Magnetic tapes are sequential storage devices, meaning that the data on the tape must be accessed one after another in a linear fashion.

Storage devices external to the computer memory are called *auxiliary storage devices.* The magnetic tape was the first of these devices. Collectively, input devices, output devices, and auxiliary storage devices became known as *peripheral devices.*

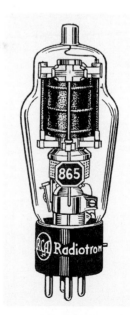

Figure 1.5 A vacuum tube
Reproduced by permission of University of Calgary

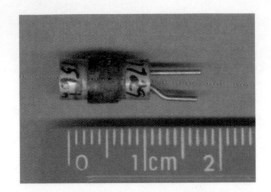

Figure 1.6
A transistor, replacing the
vacuum tube *Courtesy of Dr.
Andrew Wylie*

Second Generation (1959–1965)

The advent of the *transistor* (for which John Bardeen, Walter H. Brattain, and William B. Shockley won a Nobel Prize) ushered in the second generation of commercial computers. The transistor replaced the vacuum tube as the main component in the hardware. The transistor was smaller, more reliable, faster, more durable, and cheaper, as shown in Figure 1.6.

The second generation also witnessed the advent of immediate-access memory. When accessing information from a drum, the CPU had to wait for the proper place to rotate under the read/write head. The second generation used memory made from *magnetic cores*, tiny doughnut-shaped devices, each capable of storing one bit of information. These cores were strung together with wires to form cells, and cells were combined into a memory unit. Because the device was motionless and was accessed electronically, information was available instantly.

The *magnetic disk*, a new auxiliary storage device, was also developed during the second generation. The magnetic disk is faster than magnetic tape because each data item can be accessed directly by referring to its location on the disk. Unlike a tape, which cannot access a piece of data without accessing everything on the tape that comes before it, a disk is organized so that each piece of data has its own location identifier called an address. The read-write heads of a magnetic disk can be sent directly to the specific location on the disk where the desired information is stored.

Third Generation (1965–1971)

In the second generation, transistors and other components for the computer were assembled by hand on printed *circuit boards*. The third generation is characterized by *integrated circuits* (IC), solid pieces of silicon that contained the transistors, other components, and their connections. Integrated circuits were much smaller, cheaper, faster, and more reliable than printed circuit boards. Gordon Moore, one of the cofounders of Intel, noted that from the time of the invention of the IC, the number of circuits that could be placed on a single integrated circuit was doubling each year. This observation became known as Moore's law."[4]

Transistors also were used for memory construction. Each transistor represented one bit of information. Integrated-circuit technology allowed memory boards to be built using transistors. Auxiliary storage devices were still needed because transistor memory was volatile; that is, the information went away when the power was turned off.

The *terminal*, an input/output device with a keyboard and screen, was introduced during this generation. The keyboard gave the user direct access to the computer, and the screen provided immediate response.

Fourth Generation (1971–?)

Large-scale integration characterizes the fourth generation. From several thousand transistors to a silicon chip in the early 1970s, we moved to a whole microcomputer on a chip by the middle of the decade. Main memory devices are still made almost exclusively out of chip technology. Over the previous 40 years, each generation of computer hardware had become more powerful in a smaller package at lower cost. Moore's law was modified to say that chip density was doubling every 18 months.

By the late 1970s, the phrase *personal computer* (PC) had entered the vocabulary. Microcomputers had become so cheap that almost anyone could have one. And a generation of kids grew up playing PacMan.

The fourth generation found some new names entering the commercial market. Apple, Tandy/Radio Shack, Atari, Commodore, and Sun joined the big companies of earlier generations—IBM, Remington Rand, NCR, DEC, Hewlett Packard, Control Data, and Burroughs. The best-known success story of the personal computer revolution is that of the Apple. Steve Wozniak, an engineer, and Steve Jobs, a high-school student, created a personal computer kit and marketed it out of a garage. This was the beginning of Apple Computer, a multibillion-dollar company.

The IBM PC was introduced in 1981 and soon was followed by compatible machines manufactured by many other companies. For example, Dell and Compaq were successful in making PCs that were compatible with IBM PCs. Apple introduced its very popular Macintosh microcomputer line in 1984.

From a garage to the Fortune 500

Boyhood friends Steve Jobs and Steve Wozniak sold their respective Volkswagen van and programmable calculator to raise the money to finance their new computer company. Their first sale was 50 Apple Is, the computer that they had designed and built in a garage. In six short years Apple was listed in the Fortune 500, the youngest firm on this prestigious list. www

In the mid–1980s, larger, more powerful machines were created, and they were referred to as *workstations*. Workstations were generally for business, not personal, use. The idea was for each employee to have his or her own workstation on the desktop. These workstations were connected by cables, or *networked*, so that they could interact with one another. Workstations were made more powerful by the introduction of the RISC (reduced-instruction-set computer) architecture. Each computer was designed to understand a set of instructions, called its *machine language*. Conventional machines such as the IBM 370/168 had an instruction set of over 200 instructions. Instructions were fast and memory access was slow, so specialized instructions made sense. As memory access got faster and faster, using a reduced set of instructions became attractive. SUN Microsystems introduced a workstation with a RISC chip in 1987. Its popularity proved the feasibility of the RISC chip. These workstations were often called UNIX workstations because they used the UNIX operating system.

Because computers are still being made using circuit boards, we cannot mark the end of this generation. However, several things have occurred that so impact how we use machines that they certainly have brought in a new era. Moore's law was once again restated in the following form: "Computers will either double in power at the same price or halve in cost for the same power every 18 months."[5]

Parallel Computing

Though computers that use a single primary processing unit continue to flourish, radically new machine architectures began appearing in the late eighties. Computers that use these *parallel architectures* rely on a set of interconnected central processing units.

One class of parallel machines is organized so that the processors all share the same memory unit. In another, each central processor has its own local memory and communicates with the others over a very fast internal network.

Parallel architectures offer several ways to increase the speed of execution. For example, a given step in a program can be separated into multiple pieces, and those pieces can be executed simultaneously on several individual processors. These machines are called SIMD (single-instruction, multiple-data-stream) computers. A second class of machines can work on different parts of a program simultaneously. These machines are called MIMD (multiple-instruction, multiple-data stream) computers.

The potential of hundreds or even thousands of processors combined in one machine is enormous. And the challenge to programming is equally enormous. Software designed for parallel machines is different from software designed for sequential machines. Programmers have to rethink the ways in which they approach problem solving and programming in order to exploit parallelism.

Networking

In the 1980s, the concept of a large machine with many users gave way to a network of smaller machines connected in order to share resources such as printers, software, and data. The *Ethernet*, invented by Robert Metcalfe and David Boggs in 1973, was a cheap coaxial cable connecting the machines and a set of protocols that allowed the machines to communicate with one another. By 1979, DEC (Digital Equipment Corporation), Intel, and Xerox joined to establish Ethernet as a standard.

Workstations were designed for networking, but networking personal computers didn't become practical until a more advanced Intel chip was introduced in 1985. By 1989, Novell's Netware connected PCs together with a *file server*, a PC with generous mass storage and good input/output capability. Locating data and office automation software on the server rather than each PC having its own copy allowed for a measure of central control while giving each machine a measure of autonomy. Workstations or personal computers networked together became known as LANs (local area networks).

The *Internet* as we know it today is descended from the ARPANET, a government-sponsored network begun in the late 1960s, consisting of 11 nodes concentrated mainly in the Los Angeles and Boston areas. Like ARPANET and LANs, the Internet uses *packet switching*, a way for messages to share lines. The Internet, however, is made up of many different networks across the world that communicate by using a common protocol, *TCP/IP* (transmission-control protocol/internet protocol).

What is a protocol?

The dictionary defines a protocol as a code prescribing strict adherence to correct etiquette and procedure (as in a diplomatic exchange). Computing terminology has borrowed the word to describe the correct etiquette for computers to use when communicating with one another.

Paul E. Ceruzzi, in *A History of Modern Computing*, comments on the relationship between Ethernet and the Internet as follows:

> "If the Internet of the 1990s became the Information Superhighway, then Ethernet became the equally important network of local roads to feed it. As a descendent of ARPA research, the global networks we now call the Internet came into existence before the local Ethernet was invented at Xerox. But Ethernet transformed the nature of office and personal computing before the Internet had a significant effect." [6]

A Brief History of Computing Software

The hardware of a computer can be turned on, but it does nothing until directed by the programs that make up the computer's software. The manner in which software evolved is crucial to understanding how software works in a modern computing system.

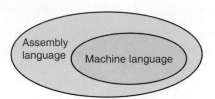

Figure 1.7 Layers of languages at the end of the first generation

First-Generation Software (1951–1959)

The first programs were written using machine language, the instructions built into the electrical circuitry of a particular computer. Even the small task of adding two numbers together used three instructions written in *binary* (1s and 0s), and the programmer had to remember which combination of binary digits means what. Programmers using machine language had to be very good with numbers and very detail-oriented. It's not surprising that the first programmers were mathematicians and engineers. Nevertheless, programming in machine language is both time-consuming and prone to errors.

Because writing in machine code is so tedious, some programmers took the time to develop tools to help with the programming process. Thus the first artificial programming languages were developed. These languages, called *assembly languages*, used mnemonic codes to represent each machine-language instruction.

Because every program that is executed on a computer eventually must be in the form of the computer's machine language, the developers of assembly language also created software *translators* to translate programs written in assembly language into machine code. A program called an *assembler* reads each of the program's instructions in mnemonic form and translates it into the machine-language equivalent. These mnemonics are abbreviated and sometimes difficult to read, but they are much easier to use than long strings of binary digits.

Those programmers who wrote tools to make programming easier for others were the first *systems programmers*. So, even in first-generation software, there was the division between those programmers who wrote tools and those programmers who used the tools. The assembly language acted as a buffer between the programmer and the machine hardware. See Figure 1.7. Sometimes, when efficient code is essential, programs today may be written in assembly language. Chapter 7 explores an example of machine code and a corresponding assembly language in detail.

Second-Generation Software (1959–1965)

As hardware became more powerful, more powerful tools were needed to use it effectively. Assembly languages were certainly a step in the right direction, but the programmer still was forced to think in terms of individual machine instructions. The second generation saw more powerful languages developed. These *high-level languages* allowed the programmer to write instructions using more English-like statements.

Two of the languages developed during the second generation are still used today. They are FORTRAN (a language designed for numerical applications) and COBOL (a language designed for business applications). FORTRAN and COBOL developed quite differently. FORTRAN started out as a simple language and grew with additional features added to it over the years. In contrast, COBOL was designed first, and then implemented. It has changed little over time.

Another language that was designed during this period that is still in use today is Lisp. Lisp differs markedly from FORTRAN and COBOL and was not widely accepted. Lisp was used mainly in artificial intelligence applications and research. Dialects of Lisp are among the languages of choice today in artificial intelligence. Scheme, a dialect of Lisp, is used at some schools as an introductory programming language.

The introduction of high-level languages provided a vehicle for running the same program on more than one computer. Each high-level language has a translating program that goes with it, a program that takes statements written in the high-level language and converts them to the equivalent machine-code instructions. In the earliest days, the high level language statements were often translated into an assembly language and then the assembly-language statements were translated into machine code. A program written in FORTRAN or COBOL can be translated and run on any machine that has a translating program called a *compiler.*

At the end of the second generation, the role of the systems programmer was becoming more distinct. Systems programmers wrote tools like assemblers and compilers; those people who used the tools to write programs were called *application programmers.* The application programmer was becoming even more insulated from the computer hardware. The software surrounding the hardware had become more sophisticated. See Figure 1.8.

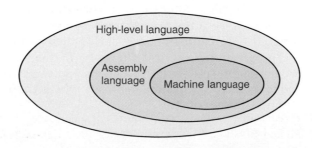

Figure 1.8
Layers of language at the end of the second generation

Third-Generation Software (1965–1971)

During the third generation of commercial computers, it became apparent that the human was slowing down the computing process. Computers were sitting idle while waiting for the computer operator to prepare the next job. The solution was to put the computer resources under the control of the computer, that is, to write a program that would determine which programs were run when. This kind of program is called an *operating system*.

During the first two generations, utility programs had been written to handle often-needed tasks. *Loaders* loaded programs into memory and *linkers* linked pieces of large programs together. In the third generation, these utility programs were refined and put under the direction of the operating system. This group of utility programs, the operating system, and the language translators (assemblers and compilers) became known as *systems software*.

The introduction of computer terminals as input/output devices gave the user ready access to the computer, and advances in systems software gave the machine the ability to work much faster. However, inputting and outputting data from keyboards and screens was a slow process, much slower than carrying out instructions in memory. The problem was how to make use of the machine's greater capabilities and speed. The solution was *time sharing*—many different users, each at a terminal, communicating (inputting and outputting) with a single computer all at the same time. Controlling the process was an operating system that organized and scheduled the different jobs.

For the users, time sharing is much like having their own machine. Each user is assigned a small slice of central processing time and then is put on hold while another user is serviced. Users generally aren't even aware that there are other users. However, if too many people try to use the system at the same time, there can be a noticeable wait for a job to be completed.

During the third generation, general-purpose application programs were being written. One example was the Statistical Package for the Social Sciences (SPSS) written in FORTRAN. SPSS had a special language, and users wrote instructions in that language as input to the program. This language allowed the user, who was often not a programmer, to describe some data and the statistics to be computed on that data.

At the beginning, the computer user and the programmer were one in the same. By the end of the first generation, programmers emerged who wrote tools for other programmers to use, giving rise to the distinction between systems programmers and applications programmers. However, the programmer was still the user. In the third generation, systems programmers were writing programs—software tools—for others to use. Suddenly there were computer users who were not programmers in the traditional sense.

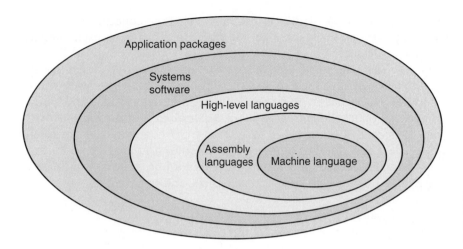

Figure 1.9
The layers of software surrounding the hardware continue to grow

The separation between the user and the hardware was growing wider. The hardware had become only a small part of the picture. A computer system—a combination of hardware, software, and the data managed by them—had emerged. See Figure 1.9. Although the layers of languages kept getting deeper, programmers continued (and still continue) to use some of the very inner layers. If a small segment of code must run as quickly as possible and take up as few memory locations as possible, it may still be programmed in an assembly language or even machine code today.

Fourth Generation (1971–1989)

The 1970s saw the introduction of better programming techniques called *structured programming*, a logical, disciplined approach to programming. The languages Pascal and Modula-2 were built on the principles of structured programming. And BASIC, a language introduced for third-generation machines, was refined and upgraded to more-structured versions. C, a language that allows the user to intersperse assembly-language statements, was also introduced. C++, a structured language that also allows the user access to low-level statements, became the language of choice in industry.

Better and more powerful operating systems also were being developed. UNIX, developed at AT&T as a research tool, has become standard in many university settings. PC-DOS, developed for IBM PC, and MS-DOS, developed for compatibles, became standards for personal computers. The operating system for the Macintosh introduced the concept of the mouse and the point-and-click graphical interface, thus changing user/computer interaction drastically.

High-quality, reasonably priced applications software packages became available at neighborhood stores. These programs allow the user with no computer experience to do a specific task. Three typical kinds of application packages are *spreadsheets*, *word processors*, and *database management systems*. Lotus 1-2-3 was the first commercially successful spreadsheet that allowed a novice user to enter and analyze all kinds of data. WordPerfect was one of the first real-word processors, and dBase IV was a system that let the user store, organize, and retrieve data.

Fifth Generation (1990–present)

The fifth generation is notable for three major events: the rise of Microsoft as a dominant player in computer software; object-oriented design and programming; and the World Wide Web.

Microsoft's Windows operating system became dominant in the PC market during this period. Although WordPerfect continued to improve, Microsoft's Word became the most used word processing program. In the mid–90s word processors, spreadsheet programs, database programs, and other application programs were bundled together into super packages called *office suites*.

Object-oriented design became the design of choice for large programming projects. Whereas structured design is based on a hierarchy of tasks, object-oriented design is based on a hierarchy of data objects. Java, a language designed by Sun Microsystems for object-oriented programming, began to rival C++.

The *World Wide Web* made it easy to use the Internet to share information around the world. A *browser* is a program that allows a user to access information from web sites worldwide. See Figure 1.10. There are two giants in the browser market: Netscape Navigator and Microsoft's Internet Explorer. Microsoft's bundling of Internet Explorer with the Windows operating system led to an antitrust suit being filed against them.

The 1980s and 1990s must be characterized most of all by the changing profile of the user. The first user was the programmer who wrote programs to solve specific problems, his or her own or someone else's. Then the systems programmer emerged who wrote more and more complex tools for other programmers. By the early 1970s, applications programmers were using these complex tools to write applications programs for nonprogrammers to use. With the advent of the personal computer, computer games, educational programs, and user-friendly software packages, many people became computer users. With the advent of the World Wide Web, web surfing has

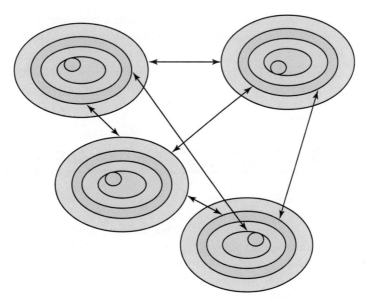

Figure 1.10
Sharing information on the
World Wide Web

become the recreation of choice, so even more people have become computer users. The user is a first-grade child learning to read, a teenager downloading music, a college student writing a paper, a homemaker planning a budget, a banker looking up a customer's loan record. The user is all of us.

In our brief history of hardware and software, we have focused our attention on traditional computers and computing systems. Paralleling this history is the use of integrated circuits, or chips, to run or regulate everything from toasters, to cars, to intensive care monitors, to satellites. Such computing technology is called an *embedded system*. Although these chips are not actually computers in the sense that we are going to study in this book, they are certainly a product of the technology revolution of the last 50 years.

Predictions

We end this brief history of computing with a few predictions about computers that didn't come true:[7]

> "I think there is a world market for maybe five computers."—Thomas Watson, chair of IBM, 1943.

> "Where ... the ENIAC is equipped with 18,000 vacuum tubes and weighs 30 tons, computers in the future may have only 1,000 vacuum tubes and weigh only 1.5 tons."—*Popular Mechanics*, 1949.

> "Folks, the Mac platform is through—totally."—John C. Dvorak, *PC Magazine*, 1998.

"There is no reason anyone would want a computer in their home."
—Ken Olson, president, chairman, and founder of Digital Equipment
Corp., 1977.

"I predict the Internet ... will go spectacularly supernova and in 1996
catastrophically collapse."—Bob Metcalfe, 3Com founder and inventor,
1995.

1.3   Computing as a Tool and a Discipline

In the previous section on the history of computer software, we pointed
out the ever-changing role of the user. At the end of the first generation,
the user split into two groups: the systems programmer who developed
tools to make programming easier and the applications programmer who
used the tools. Later applications programmers built large domain-specific
programs such as statistical packages, word processors, spreadsheets, intelligent browsers, virtual environments, and medical diagnosis applications
on top of the traditional language tools. These application programs were
in turn used by practitioners with no computer background.

So who is using the computer as a tool? Everyone, except for those who
are creating the tools for others. For these toolmakers, either computing is
a discipline (low-level tools) or the discipline of computing has made their
tools possible (applications built upon applications).

The dictionary defines *discipline* as a field of study. Peter Denning
defines the discipline of computer science as "the body of knowledge and
practices used by computing professionals in their work.... This discipline
is also called computer science and engineering, computing, and informatics."[8] He continues, "The body of knowledge of computing is
frequently described as the systematic study of algorithmic processes that
describe and transform information: their theory, analysis, design, efficiency, implementation, and application. The fundamental question underlying all of computing is, *What can be (efficiently) automated?*"

Denning states that each practitioner must be skilled in four areas: *algorithmic thinking*, in which one is able to express problems in terms of step-
by-step procedures to solve them, *representation*, in which one is able to
store data in a way that it can be processed efficiently, *programming*, in
which one is able to combine algorithmic thinking and representation into
computer software, and *design*, in which the software serves a useful
purpose.

A debate has long raged about whether computing is a mathematical
discipline, a scientific discipline, or an engineering discipline. Computing

certainly has roots in mathematical logic. The theorems of Turing tell us that certain problems cannot be solved, Boolean algebra describes computer circuits, and numerical analysis plays an important role in scientific computing. Scientific disciplines attempt to understand how their systems work. The natural sciences exist to "fill in the instruction book that God forgot to leave us." [9] Thus, computing is a scientific discipline as we build and test models of natural phenomena. As we design and build larger and larger computing systems, we are using techniques from engineering.

In 1989, a task force of computer science educators proposed a curriculum model that covered the subareas of computing from the three perspectives represented in our history: theory (mathematics); experimentation, called abstraction by computer scientists (sciences); and design (engineering). [10] Theory refers to the building of conceptual frameworks and notations for understanding relationships among objects in a domain. Experimentation (abstraction) refers to exploring models of systems and architectures within different application domains and determining whether the models predict new behaviors. Design refers to constructing computer systems that support work in different application domains.

The following table shows the subareas outlined by the task force plus three areas that have emerged since that time.

Subareas of Computer Science
Algorithms and data structures
Programming languages
Architecture
Numerical and symbolic computation
Operating systems
Software methodology and engineering
Databases and information retrieval
Artificial intelligence and robotics
Human–computer communication
Graphics
Organizational informatics
Bioinformatics

Of the 12 subject subareas, six relate to understanding and building computing tools in general: algorithms and data structures, programming languages, (computer) architecture, operating systems, software methodology and engineering, and human-computer communication. Not surprisingly, these are called *systems areas*. Six of the subareas relate to the computer's use as a tool: numerical and symbolic computation, databases and informational retrieval, artificial intelligence and robotics, graphics, organizational informatics, and bioinformatics. These areas are called *applications areas*.

Research is ongoing in both systems and applications. Systems research produces better general tools; applications research produces better tools for the domain-specific applications. There is no doubt that the relationships between the people who investigate computing topics as a discipline directly affect those who use computers as a tool. Computing research fuels the applications people use daily, and the turnaround for the technology is amazingly fast. This symbiotic relationship is more dynamic in computing than in any other discipline.

In this book we explain, at an introductory level, the ideas underlying computing as a discipline. This book does not exist to make you better users of a computer, though it should undoubtedly have that side effect. Instead, we want you to walk away with a thorough underlying knowledge of how computer systems work, where they are now, and where they may go in the future. For this reason, we examine both systems and applications.

Summary

This book is a broad study of computer systems, including the hardware that makes up the devices, the software programs executed by the machine, and the data managed and manipulated by both. Computing systems can be divided into layers, and our organization of this book follows those layers from the inside out.

The history of computing gives us the roots from which modern computing systems grew. The history of computing spans four generations, each characterized by the components used to build the hardware and the software tools developed to allow the programmer to make more productive use of the hardware. These tools have formed layers of software around the hardware.

Throughout the rest of this book, we examine the different layers that make up a computing system, beginning with the information layer and ending with the communication layer. Our goal is to give you an appreciation and understanding of all aspects of computing systems.

You may go on to study computer science in depth and contribute to the future of computing systems. Or you may go on to be application specialists within other disciplines, using the computer as a tool. Whatever your future holds, with computing systems as prevalent as they are, a fundamental understanding of how they work is imperative.

ETHICAL ISSUES

Microsoft Anti-Trust Case

In 1975, Bill Gates and Paul Allen formed a partnership and named it Microsoft. They created the business in anticipation of a future where software would be in high demand as personal computers became standard household commodities. Their vision came true, and the company that began in a Harvard University dorm room has become the world's leader in the software industry. Today, over 90% of all personal computers use Microsoft's Windows as their operating system.

Microsoft's efforts to dominate the market have led the company into a critical period that will greatly impact its future. In the early 90s, Microsoft felt that advancements made in Internet technology threatened their dominance. With the advent of the web, personal computers no longer needed to rely on their independent systems. Internet browsers were the wave of the future and Microsoft believed that the company controlling the browser market would control the industry. Shortly after Netscape introduced Navigator, an easy-to-use browser, Microsoft launched Internet Explorer. Microsoft had already licensed its software to many manufacturers; the company now attempted to prevent customers from using other browsers by threatening them with the loss of their Windows license.

In 1990, the Federal Trade Commission targeted Microsoft for possibly working with IBM to monopolize the software market. When IBM was dropped from the investigation in 1991, the focus centered on Microsoft, and in 1993 the Department of Justice took over the investigation. On July 16, 1994 an agreement was made between Microsoft and the Department of Justice in which they signed a consent decree. This decree prevented Microsoft from requiring computer manufacturers who license Windows to license Internet Explorer. Microsoft was not, however, prohibited from "integrating" products within its operating system. It was this distinction that would later become an important argument for Microsoft in the antitrust suit set against them.

The Justice Department sued Microsoft on October 20, 1997 for violating the 1994 consent decree. The Department of Justice accused Microsoft of bundling Internet Explorer with their operating system, but Microsoft denied anti-competition intentions and claimed that Internet Explorer was an integrated component of Windows. Microsoft's contention was that the packaged deal did not hurt consumers or their competition. The company stated that the browser could not be removed from the operating system without compromising its quality. The argument against Microsoft asserted that the company acted in violation of antitrust laws, which were established to protect competition. Microsoft's opponents saw the bundling of Internet Explorer as an attempt to monopolize the market by eliminating competition.

In April of 2000, the court ruled that Microsoft was indeed a monopoly, and that its bundling of Internet Explorer was in violation of antitrust laws. At that time, Judge Thomas Jackson ordered the breakup of Microsoft. Microsoft appealed the ruling and Judge Jackson's ethical conduct was investigated. It was determined that he was a biased judge. While his ruling that Microsoft is a monopoly stands, the order to split the company was thrown out. Whether the case moves to an appeals court or the Supreme Court, Microsoft's problems are far from over. In the meantime, other operating systems are struggling to obtain their share of the software market. Linux, a stable and reliable operating system, has challenged the widespread use of Windows by making its source code free and accessible. The outcome of Microsoft's antitrust case will have a great impact on the future operating systems.

Key Terms

Abstraction pg. 7

Computer hardware pg. 4

Computer software pg. 4

Computing system pg. 4

Exercises

1. What French mathematician built and sold the first gear-driven mechanical machine that did addition and subtraction?
2. Leibniz made a improvement on the machine in Exercise 1. What was the improvement?
3. Describe Babbage's contribution to the history of computers.

4. Who was considered the first programmer? Describe her contributions to the history of computers.

5. What company did Dr. Hollerith form?

6. How is data represented in an IBM card?

7. For whom is the Turing Award in computing named?

8. a. What was the first commercial computer?
   b. Who bought it?
   c. When was it sold?

9. What was the first computer used to predict the outcome of an election?

10. Some experts made early predictions that a small number of computers would handle all of mankinds computational needs. Why was this prediction faulty?

11. a. List four important facts about the first generation of hardware.
    b. List three important facts about the second generation of hardware.
    c. List three important facts about the third generation of hardware.

12. The following companies were giants in the field of computer hardware in early generations: IBM, Remington Rand, NCR, DEC, Hewlett Packard, Control Data, Burroughs, Intel, and Xerox.
    a. Which of these companies are still in business today under the same name?
    b. Which of these companies are still in business under another name?
    c. Which of these companies are no longer in business?

13. The following names were prominent in the early part of the fourth generation of computer hardware: Apple, Tandy/Radio Shack, Atari, Commodore, and Sun.
    a. Which of these companies are still in business today under the same name?
    b. Which of these companies are still in business under another name?
    c. Which of these companies are no longer in business?

14. Define SIMD and MIMD.

15. What is Ethernet?

16. What does the acronym LAN stand for?

17. Define the word *protocol* and explain how it is used in computing.

18. Distinguish between machine language and assembly language.

19. Distinguish between assembly language and high-level languages.

20. FORTRAN and COBOL were two high-level languages defined during the second generation of computer software. Compare and contrast these languages in terms of their history and their purpose.

21. Distinguish between an assembler and a compiler.

22. Distinguish between a systems programmer and an applications programmer.

23. What was the rationale behind the development of operating systems?

24. What constituted systems software?

25. What do the following pieces of software do?
    a. Loader
    b. Linker
    c. Editor

26. How was the program SPSS different from the programs that came before it?

27. Name five languages that were prominent during the fourth generation of computer software.

28. Name several typical types of fourth-generation application software.

29. Name two design techniques.

30. What do we mean by the statement that the 1980s and 1990s must be characterized by the changing profile of the user?

31. Distinguish between computing as a tool and computing as a discipline.

32. Is computing a mathematical discipline, a scientific discipline, or an engineering discipline? Explain.

33. Distinguish between systems areas and applications areas in computing as a discipline.

34. Define the word *abstraction* and relate it to the drawing in Figure 1.3.

35. Name four skills that each practitioner should master (according to Peter Denning).

36. Name the six subject subareas of computer science called systems areas that relate to understanding and building computing tools in general.

37. Name the six subject subareas of computer science called applications areas that relate to the computer's use as a tool.

38. What does SIMD stand for?

39. What does MIMD stand for?

40. What is the fundamental question underlying all of computing (according to Peter Denning)?

41. What do Joseph Jacquard and Herman Hollerith have in common?

42. Why was Ada Lovelace called the first programmer?

43. To what English poet was Ada Lovelace related?

❓ Thought Questions

1. Identify five abstractions in your school environment. Indicate what details are hidden by the abstraction and how the abstraction helps manage complexity.

2. Explain the statement "The history of computing can be traced through the ever-changing definition of the *user*."

3. Did you have a computer in the home as you were growing up? If so, how did it influence your education to this point? If not, how did the lack of one influence your education to this point?

4. In 1969 an antitrust action was filed against IBM. What was the basis of the case? How was it resolved?

5. Compare the 1969 antitrust action against IBM with the 1990s action against Microsoft.

6. Is it in the interest of the computer user that curbs be placed on multi-billion-dollar corporations like Microsoft and IBM?

The Information Layer

2 Binary Values and Number Systems

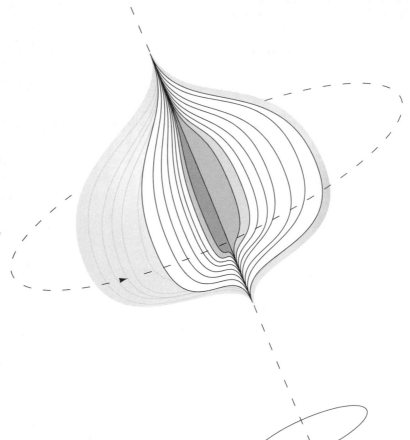

Chapter 2

Binary Values and Number Systems

Now that we've established some common terminology in Chapter 1, our exploration of computing technology can begin in earnest. This chapter describes binary values—the way in which computer hardware represents and manages information. This chapter also puts binary values in the context of all number systems, reminding us of grade school principles that we now take for granted. You probably already know many of the concepts about binary numbers described in this chapter, but you might not realize that you know them! The rules of all number systems are the same; it's just a matter of going back to those underlying concepts and applying them in a new base. By making sure we have an understanding of binary values, we pave the way to understanding how computing systems use the binary number system to accomplish their tasks.

Goals

After studying this chapter, you should be able to:

- distinguish among categories of numbers.
- describe positional notation.
- convert numbers in other bases to base ten.
- convert base-ten numbers to numbers in other bases.
- describe the relationship between bases 2, 8, and 16.
- explain the importance to computing of bases that are powers of 2.

2.1   Number Categories

Numbers come in all sorts of categories. There are natural numbers, negative numbers, rational numbers, irrational numbers, and many others that are important in mathematics but not to the understanding of computing. Let's review the relevant category definitions briefly.

First, let's define the general concept of a number: A **number** is a unit belonging to an abstract mathematical system and subject to specified laws of succession, addition, and multiplication. That is, a number is a representation of a value, and certain arithmetic operations can be consistently applied to such values.

Now let's separate numbers into categories. A **natural number** is the number 0 or any number obtained by repeatedly adding 1 to this number. Natural numbers are the ones we use in counting. A **negative number** is less than zero, and is opposite in sign to a positive number. An **integer** is any of the natural numbers or any of the negatives of these numbers. A **rational number** is an integer or the quotient of two integers—that is, any value that can be expressed as a fraction.

In this chapter we focus on natural numbers and how they are represented in various number systems. As part of that discussion we establish how all number systems relate to each other. In Chapter 3 we examine the computer representation of negative and rational numbers.

Some of the material in this chapter may be familiar to you. Certainly some of the underlying ideas should be. You probably take for granted some basic principles of numbers and arithmetic because you've become so used to them. Part of our goal in this chapter is to remind you of those underlying principles and show you that those principles apply to all number systems. Then, the idea that a computer uses binary values, 1s and 0s, to represent information should be less mysterious.

> **Number**   A unit of an abstract mathematical system subject to the laws of arithmetic
>
> **Natural number**   The number 0 and any number obtained by repeatedly adding 1 to it
>
> **Negative number**   A value less than 0, with a sign opposite to its positive counterpart
>
> **Integer**   A natural number, a negative of a natural number, or zero
>
> **Rational number**   An integer or the quotient of two integers (division by zero excluded)

2.2 Natural Numbers

How many ones are there in 943? That is, how many actual things does the number 943 represent? Well, in grade school terms you might say there are 9 hundreds plus 4 tens plus 3 ones. Or, said another way, there are 900 ones plus 40 ones plus 3 ones. So how many ones are there in 754? 700 ones plus 50 ones plus 4 ones. Right? Well, maybe. The answer depends on the *base* of the number system you are using. This answer is correct in the base-10, or decimal, number system, which is the number system we humans use every day. But that answer is not correct in other number system.

The **base** of a number system specifies the number of digits used in the system. The digits always begin with 0 and continue through one less than the base. For example, there are 2 digits in base 2: 0 and 1. There are 8 digits in base 8: 0 through 7. There are 10 digits in base 10: 0 through 9. The base also determines what the position of digits mean. When you add 1 to the last digit in the number system, you have a carry to the digit position to the left.

> **Base** The foundational value of a number system, which dictates the number of digits and the value of digit positions

Positional Notation

Numbers are written using **positional notation**. The rightmost digit represents its value times the base to the zeroth power. The digit to the left of that one represents its value times the base to the first power. The next digit represents its value times the base to the second power. The next digit represents its value times the base to the third power, and so on. You are so familiar with positional notation that you probably don't think about it. We used it instinctively to calculate the number of ones in 943.

> **Positional notation** A system of expressing numbers in which the digits are arranged in succession, the position of each digit has a place value, and the number is equal to the sum of the products of each digit by its place value[1]

$$
\begin{array}{rcrcr}
9 * 10^2 &=& 9 * 100 &=& 900 \\
+\ 4 * 10^1 &=& 4 * \ \ 10 &=& 40 \\
+\ 3 * 10^0 &=& 3 * \ \ \ \ 1 &=& \underline{\ \ 3} \\
& & & & 943
\end{array}
$$

A more formal way of defining positional notation is that the value is represented as a polynomial in the base of the number system. But what is a polynomial? A polynomial is a sum of two or more algebraic terms, each of which consists of a constant multiplied by one or more variables raised to a nonnegative integral power. When defining positional notation, the variable is the base of the number system. 943 is represented as a polynomial as follows, with x acting as the base.

$$9 * x^2 + 4 * x^1 + 3 * x^0$$

Let's express this idea formally. If a number in the base-R number system has n digits, it is represented as follows, where d_i represents the digit in the ith position in the number.

$$d_n * R^{n-1} + d_{n-1} * R^{n-2} + \cdots + d_2 * R + d_1$$

Look complicated? Let's look at a concrete example: 63578 in base 10. n is 5 (the number has 5 digits), and R is 10 (the base). The formula says that the fifth digit (last digit on the left) is multiplied by the base to the fourth power; the fourth digit is multiplied by the base to the third power; the third digit is multiplied by the base to the second power; the second digit is multiplied by the base to the first power; and the first digit is not multiplied by anything.

$$6 * 10^4 + 3 * 10^3 + 5 * 10^2 + 7 * 10^1 + 8$$

In the previous calculation, we have assumed that the number base is ten. This is a logical assumption since our number system *is* base ten. However, there is nothing about the number 943 that says it couldn't be representing a value in base 13. If so, to determine the number of ones, we would have to convert it to base 10.

The Importance of Zero

It is interesting to note that positional notation is only possible because of the concept of zero. Zero, which we usually take for granted, was the fundamental concept at the intersection of all branches of modern mathematics. As Georges Ifrah noted in his book, *The Universal History of Computing:* "To sum up, the vital discovery of zero gave the human mind an extraordinarily powerful potential. No other human creation has exercised such an influence on the development of mankind's intelligence." [2]

$$
\begin{array}{rcccccr}
9 & * & 13^2 & = & 9 * & 169 & = & 1521 \\
+ 4 & * & 13^1 & = & 4 * & 13 & = & 52 \\
+ 3 & * & 13^0 & = & 3 * & 1 & = & \underline{3} \\
& & & & & & & 1576
\end{array}
$$

Therefore, 943 in base 13 is equal to 1576 in base 10. Keep in mind that these two numbers have an equivalent value. That is, they both represent the same number of things. If a bag contains 943 (base 13) beans, and another bag contains 1576 (base 10) beans, both bags contain the exact same number of beans. Number systems just allow us to represent values in various ways.

Why would anyone want to represent values in base 13? It isn't done very often, granted, but it is sometimes helpful to understand how it works. For example, there is a computing technique called *hashing* that takes numbers and scrambles them, and one way to scramble numbers is to interpret them in a different base.

Other bases, such as base 2 (binary), are particularly important in computer processing. Let's explore these bases in more detail.

The Abacus

In our brief history of computing in Chapter 1, we mentioned the abacus as an early computing device. More specifically, the abacus is a device that uses positional notation to represent a decimal number. The beads in any one column represent the digit in that column. All columns combined represent a complete number.

Photo courtesy of Theresa DiDonato

The beads above the middle bar represent units of 5 and the beads below the bar each represent 1. Beads pushed away from the middle bar do not contribute to the number. The following diagram shows the number 27,091 represented on an abacus:

Photo courtesy of Theresa DiDonato

The user performs calculations by moving the beads in specific ways to reflect the basic arithmetic operations of addition, subtraction, multiplication, and division.

Though ancient, the abacus is still used today in many Asian cultures. In stores, a checkout clerk might use an abacus instead of an electronic cash register. Although lacking some of the advantages of electronic devices, the abacus is more than sufficient for the kinds of calculations needed for basic business transactions. And skilled users of an abacus can rival anyone with a calculator in terms of both speed and accuracy.

Children in these cultures learn rote operations on the abacus, much as you were drilled in your multiplication tables. To perform an operation on a number, the user executes a series of movements using only the thumb, pointing finger, and middle finger of one hand. These movements correspond to individual digits and depend on the operation being performed. For example, to add the digit 7 to the digit 5 already showing on the abacus, the user clears the five marker (pushes it to the top), pushes 2 onto the bar from below, and increments 1 in the next column. Though this move corresponds to the basic addition operation we do on paper, the abacus user is not thinking about the mathematics. The user is conditioned to execute a specific movement when specific digits are encountered for a specific operation. When the calculation is complete, the user reads the result as shown on the abacus.

Bi-Quinary Number Representation

The console of the IBM 650, a popular commercial computer in the late 1950s, allowed the operator to read the contents of memory using the bi-quinary system. This number representation system uses seven lights to represent the 10 decimal digits.

Photo courtesy of IBM Corporate Archives

Each digit is represented by two lights, one of the top two and one of the bottom five. If the upper-left light is on, the five other lights represent 0, 1, 2, 3, and 4, respectively, from top to bottom. If the upper-right light is on, the five other lights represent 5, 6, 7, 8, and 9. The following configuration represents the number 7:

The International Business Machine (IBM) 650 was called the Ford Tri-Motor of computers: Like the Ford Tri-Motor, old IBM 650s were shipped to Latin America where they enjoyed an extended life.

Binary, Octal, and Hexadecimal

The base-2 (binary) number system is important in computing. It is also helpful to be familiar with number systems that are powers of 2, such as base 8 (octal), and base 16 (hexadecimal). Remember that the base value specifies the number of digits in the number system. Base 10 has ten digits (0–9), base 2 has two digits (0–1), and base 8 has eight digits (0–7). Therefore, the number 943 could not represent a value in any base less than base 10, because the digit 9 doesn't exist in those bases. It is, however, a valid number in base 10 or any base higher than that. Likewise, the number 2074 is a valid number in base 8 or higher, but it simply does not exist (because it uses the digit 7) in any base lower than that.

What are the digits in bases higher than 10? We need symbols to represent the digits that correspond to the decimal values 10 and beyond. In bases higher than 10, we use letters as digits. We use the letter A to represent the number 10, B to represent 11, C to represent 12, etc. Therefore, the 16 digits in base 16 are:

0, 1, 2, 3, 4, 5, 6, 7, 8, 9, A, B, C, D, E, and F

Let's look at values in octal, hexadecimal, and binary to see what they represent in base 10. For example, let's calculate the decimal equivalent of 754 in octal (base 8). As before, we just expand the number in its polynomial form and add up the numbers.

$$
\begin{array}{rcl}
7 * 8^2 = 7 * 64 = & 448 \\
+ 5 * 8^1 = 5 * 8 = & 40 \\
+ 4 * 8^0 = 4 * 1 = & \underline{4} \\
& 492
\end{array}
$$

Let's convert the hexadecimal number ABC to decimal:

$$
\begin{array}{rcl}
A * 16^2 = 10 * 256 = & 2560 \\
+ B * 16^1 = 11 * 16 = & 176 \\
+ C * 16^0 = 12 * 1 = & \underline{12} \\
& 2748
\end{array}
$$

Note that we perform the exact same calculation to convert the number to base 10. We just use a base value of 16 this time, and we have to remember what the letter digits represent. After a little practice you won't find the use of letters as digits that strange.

Finally, let's convert a binary (base-2) number 1010110 to decimal. Once again, we perform the same steps; only the base value changes:

$$
\begin{array}{rcccccc}
  1 & * & 2^6 & = 1 & * & 64 & = 64 \\
+ 0 & * & 2^5 & = 0 & * & 32 & = 0 \\
+ 1 & * & 2^4 & = 1 & * & 16 & = 16 \\
+ 0 & * & 2^3 & = 0 & * & 8 & = 0 \\
+ 1 & * & 2^2 & = 1 & * & 4 & = 4 \\
+ 1 & * & 2^1 & = 1 & * & 2 & = 2 \\
+ 0 & * & 2^0 & = 0 & * & 1 & = \underline{0} \\
  &   &   &   &   &   & 86
\end{array}
$$

Recall that the digits in any number system go up to one less than the base value. To represent the base value in that base, you need two digits. In any base, a 0 in the rightmost position and a 1 in the second position represent the value of the base itself. So 10 is ten in base 10 and 10 is eight in base 8 and 10 is sixteen in base 16. Think about it. The consistency of number systems is actually quite elegant.

Addition and subtraction of numbers in other bases are performed exactly like they are on decimal numbers.

Arithmetic in Other Bases

Recall the basic idea of arithmetic in decimal. 0 + 1 is 1, 1 + 1 is 2, 2 + 1 is 3, and so on. Things get interesting when you try to add two numbers whose sum is equal to or larger than the base value. For example: 1 + 9. Because there isn't a symbol for 10, we reuse the same digits and rely on position. The rightmost digit reverts to 0, and there is a carry into the next position to the left. Thus 1 + 9 equals 10 in base 10.

The rules of binary arithmetic are analogous, but we run out of digits much sooner. 0 + 1 is 1, and 1 + 1 is 0 with a carry. Then the same rule is applied to every column in a larger number, and the process continues until there are no more digits to add. The example below adds the binary values 101110 and 11011. The carry value is marked above each column in color.

```
  11111      ← carry
   101110
+   11011
  1001001
```

We can convince ourselves that this answer is correct by converting both operands to base 10, adding them, and comparing the result. 101110 is 46, 11011 is 27, and the sum is 73. 101001 is 73 in base 10.

The subtraction facts that you learned in grade school were that $9 - 1$ is 8, $8 - 1$ is 7, and so on until you try to subtract a larger digit from a smaller one, such as $0 - 1$. To accomplish this, you have to "borrow one" from the next left digit of the number from which you are subtracting. More precisely, you borrow one power of the base. So in base 10, when you borrow, you borrow 10. The same logic applies to binary subtraction. Every time you borrow in a binary subtraction, you borrow 2. Here is an example with the borrowed values marked above.

```
      1
    0̸2 2   ← borrow
   111001
 −    110
   110011
```

Once again, you can check the calculation by converting all values to base 10 and subtract to see if the answers correspond.

Power of Two Number Systems

Binary and octal numbers have a very special relationship to one another: Given a number in binary, you can read it off in octal and given a number in octal, you can read it off in binary. For example, take the octal number 754. If you replace each digit with the binary representation of that digit, you have 754 in binary. That is, 7 in octal is 111 in binary, 5 in octal is 101 in binary, 4 in octal is 100 in binary, so 754 in octal is 111101100 in binary.

To facilitate this type of conversion, the table below shows counting in binary from 0 through 10 with their octal and decimal equivalents.

Binary	Octal	Decimal
000	0	0
001	1	1
010	2	2
011	3	3
100	4	4
101	5	5
110	6	6
111	7	7
1000	10	8
1001	11	9
1010	12	10

To convert from binary to octal, you start at the rightmost binary digit and mark the digits in groups of threes. Then you convert each group of three to its octal value.

111 101 100
 7   5   4

Let's convert the binary number 1010110 to octal, and then convert that octal value to decimal. The answer should be the equivalent of 1010110 in decimal, or 86.

1 010 110
1 2   6

$$1 * 8^2 = 1 * 64 = 64$$
$$+ 2 * 8^1 = 2 * 8 = 16$$
$$+ 6 * 8^0 = 6 * 1 = 6$$
$$86$$

The reason that binary can be immediately converted to octal and octal to binary is that 8 is a power of 2. There is a similar relationship between binary and hexadecimal. Every hexadecimal digit can be represented in four binary digits. Let's take the binary number 1010110 and convert it to hexadecimal by marking of the digits from right to left in groups of four.

101 0110
 5   6

$$5 * 16^1 = 5 * 16 = 80$$
$$+ 6 * 16^0 = 6 * 1 = 6$$
$$86$$

Now let's convert ABC in hexadecimal to binary. It takes four binary digits to represent each hex digit. A in hexadecimal is 10 in decimal and therefore is 1010 in binary. Likewise, B in hexadecimal is 1011 in binary, and C in hexadecimal is 1100 in binary. Therefore, ABC in hexadecimal is 101010111100 in binary.

Rather than confirming that 10001001010 is 2748 in decimal directly, let's mark it off in octal and convert the octal.

101 010 111 100
 5   2   7   4

5274 in octal is 2748 in decimal.

In the next section, we show how to convert base-10 numbers to the equivalent number in another base.

Napier's Bones, An Early Calculation Aid

Invented in 1617 by Scotsman John Napier, Napier's Bones was a set of rectangular bones (tiles) marked off with numbers at the top of the face and multiples of that number down the face of the tile. Each tile (bone) represented the multiplication table for a single digit. These bones could be lined up beside one another in a way

Reproduced by permission of University of Calgary

that allowed the user to do one-digit multiplication using only addition.

John Napier also invented the slide rule and is given credit for discovering the binary number system. For more on Napier and how to use his bones, see our Web site.

Converting from Base 10 to Other Bases

The rules for converting base-10 numbers involve dividing by the base into which you are converting the number. From this division, you get a quotient and a remainder. The remainder becomes the next digit in the new number (from right to left), and the quotient replaces the number to be converted. The process continues until the quotient is zero. Let's write the rules in a different form.

> While the quotient is not zero
>   Divide the decimal number by the new base
>   Make the remainder the next digit to the left in the answer
>   Replace the decimal number with the quotient

These rules form an *algorithm* for converting from base 10 to another base. An algorithm is a logical sequence of steps that solves a problem. We have much more to say about algorithms in later chapters. Here we show one way of describing an algorithm and show how we can apply it to perform the conversions.

The first line of the algorithm tells us to repeat the next three lines until the quotient from our division becomes zero. Let's convert the decimal number 2748 to hexadecimal. As we've seen in previous examples, the answer should be ABC.

```
     171     ← quotient
16 ⟌2748
     16
     114
     112
      28
      16
      12     ← remainder
```

The remainder (12) is the first digit in the hexadecimal answer, represented by the digit C. So the answer so far is C. Since the quotient is not zero, we divide it (171) by the new base.

```
     10      ← quotient
16 ⟌171
     16
     11      ← remainder
```

The remainder (11) is the next digit to the left in the answer, which is represented by the digit B. Now the answer so far is BC. Since the quotient is not zero, we divide it (10) by the new base.

```
     0       ← quotient
16 ⟌10
     0
     10      ← remainder
```

The remainder (10) is the next digit to the left in the answer, which is represented by the digit A. Now the answer is ABC. The quotient is zero, so we are finished, and the final answer is ABC.

Binary Values and Computers

Although some of the early computers were decimal machines, modern computers are binary machines. That is, numbers within the computer are represented in binary form. In fact, all information is somehow represented using binary values. The reason is that each storage location within a computer either contains a low-voltage signal or a high-voltage signal. Because each location can have one of two states, it is logical to equate those states to 0 and 1. A low-voltage signal is equated with a 0, and a high-voltage signal is equated with a 1. In fact, you can forget about voltages and think of each storage location as containing either a 0 or a 1. Note that a storage location cannot be empty: It must contain either a 0 or a 1.

Each storage unit is called a **binary digit** or **bit** for short. Bits are grouped together into **bytes** (8 bits), and bytes are grouped together into units called **words**. The number of bits in a word is known as the word length of the computer. For example, IBM 370 architecture in the late

Binary digit A digit in the binary number system; a 0 or a 1

Bit Short for binary digit

Byte Eight binary digits

Word A group of one or more bytes; the number of bits in a word is the word length of the computer.

Grace Murray Hopper

From 1943 until her death on New Year's Day in 1992, Admiral Grace Murray Hopper was intimately involved with computing. In 1991, she was awarded the National Medal of Technology "for her pioneering accomplishments in the development of computer programming languages that simplified computer technology and opened the door to a significantly larger universe of users."

Admiral Hopper was born Grace Brewster Murray in New York City on December 9, 1906. She attended Vassar and received a Ph.D. in mathematics from Yale. For the next 10 years, she taught mathematics at Vassar.

In 1943, Admiral Hopper joined the U.S. Navy and was assigned to the Bureau of Ordnance Computation Project at Harvard University as a programmer on the Mark I. After the war, she remained at Harvard as a faculty member and continued work on the Navy's Mark II and Mark III computers. In 1949, she joined Eckert-Mauchly Computer Corporation and worked on the UNIVAC I. It was there that she made a legendary contribution to computing: She discovered the first computer "bug"—a moth caught in the hardware.

Admiral Hopper had a working compiler in 1952, a time when the conventional wisdom was that computers could do only arithmetic. Although not on the committee that designed the computer language COBOL, she was active in its design, implementation, and use. COBOL (which stands for Common Business-Oriented Language) was developed in the early 1960s and is still widely used in the business data processing.

Admiral Hopper retired from the Navy in 1966, only to be recalled within a year to full-time active duty. Her mission was to oversee the Navy's efforts to maintain uniformity in programming languages. It has been said that just as Admiral Hyman Rickover was the father of the nuclear navy, Rear Admiral Hopper was the mother of computerized data automation in the Navy. She served with the Naval Data Automation Command until she retired again in 1986 with the rank of Rear Admiral. At the time of her death, she was a senior consultant at Digital Equipment Corporation.

During her lifetime, Admiral Hopper received honorary degrees from more than 40 colleges and universities. She was honored by her peers on several occasions, including the first Computer Sciences Man of the Year award given by the Data Processing Management Association, and the Contributors to Computer Science Education Award given by the Special Interest Group for Computer Science Education, which is part of the ACM (Association for Computing Machinery).

Admiral Hopper loved young people and enjoyed giving talks on college and university campuses. She often handed out colored wires, which she called nanoseconds because they were cut to a length of about one foot—the distance that light travels in a nanosecond (billionth of a second). Her advice to the young was, "You manage things, you lead people. We went overboard on management and forgot about the leadership."

When asked which of her many accomplishments she was most proud of, she answered, "All the young people I have trained over the years."

1970s had half words (2 bytes or 16 bits), full words (4 bytes), and double words (8 bytes).

Modern computers are often 32-bit machines (such as Intel's Pentium III processor) or 64-bit machines (such as Compaq's Alpha processors and Intel's Itanium processor). However, some microprocessors that are used in applications such as pagers are 8-bit machines. The computing machine you are using, whatever it is, is ultimately supported by the binary number system.

We have more to explore about the relationship between computers and binary numbers. In the next chapter we examine many kinds of data and see how they are represented in a computer. In Chapter 4 we see how to control electrical signals that represent binary values. And in Chapter 7 we see how binary numbers are used to represent program commands that the computer executes.

Summary

Numbers are written using positional notation, in which the digits are arranged in succession, the position of each digit has a place value, and the number is equal to the sum of the products of each digit by its place value. The place values are powers of the base of the number system. Thus, in the decimal number system, the place values are powers of 10; in the binary number system, the place values are powers of 2.

Arithmetic can be performed on numbers in any base represented in positional notation. The same number facts apply to other bases as they do to base 10. Adding 1 to the largest digit in the base causes a carry into the next position.

Base 2, base 8, and base 16 are all related because the bases are powers of 2. This relationship provides a quick way to convert between numbers in these bases. Computer hardware is designed using numbers in base 2. A low-voltage signal is equated with 0 and a high-voltage signal is equated with 1.

ETHICAL ISSUES

The Digital Divide

Over the past few years, society's dependence on computer technology has increased dramatically. The ability to communicate via e-mail and to access the Internet has become an essential part of every day life for many Americans. The U.S. Department of Commerce says that over half of U.S. households were reported to have Internet access in the year 2000. This means that the other half lack access to the Internet and/or the technological skills to use it. The term *digital divide* has come to represent this disparity between the Information Age "haves" and "have-nots."

This gap is of growing social concern. Rural communities, minority households, low-income families, and people with disabilities do not have the same Internet access as the more advantaged. In terms of education, the quantity and quality of computers and web connections in schools varies greatly across demographic regions. Furthermore, it is not enough to have the necessary hardware; teachers must have the training to use the technology and the understanding of it can enhance student learning. Programs such as the federally supported E-Rate Program, established in 1996, are responding to these inequalities within schools and libraries by providing financial discounts to needy schools.

From a global perspective, the digital divide illustrates an additional challenge that developing nations must face as they make their way into the international community. Without the necessary telecommunication infrastructures to support Internet access, emerging countries are at a serious disadvantage. Only 16 percent of the world's population utilizes 90 percent of its Internet host computers—clear evidence of this disparity. Indeed, the entire continent of Africa has fewer Internet connections than New York City. International organizations are making the technological gap between countries a top priority. The turn of the millennium saw the creation of the Digital Opportunity Task force (DOT force), an initiative designed to expand global access to computer technology. Similarly, in 2001, the UN's Task Force on Information and Communications Technology (ICT) was established to confront the digital divide and bridge the gap between nations.

The digital divide brings to light the serious impact that computer technology has on society, both domestic and global. It is an issue that the world will undoubtedly continue to address throughout the 21st century and into the next.

Key Terms

Base pg. 35	Negative number pg. 34
Binary digit pg. 43	Number pg. 34
Bit pg. 43	Positional notation pg. 35
Byte pg. 43	Rational number pg. 34
Integer pg. 34	Word pg. 43
Natural number pg. 34	

Exercises

1. Distinguish between a natural number and a negative number.
2. Distinguish between a natural number and a rational number.
3. Label the following numbers as natural, negative, or rational.
   a. 1.333333
   b. −1/3
   c. 1066
   d. 2/5
   e. 6.2
   f. π(pi)

4. How many ones are there in 891 if it is a number in each of the following bases?
   a. base 10   d. base 13
   b. base 8   e. base 16
   c. base 12

5. Express 891 as a polynomial in each of the bases in Exercise 4.

6. Convert the following numbers from the base shown to base 10.
   a. 111 (base 2)   d. 777 (base 16)
   b. 777 (base 8)   e. 111 (base 8)
   c. FEC (base 16)

7. Explain how base 2 and base 8 are related.

8. Explain how base 8 and base 16 are related.

9. Expand the table on page 40 to include the decimal numbers from 11 through 16.

10. Expand the table in Exercise 9 to include hexadecimal numbers.

11. Convert the following octal numbers to binary.
    a. 766   d. 142
    b. 101   e. 889
    c. 202

12. Convert the following binary numbers to octal.
    a. 111110110   d. 1100010
    b. 1000001   e. 111000111
    c. 010000010

13. Convert the following binary numbers to hexadecimal.
    a. 111110110
    b. 1000001
    c. 010000010
    d. 1100010
    e. 111000111

14. Convert the following octal numbers to hexadecimal.
    a. 777
    b. 605
    c. 443
    d. 521
    e. 1

15. Convert the following decimal numbers to octal.
    a. 901
    b. 321
    c. 1492
    d. 1066
    e. 2001

16. Convert the following decimal numbers to binary.
    a. 45
    b. 69
    c. 1066
    d. 99
    e. 1

17. Convert the following decimal numbers to hexadecimal.
    a. 1066
    b. 1939
    c. 1
    d. 998
    e. 43

18. If you were going to represent numbers in base 18, what symbols might you use to represent the decimal numbers 10 through 17 other than letters?

19. Convert the following decimal numbers to base 18 using the symbols you suggested in Exercise 18.
    a. 1066
    b. 99099
    c. 1

20. Perform the following binary additions.
    a. 1110011 + 11001
    b. 1111111 + 11111
    c. 1010101 + 10101

21. Perform the following octal additions.
    a. 770 + 665
    b. 101 + 707
    c. 202 + 667

22. Perform the following hexadecimal additions.
    a. 19AB6 + 43
    b. AE9 + F
    c. 1066 + ABCD

23. Perform the following binary subtractions.
    a. 1100111 − 111
    b. 1010110 − 101
    c. 1111111 − 111

24. Perform the following octal subtractions.
    a. 1066 − 776
    b. 1234 − 765
    c. 7766 − 5544

25. Perform the following hexadecimal subtractions.
    a. ABC − 111
    b. 9988 − AB
    c. A9F8 − 1492

26. Why are binary numbers important in computing?

27. A byte contains how many bits?

28. How many bytes are there in one word of a 64-bit machine?

29. Why do microprocessors such as pagers have only 8-bit words?

30. Why is important to study how to manipulate fixed-sized numbers?

? Thought Questions

1. Exercise 3 asked you to classify π as one of the options. π does not belong in any of the categories named; π (and *e)* are transcendental numbers. Look up transcendental numbers in the dictionary or in an old math book and give the definition in your own words.

2. Complex numbers are another category of numbers that are not discussed in this chapter. Look up complex numbers in a dictionary or an old math book and give the definition in your own words.

3. Many everyday occurrences can be represented as a binary bit. For example, a door is open or not open, the stove is on or off, the dog is asleep or awake. Could relationships be represented as a binary value? Discuss the question giving examples.

4. The digital divide puts those that have access to technology on one side and those that do not on the other. Do you feel that it is the right of everyone to have access to technology?

5. It will cost a great deal of money to erase the digital divide. Who do you think should be responsible for paying the cost?

6. Having access to technology is not enough; people must be taught to use the technology they have. How would you define computer literacy for each of the following groups of people?
   • high school students in an industrialized country
   • kindergarten teachers in an industrialized country
   • college graduates in an industrialized country
   • students in sub-Saharan Africa
   • college graduates in sub-Saharan Africa
   • government officials in the Andes

The Information Layer

3 Data Representation

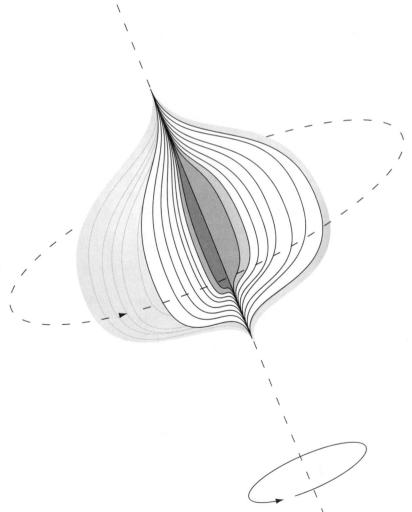

Chapter 3

Data Representation

When you go on a trip, you probably follow a road map. The map is not the land over which you travel; it is a representation of that land. The map has captured the essential information needed to accomplish the goal of getting from one place to another.

Likewise, the data we need to store and manage on a computer must be represented in a way that captures the essence of the information, and it must do so in a form convenient for computer processing. Building on the fundamental concepts of the binary number system established in Chapter 2, this chapter explores how we represent and store the various kinds of information a computer manages.

Goals

After studying this chapter, you should be able to:

- distinguish between analog and digital information.
- explain data compression and calculate compression ratios.
- explain the binary formats for negative and floating-point values.
- describe the characteristics of the ASCII and Unicode character sets.
- perform various types of text compression.
- explain the nature of sound and its representation.
- explain how RGB values define a color.
- distinguish between raster and vector graphics.
- explain temporal and spatial video compression.

3.1   Data and Computers

Without data, computers would be useless. Every task a computer undertakes deals with managing data in some way. Therefore, our need to represent and organize that data in appropriate ways is paramount.

In the not-so-distant past, computers dealt almost exclusively with numeric and textual data, but now computers are truly **multimedia** devices, dealing with a vast array of information categories. Computers store, present, and help us modify many different types of data, including:

Multimedia   Several different media types

Data compression Reducing the amount of space needed to store a piece of data

Bandwidth   The number of bits or bytes that can be transmitted from one place to another in a fixed amount of time

- Numbers
- Text
- Audio
- Images and graphics
- Video

Ultimately, all of this data is stored as binary digits. Each document, picture, and sound bite is somehow represented as strings of 1s and 0s. This chapter explores each of these types of data in turn and discusses the basic ideas behind the ways in which we represent these types of data on a computer.

We can't discuss data representation without also talking about **data compression**—reducing the amount of space needed to store a piece of data. In the past we needed to keep data small because of storage limitations. Today, computer storage is relatively cheap; but now we have an even more pressing reason to shrink our data: the need to share it with others. The Web and its underlying networks have inherent **bandwidth** restrictions that define the maximum number of bits or bytes that can be transmitted from one place to another in a fixed amount of time.

The **compression ratio** gives an indication of how much compression occurs. The compression ratio is the size of the compressed data divided by the size of the original data. The values could be in bits or characters or whatever is appropriate as long as both values are measuring the same thing. The ratio should result in a number between 0 and 1. The closer the ratio is to zero, the tighter the compression.

A data compression technique can be **lossless**, which means the data can be retrieved without losing any of the original information. Or it can be **lossy**, in which case some information is lost in the process of compaction. Although we never want to lose information, in some cases the loss is acceptable. When dealing with data representation and compression, we always face a tradeoff between accuracy and size.

Analog and Digital Information

The natural world, for the most part, is continuous and infinite. A number line is continuous, with values growing infinitely large and small. That is, you can always come up with a number larger or smaller than any given number. And the numeric space between two integers is infinite. For instance, any number can be divided in half. But the world is not just infinite in a mathematical sense. The spectrum of colors is a continuous rainbow of infinite shades. Objects in the real world move through continuous and infinite space. Theoretically, you could always close the distance between you and a wall by half, and you would never actually reach the wall.

Computers, on the other hand, are finite. Computer memory and other hardware devices have only so much room to store and manipulate a certain amount of data. We always fail in our attempt to represent an infinite world on a finite machine. The goal, then, is to represent enough of the world to satisfy our computational needs and our senses of sight and sound. We want to make our representations good enough to get the job done, whatever that job might be.

Information can be represented in one of two ways: analog or digital. **Analog data** is a continuous representation, analogous to the actual information it represents. **Digital data** is a discrete representation, breaking the information up into separate elements.

A mercury thermometer is an analog device. The mercury rises in a continuous flow in the tube in direct proportion to the temperature. We calibrate and mark the tube so that we can read the current temperature, usually as an integer such as 75 degrees Fahrenheit. However, a mercury thermometer is actually rising in a continuous manner between degrees. So at some point in time the temperature is actually 74.568 degrees

Compression ratio The size of the compressed data divided by the size of the uncompressed data

Lossless compression A technique in which there is no loss of information

Lossy compression A technique in which there is loss of information

Analog data Information represented in a continuous form

Digital data Information represented in a discrete form

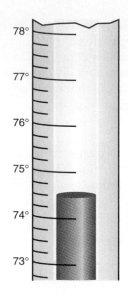

Figure 3.1
A mercury thermometer continually rises in direct proportion to the temperature

Fahrenheit, and the mercury is accurately indicating that, even if our markings are not fine enough to note such small changes. See Figure 3.1.

Analog information is directly proportional to the continuous, infinite world around us. Computers, therefore, cannot work well with analog information. So instead, we **digitize** information by breaking it into pieces and representing those pieces separately. Each of the representations we discuss in this chapter has found an appropriate way to take a continuous entity and separate it into discrete elements. Those discrete elements are then individually represented using binary digits.

Digitize   The act of breaking information down into discrete pieces

But why do we use binary? We know from Chapter 2 that binary is just one of many equivalent number systems. Couldn't we use, say, the decimal number system, with which we are already more familiar? We could. In fact, it's been done. Computers have been built that are based on other number systems. However, modern computers are designed to use and manage binary values because the devices that store and manage the data are far less expensive and far more reliable if they only have to represent one of two possible values.

Also, electronic signals are far easier to maintain if they transfer only binary data. An analog signal continually fluctuates in voltage up and down. But a digital signal has only a high or low state, corresponding to the two binary digits. See Figure 3.2.

All electronic signals (both analog and digital) degrade as they move down a line. That is, the voltage of the signal fluctuates due to environmental effects. The trouble is that as soon as an analog signal degrades,

Figure 3.2
An analog and a digital signal

information is lost. Since any voltage level within the range is valid, it's impossible to know what the original signal state was or even that it changed at all.

Digital signals, on the other hand, jump sharply between two extremes. This is referred to as **pulse-code modulation** (PCM). A digital signal can degrade quite a bit before any information is lost, because any voltage value above a certain threshold is considered a high value, and any value below that threshold is considered a low value. Periodically, a digital signal is **reclocked** to regain its original shape. As long as it is reclocked before too much degradation occurs, no information is lost. Figure 3.3 shows the degradation effects of analog and digital signals.

> **Pulse-code modulation**
> Variation in a signal that jumps sharply between two extremes
>
> **Reclock**   The act of reasserting an original digital signal before too much degradation occurs

Binary Representations

As we undertake the details of representing particular types of data, it's important to remember the inherent nature of using binary. One bit can be either 0 or 1. There are no other possibilities. Therefore, one bit can represent only two things. For example, if we wanted to classify a food as being either sweet or sour, we would need only one bit to do it. We could say that if the bit is 0, the food is sweet, and if the bit is 1, the food is sour. But if we want to have additional classifications (such as spicy), one bit is not sufficient.

To represent more than two things, we need multiple bits. Two bits can represent four things because there are four combinations of 0 and 1 that can be made from two bits: 00, 01, 10, and 11. So, for instance, if we want to represent which of four possible gears a car is in (park, drive, reverse, or neutral), we need only two bits. Park could be represented by 00, drive by 01, reverse by 10, and neutral by 11. The actual mapping between bit combinations and the thing each combination represents is sometimes irrelevant (00 could be used to represent reverse, if you prefer), though

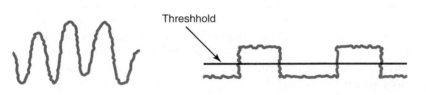

Threshhold

Figure 3.3
Degradation of analog and digital signals

1 Bit	2 Bits	3 Bits	4 Bits	5 Bits
0	00	000	0000	00000
1	01	001	0001	00001
	10	010	0010	00010
	11	011	0011	00011
		100	0100	00100
		101	0101	00101
		110	0110	00110
		111	0111	00111
			1000	01000
			1001	01001
			1010	01010
			1011	01011
			1100	01100
			1101	01101
			1110	01110
			1111	01111
				10000
				10001
				10010
				10011
				10100
				10101
				10110
				10111
				11000
				11001
				11010
				11011
				11100
				11101
				11110
				11111

Figure 3.4
Bit combinations

sometimes the mapping can be meaningful and important, as we discuss in later sections of this chapter.

If we want to represent more than four things, we need more than two bits. Three bits can represent eight things because there are eight combinations of 0 and 1 that can be made from three bits. Likewise, four bits can represent 16 things, five bits can represent 32 things, and so on. See Figure 3.4. Note that the bit combinations are simply counting in binary as you move down a column.

In general, n bits can represent 2^n things because there are 2^n combinations of 0 and 1 that can be made from n bits. Note that every time we increase the number of available bits by 1, we double the number of things we can represent.

Let's turn the question around. How many bits do you need to represent, say, 25 unique things? Well, four bits wouldn't be enough because four bits can represent only 16 things. We would have to use at least five bits, which would allow us to represent 32 things. Since we only need to represent 25 things, some of the bit combinations would not have a valid interpretation.

Keep in mind that even though we may technically need only a certain minimum number of bits to represent a set of items, we may allocate more than that for the storage of that data. There is a minimum number of bits that a computer architecture can address and move around at one time, and it is usually a power of two, such as 8, 16, or 32 bits. Therefore, the minimum amount of storage given to any type of data is in multiples of that value.

3.2 Representing Numeric Data

Numeric values are the most prevalent type of data used in a computer system. Unlike other types of data, there may seem to be no need to come up with a clever mapping between binary codes and numeric data. Since binary is a number system, there is a natural relationship between the numeric information and the binary values that we store to represent them. This is true, in general, for positive integer data. The basic issues regarding integer conversions were covered in Chapter 2 in the general discussion of the binary system and its equivalence to other bases. However, there are other issues regarding the representation of numeric information to consider at this point. Integers are just the beginning in terms of numeric data. This section discusses the representation of negative and noninteger values.

Representing Negative Values

Aren't negative numbers just numbers with a minus sign in front? Perhaps. That is certainly one valid way to think about them. Let's explore the issue of negative numbers, and discuss appropriate ways to represent them on a computer.

Signed-Magnitude Representation

You have used the **signed-magnitude representation** of numbers since you first learned about negative numbers in grade school. In the traditional

> **Sign-magnitude representation** Number representation in which the sign represents the ordering of the number (negative and positive) and the value represents the magnitude

decimal system, a sign (+ or −) is placed before a number's value, though the positive sign is often assumed. The sign represents the ordering, and the digits represent the magnitude of the number. The classic number line looks something like this, in which a negative sign meant that the number was to the left of zero and the positive number was to the right of zero.

− Negative   + Positive (sign usually omitted)

Performing addition and subtraction with signed integer numbers can be described as moving a certain number of units in one direction or another. To add two numbers you find the first number on the scale and move in the direction of the sign of the second as many units as specified. Subtraction was done in a similar way, moving along the number line as dictated by the sign and the operation. In grade school you soon graduated to doing addition and subtraction without using the number line.

There is a problem with the sign-magnitude representation: There are two representations of zero. There is plus zero and minus zero. The idea of a negative zero doesn't necessarily bother us; we just ignore negative zero entirely. However, two representations of zero within a computer can cause unnecessary complexity, so other representations of negative numbers are used. Let's examine another alternative.

Fixed-Sized Numbers

If we allow only a fixed number of values, we can represent numbers as just integer values, where half of them represent negative numbers. The sign is determined by the magnitude of the number. For example, if the maximum number of decimal digits we can represent is two, we can let 1 through 49 be the positive numbers 1 through 49 and let 50 through 99 represent the negative numbers −50 through −1. Let's take the number line and number the negative values on the top according to this scheme:

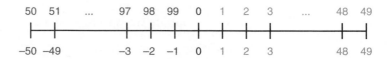

To perform addition within this scheme, you just add the numbers together and discard any carry. Adding positive numbers should be ok;

let's try adding a positive number and a negative number, a negative number and a positive number, and two negative numbers. These are shown below in sign-magnitude and in this scheme. (Note that the carries are discarded.)

Sign-Magnitude	New Scheme
5	5
+ − 6	+ 94
− 1	99
− 4	96
+ 6	+ 6
2	2
− 2	98
+ − 4	+ 96
− 6	94

What about subtraction, using this scheme for representing negative numbers? The key is in the relationship between addition and subtraction: A − B = A + (−B). We can subtract one number from another by adding the negative of the second to the first.

Sign − Magnitude	New Scheme	Add Negative
−5	95	95
− 3	− 3	+ 97
−8		92

In this example, we have assumed a fixed size of 100 values, and kept our numbers small enough to use the number line to calculate the negative representation of a number. However, there is a formula that you can use to compute the negative representation.

Negative(I) = 10^k − I, where k is the number of digits

This representation of negative numbers is called the **ten's complement**. Although humans tend to think in terms of sign and magnitude to represent numbers, the complement strategy is actually easier in some ways when it comes to electronic calculations. And since we store everything in a modern computer in binary, we use the binary equivalent of the ten's complement, called the two's complement.

Ten's complement A representation of negative numbers such that the negative of I is 10 raised to k minus I.

Two's Complement
Let's assume that a number must be represented in eight bits. To make it easier to look at long binary numbers, we make the number line vertical:

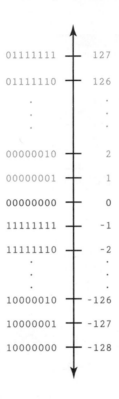

Addition and subtraction are accomplished the same way as in 10's complement arithmetic:

$$
\begin{array}{rl}
- \ 127 & 10000001 \\
+ \quad 1 & 00000001 \\
\hline
- \ 126 & 10000010 \\
\end{array}
$$

Notice that with this representation, the leftmost bit in a negative number is always a 1. Therefore, you can tell immediately whether a binary number in two's complement is negative or positive.

Number Overflow
Overflow occurs when the value that we compute cannot fit into the number of bits we have allocated for the result. For example, if each value is stored using eight bits, adding 127 to 3 would overflow:

> **Overflow**   A situation where a calculated value cannot fit into the number of digits reserved for it

```
  01111111
+ 00000011
  10000010
```

100000010 in our scheme represents −126, not +130. If, however, we were not representing negative numbers, the result would be correct.

Overflow is a classic example of the type of problems we encounter by mapping an infinite world onto a finite machine. No matter how many bits we allocate for a number, there is always the potential need to represent a number that doesn't fit. How overflow problems are handled varies by computer hardware and by the differences in programming languages.

Representing Real Numbers

In computing, we call all noninteger values (that can be represented) *real* values. For our purposes here, we define a real number as a value with a potential fractional part. That is, real numbers have a whole part and a fractional part, either of which may be zero. For example, some real numbers in base 10 are 104.32, 0.999999, 357.0, and 3.14159.

As we explored in Chapter 2, the digits represent values according to their position, and those position values are relative to the base. To the left of the decimal point, in base 10, we have the 1s position, the 10s position, the 100s position, etc. These position values come from raising the base value to increasing powers (moving from the decimal point to the left). The positions to the right of the decimal point work the same way, except the powers are negative. So the positions to the right of the decimal point are the tenths position (10^{-1} or one tenth), the hundredths position (10^{-2} or one hundredth), etc.

In binary, the same rules apply but the base value is 2. Since we are not working in base 10, the decimal point is referred to as a **radix point**, a term that can be used in any base. The positions to the right of the radix point in binary are the halves position (2^{-1} or one half), the quarters position (2^{-2} or one quarter), etc.

So how do we represent a real value in a computer? We store the value as an integer and include information showing where the radix point is. That is, any real value can be described by three properties: the sign (positive or negative one), the mantissa, which is made up of the digits in the value with the radix point assumed to be to the right, and the exponent, which determines how the radix point is shifted relative to the mantissa. A real value in base 10 can therefore be defined by the following formula:

sign * mantissa * 10^{exp}

The representation is called **floating point** because the number of digits is fixed but the radix point floats. When a value is in floating-point form, a

> **Radix point** The dot that separates the whole part from the fractional part in a real number in any base
>
> **Floating point** A representation of a real number that keeps track of the sign, mantissa, and exponent

Table 3.1 Values in decimal notation and floating-point notation (five digits)

Real Value	Floating-Point Value
12001.00	$12001 * 10^0$
−120.01	$−12001 * 10^{-2}$
0.12000	$1200 * 10^{-5}$
−123.1	$−12310 * 10^2$
1555555555	$15555 * 10^3$

positive exponent shifts the decimal point to the right, and a negative exponent shifts the decimal point to the left.

Let's look at how to convert a real number expressed in our usual decimal notation into floating point. For example, consider the number 148.69. The sign is positive, and there are two digits to the right of the decimal point. Thus, the exponent is $−2$, giving us $14869 * 10^{-2}$. Table 3.1 shows other examples. For the sake of this discussion, we assume that only five digits can be represented.

How do we convert a value in floating-point form back into decimal notation? The exponent on the base tells us how many positions to move the radix point. If the exponent is negative, we move the radix point to the left. If the exponent is positive, we move the radix point to the right. Apply this scheme to the floating-point values in Table 3.1.

Notice that in the last example in Table 3.1, we lose information. Since we are only storing five digits to represent the significant digits (the mantissa), the whole part of the value is not accurately represented in floating-point notation.

Likewise, a binary floating-point value is defined by the following formula:

$$sign * mantissa * 2^{exp}$$

Note that only the base value has changed. Of course, the mantissa would only contain binary digits. To store a floating-point number in binary on a computer, we can store the three values that define it. For example, according to a common standard, if we devote 64 bits to the storage of a floating-point value, we use 1 bit for the sign, 11 bits for the exponent, and 52 bits for the mantissa. Internally, this format is taken into account any time the value is used in a calculation or is displayed.

Scientific notation is a term with which you may already be familiar, so we mention it here. Scientific notation is a form of floating-point representation in which the decimal point is kept to the right of the leftmost digit.

Scientific notation An alternative floating-point representation

That is, there is one whole number. In many programming languages, if you print out a large real value without specifying how to print it, the value is printed in scientific notation. Because exponents could not be printed in early machines, an "E" was used instead. For example, 12001.32708 would be written as 1.200132708E+4 in scientific notation.

3.3   Representing Text

A text document can be decomposed into paragraphs, sentences, words, and ultimately individual characters. To represent a text document in digital form, we simply need to be able to represent every possible character that may appear. The document is the continuous (analog) entity, and the separate characters are the discrete (digital) elements that we need to represent and store in computer memory.

We should distinguish at this point between the basic idea of representing text and the more involved concept of word processing. When we create a document in a word processing program such as Microsoft Word, we can specify all kinds of formatting: fonts, margins, tabs, color, and so on. Many word processors also let us add art, equations, and other elements. This extra information is stored with the rest of the text so that the document can be displayed and printed the way you want it. The core issue, however, is the way we represent the characters themselves; therefore, those techniques remain our focus at this point.

There are a finite number of characters to represent. So the general approach for representing characters is to list them all and assign each a binary string. To store a particular letter, we store the appropriate bit string.

So what characters do we have to worry about? There are the 26 letters in the English language. But uppercase and lowercase letters have to be treated separately, so that's really 52 unique characters. Various punctuation characters also have to be represented, as do the numeric digits (the actual characters '0', '1', through '9'). Even the space character must have a representation. And what about languages other than English? The list of characters we may want to represent starts to grow quickly once you begin to think about it. Keep in mind that, as we discussed earlier in this chapter, the number of unique things (characters in this case) we want to represent determines how many bits we'll need to represent any one of them.

A **character set** is simply a list of characters and the codes used to represent each one. There have been several character sets used over the years, though a few have dominated. By agreeing to use a particular character set, computer manufacturers have made the processing of text data easier. We explore two character sets in the following sections: ASCII and Unicode.

Character set   A list of the characters and the codes used to represent each one

The ASCII Character Set

ASCII stands for American Standard Code for Information Interchange. The ASCII character set originally used seven bits to represent each character, allowing for 128 unique characters. The eighth bit in each character byte was originally used as a *check bit*, which helped ensure proper data transmission. Later ASCII evolved so that all eight bits were used to represent a character. This eight-bit version is formally called the Latin–1 Extended ASCII character set. The extended ASCII set allows for 256 characters and includes accented letters as well as several additional special symbols. The entire extended ASCII character set is shown in Figure 3.5.

The codes in this chart are expressed as decimal numbers, but these values get translated to their binary equivalent for storage. Note that the ASCII characters have a distinct order based on the codes used to store them. Each character has a relative position (before or after) every other character. This property is helpful in various ways. For example, note that both the uppercase and lowercase letters are in order. Therefore, we can use the character codes to help us put a list of words into alphabetical order.

Left Digit(s)	Right Digit	0	1	2	3	4	5	6	7	8	9
						ASCII					
0		NUL	SOH	STX	ETX	EOT	ENQ	ACK	BEL	BS	HT
1		LF	VT	FF	CR	SO	SI	DLE	DC1	DC2	DC3
2		DC4	NAK	SYN	ETB	CAN	EM	SUB	ESC	FS	GS
3		RS	US	□	!	"	#	$	%	&	'
4		(	)	*	+	,	–	.	/	0	1
5		2	3	4	5	6	7	8	9	:	;
6		<	=	>	?	@	A	B	C	D	E
7		F	G	H	I	J	K	L	M	N	O
8		P	Q	R	S	T	U	V	W	X	Y
9		Z	[	\	]	^	_	`	a	b	c
10		d	e	f	g	h	i	j	k	l	m
11		n	o	p	q	r	s	t	u	v	w
12		x	y	z	{			}	~	DEL		

Figure 3.5   The ASCII character set

Also note that the first 32 characters in the ASCII character chart do not have a simple character representation that you could print to the screen. These characters are reserved for special purposes such as carriage return and tab. These characters are usually interpreted in special ways by whatever program is processing the information.

The Unicode Character Set

The extended version of the ASCII character set provides 256 characters, which is enough for English but not enough for international use. This limitation gave rise to the Unicode character set, which has a much stronger international influence.

The goal of the people who created Unicode is nothing less than to represent every character in every language used in the entire world, including all of the Asian ideograms. It also represents many additional special-purpose characters such as scientific symbols.

To accomplish this, the Unicode character set uses 16 bits per character. Therefore, the Unicode character set can represent 2^{16}, or over 65 thousand, characters. Compare that to the 256 characters represented in the extended ASCII set.

The Unicode character set is gaining popularity and is used by many programming languages and computer systems today. However, the character set itself is still evolving. Not all of the available codes have been assigned to particular characters. Figure 3.6 shows a few select characters currently represented in the Unicode character set.

For consistency, Unicode was designed to be a superset of ASCII. That is, the first 256 characters in the Unicode character set correspond exactly

Code (Hex)	Character	Source
0041	A	English (Latin)
042F	Я	Russian (Cyrillic)
OE09	ฤ	Thai
13EA	ꮹ	Cherokee
211E	℞	Letterlike Symbols
21CC	⇌	Arrows
282F	⠯	Braille
345F	佄	Chinese/Japanese/Korean (Common)

Figure 3.6
A few characters in the Unicode character set

to the extended ASCII character set, including the codes used to represent them. Therefore, programs that assume ASCII values are unaffected even if the underlying system embraces the Unicode approach.

Text Compression

Alphabetic information (text) is a fundamental type of data. Therefore, it is important that we find ways to store text efficiently and transmit text efficiently between one computer and another. The following sections examine three types of text compression:

- keyword encoding
- run-length encoding
- Huffman encoding

As we discuss later in this chapter, some of the underlying ideas of these text compression techniques come into play when dealing with other types of data as well.

Keyword Encoding

Consider how often you use words such as "the," "and," "which," "that," and "what." If these words took up less space (that is, had fewer characters), our documents would shrink in size. Even though the savings on each word would be small, they are used so often in a typical document that the combined savings would add up quickly.

One fairly straightforward method of text compression is called **keyword encoding**, in which frequently used words are replaced with a single character. To decompress the document, you reverse the process: replace the single characters with the appropriate full word.

> **Keyword encoding**
> Substituting a frequently used word with a single character

For example, suppose we used the following chart to encode a few words:

Word	Symbol
as	^
the	~
and	+
that	$
must	&
well	%
those	#

Let's encode the following paragraph:

> The human body is composed of many independent systems, such as the circulatory system, the respiratory system, and the reproductive system. Not only must all systems work independently, they must interact and cooperate as well. Overall health is a function of the well-being of separate systems, as well as how these separate systems work in concert.

The encoded paragraph is:

> The human body is composed of many independent systems, such ^ ~ circulatory system, ~ respiratory system, + ~ reproductive system. Not only & each system work independently, they & interact + cooperate ^ %. Overall health is a function of ~ %-being of separate systems, ^ % ^ how # separate systems work in concert.

There are a total of 349 characters in the original paragraph including spaces and punctuation. The encoded paragraph contains 314 characters, resulting in a savings of 35 characters. The compression ratio for this example is 314/349 or approximately 0.9.

There are several limitations to keyword encoding. First, note that the characters we use to encode the keywords cannot be part of the original text. If, for example, the '$' was part of the original paragraph, the resulting encoding would be ambiguous. We wouldn't know whether a '$' represented the word "that" or if it was the actual dollar-sign character. This limits the number of words we can encode as well as the nature of the text that we are encoding.

Also, note that the word "The" in the example is not encoded by the '~' character because the word "The" and the word "the" contain different letters. Remember, the uppercase and lowercase versions of the same letter are different characters when it comes to storing them on a computer. A separate symbol for "The" would have to be used if we wanted to encode it.

Finally, note that we would not gain anything to encode words such as "a" and "I" because it would simply be replacing one character for another. The longer the word, the more compression we get per word. Unfortunately, the most frequently used words are often short. On the other hand, some documents use certain words more frequently than others depending on the subject matter. For example, we would have some nice savings if we had chosen to encode the word "system" in our example, but it might not be worth encoding in a general situation.

An extension of keyword encoding is to replace specific patterns of text with special characters. The encoded patterns are generally not complete words, but rather parts of words such as common prefixes and suffixes— "ex", "ing", and "tion," for instance. An advantage of this approach is that patterns being encoded generally appear more often than whole words (because they appear in many different words). A disadvantage, as before, is that they are generally short patterns and the replacement savings per word is small.

Run-Length Encoding

In some situations, a single character may be repeated over and over again in a long sequence. This type of repetition doesn't generally take place in English text, but often occurs in large data streams, such as DNA sequences. A text compression technique called **run-length encoding** capitalizes on these situations. Run-length encoding is sometimes called *recurrence coding*.

> **Run-length encoding**
> Replacing a long series of a repeated character with a count of the repetition

In run-length encoding, a sequence of repeated characters is replaced by a *flag character*, followed by the repeated character, followed by a single digit that indicates how many times the character is repeated. For example, consider the following string of seven repeated 'A' characters:

AAAAAAA

If we use the '*' character as our flag, this string would be encoded as:

*A7

The flag character is the indication that the series of three characters (including the flag) should be decoded into the appropriate repetitious string. All other text is treated regularly. Therefore, the following encoded string:

*n5*x9ccc*h6 some other text *k8eee

would be decoded into the following original text:

nnnnnxxxxxxxxxcccchhhhhh some other text kkkkkkkkeee

The original text contains 51 characters, and the encoded string contains 35 characters, giving us a compression ratio in this example of 35/51 or approximately 0.68.

Note that in this example the three repeated 'c' characters and the three repeated 'e' characters are not encoded. Since it takes three characters to encode a repetition sequence, it is not worth it to encode strings of two or three. In fact, in the case of two repeated characters, encoding would actually make the string longer!

Since we are using one character for the repetition count, it seems that we can't encode repetition lengths greater than nine. However, keep in mind that each character is represented by a series of bits based on some character set. For example, the character '5' is represented as ASCII value 53, which in an eight-bit binary string is 00110101. So, instead of interpreting the count character as an ASCII digit, we could interpret it as a binary number. If we do that, we can have repetition counts between 0 and 255, or even between 4 and 259 since runs of three or less are not represented.

Huffman Encoding

Another text compression technique, called **Huffman encoding**, is named after its creator, Dr. David Huffman. Why should the character "X", which is seldom used in text, take up the same number of bits as the blank, which is used very frequently? Huffman codes address this question by using variable-length bit strings to represent each character. That is, a few characters may be represented by five bits, and another few by six bits, and yet another few by seven bits, and so forth. This approach is contrary to the idea of a character set, in which each character is represented by a fixed-length bit string (such as 8 or 16).

The idea behind this approach is that if we use only a few bits to represent characters that appear often and reserve longer bit strings for characters that don't appear often, the overall size of the document being represented is small.

For example, suppose we use the following Huffman encoding to represent a few characters:

Huffman Code	Character
00	A
01	E
100	L
110	O
111	R
1010	B
1011	D

> **Huffman encoding**
> Using a variable-length binary string to represent a character so that frequently used characters have short codes

Then the word DOORBELL would be encoded in binary as:

1011110110111101001100100

If we used a fixed-size bit string to represent each character (say, 8 bits), then the binary form of the original string would be 8 characters times 8 bits or 64 bits. The Huffman encoding for that string is 25 bits long, giving a compression ratio of 25/64, or approximately 0.39.

What about the decoding process? When we use character sets, we just take the bits in chunks of 8 or 16 bits to see what character it represents. In Huffman encoding, with its variable length codes, it seems like we might get confused trying to decode a string because we don't know how many bits we should include for each character. But that potential confusion has been eliminated by the way the codes are created.

An important characteristic of any Huffman encoding is that no bit string used to represent a character is the prefix of any other bit string used to represent a character. Therefore, as we scan left to right across a bit string, when we find a string that corresponds to a character, that must be the character it represents. It can't be part of a larger bit string.

Therefore, if the following bit string is created with the previous table:

1010110001111011

it must be decoded into the word BOARD. There is no other possibility.

So how is a particular set of Huffman codes created to begin with? Well, the details of that process are a bit beyond the scope of this book, but let's discuss the underlying issue. Since Huffman codes use the shortest bit strings for the most common characters, we start with a table that lists the frequency of the characters we want to encode. Frequencies may come from counting characters in a particular document (352 E's, 248 S's, and so on) or from counting characters in a sample of text from a particular content area. A frequency table may also come from a general idea of how frequently letters occur in a particular language such as English. Using those values, we can construct a structure from which the binary codes can be read. The way the structure is created ensures that the most frequently used characters get the shortest bit strings.

3.4 Representing Audio Information

We perceive sound when a series of air compressions vibrate a membrane in our ear, which sends signals to our brain. Thus a sound is defined in nature by the wave of air that interacts with our eardrum. See Figure 3.7. To represent a sound, we must somehow represent the appropriate sound wave.

A stereo sends an electrical signal to a speaker to produce sound. This signal is an analog representation of the sound wave. The voltage in the signal varies in direct proportion to the sound wave. The speaker receives the signal and causes a membrane to vibrate, which in turn vibrates the air (creating a sound wave), which in turn vibrates the eardrum. The created sound wave is hopefully identical to the one that was captured initially, or at least good enough to please the listener.

To represent audio information on a computer, we must digitize the sound wave, somehow breaking it into discrete, manageable pieces. One

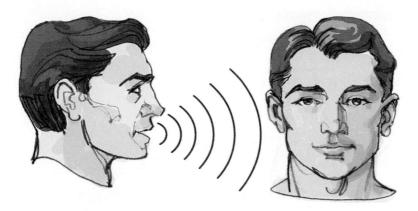

Figure 3.7
A sound wave vibrates our eardrums

way to accomplish this is to actually digitize the analog representation of the sound. That is, take the electric signal that represents the sound wave and represent it as a series of discrete numeric values.

An analog signal varies in voltage continuously. To digitize the signal we periodically measure the voltage of the signal and record the appropriate numeric value. This process is called *sampling*. Instead of a continuous signal, we end up with a series of numbers representing distinct voltage levels.

To reproduce the sound, the stored voltage values are used to create a new continuous electronic signal. The assumption is that the voltage levels in the original signal changed evenly between one stored voltage value and the next. If enough samples are taken in a short period of time, that assumption is reasonable. But certainly the process of sampling can lose information, as shown in Figure 3.8.

In general, a sampling rate of around 40,000 times per second is enough to create a reasonable sound reproduction. If the sampling rate is much

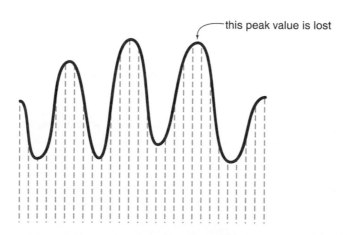

this peak value is lost

Figure 3.8
Sampling an audio signal

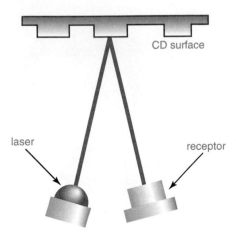

CD surface

laser

receptor

Figure 3.9
A CD player reading binary
information

lower than that, the human ear begins to hear distortions. A higher
sampling rate produces better quality sound, but after a certain point the
extra data is irrelevant because the human ear can't hear the difference.
The overall result is affected by many factors, including the quality of the
equipment, the type of sound, and the human listening.

A vinyl record album is an analog representation of the sound wave.
The needle of a record player (turntable) rides up and down in the spiral
groove of the album. The rise and fall of the needle is analogous to the
voltage changes of the signal that represents the sound.

A compact disc (CD), on the other hand, stores audio information digitally. On the surface of the CD are microscopic pits that represent binary
digits. A low intensity laser is pointed at the disc. The laser light reflects
strongly if the surface is smooth and reflects poorly if the surface is pitted.
A receptor analyzes the reflection and produces the appropriate string of
binary data, which represents the numeric voltage values that were stored
when the signal was digitized. The signal is reproduced and sent to the
speaker. This process is shown in Figure 3.9.

Audio Formats
Over the past few years there have been several popular formats for audio
information, including WAV, AU, AIFF, VQF, and MP3. All of these are
based on the storage of voltage values sampled from analog signals, but all
format the details of the information in different ways and all use various
compression techniques to one extent or another.

Currently, the dominant format for compressing audio data is MP3. The popularity of MP3 resulted mostly from a stronger compression ratio than others available at the time. Other formats may prove more efficient in the future, but for now MP3 is the general favorite. In mid–1999 the term "MP3" was searched for more than any other term and is still going strong today. Let's look at the details of the MP3 format a little more closely.

The MP3 Audio Format

MP3 is short for MPEG–2, audio layer 3 file. MPEG is an acronym for the Moving Picture Experts Group, which is an international committee that develops standards for digital audio and video compression.

MP3 employs both lossy and lossless compression. First it analyzes the frequency spread and compares it to mathematical models of human psychoacoustics (the study of the interrelation between the ear and the brain), then it discards information that can't be heard by humans. Then the bit stream is compressed using a form of Huffman encoding to achieve additional compression.

There are many software tools available on the Web to help you create MP3 files. These tools generally require that the recording be stored in some other common format, such as WAV, before that data is converted into MP3 format, significantly reducing the file size.

3.5   Representing Images and Graphics

Images such as photographs and graphics such as line drawings have common issues when it comes to their representation and compression. We first look at the general idea of representing color, then turn to the various techniques for digitizing and representing visual information.

Representing Color

Color is our perception of the various frequencies of light that reach the retinas of our eyes. Our retinas have three types of color photoreceptor cone cells that respond to different sets of frequencies. These photoreceptor categories correspond to the colors of red, green, and blue. All other colors perceptible by the human eye can be made by combining various amounts of these three colors.

Therefore, color is often expressed in a computer as an RGB (red-green-blue) value, which is actually three numbers that indicate the relative contribution of each of these three primary colors. If each number in the triple is given on a scale of 0 to 255, then 0 means no contribution of that color, and 255 means full contribution of that color. For example, an RGB

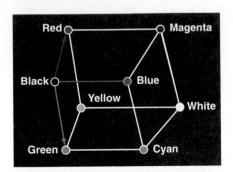

Figure 3.10
Three-dimensional color space

value of (255, 255, 0) maximizes the contribution of red and green, and minimizes the contribution of blue, which results in a bright yellow.

The concept of RGB values gives rise to a three-dimensional "color space." One way to display such a color space is shown in Figure 3.10.

The amount of data that is used to represent a color is called the *color depth*. It is usually expressed in terms of the number of bits that are used to represent its color. *HiColor* is a term that indicates a 16-bit color depth. Five bits are used for each number in an RGB value and the extra bit is sometimes used to represent transparency. *TrueColor* indicates a 24-bit color depth. Therefore, each number in an RGB value gets eight bits, which gives the range of 0 to 255 for each. This results in the ability to represent over 16.7 million unique colors.

The following chart shows a few TrueColor RGB values and the colors they represent:

RGB Value			Actual Color
Red	Green	Blue	
0	0	0	black
255	255	255	white
255	255	0	yellow
255	130	255	pink
146	81	0	brown
157	95	82	purple
140	0	0	maroon

Keep in mind that 24-bit TrueColor provides more colors than the human eye can distinguish. To reduce file sizes, a technique called *indexed color* is

Bob Bemer

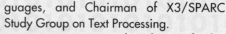

Bob Bemer has been a fixture in computing circles since 1945. His resume reads like a list of the influential computing companies of the last half-century. He worked for Douglas Aircraft, RKO Radio Pictures, the Rand Corporation, Lockheed Aircraft, Marquardt Aircraft, Lockheed Missiles and Space, IBM, Univac Division of Sperry Rand, Bull General Electric (Paris), GTE, Honeywell, and finally his own software company, Bob Bemer Software.

The predominance of aircraft manufacturers on Bemer's resume is not surprising because he studied mathematics and holds a Certificate in Aeronautical Engineering from Curtiss-Wright Technical Institute (1941). In the early days of computing, aircraft manufacturers were pioneers in using computers in industry.

During his career Bemer was active in programming language development. He developed FORTRANSET, an early FORTRAN compiler. He was actively involved in the development of the COBOL language and the CODASYL language, an early approach to data base modeling and management. In addition, he was responsible for authorizing funding for the development of SIMULA, a simulation language that introduced many object-oriented features.

Bemer was also an active participant in committees formed to bring universal standards into the new computing industry. He was U.S. representative on the IFIP Computer Vocabulary Committee, Chairman of ISO/TC97/SC5 on Common Programming Lan-

guages, and Chairman of X3/SPARC Study Group on Text Processing.

However, Bemer is best known for his work on the ASCII computer code, which is the standard internal code for 8-bit PCs today. Early on Bemer recognized that if computers were going to communicate with each other, they needed a standard code for transmitting textual information. Bemer made and published a survey of over 60 different computer codes, thus demonstrating a need for a standard code. He created the program of work for the standards committee, forced the U.S. standard code to correspond to the international code, wrote the bulk of the articles published about the code, and pushed for a formal registry of ASCII-alternate symbol and control sets to accommodate other languages.

Perhaps Bemer's most important contribution is the concept of an escape character. The escape character alerts the system processing the characters that the character(s) following the escape character change the standard meaning of the characters to follow. For example, ESC (N alerts the system that the following characters are in the Cyrillic equivalent of ASCII.

The first version of a 16-bit code called Unicode was published in October 1991. Two factors drove the need for an enlarged code: 16-bit computer architecture was becoming popular, and the expansion of the Internet and the WWW drove the need for a code that could directly include the world's alphabets. ASCII, however, has not gone away; it remains a subset of Unicode.

often used. That is, a particular application such as a browser may support only a certain number of specific colors, creating a palette from which to choose. The palette color closest to the actual color is displayed by the browser. For example, Figure 3.11 shows the Netscape Navigator's color palette.

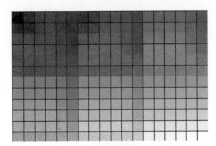

Figure 3.11
The Netscape color palette

Digitized Images and Graphics

A photograph is an analog representation of an image. It is continuous across its surface, with shades of one color blending into another. Digitizing a picture is the act of representing it as a collection of individual dots called **pixels**, a term that stands for picture elements. Each pixel is composed of a single color. The number of pixels used to represent a picture is called the **resolution**. If enough pixels are used (high resolution), and are then presented in the proper order side by side, the human eye can be fooled into thinking it's viewing a continuous picture.

Figure 3.12 shows a digitized picture, with a small portion of it magnified to show the individual pixels.

The storage of image information on a pixel-by-pixel basis is called a **raster-graphics format**. There are several popular raster file formats in use, including bitmap (BMP), GIF, and JPEG.

A *bitmap file* is one of the most straightforward graphic representations. In addition to a few administrative details, a bitmap file contains the

Pixels Individual dots used to represent a picture; stands for picture elements

Resolution The number of pixels used to represent a picture

Raster-graphics format Storing image information pixel by pixel

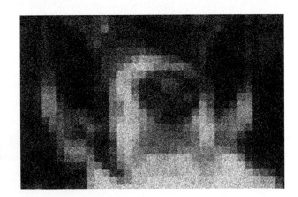

Figure 3.12 A digitized picture composed of many individual pixels Courtesy of Amy Rose

pixel color values of the image from left to right and top to bottom. A bitmap file supports 24-bit TrueColor, though usually the color depth can be specified to reduce the file size. A bitmap file may be compressed using run-length encoding as described earlier in this chapter.

The GIF format (Graphics Interchange Format), developed by CompuServe in 1987, uses indexed color exclusively to reduce file size, which limits the number of available colors to 256. If even fewer colors are required, the color depth can usually be specified to fewer bits. GIF files are best used for graphics and images with few colors, and are therefore considered optimal for line art.

The JPEG format is designed to exploit the nature of our eyes. Humans are more sensitive to gradual changes of brightness and color over distance than we are to rapid changes. Therefore, the data that the JPEG format stores averages out the color hues over short distances. The JPEG format is considered superior for photographic color images. A fairly complicated compression scheme significantly reduced file sizes.

Vector Representation of Graphics

Vector graphics is another technique for representing images. Instead of assigning colors to pixels as we do in raster graphics, a vector-graphics format describes an image in terms of lines and geometric shapes. A vector graphic is a series of commands that describe a line's direction, thickness, and color. The file sizes for these formats tend to be small because every pixel does not have to be accounted for. The complexity of the image, such as the number of items in the picture, determines the file size.

A raster graphic such as a GIF must be encoded multiple times for different sizes and proportions. Vector graphics can be resized mathematically, and these changes can be calculated dynamically as needed.

However, vector graphics is not good for representing real-world images. JPEG images are far superior in that regard, but vector graphics is good for line art and cartoon-style drawings.

The most popular vector format used on the Web today is called Flash. Flash images are stored in a binary format and require a special editor to create. A new vector format, called Scalable Vector Graphics (SVG), is under development. SVG is expressed in plain text. When the SVG format is finalized, it is likely to make vector graphics a popular approach for web-based imaging.

> **Vector graphics** Representation of an image in terms of lines and shapes

> **Einstein describes the telegraph**
> "You see, wire telegraph is a kind of very, very long cat," explained Albert Einstein. "You pull its tail in New York and his head is meowing in Los Angeles...And radio operates exactly the same way: you send signals here, they receive them there. The only difference is that there is no cat."
>
> How do you think he would describe a computer?

3.6   Representing Video

Video information is one of the most complex types of information to capture and compress to get a result that makes sense to the human eye. Video clips contain the equivalent of many still images, each of which must be compressed. The Web is full of video clips that are choppy and hard to follow. This situation will likely improve over the next few years, depending on the evolving sophistication of video compression techniques, which are referred to as video codecs.

Video Codecs

Codec stand for COmpressor/DECompressor. A **video codec** refers to the methods used to shrink the size of a movie to allow it to be played on a computer or over a network. Almost all video codecs use lossy compression to minimize the huge amounts of data associated with video. The goal therefore is not to lose information that affects the viewer's senses.

Most codecs are block oriented, meaning that each frame of a video is divided into rectangular blocks. The codecs differ in how the blocks are encoded. Some video codecs are accomplished completely in software, while others require special hardware.

Video codecs employ two types of compression: temporal and spatial. **Temporal compression** looks for differences between consecutive frames. If most of an image in two frames hasn't changed, why should we waste space to duplicate all of the similar information? A *keyframe* is chosen as the basis to compare the differences, and its entire image is stored. For consecutive images, only the changes (called *delta frames*) are stored. Temporal compression is effective in video that changes little from frame to frame, such as a scene that contains little movement.

Spatial compression removes redundant information within a frame. This problem is essentially the same as that faced when compressing still images. Spatial video compression often groups pixels into blocks (rectangular areas) that have the same color, such as a portion of a clear blue sky. Instead of storing each pixel, the color and the coordinates of the area are stored instead. This idea is similar to run-length encoding described earlier in this chapter.

Various video codecs are popular today, including Sorenson, Cinepak, MPEG, and Real Video. The details of how these codecs work are beyond the scope of this book.

Video codec   Methods used to shrink the size of a movie

Temporal compression   Movie compression technique based on differences between consecutive frames

Spatial compression   Movie compression technique based on the same compression techniques used for still images

Summary

Computers are multimedia devices that manipulate data varying in form from numbers to graphics to video. Because a computer can only manipulate binary values, all forms of data must be represented in binary form. Data is classified as being continuous (analog) or discrete (digital).

Integer values are represented by their binary equivalent, using one of several techniques for representing negative numbers, such a sign magnitude or one's complement. Real numbers are represented by a triple made up of the sign, the digits in the number, and an exponent that specifies the radix point.

A character set is a list of alphanumeric characters and the codes that represent each one. The most common character set is Unicode (16 bits for each character), which has ASCII as a subset. The 8-bit ASCII set is sufficient for English but not for other (or multiple) languages. There are various ways for compressing text so that it takes less space to store it or less time to transmit it from one machine to another.

Audio information is represented as digitized sound waves. Color is represented by three values that represent the contribution of each of red, blue, and green. There are two basic techniques for representing pictures, bitmaps and vector graphics. Video is broken up into a series of still images, each of which is represented as a picture.

ETHICAL ISSUES

Napster

In 1999, Shawn Fanning launched a file-sharing program that took the music industry by storm, rapidly gaining the praise of millions and the criticism of many. Nineteen-year-old Shawn had only recently dropped out of his first year at Northeastern University to pursue a solution to the difficulty of downloading and exchanging music over the Net. With the support of his uncle, Shawn tackled this problem with dedication and ingenuity and, in a few months, developed an answer. Shawn wrote source code that wove together a search engine, file sharing, and Internet Relay Chat, making it possible for anyone to easily access and trade music files. Napster was born, and with it a fresh controversy over intellectual property rights and privileges.

Napster worked through the direct exchange of files from one computer to another. This peer-to-peer sharing allows users to bypass a central server, access music files from computers located all over the world, and download those files. The ease of this application led to its immediate popularity, especially among college students, who used Napster more than any other age group. An additional factor in the appeal of Napster was that the user did not pay for the music. The music industry's objection to Napster stemmed from the fact that this property changes hands at no charge. Artists and labels collected no royalties when their music was copied through Napster, and they might lose prospective customers. Opponents argued that Napster infringed on copyrights and that the file-swapping service should be shut down. Napster disagreed, asserting that the music files are personal files and therefore are not the responsibility of the company.

There are some artists who supported Napster, believing that getting their music out and having people listen to it was more important than the money they could earn from it. Like many musicians, Dave Matthews, from the Dave Matthews Band, saw Napster as a new and exciting means of communicating. He said, "It is the future, in my opinion." Other musicians felt that Napster did not hurt sales, but rather helped introduce their music to people who will then buy the CDs. Still others felt strongly that Napster threatened the protection of their name and creativity. Many artists were not opposed to the idea behind Napster, but felt that Napster should obtain their permission before including their music.

The legal case that confronted Napster's facilitation of unauthorized copying has resulted in filtering and blocking programs that make certain music unavailable to users. A subscription fee to use Napster, as well as more advanced filtering technology, are among possible solutions to the Napster case. The future of music and the Internet is full of possibilities, and the resolution of this case will no doubt greatly impact what that future will hold.

Key Terms

Analog data pg. 53

Bandwidth pg. 52

Character set pg. 63

Compression ratio pg. 53

Data compression pg. 52

Digital data pg. 53

Digitize pg. 54

Floating point pg. 61

Huffman encoding pg. 69

Keyword encoding pg. 66

Lossless compression pg. 53

Lossy compression pg. 53

Exercises

1. What is data compression and why is it an important topic today?

2. What is the difference between lossless and lossy data compression?

3. Why do computers have difficulty with analog information?

4. Is a clock with a sweeping second hand an analog or a digital device? Explain.

5. What does it mean to digitize something?

6. What is pulse-code modulation?

7. How many things can be represented with:
   a. four bits.
   b. five bits.
   c. six bits.
   d. seven bits.

8. Although you have been computing simple arithmetic operations since the second grade, take the following small test to confirm that you thoroughly understand operations on signed integers.

   Evaluate the following expressions, where W is 17, X is 28, Y is −29, and Z is −13.
   a. X + Y   b. X + W   c. Z + W   d. Y + Z
   e. W − Z   f. X − W   g. Y − W   h. Z − Y

9. Use the base-ten number line to prove the solutions to the following operations, where A is 5 and B is −7.
   a. A + B
   b. A − B
   c. B + A
   d. B − A

10. Given a fixed-sized number scheme, where k in the formula for the ten's complement is 6 (see page 59), answer the following questions.

     a. How many positive integers can be represented?

     b. How many negative integers can be represented?

     c. Draw the number line showing the three smallest and largest positive numbers, the three smallest and largest negative numbers, and zero.

11. Use the number line on page 58 to calculate the following expressions, where A is −499999 and B is 3.

     a. A + B

     b. A − B

     c. B + A

     d. B − A

12. Use the formula for the ten's complement to calculate the following numbers in the scheme described in on page 59.

     a. 35768

     b. −35768

     c. −4455

     d. −12345

13. In calculating the ten's complement in Exercise 12, did you have trouble borrowing from so many zeros? Such calculations are error prone. There is a trick that you can use that makes the calculation easier and thus less prone to errors: Subtract from all 9's and then add 1. A number subtracted from all 9's is called the nine's complement of the number.

     a. Prove that the nine's complement of a number plus 1 is equal to the ten's complement of the same number.

     b. Use the nine's complement plus one to calculate the values in Exercise 12 b, c, and d.

     c. Which did you find easier to use, the direct calculation of the ten's complement or the nine's complement plus 1? Justify your answer.

14. Evaluate the following expressions, where A is 00110011 and B is 01010101

     a. A + B

     b. A − B

     c. B − A

     d. −B

     e. −(−A)

15. Is the two's complement of a number always a negative number? Explain.

16. The one's complement of a number is analogous to the nine's complement of a decimal number. Use the scheme outlined in Exercise 13 to calculate the results of Exercise 14, using the one's complement rather than the two's complement.

17. How is a real value stored in a computer?

18. Convert the rules for subtraction in a sign-magnitude system to the algorithm format.

19. How many bits would be needed to represent a character set containing 45 characters? Why?

20. How can the decimal number 175.23 be represented as a sign, mantissa, and exponent?

21. What is the main difference between the ASCII and Unicode character sets?

22. Create a keyword encoding table that contains a few simple words. Rewrite a paragraph of your choosing using this encoding scheme. Compute the compression ratio you achieve.

23. How would the following string of characters be represented using run-length encoding?

    AAAABBBCCCCCCCCDDDD hi there EEEEEEEEEFF

24. Given the following Huffman encoding table, decipher the bit strings below.

Huffman Code	Character
00	A
11	E
010	T
0110	C
0111	L
1000	S
1011	R
10010	O
10011	I
101000	N
101001	F
101010	H
101011	D

a. 1101110001011
b. 011010101010010101011111000
c. 10100100101000010001000010100110110
d. 1010001001010100010001110100 0100011

25. How do humans perceive sound?

26. Is a stereo speaker an analog or a digital device? Explain.

27. What is an RGB value?

28. What does color depth indicate?

29. How does pixel resolution affect the visual impact of an image?

30. Explain temporal video compression.

31. Describe a situation in which spatial video compression would be effective.

32. Define sampling as it relates to digitizing sound waves.

33. Which produces better sound quality, higher sampling rates or lower sampling rates?

34. What is the sampling rate per second that is enough to create reasonable sound reproduction?

35. Do vinyl record albums and compact discs record sound the same way?

36. What does an RGB value of (130, 0, 255) mean?

37. What color does an RGB value of (255, 255, 255) represent?

38. What is resolution?

39. The GIF format uses what technique?

40. What are GIF files best for?

41. How are the various video codecs alike?

42. How are the various video codecs different?

43. Name two types of video compression.

44. What do we call the perception of the various frequencies of light that reach the retinas of our eyes?

45. What is the best format for photographic color images?

46. What are the techniques called that shrink the sizes of movies?

47. What is the technique in which an application supports only a certain number of specific colors, creating a palette from which to choose?

48. What is the format that describes an image in terms of lines and geometric shapes?

49. What format stores information on a pixel-by-pixel basis?

50. What is the difference between HiColor and TrueColor?

? Thought Questions

1. Devise a number system based on base 11.
   a. Draw the number line.
   b. Show examples of addition and subtraction.
   c. Develop a representation of negative numbers based on eleven's complement.
2. Technology is changing rapidly. What changes have occurred in data compression since this book was written?
3. What are the arguments for allowing music to be shared freely over the Internet?
4. What are the arguments against allowing music to be freely shared over the Internet?
5. What is the state of music sharing over the Internet at the time you are reading this question?
6. If you were an artist, which side of the argument would you take?

The Hardware Layer

4 Gates and Circuits

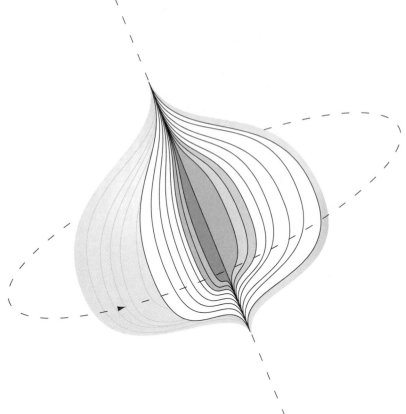

Chapter 4

Gates and Circuits

Computers are electronic devices; the most fundamental hardware elements of a computer control the flow of electricity. In a very primitive sense, we use technology to harness the power of a lightning bolt, bending it to our will so that we can perform calculations and make decisions. This chapter dances the fine line between computer science and electrical engineering, examining the most basic hardware elements in a computer.

In Chapter 2, we looked at number systems in general and at the binary number system in particular. And, as we saw in Chapter 3, the binary number system is of special interest because it is used to represent information in a computer. In this chapter, we explore how computers use electric signals to represent and manipulate those binary values.

Goals

After studying this chapter, you should be able to:

- identify the basic gates and describe the behavior of each.
- describe how gates are implemented using transistors.
- combine basic gates into circuits.
- describe the behavior of a gate or circuit using Boolean expressions, truth tables, and logic diagrams.
- compare and contrast a half adder and a full adder.
- describe how a multiplexer works.
- explain how an S-R latch operates.
- describe the characteristics of the four generations of integrated circuits.

4.1   Computers and Electricity

Any given electronic signal has a level of voltage. As we mentioned in the last chapter, we distinguish between the two values of interest (binary 0 and 1) by the voltage level of a signal. In general, a voltage level in the range of 0 to 2 volts is considered "low" and is interpreted as a binary 0. A signal in the 2- to 5-volt range is considered "high" and is interpreted as a binary 1. Signals in a computer are constrained to be within one range or the other.

A **gate** is a device that performs a basic operation on electrical signals. A gate accepts one or more input signals, and produces a single output signal. There are several specific types of gates; we examine the six most fundamental types in this chapter. Each type of gate performs a particular logical function.

Gates are combined into **circuits** to perform more complicated tasks. For example, circuits can be designed to perform arithmetic and to store values. In a circuit, the output value of one gate often serves as an input value for one or more other gates. The flow of electricity through a circuit is controlled by the carefully designed logic of the interacting gates.

There are three different, but equally powerful, notational methods for describing the behavior of gates and circuits:

- Boolean expressions
- logic diagrams
- truth tables

Gate   A device that performs a basic operation on electrical signals, accepting one or more input signals and producing a single output signal

Circuit   A combination of interacting gates designed to accomplish a specific logical function

George Boole[1]

Boolean algebra is named for its inventor, English mathematician George Boole, born in 1815. His father, a tradesman, began teaching him mathematics at an early age. But Boole was initially more interested in classical literature, languages, and religion—interests he maintained throughout his life. By the time he was 20, he had taught himself French, German, and Italian. He was well versed in the writings of Aristotle, Spinoza, Cicero, and Dante, and wrote several philosophical papers himself.

At 16 he took a position as a teaching assistant in a private school to help support his family. His work there plus a second teaching job left him little time to study. A few years later, he opened a school and began to learn higher mathematics on his own. In spite of his lack of formal training, his first scholarly paper was published in the *Cambridge Mathematical Journal* when he was just 24. In 1849, he was appointed professor of mathematics at Queen's College in Cork, Ireland. He became chair of mathematics and spent the rest of his career there. Boole went on the publish over 50 papers and several major works before he died in 1864, at the peak of his career.

Boole's *The Mathematical Analysis of Logic* was published in 1847. It would eventually form the basis for the development of digital computers. In the book, Boole set forth the formal axioms of logic (much like the axioms of geometry) on which the field of symbolic logic is built. Boole drew on the symbols and operations of algebra in creating his system of logic. He associated the value 1 with the universal set (the set representing everything in the universe) and the value 0 with the empty set, and restricted his system to these quantities. He then defined operations that are analogous to subtraction, addition, and multiplication.

In 1854, Boole published *An Investigation of the Laws of Thought, on Which Are Founded the Mathematical Theories of Logic and Probabilities*. This book described theorems built on his axioms of logic and extended the algebra to show how probabilities could be computed in a logical system. Five years later, Boole published *Treatise on Differential Equations*, followed by *Treaties on the Calculus of Finite Differences*. The latter is one of the cornerstones of numerical analysis, which deals with the accuracy of computations.

Boole received little recognition and few honors for his work. Given the importance of Boolean algebra in modern technology, it is hard to believe that his system of logic was not taken seriously until the early twentieth century. George Boole was truly one of the founders of computer science.

We examine all three types of representation during our discussion of gates and circuits.

An English mathematician named George Boole invented a form of algebra in which variables and functions take on only one of two values (0 and 1). This algebra is appropriately called **Boolean algebra**. Expressions in this algebraic notation are an elegant and powerful way to demonstrate the activity of electrical circuits. Specific operations and properties in Boolean algebra allow us to define and manipulate circuit logic using a mathematical notation. Boolean expressions come up again in our discussions of high-level programming languages in Chapter 8.

A **logic diagram** is a graphical representation of a circuit. Each type of gate is represented by a specific graphical symbol. By connecting those

Boolean algebra A mathematical notation for expressing two-valued logical functions

Logic diagram A graphical representation of a circuit; each type of gate has its own symbol.

89

symbols in various ways we can visually represent the logic of an entire circuit.

> **Truth table** A table showing all possible input values and the associated output values

A **truth table** defines the function of a gate by listing all possible input combinations that the gate could encounter, and the corresponding output. We can design more complex truth tables with sufficient rows and columns to show how entire circuits perform for any set of input values.

4.2   Gates

The gates in a computer are sometimes referred to as logic gates because they each perform one logical function. Each gate accepts one or more input values and produces a single output value. Since we are dealing with binary information, each input and output value is either 0, corresponding to a low-voltage signal, or 1, corresponding to a high-voltage signal. The type of gate and the input values determine the output value.

Let's examine the processing of the following six types of gates. After we have done so, we show how they can be combined into circuits to perform arithmetic operations.

- NOT
- AND
- OR
- XOR
- NAND
- NOR

What is nanoscience?

Nanoscience is the study of materials smaller than 100 nanometers—or 1/100th the width of a human hair strand. Scientists expect nanoscience to eventually lead to new materials that are stronger, lighter, and cheaper to make. Two nanotubes—each 10 atoms wide—have been used to create a simple circuit. "They're the only thing in the world that right now has some potential of making a switch to process information that's faster than the fastest silicon transistor," said IBM's worldwide director of physical science research Tom Theis.

"If nanotechnology has the impact we think it might have, it may well cause social and industrial rearrangements not unlike the original Industrial Revolution," said Richard W. Siegel, director of Rensselaer Nanotechnology Center in Troy, New York.[2]

There is one important note to keep in mind as you examine these gates. In this book we have colorized the logic diagram symbols for each gate to help you keep track of the various types. When we examine full circuits with many gates, the colors help you distinguish among them. Typically, however, logic diagrams are black and white, and the gates are distinguished only by their shape.

NOT Gate

A NOT gate accepts one input value and produces one output value. Figure 4.1 shows a NOT gate represented in three ways: as a Boolean expression, as its logical diagram symbol, and using a truth table. In each representation, the variable A represents the input signal, which is either 0

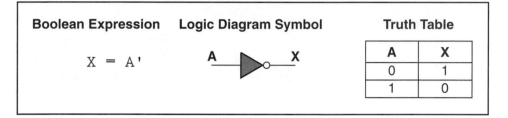

Boolean Expression	Logic Diagram Symbol	Truth Table	

X = A'

A ▷○ X

A	X
0	1
1	0

Figure 4.1 Various representations of a NOT gate

or 1. The variable X represents the output signal, whose value (also 0 or 1) is determined by the value of A.

By definition, if the input value for a NOT gate is 0, the output value is 1, and if the input value is 1, the output is 0. A NOT gate is sometimes referred to as an *inverter* because it inverts the input value.

In Boolean expressions, the NOT operation is represented by the ' mark after the value being negated. Sometimes this operation is shown as a horizontal bar over the value being negated. In the Boolean expression in Figure 4.1, X is assigned the value determined by applying the NOT operation to input value A. This is an example of an *assignment statement*, in which the variable on the left of the equal sign takes on the value of the expression on the right-hand side. Assignment statements are discussed further in Chapter 8 on high-level programming languages.

The logic diagram symbol for a NOT gate is a triangle with a tiny circle (called an *inversion bubble*) on the end. The input and output are shown as lines flowing into and out of the gate. Sometimes these lines are labeled, though not always.

The truth table in Figure 4.1 shows all possible input values for a NOT gate, as well as the corresponding output values. Since there is only one input signal to a NOT gate, and that signal can only be a 0 or a 1, those are the only two possibilities for the column labeled A in the truth table. The column labeled X shows the output of the gate, which is the inverse of the input. Note that of all three representations, only the truth table actually defines the behavior of the gate for all situations.

Keep in mind that these three notations are just different ways of representing the same thing. For example, the result of the Boolean expression

0'

is always 1, and the result of the Boolean expression

1'

is always 0. This behavior is consistent with the values shown in the truth table.

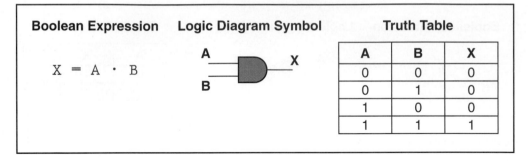

Figure 4.2   Various representations of an AND gate

AND Gate

An AND gate is shown in Figure 4.2. Unlike a NOT gate, which accepts one input signal, an AND gate accepts two input signals. The values of both input signals determine what the output signal will be. If the two input values for an AND gate are both 1, the output is 1; otherwise, the output is 0.

The AND operation in Boolean algebra is expressed using a single dot (·). Sometimes an asterisk (*) is used to represent this operator. And often the operator itself is assumed. For example A·B is often written AB.

Because there are two inputs, and two possible values for each input, there are four possible combinations of 1 and 0 that can be provided as input to an AND gate. Therefore, there are four possible situations that can occur using the AND operator in a Boolean expression:

$0 \cdot 0$ equals 0
$0 \cdot 1$ equals 0
$1 \cdot 0$ equals 0
$1 \cdot 1$ equals 1

Likewise, the truth table showing the behavior of the AND gate has four rows, showing all four possible input combinations. The output column of the truth table is consistent with results of these Boolean expressions.

OR Gate

An OR gate is shown in Figure 4.3. Like the AND gate, there are two inputs to an OR gate. If the two input values are both 0, the output value is 0; otherwise, the output is 1.

The Boolean algebra OR operation is expressed using a plus sign (+). The OR gate has two inputs, each of which can be one of two values, so as with an AND gate there are four input combinations and therefore four rows in the truth table.

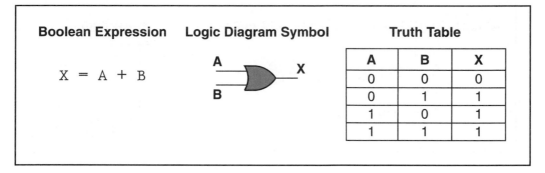

A	B	X
0	0	0
0	1	1
1	0	1
1	1	1

Boolean Expression: X = A + B

Figure 4.3   Various representations of an OR gate

XOR Gate

The XOR, or *exclusive* OR, gate is shown in Figure 4.4. An XOR gate produces 0 if its two inputs are the same, and a 1 otherwise. Note the difference between the XOR gate and the OR gate; they differ only in one input situation. When both input signals are 1, the OR gate produces a 1 and the XOR produces a 0.

Sometimes the regular OR gate is referred to as the *inclusive* OR, because it produces a 1 if either or both of its inputs is a 1. The XOR produces a 1 only if its inputs are mixed, one 1 and one 0. Think of XOR gate as saying, "When I say *or*, I mean one or the other, not both."

The Boolean algebra symbol $\oplus$ is sometimes used to express the XOR operation. However, the XOR operation can also be expressed using the other operators; we leave that as an exercise.

Note that the logic diagram symbol for the XOR gate is just like the symbol for an OR gate except that it has an extra curved line connecting its input signals.

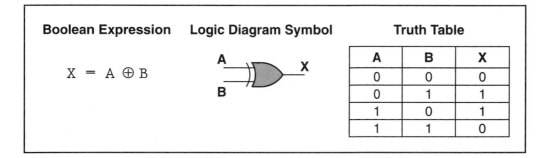

A	B	X
0	0	0
0	1	1
1	0	1
1	1	0

Boolean Expression: X = A $\oplus$ B

Figure 4.4   Various representations of an XOR gate

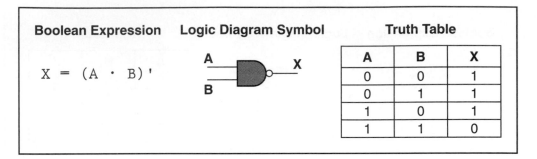

Boolean Expression	Logic Diagram Symbol	Truth Table		
		A	B	X
$X = (A \cdot B)'$		0	0	1
		0	1	1
		1	0	1
		1	1	0

Figure 4.5   Various representations of a NAND gate

NAND and NOR Gates

The NAND gate is shown in Figure 4.5 and the NOR gate is shown in Figure 4.6. They each accept two input values. The NAND and NOR gates are essentially the opposite of the AND and OR gates, respectively. That is, the output of a NAND gate is the same as if you took the output of an AND gate and put it through an inverter (a NOT gate).

There are typically no specific symbols used to express the NAND and NOR operations in Boolean algebra. Instead, we rely on their definitions to express the concepts. That is, the Boolean algebra expression for NAND is the negation of an AND operation. Likewise, the Boolean algebra expression for NOR is the negation of an OR operation.

The logic diagram symbols for the NAND and NOR are the same as those for the AND and OR except that the NAND and NOR symbols have the inversion bubble (to indicate the negation). Compare the output

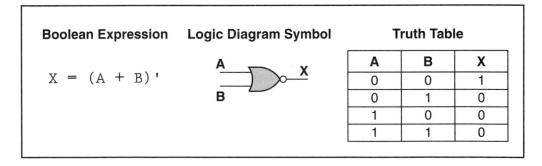

Boolean Expression	Logic Diagram Symbol	Truth Table		
		A	B	X
$X = (A + B)'$		0	0	1
		0	1	0
		1	0	0
		1	1	0

Figure 4.6   Various representations of a NOR gate

columns for the truth tables for the AND and NAND gates. They are opposite, row by row. The same is true for the OR and NOR gates.

Review of Gate Processing

We've looked at six specific types of gates. It may seem to be a difficult task to keep them straight and remember how they all work. Well, that probably depends on how you think about it. We definitely don't encourage you to try to memorize truth tables. The processing of these gates can be described briefly in general terms. If you think of them that way, you can produce the appropriate truth table any time you need it.

Let's review the processing of each gate. Some of these descriptions are in terms of what input values cause the gate to produce a 1 as output; in any other case, it produces a 0.

- A NOT gate inverts its single input value.
- An AND gate produces 1 if both input values are 1.
- An OR gate produces 1 if one or the other or both input values are 1.
- An XOR gate produces 1 if one or the other (but not both) input values are 1.
- A NAND gate produces the opposite results of an AND gate.
- A NOR gate produces the opposite results of an OR gate.

Once you keep these general processing rules in mind, all that's left is to remember the Boolean operators and the logic diagram symbols. Keep in mind that several of the logic diagram symbols are variations of each other. Also, remember that the coloring of the gates that we use in this book is to help you to keep track of the various gate types; traditionally, they are simply black and white diagrams.

Gates with More Inputs

Gates can be designed to accept three or more input values. A three-input AND gate, for example, produces an output of 1 only if all input values are 1. A three-input OR gate produces an output of 1 if any input value is 1. These definitions are consistent with the two-input versions of these gates. Figure 4.7 shows an AND gate with three input signals.

Note that there are 2^3 or 8 possible input combinations for a gate with three inputs. Recall from Chapter 3 that there are 2^n combinations of 1 and 0 for n distinct input values. This determines how many rows are needed in a truth table.

For the logic diagram symbol, we simply add a third input signal to the original symbol. For a Boolean expression, however, we repeat the AND operation to represent the third value.

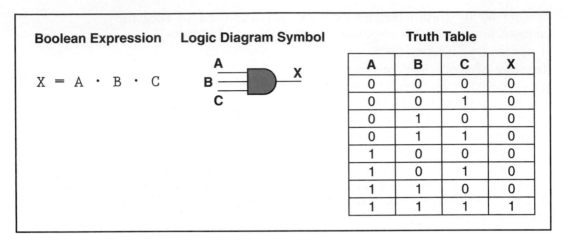

Figure 4.7   Various representations of a three-input AND gate

4.3   Constructing Gates

Before we examine how gates are connected to form circuits, let's examine, at an even more basic level, how a gate is constructed to control the flow of electricity.

Transistors

A gate uses one or more transistors to establish how the input values map to the output value. A **transistor** is a device that acts, depending on the voltage level of an input signal, either as a wire that conducts electricity or as a resistor that blocks the flow of electricity. A transistor has no moving parts, yet acts like a switch. It is made of a **semiconductor** material, which is neither a particularly good conductor of electricity, such as copper, nor a particularly good insulator, such as rubber. Usually silicon is used to create transistors.

In Chapter 1, we mentioned that the invention of transistors, in 1947 at Bell Labs, changed the face of technology, ushering in the second generation of computer hardware. Before transistors, digital circuits used vacuum tubes, which dissipated a great deal of heat and often failed, requiring replacement. Transistors are much smaller than vacuum tubes and require less energy to operate. They can switch states in a few nanoseconds. Computing, as we know it today, is largely due to the invention of the transistor.

Transistor A device that acts either as a wire or a resistor, depending on the voltage level of an input signal

Semiconductor Material such as silicon that is neither a good conductor nor insulator

Before tackling the details of transistors, let's discuss some basic principles of electricity. An electrical signal has a source, such as a battery or an outlet in your wall. If the electrical signal is *grounded*, it is allowed to flow through an alternative route to the ground (literally) where it can do no harm. A grounded electrical signal is pulled down, or reduced, to 0 volts.

A transistor has three terminals: a source, a base, and an emitter. The emitter is typically connected to a ground wire, as shown in Figure 4.8. For computers, the source produces a high value, approximately 5 volts. The base value regulates a gate that determines whether the connection between the source and ground is made. If the source signal is grounded, it is pulled down to 0 volts. If the base does not ground the source signal, it stays high.

An output line is usually connected to the source line. If the source signal is pulled to the ground by the transistor, that output signal is low, representing a binary 0. If the source signal remains high, so is that output signal, representing a binary 1.

The transistor is either on, producing a high output signal, or off, producing a low output signal. This is determined by the base electrical signal. If the base signal is high (close to a +5 voltage), the source signal is grounded, which turns the transistor off. If the base signal is low (close to a 0 voltage), the source signal stays high, and the transistor is on.

Now let's see how a transistor is used to create various types of gates. It turns out that, because the way a transistor works, the easiest gates to create are the NOT, NAND, and NOR gates. Figure 4.9 contains diagrams that show how these gates can be constructed using transistors.

The diagram for the NOT gate is essentially the same as our original transistor diagram. It only takes one transistor to create a NOT gate. The signal V_{in} represents the input signal to the NOT gate. If it is high, the

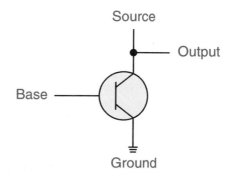

Figure 4.8
The connections of a transistor

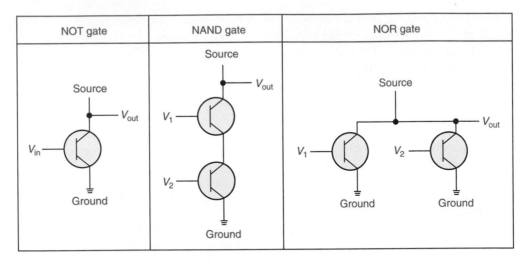

NOT gate	NAND gate	NOR gate

Figure 4.9   Constructing gates using transistors

source is grounded, and the output signal V_{out} is low. If V_{in} is low, the source is not grounded, and V_{out} is high. Thus the input signal is inverted, which is exactly what a NOT gate does.

The NAND gate requires two transistors. The input signals V_1 and V_2 represent the input to the NAND gate. If both input signals are high, the source is grounded and the output V_{out} is low. But if either input signal is low, one transistor or the other keep the source signal from being grounded and the output is high. Therefore, if V_1, or V_2, or both, carry a low signal (binary 0), the output is a 1. This is consistent with the processing of a NAND gate.

The construction of a NOR gate also requires two transistors. Once again, V_1 and V_2 represent the input to the gate. This time, however, the transistors are not connected in series. The source connects to each transistor separately. If either transistor allows the source signal to be grounded, the output is 0. Therefore, the output is high (binary 1) only when both V_1 and V_2 are low (binary 0), which is what we want for a NOR gate.

An AND gate, as we pointed out earlier in this chapter, produces output that is exactly opposite of the NAND gate. Therefore, to construct an AND gate we simply pass the output of a NAND gate through an inverter (or NOT gate). That's why AND gates are more complicated to construct than NAND gates: They require three transistors, two for the NAND and one for the NOT. The same reasoning can be made for the relationship between NOR and OR gates.

4.4 Circuits

Now that we know how individual gates work, and how they are actually constructed, let's examine how we combine gates into circuits. Circuits can be separated into two general categories. In a **combinational circuit**, the input values explicitly determine the output. In a **sequential circuit**, the output is a function of the input values as well as the existing state of the circuit. Thus, sequential circuits usually involve the storage of information.

Most of the circuits we examine in this chapter are combinational circuits, though we briefly mention sequential memory circuits as well.

Keep in mind that, as with gates, we can describe the operations of entire circuits using three notations: Boolean expressions, logic diagrams, and truth tables. They are different, but equally powerful, representation techniques.

> **Combinational circuit** A circuit whose output is solely determined by its input values
>
> **Sequential circuit** A circuit whose output is a function of input values and the current state of the circuit

Combinational Circuits

Gates are combined into circuits by using the output of one gate as the input for another. For example, consider the following logic diagram of a circuit:

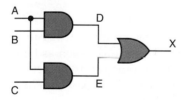

The output of the two AND gates is used as the input to the OR gate. Note that the input value A is used as input to both AND gates. The dot indicates that two lines are connected. If the intersection of two crossing lines does not have a dot, you should think of one as "jumping over" the other without affecting each other.

What does the logic diagram mean? Well, let's work backwards to see what it takes to get a particular result. For the final output X to be 1, either D must be 1 or E must be 1. For D to be 1, A and B must both be 1. For E to be 1, both A and C must be 1. Both E and D may be 1, but that isn't necessary. Examine this circuit diagram carefully; make sure that this reasoning is consistent with your understanding of the types of gates used.

Now let's represent the processing of this entire circuit using a truth table:

A	B	C	D	E	X
0	0	0	0	0	0
0	0	1	0	0	0
0	1	0	0	0	0
0	1	1	0	0	0
1	0	0	0	0	0
1	0	1	0	1	1
1	1	0	1	0	1
1	1	1	1	1	1

Because there are three inputs to this circuit, eight rows are required to describe all possible input combinations. Intermediate columns are used to show the intermediate values (D and E) in the circuit.

Finally, let's express this same circuit using Boolean algebra. A circuit is a collection of interacting gates, so a Boolean expression to represent a circuit is a combination of the appropriate Boolean operations. We just have to put the operations together in the proper form to create a valid Boolean algebra expression. In this circuit, there are two AND expressions. The output of each AND is input to the OR operation. Thus, this circuit is represented by the following Boolean expression (in which the AND operator is assumed):

(AB + AC)

When we write truth tables it is often better to label columns using these kinds of Boolean expressions, rather than arbitrary variables such as D, E, and X. That makes it more clear what each column represents. In fact, we can use Boolean expressions to label our logic diagrams as well, eliminating the need for intermediate variables altogether.

Now let's go the other way; let's take a Boolean expression and draw the corresponding logic diagram and truth table. Consider the following Boolean expression:

A(B + C)

In this expression, the OR operation is applied to input values B and C. The result of that operation is used as input, along with A, to an AND operation, producing the final result. The corresponding circuit diagram is therefore:

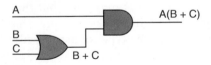

And once again, let's complete our series of representations by expressing this circuit as a truth table. Like the previous example, since there are three input values there are eight rows in the truth table:

A	B	C	B + C	A(B+C)
0	0	0	0	0
0	0	1	1	0
0	1	0	1	0
0	1	1	1	0
1	0	0	0	0
1	0	1	1	1
1	1	0	1	1
1	1	1	1	1

Pick a row from this truth table and follow the logic of the circuit diagram to make sure the final results are consistent. Try it with a few rows to get comfortable with tracing the logic of a circuit.

Now compare the final result column in this truth table to the truth table for the previous example. They are identical. We have therefore just demonstrated **circuit equivalence**. That is, both circuits produce the exact same output for each input value combination.

In fact, this situation specifically demonstrates an important property of Boolean algebra called the *distributive law*:

$$A(B+C) = AB + AC$$

That's the beauty of Boolean algebra: It allows us to apply provable mathematical principles to help us design logical circuits. The following chart shows a few of the properties of Boolean algebra:

> **Circuit equivalence**
> The same output for each corresponding input-value combination for two circuits

Property	AND	OR
Commutative	AB = BA	A + B = B + A
Associative	(AB)C = A(BC)	(A + B) + C = A + (B + C)
Distributive	A(B + C) = (AB) + (AC)	A + (BC) = (A + B)(A + C)
Identity	A1 = A	A + 0 = A
Complement	A(A') = 0	A + (A') = 1
DeMorgan's law	(AB)' = A' OR B'	(A + B)' = A'B'

These properties are consistent with our understanding of gate processing, and with the truth table and logic diagram representations. For instance, the commutative property, in plain English, says that the order of the input signals doesn't matter, which is true. (Verify it using the truth tables of individual gates.) The complement property says that if we put a signal and its inverse through an AND gate, we are guaranteed to get 0, but if we put a signal and its inverse through an OR gate, we are guaranteed to get 1.

There is one very famous—and useful—theorem in Boolean algebra called *DeMorgan's law*. This law states that the NOT operator applied to the AND of two variables is equal to the NOT applied to each of the two variables with an OR between. That is, inverting the output of an AND gate is equivalent to inverting the individual signals first, then passing them through an OR gate:

$(AB)' = A'\ OR\ B'$

The second part of the law is that the NOT operator applied to the OR of two variables is equal to the NOT applied to each of the two variables with an AND between. Again, expressed in circuit terms: inverting the output of an OR gate is equivalent to inverting both signals first, then passing them through an AND gate:

$(A + B)' = A'B'$

DeMorgan's law and other Boolean algebra properties provide a formal mechanism for defining, managing, and evaluating logical circuit designs.

DeMorgan's law, named for Augustus DeMorgan

DeMorgan, a contemporary of George Boole, was the first professor of mathematics to the University of London in 1828, where he continued to teach for 30 years. He wrote elementary texts on arithmetic, algebra, trigonometry, and calculus as well as papers on the possibility of establishing a logical calculus and the fundamental problem of expressing thought by means of symbols. DeMorgan did not discover the laws bearing his name, but he is credited with formally stating them as they are known today.

Adders

Perhaps the most basic operation a computer can perform is to add two numbers together. At the digital logic level, this addition is performed in binary. Chapter 2 contains a discussion of this process. These types of addition operations are carried out by special circuits called, appropriately, **adders**.

Like addition in any base, the result of adding two binary digits could produce a *carry value*. Recall that $1 + 1 = 10$ in base two. A circuit that computes the sum of two bits and produces the correct carry bit is called a **half adder**.

Let's consider all possibilities when adding two binary digits A and B: If both A and B are 0, the sum is 0 and the carry is 0. If A is 0 and B is 1, the sum is 1 and the carry is 0. If A is 1 and B is 0, the sum is 1 and the carry

Adder   An electronic circuit that performs an addition operation on binary values

Half adder   A circuit that computes the sum of two bits and produces the appropriate carry bit

is 0. If both A and B are 1, the sum is 0 and the carry is 1. This yields the following truth table:

A	B	Sum	Carry
0	0	0	0
0	1	1	0
1	0	1	0
1	1	0	1

Note that in this case we are actually looking for two output results, the sum and the carry. So our circuit has two output lines.

If you compare the sum and carry columns to the output of the various gates, you see that the sum corresponds to the XOR gate and the carry corresponds to the AND gate. Thus, the following circuit diagram represents a half adder:

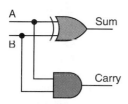

Test this diagram by assigning various combinations of input values and determining what two output values will be produced. Do the results follow the rules of binary arithmetic? They should. Now compare your results to the corresponding truth table. They should match there also.

What about the Boolean expression for this circuit? Since the circuit produces two distinct output values, we represent it using two Boolean expressions:

sum = A $\oplus$ B
carry = AB

Note that a half adder does not take into account a possible carry value *into* the calculation (carry-in). That is, a half adder is fine for adding two single digits, but it cannot be used as is to compute the sum of two binary values with multiple digits each. A circuit called a **full adder** takes the carry-in value into account.

We can use two half adders to make a full adder. How? Well, the input to the sum must be the carry-in and the sum from adding the two input

Full adder A circuit that computes the sum of two bits, taking an input carry bit into account

Logic Diagram

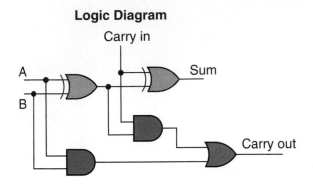

Truth Table

A	B	Carry-in	Sum	Carry-out
0	0	0	0	0
0	0	1	1	0
0	1	0	1	0
0	1	1	0	1
1	0	0	1	0
1	0	1	0	1
1	1	0	0	1
1	1	1	1	1

Figure 4.10   A full adder

values. That is, we add the sum from the half adder to the carry-in. Both of these additions have a carry out. Is it possible for both of these carry-outs to be 1, thus having a further carry? Fortunately, no. Look at the truth table for the half adder. There is no case where the sum and carry are both 1.

The logic diagram and the truth table for the full adder are shown in Figure 4.10. Keep in mind that there are three inputs to this circuit: the original two digits (A and B) and the carry-in value. Thus the truth table has eight rows. We leave the corresponding Boolean expression as an exercise.

To add two eight-bit values, we can duplicate a full-adder circuit eight times. The carry-out from one place value is used as the carry-in to the next highest place value. The value of the carry-in for the rightmost bit position is assumed to be zero, and the carry-out of the leftmost bit position is discarded (potentially creating an overflow error).

There are various ways to improve on the design of these adder circuits, but we do not explore them in any more detail in this text.

Multiplexers

Multiplexer A circuit that uses a few input control signals to determine which of several input data lines is routed to its output

A **multiplexer** (often referred to as a *mux*) is a general circuit that produces a single output signal. The output is equal to one of several input signals to the circuit. The multiplexer selects which input signal is used as an output signal based on the value represented by a few more input signals, called *select signals* or *select control lines*.

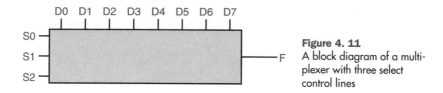

Figure 4. 11
A block diagram of a multiplexer with three select control lines

Let's look at an example. A block diagram of a mux is shown in Figure 4.11. The control lines S0, S1, and S2 determine which of eight other input lines (D0 through D7) are routed to the output (F).

The values of the three control lines, taken together, are interpreted as a binary number, which determines which input line to route to the output. Recall from Chapter 2 that three binary digits can represent eight different values: 000, 001, 010, 011, 100, 101, 110, and 111. Note that these values simply count in binary from 0 to 7, which correspond to our output values D0 through D7. So if S0, S1, and S2 are all 0, the input line D0 would be the output from the mux. If S0 is 1, S1 is 0, and S2 is 1, then D5 would be output from the mux.

The following truth table shows how the input control lines determine the output for this multiplexer:

S0	S1	S2	F
0	0	0	D0
0	0	1	D1
0	1	0	D2
0	1	1	D3
1	0	0	D4
1	0	1	D5
1	1	0	D6
1	1	1	D7

The block diagram in Figure 4.11 hides a fairly complicated circuit to carry out the logic of a multiplexer. Such a circuit could be shown using eight three-input AND gates and one eight-input OR gate. We won't get into the details of the circuit in this book.

A multiplexer can be designed with various numbers of input lines and corresponding control lines. In general, the binary values on n input control lines are used to determine which of 2^n other data lines are selected for output.

A circuit called a *demultiplexer* (or *demux*) performs the opposite operation. That is, it takes a single input and routes it to one of 2^n outputs, depending on the values of the n control lines.

4.5   Circuits as Memory

Another important role of digital circuits is that they can be used to store information. These circuits form a sequential circuit, because the output of the circuit is also used as input to the circuit. That is, the existing state of the circuit is used in part to determine the next state.

Many types of memory circuits have been designed. We examine only one type in this book: the *S-R latch*. An S-R latch stores a single binary digit (1 or 0). There are several ways an S-R latch circuit could be designed using various kinds of gates. One such circuit, using NAND gates, is pictured in Figure 4.12.

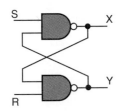

Figure 4.12
An S-R latch

The design of this circuit guarantees that the two outputs X and Y are always complements of each other. That is, when X is 0, Y is 1, and vice versa. The value of X at any point in time is considered to be the current state of the circuit. Therefore, if X is 1, the circuit is storing a 1; if X is 0, the circuit is storing a 0.

Recall that a NAND gate produces an output of 1 unless both of its input values are 1. Each gate in this circuit has one external input (S or R) and one input coming from the output of the other gate. Suppose the current state of the circuit is storing a 1 (that is, X is 1). And suppose both S and R are 1. Then Y remains 0 and X remains 1. Now suppose that the circuit is currently storing a 0 (X is 0), and that R and S are again 1. Then Y remains 1 and X remains 0. Therefore, no matter which value is currently being stored, if both input values S and R are 1, the circuit keeps its existing state.

This explanation demonstrates that the S-R latch maintains its value as long as S and R are 1. How does a value get stored in the first place? We set the S-R latch to 1 by momentarily setting S to 0 while keeping R at 1. If S is 0, X becomes 1. As long as S is returned to 1 immediately, the S-R latch remains in a state of 1. We set the latch to 0 by momentarily setting R to 0 while keeping S at 1. If R is 0, Y becomes 0, so X becomes 0. As long as R is immediately reset to 1, the circuit state remains 0.

Therefore, by carefully controlling the values of S and R, the circuit can be made to store either value. By scaling this idea to larger circuits, memory devices with larger capacities can be designed.

4.6 Integrated Circuits

An **integrated circuit** (also called a *chip*) is a piece of silicon on which multiple gates have been embedded. These silicon pieces are mounted on a plastic or ceramic package with pins along the edges that can be soldered onto circuit boards or inserted into appropriate sockets. Each pin connects to the input or output of a gate, or to power or ground.

Integrated circuits (IC) are classified by the number of gates contained in them. These classifications also reflect the historical development of IC technology:

> **Integrated circuit (also chip)** A piece of silicon on which multiple gates have been embedded

Abbreviation	Name	Number of Gates
SSI	Small-Scale Integration	1 to 10
MSI	Medium-Scale Integration	10 to 100
LSI	Large-Scale Integration	100 to 100,000
VLSI	Very-Large-Scale Integration	more than 100,000

An SSI chip has a few independent gates, such as the one shown in Figure 4.13. This chip has 14 pins: eight for inputs to gates, four for output of the gates, one for ground, and one for power. Similar chips can be made with different gates.

How can a chip have more than 100,000 gates on it? That would imply the need for 300,000 pins! The key is that the gates on a VLSI chip are not independent as they are in small-scale integration. VLSI chips embed

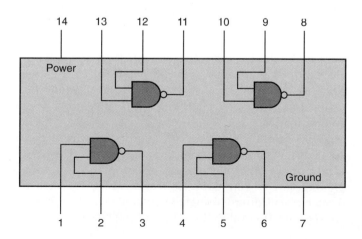

Figure 4.13
An SSI chip containing independent NAND gates

circuits with a high gate-to-pin ratio. That is, many gates are combined to create complex circuits that require only a few input and output values. Multiplexers are an example of this type of circuit.

4.7   CPU Chips

The most important integrated circuit in any computer is the Central Processing Unit, or CPU. The processing of a CPU is discussed in the next chapter, but it is important to recognize at this point that the CPU is, in one sense, merely an advanced circuit with input and output lines.

Each CPU chip has a large number of pins through which essentially all communication in a computer system occurs. This communication connects the CPU to memory and I/O devices, which are themselves, at fundamental levels, advanced circuits.

The explanation of CPU processing and its interaction with other devices take us to another level of computer processing, sometimes referred to as *component architecture*. Though still primarily focused on hardware, computer component architecture applies the principle of abstraction once again, allowing us to temporarily ignore the details of the gates and circuits we've discussed in this chapter and bring us ever closer to a complete understanding of computer processing.

Summary

We've discussed in this chapter how a computer operates at its lowest level by controlling the flow of electricity. Since we are dealing with digital computers that use binary information, we concern ourselves only with two voltage ranges that we interpret as binary 1 or 0. The flow of electricity is guided by electronic devices called gates, which perform basic logical operations such as NOT, AND, and OR. A gate is created using one or more transistors, an invention which revolutionized computing.

Gates can be combined into circuits, in which the output of one gate serves as an input to another. By designing these circuits carefully, we create devices that perform more complex tasks such as adding, multiplexing, and storing data. Collections of gates, or complete circuits, are often embedded into a single integrated circuit, or chip, which leads to the concept of a Central Processing Unit (CPU).

ETHICAL ISSUES

E-mail Privacy

Have you ever written an important message, submitted your resume, or complained about your roommate over e-mail? Would you have handled it differently if you knew that strangers, administrators, or your roommate could read your message? Once a tool for only the most computer literate, today e-mail is a standard means of communication for millions of people. Many users, however, incorrectly assume that only those who are intended to read their correspondence have access to its content. With an illusion of privacy, people e-mail personal letters that they would never want anyone else to read, or send confidential information that could be compromising if it fell into the wrong hands. On its path from sender to recipient, e-mail travels from server to server and can be read more easily than a postcard. E-mail security has become the center of many debates that search for a common ground between individual rights, corporate rights, and computer technology.

Many companies who rely on e-mail for much of their communication now have policies that outline where e-mail privacy ends and e-mail monitoring begins. Supporters of e-mail monitoring state that all correspondence through a company's server belongs to the company and therefore the company has the right to access it at will. They argue that surveillance prevents employees from abusing their e-mail access and allows the employer more control over correspondences for which the company could be held liable. Opponents explain that e-mail monitoring creates an atmosphere of mistrust and disrespect, and that surveillance is an unnecessary obstruction of employee autonomy.

The privacy issues that surround e-mail extend beyond company policies. For example, in July of 2000 the United Kingdom passed the Regulation of Investigatory Powers bill, giving the government access to all Internet correspondence. Internet Service Providers must route all e-mail through governmental headquarters, and government officials have access to all encryption keys that are used to protect and secure e-mails.

Even after an e-mail has reached its destination an unintended audience can read its contents. The forwarding feature provided by most e-mail services gives the recipient the ability to pass on e-mail without the author's knowledge. Research shows that people consider reading someone else's e-mail as less of an invasion of privacy than reading someone's ordinary mail. This belief, along with eavesdropping and monitoring, compromises the security of e-mail correspondence.

Key Terms

Adder pg. 102

Boolean algebra pg. 89

Circuit pg. 88

Circuit equivalence pg. 101

Combinational circuit pg. 99

Full adder pg. 103

Gate pg. 88

Half adder pg. 102

Integrated circuit (also chip)
  pg. 107

Logic diagram pg. 89

Multiplexer pg. 104

Semiconductor pg. 96

Sequential circuit pg. 99

Transistor pg. 96

Truth table pg. 90

Exercises

1. How is voltage level used to distinguish between binary digits?

2. Distinguish between a gate and a circuit.

3. What are the three notational methods for describing the behavior of gates and circuits?

4. Characterize the notations asked for in Exercise 3.

5. How many input signals can a gate receive and how many output signals can a gate produce?

6. Name six types of gates.

7. Give the three representations of a NOT gate and say in words what NOT means.

8. Give the three representations of an AND gate and say in words what AND means.

9. Give the three representations of an OR gate and say in words what OR means.

10. Give the three representations of an XOR gate and say in words what XOR means.

11. Give the three representations of a NAND gate and say in words what NAND means.

12. Give the three representations of a NOR gate and say in words what NOR means.

13. Why are there no logic diagram symbols for the NAND and NOR gates?

14. Draw and label the symbol for a three-input AND gate; then show its behavior with a truth table.

15. Draw and label the symbol for a three-input OR gate; then show its behavior with a truth table.

16. What is used in a gate to establish how the input values map to the output value?

17. How does a transistor behave?

18. Of what is a transistor usually made?

19. What happens when an electric signal is grounded?

20. What are the three terminals in a transistor and how do they operate to produce an output?

21. How many transistors does it take for each of these gates?
   a. NOT
   b. AND
   c. NOR
   d. OR
   e. XOR

22. Draw a transistor diagram for an AND gate. Explain the processing.

23. Draw a transistor diagram for an OR gate. Explain the processing.

24. How can gates be combined into circuits?

25. What are the two general categories of circuits and how do they differ?

26. Draw a circuit diagram corresponding to the following Boolean expression:

$(A + B)(B + C)$

27. Draw a circuit diagram corresponding to the following Boolean expression:

$(AB + C)D$

28. Draw a circuit diagram corresponding to the following Boolean expression:

$A'B + (B+C)'$

29. Draw a circuit diagram corresponding to the following Boolean expression:

(AB)′ + (CD)′

30. Show the behavior of the following circuit with a truth table:

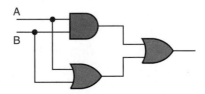

31. Show the behavior of the following circuit with a truth table:

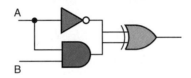

32. Show the behavior of the following circuit with a truth table:

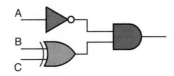

33. Show the behavior of the following circuit with a truth table:

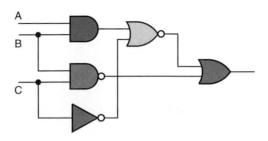

34. What is circuit equivalence?

35. Name six properties of Boolean algebra and explain what each means.

36. Differentiate between a half adder and a full adder.

37. What is the Boolean expression for a full adder?

38. What is a multiplexer?

39. **a.** Circuits used for memory are which type of circuits?
    b. How many digits does an S-R latch store?
    c. The design for an S-R latch shown in Figure 4.12 guarantees what about the outputs X and Y?

40. What is an integrated circuit or chip?

41. Define the abbreviations SSI, MSI, LSI, and VLSI.

42. In the chip shown in Figure 4.13, what are the pins used for?

43. Draw a circuit using two full adders that adds two two-bit binary values.

44. How can the XOR operation be expressed using other operators?

? Thought Questions

1. Throughout this chapter we have used Boolean expressions, truth tables, and logic diagrams to describe the same behavior. Is the relationship among these notational methods clear to you? Which do you find is the most intuitive? Which do you find the least intuitive?

2. There are many situations that can be described by the ideas in this chapter, for example, the operation of a single light switch or a light that has two switches. Can you think of other everyday occurrences that can be described by the notational methods presented in this chapter?

3. Have you ever sent e-mail to someone only to regret it immediately? Do you find that you would say something in e-mail that you would never say in person? Consider the premise "E-mail has lowered the civility of personal discourse." Do you agree or disagree?

4. If a person sends e-mail from a school computer or a business computer, should that message be considered private? Does the institution or person that owns the computer from which e-mail is sent have a right to inspect the message?

5. Do you consider reading someone else's e-mail as less of an invasion of privacy than reading someone's ordinary mail?

The Hardware Layer

5 Computing Components

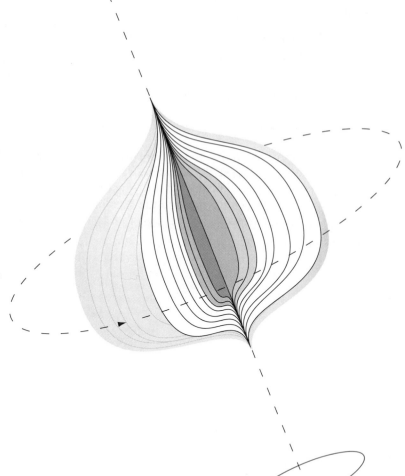

Chapter 5

Computing Components

Chapter 2 described the binary number system in which all information is represented on a computer. Chapter 4 described how we control electricity at a fundamental level to manage binary values. Now we can describe the primary components of a computer, which capitalize on these technologies. These primary components are like Lego pieces; they can be combined to build a variety of different computers, just as Legos can form a variety of buildings.

Although these components, such as main memory and the Central Processing Unit, are often thought of as the most fundamental parts of a computer, we know that they are abstractions of even more fundamental concepts.

Goals

After studying this chapter, you should be able to:

- read an ad for a computer and understand the jargon.
- list the components and their function in a von Neumann machine.
- describe the fetch-decode-execute cycle of the von Neumann machine.
- describe how computer memory is organized and accessed.
- name and describe different auxiliary storage devices.
- define three alternative parallel computer configurations.

5.1   Individual Computer Components

Computing, more than most fields, has its own special jargon and acronyms. We begin this chapter by translating an ad for a desktop computer. We then examine the components of a computer as a logical whole before looking at each component in some detail.

Consider the following ad for a desktop computer, as if it were real.

Dell™ Dimension 8100™ Series
The Advanced Performance, Smart Value Desktop

- Intel® Pentium® IV Processor at 866 MHz
- 128MB SDRAM at 1.4 GHz
- 40GB Ultra ATA-100 Hard Drive (7200 RPM)
- 17" (16.0" vis, .28dpi) E770 Monitor
- 16MB ATI Range™ 128 Pro Graphics
- 48X Max CD-ROM Drive
- FREE 8X/4X/32X CD-RW Drive
- SB Live! Value Digital

- FREE 8X/4X/32X CD-RW Drive
- SB Live! Value Digital
- Altec Lansing® ACS-340™ Speakers with Subwoofer
- V.90 56K Capable PCI Telephony Model for Windows®
- MS® Works Suite 2001 MS® Windows® Me
- 3-Yr Limited Warranty 1-Yr-at Home Service
- 1 Year of Dellnet™ by MSN® Internet Access Included

There are two important and interesting things about this ad: The average person hasn't the foggiest idea what it all means, and by the time you are reading it, the machine that it describes will be obsolete. In this chapter, we try to interpret the acronyms; we can't do anything about the speed at which computer hardware and software change.

Before we go on to describe computer components in the abstract, let's go through this ad and decipher the acronyms. After this exercise, we go through all of the material again in more depth, so don't be concerned if the terms seem confusing. You'll see all of them defined again later.

The first line describes the central processor inside the computer. This description tells you how powerful the computer is. The central processor is an Intel Pentium IV processor. We mentioned in the last chapter that this is a common 32-bit processor. The 1.4 GHz tells how fast the processor is. The abbreviation G is short for Giga, which in computer terms stands for 10^9. Hz stands for hertz, a unit of frequency equal to one cycle per second, named for Heinrich R. Hertz. Therefore, the speed of this processor is 1,400,000,000 cycles per second. (Faster is better.)

The next line describes the memory that comes with the machine, called the main memory. 128MB tells you how much memory comes with the computer: 128,000,000 bytes. SDRAM stands for static dynamic random-access memory. Random access means that each word of memory can be directly accessed, rather than having to begin at the beginning and access each word in turn until you get to the one you want. 133 MHz says that memory can be accessed at 133,000,000 cycles per second. A quote attributed to Bill Gates, Microsoft chair, in 1981 did not prove to be very accurate: "640K ought to be enough for anybody."[1] (Faster is better.)

The next line describes the hard disk drive, which is the common name for the disk that is a secondary (also called auxiliary) storage device. The disk drive is installed within the box housing everything but the screen, keyboard, and mouse. 40GB specifies the number of bytes of storage, (the G stands for Giga, which is 10^9.) so this machine has 40,000,000,000 bytes of storage. Ultra ATA-100 is the name of the drive's manufacturer. 7,200 RPM specifies how fast the disk revolves. The speed of accessing a particular location in main memory is measured in MHz; the access speed of a hard disk is measured in terms of revolutions per minute. As you can guess from the numbers, accessing main memory is much, much faster than accessing information on a disk. (Faster is better.)

The next line describes the monitor. E770 is the kind of monitor; 17″ is the diagonal measurement of the screen. Parenthetically, it states that the visible part of the screen is 16.0″, with a dp (dot pitch) of .28. The dot pitch refers to the size of the dots on the screen. (Smaller is better.) The next line describes a special video adapter to improve the graphics capability of the machine.

A CD-ROM drive comes with the machine. CD-ROM stands for compact disk, read-only memory. Read-only means that you can read from disks in the drive, but you cannot change any of the information on the disk. The compact disks look just like any CD in your music collection. And, in fact, if you have this drive, you can play any of your CDs on the computer. 48X Max is a measure of how fast information can be accessed on the drive. The X stands for the speed of a standard audio CD player.

As an added bonus with this machine, a free CD-RW drive is installed. A CD-RW is a CD disk drive that also allows you to write information on the disk as well as read information from it. 8X/4X/32X is a measure of the read/write speed on the disk. (Bigger is better.)

The next two lines describe the sound system that is installed within the computer. If you are into computer music, the sound card and the speakers are important. For some people, a computer is as much an audio system as it is a computing device. There is also usually a small internal speaker built into the computer for basic audio beeps and pings.

The modem is described next. The modem is one type of device that allows you to connect to the Internet. V.90 is an International Standards technical specification. 56K Capable means that the modem is capable of processing 56,000 bytes per second. (K stands for kilo: 10^3.) A footnote in the ad (not shown) states that the download speeds are limited to 53K per second and upload speeds are about 30K per second and that these speeds vary by manufacturer and line conditions. Download means information coming from the Internet to your computer; upload means information going from your computer to the Internet. PCI Telephony Modem for Windows means that the modem is configured to work with the Windows Operating System.

The next two lines describe the software that comes installed with the system and the warranty. MS Works Suite 2001 stands for a collection of programs from Microsoft that include a word processor, a spreadsheet program, a data management program, and a display presentation program. The last line says that one year of Internet access is provided by MSN, an Internet service provider.

Within this ad, there are eleven trademarked names: eight marked with an ® and three marked with a ™. Intel and Pentium are registered trademarks of the Intel Corporation. MS, Microsoft, MSN, and Windows are registered trademarks of Microsoft Corporation.

Within this ad, three size measures that are powers of ten have been used. Let's summarize the prefixes that refer to powers of ten that are used frequently in computing.

Putting sizes in perspective

Admiral Grace Murray Hopper demonstrated the relative sizes of computer jargon by displaying a coil of wire nearly 1,000 feet long, a short piece of wire about as long as your forearm, and a bag containing grains of pepper. She would point out that the wire coil was the distance traveled by an electron along the wire in the space of a microsecond. The short piece of wire was the distance traveled by an electron along the wire in the space of a nanosecond. The grains of pepper represented the distance traveled by an electron in a picosecond. She would admonish the members of her audience to remember their nanoseconds.

Multiple of ten	Prefix	Abbreviation	Derivation
10^{-12}	pico	p	Spanish for little
10^{-9}	nano	n	Greek for dwarf
10^{-6}	micro	μ	Greek for small
10^{-3}	milli	m	Latin for thousand
10^{3}	kilo	K	Greek for thousandth
10^{6}	mega	M	Greek for large
10^{9}	giga	G	Greek for giant
10^{12}	tera	T	Greek for monster

We now move from the specific to the general. In the next several sections we look at each of the pieces of hardware that make up a computer from the logical level, rather than from a specific computer configuration.

5.2   Stored-Program Concept

A major defining point in the history of computing was the realization in 1944–45 that data and instructions to manipulate the data are logically the same and could be stored in the same place. The computer design built around this principle, which became known as the *von Neumann architecture*, is still the basis for computers today. Although the name honors John von Neumann, a brilliant mathematician who worked on the construction of the atomic bomb, the idea probably originated with J. Presper Eckert and John Mauchly, two other early pioneers who worked on the ENIAC at the Moore School at the University of Pennsylvania during the same time period.

von Neumann Architecture

Another major characteristic of the von Neumann architecture is that the units that process information are separate from the units that store information. This characteristic leads to the following five components of the von Neumann architecture, shown in Figure 5.1.

- The memory unit that holds both data and instructions

Does it matter who was the father of the modern computer?

All of the people involved in the research and development of electronic computing devices in the late 1930s and 1940s undoubtedly contributed to the computer as we know it. This list includes John Atanasoff, Clifford Berry, and Konrad Zuse, in addition to von Neumann, Eckert, and Mauchly.

In 1951 Sperry Rand bought the patent for the ENIAC and its underlying concepts and began charging royalties to other computer manufacturers. Not wanting to pay royalties, Honeywell researched the history of modern computers and presented evidence that the work of John Atanasoff at Iowa State College had directly influenced Mauchley and Eckert. Because of this evidence, the patent for the ENIAC was invalidated in 1973. See the web site for more information.

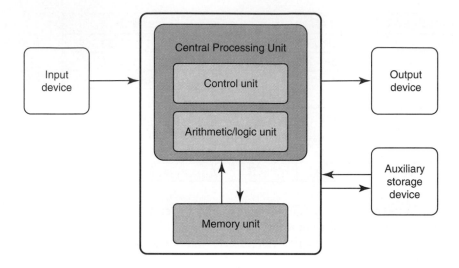

Figure 5.1 The von Neumann architecture

- The arithmetic/logic unit that is capable of performing arithmetic and logic operations on data
- The input unit that moves data from the outside world into the computer
- The output unit that moves results from inside the computer to the outside world
- The control unit that acts as the stage manager to ensure that all the other components act in concert

Memory

Recall from the discussion of number systems that each storage unit, called a bit, is capable of holding a one or a zero and that these bits are grouped together into bytes (8 bits) and that bytes are grouped together into words. Memory is a collection of cells, each with a unique physical address. We use the generic word *cell* here rather than byte or word, because the number of bits in each addressable location, called the memory's **address-ability**, varies from one machine to another. However, most computers are byte-addressable today.

The ad in the previous section describes a memory of 128,000,000 bytes. This means that each of the 128M bytes is uniquely addressable. Therefore, the addressability of the machine is 8 bits. The machine being described could have as many as 4,294,967,296 bytes of memory, but only 128MB are being provided. Where did that figure of possible number of bytes come from? It is 2^{32}. The Pentium IV processor mentioned in the ad is a 32-bit machine. This means that the processor can distinguish 2^{32}

> **Addressability** The number of bits stored in each addressable location in memory

John Vincent Atanasoff

John Vincent Atanasoff was born in Hamilton, New York, on October 4, 1903, one of nine children. When he was about ten, his father bought a new slide rule. After reading the instructions, John Vincent became more interested in the mathematics involved than in the slide rule itself. His mother picked up on his interest and helped him study his father's old college algebra book. He continued his interest in mathematics and science and graduated from high school in two years. His family moved to Old Chicara, Florida where John Vincent graduated from the University of Florida in 1925 with a degree in electrical engineering because the university didn't offer a degree in theoretical physics. A year later, he received a Master's degree in mathematics from Iowa State College. In 1930, after receiving his Ph.D. in theoretical physics, he returned to Iowa State College as an assistant professor in mathematics and physics.

Dr. Atanasoff became interested in finding a machine that could do the complex mathematical work he and his graduate students were doing. He examined computational devices in existence at that time, including the Monroe calculator and the IBM tabulator. Upon concluding that these machines were too slow and inaccurate, he became obsessed with finding a solution. He said that at night in a tavern after a drink of bourbon he began generating ideas of how to build this computing device. It would be electronically operated and would compute by direct logical action rather than enumeration, as in analog devices. It would use binary numbers rather than decimal numbers, condensers for memory, and a regenerative process to avoid lapses due to leakage of power.

In 1939, with a $650 grant from the school and a new graduate assistant named Clifford Berry, Dr. Atanasoff began work on the first prototype of the Atanasoff Berry Computer (ABC) in the basement of the physics building. The first working prototype was demonstrated that year.

In 1941, John Mauchly, a physicist at Ursinus College whom Dr. Atanasoff had met at a conference, came to Iowa State to visit the Atanasoffs and see a demonstration of the ABC machine. After extensive discussions, Mauchly left with papers describing its design. Mauchly and J. Presper Eckert continued their work on a computation device at the Moore School of Electrical Engineering at the University of Pennsylvania. Their machine, the ENIAC, completed in 1945, became known as the first computer.

Dr. Atanasoff went to Washington in 1942 to become director of the Underwater Acoustics Program at the Naval Ordnance Laboratory, leaving the patent application for the ABC computer in the hands of the Iowa State attorneys. The patent application was never filed and the ABC was eventually dismantled without either Atanasoff or Berry being notified. After the war, Dr. Atanasoff was chief scientist for the Army Field Forces and director of the Navy Fuse program at the Naval Ordnance Laboratory.

In 1952, Dr. Atanasoff established The Ordnance Engineering Corporation, a research and engineering firm, which was later sold to Aerojet General Corporation. He continued to work for Aerojet until he retired in 1961.

Meanwhile, in 1947 Mauchly and Eckert applied for the patent on their ENIAC computer. Sperry Rand bought the patent, and when it was issued in 1964, began to collect royalties. Honeywell declined to pay and Sperry Rand brought suit. The subsequent trial lasted 135 working days and filled more than 20,000 pages of transcript from the testimony of 77 witnesses, including Dr. Atanasoff. Judge Larson found that Mauchly and Eckert "did not themselves first invent the automatic electronic digital computer, but instead derived that subject matter from one Dr. John Vincent Atanasoff."

In 1990 President George Bush acknowledged Dr. Atanasoff's pioneering work by awarding him the National Medal of Technology. Dr. Atanasoff died on June 15, 1995.

different memory addresses. Notice the relationship between the bits in the processor and the number of different addresses: n bits can address 2^n different locations.

The cells in memory are numbered consecutively beginning with 0. For example, if the addressability is 8, and there are 256 cells of memory, the cells would be addressed as follows:

Address	Contents
00000000	11100011
00000001	10101001
⋮	⋮
11111100	00000000
11111101	11111111
11111110	10101010
11111111	00110011

What are the contents of address 11111110? The bit pattern stored at that location is 10101010. What does it mean? We can't answer that question in the abstract. Does location 11111110 contain an instruction? A integer with a sign? A two's complement value? Part of an image? Without knowing what the contents represent, we cannot determine what it means: It is just a bit pattern. We must apply an interpretation on any bit pattern to determine the information it represents.

When referring to the bits in a byte or word, the bits are numbered from right to left beginning with zero. The bits in address 11111110 above are numbered as follows:

7	6	5	4	3	2	1	0	⟵ Bit position
1	0	1	0	1	0	1	0	⟵ Contents

Arithmetic/logic unit
The computer component that performs arithmetic operations (addition, subtraction, multiplication, division) and logical operations (comparison of two values)

Arithmetic/Logic Unit

The **arithmetic/logic unit (ALU)** is capable of performing basic arithmetic operations such as adding, subtracting, multiplying, and dividing two numbers. This unit is also capable of performing logical operations such as AND, OR, and NOT. The ALU operates on words; thus the word length of a computer is the size of the quantities processed by the ALU. The word length of the Pentium IV is 32 bits or 4 bytes.

Who Was Herman Hollerith?

In 1889 the United States Census Bureau realized that unless they found a better way to count the 1890 census, the results might not be tabulated before the next required census in 1900. Herman Hollerith had designed a method of counting based on cards with holes

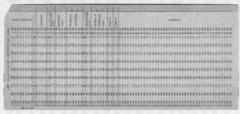

Courtesy of Douglas W. Jones at the University of Iowa

punched in them. This method was used for tabulating the census and the cards became known as Hollerith cards. Hollerith's electrical tabulating system led to the founding of the company known today as IBM. See the book's Web site for more information.

Most modern ALUs have a small amount of special storage units called **registers**. These registers contain one word and are used to store information that is needed again immediately. For example, in the calculation of

One * (Two + Three)

Two is first added to Three and the result is then multiplied by One. Rather than storing the result of adding Two and Three in memory and then retrieving it to multiply it by One, the result is left in a register and the contents of the register is multiplied by One. Access to registers is much faster than access to memory locations.

> **Register** A small storage area in the CPU used to store intermediate values or special data

Input/Output Units

All of the computing power in the world wouldn't be useful if we couldn't input values into the calculations from outside or report to the outside the results of the calculations. Input and output units are the channels through which the computer communicates with the outside world.

An **input unit** is a device through which data and programs from the outside world are entered into the computer. The first input units interpreted holes punched on paper tape or cards. Modern-day input devices include the terminal keyboard, the mouse, and scanning devices used at supermarkets.

An **output unit** is a device through which results stored in the computer memory are made available to the outside world. The most common output devices are printers and video display terminals.

> **Input unit** A device that accepts data to be stored in memory
>
> **Output unit** A device that prints or otherwise displays data stored in memory or makes a permanent copy of information stored in memory or another device

123

Control Unit

Control unit   The computer component that controls the actions of the other components in order to execute instructions in sequence

Instruction register (IR)   The register that contains the instruction currently being executed

Program counter (PC)   The register that contains the address of the next instruction to be executed

CPU   A combination of the arithmetic/logic unit and the control unit; the "brain" of a computer that interprets and executes instructions.

Bus   A set of wires that connect all major sections of a machine through which data flows

Motherboard   The main circuit board of a personal computer

The **control unit** is the organizing force in the computer, for it is in charge of the fetch-execute cycle, discussed in the next section. There are two registers in the control unit. The **instruction register** (**IR**) contains the instruction that is being executed, and the **program counter** (**PC**) contains the address of the next instruction to be executed.

Because the ALU and the control unit work so closely together, they are often thought of as one unit called the **Central Processing Unit**, or CPU.

Figure 5.2 shows the flow of information through the parts of a von Neumann machine. The parts are connected to one another by a collection of wires called a **bus** through which data travels within the computer. You can think of a bus as a highway through which data flows. The data may flow in different ways, but this is a common example.

In a personal computer, the components in a von Neumann machine reside physically in a printed circuit board called the **motherboard**. The motherboard also has connections for attaching other devices to the bus, such as a mouse, a keyboard, or additional storage devices. (See the section on Secondary Storage Devices later in the chapter.)

The Fetch-Execute Cycle

Before looking at *how* a computer does what it does, let's look at *what* it can do. The definition of a computer outlines its capabilities: A computer is a device that can store, retrieve, and process data. Therefore, the instructions that we give to the computer all relate to storing, retrieving, and processing data. In Chapter 8, we look at various languages that we can use to give instructions to the computer. For our examples here, we use simple English-like instructions.

Recall the principal of the von Neumann machine: Data and instructions are stored in memory and treated alike. This means that instructions and data are both addressable. Instructions are stored in contiguous memory locations; data to be manipulated are stored together in a different part of memory. To start the fetch-execute cycle, the address of the first instruction is loaded into the program counter.

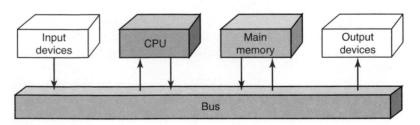

Figure 5.2
Data flow through a von Neumann machine

The steps in the processing cycle are:

- Fetch the next instruction.
- Decode the instruction.
- Get data if needed.
- Execute the instruction.

Let's look at each of these steps in more detail. The process starts with the address in memory of the first instruction being stored in the program counter.

Fetch the Next Instruction

The program counter (PC) contains the address of the next instruction to be executed, so the control unit goes to the address in memory specified in the PC, makes a copy of the contents, and places the copy in the instruction register. At this point the instruction register contains the instruction to be executed. Before going on to the next step in the cycle, the program counter must be updated to hold the address of the next instruction to be executed when the current instruction has been completed. Because the instructions are stored contiguously in memory, adding 1 to the program counter should put the address of the next instruction into the PC. So the control unit increments the program counter. It is possible that the PC may be changed later by the instruction being executed.

Accessing memory takes one cycle. The computer in the ad at the beginning of this chapter can access memory at 133,000,000 cycles per second, so one access takes 7.5 nanoseconds or 7.5 billionths of a second. Is that fast?

Decode the Instruction

In order to execute the instruction in the instruction register, the control unit has to determine what instruction it is. It might be an instruction to access data from an input device, to send data to an output device, or to perform some operation on a data value. At this phase, the instruction is decoded into control signals. That is, the logic of the circuitry in the CPU determines which operation is to be executed. This step shows why a computer can only execute instructions that are expressed in its own machine language. The instructions themselves are literally built into the circuits.

Get Data If Needed

It may be that the instruction to be executed requires additional memory accesses in order to complete its task. For example, if the instruction says

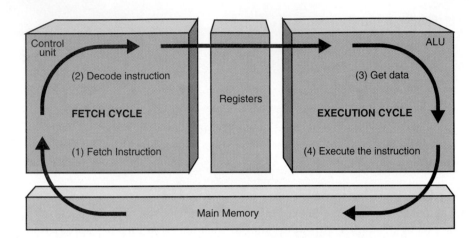

Figure 5.3
The fetch-execute cycle

to add the contents of a memory location to a register, the control unit must get the contents of the memory location.

Execute the Instruction
Once an instruction has been decoded and any operands (data) fetched, the control unit is ready to execute the instruction. Execution involves sending signals to the arithmetic/logic unit to carry out the processing. In the case of adding a number to a register, the operand is sent to the ALU and added to the contents of the register.

When the execution is complete, the cycle begins again. If the last instruction was to add a value to the contents of a register, the next instruction probably says to store the results into a place in memory. However, the next instruction might be a control instruction: an instruction that asks a question about the result of the last instruction and perhaps changes the contents of the program counter.

Figure 5.3 summarizes the fetch-execute cycle.

Hardware has changed dramatically in the last half-century, yet the von Neumann machine is still the basis of most computers today. As Alan Perlis, a well-known computer scientist, said in 1981, "Sometimes I think the only universal in the computing field is the fetch-execute cycle." [2] This statement is still true today, 20 years later.

RAM and ROM

We said previously that RAM stands for **R**andom **A**ccess **M**emory. RAM is memory in which each cell (usually byte) can be directly accessed. Inherent in the idea of being able to access each location is the ability to *change* the contents of each location. That is, storing something else into that place can change the bit pattern in each cell.

Recall that data and instructions reside in main memory and are treated alike. This means that an instruction could be changed while a program is executing. How can this happen? There could be an instruction to take the contents of the location that contains an instruction, add or subtract a value from it, and return it to the same location. There are times that you might actually want to do this. However, inadvertently changing a program can be very costly. ROM memory solves this problem.

ROM stands for **R**ead **O**nly **M**emory. The contents in locations in ROM cannot be changed. Their contents are permanent and cannot be changed by a stored operation. Placing the bit pattern in ROM is called *burning*. The bit pattern is burned either at the time the ROM is manufactured or at the time the computer parts are assembled.

RAM and ROM are differentiated by another very basic property. RAM is volatile; ROM is not. This means that RAM does not retain its bit configuration when the power is turned off, but ROM does. The bit patterns within ROM are permanent. Because ROM is stable and cannot be changed, it is used to store the instructions that the computer needs to start itself. Frequently used software is also stored in ROM to keep from having to read the software in each time the machine is turned on.

Main memory usually contains some ROM along with the general purpose RAM. Note that ROM is also random access. It has been suggested that RAM be called RWM for read/write memory, because all main memory is random access, but the term is already in common use.

Secondary Storage Devices

The von Neumann architecture that we have just examined is hypothetical. We have described the five parts that any computer built using this design must have. An input device is the means by which data and programs are entered into the computer and stored into memory. An output device is the means by which results are sent back to the user. Because most of main memory is volatile and limited, it is essential that there be other types of storage devices where programs and data can be stored when they are no longer being processed or the machine is not turned on. These other types of storage devices (other than main memory) are called *secondary* or *auxiliary* storage devices. Because data must be read from them and written to them, each secondary storage device is also an input and an output device.

Secondary storage devices can be installed within the computer box at the factory or added later as needed. Because these storage devices can store large quantities of data, they are also known as mass storage devices. For example, the hard disk drive that comes with the computer in the ad can store 40,000,000,000 bytes as opposed to 133,000,000 bytes in main memory.

In the next sections we look at several secondary storage devices.

Magnetic Tape

We mentioned card readers and card punches as very early input/output devices. Paper tape readers were the next input/output devices. Although paper tapes, like cards, are permanent, they do not contain much data. The first truly mass auxiliary storage device was the *magnetic tape drive*. A magnetic tape drive is like a tape recorder and is most often used to back up (make a copy of) the data on a disk in case the disk is ever damaged. Tapes come in several varieties, from small streaming-tape cartridges to large reel-to-reel models.

Tape drives have one serious drawback: In order to access data in the middle of the tape, all the data before the one you want must be accessed and discarded. Although the modern streaming-tape systems have the capability of skipping over segments of tape, the tape must physically move through the read/write heads. Any physical movement of this type is time-consuming. See Figure 5.4.

Magnetic Disks

A *disk drive* is a cross between a compact disk player and a tape recorder. A read/write head (similar to the record/playback head in a tape recorder) travels across a spinning magnetic disk, retrieving or recording data. Like a compact disk, the heads travel directly to the information desired, and like a tape, the information is stored magnetically.

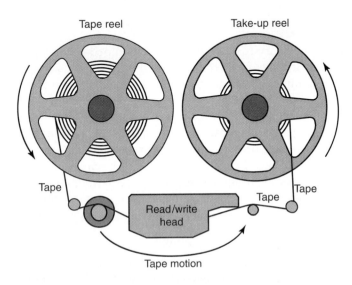

Figure 5.4
A magnetic tape

A magnetic tape storage mechanism

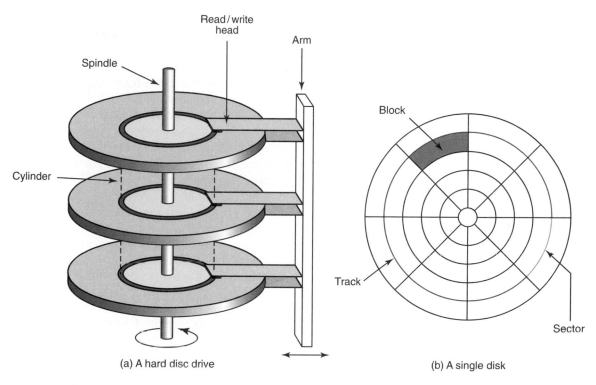

(a) A hard disc drive   (b) A single disk

Figure 5.5   The organization of a magnetic disk

Disks come in several varieties, but they all use a thin disk made out of magnetic material. The surface of each disk is logically organized into **tracks** and **sectors**. Tracks are concentric circles around the surface of the disk. Each track is divided into sectors. Each sector holds a **block** of information as a continuous sequence of bits. (See Figure 5.5.) Although the tracks nearer the center look smaller, each track has the same number of sectors, and each sector has the same number of bits. The blocks of data nearer the center are just more densely packed. The actual number of tracks per surface and the number of sectors per track vary, but 512 bytes or 1024 bytes are common. (The power of two strikes again.) The location of the tracks and sectors are marked magnetically when a disk is formatted; they are not physically part of the disk.

The read/write head in a disk drive is positioned on an arm that moves from one track to another. An input/output instruction specifies the track and sector. When the read/write head is over the proper track, it waits

Track   A concentric circle on the surface of a disk

Sector   A section of a track

Block   The information stored in a sector

until the appropriate sector is beneath the head and the block of information in the sector is then accessed. This process gives rise to four measures of a disk drive's efficiency: **seek time**, **latency**, **access time**, and **transfer rate**. Seek time is the time it takes for the read/write head to get positioned over the specified track. Latency is the time it takes for the specified sector to spin to the read/write head. The average latency is one-half the time for a full rotation of the disk. For this reason, latency is also called rotation delay. Access time is the sum of seek time and latency. Transfer rate is the rate at which data is transferred from the disk to memory.

Now, let's look at some of the varieties of disks. One classification of disk is hard versus floppy. These terms refer to the flexibility of the disk itself. The original floppy disk, introduced in the 1970s, was 8″ in diameter and very floppy. By the time of the rise in personal computers in the late 1970s, the floppy disk had been reduced in size to 5–1/2″ in diameter. Today's generic "floppy" disks are 3–1/2″ in diameter, encased in a hard plastic cover, and capable of storing 1.44 MB of data. Newer machines do not automatically have built-in drives for these disks as they did a few years ago, but they are still popular and drives for them can be added. There are newer specialized disks available today, such as the Zip disk and its associated drive. A Zip disk stores up to several hundred MB on a single hard disk, but is much more expensive.

Hard disks, the disks on the hard drive that comes with the computer, consist of several disks—this sounds strange, so let's explain. Let's call the individual disks platters. Hard disks consist of several platters attached to a spindle that rotates. Each platter has its own read/write head. All of the tracks that line up under one another are called a **cylinder**, which is also shown in Figure 5.5. An address in a hard drive is the cylinder number, the surface number, and the sector. Hard drives rotate at a much higher speed than floppy drives, and the read/write heads don't actually touch the surface of the platters but, rather, float above them. The advertisement that we examined at the beginning of the chapter specified that the hard drive disk rotated 7,200 revolutions per minute. Compare this speed to the average floppy disk drive, which revolves the floppy disk at a tenth of that speed. For this reason, we talk about hard disk transfer rates using megabytes per second and floppy disk transfer rates using kilobytes per seconds.

Compact Disks

The world of compact disks and their drivers looks like acronym soup. The ad we examined used two acronyms: CD-ROM and CD-RW. In addition, we have to decipher CD-DA, CD-WORM, and DVD. And we are sure that by the time you are done reading this book, there will be many more.

Seek time   The time it takes for the read/write head to get positioned over the specified track

Latency   The time it takes for the specified sector to be in position under the read/write head

Access time   The time it takes for a block to start being read; the sum of seek time and latency.

Transfer rate   The rate at which data moves from the disk to memory

Cylinder   The set of concentric tracks on all surfaces

Let's look for a moment at the acronym CD. CD, of course, stands for compact disk—you probably have a collection of them with recorded music. A CD drive uses a laser to read information stored optically on a plastic disk. Rather than having concentric tracks, there is one track that spirals from the inside out. Like other disks, the track is broken into sectors. Unlike magnetic disks where the tracks near the center are more densely packed, a CD has the data evenly packed over the whole disk, thus more information is stored in the track on the outer edges and read in a single revolution. In order to make the transfer rate consistent throughout the disk, the rotation speed varies depending on the position of the laser beam.

The other letters attached to CD refer to various properties of the disk, such as formatting, and whether or not the information on them can be changed. CD-DA is the format used in audio recordings: CD-DA stands for **C**ompact **D**isk-**D**igital **A**udio. Certain fields in the format are used for timing information. A sector in a CD-DA contains 1/75 of a second of music.

CD-ROM is the same as CD-DA but the disk is formatted differently. Data is stored in the sectors reserved for timing information in CD-DA. ROM stands for **R**ead-**O**nly **M**emory. As we said when we described the CD-ROM that was in the ad, read-only memory means that the data is permanent on the disk and cannot be changed. A sector on a CD-ROM contains 2KB of data. The CD-ROM drive described in the ad gave the transfer rate, but did not give the capacity of a disk read by the drive. However, the capacity is in the neighborhood of 600 MB.

DVD is a newer technology that can store up to 10 GB. DVD, which stands for **D**igital **V**ersatile **D**isk, can store multi-media presentations that combine audio and video. As you probably know, movies are now available on DVDs.

The acronym CD-WORM stands for **W**rite **O**nce, **R**ead **M**any. This technology allows a CD to be recorded after its manufacture. This format is used typically for archiving data, where the data is not to be changed after being recorded. Then, finally, the acronyms RW or RAM mean that the disk can be both read from and written to.

> ### NASA Backup Computers
>
> In the early days of manned space flights, NASA used a backup system composed of three mainframe computers, each of which calculated exactly the same thing. If one computer failed, there were still two computers carrying out the necessary calculations. If two computers failed, there was still one computer left to do the necessary processing. If three computers failed—well, fortunately that never happened.

5.3 Non-von Neumann Architectures

The linear fetch-execute cycle of the von Neumann architecture still dominates the technology today. However, since 1990, alternative parallel-

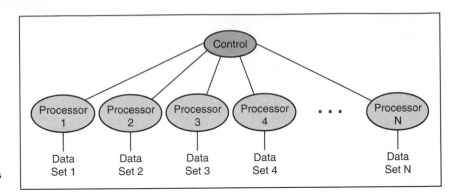

Figure 5.6
Processors in a synchronous computing environment

processing systems have entered the marketplace. They have the potential to process much more data at much higher speeds.

One approach to parallelism is to have multiple processors apply the same program to multiple data sets. In this approach, processors often execute the same instructions at the same time; that is, a common program is run at each processor. This approach is called **synchronous processing** and is effective when the same process needs to be applied to many data sets. See Figure 5.6. This approach is similar to that of the NASA backup system in which three computers do the same thing as a security measure. However, here there are multiple processors applying the same process to different data sets in parallel.

Another configuration arranges processors in tandem, where each processor contributes one part to an overall computation. This approach is called **pipelining**, and is reminiscent of an assembly line. When this organization is applied to data, the first processor does the first task. Then the second processor starts working on the output from the first processor, while the first processor applies its computation to the next data set. Eventually, each processor is working on one phase of the job, each getting material or data from the previous stage of processing, and each in turn handing over its work to the next stage. See Figure 5.7.

Synchronous processing Multiple processors apply the same program in lock-step to multiple data sets

Pipelining processing Multiple processors arranged in tandem, where each contributes one part of an overall computation

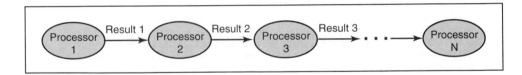

Figure 5.7   Processors in a pipeline

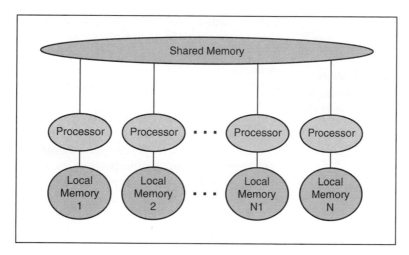

Figure 5.8
A shared-memory configuration of processors

In the first example, each processor is doing the same thing to a different data set. For example, each processor might be computing the grades for a different class. In the second example, each processor is contributing to the grade for the same class. The third approach is to have different processors doing different things with different data. This configuration allows processors to work independently much of the time, but introduces problems of coordination among the processors. This leads to a configuration where the processors each have a local memory and a shared memory. The processors use the shared memory for communication, and the configuration is thus called a **shared-memory** configuration. See Figure 5.8.

Shared memory
Multiple processors share a global memory

5.4   Interpreting Ads

Walter S. Mossberg, a columnist for *The Wall Street Journal*, listed items to watch out for when shopping for a personal computer.[3] Here are a few of his points that are relevant to the jargon in computer ads.

Increased processor speed does not necessarily mean better performance in tasks such as web surfing, e-mail, and word processing as long as the machine has sufficient memory. That is, the more memory you have, the less powerful the processor needs to be. Be aware, however, that the total memory that comes with a computer may not be available to the user. In lower-priced machines, memory may be siphoned off to power the video processor. For example, in a 64MB shared-memory machine, only 54 to 60MB may be available for programs.

The X used in rating CD-ROMs stands for the speed of a standard audio CD player. When evaluating the CD-ROM, be aware that the higher speeds listed for CD-ROMs are usually attainable only when retrieving data from certain parts of the CD. The speed stated is not an average. Therefore, faster may not be better in terms of the added cost.

Summary

The components that make up a computer cover a wide range of devices. They each have characteristics that dictate how fast, large, and or efficient they are. Furthermore, they each play an integral role in the overall processing of the machine.

The world of computing is filled with jargon and acronyms. The speed of a processor is specified in GHz (gigahertz), the amount of memory is specified in MB (megabytes), external storage devices are specified in GB (gigabytes), and a monitor is specified in db (dot pitch). Intel and Pentium are registered trademarks of Intel Corporation; MS, Microsoft, MSN, and Windows are registered trademarks of Microsoft Corporation.

The von Neumann architecture is the underlying architecture of most of the computers today. It has five main parts: memory, the arithmetic/logic (ALU) unit, input devices, output devices, and the control unit. The fetch-execute cycle, under the direction of the control unit, is the heart of the processing. In this cycle, instructions are fetched from memory, decoded, and executed.

RAM and ROM are acronyms for two types of computer memory. RAM stands for random-access memory; ROM stands for read-only memory. The values stored in RAM can be changed; those in ROM cannot.

Secondary storage devices are essential to a computer system. These devices save data when the computer is not running. Magnetic tape and magnetic disk are two common types of secondary storage.

Although von Neumann machines are by far the most common, there are other architectures. For example, there are machines with more than one processor so that calculations can be done in parallel, thus speeding up the processing.

ETHICAL ISSUES

Facial Recognition/Privacy

Forgot your password? Not a problem! Lost your ID? No need to worry! Soon, your face may be the only key you need to access ATMs, enter secure buildings, or log on to your e-mail. Facial recognition technology, until recently relegated to the realm of science fiction, is now becoming a central security feature for companies and organizations all over the world.

Facial recognition is an identity verification technique that matches the structure of a person's face to his/her picture with over 99% accuracy. While only recently gaining the public's attention, facial recognition technology has been in development for well over a decade and has been used for commercial purposes since 1997. It is a branch of biometrics, an increasingly popular method of identity verification that is more reliable than traditional codes, pictures, and passwords. Biometric technology takes unique physical characteristics, such as fingerprints, eyes, ears, or faces, and compares them with a database developed for identification purposes. Unlike handprints and iris scans, "faceprints" are obtained in a nonintrusive manner, and the scanning and matching system is less expensive than other techniques.

To obtain a faceprint, cameras scan the peaks and valleys of features, called nodal points. The face contains over 80 nodal points, but only 14 to 22 stable nodal points are needed for a successful match. Stable nodal points are those that do not fluctuate with weight or expression, such as eye socket depth. Once a faceprint is obtained, it is compared to a database of images.

Because of its speed and accuracy, facial recognition software has become popular in casinos as a means to identify known cardsharps. The technology has also been used as a security precaution to spot known terrorists in international airports. Tampa, Florida is one of the first cities to use facial recognition in a public setting in an effort to reduce crime rates. In the 2001 Super Bowl, Tampa officials scanned the faces of the 100,000 spectators and compared each with its database of known felons.

Was this an invasion of privacy? Football fans did not give permission for their faces to be scanned, but proponents of the use of these techniques note that permission is not obtained by stores and malls who use video surveillance cameras for similar purposes either. Opponents feel that this surveillance technique violates individual rights to privacy. These critics oppose both clandestine capture (the scanning of faces without consent) and tracking (the use of this technology to monitor a person's movements). Privacy advocates, such as the Electronic Privacy Information Center, are concerned that this Big Brother technology takes away an individual's right to anonymity and an individual's control over his/her personal information. Users of these techniques, however, assert that only public offenders and missing children, whose photographs are in the databases, are affected.

Key Terms

Access time pg. 130

Addressability pg. 120

Arithmetic/logic unit pg. 122

Block pg. 129

Bus pg. 124

Control unit pg. 124

CPU pg. 124

Cylinder pg. 130

Input unit pg. 123

Instruction register (IR) pg. 124

Latency pg. 130

Motherboard pg. 124

Output unit pg. 123

Pipelining processing pg. 132

Program counter (PC) pg. 124

Register pg. 123

Sector pg. 129

Seek time pg. 130

Shared memory pg. 133

Synchronous processing pg. 132

Track pg. 129

Transfer rate pg. 130

Exercises

1. Define the following terms.
   a. Pentium III processor
   b. hertz
   c. random-access memory

2. What is the word length in the Pentium IV processor?

3. What does it mean to say that a processor is 1.4 GHz?

4. What does it mean to say that memory is 133 MHz?

5. How many bytes of memory are in the following machines?
   a. 128MB machine
   b. 256MB machine

6. Define RPM and discuss what it means in terms of speed of access to a disk.

7. Define the following terms and give their abbreviation.
    a. pico
    b. nano
    c. micro
    d. milli

8. Define the following terms and give their abbreviation.
    a. kilo
    b. mega
    c. giga
    d. tera

9. Give the derivation of the terms in Exercises 7 and 8.

10. What is the stored-program concept and why is it important?

11. What does "units that process information are separate from the units that store information" mean in terms of a computer architecture?

12. Name the components of a von Neumann machine.

13. What is the addressability of an 8-bit machine?

14. What is the function of the ALU?

15. Which component in the von Neumann architecture acts as the stage manager. Explain.

16. Punched cards and paper tape were early input/output mediums. Discuss their advantages and disadvantages.

17. What is an instruction register? What is its function?

18. What is a program counter? What is its function?

19. List the steps in the fetch-execute cycle.

20. Explain what is meant by "fetch an instruction."

21. Explain what is meant by "decode and instruction."

22. Explain what is meant by "execute an instruction."

23. Compare and contrast RAM and ROM memory.

24. What is a secondary storage device? Why are such devices important?

25. Discuss the pros and cons of using magnetic tape as a storage medium.

26. Draw one surface of a disk showing the tracks and sectors.

27. Define what is meant by a block of data.

28. What is a cylinder?

29. Define the steps that a hard disk drive goes through to transfer a block of data from the disk to memory.

30. Distinguish between a compact disk and a magnetic disk.

31. Define the following acronyms.
    a. CD
    b. CD-ROM
    c. CD-DA
    d. CD-RW
    e. DVD

32. Compare the transfer rates of a hard disk and a floppy disk.

33. Compare the storage capacity of a hard drive and a floppy disk.

34. Compare the storage capacity of a generic floppy disk and a zip disk.

35. Look in your local newspaper for an ad for a desktop computer. How many acronyms did you recognize? How many did you not recognize?

36. Call the manufacturer of the computer that was advertised in Exercise 35 and get the definitions of the acronyms that you did not recognize.

37. Describe a parallel architecture that uses synchronous processing.

38. Describe a parallel architecture that uses pipeline processing.

39. How does a shared-memory parallel configuration work?

40. How many different memory locations can a 16-bit processor access?

41. In discussing the computer ad, we used the expression "Faster is better" three times. Explain what it means in each case.

42. In discussing the computer ad, we used the expression "Smaller is better" in relation to the monitor. Explain.

43. In discussing the computer ad, we used the expression "Bigger is better" in relation to the compact disk. Explain.

44. Keep a diary for a week of how many times the terms hardware and software appear in television commercials.

45. Take a current ad for a desktop computer and compare that ad with the one shown at the beginning of this chapter.

46. What is the common name for the disk that is a secondary storage device?

47. To what does the expression *dot pitch* refer?

48. What is a modem?

49. Which are faster, download seeds or upload speeds?

50. What is included in MS Works Suite 2001?

? Thought Questions

1. Would octal or hexadecimal be a better way to refer to the addresses in a 16-bit processor? Justify your answer.

2. Relate the concept of a program to the fetch/execute cycle of the von Neumann machine.

3. Personal computers originally came equipped with one, then two floppy drives. After that, floppy drives became optional as CD drives became standard. What do you think will be the standard personal computer of the future?

4. After the September 11 hijackings and subsequent suicide attacks, there was talk of using biometric technology for airport screening. What do you think of this use of biometrics? Would it make air travel more secure?

5. Must citizens give up privacy for security? What are the pros and cons of this issue?

The Programming Layer

6 Problem Solving and Algorithm Design

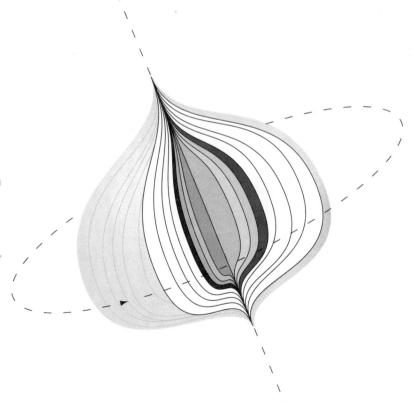

Problem Solving and Algorithm Design

Chapter 6 is the first chapter in the programming layer. In Chapters 2 and 3 we have covered the basic information necessary for understanding a computing system, including number systems and how to represent different types of information in a computer. In Chapters 4 and 5 we have covered the hardware components of a computer. Now the emphasis changes from what a computer system is to how to use one.

In this chapter we examine ways to solve problems and how to write the solutions (algorithms) in a shorthand called *pseudocode*. These pseudocode solutions are like recipes. Just as a recipe is a set of instructions for cooking a particular food dish, a pseudocode algorithm is a set of instructions for how to solve a particular problem. In subsequent chapters in this layer, we cover translating a pseudocode solution into a programming language that can be run on a computer.

Goals

After studying this chapter, you should be able to

- determine whether a problem is suitable for a computer solution.
- describe the computer problem-solving process and relate it to Polya's How to Solve It list.
- distinguish between following an algorithm and developing one.
- apply top-down design methodology to develop an algorithm to solve a problem.
- define the key terms in object-oriented design.
- apply object-oriented design methodology to develop a collection of interacting objects to solve a problem.
- discuss the following threads as they relate to problem solving: information hiding, abstraction, naming things, and testing.

6.1   Problem Solving

What do the words *problem solving* mean to you? Do they evoke images of a child drearily working on a photocopied math worksheet? Of a farmer trying to get his hay in before the storm comes? Of your mother trying to make the budget balance with the increase in college tuition? Of Albert Einstein wrestling with the theory of relativity? Of you trying to get the seven people you asked to the game into your four-seater car? Of your girlfriend or boyfriend who seems to be drifting away? Of the address list that you promised to organize for your club yesterday? Of the troubles in Northern Ireland? Of India and Pakistan?

A dictionary defines a problem as a question raised for inquiry, consideration, or solution. In mathematics, a problem is usually a situation to resolve with well-defined mathematical principles. Another definition says that a problem is an intricate unsettled question or a source of perplexity, distress, or vexation. Solving is defined as finding a solution for something such as a problem. Putting these definitions together, **problem solving** is the act of finding a solution to a perplexing, distressing, vexing, or unsettled question.

Certainly, all of the problems in the first paragraph meet this definition. However, only some of them are of interest in the context of computing. The computer cannot be used, at least directly, to help the farmer with his hay, the squeezing of additional people into a car, the girl with the drifting boyfriend, the centuries-old conflict between Catholics and Protestants in Northern Ireland, or the religious and territorial conflicts between India

Problem solving The act of finding a solution to a perplexing question

and Pakistan. The computer cannot be used to solve problems involving physical activity or emotions.

Furthermore, the computer can do nothing without being told what to do. A computer is not intelligent. It cannot analyze a problem and come up with a solution. A human (the *programmer*) must analyze the problem, develop the instructions for solving the problem (the *program*), and then have the computer carry out the instructions.

What's the advantage of using a computer if it can't solve problems? Well, once we have written a solution for the computer, the computer can repeat the solution very quickly and consistently, again and again, for different situations and data. The computer frees people from repetitive and boring tasks.

The computer can be used to make the math worksheet more interesting (and less dreary) by letting the student interact with a computer-based worksheet. The student can see the worksheet on the screen and enter the solutions. The program can check the answers and give feedback to the student. The computer can be used to help your mother with her budget by taking over the time-consuming task of keeping track of the finances. There are many commercial software packages available to provide this help.

Who knows how much time would have been saved if Einstein had had access to one of today's supercomputers with enhanced mathematical capabilities. What about your address list? There are many packages available to help with organizing information such as address lists. In addition, it is a relatively simple task to write a program to handle a specific address list. Any second-year computer science student could write a simple version within a week.

How to Solve Problems

In 1945, G. Polya wrote a little book entitled *How to Solve It: A New Aspect of Mathematical Method*.[1] Although this book was written over 50 years ago when computers were only experimental—it remains the classic description of the problem-solving process. The process is summarized in Figure 6.1.

What has made Polya's book a classic is that his How to Solve It list is quite general. Although it was written in the context of solving mathematical problems, we can replace the words *unknown* with *problem*, *data* with *information*, and *theorem* with *solution*, and the list becomes applicable to all types of problems. Of course, it is the second step—finding the connection between the information and the solution—that is at the heart of problem solving. Let's look at several strategies suggested by Polya's list.

Ask Questions

If you are given a problem or task verbally, you typically ask questions until what you are to do is clear. You ask when, why, and where until your task is completely specified. If your instructions are written, you

HOW TO SOLVE IT

UNDERSTANDING THE PROBLEM

First.
You have to *understand* the problem.

What is the unknown? What are the data? What is the condition?
Is it possible to satisfy the condition? Is the condition sufficient to determine the unknown? Or is it insufficient? Or redundant? Or contradictory?
Draw a figure. Introduce suitable notation.
Separate the various parts of the condition. Can you write them down?

DEVISING A PLAN

Second.
Find the connection between the data and the unknown. You may be obliged to consider auxiliary problems if an immediate connection cannot be found. You should obtain eventually a *plan* of the solution.

Have you seen it before? Or have you seen the same problem in a slightly different form?
Do you know a related problem? Do you know a theorem that could be useful?
Look at the unknown! And try to think of a familiar problem having the same or a similar unknown.
Here is a problem related to yours and solved before. Could you use it? Could you use its result? Could you use its method? Should you introduce some auxiliary element in order to make its use possible? Could you restate the problem? Could you restate it still differently? Go back to definitions.
If you cannot solve the proposed problem, try to solve first some related problem. Could you imagine a more accessible related problem? A more general problem? A more special problem? An analogous problem? Could you solve a part of the problem? Keep only a part of the condition, drop the other part; how far is the unknown then determined; how can it vary? Could you derive something useful from the data? Could you think of other data appropriate to determine the unknown? Could you change the unknown or the data, or both if necessary, so that the new unknown and the new data are nearer to each other? Did you use all the data? Did you use the whole condition? Have you taken into account all essential notions involved in the problem?

CARRYING OUT THE PLAN

Third.
Carry out your plan.

Carrying out your plan of the solution, *check each step.* Can you see clearly that the step is correct? Can you prove that it is correct?

LOOKING BACK

Fourth.
Examine the solution obtained.

Can you *check the result?* Can you check the argument? Can you derive the result differently? Can you see it at a glance? Can you use the result, or the method, for some other problem?

Figure 6.1   Polya's How to Solve It list. *Polya, George; How to Solve it. Copyright © 1945 renewed 1973 by Princeton University Press. Reprinted by permission of Princeton University Press.*

might put question marks in the margin, underline a word, a group of words, or a sentence, or in some other way indicate the parts of the task that are not clear. Perhaps your questions may be answered in a later paragraph, or you might have to discuss them with the person giving you the task. If the task is one that you set for yourself, this sort of questioning might not be verbal, but instead takes place on the subconscious level.

George Polya

George Polya was born in Budapest on December 13, 1887. Although he became known as a world famous mathematician, he did not show an early interest in mathematics. His lack of interest might be explained by his memory of three high school mathematics teachers: "two were despicable and one was good."

In 1905, Polya entered the University of Budapest, where he studied law at the insistence of his mother. After one very boring semester, he decided to study languages and literature. He earned a teaching certificate in Latin and Hungarian—and never used it. He became interested in philosophy and took courses in math and physics as part of his philosophy studies. He settled on mathematics, commenting that "I am too good for philosophy and not good enough for physics. Mathematics is in between." He received his Ph.D. in mathematics in 1912, which launched his career.

Polya did research and taught at the University of Göttingen, the University of Paris, and the Swiss Federation of Technology in Zurich. While in Zurich he interacted with John von Neumann, about whom he said, "Johnny was the only student I was ever afraid of. If, in the course of a lecture, I stated an unsolved problem, the chances were he'd come to me as soon as the lecture was over, with the complete solution in a few scribbles on a slip of paper."

Like many Europeans of that era, he moved to the United States in 1940 because of the political situation in Germany. After teaching at Brown University for two years, he moved to Palo Alto to teach at Stanford, where he remained for the rest of his career.

Polya's research and publications encompassed many areas of mathematics, including number theory, combinatorics, astronomy, probability, integral functions, and boundary value problems for partial differential equations. The George Polya Prize is given in his honor for notable application of combinatorial theory.

Yet, for all George Polya's contributions to mathematics, it is his contribution to mathematics education for which he was the most proud and for which he will be the most remembered. His book, *How to Solve It*, published in 1945, sold over a million copies and was translated into 17 languages. In this book, Polya outlines a problem-solving strategy designed for mathematical problems. The generality of the strategy makes it applicable to all problem solving, however. Polya's strategy is the basis of the computer problem-solving strategy outlined in this text. *Mathematics and Plausible Reasoning*, published in 1954, was another book dedicated to mathematics education. He not only wrote about mathematics education, but also took an active interest in the teaching of mathematics. He was a regular visitor to the schools in the Bay Area and visited most of the colleges in the western states. The Math Center at the University of Idaho is named for him.

On September 7, 1985, George Polya died in Palo Alto at the age of 97.

Some typical questions you should be asking are as follows:

- What do I know about the problem?
- What is the information that I have to process in order the find the solution?
- What does the solution look like?
- What sort of special cases exist?
- How will I recognize that I have found the solution?

Look for Familiar Things

You should never reinvent the wheel. If a solution exists, use it. If you've solved the same or a similar problem before, just repeat the successful solution. We usually don't consciously think, "I have seen this before, and I know what to do," we just do it. Humans are good at recognizing similar situations. We don't have to learn how to go to the store to buy milk, then to buy eggs, then to buy candy. We know that going to the store is always the same and only what we buy is different.

Recognizing familiar situations is particularly useful in computing. In computing, you see certain problems again and again in different guises. A good programmer sees a task, or perhaps part of a task (a subtask), that has been solved before and plugs in the solution. For example, finding the daily high and low temperatures in a list of temperatures is exactly the same problem as finding the highest and lowest grades in a list of test scores. You want the largest and smallest values in a set of numbers.

Divide and Conquer

We constantly break up a large problem into smaller units that we can handle. The task of cleaning the house or apartment may seem overwhelming. The task composed of cleaning the living room, the dining room, the kitchen, the bedrooms, and the bathroom seems more manageable. This principle is especially relevant to computing. We break up a large problem into smaller pieces that we can solve individually.

This approach applies the concept of abstraction that we discussed in Chapter 1—cleaning the house is a large, abstract problem made up of the subtasks defined by cleaning the individual rooms. Cleaning a room can also be thought of as an abstraction of the details of straightening the dresser, making the bed, vacuuming the floor, and so on. Tasks are divided into subtasks, which can be divided further into sub-subtasks and so forth. The divide-and-conquer approach can be applied over and over again until each subtask is manageable.

Applying These Strategies

Now let's apply these strategies (called *heuristics*) to a specific problem: How do we get to the party next Saturday at Sally's house?

Questions: Where is Sally's house? Where are we coming from? What is the weather like (or likely to be like)? Will we be walking? Driving a car? Taking a bus? Once these questions have been answered, you can begin to plan the solution.

If it is raining, the car is in the shop, and the busses have stopped, the best solution might be to call a taxi and give the driver Sally's address.

If we are driving, we look at a map and see that Sally's address is six blocks west of the building where we work, so the first part of the solution might be to repeat what we do each morning to get to work (providing we are leaving from home). The next part would be to turn west and go six blocks. If we have trouble remembering how many blocks we have driven, we might take a pencil and make a hash mark on a piece of paper each time we cross a street. Though hash marking might be stretching the human solution a little too much, this is a technique used frequently in a computer solution. To repeat a process ten times, we have to write the instructions to count each time the process is done and check to see when the count reaches 10. In computing, this process is called *repetition* or *looping*.

If we need to write the directions for other people, some of whom would be leaving from one place and some from another, we would have to write two sets of directions prefaced by a question: Where are you coming from? If you are coming from place A, follow the first set of directions; otherwise, follow the second set of directions. In computing, this process is called *conditional processing*.

Coming up with a step-by-step procedure for solving a particular problem is not always cut and dried. In fact, it is usually a trial-and-error process requiring several attempts and refinements. We test each attempt to see if it truly solves the problem. If it does, fine. If it doesn't, we try again.

Algorithms

The last sentence in the second step in Polya's list says that you should eventually obtain a plan of the solution. In computing, the plan is called an **algorithm**. An algorithm is set of instructions for solving a problem or subproblem in a finite amount of time using a finite amount of data. Implicit in this definition is that the instructions are unambiguous. In computing, we must make certain conditions explicit that are implicit in human solutions. For example, in everyday life we would not consider a solution that takes forever to be much of a solution. We would also reject

Algorithm Unambiguous instructions for solving a problem or subproblem in a finite amount of time using a finite amount of data

a solution that requires us to process more information than we are capable of processing. These constraints must be explicit in a computer solution, so the definition of an algorithm includes them.

The third step in Polya's list is to carry out the plan, that is, to test the solution to see if it solves the problem. The fourth step is to examine the solution for future applicability.

Computer Problem-Solving

In computing, there are three phases in the problem-solving process: the *algorithm development phase*, the *implementation phase*, and the *maintenance phase*. See Figure 6.2. The output from the algorithm development phase is a plan for a general solution to the problem. The output from the second phase is a working computer program that implements the algorithm, that is, a specific solution to the problem. There is no output from the third phase, unless errors are detected or changes need to be made. If so, these errors or changes are sent back either to the first phase or second phase, whichever is appropriate. See Figure 6.3.

Notice that all of Polya's phases are included in this outline of how we solve problems using the computer. The first step is always to understand the problem. You cannot write a computer solution to a problem you don't understand. The next step is to develop a plan—an algorithm—for the solution. There are various techniques for expressing algorithms. We introduced one, shown in the box on the next page, when we were describing how to convert numbers from base 10 to other bases.

Algorithm Development Phase
    Analyze   Understand (define) the problem.
    Propose algorithm Develop a logical sequence of steps to be used to solve the problem.
    Test algorithm   Follow the steps as outlined to see if the solution truly solves the problem.

Implementation Phase
    Code   Translate the algorithm (the general solution) into a programming language.
    Test   Have the computer follow the instructions. Check the results and make corrections until the answers are correct.

Maintenance Phase
    Use   Use the program.
    Maintain   Modify the program to meet chaining requirements or to correct any errors.

Figure 6.2 The computer problem-solving process

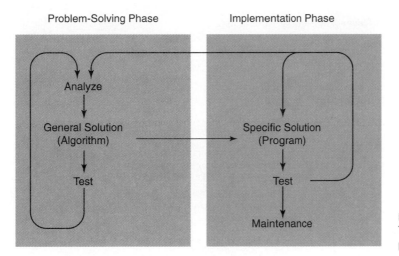

Problem-Solving Phase   Implementation Phase

Analyze

General Solution
(Algorithm)

Specific Solution
(Program)

Test

Test

Maintenance

Figure 6.3
The interaction between
problem-solving phases

> While (the quotient is not zero)
>   Divide the decimal number by the new base
>   Make the remainder the next digit to the left in the answer
>   Replace the original decimal number with the quotient

This form for presenting algorithms, called *pseudocode*, uses a mixture of English and formatting to make the steps in the solution explicit. Whatever form you use for your algorithm, you must test it by examining it carefully to be sure that it does solve the problem.

The next step is to implement the plan in a way that the computer can execute it and test the results. In Polya's list, the human executes the plan and evaluates the results. In a computer solution, a program is written expressing the plan in a language that the computer can execute. But it is the human who takes the results of the computer program and checks them to be sure that they are correct. The maintenance phase maps to Polya's last stage, where the results are examined and perhaps modified.

Following an Algorithm

Although you work with algorithms all the time, most of your experience with them is in the context of *following* them. You follow an algorithm every time you follow a recipe, play a game, assemble a toy, or take medicine. Let's look at a recipe and see how this fits the description of an algorithm. See Figure 6.4.[2]

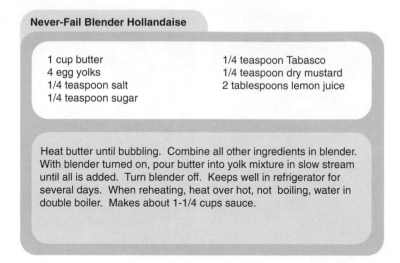

Figure 6.4
A recipe for Hollandaise sauce

To be an algorithm, the steps must solve a problem. In this case the problem is preparing a Hollandaise sauce, a wonderful mayonnaise-type sauce used on steak or for Eggs Benedict. Are the directions in a step-by-step fashion that someone can follow? Is there a finite amount of data—ingredients, in this case? Can it be made in a finite amount of time? Provided that the stove is working, the butter will eventually bubble. So we can answer yes to all three questions. This is definitely an algorithm. Of course, it is easier to follow an algorithm than it is to devise one.

Let's reorganize this recipe and present it in the algorithm format we used previously.

Put butter in a pot
Turn on burner
Put pot on the burner
While (NOT bubbling)
    Leave pot on the burner
Put other ingredients in the blender
Turn on blender
While (more butter)
    Pour butter into blender in slow stream
Turn off blender

As we said in Chapter 5, computing has its jargon; so does cooking. *Repeat* and *While* are terms that have meaning within the context of programming. *Bubbling* is a term that any cook recognizes.

In our recipe analogy, someone else undertook the algorithm development phase and, hopefully, the implementation phase, including the testing. When we make the Hollandaise sauce, we are in the maintenance phase. We are using a recipe that someone else developed and tested.

Developing an Algorithm

We looked briefly at developing an algorithm when we looked at applying the problem-solving strategies to the problem of giving directions. We asked questions and looked at several alternatives. Humans are involved in the problem-solving process every day. In fact, we do it so often that it has become instinctive. We go from one step to the next in Polya's list every day without being conscious of it. It is only when we have a big problem to solve that we take time to examine what we are doing and become aware of the transition between stages.

In computing, the implementation phase involves translating the plan into a form that the computer can use to execute it. In order to make this translation, the plan must be in a suitable form. Therefore, we must develop a methodology that begins with the problem statement and hopefully ends with the plan—an algorithm—in a form that can be translated. We talk about the process of converting the algorithm into a *program*, the form that the computer can execute, in a later chapter. Here we are interested in outlining a reliable process.

There are two methodologies that are currently used: *top-down design* (also called *functional decomposition)* and *object-oriented design* (OOD). We introduce top-down design first because it mirrors how we solve problems in general. We cover object-oriented design, a newer methodology, later in the chapter. In recent years OOD has become very popular in the computing world. Both of these methodologies are based on the divide-and-conquer strategy.

6.2 Top-Down Design

The **top-down design** process starts by breaking the problem into a set of subproblems. Then, each subproblem is divided into subproblems. This process continues until each subproblem is defined at a level basic enough so that further decomposition is not necessary. We are creating a hierarchical structure, also known as a tree structure, of problems and subproblems, called **modules**. Modules at one level can call on the services of

Top-down design A technique for developing a program in which the problem is divided into more easily handled subproblems, the solutions of which create a solution to the overall problem

Module A self-contained collection of steps that solves a problem or subproblem

modules at a lower level. These modules are the basic building blocks of our algorithm.

The goal of dividing our problem into subproblems, modules, or segments is to be able to solve each module fairly independently of the others. In a computing context, one module could read data values, another could sum the values, another could print the sum, while still another compares the sum to the previous week's totals.

The design tree contains successive levels of refinement (see Figure 6.5). The top, or level 0, is our functional description of the problem; the lower levels are our successive refinements. So how do we divide the problem into modules?

Well, let's think for a moment how humans usually approach any big problem. We spend some time thinking about the problem in an overall sort of way, then we jot down the major steps. We then examine each of the major steps, filling in the details. If we don't know how to accomplish a specific task, we go to the next one, planning to come back and take care of the one we skipped later when we have more information. What are we doing? We are dividing the problem into subproblems; we are using the divide-and-conquer strategy.

This is exactly the process you should be using in designing an algorithm. Write down the major steps. This then becomes your main module.

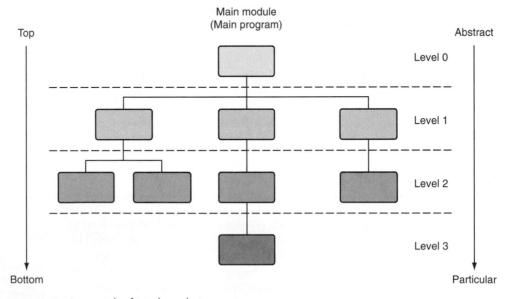

Figure 6.5   An example of top-down design

Begin to develop the details of the major steps as level 1 modules. If you don't know how to do something, or feel overwhelmed by details, give the task a name and go on. The name can be expanded later as a lower module.

This process continues for as many levels as it takes to expand every task to the smallest details. A step that needs to be expanded is an **abstract step**. A step that does not need to be expanded is a **concrete step**. If a task is cumbersome or difficult, defer its details to a lower level. This process can be applied to the troublesome subtasks. Eventually, the whole problem is broken up into manageable units.

Writing a top-down design is similar to writing an outline for an English paper. The domain of computing is new, but the process is one you have done all your life.

Abstract step   An algorithmic step for which some details remain unspecified

Concrete step   A step for which the details are fully specified

A General Example

Let's apply this top-down design process to the pleasant task of planning a large party. A little thought reveals that there are two main tasks: inviting the people and preparing the food. (We ignore cleaning the house in this example.)

One approach to inviting the people would be to reach for the phone book and start calling our friends. However, we would soon be confused as to whom we had reached, whose line was busy, whose answering machines we left messages on, and who had said what. A much better approach would be to make a list of those we wished to invite, then put the list aside and check it over the next day to see which of our best friends we had forgotten.

Then with the list in hand we can go through and fill in the telephone numbers. Now we begin to call and mark down the messages left and the responses. It may take a while to reach everyone, but we know where we stand. By the time we have an estimate of numbers, we can start planning the food.

Heaven help us if we just run in and start cooking! Without prior planning the job would be overwhelming. Instead, let's break down this task into planning the menu and preparing the food.

We can save a lot of time and effort in this task if we take advantage of what others have done and look at suggested menus in cookbooks. (In computing, we would look in the literature to see if algorithms already exist to solve this subproblem.) As we choose a menu, we can put off a careful examination of the recipes until later. The time to do that is when we are preparing the shopping list. Our goal is to defer details until the appropriate time to handle them.

The tree diagram in Figure 6.6 shows the process we have broken down so far. Note that a module at each level expands a task or step at the level

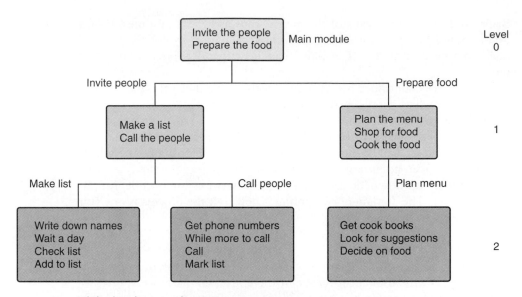

Figure 6.6   Subdividing the party planning

above. As humans we could probably take the level 2 modules and do them from this description. In computing, we would have to break them down into much finer detail. For example, *Write down names* would have to be at the following level of detail:

Do you have paper?
    No, get paper.
Do you have a pen?
    No, get a pen.
Pick up pen.
Put pen to paper.
etc.

Our top-down design for giving a party might be quite different. If we had a great little delicatessen down the block, we could let them cater the party. Then the main module would be:

Invite the people
Call the delicatessen

To summarize, the main module specifies the names of tasks. Each name of a task needs to be expanded at a lower level unless the task is completely specified. This is true of each level. There are as many modules at level 1 as there are names of tasks at level 0 that are not completely specified, and so on for each successive level.

A Computer Example

Let's leave the social analogy now and look at the process applied to a problem whose solution can be implemented in a computer. We can use English sentences or pseudocode to express our algorithms. The algorithm format that we have used is an example of pseudocode. As we go along we introduce certain English words that have special meaning in our pseudocode. For example, we used the words While and Repeat to express that certain statements were to be repeated. We use the word If to indicate that we are asking a question and only one of two statements or groups of statements will be used.

We said previously that the computer could be used to help with an address list. Let's collect all the scraps of paper and business cards that are stuck in various places and create a list of names, addresses, telephone numbers, and e-mail addresses, in alphabetical order by last name. The first step is to formulate the problem statement.

Problem: Create an address list that includes each person's name, address, telephone number, and e-mail address. This list should then be printed in alphabetical order. The names to be included in the list are on scraps of paper and business cards.

Surprisingly, the starting point in solving a computer problem is to ask how we would do the task by hand. Why? Because if we cannot do the task by hand, we do not understand it well enough to begin writing the algorithm. In this case, the first step would be to round up all the scraps of paper and cards from various pockets and wallets and sit down at a desk.

The next step in the by-hand solution is to take a writing tablet and jot down each name. If the address, telephone number, and/or e-mail are with the name, add this information to the list. Once we have recorded all the information we have, we can look up the missing information. Once all of the information is on our tablet, we put the names into alphabetical order. As often happens, our by-hand solution serves as a model for the computer solution. Instead of using a tablet, we enter the information into a list kept in the computer. After the list of information is entered, the computer goes through it and finds where information is missing and requests that missing information be entered. When all the data is complete, the list is sorted. We can now write our main module, substituting list for tablet.

Main	Level 0
Enter names into list	
Fill in missing data	
Put list into alphabetical order	
Print the list	

Now we must further specify the first task: Enter names into list. As we indicated, the human must gather the information beforehand. The process of entering the names involves the human keying in the names. This can be done in an interactive fashion, where the computer gives a prompt for information (data) to be entered and the user keys in the information as prompted, or the data can be entered beforehand and the computer just reads it from disk. Let's have this algorithm enter the data interactively. Note that we have talked about using shorthand for entering the names and the associated data.

Enter names into list	Level 1
Prompt for and enter names includes other data as well	
Insert names into list	

In the last paragraph, we used the words *information* and *data*. These are common words, and we've used them interchangeably until now. But let's take a detour before we go on to the next module and define them more precisely in the computing context. There are various definitions in the literature, but these are the ones we use in this text: **Information** is any knowledge that can be communicated; **data** is information in a form that a computer can use. So in the context of this algorithm, we gather the information together and enter the data.

We now have a choice: We can decompose the second task at level 0 or the first task at level 1. Let's continue working down the tree rather than across the tree. That is, let's finish with entering the names before we start looking at inputting the missing information. Prompting for and entering names involves telling the person entering the data exactly how to input each piece of data. We also need to indicate what to do if there is no information about one of the fields. For example, if an address is not known at this time, what should be entered? Let's tell the person entering the data to

Information Any knowledge that can be communicated

Data Information in a form that a computer can use

just press the return key if there is no data for an item. We need to enclose these instructions within a loop.

Prompt for and enter names   Level 2

Write "To any of the prompts below, if the information is not known, just
    press return."
While (more names)
    Write "Enter the last name, a comma, a blank, and the first name;
        press return."
    Read lastFirst
    Write "Enter street number and name; press return."
    Read street
    Write "Enter city, a comma, a blank, and state; press return."
    Read cityState
    Write "Enter area code and 7-digit number; press return."
    Read telephone
    Write "Enter e-mail; press return."
    Read eMail

Determining when there are more names to enter is easy in a by-hand algorithm: The stack of papers and cards is empty. Determining how to do it in a computer algorithm is more difficult. Let's assume that the level of detail is sufficient.

What do Write and Read mean? These are special words that we use with algorithms to stand for "put information on the screen" and "get the data that the user has entered." Remember from the discussion of von Neumann machines that there are input devices, which allow us to enter data from the outside world into memory, and there are output devices, which allow us to display data so that the world outside the computer can see it.

We have used some shorthand in this subalgorithm that needs clarifying. We have called the information about a person name. Name is actually a collection of four pieces of data, called fields. We use the following names for these fields: lastFirst for the name itself, street for the street address, cityState for the city and state, telephone for the 10-digit telephone number, and eMail for the e-mail address. These names are called *identifiers*. In the next two chapters, we describe how these fields become associated with memory locations and how the input data becomes the contents of these places. For the moment, you can defer these details until later.

Now that we have the names and associated data, we can insert the data into the list. Do we need to further refine the Insert names into list module? The answer can be either no or yes, depending on the language into which we are going to translate the algorithm. We discuss the languages into which algorithms are translated in the next chapter. For this example, let's assume that the level of detail is sufficient for this module.

So now, we go back to the second level 0 module: Fill in missing data. The algorithm must go through each of the names and determine whether any data is missing. If data is missing, the user must be prompted to enter the missing data. We express this process by using the word If with an expression in parentheses. If the expression is true, the indented process is carried out; if the expression is not true, the indented process is skipped. So we must check each of the four data items to see if data is missing. How does the algorithm determine if a data item is missing? That's not our problem at this level. We can defer these details to a later refinement. We can also defer until later how we access each item in the list. Here we just say to get a name from the list.

Fill in missing data   Level 1

Write "To any of the prompts below, if the information is still not known,
    just press return."
Get a name from the list
While there are more names
  Get a lastFirst
  Write lastFirst
  If (street is missing)
    Write "Enter street number and name; press return."
    Read street
  If (telephone is missing)
    Write "Enter area code and 7-digit number; press return."
    Read telephone
  If (eMail is missing)
    Write "Enter e-mail; press return."
  Get a name from the list

The next module to be specified is Put list in alphabetical order. In computing terms, alphabetizing a list is called **sorting** the list. If the contents of the list are numbers, they are put into numeric order. If the contents of the list are strings, as they are in this case, they are put in alphabetic order. Sorting algorithms abound in the literature, so we can just use one of them. We do have to specify what field we want to use for the **sort key**. If the data that we want to sort is made up of more than one field, the sort key is the field on which we want to order the list. In our case, the sort key is the person's name, which we call lastFirst.

Sorting Putting a list of items in order, either numerically or alphabetically

Sort key The field to be used in the ordering

The last module is Print the list. This task requires us to loop through the list, printing each item.

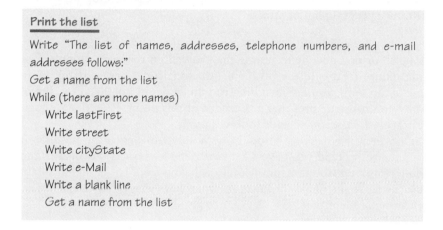

Here is the tree structure for this algorithm. The tasks in blue need to be further specified in a module at a lower level.

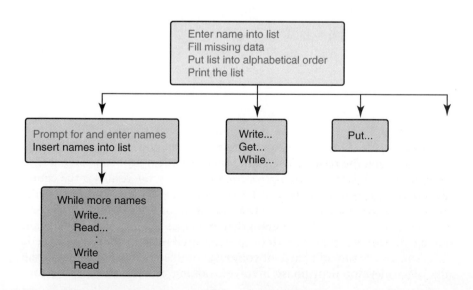

Summary of Methodology

The top-down methodology can be broken down into four major steps:

1. Analyze the Problem

Understand the problem! List the information you have to work with. This information is probably going to be the data in the problem. Specify what the solution is to look like. If it is a report, specify the format. List any assumptions that you are making about the problem or the information. Think. How would you solve the problem by hand? Develop an overall algorithm or general plan of attack.

2. Write the Main Module

Use English or pseudocode to restate the problem in the main module. Use module names to divide the problem into functional areas. If the main module is too long, you are including too much detail for this level. Introduce any control structures that are needed at this point. Re-sequence logically, if needed. Postpone details to lower levels.

Don't worry if you don't know how to solve an unwritten module at this point. Just pretend you have a "smart friend" who has the answer and postpone thinking about it until later. All you have to do in the main module is to give the names of lower-level modules that solve certain tasks. Use meaningful identifiers.

3. Write the Remaining Modules

There is no fixed number of levels. Modules at one level can specify more modules at lower levels. Each module must be complete although it references unwritten modules. Do successive refinements through each module until each statement is a concrete step.

4. Re-Sequence and Revise as Necessary

Plan for change. Don't be afraid to start over. Several attempts and refinements may be necessary. Try to maintain clarity. Express yourself simply and directly.

Testing the Algorithm

Both Polya's list and the model of computer problem solving have testing as an integral part. Of course, Polya doesn't use the word *test*; his list talks about checking the results. The goal of mathematical problem solving is to produce a specific answer to a problem, so checking the results is the equivalent of testing the process by which the answer was derived. If the answer is correct, the process is correct. However, the goal of computer problem solving is the *process*. The program that embodies the process is used again and again with different data, so the process itself must be tested or verified.

Testing occurs in all phases of computer problem solving. Testing at the algorithm development phase involves looking at each level of the top-down design and saying, "If the levels below this are correct, does this level do what needs to be done?" Let's apply this strategy to test the address list solution. Here is the problem statement: Create an address list that includes each person's name, address, telephone number, and e-mail address. This list should then be printed in alphabetical order. The names to be included in the list are on scraps of paper and business cards.

The main module consists of four steps: entering the names, filling in the missing data, putting the list into alphabetical order, and printing the list. We make the assumption that each of the four tasks is correctly carried out, and ask the question: Does the correct completion of these four tasks solve the problem? The names are entered in the first task, so all of the names are present. The second module fills in all the missing data, so the list is complete. The third module sorts the names into alphabetical order. The fourth module prints the names. Because the third sorts the names, the fourth task prints them in alphabetical order. At the completion of the fourth task, we have an alphabetical listing of the names and associated information.

Now we must repeat the process with the next level modules. Entering names into the list is broken down into two steps: prompting for and entering names and inserting the names into the list. We make the assumption that these tasks are correctly carried out and ask the question: Does the correct completion of these two tasks correctly solve the first step in the main module? If the names are correctly entered into the machine and then correctly put in the list, the names are in the list. We now have a choice of going down into the tree structure or across the same level. Let's verify that the names are properly prompted for and entered. This is a longer module, so it is repeated below.

Prompt for and enter names   Level 2

Write "To any of the prompts below, if the information is not known, just
    press return."
While (there are more names)
  Write "Enter the last name, a comma, a blank, and the first name;
    press return."
    Read lastFirst
    Write "Enter street number and name; press return."
    Read street
    Write "Enter city, a comma, a blank, and state; press return."
    Read cityState
    Write "Enter area code and 7-digit number; press return."
    Read telephone
    Write "Enter e-mail; press return."
    Read eMail

The first step tells us what to do if there is missing data. The next sets up a looping situation that continues as long as there is more data to be read. The first step in the loop describes how the name is to be entered; the next step reads the data. We assume that the user enters the data correctly and that the read executes correctly; therefore, the name is stored in the lastFirst part of the name. The same logic can be applied to the next three pairs of statements. The first specifies how the user is to input the data; the second reads the data. We have now verified this module. We ask you to finish verifying this design in the exercises.

The process we have used is a *top-down testing*. We assume that lower modules are correct and verify the main module. Then we take each first-level module and repeat the process. Then we take each second-level module and repeat the process. Alternately, we can take one first-level module and verify it and all its submodules before going to the second first-level module. This continues until all the modules have been verified. An alternative approach is *bottom-up testing*. Bottom-up testing starts by verifying the lowest-level modules first, and working toward the top of the design tree.

This process that we used to verify this design is called **desk checking**. We sit at a desk with a pencil and paper and work through the design. It is useful to take actual data values and trace what happens to them as we reason about the design. For example, we can take a few names, some with all the information and some with only partial values, and follow the design by hand.

Teams of programmers develop most professional computer programs. A verification method analogous to desk checking that is used by teams is a **walk-through**. A walk-through is a manual simulation of the design by the team members. They take sample data values and simulate the design using the sample data. Another team-oriented technique is an **inspection**. In this technique, the design is handed out in advance, and one person (not the designer) reads the design line by line while the others point out errors. These activities are carried out in as nonthreatening a manner as possible. The goal is not to criticize the design or the designer, but to remove defects in the product. Sometimes it is difficult to remove the natural human emotion of pride from this process, but the best teams adopt a policy of *egoless programming*.

Desk checking
Tracing the execution of a design on paper

Walk-through A manual simulation of a design, performed by a team

Inspection A verification method in which one member of the team reads the design line by line and the others point out errors

6.3   Object-Oriented Design

We said that we were going to cover top-down design first because it mirrors more the way humans solve problems. As you can see, a top-down solution produces a hierarchy of tasks. Object-oriented design is a problem-solving methodology that produces a solution to a problem in terms of self-contained entities called *objects*, which are composed of both data and operations that manipulate the data. Object-oriented design focuses on the objects and their interactions within a problem.

Object Orientation

Data and the algorithms that manipulate the data are bundled together in the object-oriented view, thus making each object responsible for its own manipulation (behavior). Underlying object-oriented design (OOD) are the concepts of *classes* and *objects*.

An **object** is a thing or entity that makes sense within the context of the problem. For example, if the problem relates to information about students, a student would be a reasonable object in the solution. A group of similar objects is described by an **object class**, or **class** for short. Although no two students are identical, students do have properties and behaviors in common. Students are male or female humans who attend courses at a school (at least most of the time). Therefore, students would be a class. The word *class* refers to the idea of classifying objects into related groups and describing their common characteristics. Therefore, a class describes the properties and behaviors that objects of the class exhibit. Any particular object is an instance (concrete example) of the class.

Object-oriented problem solving involves isolating the classes within the problem. Objects communicate with each other by sending messages (invoking each other's subprograms). A class contains **fields** that represent the properties and behaviors of the class. A field can contain data value(s) and/or methods (subprograms). A **method** is a named algorithm that manipulates the data values in the object. A class in the general sense is a pattern for what an object looks like (data) and how it behaves (methods).

Object An entity or thing that is relevant in the context of a problem

Object class or **class** A description of a group of objects with similar properties and behaviors

Fields Named items in a class; can be data or subprograms

Method A named algorithm that defines one aspect of the behavior of a class

Relationships between Classes

Object classes can relate to one another in three ways. The first relationship is that a class can contain an instance of another class as a field. This relationship is called **containment**. This is a "part-of" or "contains" relationship. An address class may be part of the definition of a student class; therefore, a student object may contain an address object.

A second relationship is that a class can inherit from another class. **Inheritance** is a property of object-oriented design in which classes can inherit data and behavior from other classes. This relationship is an "is-a" relationship. A *super class* is a class being inherited from; a *derived class* is a class doing the inheriting. Classes form an inheritance hierarchy. In the hierarchy, objects become more specialized the lower in the hierarchy we

Containment A mechanism whereby one class contains an object of another class as a field

Inheritance A mechanism by which one class acquires the properties—data fields and methods—of another class

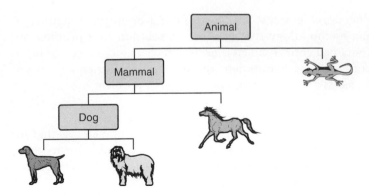

Figure 6.7
An example of inheritance

go. Classes lower down in the hierarchy inherit all the behaviors and data of their parent superclass.

For example, Maggie, the brown pet, is an instance of the class Labrador. A Labrador is a dog, a dog is a mammal, and a mammal is an animal. Therefore, Maggie inherits all the characteristics of animals, mammals, dogs, and Labradors: She is an affectionate, big brown animal that nursed her puppies. See Figure 6.7. Another example would be a student. A student is a person, so he or she can inherit all the properties of people and add the behavior of going to school.

The third way that classes can relate to one another is through collaboration. One class can call upon another class to provide information or a service. A student class can call on the services of a library class to check out a book. Note that all classes can collaborate with one another, even those that are related through containment or inheritance.

Top-down design is a problem-solving methodology based on breaking a problem into successively smaller tasks until each task is a concrete step that can be coded in a programming language. This structured design view sees each module as a step in the overall process. Thus, top-down design decomposes the problem into algorithmic steps. Object-oriented design is based on looking for the objects in the problem rather than tasks to be solved. Thus, object-oriented design decomposes the problem according to the key abstractions in the problem domain.

Object-Oriented Design Methodology

There are four stages to the decomposition process that we present. *Brainstorming* is the stage in which we make a first pass at determining the classes in the problem. *Filtering* is the stage in which we go back over the proposed classes determined in the brainstorming stage to see if any can be combined or if any are missing. Each class that survives the filtering stage is recorded on a 5-by-8 card with appropriate headings, called a *CRC card*.

Scenarios is the stage in which the behavior of each class is determined. Because each class is responsible for its own behavior, we call the behaviors *responsibilities*. In this stage, "what if" questions are explored to be sure that all situations are examined. When all of the responsibilities of each class have been determined, they are recorded on the class's CRC card, along with the names of any other classes with which it must collaborate (interact) to complete its responsibility. *Responsibility algorithms*, the last stage, is where the algorithms are written for each of the responsibilities outlined on the CRC cards. Now you can see where the term CRC comes from: Class, Responsibility, and Collaboration.

Origin of CRC cards

CRC cards were first introduced by Kent Beck and Ward Cunningham at a conference on "Object-Oriented Systems, Languages and Applications" in 1989. This simple card technique has now been endorsed by many prominent software developers as a means of getting started analyzing the problem domain. These advocates include Grady Booch, Ed Yourdon, Rebecca Wirfs-Brock, and Adele Goldberg.[3]

Class Name:	Superclass:	Subclasses:
Responsibilities	**Collaborations**	

Let's look at each of these stages in a little more detail.

Brainstorming

What is *brainstorming*? The dictionary defines it as a group problem-solving technique that involves the spontaneous contribution of ideas from all members of the group.[4] Brainstorming brings to mind a movie or TV show where a group of bright young people tosses around ideas about an advertising slogan for the latest revolutionary product. This picture seems at odds with the traditional picture of a computer analyst working alone in a closed, windowless office for days who finally jumps up shouting "Ah ha!" As computers have gotten more powerful, the problems that can be solved have gotten more and more complex, and the picture of the genius locked in a windowless room has become obsolete. Solutions to complex problems need new and innovative solutions based on collective "Ah ha!"s.

Belin and Simone list four principles of successful brainstorming.[5] First and foremost, all ideas are potential good ideas. It is imperative that the members of the group don't censor their own ideas or make judgments out of hand on others' ideas. The next principle relates to pace: Think fast and furiously first, and ponder later. The faster the pace at first, the better the creative juices flow. Thirdly, give every voice a turn. To slow down those predisposed to hog the conversation and spur those reluctant to talk, use a rotation. Continue the pattern until team members are truly forced to "pass" because they are out of ideas. Lastly, a little humor can be a powerful force. Humor helps convert a random group into a cohesive team.

In the context of object-oriented problem solving, brainstorming is a group activity designed to produce a list of candidate classes to be used to solve a particular problem. Belin and Simone point out that although each project is different and each team has a different personality, the following four steps are a good general approach.

Step 1 is to review brainstorming principles at the beginning of the meeting to remind everyone that this is a group activity and personal style should be put aside. Step 2 is to state specific session objectives such as: "Today we want to come up with a list of candidate classes for the student project," or "Today we want to determine the classes that are active during the registration phase." Step 3 is to use a round-robin technique to allow the group to proceed at an even tempo but give people enough time to think. Each person should contribute a possible object class to the list. A facilitator should keep the discussion on target, and a scribe should take notes. The brainstorming stops when each person in the group has to "pass" because he or she cannot think of another class to suggest. Step 4 of Belin and Simone's process is to discuss the classes and select the final list of classes. We prefer to think of this stage as separate from brainstorming and discuss it in the next section.

Just as the people brainstorming for an advertising slogan know something of the product before the session, brainstorming for classes requires that the participants know something about the problem. Each participant should be familiar with the requirements document and any correspondence relating to the technical aspects of the project. If there seem to be ambiguities, participants should conduct interviews to clarify these points before the brainstorming sessions. Each team member should enter the brainstorming sessions with a clear understanding of the problem to be solved. No doubt during the preparation, each team member will have generated his/her own preliminary list of classes.

Filtering

The brainstorming session produces a tentative list of classes. The next phase is to take the tentative list of classes and determine which are the core classes in the problem solution. There may be two classes on the list that are actually the same thing. These duplicate classes usually arise because people within different parts of an organization use different names for the same concept or entity. There may be two classes in the list that have many common attributes and behaviors. The common parts should be gathered together into a superclass with the two classes inheriting the common properties and adding the properties that are different.

There may be classes that really don't belong in the problem solution. For example, if we are simulating a calculator, we might list the user as a possible class. However, the user is not within the simulation as a class; the user is an entity outside the problem that provides input to the simulation. Another possible class might be the *on* button. However, a little thought shows that the *on* button is not part of the simulation; it is what starts the simulation program running.

As the filtering is completed, CRC cards should be written for each of the classes that have survived to this stage.

Scenarios

The goal of this phase is to assign responsibilities to each class. What are responsibilities? They are the tasks that each class must perform. Responsibilities are eventually implemented as subprograms. At this stage we are interested only in *what* the tasks are, not in how they might be carried out.

There are two types of responsibilities: what a class must know about itself (knowledge) and what a class must be able to do (behavior). A class *encapsulates* its data (knowledge); objects in one class cannot directly access data in another class. **Encapsulation** is the bundling of data and actions in such a way that the logical properties of the data and actions are separated from the implementation details. Encapsulation is a key to abstraction. However, each class has the responsibility of making data (knowledge) available to other classes that need it. Therefore, each class has responsibility for knowing the things about itself that others need to know. For example, a student class should "know" its name and address. The responsibilities for this knowledge might be called *know name* and *know address*. Whether the address is kept in the student class or whether the student class must ask some other class to access the address is irrelevant at this stage. The important fact is that the student class knows its own address.

The responsibilities for behavior look more like the tasks we described in top-down design. For example, a responsibility might be for the student class to calculate its grade point average gpa. In top-down design, we would say that a task is to calculate the gpa given the data. In object-oriented design, we say that the student class is responsible for calculating its own gpa. The

Encapsulation
Bundling data and actions so that the logical properties of data and actions are separated from the implementation details

Figure 6.8
A scenario walk-through in progress

distinction is both subtle and profound. The final code for the calculation may look the same, but it is executed in different ways. In a program based on a top-down design, the program calls the subprogram that calculates the gpa, passing the student object as a parameter. In an object-oriented program, a message is sent to the object of the class to calculate its gpa. There are no parameters because the object to which the message is sent knows its own data.

The name for this phase gives a clue as to how to go about assigning responsibilities to classes. The team uses play acting to test different scenarios. Each member of the team plays the role of one of the classes. Scenarios are "what if" scripts that allow participants to act out different situations. When a class has been sent a message, the actor holds up the CRC card and responds to the message, sending messages to others as needed. As the scripts are being acted out, missing responsibilities are unearthed and unneeded responsibilities are detected. Sometimes the need for new classes surfaces. Although waving cards in the air when "you" are active may be a little embarrassing at first, team members quickly get into the spirit of the action when they see how effective the technique is. See Figure 6.8.

The output from this phase is a set of CRC cards representing the core classes in the problem solution. The responsibilities for each class are listed on the card, along with the classes with which a responsibility must collaborate.

Responsibility Algorithms
Eventually, the algorithms must be written for the responsibilities. Because of the process of focusing on data rather than actions in the object-

oriented view of design, the algorithms for carrying out responsibilities tend to be fairly short. For example, the knowledge responsibilities usually just return the contents of one of an object's variables, or send a message to another object to retrieve it. Action responsibilities are a little more complicated, often involving calculations. Thus, the top-down method of designing an algorithm is usually appropriate for designing responsibility algorithms.

Final Word

To summarize, top-down design methods focus on the *process* of transforming the input into the output, resulting in a hierarchy of tasks. Object-oriented design focuses on the *data objects* that are to be transformed, resulting in a hierarchy of objects. Grady Booch puts it this way: "Read the specification of the software you want to build. Underline the verbs if you are after procedural code, the nouns if you aim for an object-oriented program." [6]

We propose that you circle the nouns and underline the verbs. The nouns become objects; the verbs become operations. In a top-down design, the verbs are the primary focus; in an object-oriented design, the nouns are the primary focus.

General Example

We first applied the top-down process to planning a big party. Let's now reevaluate the party problem with our object-oriented process using our four-stage methodology.

Brainstorming and Filtering

It is a little difficult to brainstorm with one person or even two, so we must simulate brainstorming and filtering with words. What are the possible objects? There must be the host or hostess, the guests, the menu, and the food. Where is the party going to be? We need an address object. Are the invitations to be done by phone or by invitation? Let's assume by written invitation, so we have invitation objects.

If we are going to send invitations, we need a list of people to which to send them. A list would be a *container* object: an object that contains other objects. In order to prepare the food, we need to know how many people are coming. This means that we need two containers: one for the list of those to whom invitations are sent and one for those who are coming.

Can we combine any of these objects into one class? A host or hostess is no different from the guests except he/she starts the process by inserting names into the invitation list. Can we combine them into one class? Let's assume that there is a person class of which the host or hostess and the guests are objects. For the moment let's assume that there is one list class with two objects: one for the invitation list and one for the guest list. Here is the list of possible classes at this stage.

Scenarios

What are the scenarios that occur? Let's begin with sending the invitations. Whose responsibility is it to send the invitations? The host or hostess. So send invitations must be added as a responsibility to the person class. No, that's not right. It isn't reasonable for all people to have this responsibility. Let's make the host/hostess be an object of a class that is derived from the person class with the added responsibility of sending the invitations. With what classes must the host/hostess class interact (collaborate)? The invitation class, the person class, and the list class. The CRC for the host/hostess class looks like this so far.

Class Name: Host/Hostess	Superclass: Person	Subclasses:
Responsibilities	**Collaborations**	
Send invitations	Invitation, Person, List	

Another scenario would involve the person class responding to an invitation. How would we simulate a person responding to an invitation? A message would be sent to the person asking him or her to respond if free on a certain date. Thus, the responsibility would be to respond if free with a parameter that represents the date. Oops, this scenario shows that we forgot the date object. How can a person carry out this responsibility? A person object must look at its calendar.... Each person needs to collaborate with a calendar object, so we need a calendar class. Should every person have this responsibility? No, probably not. Let's derive another class from person called guest.

Class Name: *Guest*	Superclass: *Person*	Subclasses:
Responsibilities		**Collaborations**
Respond to invitation (date)		*Date, calendar*

We leave this general example at this stage and go on to a more concrete example.

Computer Example

Once again, let's repeat the problem-solving process for a previous example, except this time using an object-oriented approach. To refresh your memory:

Problem: Create an address list that includes each person's name, address, telephone number, and e-mail address. This list should then be printed in alphabetical order. The names to be included in the list are on scraps of paper and business cards.

Brainstorming and Filtering
Let's try circling the nouns and underlining the verbs.

Create an address list that includes each person's name, address, telephone number, and e-mail address. This list should then be printed in alphabetical order. The names to be included in the list are on scraps of paper and business cards.

The first pass at a list of classes would include the following:

Three of these classes are the same: the two references to *list* and one reference to *address list*. The two references to *address* are not the same. There is an address class with street, city, and so forth, and an e-mail address. *Order* is a noun, but what is an *order class*? This is actually describing how the list class should print its items. Therefore, we discard it as a class. *Name* and *names* should be combined into one class. *Scraps, paper,* and *cards* describe objects that contain the data in the real world. They have no counterpart within the design. Our filtered list is shown below.

The verbs in the problem statement give us a head start on the responsibilities: *create, print,* and *include*. Like *scraps, paper,* and *cards, include* is an instruction to someone preparing the data and has no counterpart within the design. However, this does indicate that we must have an object that inputs the information to be put on the list. Exactly what is this information? It is the name, address, telephone, and e-mail address of each person on the list. But this train of thought leads to the discovery that we have missed a major clue in the problem statement. A possessive adjective, person's, actually names a major class; name, address, telephone, and e-mail are classes that help define (are contained within) a person class.

Now we have a design choice. Should the person class use the input object(s) to initialize itself or should the input object create the person object with the appropriate data? Let's let the person class be responsible for initializing itself. The person class must also be responsible for printing itself.

Does the person class collaborate with any other class? This depends on how we decide to represent the data in the person class. Do we represent name, address, telephone, and e-mail as simple data items within person or do we represent each as a class? Let's temporarily represent each as a class. We may rethink this when we implement the design in a programming language. Let's make each class responsible for initializing and printing itself.

Class Name: *Person*	Superclass:	Subclasses:
Responsibilities	**Collaborations**	
Initialize itself (name, address, telephone, e-mail)	Name, Address, Telephone, E-mail	
Print	Name, Address, Telephone, E-mail	

Class Name: *Name*	Superclass:	Subclasses:
Responsibilities	**Collaborations**	
Initialize itself (name)	String	
Print itself	String	

Class Name: Address	Superclass:	Subclasses:
Responsibilities	**Collaborations**	
Initialize itself (street, city, state)	String	
Print itself	String	

Class Name: Telephone	Superclass:	Subclasses:
Responsibilities	**Collaborations**	
Initialize itself (number)	String	
Print itself	String	

Class Name: E-mail	Superclass:	Subclasses:
Responsibilities	**Collaborations**	
Initialize itself (e-mail)	String	
Print itself	String	

What about the list object? Should the list keep the items in alphabetical order or should the list sort the items before printing them? Each language in which we might implement this design has a library of container classes available for use. Let's use one of these, which keeps the list in alphabetic order. This library class should also print the list. We can create a CRC card for this class, but mark that it most likely will be implemented using a library class.

Class Name:	Superclass:	Subclasses:
SortedList (from library)		

Responsibilities	Collaborations
Insert (person)	Person
Print	Person

Responsibility Algorithms

Person class   There are two responsibilities to be decomposed: initialize and print. Because each of the fields of the class is a class, we can just let each initialize and print itself.

Initialize

```
name.Initialize()
address.Initialize()
telephone.Initialize()
email.Initialize()
```

Print

```
name.Print()
address.Print()
telephone.Print()
email.Print()
```

Name class   This class has the same two responsibilities: *initialize* and *print*; however, the algorithms are different. For Initialize, the user must be prompted to enter the name and the algorithm must read the name. For Print, the first and last names must be output with appropriate labels.

Initialize

"Enter the first name."
Read a string into firstName
"Enter the last name."
Read a string into lastName

Print

Print line "First name: " + firstName
Print line "Last name: " + lastName

Address, Telephone, and E-mail classes   The algorithms for the responsibilities for these classes are mirror images of the algorithms for class Name.

We stop the design at this point. Go back to the beginning of Chapter 6 and look at the top-down design for the same problem. The designs are quite different. Is one better than the other? Well, the object-oriented design has created several classes that might be useful in other contexts. *Reusability* is one of the great advantages of an object-oriented design. Classes designed for one problem can be used in another, because each class is self-contained; that is, each class is responsible for its own behavior.

6.4   Important Threads

In this chapter, we have mentioned several topics in passing that are important not only in problem-solving but in computing in general. Let's review some of the common threads discussed in this chapter.

Information Hiding

Several times we have used the idea of deferring the details. We have used it in the context of giving a name to a task and not worrying about how the task is to be implemented until later. The details of the implementation are deferred to a later time. Deferring the details in a design has distinct advantages. The details of a design are hidden from the higher levels. The designer sees just the details that are relevant at a particular level of the design. This practice, called **information hiding**, makes the details at a lower level inaccessible during the design of the higher levels.

This practice must seem very strange! Why shouldn't the details be accessible while the algorithm is being designed? Shouldn't the designer know everything? No. If the designer knows the low-level details of a module, he/she is more likely to base the module's algorithm on these details. And it is these low-level details that are more likely to change. If they do, then the entire module has to be rewritten.

The advantage of using information hiding when writing algorithms becomes more evident when we look at translating the algorithm into a computer language, so we return to this thread later.

> **Information hiding** The practice of hiding the details of a module with the goal of controlling access to the details of the module

Abstraction

Abstraction and information hiding are two sides of the same coin. Information hiding is the practice of hiding details; abstraction is the result with the details hidden. As we said in Chapter 1, an abstraction is a model of a complex system that includes only the details essential to the viewer. Take, for example, Daisy, the English Spaniel. To her owner she is the household pet, to a hunter she is a bird dog, and to the vet she is a mammal. Her owner sees her wagging tail, hears her yelp when she gets left outside, and see the hair she leaves everywhere. The hunter sees a finely trained helper who knows her job and does it well. The vet sees all of the organs, flesh, and bones of which she is composed. See Figure 6.9.

> **Abstraction** A model of a complex system that includes only the details essential to the viewer

Figure 6.9
Different views of the same concept

In algorithm design, a module at a higher level is an abstraction of those modules underneath it. We see later when we examine translating an algorithm that there are two major kinds of abstraction in computing. **Data abstraction** refers to the view of data; it is the separation of the logical view of data from its implementation. For example, your bank's computer may represent numbers in 2's complement or 1's complement, but this distinction is of no concern to you as long as your bank statements are accurate. **Procedural abstraction** refers to the view of actions; it is the separation of the logical view of an action from its implementation. For example, when you hit the brakes of your car, the car stops (hopefully). How pressing the brake makes the car stop is immaterial to you—as long as you stop.

> **Data abstraction**   The separation of the logical view of data from its implementation
>
> **Procedural abstraction** The separation of the logical view of an action from its implementation
>
> **Control abstraction** The separation of the logical view of a control structure from its implementation
>
> **Control structure**   A statement used to alter the normally sequential flow of control

There is a third kind of abstraction in computing, called **control abstraction**. Control abstraction refers to the view of a *control structure*; it is the separation of the logical view of a control structure from its implementation. We have used several control structures in our algorithms. For example, While and If are control structures. While lets us indicate that we want to repeat an action; If let's us indicate that we want to make a choice. In an algorithm the steps flow sequentially. We follow the first step, the second step, and so forth. A **control structure** lets us alter this sequential flow of control. How these control structures are implemented in the languages into which we might translate an algorithm is immaterial to the design of the algorithms.

Abstraction is the most powerful tool people have for managing complexity. This statement is true in computing as well as real life.

Naming Things

When we write algorithms, we use shorthand to stand for the tasks and information with which we are dealing. We give names to data and processes. These names are called *identifiers*. For example, we used lastFirst to stand for the last name, comma, first name. We used street to stand for street name and number. We also gave names to tasks. For example, we said Get a name from the list, which stands for accessing a name and all the information associated with that name.

When we get to the stage where we translate an algorithm into a program in a language that a computer can execute, we may have to modify the identifiers. Each language has its own rules about forming identifiers. So there is a two-stage process: Data and actions are given names in the algorithm, then these names are translated into identifiers that meet the rules of the computer language. Notice that giving identifiers to information and actions is a form of abstraction.

Programming Languages

We have used the expression "a language that a computer can execute" several times. Let's be more precise. We know from our discussion of the von Neumann machine that the CPU takes instructions one at a time and executes them. The instructions that a computer can execute directly are those that are built into the hardware. However, instructions written in a **programming language** can be *translated* into the instructions that a computer can execute directly. A programming language is an artificial language, made up of symbols, special words, and a set of rules, used to construct a **program**—that is, to express a meaningful sequence of instructions for a computer.

Programming languages come in many forms and many levels of complexity, but they all are made up of two parts: **syntax**, the part that says how the instructions of the language can be put together, and **semantics**, the part that says what the instructions mean.

In this chapter we have looked at problem solving and algorithm design; in the next chapter we look at implementing an algorithm in a program. The process of translating an algorithm into a program is called *coding*.

Programming language A set of rules, symbols, and special words used to construct a program—that is, to express a sequence of instructions for a computer

Program A sequence of instructions written to perform a specified task

Syntax The formal rules governing the construction of valid instructions

Semantics The set of rules that gives the meaning of instructions in a language

Testing

We have demonstrated testing at the algorithm phase. Testing at the implementation phase involves running the program with various data designed to test all parts of the program. We discuss the theory of testing at these stages in later chapters. However, everything we have said about testing at the design phase is applicable at all the other stages.

Summary

Polya in his classic *How to Solve It* outlined a problem-solving strategy for mathematical problems. This strategy can be applied to all problems including those for which a computer program is to be written. These strategies include asking questions, looking for familiar things, and dividing and conquering; when these are applied, they should lead to a *plan* for solving a problem. In computing, such a plan is called an *algorithm*.

Humans have more experience following algorithms (plans) than designing them. In this chapter, the top-down design methodology is outlined and applied to a general problem and to a problem for which a computer program is to be written. This methodology is based on breaking a task into smaller and smaller subtasks until the implementation of each subtask is obvious. Testing must be applied at each stage of the process to ensure that the results are correct.

Object-oriented design focuses on determining the objects within a problem, and abstracting (grouping) the objects into classes based on like properties and behaviors. Classes and objects can relate to each other in three ways: containment, inheritance, and collaboration. Containment is a *has a* relationship, where a class contains an object of another class. Inheritance is an *is a* relationship, where one class inherits the properties and behaviors of another class. Collaboration is a *works with* relationship, where one class calls upon another class for information or a service.

There are four stages to object-oriented decomposition:

- *Brainstorming*, in which we make a first pass at determining the classes in the problem
- *Filtering*, in which we review the proposed classes
- *Scenarios*, in which the responsibilities of each class are determined
- *Responsibility algorithms*, in which the algorithms are written for each of the responsibilities

There are four major threads presented in this chapter that permeate computing: information hiding, abstraction, naming things, and testing. Information hiding is the process of hiding details of a subtask. Abstraction is the result of hiding the details. For example, we hide the details of a car under the body, and the body is the abstraction for the car. We give names to data and tasks so that we can talk about them. The names become the abstractions for the data and tasks. When we solve non-computer-related problems, we carry out the solution ourselves and thus know whether we have solved the problem or not. If the result of the problem solving is a computer program, we must test each algorithm thoroughly to be sure that the program gives the correct answer when (and each time) it is executed.

ETHICAL ISSUES

Plagiarism

Plagiarism is by no means a new ethical concern in the academic world. Since the advent of term papers, students have successfully (and not so successfully) handed in well-researched papers written by someone else. Students have purchased papers from friends, recycled old essays, and copied directly from articles and encyclopedias. Professors have always faced the challenge of discriminating between original compositions and plagiarized work, but today they are confronted with an additional obstacle. Students today have access to the Web;

and with the Web, these students have millions upon millions of term papers available for their use with a simple click of a mouse.

Web sites such as fastpapers.com and planetpapers.com serve as online paper mills, where students can download documents and submit them as their own. This form of cyber cheating has revolutionized plagiarism, and professors are struggling to keep up. Studies show that on any given assignment, approximately 30% of all students plagiarize. It is natural and appropriate, of course, for students to quote from and cite outside sources in their academic papers. Plagiarism occurs when a student uses another person's intellectual property improperly and fails to give credit to the original author. Most schools have severe consequences for students who plagiarize, violating honor codes, and compromising their own integrity.

Digital plagiarism is particularly difficult to detect since there is no visible difference between papers that have been downloaded and printed and those that were typed and printed. Furthermore, the wide selection of online papers allows students to select works on specific topics that are written at the appropriate intellectual level. Still, professors have developed ways to uncover web-based plagiarism. Some enter key phrases into search engines when they suspect that a student has handed in a paper that was not his or her own work. Others use sites like plagiarism.org, which takes an uploaded portion of text and compares it to thousands of papers that exist online. Students also cut and paste portions of different scholarly works to piece together a paper, but search engines are useful in detecting these copyright violations as well.

While digital plagiarism is a growing concern at schools around the world, the Web also fosters plagiarism that extends beyond the academic world. For example, lifting graphics and images from one page and including them in another site without seeking permission violates copyright laws. The ethics are less clear on issues such as copying someone's HTML source code and using that code to define the layout of the content of another web page without prior permission. In the future, copyright laws will have to be clarified to take into consideration situations brought about by the growing popularity of the Web.

Key Terms

Exercises

1. List the four steps in Polya's How-To-Solve-It list.
2. Describe the four steps listed in Exercise 1 in your own words.
3. List the problem-solving strategies discussed in this chapter.
4. Apply the problem-solving strategies to the following situations.
   a. Buying a toy for your four-year-old cousin
   b. Organizing an awards banquet for your soccer team
   c. Buying a dress or suit for an awards banquet at which you are being honored
5. Examine the solutions in Exercise 4 and determine three things they have in common.
6. What is an algorithm?
7. Write an algorithm for the following tasks.
   a. Making a peanut butter and jelly sandwich
   b. Getting up in the morning
   c. Doing your homework
   d. Driving home in the afternoon
8. List the three phases of the computer problem-solving model.
9. How does the computer problem-solving model differ from Polya's?
10. Describe the steps in the algorithm development phase.
11. Describe the steps in the implementation phase.
12. Describe the steps in the maintenance phase.
13. Look up a recipe for chocolate brownies in a cookbook and answer the following questions.

a. Is the recipe an algorithm? Justify your answer.
b. Organize the recipe as an algorithm, using pseudocode.
c. List the words that have meaning in computing.
d. List the words that have meaning in cooking.
e. Make the cookies and take them to your professor.

14. We said that following a recipe is easier than developing one. Go to the supermarket and buy a vegetable that you have not cooked (or eaten) before. Take it home and develop a recipe. Write your recipe and your critique of the process. (If it is good, send it to the authors.)

15. Describe the top-down design process.

16. Differentiate between a concrete step and an abstract step.

17. Write a top-down design for the following tasks.
    a. Buying a toy for your four-year-old cousin
    b. Organizing an awards banquet for your soccer team
    c. Buying a dress or suit for an awards banquet at which you are being honored

18. Write a top-down design for the following tasks.
    a. Calculating the average of ten test scores
    b. Calculating the average of an unknown number of test scores
    c. Describe the differences in the two designs.

19. Write a top-down design for the following tasks.
    a. Finding a telephone number in the phone book
    b. Finding a telephone number on the Internet
    c. Finding a telephone number on a scrap of paper that you have lost
    d. Describe the similarities and differences among these designs.

20. Distinguish between information and data.

21. Write a top-down design for sorting a list of names into alphabetical order.

22. a. Why is information hiding important?
    b. Name three examples of information hiding that you encounter every day.

23. An airplane is a complex system.
    a. Give an abstraction of an airplane from the view of a pilot.
    b. Give an abstraction of an airplane from the view of a passenger.
    c. Give an abstraction of an airplane from the view of the cabin crew.
    d. Give an abstraction of an airplane from the view of a maintenance mechanic.
    e. Give an abstraction of an airplane from the view from the airline's corporate office.

24. List the identifiers and whether they named data or actions for the designs in Exercise 17.

25. List the identifiers and whether they named data or actions for the designs in Exercise 18.

26. List the identifiers and whether they named data or actions for the designs in Exercise 19.

27. Finish the verification of the address list example.

28. Take some sample data and desk check the address list example with actual values.

29. Verify the designs in Exercise 17 using a walkthrough.

30. Verify the designs in Exercise 18 using an inspection.

31. Verify the designs in Exercise 19 using top-down reasoning.

32. Distinguish between an object and an object class.

33. Distinguish between a field and a method.

34. How can objects relate to one another?

35. Discuss the differences between a top-down design and an object-oriented design.

36. We outlined a strategy for developing an object-oriented decomposition.
    a. List the four stages.
    b. Outline the characteristics of each stage.
    c. What is the output from each of the four stages?
    d. Are the stages independent? Explain.

Apply the four-stage design strategy to each of the problems in Exercises 37 through 41.

37. Design the CRC cards for an inventory system for a car dealership, using brainstorming, filtering, and scenarios.

38. Design the CRC cards for a database for a zoo, using brainstorming, filtering, and scenarios.

39. Distinguish between data abstraction and procedural abstraction.

40. What is a programming language?

41. Distinguish between syntax and semantics.

Thought Questions

1. Distinguish between a program that the CPU can execute directly and a program that must be translated.

2. Top-down design and object-oriented design both create scaffolding that is used to write a program. Isn't all this scaffolding just a waste of effort? Is it ever used again? Of what value is it after the program is up and running?

3. Which of the problem-solving strategies do you use the most? Can you think of some others that you use? Would they be appropriate for computing problem solving?

4. A friend who is taking a course that you took last year comes to you and asks to see the term paper you wrote for the class last year. Would you let her see it? If you know that she would copy it, would you let her have it? What are the moral issues involved in letting a friend see material you submitted for a current course? A previous course?

5. Friends who are taking a programming course with you say that they have found a web site with solutions to the programming assignments in the textbook. What would you do? Would you tell the instructor? Would you look at the solutions? Would you turn in a solution as your own?

6. You find a great home page on a web site. What are the ethical issues involved with downloading the source code and replacing your name and information on the page and using it on your home page?

The Programming Layer

7 Low-Level Programming Languages

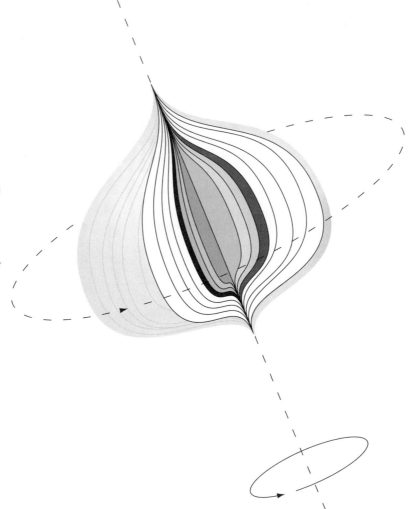

Chapter 7

Low-Level Programming Languages

In the last chapter we examined problem solving, both how humans solve problems in general and how humans must approach problems in which the computer plays a part in the solution. The first phase, in both cases, is to come up with a plan or algorithm. In Polya's How To Solve It list, the human executes the plan and evaluates the results. In a computer solution, we write a program that expresses the plan in a programming language.

In the last chapter we introduced the concept of pseudocode as a way to express algorithms. In this chapter, we begin to examine the programming languages into which we translate our pseudocode. Recall that just as each lock has a specific key that opens it, each type of computer has a specific set of operations that it can execute, called the computer's machine language. We begin our discussion of programming languages with machine code. Because we never write a program in a vacuum, the language presentation and appropriate pseudocode is intertwined within this chapter.

Goals

After studying this chapter, you should be able to

- list the operations that a computer can perform.
- discuss the relationship between levels of abstraction and the determination of concrete algorithm steps.
- describe the important features of the Pep/7 virtual machine.
- distinguish between immediate mode addressing and direct addressing.
- convert a simple algorithm into a machine-language program.
- distinguish between machine language and assembly language.
- describe the steps in creating and running an assembly-language program.
- convert a simple algorithm into an assembly-language program.
- distinguish between instructions to the assembler and instructions to be translated.
- describe two approaches to testing.
- design and implement a test plan for a simple assembly-language program.

7.1   Computer Operations

Both our notations for expressing algorithms and the programming languages we use to implement algorithms must mirror the types of operations that a computer can perform. So let's begin our discussion by repeating the definition of a computer: A computer is a programmable electronic device that can store, retrieve, and process data.

The operational words are *programmable*, *store*, *retrieve*, and *process*. In a previous chapter we pointed out the importance of the realization that data and instructions to manipulate the data are logically the same and can be stored in the same place. That is what the word *programmable* means here. The instructions that manipulate data are stored within the machine along with the data. To change what the computer does to the data, we change the instructions.

Store, retrieve, and process are actions that the computer can perform on data. That is, the instructions that the control unit executes can store data into the memory of the machine, retrieve data from the memory of the machine, and process the data in some way in the arithmetic/logic unit. The word "process" is very general. At the machine level, the processing involves performing arithmetic and logical operations on data values.

Where does the data that gets stored in the computer memory come from? How does the human ever get to see what is stored there, such as the results of some calculation? There are other instructions that specify the interaction between an input device and the CPU and between the CPU and an output device.

7.2 Levels of Abstraction

When we described the problem-solving process in Chapter 6, we said that an abstract step is one for which some details remain unspecified and a concrete step is one for which the details are fully specified. How do we know when a step is concrete? The answer depends on the programming language in which we are going to express our algorithm.

In our address example in Chapter 6, we assumed that the task or step Sort list on lastFirst field was fully specified but that step Print the list was not. There are programming languages in which these assumptions are true. But there are also programming languages in which step Sort list on lastFirst field is abstract, and Print the list is concrete. Furthermore, there are languages in which both steps are concrete and in which both steps are abstract.

In this chapter and the next we look more at how to write algorithms in pseudocode and how to translate the pseudocode into a programming language. We begin with *machine language*, the language that comes with the hardware, graduate to *assembly language*, the lowest-level programming language, and finally move up to a *high-level language* in the next chapter. At each stage, the languages themselves become more abstract; that is, they allow us to express more and more complex processing with one statement. As you might expect, this move from the concrete to the abstract mirrors the history of software development.

7.3 Machine Language

As we pointed out in Chapter 1, the only programming instructions that a computer actually carries out are those written using **machine language**, the instructions built into the hardware of a particular computer. Initially, humans had no choice but to write programs in machine language because other programming languages had not yet been invented.

So how are computer instructions represented? Recall that every processor type has its own set of specific machine instructions. These are the only instructions the processor can actually carry out. Since there are a finite number of instructions, the processor designers simply list the instructions and assign them a binary code that is used to represent them.

Machine language
The language made up of binary-coded instructions that is used directly by the computer

This is similar to the approach taken when representing character data, as described in Chapter 3.

The relationship between the processor and the instructions it can carry out is completely integrated. The electronics of the CPU inherently recognize the binary representations of the specific commands. So there is no actual list of commands the computer must consult. The CPU embodies the list in its design.

Each machine-language instruction does only one very low-level task. Each small step in a process must be explicitly coded in machine language. Even the small task of adding two numbers together uses three instructions written in binary, and the programmer has to remember which combination of binary digits correspond to which instruction. As we mentioned in Chapter 1, machine-language programmers have to be very good with numbers and very detail-oriented.

However, we can't leave you with the impression that only mathematicians can write programs in machine language. In fact, very few programs are written in machine language today, primarily because they are an inefficient use of a programmer's time. Most programs are written in higher-level languages and then translated into machine language, a process we describe later in this chapter. However, everyone should experience what those early pioneers felt when they wrote the first programs in the machine code of a specific machine. This experience emphasizes the basic definition of a computer and makes you appreciate the ease with which you interact with a computer today.

Pep/7: A Virtual Computer

By definition, machine code differs from machine to machine. That is, each type of CPU has its own machine language that it understands. So how can we give each of you the experience of using machine language when you may be working on different machines? We solve that problem by using a **virtual computer**. A virtual computer is a hypothetical machine, in this case one that is designed to contain the important features of real computers that we want to illustrate. Pep/7, designed by Stanley Warford, is the virtual machine that we use here.[1]

Pep/7 has 32 machine-language instructions. This means that a program for Pep/7 must be a sequence made of up of a combination of these 32 instructions. Don't panic: We are not going to ask you to understand and remember 32 sequences of binary bits. We are only going to examine a few of these instructions, and we are not going to ask you to memorize any of them.

Important Features Reflected in Pep/7

The memory unit of the Pep/7 is made up of 4,096 bytes of storage. The bytes are numbered from 0 through 4,095 decimal. Recall that each byte contains 8 bits, so we can describe the bit pattern in a byte using two hexadecimal digits.

Virtual computer (machine) A hypothetical machine designed to illustrate important features of a real machine

(Refer back to Chapter 2 for more information on hexadecimal digits.) The word length in Pep/7 is 2 bytes, or 16 bits. Thus the information that flows into and out of the ALU (arithmetic/logic unit) is 16 bits in length.

Recall from Chapter 5 that a register is a small area of storage in the arithmetic/logic unit of the CPU used to hold special data and intermediate values. Pep/7 has seven registers, four of which we focus on at this point:

- The program counter (PC), which contains the address of the next instruction to be executed
- The instruction register (IR), which contains a copy of the instruction being executed
- The index register (X register)
- The accumulator (A register)

The index register and the accumulator are used to hold data and the results of operations; these are the special storage registers referred in Chapter 5 in the discussion of the ALU.

We realize that this is a lot of detailed information, but don't despair! Remember that our goal is to give you a feel for what is actually happening at the lowest level of computer processing. By necessity, that processing keeps track of many details.

Figure 7.1 shows a diagram of Pep/7's CPU and memory. Notice that the addresses in memory are in red. This color is to emphasize that the addresses

Pep/7's CPU

A register (accumulator)

X register

Program counter (CP)

Instruction register (IR)

Pep/7's Memory

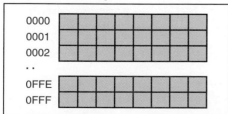

0000
0001
0002
· ·
0FFE
0FFF

Figure 7.1
Pep/7's architecture

themselves are not stored in memory, but that they *name* the individual bytes of memory. We refer to any particular byte in memory by its address.

Before we go on, let's review some aspects of binary and hexadecimal numbers. The largest decimal value that can be represented in a byte is 255. This occurs when all of the bits are 1's: 11111111 in binary is FF in hexadecimal and 255 in decimal. The largest decimal value that can be represented in a word (16 bits) is 65,535. This occurs when all 16 bits are 1's: 1111111111111111 in binary is FFFF in hexadecimal and 65,535 in decimal. If we represent both positive and negative numbers, we lose a bit in the magnitude (because one is used for the sign), so we can represent values ranging from −7FFF to +7FFF in hexadecimal, which is from −32,767 to +32,767 in decimal.

This information is important when working with the Pep/7 machine. The number of bits we have available determines the size of the numbers we can work with.

Instruction Format

We have talked about instructions going into the instruction register, being decoded, and being executed. Now we are ready to look at a set (or subset) of concrete instructions that a computer can execute. But first, we need to examine the format of an instruction in Pep/7.

Figure 7.2 shows the format for an instruction in Pep/7. There are two parts to an instruction: the 8-bit *instruction specifier* and (optionally) the 16-bit *operand specifier*. The instruction specifier (the first byte of the instruction) indicates what operation is to be carried out, such as 'Add a number' to a value already stored in a register, and how to interpret just where the operand is. The operand specifier (the second and third bytes of

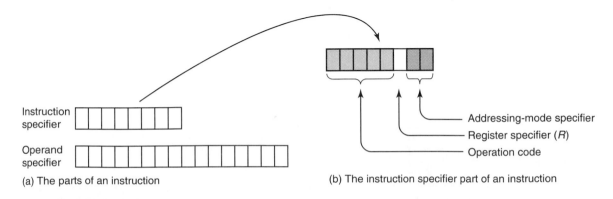

Instruction specifier

Operand specifier

(a) The parts of an instruction

Addressing-mode specifier

Register specifier (*R*)

Operation code

(b) The instruction specifier part of an instruction

Figure 7.2 The Pep/7 instruction format

the instruction) holds either the operand itself or the address of where the operand is. Some instructions do not use the operand specifier.

The instruction specifier is made up of several sections: the operation code, the register specifier, and the addressing-mode specifier. The *operation code* is 5 bits long (shaded green). The bit string in the operation code specifies which instruction is to be carried out. You may have predicted that the operation code would be 5 bits when we said that Pep/7 had 32 instructions: There are 32 unique patterns using 5 bits.

The 1-bit *register specifier* is 0 if register A (the accumulator) is involved in the operation and 1 if register X (the index register) is involved. The register specifier is not color coded.

The 2-bit *addressing-mode specifier* (shaded light blue) says how to interpret the operand part of the instruction. If the addressing mode is 00, the operand is in the operand specifier of the instruction. This addressing mode is called *immediate* (i). If the addressing mode is 01, the operand is the memory address named in the operand specifier. This addressing mode is called *direct* (d). (There are two other addressing modes that we do not cover here.) The distinction between the immediate addressing mode and the direct addressing mode is very important because it determines where the data involved in the operation is stored or is to be stored. See Figure 7.3. Locations that contain addresses are shaded in red; operands are shaded gray.

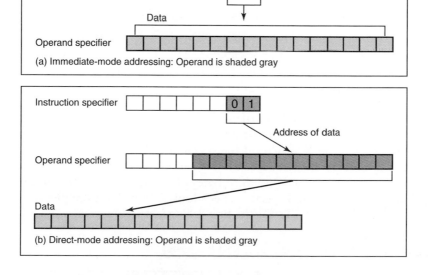

Figure 7.3
Difference between immediate-mode and direct-mode addressing

Opcode	Meaning of Instruction
00000	Stop execution
00001	Load operand into a register (either A of X)
00010	Store the contents of register (either A or X) into operand
00011	Add the operand to register (either A or X)
00100	Subtract the operand from register (either A or X)
11011	Character input to operand
11100	Character output from operand

Figure 7.4
Subset of Pep/7 instructions

Instructions that do not have an operand (data to be manipulated) are called *unary instructions*, and do not have an operand specifier. That is, unary instructions are only one byte long rather than three bytes long.

Some Sample Instructions
Let's look at some specific instructions in isolation and then put them together to write a program. Figure 7.4 contains the 5-bit *operation code* (or *opcode*). Recall that the operation code is in the leftmost 5 bits of the instruction specifier, the 6th bit specifies the register used (if any), and address mode specifier is in the remaining 2 bits.

00000 *Stop execution*   During the fetch/execute cycle, when the operation code is all zeros, the program halts. Stop is a unary instruction, so it only occupies one byte. The three rightmost bits in the byte are ignored.

00001 *Load operand into register*   This instruction loads one word (two bytes) into a register. The register specifier and the mode specifier determine where the word is and into which register the contents is loaded. Thus, the load opcode has different meanings depending on the register specifier and the addressing-mode specifier. Recall that the register specifier specifies which register (if any) is involved. In this case, it specifies the register into which the operand is to be loaded: the A register if the specifier is 0, and the X register if the specifier is 1. The mode specifier determines whether the value to be loaded is in the operand part of the instruction (the second and third bytes of the instruction) or is in the place named in the operand specifier. Let's look at concrete examples of each of these combinations. Here is the first 3-byte instruction.

Instruction specifier | 0 | 0 | 0 | 0 | 1 | 0 | 0 | 0 |

Operand specifier | 0 | 0 | 0 | 0 | 0 | 0 | 0 | 0 | 0 | 0 | 0 | 0 | 0 | 1 | 1 | 1 |

The register specifier is 0, which refers to the A register, and the addressing mode is immediate, meaning that the value to be loaded is in the operand specifier. That is, the data is in the operand specifier; thus it is shaded gray. After execution of this instruction, the contents of the second and third bytes of the instruction (the operand specifier) would be loaded into the A register (the accumulator). That is, the A register would contain 0007 and the original contents of A would be lost.

To simplify the discussion, from here on we represent all numbers in hexadecimal (except the bit strings in the registers). We specify leading zeros on addresses but not on numeric values.

Here is another load instruction.

Instruction specifier | 0 | 0 | 0 | 0 | 1 | 1 | 0 | 0 |

Operand specifier | 0 | 0 | 0 | 0 | 0 | 0 | 0 | 0 | 0 | 0 | 0 | 1 | 1 | 1 | 1 | 1 |

The register specifier is 1, which refers to the X register, and the addressing mode is immediate. Thus, the data to be loaded into the X register is stored in the operand specifier itself. After the execution of this instruction, the X register would contain 1F. Note that the original contents of the X register would be lost.

Here is a third load instruction.

Instruction specifier | 0 | 0 | 0 | 0 | 1 | 0 | 0 | 1 |

Operand specifier | 0 | 0 | 0 | 0 | 0 | 0 | 0 | 0 | 0 | 0 | 0 | 1 | 1 | 1 | 1 | 1 |

The register specifier is 0 and the addressing mode is direct. Direct-mode addressing means that the operand itself is not in the operand specifier (second and third bytes of the instruction); instead, the operand specifier holds the address specifying where the operand is in memory. Thus, when this instruction is executed, the contents of *location* 001F would be loaded into the A register. Note that we have shaded the bits that represent a memory address in red just as we have used red for other addresses. The A register holds a word (2 bytes), so when an address is used to specify a word (rather than a single byte) as in this case, the address given is the left-most byte in the word. Thus, the content of adjacent locations 001F and 0020 are loaded into the A register. The contents of the operand (001F and 0020) are not changed.

Here is the fourth, and last, combination.

Instruction specifier | 0 | 0 | 0 | 0 | 1 | 1 | 0 | 1 |

Operand specifier | 0 | 0 | 0 | 0 | 0 | 0 | 0 | 0 | 0 | 0 | 0 | 1 | 1 | 1 | 1 | 1 |

Because the register specifier is 1, the contents of word 001F (bytes 001F and 0020) would be loaded into register X. Otherwise, this instruction is identical to the one before it.

00010 *Store register to operand*   This instruction stores the contents of either the A register or the X register into the location specified in the operand, which is either the operand itself or the place named in the operand.

Instruction specifier | 0 | 0 | 0 | 1 | 0 | 0 | 0 | 1 |

Operand specifier | 0 | 0 | 0 | 0 | 0 | 0 | 0 | 0 | 0 | 0 | 0 | 0 | 1 | 0 | 1 | 0 |

This instruction stores the contents of the A register into the word beginning at location 000A. It is invalid to have an addressing mode of immediate with a store opcode; that is, we cannot try to store the contents of a register into the operand specifier.

00011 *Add operand to register*   Like the Load operation, the Add operation uses both the register specifier and the addressing mode specifier, giving alternative interpretations. The four alternatives for this instruction are shown below with the explanation following each instruction.

Instruction specifier | 0 | 0 | 0 | 1 | 1 | 0 | 0 | 0 |

Operand specifier | 0 | 0 | 0 | 0 | 0 | 0 | 1 | 0 | 0 | 0 | 0 | 0 | 1 | 0 | 1 | 0 |

The contents of the second and third bytes of the instruction (the operand specifier) are added to the contents of the A register (20A in hex). Thus we have shaded the operand specifier to show that it is data.

Instruction specifier | 0 | 0 | 0 | 1 | 1 | 1 | 0 | 0 |

Operand specifier | 0 | 0 | 0 | 0 | 0 | 0 | 1 | 0 | 0 | 0 | 0 | 0 | 1 | 0 | 1 | 0 |

The contents of the second and third bytes of the instruction (the operand specifier) are added to the contents of the X register.

Instruction specifier | 0 | 0 | 0 | 1 | 1 | 0 | 0 | 1 |

Operand specifier | 0 | 0 | 0 | 0 | 0 | 0 | 1 | 0 | 0 | 0 | 0 | 0 | 1 | 0 | 1 | 0 |

The contents of the operand specified in the second and third bytes of the instruction (location 020A) are added into the A register.

Instruction specifier | 0 | 0 | 0 | 1 | 1 | 1 | 0 | 1 |

Operand specifier | 0 | 0 | 0 | 0 | 0 | 0 | 1 | 0 | 0 | 0 | 0 | 0 | 1 | 0 | 1 | 0 |

The contents of the operand specified in the operand specifier (020A in hex) are added to the X register.

00100 *Subtract the operand*   This instruction is just like the Add operation except the operand is subtracted from the specified register rather than added. Like the Load and the Add, there are variations of this instruction depending on the register specifier and the addressing mode.

11011 *Character input to operand*   This instruction allows the program to enter an ASCII character from the input device while the program is running. Only direct addressing is allowed, so the character is stored in the address shown in the operand specifier.

Instruction specifier | 1 | 1 | 0 | 1 | 1 | 0 | 0 | 1 |

Operand specifier | 0 | 0 | 0 | 0 | 0 | 0 | 0 | 0 | 0 | 0 | 0 | 0 | 1 | 0 | 1 | 0 |

This instruction reads an ASCII character from the input device and store it into location 000A.

11100 *Character output from operand*   This instruction sends an ASCII character to the output device while the program is running. The register specifier is ignored, but the addressing may be either immediate or direct.

Instruction specifier | 1 | 1 | 1 | 0 | 0 | 0 | 0 | 0 |

Operand specifier | 0 | 0 | 0 | 0 | 0 | 0 | 0 | 0 | 1 | 0 | 0 | 0 | 0 | 0 | 1 |

Because immediate addressing is specified, this instruction writes out the ASCII character stored in the operand specifier. The operand specifier contains 1000001, which is 41 in hex and 65 in decimal. The ASCII character corresponding to that value is 'A', so the letter A is written to the screen.

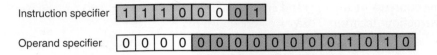

Because direct addressing is used, this instruction writes out the ASCII character stored in the location named in the operand specifier, location 000A. What is written? We can't say unless we know the contents of byte 000A. The ASCII character corresponding to whatever is stored at that location is printed.

7.4   A Program Example

Let's look at an example using machine language. Programs are written to solve problems, so we first begin with the problem and the algorithm to solve it.

Problem and Algorithm

Let's start with a very simple problem; let's write "Hello" on the screen. The algorithm is easy.

> Write "Hello"

Is this a concrete step? It certainly would be if we were going to implement it in a high-level programming language. However, it is not a concrete step in machine language. Let's further specify it by writing each letter separately.

> **Write "Hello"**
>
> Write "H"
> Write "e"
> Write "l"
> Write "l"
> Write "o"

Are these concrete steps? Not in machine language. We have to convert the letters to their ASCII representation.

Write "H"

Write 48 (hex)

Write "e"

Write 65 (hex)

Write "l"

Write 6C (hex)

Write "l"

Write 6C (hex)

Write "o"

Write 6F (hex)

Now each of these steps is a concrete step.

A Program

We are now ready to write a machine-language program to implement the algorithm to write "Hello" on the screen. There are six instructions in this program: five to write out a character and one to indicate the end of the process. The instruction to write a character on the screen is 11100, the 'Character output from operand' operation. Should we store the characters in memory and write them using direct addressing or just store them in the operand specifier and use immediate addressing? Let's write it both ways and see the difference. We use immediate addressing first. This means that the addressing-mode specifier is 01 and the ASCII code goes into the third byte of the instruction.

Module	Binary Instruction	Hex Instruction
Write "H"	11100000 0000000001001000	E0 0048
Write "e"	11100000 0000000001100101	E0 0065
Write "l"	11100000 0000000001101100	E0 006C
Write "l"	11100000 0000000001101100	E0 006C
Write "o"	11100000 0000000001101111	E0 006F
Stop	00000000	00

The machine-language program is shown in binary in the second column and in hexadecimal in the third column. Note that we need to construct the operation specifier in binary because it is made up of a 5-bit opcode, a 1-bit register specifier, and a 2-bit addressing-mode specifier. Once we have the complete eight bits, we can convert it to hexadecimal. We could construct the operand specifier directly in hexadecimal.

Hand Simulation

Let's simulate this program's execution by following the steps of the fetch/execute cycle. Such traces by hand really drive home the steps that the computer carries out.

Recall the four steps in the fetch-execute cycle:

- Fetch the next instruction (from place named in the program counter).
- Decode the instruction (and update program counter).
- Get data (operand) if needed.
- Execute the instruction.

There are six instructions in our program. Let's assume that they are in contiguous places in memory with the first instruction stored in memory locations 0000–0002. Execution begins by loading 0000 into the program counter (PC). At each stage of execution, let's examine the PC (program counter) and the IR (instruction register). The program does not access the A register or the X register, so we do not bother to show them. At the end of the first fetch, the PC and the IC look like this. (We continue to use color to emphasize addresses, opcode, address-mode specifier, and data.)

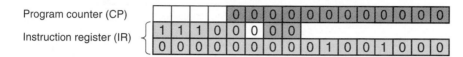

Program counter (CP)

Instruction register (IR)

The instruction is decoded as a 'Write character to output' instruction with immediate mode addressing. Because this instruction takes three bytes, the PC is incremented by three. The data is retrieved from the operand specifier in the IR, and the instruction is executed. "H" is written on the screen. The second fetch is executed and the PC and IR are as follows:

Program counter (CP)

Instruction register (IR)

The instruction is decoded as another 'Write character to output' instruction with immediate mode addressing. The instruction takes three bytes, so the PC is again incremented by three. The data is retrieved, the instruction is executed, and "e" is written on the screen. The next three instructions are executed exactly the same way. After the "o" has been written, the PC and IR look as follows:

Program counter (CP)

Instruction register (IR)

The opcode is decoded as a Stop instruction. The contents of the addressing mode and the operand specifier are ignored. The fetch-execute cycle stops.

Pep/7 Simulator

Remember that the instructions are written in the Pep/7 machine language, which doesn't correspond to any particular CPU's machine language. We have just hand-simulated the program. Can we execute it on the computer? Yes, we can. Pep/7 is a virtual (hypothetical) machine, but we have a *simulator* for the machine. That is, we have a program that behaves just like the Pep/7 virtual machine behaves. To run a program, we enter the hexadecimal code, byte by byte with blanks between each, and end the program with zz. The simulator recognizes two z's as the end of the program. Here is a screen shot of the Pep/7 machine-language program, followed by a screen shot of the output window.

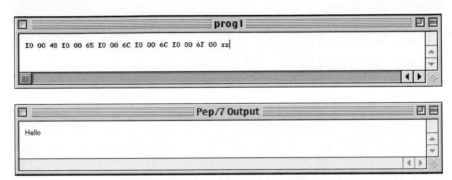

Let's go through the steps required to go from the algorithm to the output. We assume that the Pep/7 simulator has been installed. We begin by opening a new file into which we enter our program. The File menu on the menu bar allows us to do this. The menu bar looks like this:

File   Edit   Info   Dev   Tools   Controls   Obx   Tut   Pep7   Windows   Help

We then key in the program as shown above and save the file, thus giving it a name.

The next step is to load this program into the memory of the Pep/7 virtual machine and execute it. Under the Pep7 pull-down menu, there are several options. The second is *Load*, the one we need. When *Load* is clicked, a piece of software called the **loader** takes the program and loads it into memory beginning in location 00000. Here is what Pep/7's memory looks like when the loader has finished. Although memory is one long stream of bytes, we show it here in groups of three because each instruction except the Stop instruction takes three bytes.

Loader   A piece of software that takes a machine language program and places it into memory

Address			
00	E0	00	48
03	E0	00	65
06	E0	00	6C
09	E0	00	6C
0C	E0	00	6F
0F	00		

The fetch-execute cycle begins with the instruction in location 0000, which is where the first instruction has been loaded. To start the fetch-execute cycle, we go back to the same pull-down menu (Pep7) and click on *Execute*. We could have done the loading and executing in one step by clicking on *Load/Execute*.

The loader that puts the program into memory is very exacting. The instructions must be in hexadecimal with exactly one blank between each byte. If we mistype the program, say, by forgetting the blank before the zz, the loader gives the following message.

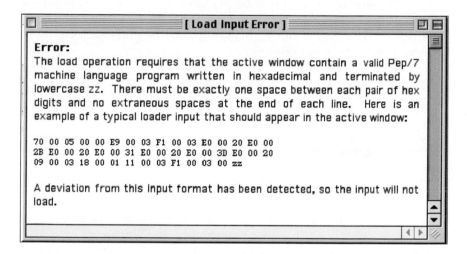

An Alternate Program for the Same Algorithm

In the last section we encoded the algorithm using immediate-mode addressing. The ASCII code for each character to be output was stored directly into the third byte of the 'Character output from operand' instruction that would write out the character. Now, let's code the program using direct addressing. That is, the operand specifier for each 'Character output from operand' instruction should contain the *address* of the character to be output rather than the character itself. Therefore, we must change the instruction specifier from

```
11100000 (E0 hex)
```

to

```
11100001 (E1 hex)
```

We must also change the operand specifier from the ASCII character to the *address* describing where the ASCII character is stored in memory. How do we know what the address is? We must store the character in a byte and then put the address of that byte into the output instruction. This sounds more complicated than it is.

Look back at the map of memory after the program is loaded. There are 16 bytes used in the program. We must store the characters in "Hello" in successive bytes beginning with the 17th byte (address 10 in hex). Then the first instruction has 10 (17 decimal) in the second byte of its operand specifier. The second instruction has 11 (18 decimal) in the second byte of its operand specifier, and so forth. Now all we have to do is store the ASCII code for the characters. And that turns out to be easy. We just insert the hexadecimal for each character between the Stop instruction and the zz. Here is the screen shot of this revised program. The output is exactly the same as from the previous versions.

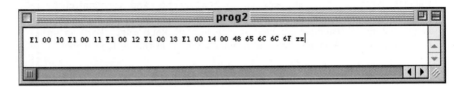

An Enhanced Version of "Hello"

Before we leave machine language, let's add another feature to our program. Let's use the 'Character input to operand' command to read in an initial and print it following "Hello". Any enhancement means going back to update the algorithm.

Because we are reading and writing one character at a time, these steps are concrete steps in machine language. However, we must do some calculation before we actually write the machine-language instruction. We used the identifier initial to stand for the character read in; actually, initial refers to the place in memory to store the character and the place in memory from which we wish to write out the character. In many languages, we can actually use an identifier and let the translating system determine the place in memory to use. In machine language, we must specify the memory address ourselves.

The Read and Write can be converted directly into machine-language statements 'Character input' and 'Character output'. The 'Character input' to operand allows only direct addressing, so the character is stored into the place named in the third byte of the input instruction. How do we know where to tell the instruction to put the character? Well, since the next statement is going to write out that character, let's just store the character directly into the third byte of the next instruction, which is the 'Character output' instruction, and mark the 'Character output' instruction to use immediate addressing.

But we must know where the 'Character input' instruction is going to be placed before we can determine where the 'Character output' instruction is going. In the original version of the program, we know that the Stop command was stored into location 0F. Our enhancements go before the Stop instruction, so the 'Character input' instruction goes into locations 0F, 10, and 11. The 'Character output' instruction goes into the next three locations: 12, 13, and 14. Therefore, the 'Character input' instruction must have 14 in its third byte; that is, the input character must be stored into location 14. When the 'Character output' instruction is executed, the character stored in location 14 is written out.

Module	Binary Instruction	Location	Hex Instruction
Write "H"	11100000 0000000001000101	00 01, 02	E0 0048
...			
Get initial	11011001 0000000000010100	0F 10, 11	D9 0014
Write initial	11100000 0000000000000000	12 13, 14	E0 0000
Stop	00000000	15	00

Here is a copy of the screen with the input program, followed by a copy of the output screen.

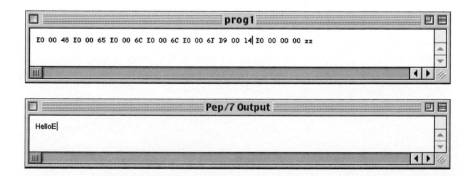

John von Neumann

John von Neumann was a brilliant mathematician, physicist, logician, and computer scientist. Legends have been passed down about his astonishing memory and the phenomenal speed at which von Neumann solved problems. He used his talents not only for furthering his mathematical theories, but also for memorizing entire books and reciting them years after he had read them. But ask a highway patrolman about von Neumann's driving ability and he would be likely to throw up his hands in despair; behind the wheel, the mathematical genius was as reckless as a rebel teenager.

John von Neumann was born in Hungary in 1903, the oldest son of a wealthy Jewish banker. He was able to divide 8-digit numbers in his head by the age of 6. He entered high school by the time he was 11, and it wasn't long before his math teachers recommended he be tutored by university professors. He enrolled at the University of Berlin in 1921 to study chemistry as a compromise with his father, who wanted him to study something that would allow him to make money. He received his diploma in chemical engineering from the Technische Hochschule in Zürich in 1926. In the same year, he received his doctorate in mathematics from the University of Budapest, with a thesis on set theory. During the period from 1926 to 1929 von Neumann lectured at Berlin and at Hamburg while holding a Rockefeller fellowship for postdoctoral studies at the University of Göttingen.

von Neumann came to the United States in the early 1930s to teach at Princeton, while still keeping his academic posts in Germany. He resigned the German posts when the Nazis came to power; he was not, however, a political refugee as so many were at that time. While at Princeton, he worked with the talented and as-yet-unknown British student Alan Turing. He continued his brilliant mathematical career, becoming editor of *Annals of Mathematics* and co-editor of *Compositio Mathematica*. During the war von Neumann was hired as a consultant for the U.S.

Armed Forces and related civilian agencies because of his knowledge of hydrodynamics. He was also called upon to participate in the construction of the atomic bomb in 1943. It was not surprising that, following this work, President Eisenhower appointed him to the Atomic Energy Commission in 1955.

Even though bombs and their performance fascinated von Neumann for many years, a fortuitous meeting in 1944 with Herbert Goldstine, a pioneer of one of the first operational electronic digital computers, introduced the mathematician to something more important than bombs—computers. von Neumann's chance conversation with Goldstine in a train station sparked a new fascination for him. He started working on the stored program concept and concluded that internally storing a program eliminated the hours of tedious labor required to reprogram computers (in those days). He also developed a new computer architecture to perform this storage task. In fact, today's computers are often referred to as von Neumann machines because the architectural principles he described have proven so tremendously successful. Changes in computers over the past 40 years have been primarily in terms of the speed and composition of the fundamental circuits, but the basic architecture designed by von Neumann has persisted.

During the 1950s, von Neumann was a consultant for IBM, where he reviewed proposed and ongoing advanced technology projects. One such project was John Backus's FORTRAN, which von Neumann reportedly questioned, asking why anyone would want more than one machine language. In 1957, von Neumann died of bone cancer in Washington, D.C. at the age of 54. Perhaps his work with the atomic bomb resulted in the bone cancer that caused the death of one of the most brilliant and interesting minds of the twentieth century.

Where did the E come from? It is the first character in the machine-language program! The Pep/7 system is expecting input from the active screen. We must load the program and then create a new screen and write the character we wish to input. Now when we click on *Execute*, the program works as we expected. Here is the output screen after entering the character N in a separate window.

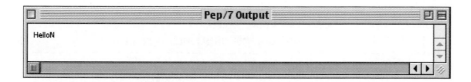

You are asked in the exercises to insert a blank before the initial to make the output more readable.

Notice in all of these programs that the instructions and the data that is being manipulated are both stored in memory, demonstrating the principles of the von Neumann architecture.

7.5 Assembly Language

As we pointed out in Chapter 1, the first tools developed to help the programmer were assembly languages. **Assembly languages** assign mnemonic letter codes to each machine-language instruction. The programmer uses these letter codes in place of binary digits. The instructions in an assembly language are much like those we would use to tell someone how to do a calculation on a handheld calculator.

Because every program that is executed on a computer eventually must be in the form of the computer's machine language, a program called an **assembler** reads each of the instructions in mnemonic form and translates it into the machine-language equivalent. And because each type of computer has a different machine language, there are as many assembly languages and translators as there are types of machines.

> **Assembly language** A low-level programming language in which a mnemonic represents each of the machine-language instructions for a particular computer
>
> **Assembler** A program that translates an assembly-language program in machine code

Pep/7 Assembly Language

The goal of this section is not to make you assembly-language programmers; it is to make you appreciate the advantages of assembly-language programming over machine coding. With this goal in mind, we cover only a few of Pep/7's assembly-language features. Let's begin by examining the same operations we looked at in the last sections. In Pep/7's assembly language, there is a different opcode for each register, the operand is specified by "h#" and the hexadecimal value, and the addressing mode specifier is indicated by the letters i or d.

Mnemonic	Operand, Mode Specifier	Meaning of Instruction
STOP		Stop execution
LOADA	h#008B,i	Load 008B into register A
LOADA	h#008B,d	Load the contents of location 8B into register A
LOADX	h#008B,i	Load 008B into register X
LOADX	h#008B,d	Load the contents of 8B into register X
STOREA	h#008B,d	Store the contents of register A into location 8B
STOREX	h#008B,d	Store the contents of register X into location 8B
ADDA	h#008B,i	Add 008B to register A
ADDA	h#008B,d	Add the contents of location 8B to register A
ADDX	h#008B,i	Add 008B to register X
ADDX	h#008B,d	Add the contents of location 8B to register X
SUBA	h#008B,i	Subtract 008B from register A
SUBA	h#008B,d	Subtract the contents of location 8B from register A
SUBX	h#008B,i	Subtract 008B from register X
SUBX	h#008B,d	Subtract the contents of location 8B from register X
CHARI	h#008B,d	Read a character and store it into byte 8B
CHARO	c#/B/,i	Write the character B
	h#008B,d	Write the character stored in byte 0B
DECI	h#008B,d	Read a decimal number and store it into location 8B
DECO	h#008B,i	Write the decimal number 139 (8B in hex)
DECO	h#008B,d	Write the decimal number stored in 8B

Did you wonder why we didn't do any arithmetic in machine language? Well, the output was defined only for characters. If we had done arithmetic, we would have had to convert the numbers to character form to see the results, and this is more complex than we wished to get. However, the Pep/7 assembly language has mnemonics DECI and DECO, which allow us to do decimal input and output.

Pseudo-Operations

In a machine language program, every instruction is stored in memory and then executed. Beginning with assembly languages, most programming languages have two kinds of instructions: instructions to be translated and instructions to the translating program. Here are a few useful *assembler directives* for the Pep/7 assembler; that is, instructions to the assembler.

Pseudo-Op	Operand	Meaning
.ASCII	/.../	Store the characters between the //'s into memory
.BLOCK	d#3	Generate three bytes of storage and set each byte to zero
.WORD .WORD	d#5 h#0105	Generate a word with the decimal value 5 stored in it Generate a word with the hexadecimal value 0105 stored in it
.END		Signals the end of the assembly-language program

Assembly-Language Versions of Previous Program
Program 1 (immediate addressing)   Let's take a look at the algorithm again. Recall that it writes "Hello" on the screen.

Write "Hello"

Write "Hello"

Write "H"
Write "e"
Write "l"
Write "l"
Write "o"

For our machine-language program, we had to further specify each step in this module. Because the assembly language allows us to directly specify the character to be output, this module is concrete if we use assembly language rather than machine language. Each step in this module can be coded directly. Assembly language allows us to add a **comment** beside the instruction. A comment is text written for the human reader of the program that explains what is happening. Comments are an essential part of writing any program. The assembler ignores everything from the semicolon through the end of the line. Here is our assembly language program with appropriate comments.

Comment   Explanatory text for the human reader

```
CHARO C#/H/,i ;Output 'H'
CHARO C#/e/,i ;Output 'e'
CHARO C#/l/,i ;Output 'l'
CHARO C#/l/,i ;Output 'l'
CHARO C#/o/,i ;Output 'o'
STOP
.END
```

The result of running the Assemble option on the Pep7 menu is shown in the following screen.

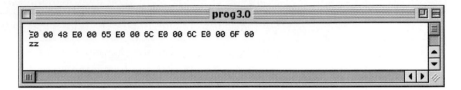

Compare this screen with the machine-language program. They are identical. The output from the assembler is a machine-language version of the program. Once we have the machine-language program, we execute it just as we did with the machine-language version we loaded. We can also get an assembler listing as shown below by clicking the *Assembler Listing* option on the Pep7 menu.

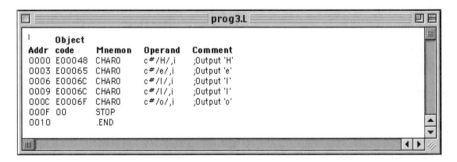

The process is illustrated in Figure 7.5. The input to the Assembler is a program written in assembly language. The output from the Assembler is a program written in machine code. You can see why the creation of assembly language was an important step in the history of programming languages. It removed much of the details of machine-language programming by abstracting the instructions into words. It added a step to the process of executing a program (the translation of assembly to machine code), but that extra step is well worth the effort because it has made the programmer's life so much easier.

Figure 7.5   Assembly process

The Rosetta Stone as a Translation System

The Rosetta stone was unearthed by Napoleon's troops in 1799. The stone contained a proclamation marking the first anniversary of the coronation of Ptolemy V, inscribed in three languages: hieroglyphics, demonic (a cursive version of hieroglyphs), and Greek. Thomas Young, a British physi-

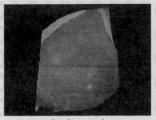

© Copyright The British Museum

cist, and Francois Champollion, a French Egyptologist, were able to decipher the ancient Egyptian languages using the Greek as a guide. Thus, the Rosetta stone provided the key that unlocked the translation of Egyptian hieroglyphics.

Program 1 with direct addressing   What about the version of program 1 that used direct addressing rather than immediate addressing? We can code it from the same algorithm, but it is more complex. Recall that when using direct addressing we must specify the location in which the character we wish to output is stored. We still have to figure out that address, but we can store the characters there more easily than we did in machine language. We put the .ASCII pseudocode operation immediately below the STOP, so that the characters of "Hello" are stored beginning at location 0010.

```
CHARO h#0010,d ;Output 'H'
CHARO h#0011,d ;Output 'e'
CHARO h#0012,d ;Output 'l'
CHARO h#0013,d ;Output 'l'
CHARO h#0014,d ;Output 'o'
STOP
.ASCII /Hello/ ;Store 'Hello' into proper places
.END
```

Here is the screen shot of the assembler listing and the assembled version of the program. Compare the assembled version with the machine language version found on page 204.

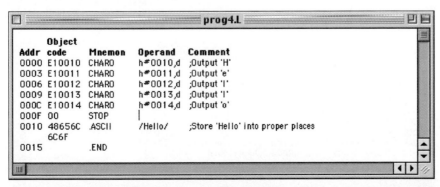

Program 1 enhanced version   Now let's code the enhanced version of the program, where we read in an initial and write it out following 'Hello'. Rather than enhance the immediate-addressing-mode version, let's use the direct-addressing-mode version previously shown. We need to insert a CHARI instruction and a CHARO instruction before the STOP. This means that the characters to be printed must be moved two instructions further down in memory, changing the address of each by 6 bytes. Thus the operands of the CHARO statements must be increased by 6. The only tricky part is to remember that 14 plus 6 is 1A, not 20.

```
CHARO h#16,d ;Output 'H'
CHARO h#17,d ;Output 'e'
CHARO h#18,d ;Output 'l'
CHARO h#19,d ;Output 'l'
CHARO h#1A,d ;Output 'o'
CHARI h#14,d ;Input an initial
CHARO h#00,i ;Output initial
STOP
.ASCII /Hello/ ;Store 'Hello' into proper places
.END
```

Screen shots of the assembler listing and the machine-language program are shown below. Compare the machine code generated with the machine code for the enhanced version. The output is the same, but the programs are different. Be sure that you understand why they are different.

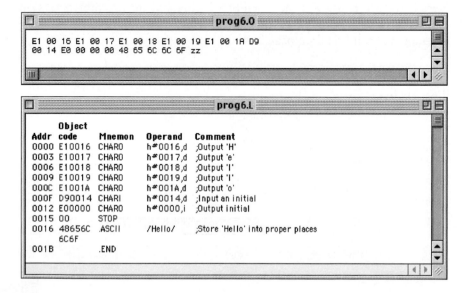

A New Program

Let's make a step up in complexity and write a program to read in three numbers and write out their sum. How would we do this task by hand? If we had a calculator, we would first clear the total; that is, set the sum to zero. Then we would get the first number and add it to the total, get the second number and add it to the total, and finally get the third number and add it to the total. The result would be what is in the accumulator of the calculator. We can model the program on this algorithm.

Set sum to 0
Read num1
Add num1 to sum
Read num2
Add num2 to sum
Read num3
Add num3 to sum
Write sum

The first step is concrete: It involves setting a place in memory to zero. In fact, all of these statements look concrete. The most complex problem is that there are four identifiers that we must associate with places in memory, and this requires knowing how many places the program itself takes—that is, if we put the data at the end of the program. Let's make this process easier by putting our data before the program. We can start associating identifiers with memory locations beginning with location 0001 and have the fetch-execute cycle skip over these places to continue with the program. In fact, we can assign identifiers to the memory locations and use these names later in the program. We set up space for the sum using the .WORD pseudocode so that we can set the contents to 0. We set up space for the three numbers using the .BLOCK pseudocode.

```
sum:   .WORD d#0      ;set up word with zero as the contents
num1:  .BLOCK d#2      ;set up a two byte block for num1
num2:  .BLOCK d#2      ;set up a two byte block for num2
num3:  .BLOCK d#2      ;set up a two byte block for num3
```

We can refer to these identifiers, and the assembler substitutes the addresses. Now all of the steps are concrete. The first step in the algorithm is to set the sum to zero. This is already done by the .WORD pseudo-op. The next two steps are repeated three times: Read a number and Add number to sum. Oops, there is a necessary step not in the algorithm: We must clear the accumulator. We can either load *sum* into the accumulator first (to set it to zero) or we can load the first number into the accumulator rather than adding it in. Since we have made sure that *sum* is zero, let's load it in first. So, after reading and adding three numbers, we must write out the sum. Oops, another missing step. We must store the accumulator into *sum* in order to write it out.

Here is our completed program. Note that we had to have a statement that branches around the data values as the first statement. That is, execution begins with the instruction stored in location 0000. We have put the data at the beginning of the program rather than the instructions that operate on the data. Thus, we must have an instruction stored in location 0000 that puts the location of the first instruction in the program into the program counter. The BR instruction does this. BR, followed by Main, stores the address associated with the name Main into the program counter, so that the instruction stored in Main is then loaded into the instruction register and executed. We have also lined the statements up so that they are easier to read.

```
        BR Main          ;branch to location Main
sum:    .WORD d#0        ;set up word with zero as the contents
num1:   .BLOCK d#2       ;set up a two byte block for num1
num2:   .BLOCK d#2       ;set up a two byte block for num2
num3:   .BLOCK d#2       ;set up a two byte block for num3
Main:   LOADA sum,d      ;load a copy of sum into accumulator
        DECI num1,d      ;read and store a decimal number in num1
        ADDA num1,d      ;add the contents of num1 to accumulator
        DECI num2,d      ;read and store a decimal number in num2
        ADDA num2,d      ;add the contents of num2 to accumulator
        DECI num3,d      ;read and store a decimal number in num3
        ADDA num3,d      ;add the contents of num2 to accumulator
        STOREA sum,d     ;store contents of the accumulator into sum
        DECO sum,d       ;output the contents of sum
        STOP             ;stop the processing
        .END             ;end of the program
```

Here is the machine code and the assembler listing for this program. Look it over carefully to be sure you understand how the program works.

```
┌──────────────────────────────── prog7.0 ─────────────────────┐
│ 70 00 0B 00 00 00 00 00 00 00 00 09 00 03 E9 00              │
│ 05 19 00 05 E9 00 07 19 00 07 E9 00 09 19 00 09              │
│ 11 00 03 F1 00 03 00 zz                                      │
└──────────────────────────────────────────────────────────────┘
```

```
┌─────────────────────────────── prog8.L ─────────────────────────────┐
│          Object                                                      │
│  Addr   code    Symbol    Mnemon    Operand    Comment               │
│  0000  700008            BR         Main       ;branch to location Main        │
│  0003  0000     sum:     .WORD      d≠0        ;set up word with zero as the contents    │
│  0005  00       num1:    .BLOCK     d≠1        ;set up a one byte block for num1         │
│  0006  00       num2:    .BLOCK     d≠1        ;set up a one byte block for num2         │
│  0007  00       num3:    .BLOCK     d≠1        ;set up a one byte block for num3         │
│  0008  090003   Main:     LOADA     sum,d      ;load a copy of sum into accumulator      │
│  000B  E90005            DECI       num1,d     ;read and store a decimal number in num1  │
│  000E  190005            ADDA       num1,d     ;add the contents of num1 to accumulator  │
│  0011  E90006            DECI       num2,d     ;read and store a decimal number in num2  │
│  0014  190006            ADDA       num2,d     ;add the contents of num2 to accumulator  │
│  0017  E90007            DECI       num3,d     ;read and store a decimal number in num3  │
│  001A  190007            ADDA       num3,d     ;add the contents of num2 to accumulator  │
│  001D  110003            STOREA     sum,d      ;store contents of the accumulator into sum │
│  0020  F10003            DECO       sum,d      ;output the contents of sum               │
│  0023  00                STOP                  ;stop the processing                      │
│  0024                    .END                  ;end of the program                      │
│                                                                      │
│                                                                      │
│  Symbol      Value           Symbol     Value                        │
│  Main        0008            num1       0005                         │
│  num2        0006            num3       0007                         │
│  sum         0003                                                    │
└──────────────────────────────────────────────────────────────────────┘
```

7.6   Other Important Threads

In the last chapter, we talked about threads that are important in computing: information hiding, abstraction, naming things, programming languages, and testing. All of these threads have appeared in this chapter, emphasizing how intertwined they all are.

At the machine-language level, there is very little information hiding going on. Every little detail must be explicitly taken care of. One bit of information was hidden: Pep/7 uses 2's complement to represent negative numbers, but we did not need to know this to use the machine language. (See Chapter 2 to refresh your memory about 2's complement.) When we move up to the assembly-language level, we can hide some of the details using the abstractions that the language provides. For example, we are able to set up a block of storage and give the first byte in the block a name by which we can refer to the block. We can associate a word of storage with a name and store a value into the word. We can give an instruction a name and branch to the instruction. These examples of abstraction involve giving names to data or actions. The idea that we can give a name to an action as we did with the instruction we called Main that loads the sum into the accumulator is an extremely important concept, upon which we dwell at some length in later chapters.

Testing

We briefly tested our programs by executing them to see if they produced the output we expected. However, there is far more to testing than just running the program once. Let's look at testing in more detail in the context of the last program. The program reads in three numbers and prints their sum. Testing at the design phase is a simple matter because every step at the top level is a concrete step. How do we test a specific program to determine its correctness? We design and implement a **test plan**. A test plan is a document that specifies how many times and with what data the program must be run in order to thoroughly test the program. Each set of input data values is called a *test case*. The test plan should list the reason for choosing the data, the data values, and the expected output from each case.

The test cases should be chosen carefully. There are several approaches to testing that can guide in the process. A **code-coverage** approach designs test cases to ensure that each statement in the program is executed. Because the code is visible to the tester, this approach is also called **clear-box testing**. **Data-coverage testing** is another approach; it designs test cases to ensure that the limits of the allowable data are covered. Because this approach is based solely on input data and not the code, it is also called **black-box testing**. Often testing is a combination of these two approaches.

Test-plan implementation involves running each of the test cases described in the test plan and recording the results. If the results are not as expected, we must go back to our design and find and correct the error(s). The process stops when each of the test cases gives the expected results. Note that an implemented test plan gives us a measure of confidence that the program is correct; however, all we know for sure is that our program works correctly on the test cases. Therefore, the quality of the test cases is extremely important.

In the case of the program that reads in three values and sums them, a clear-box test would just include three data values. There are no conditional statements in this program to test with alternate data. However, a clear-box test would not be sufficient here. We need to try both negative and positive data values. The numbers that are being read in are stored in one word. The problem does not limit values to $\pm 2^{15}-1$, but our implementation does. We should also try values at the limits of the size of the allowed input in the test plan, but because they are being summed, we need to be sure the sum does not exceed $\pm 2^{15}-1$.

Test plan   A document that specifies how a program is to be tested

Code-coverage (clear-box) testing   Testing a program or subprogram based on covering all the statements in the code

Data-coverage (black-box) testing   Testing a program or subprogram based on the possible input values, treating the code as a black box

Test-plan implementation   Using the test cases specified in a test plan to verify that a program outputs the predicted results

Reason for Test Case	Input Values	Expected Output	Observed Output
Assumption: Input values are no greater than $2^{15}-1$ or less than -2^{15}.			
Input three positive numbers	4, 6, 1	11	
Input three negative numbers	−4, −6, −1	−11	
Input mixed numbers	4, 6, −1	9	
	4, −6, 1	−1	
	−4, 6, 1	3	
Large numbers	32767, −1, +1	32767	

To implement this test plan, the program is run six times, once for each test case. The results are then written in the Observed Output column.

When running the enhanced "Hello" program, we loaded the program and then made a file with the input as the active file before we ran the program. Another alternative is to use interactive input. Interactive input is where the program tells the user to key in the input data as the program is running. If we choose *Execution Input* on the Pep7 menu, we see the following screen:

We click the button by *Interactive Input From Keyboard* and the *OK* button. When we run the program to implement the test cases, we get a window that asks us to input the data.

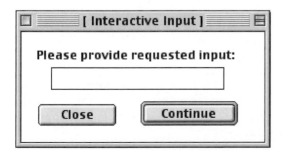

We key in a number and press *Continue*. This screen appears twice more. If the first number we key in is 4, the second is 6, and the third is 1, we get the following output.

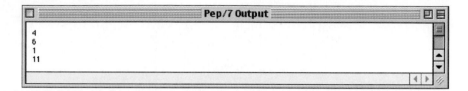

The input is shown along with the output from the program. The first test case runs correctly. You are asked to finish implementing the test plan in the exercises.

Summary

A computer can store, retrieve, and process data. A user can enter data into the machine, and the machine can display data so that the user can see it. At the lowest level of abstraction, instructions to the machine directly relate to these five operations.

A computer's machine language is the set of instructions that the machine's hardware is built to recognize and execute. Machine-language programs were written by entering a series of these instructions in their binary form. The Pep/7 is a virtual computer with two registers (A and X) and two-part instructions. One part of the instruction tells what action the instruction performs, and the other part specifies the location of the data to be used (if any). Programs written using the Pep/7 instruction set can be run using a simulator, a program that behaves like the Pep/7 computer.

The Pep/7 assembly language is a language that allows the user to enter mnemonic codes for each instruction rather than binary numbers. Programs written in assembly language are translated into their machine-language equivalents, which are then executed using the Pep/7 simulator.

Programs, like algorithms, must be tested. Code-coverage testing involves determining the input to the program by looking carefully at the program's code. Data-coverage testing involves determining the input by considering all possible input values.

ETHICAL ISSUES

Software Piracy, Copyrighting

Have you ever upgraded your operating system by borrowing the latest software from a friend? Or, when you spent only $50 to purchase sophisticated software, did you ignore your suspicion that this "steal" was too good to be true? The alarmingly casual attitude towards duplicating, downloading, and reselling software has made software piracy a critical issue for the computer industry. Research conducted by Business Software Alliance indicated that, globally, 11.5 billion dollars were lost in the year 2000 to pirated software. At a rate of 24%, the United States has the lowest piracy rate in the world, but that percentage represents over 2.4 billion dollars in lost revenue to software companies. Software piracy is the unlawful reproduction of copyrighted software, or a violation of the terms of the agreement stated in the software's license. A software license is a document that outlines the terms by which the user may use the software purchased. When you lend software to a friend, or download software onto multiple computers, you are failing to adhere to the license agreement and are, in fact, breaking the law.

Why is software copyrighted? Unlike an idea or written work, software has functionality. This unique quality distinguishes software from other forms of intellectual property and complicates its need for copyrighting. Richard Stallman, President of the Free Software Foundation, argues that assigning copyrights to software hinders its development and that requiring licensing fees makes software cost-prohibitive for many people. Both of these negative consequences suggest to many people that standard copyrighting is not the best approach for software. Advocates of open-source code believe that a program's original source code should be in the public domain. Open-source code is code that anyone can download, and therefore anyone can rewrite portions of the program, thereby participating in the software's evolution. While a number of programs, like the LINUX operating system, have open-source code, companies like Microsoft chose to protect their code.

Respecting the copyrights of software, if it is not open code, is important from a number of perspectives. Research shows that in one year 107,000 jobs were lost in the United States because of pirated software. "Softlifting," or duplicating software from a friend's copy, contributes as much to this piracy problem as counterfeiting and "hard disk loading," which is the unauthorized installation of software into a computer's hard drive before it is sold. Using pirated software also puts the user at risk by exposing him or her to potential software viruses. The person who freely "borrows" software from a friend is actually stealing, and this action has significant ramifications.

Key Terms

Assembler pg. 207

Assembly language pg. 207

Code-coverage (clear-box) testing
   pg. 216

Comment pg. 209

Data-coverage (black-box) testing
   pg. 216

Loader pg. 202

Machine language pg. 189

Test plan pg. 216

Test-plan implementation
   pg. 216

Virtual computer (machine)
   pg. 190

Exercises

1. What does it mean when we say that a computer is a *programmable* device?

2. List five operations that any machine language must include.

3. The distinction between concrete and abstract steps in algorithms is not always clear-cut. Discuss this dilemma and give concrete examples to support your discussion.

4. What is a virtual machine? Discuss this definition in terms of the Pep/7 computer.

5. We said that you should have guessed that a Pep/7 instruction would use 5 bits when we said that there were 32 instructions. Explain.

6. Describe the features of the Pep/7 CPU that we covered in this chapter.

7. We covered only two of the four addressing modes. If we had not stated this explicitly, could you have deduced that this was true? Explain.

8. Where is the data (operand) if the address mode specifier is
   a. 00
   b. 01

9. Distinguish between the IR (instruction register) and the PC (program counter).

10. How many bits are required to address the Pep/7 memory?

11. How many more cells could be added to memory without having to change the instruction format? Justify your answer.

12. Some Pep/7 instructions are unary, taking only one byte. Other instructions require three bytes. Given the instructions that we have covered in this chapter, would it be useful to define instructions that require only two bytes?

Given the following state of memory (in hexadecimal), answer Exercises 13 through 19.

    0001 A2

    0002 11

    0003 FF

13. What are the contents of the A register after the execution of this instruction?

    00001000 00000000 00000011

14. What are the contents of the A register after the execution of this instruction?

    00001001 00000000 00000011

15. What are the contents of the X register after the execution of this instruction?

    00001101 00000000 00000011

16. What are the contents of the A register after the execution of the following two instructions?

    00001001 00000000 00000001
    00011000 00000000 00000001

17. What are the contents of the A register after the execution of the following two instructions?

    00001000 00000000 00000001
    00011001 00000000 00000010

18. What are the contents of the A register after the execution of the following two instructions?

    00001001 00000000 00000011
    00100001 00000000 00000010

19. What are the contents of the X register after the execution of the following two instructions?

    00001101 00000000 00000011
    00100101 00000000 00000010

20. If the input character is A, what is the result of executing the following two instructions?

    0001 11011001 00000000 00000110
    0004 11100000 00000000 00001010

21. If the input character is A, what is the result of executing the following two instructions?

    ```
    0001 11011001 00000000 00000110
    0004 11100001 00000000 00001010
    ```

22. Write the algorithm for writing your name, given that the implementation language is Pep/7 machine code.

23. Write the machine-language program to implement the algorithm in Exercise 22.

24. Write the algorithm for writing out your name, given that the implementation language is Pep/7 assembly language.

25. Write the assembly-language program to implement the algorithm in Exercise 23.

26. Rewrite the enhanced "Hello" program so that a blank is printed before the initial.

27. Distinguish between the Pep/7 menu options *Load*, *Load/Execute*, and *Execute*.

28. The following program seems to run, but does strange things with certain input values. Can you find the bug?

    ```
    BR Main
    sum:    .WORD d#0
    num1:   .BLOCK d#1
    num2:   .BLOCK d#1
    num3:   .BLOCK d#1
    Main:   LOADA sum,d
            DECI num1,d
            ADDA num1,d
            DECI num2,d
            ADDA num2,d
            DECI num3,d
            ADDA num3,d
            STOREA sum,d
            DECO sum,d
            STOP
            .END
    ```

29. Correct the code in Exercise 28 and run the test plan outlined in the chapter.

30. Finish executing the test plan for the algorithm in the text that reads and sums three values.

31. Write an algorithm that reads in three values and writes out the result of subtracting the second value from the sum of the first and the third values.

32. Implement the algorithm in Exercise 31 as an assembly-language program.

33. Write and implement a test plan for the program in Exercise 31.

34. Design and implement an algorithm that reads four values and prints the sum.

35. Is the test plan for a machine language program valid for the same solution written in assembly language? Explain your answer.

36. Distinguish between the pseudocode instructions .BLOCK and .WORD.

37. Distinguish between assembly language pseudocode instructions and mnemonic instructions.

38. Distinguish between test plans based on code coverage and data coverage.

39. Explain the meaning of the Pep/7 menu option Execution Input.

? Thought Questions

1. Would you like to do assembly-language programming? Can you think of any personality types that would be suited for such detail work?

2. The translation process has been demonstrated by showing the machine-language program that is the result of the assembly-language program. Look carefully at the solution of Exercise 32. Think about the steps that the assembler program must execute. Do you think that the translation can be made by looking at each assembly-language instruction once or must each one be examined twice? Convince a friend that you are right.

3. If a person has two computers of the same kind, is it ethical to buy one copy of a software package and install it on both machines? What are the arguments on the yes side? What are the arguments on the no side?

4. Daniel Bricklin, whose biography appears in Chapter 12, did not patent (or copyright) his software, believing that software should not be proprietary. As a result he lost a great deal of possible royalties. Do you consider his actions to be visionary or naive?

5. The Free Software Foundation is a tax-exempt charity that raises funds for work on the GNU Project. GNU software is free. Go to the Web and find out their philosophy. Compare GNU products with those of manufacturers such as Microsoft and Sun.

6. If you continue with computing and become a programmer, which side of this argument would you take: Should software be copyrighted or should it be free?

The Programming Layer

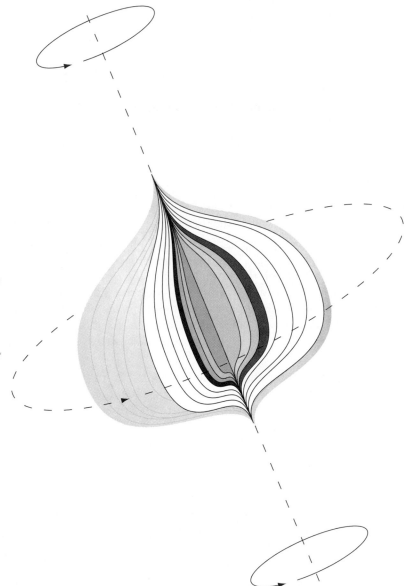

Karibu Welcome
WILLKOMMEN
Bienvenido
Welkom *Benvenuto*

8 High-Level Programming Languages

Chapter 8

High-Level Programming Languages

In Chapter 1, we examined how the layers of languages were built up over time around the hardware to make computing easier for the applications programmer. In the last chapter, we looked at machine code and then at an assembly language that allows the programmer to use mnemonics to represent instructions rather than numbers.

Assembly languages are a step in the right direction, but the programmer still must think in terms of individual machine instructions. High-level programming languages were developed to be closer to how humans think and communicate. Because computers can only execute machine code, translators were developed to translate programs written in these high-level languages into machine code.

In this chapter, we look first at the translation process itself, then we present four differing views of high-level programming languages. This chapter then goes on to examine the functionality that high-level languages give the programmer. Just as the concept of "welcome" can be expressed in different languages, the functionality we describe can be expressed in different languages. We give concrete examples in four high-level languages: Ada, C++, Java, and Visual Basic .NET.

Goals

After studying this chapter, you should be able to

- describe the translation process and distinguish between assembly, compilation, interpretation, and execution.
- name four distinct programming paradigms and name a language characteristic of each.
- describe the following constructs: stream input and output, selection, looping, and subprograms.
- construct Boolean expressions and describe how they are used to alter the flow of control of an algorithm.
- define the concepts of a data type and strong typing.
- explain the concept of a parameter and distinguish between value and reference parameters.
- describe two composite data-structuring mechanisms.
- name, describe, and give examples of the three essential ingredients of an object-oriented language.

8.1   Translation Process

Recall from the last chapter that a program written in assembly language is input to the assembler, which translates the assembly-language instructions into machine code. The machine code, which is the output from the assembler, is then executed. Figure 7.5 depicts the assembly process. The Pep/7 simulator produced a window showing the assembly-language statement, the translated machine code, and the address in memory into which the machine instruction is stored. This listing makes the assembly process very clear. The hallmark of an assembly language is that each assembly-language instruction is translated into one machine-language instruction.

Compilers

The algorithms that translate assembly-language instructions into machine code are very simple because assembly languages are very simple. By simple we mean that each instruction carries out a fundamental operation. High-level languages provide a richer set of instructions that makes the programmer's life even easier, but because the constructs are more abstract, the translation process is more difficult. Programs that translate programs written in a high-level language are called **compilers**. In the early days, the output of a compiler was an assembly-language version of the

> **Compiler** A program that translates a high-level language program into machine code

Figure 8.1   Compilation process

program, which then had to be run through an assembler to finally get the machine-language program to execute. As computer scientists began to have a deeper understanding of the translation process, compilers became more sophisticated and the assembly-language phase was often eliminated. See Figure 8.1.

A program written in a high-level language can be run on any computer that has an appropriate compiler for the language. Note that a compiler is a program; therefore, there must be a machine-code version of the compiler for a particular machine in order to be able to compile a program. Thus, to be able to be used on multiple types of machines, each high-level language must have many compilers for that language.

Interpreters

An **interpreter** is a translating program that translates and executes the statements in sequence. Unlike an assembler or compiler that produces machine code as output, which is then executed in a separate step, an interpreter translates a statement and then immediately executes the statement. Interpreters can be viewed as *simulators* for the language in which a program is written. As Terry Pratt in his classic text on programming languages points out, both a translator and a simulator accept programs in a high-level language as input. The translator (assembler or compiler) simply produces an equivalent program in the appropriate machine language, which must then be run. The simulator executes the input program directly.[1]

Second-generation high-level languages came in two varieties: those that were compiled and those that were interpreted. FORTRAN, COBOL, and ALGOL were compiled; Lisp, SNOBOL4, and APL were interpreted. Because of the complexity of the software interpreters, programs in interpreted languages usually ran much more slowly than compiled programs. As a result, the trend was towards compiled languages until the advent of Java.

Java was introduced in 1996 and swept the computing community by storm. In the design of Java, portability was of primary importance. To

> **Interpreter**   A program that inputs a program in a high-level language and directs the computer to perform the actions specified in each statement

> **Bytecode** A standard machine language into which Java source code is compiled

achieve optimum portability, Java is compiled into a standard machine language called **Bytecode**. How can there by a *standard machine language*? A software interpreter called the JVM (Java Virtual Machine) takes the Bytecode program and executes it. That is, Bytecode is not the machine language for any particular hardware processor. Any machine that has a JVM can run the compiled Java program.

Be aware of the difference between the portability achieved by standardized high-level languages and the portability achieved by translating Java into Bytecode and then interpreting it on a JVM. A program written in a high-level language can be compiled and run on any machine that has the appropriate compiler. The program is translated into machine code that is directly executed by a computer. A Java program is compiled into Bytecode and the compiled Bytecode program can be run on any machine that has a JVM interpreter. That is, the output from the Java compiler is interpreted, not directly executed. See Figure 8.2. Java is always translated into Bytecode. In addition, there are compilers for other languages that translate the language into Bytecode rather than machine code. For example, there are versions of Ada compilers that translate Ada into Bytecode.

UCSD's p-system predates Bytecode

In the 1970's the University of California at San Diego had a system that executed p-code, a language very similar to Bytecode. Programs written in Pascal and FORTRAN were translated into p-code, which could be executed on any hardware with a p-code interpreter.

The JVM is a virtual machine, just like Pep/7, discussed in Chapter 7. We defined a virtual machine as a hypothetical machine designed to illustrate important features of a real machine. The JVM is a hypothetical machine designed to execute Bytecode.

8.2   Programming Language Paradigms

What is a *paradigm*? The American Heritage Dictionary of the English Language gives two definitions that relate to how we, in computing, use the term: "One that serves as a pattern or model" and "A set of assumptions, concepts, values, and practices that constitute a way of viewing reality for the community that shares them, especially in an intellectual discipline."[2] In Chapter 1, we outlined the history of software development listing some of the programming languages that developed in each generation. Another way to view programming languages is to look at the ways different languages reflect differing views of reality; that is, to look at the different paradigms represented.

The von Neumann model of sequential instructions that operate on values in memory greatly influenced the most common model of a

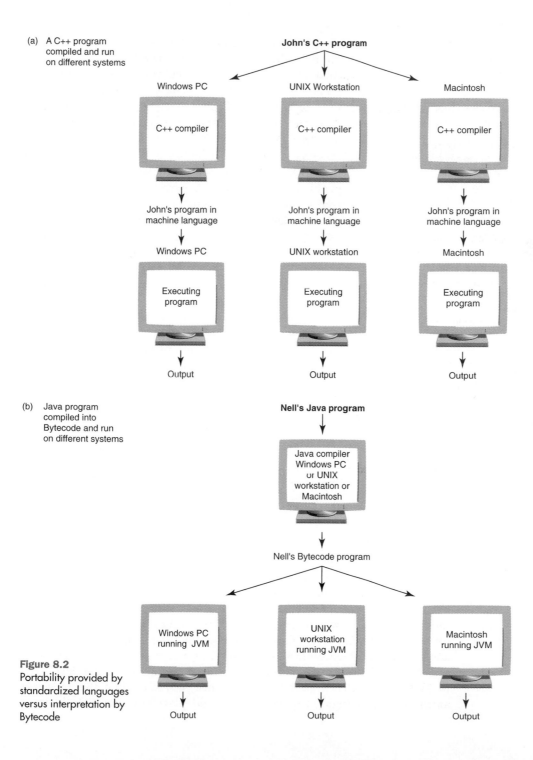

(a) A C++ program compiled and run on different systems

John's C++ program

Windows PC — C++ compiler → John's program in machine language → Windows PC — Executing program → Output

UNIX Workstation — C++ compiler → John's program in machine language → UNIX workstation — Executing program → Output

Macintosh — C++ compiler → John's program in machine language → Macintosh — Executing program → Output

(b) Java program compiled into Bytecode and run on different systems

Nell's Java program

Java compiler Windows PC or UNIX workstation or Macintosh

Nell's Bytecode program

Windows PC running JVM → Output

UNIX workstation running JVM → Output

Macintosh running JVM → Output

Figure 8.2
Portability provided by standardized languages versus interpretation by Bytecode

┌─────────────────────────┐

?

The word *paradigm* has changed over the years.

The 1977 *Webster's New Collegiate Dictionary* defines *paradigm* as "an example or pattern, an outstanding example of an archetype, or an example of a conjugation or declension of a word." There is no mention of a community of views. A search of the Internet in 2001 found many relevant definitions, including: "A pattern or an example of something." The word also connotes the ideas of a mental picture and pattern of thought. Thomas Kuhn uses the word to mean the model that scientists hold about a particular area of knowledge. Kuhn's famous book, *The Structure of Scientific Revolutions*, is his view of the stages through which a science goes in getting from one paradigm to the next.[3] The generally accepted perspective of a particular discipline at a given time; "he framed the problem within the psychoanalytic paradigm."[4] "A model or frame of reference. Radical transformation in the way of looking at an issue or problem."[5]

└─────────────────────────┘

programming language: the *imperative* or *procedural* model. The dominant languages used in industry throughout the history of computing software come from this paradigm. These languages include FORTRAN, COBOL, BASIC, C, Pascal, Ada, and C++. In this paradigm, the languages allow the programmer to express algorithms as a hierarchy of tasks as described in Chapter 6. That is, the program describes the processing necessary to solve the problem. The imperative paradigm is thus characterized by sequential execution of instructions, the use of variables that represent memory locations, and the use of assignment statements that change the values of these variables.[6]

Another model of computation is the *functional* model, which is based on the mathematical concept of the function. Computation is expressed in terms of the evaluation of functions. The solution to a problem is expressed in terms of function calls. The basic mechanism is the evaluation of functions; there are no variables and no assignment statements. For example, the addition of two values would be expressed this way:

(+ 30 40)

where the parentheses represent an expression to be evaluated by applying the first item (which must be a function) to the rest of the list. Thus, this expression is evaluated by applying the addition function to the next two numbers and returns the value 70. There is no looping construct; repetition is expressed in terms of recursive function calls. (Recursion is discussed later in this chapter.) The most well-known languages in the functional paradigm are LISP, Scheme (a derivative of LISP), and ML.

Logic programming is a third programming paradigm. Logic programming is based on the principles of symbolic logic. The model is of a set of facts about objects and a set of rules about the relationships among the objects. A program then consists of asking questions about the objects and their relationships, which can be deduced from the facts and the rules. The underlying problem-solving algorithm uses the rules of logic to deduce the answer from the facts and rules.

PROLOG is a third-generation logic programming language developed in France in 1970. It rose to prominence in 1981 when the Japanese announced that logic programming would play be major role in their fifth-generation computer. A PROLOG program is made up of three types of statements. One type declares facts about objects and their relationships with and to each other. Another type defines rules about objects and their relationships. A third type then asks questions about the objects and their relationships.[7]

LISP and PROLOG are both used in artificial intelligence applications described in Chapter 13. As you can see, programs in these languages have little resemblance to the von Neumann architecture reflected in languages in the imperative paradigm.

The fourth paradigm is the *object-oriented* paradigm. The object-oriented view is one of a world of interacting objects. Each object has responsibility for its own actions. In the imperative paradigm, data objects are considered passive and are acted upon by the program. In the object-oriented paradigm, objects are active. Objects and the code that manipulates them are bundled together, thus making each object responsible for its own manipulation. These languages allow the programmer to express algorithms using a hierarchy of objects, as described in Chapter 6.

SIMULA and Smalltalk were the first two object-oriented programming languages. Although C++ is considered by some to be an object-oriented language, we view it as an imperative language with some object-oriented features. On the other hand, Java, a relatively new language (released in 1996), is an object-oriented language with some imperative features.

We first discuss the functionality of imperative languages, then cover the functionality of object-oriented languages.

8.3   Functionality of Imperative Languages

In Chapter 6, we looked at problem solving in general and problem solving in which the solution is implemented on a computer. We mentioned that there are two processes that we used in designing algorithms: selection and iteration (looping). However, we did not implement either of these constructions in assembly language. We could have done so, but the implementation is very detailed and beyond the scope of what we wanted to cover with assembly languages. In high-level languages, selection and iteration are very easy. First we introduce the concept of a Boolean expression, which is the construct that high-level languages use to make choices. Then we examine constructs that high-level languages provide to make programming easier and safer.

Boolean Expressions

In Chapter 6, we wrote an algorithm to create an address list that includes each person's name, address, telephone number, and e-mail address. One of the subalgorithms was to fill in missing data that had not been entered originally. Let's look at this module.

Fill in missing data   Level 1

Write "To any of the prompts below, if the information is still not known, just
        press return."
Get a name from the list
While (there are more names)
    Get a lastFirst
    Write lastFirst
    If (street is missing)
        Write "Enter street number and name; press return."
        Read street
    If (telephone is missing)
        Write "Enter area code and 7-digit number; press return."
        Read telephone
    If (e-Mail is missing)
        Write "Enter e-mail; press return."
Get a name from the list

There is one loop and three selection statements in this algorithm. We continue looping while there are more names. If a street, telephone number, or e-mail address is missing, the algorithm asks for this information. Notice how these questions are phrased:

(there are more names)
(street is missing)
(telephone is missing)
(eMail is missing)

Each phrase is actually a statement. If the statement is true, the answer to the question is true. If the statement is not true, the answer to the question is false. Making statements and then testing to see if they are true or false is how programming languages ask questions. These statements are called *assertions* or *conditions*. When we are writing algorithms, we make assertions in English-like statements. When the algorithms are translated into a high-level programming language, the English-like statements are rewritten as Boolean expressions.

What is a *Boolean expression*? In Chapter 4, we introduced the concept of Boolean operations when we discussed gates and circuits. Here we are using them at the logical level rather than the hardware level. A **Boolean expression** is a sequence of identifiers, separated by compatible operators, that evaluates to *true* or *false*. A Boolean expression can be

- a Boolean variable.
- an arithmetic expression followed by a relational operator followed by an arithmetic expression.
- a Boolean expression followed by a Boolean operator followed by a Boolean expression.

Yes, but what is a Boolean variable? In fact, what is a variable? In the algorithms we have written, we have used identifiers to name places that represent values in the algorithm. For example, *street* represents a street address, and *telephone* represents a telephone number. In Pep/7 programs, we chose a location in memory for each identifier and stored appropriate values into those locations. A **variable** is a location in memory that is referenced by an identifier that contains a data value. Thus, a Boolean variable is a location in memory that can contain either `true` or `false`*.

A relational operator between two arithmetic expressions is asking if the relationship exists between the two expressions. For example,

xValue < yValue

is making the assertion that *xValue* is less than *yValue*. If *xValue* is less than *yValue*, then the result of the expression is *true*; if *xValue* is not less than *yValue*, then the result is *false*.

The relational operators are listed in the following table, along with the symbols that various high-level languages use to represent the relation.

Relationship	Symbol
equal to	= or ==
not equal to	<> or != or /=
less than or equal to	<=
greater than or equal to	>=
less than	<
greater than	>

Boolean expression   A sequence of identifiers, separated by compatible operators, that evaluates to true or false

Variable   A location in memory, referenced by an identifier, that contains a data value

---

*When referring to code in a specific language or to what is actually stored in memory, we use a monospace (code) font.

Recall that Boolean operators are the special operators AND, OR, and NOT. The AND operator returns `true` if both expressions are true and `false` otherwise. The OR operator returns `false` if both expressions are false and `true` otherwise. The NOT operator changes the value of the expression. These operations are consistent with the functionality of the gates in Chapter 4. At that level we were referring to the flow of electricity and the representation of individual bits. At this level the logic is the same, but we can talk in terms of a statement either being true or false.

Strong Typing

When working in an assembly language, we assign identifiers to memory locations with no regard as to what is to be stored into the locations. Most high-level languages require you to state what can be stored in a place when you associate it with an identifier. If a statement in a program tries to store a value into a variable that is not the proper type, an error message is issued. The requirement that only a value of the proper type can be stored into a variable is called **strong typing**.

In the next sections we look at common types of data values and how high-level languages allow you to associate locations with identifiers. Each of these data types has certain operations that legally can be applied to values of the type. A **data type** is a description of the set of values and the basic set of operations that can be applied to values of the type.

Strong typing Each variable is assigned a type, and only values of that type can be stored in the variable

Data type A description of the set of values and the basic set of operations that can be applied to values of the type

Consider the word *bow*.

A word is a sequence of symbols taken from the alphabet. Some sequence or patterns of symbols have been assigned meanings, others have not (for example, the symbols *ceba* don't form a meaningful word in the English language). But *bow* is an English word. However, it can mean different things: part of a ship, something a little girl wears in her hair, something you play the violin with, or the act of bending from the waist. We can differentiate between the meanings based upon the context of the word, just as a compiler can differentiate based on the surrounding syntax.

Data Types

Data are the physical symbols that represent information. Inside a computer both data and instructions are just binary bit patterns. The computer executes an instruction because the address of the instruction is loaded into the program counter and the instruction is then loaded into the instruction register. That same bit pattern that is executed can also represent an integer number, a real number, a character, or a Boolean value. The key is that the computer interprets the bit pattern to be what it expects it to be.

For example, in Pep/7 the instruction for Stop is a byte of all zero bits. When this instruction is loaded into the Instruction Register, the program halts. A byte of all zero bits can also be interpreted as an 8-bit binary number containing the value 0. If the location containing all zero bits is added to the contents of a register, the value is interpreted as a number.

Most high-level languages have four distinct data types built into the language: integer numbers, real numbers, characters, and Boolean values.

Integers   The integer data type represents a range of integer values from the smallest to the largest. The range varies depending upon how many bytes are assigned to represent an integer value. Some high-level languages provide several integer types of different sizes, which allows the user to choose the one that fits the data in a particular problem.

The operations that can be applied to integers are the standard arithmetic and relational operators. Addition and subtraction are represented by the standard symbols + and −. Multiplication and division are usually represented by * and /. Depending on the language, integer division may return a real number or the integer quotient. Some languages have two symbols for division, one that returns a real result and one that returns the integer quotient. Most languages also have an operator that returns the integer remainder from division. This operator is called the *modulus operator*, but it may or may not act as the mathematical modulus operator. The relational operators are represented by the symbols shown in the table in the previous section.

Reals   The real data type also represents a range from the smallest to the largest value with a given precision. Like the integer data type, the range varies depending on the number of bytes assigned to represent a real number. Many high-level languages have two sizes of real numbers. The operations that can be applied to real numbers are the same as those that can be applied to integer numbers. However, you must be careful when applying the relational operators to real values, because real numbers are often not exact. For example, 1/3 + 1/3 + 1/3 in computer arithmetic is not necessarily 1.0. In fact, 1/10 * 10 is not 1.0 in computer arithmetic.

Characters   In Chapter 3, we said that it takes one byte to represent characters in the ASCII character set and two bytes to represent characters in the Unicode character set. Our English alphabet is represented in ASCII, which is a subset of Unicode. Applying arithmetic operations to characters doesn't make much sense, and many strongly typed languages do not allow you to do so. However, comparing characters does make sense, so the relational operators can be applied to characters. The meaning of "less than" and "greater than" when applied to characters is "comes before" and "comes after" in the character set. The character 'A' is less than 'B', 'B' is less than 'C', and so forth. The character '1' (not the number) is less than '2', '2' is less than '3', and so forth. If you want to compare 'A' to '1', you must look up the relationship between these two characters in the character set you are using.

Boolean   As we said in the previous section, the Boolean data type consists of two values: `true` and `false`. Not all high-level languages support the Boolean data type. If a language does not, then you can simulate Boolean values by saying that the Boolean value `true` is represented by 1 and `false` is represented by 0.

Integers, reals, characters, and Booleans are called simple or atomic data types, because each value is distinct and cannot be subdivided into parts. In a later section, we discuss *composite* data types: data types made up of a collection of values. The *string* data type is a data type with some of the properties of a composite type but is often considered a simple data type.

Strings   A string is a sequence of characters considered as one data value. For example,

`"This is a string."`

is a string containing 17 characters: one uppercase letter, 12 lowercase letters, three blanks, and a period. The operations defined on strings vary from language to language. They include concatenation of strings and comparison of strings in terms of lexicographic order. Other languages provide a complete array of operations, such as taking a substring of a given string or searching a given string for a substring.

Note that we have used single quotes to enclose characters and double quotes to enclose strings. Some high-level languages use the same symbol, thus not distinguishing between a character and a string with one character.

Declarations

As we pointed out in the last chapter, most programming languages have two kinds of instructions: instructions to be translated and instructions to the translating program. We called the instructions to the assembler *directives* because they were directed to the Pep/7 assembler. Most of the instructions to the translating system have to do with naming things. In high-level languages, these instructions are called *declarations*. A **declaration** is a statement that associates an identifier with a variable, an action, or some other entity within the language that can be given a name so that the programmer can refer to that item by name. In this section we discuss how a variable is declared. Later we look at how actions are given names.

In the Pep/7 assembly language of Chapter 7, we were able to give a location a name and store a value into that location. At the assembly-language level, the programmer deals with specific memory locations.

> **Declaration** A statement that associates an identifier with a variable, an action, or some other entity within the language that can be given a name so that the programmer can refer to that item by name

In a high-level language, we do not have to be concerned with where in memory a variable is stored. We just list the identifier and specify the data type of what is to be stored there. The syntax for variable declarations varies from language to language. The following table shows how to declare the same four variables in three different languages. To make it more interesting, let's use a real number for one of the variables.

Language	Variable Declaration
| Ada | ```
sum : Float := 0; --set up word with 0 as contents
num1: Integer;     --set up a two-byte block for num1
num2: Integer;     --set up a two-byte block for num2
num3: INTEGER;     --set up a two-byte block for num3
. . .
num1:= 1;
``` |
| VB.NET | ```
Dim sum As Single = 0.0F ' set up word with 0 as contents
Dim num1 As Integer ' set up a two-byte block for num1
Dim num2 As Integer ' set up a two-byte block for num2
Dim num3 As Integer ' set up a two-byte block for num3
. . .
num1 = 1
``` |
| C++/Java | ```
float sum = 0.0;    // set up word with 0 as contents
int num1:           // set up a two-byte block for num1
int num2:           // set up a two-byte block for num2
int num3:           // set up a two-byte block for num3
num1 = 1;
``` |

These examples illustrate some differences among high-level languages. VB.NET uses a reserved word to signal a declaration. A **reserved word** is a word in a language that has special meaning; it cannot be used as an identifier. Dim is a reserved word in VB.NET used to declare variables. Ada, C++, and Java do not use a reserved word for this purpose. Ada, C++, and Java use the semicolon to end a statement in the language; VB.NET uses the end of the line or the *comment symbol*. The comment symbols are different in each of these languages. Recall that Pep/7 uses a semicolon to signal that what follows is a comment.

Notice that the reserved word for integer numbers is capitalized differently in the Ada example. Ada is not a **case-sensitive** language. This means that uppercase and lowercase letters are considered the same. C++, Java, and VB.NET are case sensitive. Two copies of the same identifier, capitalized differently, are considered different words. Thus, Integer,

Reserved word A word in a language that has special meaning; it cannot be used as an identifier.

Case sensitive Uppercase and lowercase letters are not consider the same; two identifiers with the same spelling but different capitalization are considered to be two distinct identifiers.
```

INTEGER, InTeGeR, and INTeger are considered one identifier in Ada, but four different identifiers in C++ and VB.NET. In C++ and Java, the reserved word `int` is used for integer numbers and `float` for single-precision real numbers. Ada uses `Float` for real numbers, but VB.NET uses `Single` and `Double` for its two versions of real numbers.

Each of these languages allows us to store an initial value in the location assigned to the identifier by placing the assignment operator and a value immediately following the declaration. A value can be stored in a variable with an assignment statement. An **assignment statement** is an action statement (not a declaration) that says to evaluate the expression on the right-hand side of the symbol and store that value into the place named on the left-hand side. Ada uses `:=` as the assignment operator; VB.NET, C++, and Java use the `=`.

Are these differences important? They are if you are writing a program in one of these languages. However, they are just syntactic issues, that is, different ways of doing the same thing. The important concept is that an identifier is associated with (1) a place in memory and (2) a data type.

A variable by definition is a place in memory where the contents can change. There are times in our programs when we want to associate an identifier with a value that cannot change. Such a place is called a **named constant**. Once a named constant has been declared, any attempt to store another value into that place causes an error. The following table shows how to declare the same three named constants in Ada, VB.NET, C++, and Java.

> **Assignment statement**
> A statement that stores the value of an expression into a variable
>
> **Named constant**   A location in memory, referenced by an identifier, that contains a data value that cannot be changed

	Constant Declaration

Ada	`Comma     : constant Character := ',';`
	`Message   : constant String := "Hello";`
	`Tax_Rate : constant Float := 8.5;`

VB.NET	`Const WORD1 As Char = ","c`
	`Const MESSAGE As String = "Hello"`
	`Const TaxRate As Double = 8.5`

C++	`const char COMMA = ',';`
	`const string MESSAGE = "Hello";`
	`const double TAX_RATE = 8.5;`

Java	`final char COMMA = ',';`
	`final String MESSAGE = "Hello";`
	`final double TAX_RATE = 8.5;`

In the exercises, we ask you to compare the syntactic differences that surface in these examples.

The use of uppercase and lowercase in identifiers is part of the culture of a language. In our examples, we have tried to stay with the style that is common within the language's culture. For example, most C++ programmers use all uppercase for named constants and begin variable names with lowercase, while Ada and VB.NET programmers tend to begin variable names with uppercase letters.

Input/Output Structures

In our pseudocode algorithms we have used the expressions Read and Write to indicate that we were interacting with the environment outside the program. Read was for getting a value from outside the program and storing it into a variable inside the program, and Write was for displaying a message for the human to see.

Machine-language instructions for input and output are very primitive. The Pep/7 machine had two instructions: one wrote out one character and the other read in one character. The Pep/7 assembly language provided slightly more functionality by providing instructions to read and write decimal numbers.

High-level languages view input data as a stream of characters divided into lines. How the characters are interpreted depends on the data types of the places into which the values are to be stored. There are three parts to any input statement: the declaration of the variables into which data are to be placed, the input statement with the names of the variables to be read, and the data stream itself. For example, look at the algorithm that inputs three values.

```
Read name, age, hourlyWage
```

The variables name, age, and hourlyWage would have to be declared along with their respective data types. Let's assume the types are string, integer, and real. The input statement would list the three variables. Processing would proceed as follows. The first data item on the input stream would be assumed to be a string, because name is of type string. The string would be read and stored into name. The next variable is an integer, so the read operation expects to find an integer next in the input stream. This value is read and stored in age. The third variable is a real number, so the read operation expects to find a real value next on the input stream.

The input stream may be from the keyboard or a data file, but the process is the same. The order in which the variables are listed on the input statement must be the same as the order in which the values occur in the input stream. The types of the variables being input determine how the characters in the input stream are interpreted. That is, the input stream is just a series of ASCII (or Unicode) characters. The type of the variable into which the next value is to be stored determines how a sequence of characters is interpreted. For simplicity, let's assume that the input statement assumes that a blank separates each data value. For example, given the following data stream

```
Maggie 10 12.50
```

"Maggie" would be stored in *name*; 10 would be stored in *age*, and 12.50 would be stored in *hourlyWage*. Both 10 and 12.50 are read in as characters and converted to integer and real, respectively.

Output statements create streams of characters. The items listed on the output statement can be literal values or variable names. Literal values are numbers or strings written explicitly in the output statement (or any statement for that matter). The values to be output are processed one at a time by looking at the type of the identifier or literal. The type determines how the bit pattern is to be interpreted. If the type is a string, the characters are written into the output stream. If the bit pattern is a number, the number is converted to the characters that represent the digits and the characters are written out.

Regardless of the syntax of input/output statements or where the input/output streams are, the key to the processing is in the data type that determines how characters are to be converted to a bit pattern (input) and how a bit pattern is to be converted to characters (output).

We do not give examples of input/output statements because the syntax is often quite complex and differs so widely among high-level languages.

Control Structures

In the last Pep/7 program in Chapter 7, the first statement in the program is a branch instruction around the data to the first statement to be executed.

```
BR   Main      ;branch to location Main
```

In machine language, and later in assembly language, the only way to alter the sequential order in which instructions were executed was to branch to another location, where the sequential process would resume. The branch was the only *control structure*. A **control structure** is an instruction that determines the order in which other instructions in a program are executed.

In a seminal article, "Notes on Structured Programming," published in 1972, Edsger W. Dijkstra pointed out that programmers should be precise

Control structure An instruction that determines the order in which other instructions in a program are executed

Edsger Dijkstra[8]

Every field of human endeavor has its leading contributors who are acclaimed for their theoretical insights, extensions of fundamental ideas, or innovative changes that have redefined the subject. Just as Beethoven, Schubert, Mozart, and Hayden ring true in the world of classical music, and the Beatles, Rolling Stones, and the Who stand out in rock-'n'-roll, Edsger Dijkstra has a place reserved for him in the computer language hall of fame.

Born to a Dutch chemist in Rotterdam in 1930, Dijkstra grew up with a formalist predilection toward the world. While studying at the University of Leiden in the Netherlands, he attended a summer course on programming in Cambridge, England, and became fascinated with programming. He took a part-time job at the Mathematical Centre in Amsterdam in 1952, and he continued to work there after his graduation. He came to the United States in the early 1970s as a research fellow for Burroughs Corporation, and in September of 1984 he came to The University of Texas at Austin, where he held the Schlumberger Centennial Chair in Computer Sciences. He retired in November of 1999.

One of the Dijkstra's most famous contributions to programming was his strong advocacy of structured programming principles. Dijkstra observed that programs written with *goto* statements often turned into a rat's nest of jumping back and forth among disorganized, ad hoc sections of programs, making the programs difficult to understand even for the authors—not to mention the colleagues who might later be asked to maintain the program. Dijkstra argued that the *goto* was not the be-all and end-all of control structures, and he strongly encouraged the use of iterative, or looping, constructs that clearly bracket the scope of branching in a program and effectively self document the program. Dijkstra claimed that adhering to these structured programming principles would make programs far easier to understand and maintain and less likely to contain errors.

Beyond his clear theoretical contributions, Dijkstra is an interesting character in the computing world. He has developed a reputation for speaking his mind, often in inflammatory or dramatic ways that most of us can't get away with. For example, Dijkstra once remarked that "the use of COBOL cripples the mind; its teaching should therefore be regarded as a criminal offence." Not one to single out only one language for his criticism, he also said that "it is practically impossible to teach good programming to students that have had a prior exposure to BASIC; as potential programmers they are mentally mutilated beyond hope of regeneration." Some people find his message cogent and feel that his manner is politically necessary to make his point. Others, aware of the historical development of languages and the contexts in which they were designed, appreciate his message but find his manner a bit strident.

Besides his work in language design, Dijkstra is also noted for his work in proofs of program correctness. The field of program correctness is an application of mathematics to computer programming. Researchers are trying to construct a language and proof technique that might be used to certify unconditionally that a program will perform according to its specifications—entirely free of bugs. Needless to say, whether your application is customer billing or flight control systems, this claim would be extremely valuable.

In 1972 the Association for Computing Machinery acknowledged Dijkstra's rich contributions to the field by awarding him the distinguished Turing Award. The citation for the award read:

> "Edsger Dijkstra was a principal contributor in the late 1950's to the development of the ALGOL, a high level programming language which has become a model of clarity and mathematical rigor. He is one of the principal exponents of the science and art of programming languages in general, and has greatly contributed to our understanding of their structure, representation, and implementation. His fifteen years of publications extend from theoretical articles on graph theory to basic manuals, expository texts, and philosophical contemplations in the field of programming languages."

In 1989 SIGCSE, the Special Interest Group for Computer Science Education, honored him with its award for Outstanding Contributions to Computer Science Education.

and disciplined, that they should use only selected control structures. This article and the others published with it introduced the era of *structured programming*.[9] Each logical unit of a program should have just one entry and one exit. The program should not jump randomly in and out of logical modules. Although programs could be designed in this way in assembly language using instructions that branch to other parts of the program, high-level languages introduced control constructs that made this discipline easy to follow. These constructs are selection statements, looping statements, and subprogram statements. Unrestricted branching statements were no longer necessary.

With the advent of windows on the screen and input using a mouse, a fifth basic control structure was introduced: asynchronous processing. In the next sections we introduce these concepts at the logical level.

Sequence

The concept of one instruction following another in physical sequence is still the underlying structure of an imperative program. Statements are executed in sequence until an instruction is encountered that changes this sequencing.

Selection Statements

Selection statements come in two basic varieties: the *if* statement and the *case* (or *switch*) statement for multi-way branching.

if statements   The *if* statement allows the program to test the state of the program variables using a Boolean expression. If the Boolean expression returns `true`, no instruction, one instruction, or a sequence of instructions is executed. If the Boolean expression returns `false`, no instruction, another instruction, or another sequence of instructions is executed. Figure 8.3 illustrates this flow of control.

Let's look at a concrete example. If a variable within the program represents a temperature (`temperature`), let's compare the value in order to determine the appropriate clothes to wear. Let's first state the algorithm in pseudocode, and then look at how the algorithm would be converted into a high-level language.

```
If (temperature > 75)
    Write "No jacket is necessary"
Else
    Write "A light jacket is appropriate"
```

The following table shows how Ada, VB.NET, and C++ would implement this algorithm.

Language	if Statement
| Ada | ```
if Temperature > 75 then
   Put(Item => "No jacket is necessary")
else
   Put (Item => "A light jacket is appropriate");
end if;
``` |
| VB.NET | ```
if (Temperature > 75) Then
   MsgBox("No jacket is necessary")
Else
   MsgBox("A light jacket is appropriate")
End if
``` |
| C++ | ```
if (temperature > 75)
   cout << "No jacket is necessary";
else
   cout << "A light jacket is appropriate";
``` |
| Java | ```
if (temperature > 75)
   System.out.print("No jacket is necessary");
else
   System.out.print("A light jacket is appropriate");
``` |

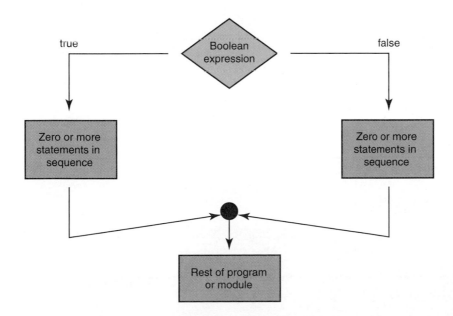

Figure 8.3   Flow of control of the *if* statement

The true branch is known as the *then* branch, but as you can see from the table, the branch may or may not be labeled as such. The false branch is called the *else* branch and is labeled as such in each of these examples. The great variety in how information is written for the human to see is demonstrated in the different way that the strings are written.

In our description of the behavior of the *if* statement we said that either branch could have none, one, or a sequence of instructions. If the sequence is empty, then the *else* branch is just not there. The example earlier shows how to write the code if there is just one instruction, but how do we write a sequence of instructions? High-level languages all have a way of considering a sequence of instructions as a single group. Let's add a second output statement to the *else* branch of our algorithm and see how these three languages handle it.

Language	if Statement

Ada	<pre>if Temperature > 75 then
	  Put(Item => "No jacket is necessary");
	else
	  Put (Item => "A light jacket is appropriate");
	  Put (Item => "but not necessary");
	end if;</pre>

VB.NET	<pre>if (Temperature > 75) Then
	  MsgBox("No jacket is necessary")
	Else
	  MsgBox("A light jacket is appropriate")
	  MsgBox("but not necessary")
	End if</pre>

C++	<pre>if (temperature > 75)
	  cout << "No jacket is necessary";
	else
	{
	  cout << "A light jacket is appropriate";
	  cout << "but not necessary";
	}</pre>

Java	<pre>if (temperature > 75)
	  System.out.print(No jacket is necessary");
	else
	{
	  System.out.print("A light jacket is appropriate");
	  System.out.print("but not necessary");
	}</pre>

Instructions considered as a single group are called a *compound statement*. Ada and VB.NET use reserved words to end a construct, so no special grouping is necessary. C++ and Java group statements within curly braces. They call this grouping a *block*.

Because we only get to the *else* branch if the Boolean expression is *not* true, we can make use of the information to ask a series of questions. Let's alter and expand the algorithm with a finer grain on our temperature problem.

```
If (temperature > 90)
     Write "Texas weather: wear shorts"
Else If (temperature > 70)
     Write "Ideal weather: short sleeves are fine"
Else if (temperature > 50)
     Write "A little chilly: wear a light jacket"
Else If (temperature > 32)
     Write "Philadelphia weather: wear a heavy coat"
Else
     Write "Stay inside"
```

The only way to get to the second *if* statement is if the first expression is not true, so if the second expression is true, you know that the temperature is between 71 and 90. If the first and second expressions are not true and the third is, then the temperature is between 51 and 70. The same reasoning leads to the conclusion that Philadelphia weather is between 33 and 50, and "Stay inside" is written if the temperature is less than or equal to 32. Any one of the branches can contain a sequence of statements.

case statement   The *if* is the workhorse of the selection statements. In fact, you don't need another selection statement, but for convenience, many high-level languages include a *case* (or *switch*) statement that allows us to make multiple-choice decisions easier, provided the choices are discrete. Because the temperature problem was based on ranges of values rather than on explicit values, it could not be implemented in a *case* statement.

Let's look at an example that is a subalgorithm in a calculator program. You have two data values and you need to determine which arithmetic operator is to be applied between them. The operator is stored in character form in operator. The algorithm for determining which operator to apply is shown here.

```
CASE operator OF
'+'  :  Set answer to one + two
'-'  :  Set answer to one – two
'*'  :  Set answer to one * two
'/'  :  Set answer to one / two
```

The value stored in variable *operator* is compared with the symbol on each successive line. When a match if found, the statement on the other side of the colon is executed and control passes to the statement following the *case* statement. If there is no match, none of the statements are executed. Because the *case* is not necessary, we do not examine how it is translated into a specific language.

Looping Statements

We introduced the concept of repeating a sequence of statements in Chapter 6. The subalgorithm that we repeated earlier in this chapter has the expression:

```
While (there are more names)
```

The processing is repeated until all the names have been processed. That is, the sequence of statements is repeated as long as the expression is true. When the expression becomes false, the processing continues with the statements immediately following the loop. We used indentation in the algorithm to show the statements included in the loop. Later we show how a loop is implemented in Ada, VB.NET, C++, and Java. A *while* statement, like an *if* statement, alters the normal sequential flow of a program. The behavior is described in Figure 8.4.

Note that an *if* statement is used to make a choice between two courses of action; the *while* statement is used to repeat a course of action. Before we look at how different high-level languages express the *while* statement, let's look at two distinct types of repetitions.

Count-controlled loops   A count-controlled loop is one that repeats a specified number of times. The looping mechanism simply counts each time the process is repeated, then tests to see if it's finished before beginning again. There are three distinct parts to this kind of loop, which makes

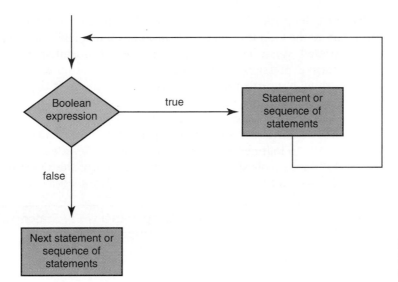

Figure 8.4
Flow of control of *while* statement

use of a special variable called a *loop control variable*. The first part is initialization: The loop control variable is initialized to some starting value. The second part is testing: Has the loop control variable reached a predetermined value? The third part is incrementation: The loop control variable is incremented by one. The following algorithm repeats a process limit times.

Set count to 1	Initialize count to 1
While (count <= limit)	Test
...	Body of the loop
Set count to count + 1	Increment
...	Statement(s) following loop

count is the loop control variable. It is set to 1 outside the loop. The while tests the expression count <= limit and executes the loop body as long as the expression is true. The last statement in the loop increments the loop control variable count. How many times does the loop execute? The loop executes when count is 1, 2, 3, ... limit. So the loop executes limit times. The initial value of the loop control variable and the relational operator used in the Boolean expression determine the number of times the loop executes.

The *while* loop is called a pretest loop. This means that the testing takes place before the loop is executed. If the condition is false initially, the loop is not entered. What happens if the incrementation statement is omitted? The Boolean expression never changes. If the expression was false to begin with, nothing happens; the loop is just not executed. If the expression is true to begin with, the expression never changes, so the loop executes forever. Actually, most computing systems have a timer, so the program would not actually run forever. The program would halt with an error message. A loop that never terminates is called an *infinite loop*.

The following table shows the implementation of the algorithm in Ada, VB.NET, C++, and Java.

Language	Count-Controlled Loop with a while Statement
| Ada | ```
Count = 1;
while Count <= Limit loop
   . . .
   Count = Count + 1;
end loop;
``` |
| VB.NET | ```
Count = 1
While (count <= limit)
   . . .
   count = count + 1
End While
``` |
| C++/Java | ```
count = 1;
while (count <= limit)
{
   . . .
   count++;
}
``` |

Incrementing the content of a variable by one is such a common operation that C++ and Java provide a shortcut. In these languages, *count++* is a short cut for the statement *count = count + 1*.

Event-controlled loops Loops in which the number of repetitions is controlled by an event that occurs within the body of the loop itself are called event-controlled loops. To implement an event-controlled loop using a *while* statement, there are again three parts to the process. The event must be initialized, the event must be tested, and the event must be updated.
```

A count-controlled loop is very straightforward: The process is repeated a specified number of times. The event-controlled loop is less clear-cut. It may not be immediately apparent what the event should be. Let's look at a couple of examples. First, let's read and sum input data values until we read a negative value. What is the event? An input value is positive. How do we initialize the event? We read the first data value. We test the value to determine if it is positive and enter the loop if it is. How do we update the event? We read the next data value. Here is the algorithm.

```
Read a value           Initialize event
While (value >= 0)     Test event
    ...                Body of loop
        Read a value   Update event
...                    Statement(s) following loop
```

Now let's write the algorithm for reading and summing positive values until ten have been counted. Ignore zero or negative values. What is the event? The number of positive values read and summed. The means that we must keep a count of the number of positive values as we read them; let's call it *posCount*. How do we initialize the event? We set *posCount* to 0. We test *posCount* against ten, and exit the loop when *posCount* reaches 11. How do we update the event? We increment *posCount* each time we read a positive value.

```
Set sum to 0               Initialize sum to zero
Set posCount to 0          Initialize event
While (posCount <= 10)     Test event
    Read a value
    If (value > 0)                  Test to see if event should be updated
        Set posCount to posCount + 1    Update event
        Set sum to sum + value          Add value into sum
...                                 Statement(s) following loop
```

Many languages have two additional looping structures. We said that the *while* structure is a pretest loop. Another type of looping structure is one where the testing occurs at the end of the loop. These loops are called *posttest* loops, for obvious reasons. Posttest loops always execute the loop body at least once. Although any loop can be implemented using the *while* construct, there are times where you know that the loop executes once, so a posttest loop would be appropriate. (Posttest loops are often called *repeat* loops.) The second additional structure is one designed for count-controlled loops where the initializing, testing, and incrementation are included in the loop construct itself. These loops are often called *for* loops.

Subprogram Statements

When doing algorithms in Chapter 6, we gave a name to a task at one level and then expanded the task at a lower level. The same idea holds in programming languages. We can give a section of code a name and use that name as a statement in another part of the program. When the name is encountered, the processing in the other part of the program halts while the named code is executed. When the named code finishes executing, processing resumes with the statement just below where the name occurred. The place where the name of the code appears is called the *calling unit*.

There are two basic forms of subprograms: One is just named code that does a particular task; the other does a task but also returns a single value to the calling unit. The first is used as a statement in the calling unit; the second is used in an expression in the calling unit where the returned value is then used in the evaluation of the expression. These subprograms have been called by many names. FORTRAN calls them subroutines and functions. Ada calls them procedures and functions. C++ calls the first a void function and the second a value-returning function. Java calls both of them methods. But regardless of what subprograms are called, they are powerful tools for abstraction. The listing of a named subprogram allows the reader of the program to see that a task is being done without having to be bothered with the details of the task's implementation. See Figure 8.5.

Many subprograms come as part of a high-level language or part of the library that comes with the language. For example, mathematical problems often need to calculate trigonometric functions. Subprograms that calculate these values are available in most high-level languages in one way or another. When a program needs to calculate one, the programmer looks up the name of the subprogram that calculates the value and just calls the subprogram to do the calculation.

> **Parameter list** A mechanism for communicating between two parts of a program

Parameter passing   There are times when the calling unit needs to give information to the subprogram to use in its processing. The method of communication used in high-level languages is called a *parameter list*. A **parameter list** is a list of the identifiers with which the subprogram is to

(a) Subprogram A does its task and calling unit continues with next statement

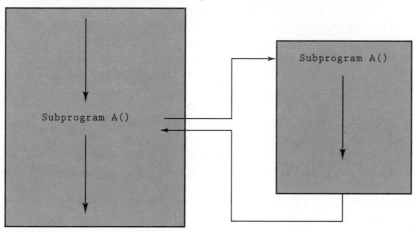

(b) Subprogram B does its task and returns a value that is added to 5 and stored in x

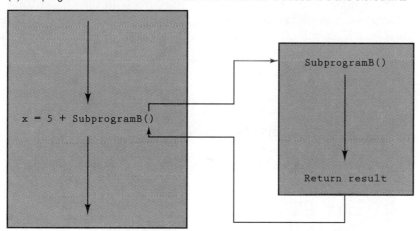

Figure 8.5
Subprogram flow of control

work, along with the types of each identifier placed in parentheses beside the subprogram name. Because a subprogram is defined before it is called, it does not know with which variables from the calling unit it is to work. To solve this dilemma, we specify a list of variable names with associated types in parentheses beside the subprogram name. These identifiers are called **parameters**. When the subprogram is called, the calling unit lists the subprogram name followed by a list of identifiers in parentheses. These

Parameters The identifiers listed in parentheses beside the subprogram name; sometimes they are called *formal parameters.*

Arguments The identifiers listed in parentheses on the subprogram call; sometimes they are called *actual parameters*.

identifiers are called **arguments**. The arguments represent actual variables in the calling unit with which the subprogram is to work.

You can think of a parameter as being a dummy identifier that is used within a subprogram. When a subprogram is called, the calling unit sends the names of the actual identifiers to the subprogram. The action in the subprogram is defined using the parameters. When the action takes place, the arguments are substituted one by one for the parameters. The substitution can be done in several ways, but the most common is by position. The first argument substitutes for the first parameter, the second argument substitutes for the second parameter, and so on.

The substitution mechanism acts like a message board. When a subprogram is called, a list of the arguments is given to the subprogram (put on the subprogram's message board). The arguments tell the subprogram where to find the values it is supposed to use. When a parameter is used in the body of the subprogram, the subprogram accesses it through a relative position on the message board. That is, the subprogram looks for its first parameter in the first position on the message board and for its second parameter in the second position on the message board. See Figure 8.6.

There must be the same number of arguments in the call as there are parameters in the subprogram heading, and the parameters and arguments must match up in both position and data type. Because the arguments and parameters are matched by position, their names don't have to be the

List   Parameter
                                              List

Figure 8.6
Passing parameters

same. This is very helpful when a subprogram is called more than once, with different arguments in each call. Parameters passed in this fashion are often called *positional parameters.*

Value and reference parameters   There are two basic ways of passing parameters: by value and by reference (or address). If a parameter is a **value parameter**, the calling unit gives a *copy* of the argument to the subprogram. If a parameter is a **reference parameter**, the calling unit gives the *address* of the argument to the subprogram. This difference means that a subprogram cannot change the content of an argument that is passed to a value parameter. The subprogram can modify the copy, but the original variable is not changed. In contrast, any argument passed by the calling unit to a reference parameter can be changed by the subprogram because the subprogram is manipulating the actual variable, not a copy of it.

> **Value parameter** A parameter that expects a copy of its argument to be passed by the calling unit (put on the message board)
>
> **Reference parameter** A parameter that expects the address of its argument to be passed by the calling unit (put on the message board)

Think of the difference this way: To access a reference parameter, the subprogram accesses the contents of the *address* listed on the message board. To access a value parameter, the subprogram accesses the contents of the place on the message board itself. Clearly, both the calling unit and the subprogram must know which parameter/argument is to be passed by value and which is to be passed by reference. Not all high-level languages allow both kinds of parameters, but those that do have some syntactic schemes to label parameters as value or reference.

The following table shows how VB.NET and C++ define a subprogram that does not return a single value. There are two integer value parameters and one real reference parameter. Again, this is to give you a flavor for the variety of syntax that abounds in high-level languages, not to make you competent in writing this construct in any of them. The ampersand (&) used in C++ is not a typo; it signals that *three* is a reference parameter.

Language	Subprogram Declaration

VB.NET	```Public Sub Example(ByVal one As Integer,```
	``` ByVal two As Integer,```
	``` ByRef three As Single)```
	``` ...```
	```End Sub```

C++/Java	```void Example(int one; int two; float& three)```
	```{```
	``` ...```
	```}```

We do not show a Java example because Java handles memory very differently from the other three and has only value parameters. We do not show an Ada example because the compiler is free to select the most efficient parameter-passing mechanism for the given hardware or Bytecode virtual machine.

Before we leave subprograms, let's look at an example that illustrates the difference between value and reference parameters. Let's write an algorithm that swaps the contents of two places in memory. Let's call them *data1* and *data2*. This sounds easy enough: We just store *data1* into *data2* and *data2* into *data1*. Right? Well, not exactly. If we do this, we end up with both variables containing what was originally in *data1*. We need an intermediate variable in which to store the contents of *data2* before we copy *data1* into it. We call this intermediate variable a *local* variable. It is only needed for a short while. We put the subprogram name on top of the algorithm box along with its parameters.

Swap (Integer item1, Integer item2)
Integer temp   Declare local variable
Set temp to item2
Set item2 to item1
Set item1 to temp

Now let's say that the calling unit (the part of the program that wants the contents of the two places exchanged) calls *Swap* with *data1* and *data2* as parameters.

Swap (data1, data2)

Now let's say that *data1* is stored in location 0002 and *data2* is stored in location 0003. They contain the values 30 and 40, respectively. Figure 8.7 shows the content of the message board when the parameters are passed by value and passed by reference. When a parameter is a value parameter, the subprogram knows to manipulate the value on the message board. When a parameter is a reference parameter, the subprogram knows to manipulate the contents of the address on the message board. Should the parameters for subprogram *Swap* be value or reference parameters?

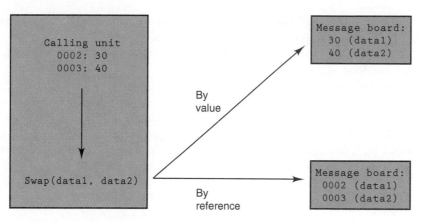

Figure 8.7
Difference between value parameters and reference parameters

Recursion

When a subprogram invokes itself, the call is known as a *recursive* call. **Recursion**—the ability of a subprogram to call itself—is an alternative control structure to repetition (looping). Rather than use a looping statement to execute a program segment, the program uses a selection statement to determine whether to repeat the code by calling the subprogram again or to stop the process.

> **Recursion** The ability of a subprogram to call itself

Each recursive solution has at least two cases: the *base case* and the *general case*. The base case is the one to which we have an answer; the general case expresses the solution in terms of a call to itself with a smaller version of the problem. Because the general case solves a smaller and smaller version of the original problem, eventually the program reaches the base case, where an answer is known and the recursion stops.

Associated with each recursive problem is some measure of the size of the problem. The size must get smaller with each recursive call. The first step in any recursive solution is to determine the *size factor*. If the problem involves a numerical value, the size factor might be the value itself. For example, a classic recursive problem is the factorial. The factorial of a number is defined as the number times the product of all the numbers between itself and 0: $N! = N * (N - 1)!$. The factorial of 0 is 1. The size factor is the number for which we are calculating the factorial. We have a base case, Factorial(0) is 1, and we have a general case, Factorial(N) is N * Factorial(N − 1). An *if* statement can evaluate N to see if it is 0 (the base case) or greater than 0 (the general case). Because N is clearly getting smaller with each call, the base case is reached.

What happens if the argument is a negative number? The subprogram just keeps calling itself until the run-time support system runs out of memory. This situation is called *infinite recursion* and is equivalent to an infinite loop.

Recursion is a very powerful and elegant tool. However, not all problems can easily be solved recursively, and not all problems that have an obvious recursive solution should be solved recursively. But there are many problems for which a recursive solution is preferable. If the problem statement logically falls into two cases, a base case and a general case, recursion is a viable alternative.

Asynchronous Processing

Most of you have grown up in the windows generation. Notice that the w is not uppercase. We are not talking about the Microsoft Windows operating system, but the concept that input and output can be accomplished through windows on the screen. At a minimum you can get rid of a window by clicking a box in the corner of the window. "Clicking" is the magic word. Whether you are clicking on the corner of a window or clicking on a button on the screen, you expect something to happen when you do this. *Clicking* has become a major form of input to the computer. In fact, for many applications, filling in boxes and clicking on buttons to say the input is ready has become the major form of input.

In traditional stream processing, an input statement is executed in the sequence in which it is encountered. Here are the first three statements in the algorithm:

```
Write "To any of the prompts below, if the information is still not known,
        just press return."
Get a name from the list
While (there are more names)
....
```

We expect these statements to be executed in sequence. Output is written to a window, a name is read from the input stream, and the while loop is executed. Stream input and output is within the sequential flow of the program.

Mouse clicking, on the other hand, is not within the sequence of the program. A user can click a mouse at any time during the execution of a program. The program must recognize when a mouse click has occurred, process the mouse click, and then continue. This type of processing is called **asynchronous**, which means "not at the same time." The mouse can be clicked at any time; it is not synchronized with any other instructions.

Asynchronous processing is also called *event-driven* processing. The processing is under the control of events happening outside the sequence of program instructions.

Asynchronous processing is used frequently in Java and VB.NET, but less so in the other languages. Although Ada does use asynchronous processing extensively in embedded systems such as Flight Management Systems software, where the events are such things as button and switch changes made in the cockpit, sensors onboard the aircraft, and signals from navigation aids on the ground.

Asynchronous Not occurring at the same moment in time as some specific operation of the computer; in other words, not synchronized with the program's actions.

Nested Logic

The statements to be executed or skipped in any control statement can be simple statements or blocks (compound statements). There is no constraint on what the statements can be. This means that the statement to be skipped or repeated can contain a control structure. Selection statements can be nested within looping structures; looping structures can be nested within selection statements. Selection and looping statements can be nested within subprograms, and subprogram calls can be nested within looping or selection structures.

Composite Data Types

The data types described previously were atomic, with the possible exception of the string. In this section, we describe three mechanisms for collecting data items together and accessing the items individually or as a collection.

Records

A record is a named *heterogeneous* collection of items in which individual items are accessed by name.[10] Heterogeneous means that the elements in the collection can be of various types. Each item is given an identifier and a type. The operations allowed on a record are passing a record as a parameter to a subprogram and individual component access. Records are good for bundling items together that relate to the same object. For example, we read in a name, an age, and an hourly wage. The three items could be bound together into a record. Let's look at how a record type is declared in our three languages.

Language	Record Type Declaration

Ada	```type Name_String is String (1..10);```
	```type Employee_Type is```
	``` record```
	``` Name : Name_String;```
	``` Age : Integer range 0..100;```
	``` Hourly_Wage : Float range 1.0..5000.0;```
	```end record;```

VB.NET	```Structure Employee```
	``` Dim Name As String```
	``` Dim Age As Integer```
	``` Dim HourlyWage As Single```
	```End Structure```

C++	```struct EmployeeType```
	```{```
	``` string name;```
	``` int age;```
	``` float hourlyWage;```
	```};```

Although the syntax is quite different, three elements are present: A record type is defined with a name and three variable names are defined with their data types. Notice that Ada allows the programmer to declare a range of a numeric data types. The Age field is defined as a reasonable subrange of the integers. If the program tries to store a value outside that range into Age, an error occurs. Hourly_Wage is defined as a reasonable subrange of the reals. This is a very nice safety feature in the language.

How do you access the fields within a record? Well, first you have to declare a record to be of the record type, and then you can access the fields within the record variable. The syntax for declaring a record variable and the accessing mechanism for the variables is shown on the next page.

Language	Record Variable Declaration and Usage
| Ada | ```
An_Employee : Employee_Type;
...
  An_Employee.Name = "Sarah Gale";
  An_Employee.Age = 32;
  An_Employee.Hourly_Wage = 95.00;
``` |
| VB.NET | ```
Dim AnEmployee As EmployeeType
...
  AnEmployee.Name = "Sarah Gale"
  AnEmployee.Age = 32
  AnEmployee.HourlyWage  95.00
``` |
| C++ | ```
EmployeeType anEmployee;
...
  anEmployee.name = "Sarah Gale";
  anEmployee.age = 32;
  anEmployee.hourlyWage = 95.00;
``` |

`Employee_Type` is a record type; `An_Employee` is a record variable. `An_Employee` can be passed as a parameter, and the items within it can be accessed by giving their individual names. In our three examples, each name is a combination of the record name and the item name with a dot in between. Some languages allow the items within a record to be a subprogram. We look at how this is done when we look at the additional functionality of object-oriented languages in the next section.

Arrays

An array is a named collection of homogeneous items in which individual items are accessed by their place within the collection. The place within the collection is called an *index*. Some languages call the first place in the collection the 0th item and some languages allow the programmer to name how the items are to be addressed; that is, the first item might be called the *a*th item. When declaring an array, it is customary to tell the system how many items are in the collection, and the data type of each. Let's look at the syntax necessary to declare an array of 10 integer items.
```

Language	Array Declaration
Ada	`type Index_Range is range 1..10;` `type Ten_Things is array (Index_Range) of Integer;`
VB.NET	`Dim TenThings(10) As Integer`
C++/Java	`int tenThings[10];`

[0]	1066
[1]	1492
[2]	1668
[3]	1945
[4]	1972
[5]	1510
[6]	999
[7]	1001
[8]	21
[9]	2001

Figure 8.8
Array variable
`tenThings` accessed
from `0..9`

Ada allows the programmer to specify how the ten items are to be accessed. In this example `Index_Range` is defined as `1..10` and is used to define the array. The result of this combination of statements is that an array of ten items is defined and is to be accessed using an index that ranges from `1..10`. In VB.NET, C++, and Java, the declaration specifies the number of elements in the array, but the accessing occurs using the values `0` to `9`. Let's look at a drawing of this array with values already stored in the individual cells. See Figure 8.8.

An array variable can be passed as a parameter and each individual cell can be accessed. How are the individual places in the array accessed? By giving the array name followed by an index. Here is how the three languages access the third and the last (tenth) cell.

Language	Array Access
Ada	`Put(Item => Ten_Things(3));` `Put(Item => Ten_Things(10));`
VB.NET	`MsgBox(TenThings(2))` `MsgBox(TenThings(9))`
C++	`cout << TenThings[2];` `cout << TenThings[9];`
Java	`System.out.print(tenThings[2]);` `System.out.print(tenThings[9]);`

A variable in a record and a variable in an array are treated exactly like any other variable. Only the accessing is different. In a record, variable access is by name; in an array, variable access is by an index that specifies which item in the collection you want.

8.4 Functionality of Object-Oriented Languages

There are three essential ingredients in an object-oriented language: *encapsulation*, *inheritance*, and *polymorphism*. These ingredients foster reuse, thus reducing the cost of building and maintaining software. Let's look at each of these ingredients.

Encapsulation

In Chapter 6, we talked about important threads running through the discussion. Two of them were *information hiding* and *abstraction*. Recall that information hiding is the practice of hiding the details of a module with the goal of controlling access to the details. We said that abstraction was a model of a complex system that includes only the details essential to the viewer. We defined three types of abstraction, but the definitions of each began and ended with the words "The separation of the logical view of ... from its implementation details." Abstraction is the goal; information hiding is a technique used to achieve the goal.

Encapsulation is a language feature that enforces information hiding. It is a feature that hides a module's implementation in a separate block with a formally specified interface. An object knows things about itself, but not about any other object. If one object needs information about another object, it must request that information from that object.

The construct used to provide encapsulation is called a *class*. Just as the concept of the class dominates object-oriented design, the class concept is the major feature of Java and other object-oriented languages. Unfortunately, the related definitions are not standard across the phases of design and implementation. In the design (problem-solving) phase, an **object** is a thing or entity that makes sense within the context of the problem. In the implementation phase, a **class** is a language construct that is a pattern for an object and provides a mechanism for encapsulating the properties and actions of the object class. To get an object that fits the pattern, we **instantiate** the class, by using an operator that takes the class name and returns an instance of the class.

Syntactically, a class is like a record, as described earlier, in that it is a heterogeneous composite data type. However, records have traditionally been considered passive structures and have only in recent years had subprograms as fields. The class, on the other hand, is an active structure, and almost always has subprograms as fields. The only way to manipulate the data fields is through the methods (subprograms) defined in the class.

Encapsulation A language feature that enforces information hiding

Object class or Class (problem-solving phase) A description of a group of objects with similar properties and behaviors

Object (problem-solving phase) An entity or thing that is relevant in the context of a problem

Object (implementation phase) An instance of a class

Class (implementation phase) A pattern for an object

Instantiate To create an object from a class

The fields in a record have traditionally been accessible to all by default; the fields in a class are usually private by default. That is, none of the fields (data) and subprograms of an object of a particular class can be accessed by an object of another class unless the field is marked *public*. If a class needs to make a method available to be called by an object of another class, the class must explicitly specify that the method is *public*.

private and *public* are called access modifiers. They specify whether or not code outside the class can access a class's fields. Some languages have additional access codes that further modify what code can access a class's fields. The class's methods that others use to modify the class's variables are marked *public*; the class's variables are marked *private*, either by default or by the use of the access code *private*.

Because actions and properties are combined within a class, classes designed for one application can often be used within another application. For example, once a class that represents time has been written and tested, it can be used in any application that requires a time object.

Inheritance

Object-oriented languages must have a construct that supports inheritance as described in the section on OOD. Let's say we define a class People to represent a person with data fields to represent such things as name, address, and telephone number. In an object-oriented language, we can define a class Student, which inherits all the properties of class People and adds additional data fields to hold the local address and telephone number. Objects of class People have only one address and phone number, but objects of class Student have two: one inherited from class People and one defined within class Student. An object can be of class People alone, but if an object is of class Student, it also has all the properties and behaviors of class People. We say that class Student is derived from class People.

Inheritance fosters reuse by allowing an application to take an already-tested class and derive a class from it that inherits the properties the application needs. Necessary additional properties and methods can then be added to the derived class.

Polymorphism The ability of a language to have duplicate method names in an inheritance hierarchy and to apply the method that is appropriate for the object to which the method is applied

Polymorphism

Suppose both class People and class Student have a method named printAddress. The method in class People prints the address defined in its class, and the method in class Student prints the address defined in its class. Here are two methods with the same name but different implementations. The ability of a language to handle this apparent ambiguity is called **polymorphism**. How does the language know which method is meant when printAddress is invoked by the calling unit? Methods that are part of a class are applied to an instance of the class by the calling unit. The class of object to which the method is applied determines which `print-Address` method is used.

For example, if we had `jane` as an instance of class `Person` and `jack` as an instance of class `Student`, `jane.printAddress()` would invoke the method defined in class `Person` and `jack.printAddress()` would print the address defined in class `Student`.

Inheritance and polymorphism combined allow the programmer to build useful hierarchies of classes that can be reused in different applications.

You can think of the problem-solving phase as mapping the objects in the real world into classes, which are descriptions of the categories of objects. The implementation phase takes the descriptions of the categories (classes) and creates instances of the classes that simulate the objects in the problem. The interactions of the objects in the program simulate the interaction of the objects in the real world of the problem. See Figure 8.9.

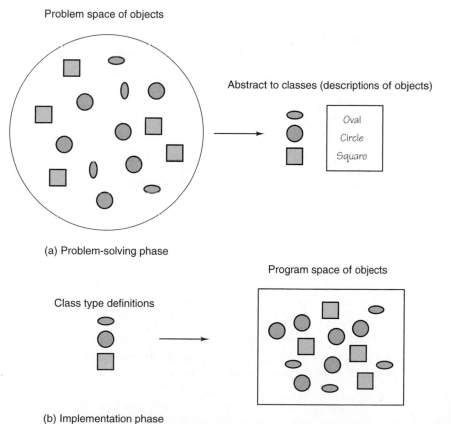

Problem space of objects

Abstract to classes (descriptions of objects)

Oval
Circle
Square

(a) Problem-solving phase

Class type definitions

Program space of objects

(b) Implementation phase

Figure 8.9 Mapping of problem into solution

Summary

An assembler translates an assembly-language program into machine code. A compiler translates a program written in a high-level language into either assembly language (to be later translated into machine code) or into machine code. An interpreter is a program that translates the instructions in a program and executes them immediately. An interpreter does not output machine-language code.

There are four models of high-level programming languages: procedural (imperative), functional, logic, and object-oriented. The imperative model describes the processing to be done. The functional model is based on the mathematical concept of a function. The logic model is based on mathematical logic. The object-oriented model is based on the concept of interacting objects, each taking responsibility for its own actions.

A Boolean expression is an assertion about the state of a program. If the assertion is true, the Boolean expression is true. If the assertion is false, the Boolean expression is false. Boolean expressions are used to allow a program to execute one section of code or another (conditional statements) and to repeat a section of code (looping statements). Recursion, the action of a subprogram executing itself, is an alternative to looping.

Each variable in a program is defined to be a certain data type. Strong typing means that only values of that data type can be stored into that variable. Storing a value into a variable is called assigning the value to the variable (assignment statements).

Actions can be given names (subprograms), and the actions are performed when the name appears as a statement or in an expression (procedures and functions) in another part of the program. Information is passed back and forth from the subprogram to the calling unit by parameter lists, which are lists of variables and/or constants in parentheses beside the subprogram name.

Collections of data can be given names (records and arrays). Items within the collection are accessed by name (records) or by position within the collection (arrays).

Object-oriented programming languages have three essential ingredients:

- *Encapsulation*, a language feature that enforces information hiding that is implemented using the class construct
- *Inheritance*, a language feature that allows one class to inherit the property and behavior of another class
- *Polymorphism*, the ability of a language to disambiguate between operations with the same name

ETHICAL ISSUES

Hacking

The phrase *computer hacker* has changed over the last forty years. In the 1960s hackers were perceived as skilled computer wizards whose curiosity would lead to technological advancements. Today, the term hacker has a more negative connotation and invokes the image of malicious kids who get a thrill from defacing Web sites or professional criminals who wreak havoc on the 'Net. These perceptions, however, fuelled by some of the media, are often far from the truth.

Although the term hacker still has both positive and negative connotation, *hacking* does not. Hacking refers to the trespassing or accessing of a Web site without authorization. Unauthorized entry can led to legal consequences, particularly if a hacker is deliberately violating the website's right to privacy. The Computer Fraud and Abuse Act states that purposefully entering a site without authority and intentionally accessing classified information is unlawful. Whether the hackers damage the content or leave the site untouched, their ability to infiltrate secure systems is powerful and disturbing. One study asserts that 59% of all company-owned Web sites were hacked during 1997.

In the famous *New York Times* hacking incident that occurred on September 13, 1998, hackers broke into the newspaper's Web site and replaced the page with pornographic material and a threatening message. Security breaches like this one have led companies such as Honeynet to design decoy PCs with different levels of security to tempt hackers. When these "honeypots" are hacked, the researchers are able to gather information about hacking and are then able to apply that knowledge to the development of better security systems.

Some hackers who penetrate secure Web sites subscribe to the belief that all information should be free and accessible. Others see themselves as taking an important role in protecting Web sites and feel that by gaining access to a site, they are identifying vulnerabilities in the security program. Still others, motivated by boredom and seeking entertainment, engage in recreational hacking and leave the sites they visit unchanged.

Can trespassing onto someone's Web site be considered parallel to trespassing onto someone's physical property? Opponents of this parallel are quick to point out the unclear boundaries and the ambiguity of ownership in cyberspace. As hacking becomes more prominent, society finds itself questioning the fine line between the free access to information and the rights of individual or corporate privacy.

Key Terms

Arguments pg. 252

Assignment statement pg. 238

Asynchronous pg. 257

Boolean expression pg. 233

Bytecode　pg. 228

Case sensitive pg. 237

Class pg. 261

Compiler pg. 226

Control structure pg. 240

Data type pg. 234

Declaration pg. 236

Encapsulation　pg. 261

Instantiate pg. 261

Interpreter pg. 227

Named constant pg. 238

Object (implementation phase)　pg. 261

Object (problem-solving phase)　pg. 261

Object class *or* Class pg. 261

Parameter list pg. 250

Parameters pg. 251

Polymorphism pg. 262

Recursion pg. 255

Reference parameter pg. 253

Reserved word　pg. 237

Strong typing pg. 234

Value parameter pg. 253

Variable pg. 233

Exercises

1. What is the hallmark of an assembly language?
2. Distinguish between an assembler and a compiler.
3. Distinguish between a compiler and an interpreter.
4. Compare and contrast an assembler, a compiler, and an interpreter.
5. Describe the portability provided by a compiler.
6. Describe the portability provided by the use of Bytecode.
7. Describe the process of compiling and running a Java program.
8. Discuss the word *paradigm* as it relates to computing.
9. Name four programming language paradigms and give an example language in each.

10. What are the characteristics of the imperative paradigm?

11. What are the characteristics of the functional paradigm?

12. What are the characteristics of the logic paradigm?

13. How does the view of an object-oriented program differ from the view of an imperative program?

14. How do you ask questions in a programming language?

15. What is a Boolean variable?

16. What is a Boolean expression?

17. Given Boolean variables one, two, and three, write an assertion for each of the following questions.
    a. Is one greater than both two and three?
    b. Is one greater than two, but less than three?
    c. Are all three variables greater than zero?
    d. Is one less than two or one less than three?
    e. Is two greater than one and three less than two?

18. Write the operation table for Boolean operation AND.

19. Write the operation table for Boolean operation OR.

20. Write the operation table for Boolean operation NOT.

21. What is a data type?

22. What is strong typing?

23. Define the following data types.
    a. integer
    b. real
    c. character
    d. Boolean

24. Is the string data type an atomic data type? Justify your answer.

25. If the same symbol is used for both single characters and strings, how can you distinguish between a single character and a one-character string?

26. What is a declaration?

27. Fill in the following table showing the appropriate syntactic marker or reserved word for the language shown based on your observation of the table on page 237.

Language	Ada	VB.NET	C++	Java
Comments				
End of statement				
Assignment statement				
Real data type				
Integer data type				
Beginning of declaration(s)				

28. How do the .WORD and .BLOCK assembler directives in the Pep/7 assembly language differ from the declarations in high-level languages?

29. Distinguish between instructions to be translated and instructions to the translating program.

30. Consider the following identifiers: Address, ADDRESS, AddRess, Name, NAME, NamE.
  a. How many different identifiers are represented if the language is Ada?
  b. How many different identifiers are represented if the language is VB.NET?
  c. How many different identifiers are represented if the language is C++?

31. Differentiate between a variable and a named constant.

32. Explain what is meant by *stream input.*

33. The example of stream input assumed that blanks were used to separate data items in the stream. Is a separator necessary? Justify your answer.

34. age, weight, and height are three integer variables and a read statement says to input them in that order. Given the following input stream (commas are separators),

123,60,23

what is stored?

a. In *age*?

b. In *weight*?

c. In *height*?

d. Do the values stored in the variables seem reasonable?

e. If not, how would you correct the problem?

35. Write the stream-input algorithm in pseudocode.

36. Write the stream-output algorithm in pseudocode.

37. Explain the operation of the sequence control structure.

38. Explain the flow of control of the *if* statement.

39. Fill in the following table showing the appropriate syntactic marker(s) or reserved word for the language shown based on your observation of the tables on pages 238, 243, and 244.

Language	Ada	VB.NET	C++	Java
Declaring a character variable				
Declaring a named constant				
Boolean expression in *if* statement				
true branch of an *if* statement				
false branch of an *if* statement				
compound statement or block				

40. How does a *case* statement differ from an *if* statement?
41. What is the flow of control in a *while* statement?
42. Why is a *while* statement called a pretest loop?
43. What are the three steps in a count-controlled loop?
44. What are the three steps in an event-controlled loop?
45. Distinguish between a count-controlled loop and an event-controlled loop.
46. Fill in the following table showing the appropriate syntactic marker(s) or reserved word for the language shown based on your observation of the table on page 248.

Language	Ada	VB.NET	C++	Java
Boolean expression in a *while* statement				
Body of the *while* statement				
Statement that increments *count*				

47. What is recursion?
48. How does recursion act as a repetition structure?
49. A looping structure uses a _____ statement; a recursive structure uses a _____ statement.
50. Explain the statement, "Subprograms are a powerful tool for abstraction."
51. Describe two kinds of subprograms.
52. Distinguish between the way in which the name of a subprogram appears in the calling unit in the two kinds of subprograms described in Exercise 51.

53. Describe how a parameter list is used to communicate information from the calling unit to the subprogram.

54. Distinguish between a parameter and an argument.

55. Distinguish between a value parameter and a reference parameter.

56. Fill in the following table showing the appropriate syntactic marker(s) or reserved word for the language shown based on your observation of the table on page 253.

Language	VB.NET	C++
Separate paramenters from one another		
Define a value parameter		
Define a reference parameter		
Body of a subprogram		

57. What is the result of executing subprogram Swap if the parameters are value parameters?

58. What is the result of executing subprogram Swap if the parameters are reference parameters?

59. What is the result of executing subprogram Swap if one of the parameters is a value parameter and one of the parameters is a reference parameter?

60. How did the invention of the mouse change programming?

61. Distinguish between an atomic data type and a composite data type.

62. Name two composite data types and describe how their accessing mechanisms differ.

63. What is meant by a *homogeneous* structure?

64. What is meant by a *heterogeneous* structure?

65. What three elements must be present in the definition of a record?

66. How do Ada, VB.NET, and C++ express the three elements outlined in Exercise 65?

67. Although Ada, VB.NET, and C++ are quite different in many ways, they all access the fields of a record in the same way. Describe this syntax.

68. Ada uses a range of index values to define and array, but VB.NET and C++ specify the number of places in the array. Explain.

69. Examine the following three array declarations:

```
type Index is range -1..10;
type Data_Array is array (Index) of Integer;
Data : Data_Array;                    -- Ada
Dim data(11) As Integer               ' VB.NET
int data[11];                         // C++
```

Are the arrays declared the same? Justify your answer.

70. Access the last element in the arrays declared in Exercise 69
   a. in Ada.
   b. in VB.NET.
   c. in C++.

71. Distinguish between the definition of an object in the design phase and in the implementation phase.

72. Distinguish between the definition of a class in the design phase and in the implementation phase.

73. We say that a record is passive, but a class is active. Explain.

74. List and define the three ingredients necessary in an object-oriented language.

? Thought Questions

1. The languages used as examples in this chapter originated in quite different ways. Ada was designed by a team of designers for the Department of Defense. VB.NET is Microsoft's latest version of Visual Basic. C++ was developed at Bell Labs as a systems-programming language, and Java was designed at Sun Microsystems. Speculate how the language's background has influenced the language.

2. Go to a computer store and price compilers for these languages. Does the language's origins influence the cost of a compiler? Was there more than one compiler for all of the languages? Again, what does this tell you about the language?

3. Microsoft has developed a language called C# designed to compete directly with Java. Things happen so rapidly in the world of computing. Is C# in the marketplace as you read this book? There were rumblings about another antitrust suite against Microsoft over C#. Did this happen?

4. The word "hacker" used to be complimentary, describing a programmer who buried his or her head in the code, only coming up for air in the morning. A hacker would write very sophisticated programs almost overnight. Now the term has come to refer to someone with malicious intent. What connotations does the word have for you?

5. Is it logical to speak of privacy in relation to Web sites when most of them are created to advertise a product or service?

6. Altering someone's Web site is illegal. Should it be illegal to enter a secure site just to show you can do it?

The Programming Layer

9 Abstract Data Types and Algorithms

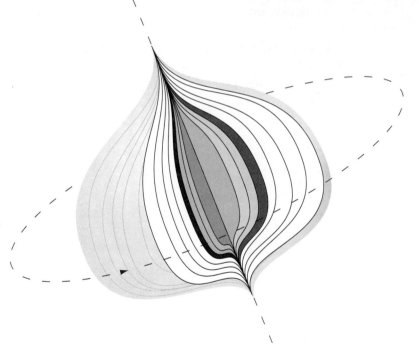

Chapter 9

Abstract Data Types and Algorithms

Computer science is sometimes defined as the study of algorithms and their efficient implementation in a computer. The focus of this chapter is the definition of useful abstract objects for modeling information in a program and the algorithms that manipulate these objects. Just as a roll-top desk organizes data into cubbyholes, there are logical structures appropriate for representing different types of data in a program.

We first look at the concept of an *abstract data type* (ADT), look at two distinct types of implementations, and then discuss a useful collection of ADTs from the logical point of view. That is, we examine the operations on these objects at the logical level; we do not implement them in code.

One of the abstract structures that we discuss in this chapter is the *list*. We develop algorithms for manipulating items in a list. Once these algorithms exist we can use them in any problem involving items in a list. Thus, the final implementation language is immaterial: We can stop the algorithm decomposition at the stage of manipulating the items in a list.

Goals

After studying this chapter, you should be able to

- define an abstract data type and discuss its role in algorithm development.
- distinguish between a data type and a data structure.
- distinguish between an array-based implementation and a linked implementation.
- distinguish between an array and a list.
- distinguish between an unsorted list and a sorted list.
- distinguish between a selection sort and a bubble sort.
- describe the Quicksort algorithm.
- apply the selection sort, the bubble sort, and the Quicksort to a list of items by hand.
- apply the binary search algorithm.
- distinguish between the behavior of a stack and a queue.
- draw the binary search tree that is built from inserting a series of items.
- demonstrate your understanding of the algorithms in this chapter by hand simulating them with a sequence of items.

9.1   Abstract Data Types

We have used the term *data type* in several chapters. You know what a data type is: It is a set of values and the basic operations that can be applied to values of that type. Let's take that idea a step further. An **abstract data type** is a data type whose properties (data and operations) are specified independently of any particular implementation. Remember that the goal in design is to reduce complexity through abstraction. If we can define useful structures and the operations that manipulate them at the logical level, we use them as if they exist when we need them in our designs.

To put the concept of an ADT into context, we need to look at how we view data. In computing, we view data from three perspectives: the application level, the logical level, and the implementation level.

The application (or user) level is the view of the data within a particular problem. If we look at object-oriented problem solving, this level represents objects within a particular problem. This view sees data objects in terms of specific properties and behaviors.

The logical (or abstract) level is an abstract view of the data values (the domain) and the set of operations to manipulate them. In object-oriented

> **Abstract data type (ADT)** A data type whose properties (data and operations) are specified independently of any particular implementation

problem solving, this level represents the classes abstracted from the objects in the application level. This view sees data objects as groups of objects with similar properties and behaviors. This level can be represented as CRC cards (discussed in Chapter 6) along with the responsibility algorithms that define the behavior of the ADT.

The implementation level is a specific representation of the structure to hold the data items and the coding of the operations in a programming language. This view sees the properties represented as specific data fields and behaviors represented as methods implemented in code. This level is concerned with **data structures**, the implementation of a composite data fields in an abstract data type.

> **Data structure** The implementation of a composite data field in an abstract data type

The abstract data types that we examine in this chapter are those that history and experience have shown come up again and again in real-world problems. These ADTs are **containers** in which data items are stored, and each exhibits specific behaviors. They are called containers because their sole purpose is to hold other objects.

> **Containers** Objects whose role is to hold and manipulate other objects

9.2 Implementation

Yes, we know; we said that we would not look at the implementations for the algorithms in this chapter—and we won't look at code. However, we do look at two distinct kinds of implementations from the logical level. These distinctions remain constant across programming languages. The implementations can be *array based* or they can be *linked*. We look at the algorithms that depend on the implementation in the next sections—still from the logical level, however.

There are several pseudocode expressions that we use in our algorithms that mean very different things in an array-based implementation and a linked implementation. They are Put item, Remove item, Get next item, and More items. The first two are considered *transformer* operations, because they change the state of a container. The third is an *iterator*, an operation that allows access to all of the components one-at-a-time. The fourth is an *observer* operation: It asks if we have looked at all of the items. We look at what each means logically in the different implementations. In later algorithms, we consider each to be a concrete step.

Array-Based Implementations

Recall from Chapter 8 that an array is a named collection of homogeneous items in which individual items are accessed by their place within the collection. The place within the collection is called an *index*. An **array-based implementation** uses an array to store the items in the container. We are not saying that an array and the container are the same; we are

> **Array-based implementation** An implementation of a container in which the items are stored in an array

saying that an array can be used to hold the items in the container. Items in a container can be unordered or they can be ordered in some fashion. If there is no ordering on the item in the container, we call the container *unsorted*. If there is an ordering, we call the container *sorted*. In this discussion we use the term *list* to mean a generic kind of container. Later we discuss the list as a specific kind of container by describing a set of behaviors.

Figure 9.1 shows a list. A list is made up of a length variable and an array to hold the list items. All processing of the logical list is done from the 0th position in the array variable list through the length − 1 position.

In an unsorted list, the component that comes before or after an item has no semantic relationship with it. It only shows the order in which the items were stored. In a sorted list, the items are arranged in such a way that the component that comes before or after an item has a semantic relationship with that item. For example, a grade list can be a random list of numbers or sorted by value. Figures 9.2 and 9.3 show an unsorted list of grades and a sorted list of grades, respectively.

In an array-based implementation, accessing the first item is accessing the list[0] position. In order to move through the items in the list, we need an integer variable that starts at 0 and stops when its value is length. Be careful: Keep in mind that the array goes from index 0 through index MAX_LENGTH − 1; the container goes from index 0 through length − 1. Forgetting this is a common cause for errors in programming.

Put item means that given an index, shift the items that follow down one slot in the array and store the item at the index position.

Remove the item means that given an index, shift the items that follow up one slot in the array.

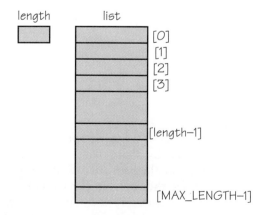

Figure 9.1
A list

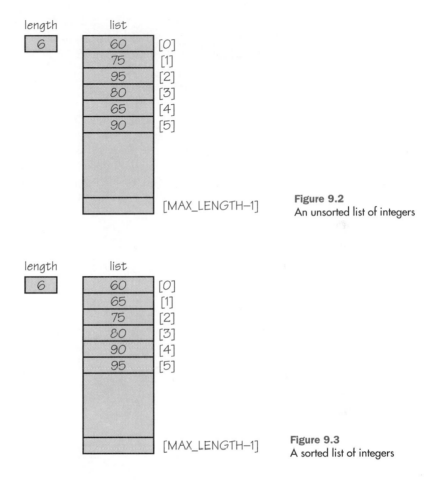

Figure 9.2
An unsorted list of integers

Figure 9.3
A sorted list of integers

Get next item means to increment the value used as an index and access that indexed position.

More items means that the variable used as an index is less than length − 1.

Linked Implementation

A **linked implementation** is based on the concept of a *node*. A node is made up of two pieces of data: the item that the user wants in the list and a pointer to the next node in the list. A pointer to the first node in a list is saved in a named variable, called the external pointer to the container (list). The pointer variable of the last node in the list contains a symbol that means the end of the list, usually null. Figure 9.4 shows the anatomy of a linked list.

Linked implementation
An implementation of a container where the items are stored together with information on where the next item can be found

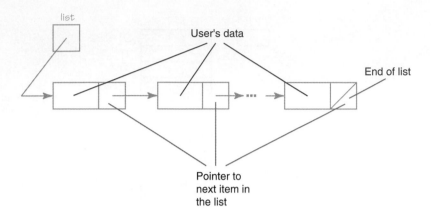

Figure 9.4
Anatomy of a linked list

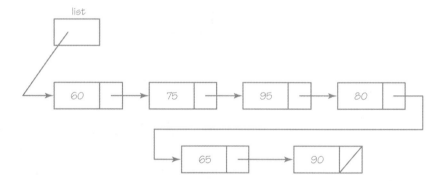

Figure 9.5
An unsorted linked list

Figures 9.5 and 9.6 display the lists in Figures 9.2 and 9.3, respectively.

We call the user's information the *info* part of the node and the pointer the *next* part of the node. In an array-based list, we access each item by using a variable that ranges from 0 through length – 1. In a linked list we use a variable of the same type as the next part of the node; let's call it current. current is initialized to list, the first node in the list. info(current) accesses the user's data in the node and next(current) accesses the pointer part of the node. To move to the next node in the list, we set current to next(current). The last item has been accessed when current is equal to null.

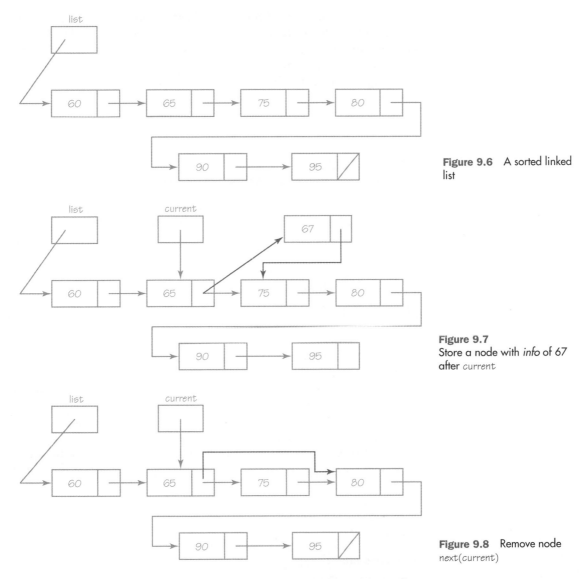

Figure 9.6 A sorted linked list

Figure 9.7 Store a node with *info* of 67 after current

Figure 9.8 Remove node next(current)

Put item means given current, insert a new node with item in the *info* part of the node between current and next(current). See Figure 9.7.

Remove item means given current, remove the next(current). See Figure 9.8.

Get next item means to set current to next(current).

More items means that current does not contain null.

Linked lists are also called *unbounded* lists because the nodes are created at run time. The only limit on the number of nodes is the size of memory. In a linked list, it is not necessary to keep track of the number of items in the list explicitly, because you can always count the number of nodes. In contrast, the length must be explicitly kept in an array-based implementation.

9.3   Lists

Lists occur as naturally in programming as they do in real life. We manipulate guest lists, grocery lists, class lists, and things-to-do lists. The list of lists is endless. Three properties characterize lists: The items are homogeneous, the items are linear, and lists have varying length. By linear we mean that each item except the first has a unique component that comes before it and each item except the last has a unique component that comes after it. For example, if there are at least three items in a list, the second item comes after the first and before the third.

Basic List Operations

There are various kinds of lists depending on the behaviors the list exhibits. Let's start with a minimal set of operations. What are the operations that we do with, say, a "to-do" list? Well, starting with an empty list, we put things on the list, and we cross items off the list. In computer terms this means we must be able to add entries to and delete entries from the list. Our "to-do" list is on a piece of paper we hold in our hand, so we can see the items on the list. The analogy for a list in the computer would be to require the list to print itself. We said that one of the characteristics of a list is that it has length. That is, the list knows how many items are stored within it. So our computerized list must be able to do the following:

- create itself
- insert an item
- delete an item
- print itself
- know the number of items it contains

CRC cards are a good way to represent ADTs. Although the terminology is object-oriented, it easily can be translated into a functional representation.

Class Name: *List*	Superclass:	Subclasses:
Responsibilities	**Collaborations**	
Initialize itself		
Insert (item)	*ItemClass*	
Delete (item)	*ItemClass*	
Print	*ItemClass*	
Know Length returns integer		
. . .		

Notice in this CRC card that we said that the list collaborates with Item-Class. We don't know what it is, but because items are being put on the list, the list must collaborate with the class of which the items are objects. We are writing this CRC card for a *generic* list. A **generic data type** (or **class**) is one in which the operations are specified but the type or class of the objects being manipulated is not.

The responsibility algorithms are quite straightforward. Initializing a list is equivalent to setting the length to zero. The act of inserting and deleting an item must increment and decrement the length, respectively. As we write the algorithms, we continue to put abstract steps in blue. The steps that we outlined in the previous section we put in red to remind you that they are different in each implementation.

> **Generic data type (class)**   A data type (or class) in which the operations are defined but the type or class of the objects being manipulated is not

Initialize

Set length to zero

Insert(item)

Find where the item belongs
Put the item there
Increment length

Delete(item)

Find the item
Remove the item
Decrement length

Print

While (more items)
     Get next item
      Print item

Know Length

return length

Constraints on the Print operation break the list into subcategories. Should the items be printed in the order in which they are inserted? Should the items be printed in order by some information in the items themselves? Answering yes to the first question leads to an unsorted list. Answering yes to the second question leads to a sorted list. How can we consider Print item concrete when we know nothing about the items on the list? That's just it. We consider this list to be generic so each item on the list must know how to print itself. Print item just tells the item to print itself.

Before we continue with the decomposition of the responsibility algorithms in the two subcategories, let's spend a moment on the implication of the Find the item in the Delete operation. Finding an item means that the class to which an item belongs has a way of recognizing a match. It is not the responsibility of the list to know what a match is; it is the responsibility of ItemClass. We need to make this assumption explicit somewhere. Let's add an assumption to the CRC card that ItemClass must provide a *compareTo* method and indicate what the results must be. Java has a `compareTo` method defined on items of class `String` and other classes in the Java Library. Let's use that definition. We also need *compareTo* in the Find where item belongs in the sorted list.

Class Name: *List*	Superclass:	Subclasses:
Responsibilities	**Collaborations**	
Initialize itself		
Insert (item)	*ItemClass**	
Delete (item)	*ItemClass*	
Print	*ItemClass*	
Know Length returns integer		

.
 .
 .
	**Assumption: ItemClass must provide compare To method:
	 item1.compare To(item2)
	   <0: item1 < item2
	     0: item1 equals item2
	   >0: item1 > item2*	

The step Find where the item belongs is decomposed differently in these two subcategories. If the list is printed in the order in which the items are inserted (unsorted), the logical place for each item is at the end of the list. This is certainly efficient in the array-based implementation because the item would go into the length position. However, in the linked implementation, the end of the list can only be accessed by traversing the entire list. It would be more efficient to put each new item at the beginning of the list, but the Print would have them in reverse order rather than the order in which they were entered.

Find where the item belongs (Unsorted)

Item belongs at length

We said that a sorted list was one in which the items were printed in order based on some information within the items on the list. This means that the list must be kept such that the Get an item within the print method gets the appropriate item to print. Thus, the Insert operation must place the items in the list in the proper order. The list doesn't have to know anything about the fields of ItemClass. The compareTo method gives enough information.

To see how this works, let's look at an example. Let's say we are keeping numbers in numeric order. The list so far contains the following values:

23, 46, 75, 1066, 1492, 2001

and we want to insert 998. Compare 998 to 23 and it is larger, so we compare 998 with the next value. 998 is larger than 46, so we compare 998 with the next value. 998 is larger than 75, so we compare 998 with the next value. 998 is less than 1066, so 998 goes in the list just before 1066. We begin with the first item in the list and compare the value to be inserted. As long as the value we are inserting is greater than the next value in the list, we keep moving down the list. When we find a place where the value to be inserted is less than the value in the list, we have found the insertion place.

Find where the item belongs (Sorted)

Set tempItem to the first item
While (item.compareTo(tempItem) > 0)
    Set tempItem to next item
Item belongs at tempItem

Find the item in the Delete algorithm is decomposed using the compareTo method. But before we write the algorithm, we must ask exactly what we mean by Delete. Can we assume that the item to be deleted is there? Do we delete the item only if it is there? Do we delete all copies of the item? Do we delete only the first copy? The answers to these questions lead to different meanings of the Delete operation. Going back to our "to-do" list, the obvious meaning is: "The item is there; delete it." We write the algorithm assuming this meaning. However, you should be aware that even an operation as simple as Delete can have more than one meaning, and the documentation of the operation must indicate the meaning being implemented in the algorithm. Delete has one abstract step, Find the item.

Find the item

Set tempItem as first item
While (item.compareTo(tempItem) not equal to 0)
    Set tempItem to next item

Additional List Operations

What other operations do we do on our "to-do" list? Do you ever look to see if an item is on the list in order to add an item if it isn't? Do you ever look to see if the list is empty? Is full? These operations are called *observer* operations because they observe the state of the list. Let's examine the algorithm to determine if an item is in the list. This method should be a Boolean method. We have to start at the beginning of the list and compare each item in the list to the one passed as a parameter. Once we find a match we return true. If we reach the end of the list without having found a match, we return false.

IsThere(item)

Set templtem to the first item
While (more items)
    If (templtem.compareTo(item) is equal to 0)
        return true
    Else
        Set templtem to next item
Return false

This algorithm is called a *sequential* search for obvious reasons. We begin at the first item and examine them in order. You are asked to complete the algorithms for the other observer operations in the exercises at the end of this chapter.

In the next sections we examine algorithms that transform an unsorted list into a sorted one. Then we look at the *binary search* algorithm, a faster searching algorithm that we can use if we know the list is sorted and the implementation is array based.

9.4 Sorting

We all know what sorting is. We sort our sock drawers, our bookshelves, even our priorities. Sorting is putting things in order. In computing, transforming an unsorted list into a sorted list is a common and useful operation. Whole books have been written about various sorting algorithms, as well as algorithms for searching a sorted list to find a particular element. The goal is to come up with better, more efficient, sorts. Because sorting a large number of elements can be extremely time-consuming, a good sorting algorithm is very desirable. This is one area in which programmers are sometimes encouraged to sacrifice clarity in favor of speed of execution.

In this section we present several quite different sorting algorithms to give you a flavor of how many different ways there are to solve the same problem. The language of sorting algorithms uses array-based notation because each item to be sorted must be accessed directly by its index, not through the item before it. In the sections that follow, we use *compareTo* to compare two items.

Selection Sort

The selection sort algorithm is probably the easiest because it mirrors how we would sort a list of values if we had to do it by hand. If you were handed a list of names and asked to put them in alphabetical order, you might use this general approach:

1. Find the name that comes first in the alphabet, and write it on a second sheet of paper.
2. Cross out the name on the original list.
3. Continue this cycle until all the names on the original list have been crossed out and written onto the second list, at which point the second list is sorted.

This algorithm is simple, but it has one drawback: It requires space for two complete lists. Although we have not talked about memory-space considerations, this duplication is clearly wasteful. A slight adjustment to this manual approach does away with the need to duplicate space, however. As you cross a name off the original list, a free space opens up. Instead of writing the minimum value on a second list, exchange it with the value currently in the position where the crossed-off item should go. Our "by-hand list" is represented in an array. Let's look at an example—sorting the five-element list shown in Figure 9.9. Because of this algorithm's simplicity, it is usually the first sorting method that students learn.

Let's think of the list as containing two parts: the unsorted part (not shaded) and the sorted part (shaded). Each time we put an item into its

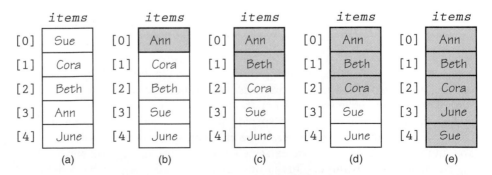

Figure 9.9 Example of selection sort (sorted elements are shaded)

proper place, we are shrinking the unsorted part and extending the sorted part. Sorting begins with all of the list items in the unsorted part and ends with all of the list items in the sorted part.

Selection Sort

Set current to the index of first item in the list
While (not sorted yet)
    Find the index of the smallest unsorted item
    Swap the current item with the smallest unsorted one
    Incrementing current to shrink unsorted part

There are only two abstract steps: determining when the list is sorted and finding the index of the smallest element. Moving from Figure 9.9(d) to 9.9(e) added the last two items to the shaded part of the list. This is always the case because when the smaller of the last two is determined and put into its proper place, the last one is also in its proper place. Thus, the loop continues as long as current is less than the length of list − 1.

No sorted yet

current < length − 1

How would you find the name that comes first in the alphabet in the unsorted portion if you were doing it by hand? You see (and mentally record) the first one and then scan down the list until you see one that comes before the first one. You remember this smaller one and continue scanning the list looking for a name that comes before this one in the alphabet. The process of remembering the smallest so far until you find a smaller one is repeated until you reach the end of the list. This by-hand algorithm is exactly the one we use here. Only we must remember the index of the smallest because we are going to swap that item with the item in the current position. So in terms of our list, we look for the smallest in the unsorted portion, which runs from current through length − 1.

Find the index of the smallest

Set indexOfSmallest to current
For index going from current + 1 to length −1
    If (list[index].compareTo(list[indexOfSmallest]) < 0)
        Set indexOfSmallest to index

Bubble Sort

The bubble sort is a selection sort that uses a different scheme for finding the minimum value. Starting with the last list element, we compare successive pairs of elements, swapping whenever the bottom element of the pair is smaller than the one above it (Figure 9.10a). In this way the smallest element "bubbles up" to the top of the list. Each iteration puts the smallest unsorted item into its correct place using the same technique, but it also makes changes in the locations of the other elements in the array (Figure 9.10b).

Before we write this algorithm, we must make an observation: Bubble sort is the slowest of all the sorting algorithms. Why then do we bother to mention it? Because it is the only sorting algorithm that can recognize when it is already sorted. Let's apply the algorithm to an already sorted list. See Figure 9.11.

We compare Phil with John and do not swap. We compare John with Jim and do not swap. We compare Jim with Bob and do not swap. We

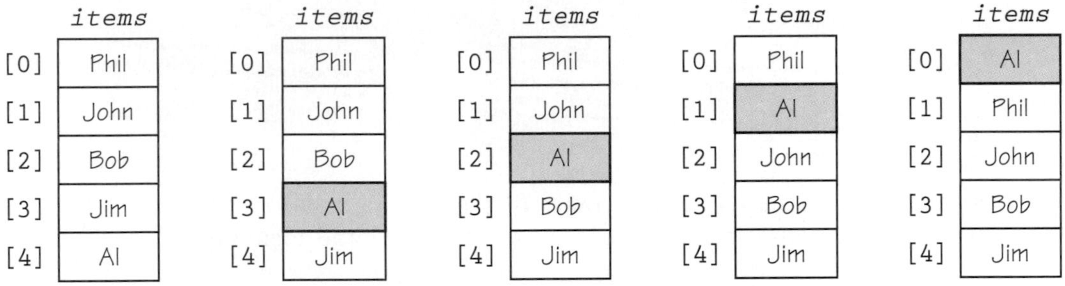

a) First iteration (Sorted elements are shaded.)

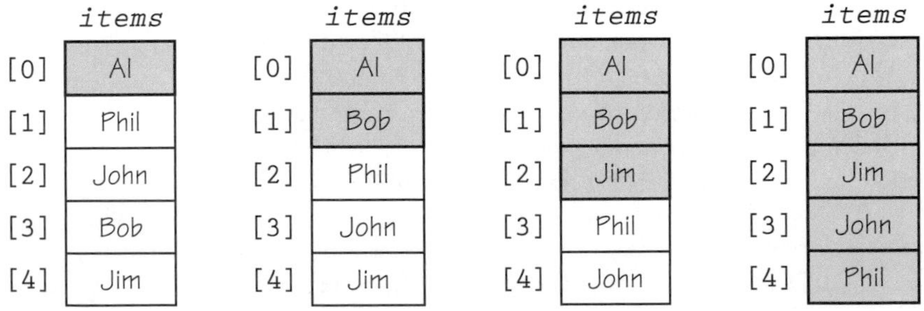

b) Remaining iterations (Sorted elements are shaded.)

Figure 9.10   Example of a bubble sort

compare *Bob* with *Al* and do not swap. If no values are swapped during an iteration, then the list is sorted. We set a Boolean variable to *false* before we enter the loop and set it to *true* if a swap occurs. If the Boolean variable is still *false*, then the list is sorted.

Compare the processing of bubble sort to selection sort on an already sorted list. Selection sort makes no attempt to determine if the list is sorted; therefore, we will go through the entire algorithm.

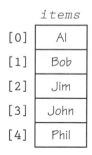

Figure 9.11
Example of an already sorted list.

Bubble Sort

Set current to index of first item in the list
Do
    Set swap to false
    "Bubble up" the smallest item in unsorted part
    Increment current to shrink the unsorted portion
While (not yet sorted AND swap)

Bubble up

For index going from length − 1 down to current + 1
    If (list[index].compareTo(list[index − 1]) < 0)
        Swap list[index] and list[index − 1]
        Set swap to true

We used a posttest loop because at least one iteration is necessary to determine that the list is sorted even if the list is sorted to begin with.

Quicksort

The Quicksort algorithm, developed by C. A. R. Hoare, is based on the idea that it is faster and easier to sort two small lists than one larger one. The name comes from the fact that, in general, Quicksort can sort a list of data elements quite rapidly. The basic strategy of this sort is to divide and conquer.

If you were given a large stack of final exams to sort by name, you might use the following approach: Pick a splitting value, say L, and divide the stack of tests into two piles, A–L and M–Z. (Note that the two piles do not necessarily contain the same number of tests.) Then take the first pile and subdivide it into two piles, A–F and G–L. The A–F pile can be further broken down into A–C and D–F. This division process goes on until the piles are small enough to be easily sorted by hand. The same process is applied to the M–Z pile.

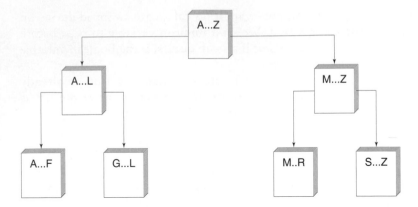

Figure 9.12
Ordering a list using the
Quicksort algorithm

Eventually all the small sorted piles can be stacked one on top of the other to produce a sorted set of tests. See Figure 9.12.

This strategy is based on recursion—on each attempt to sort the stack of tests, the stack is divided, and then the same approach is used to sort each of the smaller stacks (a smaller case). This process goes on until the small stacks do not need to be divided further (the base case). The parameter list of the *Quicksort* algorithm reflects the part of the list that is currently being processed.

Quicksort(first, last)

IF (there is more than one item in list[first]..list[last])
Select splitVal
Split the list so that
     list[first]..list[splitPoint−1] <= splitVal
     list[splitPoint] = splitVal
     list[splitPoint+1]..list[last] > splitVal
Quicksort the left half
Quicksort the right half

How do we select splitVal? One simple solution is to use whatever value is in list[first] as the splitting value. Let's look at an example using list[firstl as splitVal.

splitVal = 9

9	20	6	10	14	8	60	11

[first]   [last]

After the call to Split, all the items less than or equal to splitVal are on the left side of the list and all of those greater than splitVal are on the right side of the list.

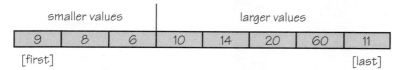

smaller values			larger values				
9	8	6	10	14	20	60	11

[first]   [last]

The two "halves" meet at splitPoint, the index of the last item that is less than or equal to splitVal. Note that we don't know the value of splitPoint until the splitting process is complete. We can then swap splitVal (list[first]) with the value at list[splitPoint].

smaller values			larger values				
6	8	9	10	14	20	60	11

[first]   [split-   [last]
               Point]

Our recursive calls to Quicksort use this index (splitPoint) to reduce the size of the problem in the general case.

Quicksort(first, splitPoint − 1) sorts the left "half" of the list. Quicksort(split-Point + 1, last) sorts the right "half" of the list. (The "halves" are not necessarily the same size.) splitVal is already in its correct position in list[splitPoint].

What is the base case? When the segment being examined has only one item, we do not need to go on.

We must find a way to get all of the elements equal to or less than splitVal on one side of splitVal and the elements greater than splitVal on the other side. We do this by moving a pair of the indexes from the ends toward the middle of the list, looking for items that are on the wrong side of the split value. When we find pairs that are on the wrong side, we swap them and continue working our way into the middle of the list.

```
Set left to first + 1
Set right to last
Do
      Increment left until list[left] > splitVal OR left > right
      Decrement right until list[right] < splitVal OR left > right
      Swap list[left] and list[right]
While (left <= right)
Set splitPoint to right
Swap list[first] and list[right]
```

Tony Hoare[1]

Tony Hoare's interest in computing was awakened in the early '50s, when he studied philosophy (together with Latin and Greek) at Oxford University, under the tutelage of John Lucas. He was fascinated by the power of mathematical logic as an explanation of the apparent certainty of mathematical truth. During his National Service (1956–1958), he studied Russian in the Royal Navy. Then he took a qualification in statistics, and incidentally a course in programming given by Leslie Fox. In 1959, as a graduate student at Moscow State University, he studied the machine translation of languages (together with probability theory) in the school of Kolmogorov. To assist in efficient look-up of words in a dictionary, he discovered the well-known sorting algorithm Quicksort.

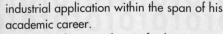

On return to England in 1960, he worked as a programmer for Elliott Brothers, a small scientific computer manufacturer. He led a team (including his later wife, Jill) in the design and delivery of the first commercial compiler for the programming language Algol 60. He attributes the success of the project to the use of Algol itself as the design language for the compiler, although the implementation used decimal machine code. Promoted to the rank of Chief Engineer, he then led a larger team on a disastrous project to implement an operating system. After managing a recovery from the failure, he moved as Chief Scientist to the computing research division, where he worked on the hardware and software architecture for future machines.

These machines were cancelled when the company merged with its rivals, and in 1968 Tony took a chance to apply for the Professorship of Computing Science at the Queen's University, Belfast. His research goal was to understand why operating systems were so much more difficult than compilers, and to see if advances in programming theory and languages could help with the problems of concurrency. In spite of civil disturbances, he built up a strong teaching and research department, and published a series of papers on the use of assertions to prove correctness of computer programs. He knew that this was long-term research, unlikely to achieve industrial application within the span of his academic career.

In 1977 he moved to Oxford University, and undertook to build up the Programming Research Group, founded by Christopher Strachey. With the aid of external funding from government initiatives, industrial collaborations, and charitable donations, Oxford now teaches a range of degree courses in Computer Science, including an external master's degree for software engineers from industry. The research of his teams at Oxford pursued an ideal that takes provable correctness as the driving force for the accurate specification, design, and development of computing systems, both critical and non-critical. Well-known results of the research include the Z specification language, and the CSP concurrent programming model. A recent personal research goal has been the unification of a diverse range of theories applying to different programming languages, paradigms, and implementation technologies.

Throughout more than thirty years as an academic, Tony has maintained strong contacts with industry, through consultation, teaching, and collaborative research projects. He took a particular interest in the sustenance of legacy code, where assertions are now playing a vital role, not for his original purpose of program proof, but rather in instrumentation of code for testing purposes. On reaching retirement age at Oxford, he welcomed an opportunity to return to industry as a senior researcher with Microsoft Research in Cambridge. He hopes to expand the opportunities for industrial application of good academic research, and to encourage academic researchers to continue the pursuit of deep and interesting questions in areas of long-term interest to the software industry and its customers.

The above biographical sketch was written by Sir Tony Hoare himself and reprinted with his permission. What he does not say is that he received the Turing Award in 1980 for his fundamental contributions to the definition and design of programming languages and was awarded a Knighthood in 1999 for his services to education and computer science.

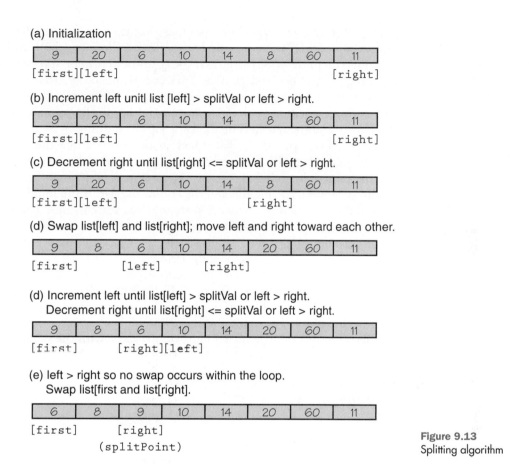

(a) Initialization

9	20	6	10	14	8	60	11

`[first][left]`   `[right]`

(b) Increment left unitl list [left] > splitVal or left > right.

9	20	6	10	14	8	60	11

`[first][left]`   `[right]`

(c) Decrement right until list[right] <= splitVal or left > right.

9	20	6	10	14	8	60	11

`[first][left]`   `[right]`

(d) Swap list[left] and list[right]; move left and right toward each other.

9	8	6	10	14	20	60	11

`[first]`   `[left]`   `[right]`

(d) Increment left until list[left] > splitVal or left > right.
    Decrement right until list[right] <= splitVal or left > right.

9	8	6	10	14	20	60	11

`[first]`   `[right][left]`

(e) left > right so no swap occurs within the loop.
    Swap list[first and list[right].

6	8	9	10	14	20	60	11

`[first]`   `[right]`
        `(splitPoint)`

Figure 9.13
Splitting algorithm

Figure 9.13 shows an example of this algorithm.

9.5 Binary Search

A **sequential search** of a list begins at the beginning of the list and continues until the item is found or the entire list has been searched without finding the item. A binary search looks for an item in a list using a different strategy. The binary search is based on this same divide-and-conquer strategy that we used in the Quicksort.

Sequential search
Looking for an item from the beginning of the list

The **binary search** algorithm assumes that the items in the list being searched are sorted and either finds the item or eliminates half of the list with one comparison. Rather than looking for the item starting at the beginning of the list and moving forward sequentially, the algorithm begins at the middle of the list in a binary search. If the item for which we are searching is less than the item in the middle, we know that the item won't be in the second half of the list. So we continue by searching the data in the first half of the list. Once again we examine the "middle" element (which is really the item 25% of the way into the list). If the item for which we are searching is greater than the item in the middle, continue searching between the middle and the end of the list. If the middle item is equal to the one for which you are searching, the search stops. The process continues with each comparison cutting in half the portion of the list where the item might be. The process stops when the item is found or when the portion of the list where the item might be is empty.

This process sounds recursive. We stop when we find the item or when we know it isn't there (base cases). We continue to look for the item in the section of the list where it will be if it is there. In the Quicksort algorithm, indexes that represented the portion of the list being sorted were parameters to the algorithm. We must do the same with the binary search algorithm.

```
Boolean Binary Search (first, last)

If (last > first)
      return false
Else
      Set middle to (first + last)/ 2
      Set result to list[middle].compareTo(item)
      If ( result is equal to 0)
            return true
      Else
            If (result < 0)
                  Binary Search (first, middle – 1)
            Else
                  Binary Search (middle + 1, last)
```

The original call to this algorithm would have first as 0 and last as length − 1. Figure 9.14 shows a trace of the binary search algorithm looking for *cat*, *fish*, and *zebra*.

[0]	ant
[1]	cat
[2]	chicken
[3]	cow
[4]	deer
[5]	dog
[6]	fish
[7]	goat
[8]	horse
[9]	camel
[10]	snake

Searching for cat

BinarySearch(0, 10)	middle: 5	cat < dog	
BinarySearch(0, 4)	middle: 2	cat < chicken	
BinarySearch(0, 1)	middle: 0	cat > ant	
BinarySearch(1, 1)	middle: 1	cat = cat	**Return: true**

Searching for fish

BinarySearch(0, 10)	middle: 5	fish > dog	
BinarySearch(6, 10)	middle: 8	fish < horse	
BinarySearch(6, 7)	middle: 6	fish = fish	**Return: true**

Searching for zebra

BinarySearch(0, 10)	middle: 5	zebra > dog	
BinarySearch(6, 10)	middle: 8	zebra > horse	
BinarySearch(9, 10)	middle: 9	zebra > camel	
BinarySearch(10, 10)	middle: 10	zebra > snake	
BinarySearch(11, 10)		last > first	**Return: false**

Figure 9.14
Trace of the binary search

Table 9.1 Average Number of Comparisons

Length	Sequential search	Binary search
10	5.5	2.9
100	50.5	5.8
1,000	500.5	9.0
10,000	5000.5	12.0

Is the binary search algorithm really faster than the sequential search algorithm? Table 9.1 shows the number of comparisons required on average to find an item using a sequential search and using a binary search. If the binary search is so much faster, why don't we always use it? More computation is required for each comparison because we must calculate the middle index. Also, the list must be in sorted order and must be implemented using an array-based implementation. If the list is already sorted, uses an array-based implementation, and the number of items is over 20, use a binary search algorithm.

9.6   Stacks and Queues

Stacks and queues are abstract data types that are often thought of as a pair—like peanut butter and jelly or horse and carriage. Why this is so must be more historical than anything else, because they have quite different behaviors.

Stacks
A stack is an abstract data type in which accesses are made at only one end. You can insert an item as the first one and you can remove the first one. This ADT models many things in real life. Accountants call it LIFO, which stands for Last In First Out. The plate holder in a cafeteria has this property. We can only take the top plate. When we do, the one below rises to the top so the next person can take one. Canned goods on a grocer's shelf exhibit this property. When we take the first can in a row, we are taking the last can put in that row.

Another way of stating the accessing behavior of a stack is that the item removed is the item that has been in the stack the shortest time. Viewing a stack from this perspective is more abstract. The insert has no constraints, the entire LIFO behavior is specified in the removal operation.

The mental image of the cafeteria plates has left an imprint on the traditional names used for the insert and delete operations. The insert is called Push and the delete is called Pop. We Push and item onto the stack and Pop an item off the stack. A stack does not have the property of length, so there is no operation that returns the number of items on the stack. We do need operations that determine whether a stack is Empty because trying to Pop an item when the stack is empty is an error.

Let's look at a case in which we use a stack. When we were designing the insertion algorithm for the sorted list, we said that putting the item into the last slot was efficient for the array-based implementation but not for the linked implementation. The obvious place to put each new item in the linked implementation is at the beginning of the list, but the list would be in reverse order. Let's assume that the insert puts the item at the beginning of the list and uses a stack to print a list in reverse order. That is, if the list is in reverse order and we print it in reverse order, the list should be ordered appropriately. Right? Let's try it.

Print list

```
While (more items)
    Get an item
    Push item
While (NOT IsEmpty)
    Pop item
    Print item
```

If items

90, 65, 80, 95, 75, 60

are entered into a linked implementation of an unordered list with each item going at the front of the list, the list would look like the one in Figure 9.5. The first item is accessed and put onto the stack, the second item is accessed and put on the stack, and so on. When the last item has been added to the stack, the contents of the stack look like this:

```
Top of stack ────────▶   60
                         75
                         95
                         80
                         65
Bottom of the stack ──▶  90
```

Now we *Pop* off one item at a time and print it. The first item printed is 60, the next item printed is 75, and so on. The original list has now been printed in reverse order using the stack. Any sequence of items put on the stack comes off in reverse order.

Queues

Queues are an abstract data type in which items are entered at one end and removed from the other end. Accountants call this FIFO, for First In First Out. This sounds like a waiting line in a bank or supermarket. Indeed, queues are used to simulate this type of situation. Insertions are made at the *rear* of the queue and deletions are made from the *front* of the queue.

Another way of stating the accessing behavior of a queue is that the item removed is the item that has been in the queue the longest time. Viewing a queue from this perspective is more abstract. Like the stack, the insert has no constraints; the entire FIFO behavior is specified in the removal operation. Unfortunately, there is no standard queue terminology relating to the insertion and deletion operations. *Enqueue, Enque, Enq, Enter,* and *Insert* are used for the insertion operation. *Dequeue, Deque, Deq, Delete,* and *Remove* are used for the deletion operation.

Implementation

Stacks and queues are often visualized as linked structures. The stack has only one external pointer and it points to the top of the stack. The queue needs two external pointers, one to the front of the queue and one to the rear. See Figure 9.15. Stacks and queues may also be implemented in array-based fashion.

It is important to note that the stack and the queue take no parameter for the deletion operation. Each knows where the next object to be deleted is; there is no choice.

9.7   Trees

ADTs such as lists, stacks, and queues are linear in nature. Only one relationship in the data is being modeled. Items are next to each other in a list or are next to each other in terms of time in a stack or queue. More complex relationships require more complex structures. Take, for example,

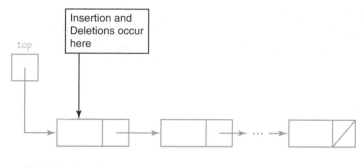

(a) A linked stack

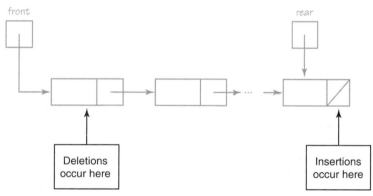

(b) A linked queue

Figure 9.15 Stack and queue visualized as linked structures

family relationships. If we want to model family relationships in a program, a hierarchical structure would be needed. At the top of the hierarchy would be the parents, the children would be at the next level, the grandchildren at the next level, and so on.

These hierarchical structures are called *trees*, and there is a rich mathematical theory relating to them. However, in computing we usually restrict our discussion to *binary trees*. These are trees that are restricted to each node having no more than two children.

Binary Trees

The vocabulary of trees uses the same vocabulary that we introduced in relation to the linked implementation. Every position in the tree is a *node*, which contains both the user's data and information on where to go to get the next node.

From the computing perspective a **binary tree** is a container object in which each node is capable of having two successor nodes, called *children*. Each of the children, being nodes in the binary tree, can also have up to two child nodes, and these children can also have up to two children, and so on, giving the tree its branching structure. The beginning of the tree is a unique starting node called the **root**, which is not the child of any node. See Figure 9.16.

The external pointer *tree* points to the root node in the tree. Each node in the tree may have zero, one, or two children. The node to the left of a node, if it exists, is called its *left child*. For example, in Figure 9.16, the left child of the root node contains the value 2. The node to the right of a node, if it exists, is its *right child*. The right child of the root node in the example contains the value 3. If a node has only one child, the child could be on either side, but it is always on one particular side. The root node is the parent of the nodes containing 2 and 3. (Earlier textbooks used the terms left son, right son, and father to describe these relationships.) If a node in the tree has no children, it is called a *leaf*. For instance, the nodes containing 7, 8, 9, and 10 are **leaf nodes**.

In addition to specifying that a node may have up to two children, the definition of a binary tree states that a unique path exists from the root to every other node. This means that every node (except the root) has a unique (single) parent.

Each of the root node's children is itself the root of a smaller binary tree, or subtree. The root node's left child, containing 2, is the root of its *left subtree*, while the right child, containing 3, is the root of its *right subtree*. In fact, any node in the tree can be considered the root node of a subtree. The subtree whose root node has the value 2 also includes the nodes with values 4 and 7. These nodes are the *descendants* of the node

> **Binary tree**   A container object with a unique starting node called the *root*, in which each node is capable of having two child nodes, and in which a unique path exists from the root to every other node
>
> **Root**   The top node of a tree structure; a node with no parent
>
> **Leaf node**   A tree node that has no children

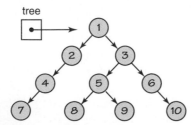

Figure 9.16
A binary tree

containing 2. The descendants of the node containing 3 are the nodes with the values 5, 6, 8, 9, and 10. A node is the *ancestor* of another node if it is the parent of the node or the parent of some other ancestor of that node. (Yes, this is a recursive definition.) The ancestors of the node with the value 9 are the nodes containing 5, 3, and 1. Obviously, the root of the tree is the ancestor of every other node in the tree.

The *level* of a node refers to its distance from the root. If we designate the level of the root as 0 (zero), the nodes containing 2 and 3 are Level 1 nodes, the nodes containing 4, 5, and 6 are Level 2 nodes, and the nodes containing 7, 8, 9, and 10 are Level 3 nodes.

The maximum level in a tree determines its *height*. Because we are referring to a binary tree, the maximum number of nodes at any level N is 2^N. Often, however, levels do not contain the maximum number of nodes. For instance, in Figure 9.16, Level 2 could contain four nodes, but because the node containing 2 in Level 1 has only one child, Level 2 contains three nodes. Level 3, which could contain eight nodes, has only four. The maximum number of nodes in a tree of height N is $2^{N+1} - 1$. Thus, the maximum number of nodes possible in the tree in Figure 9.16 is 15 compared to the actual number there, which is 10.

We could make many differently shaped binary trees out of the ten nodes in this tree. Two variations are illustrated in Figure 9.17. It is easy to see that the maximum number of levels in a binary tree with N nodes is N. What is the minimum number of levels? If we fill the tree by giving every node in each level two children until we run out of nodes, the tree has $\log_2 N + 1$ levels (Figure 9.17a). Demonstrate this to yourself by drawing "full" trees with 8 [$\log_2(8) = 3$] and 16 [$\log_2(16) = 4$] nodes. What if there are 7, 12, or 18 nodes?

Binary Search Trees

A *binary search tree* has the shape property of a binary tree; that is, a node in a binary search tree can have zero, one, or two children. In addition, a binary search tree has a semantic property among the values in the nodes in the tree: The value in any node is greater than the value in any node in its left subtree and less than the value in any node in its right subtree. See Figure 9.18.

Earlier in this chapter we described the binary search algorithm for searching in a list. We pointed out that, unfortunately, the binary search algorithm couldn't be applied to a linked implementation of a list. A binary search tree gives the flexibility of a linked implementation of a list and the speed of a binary search.

Searching a Binary Search Tree

Let's search for the value 18 in the tree in Figure 9.18. We compare 18 with 15, the value in the root node. 18 is greater than 15, so we know that if 18 is in the tree it will be in the right subtree of the root. Note the

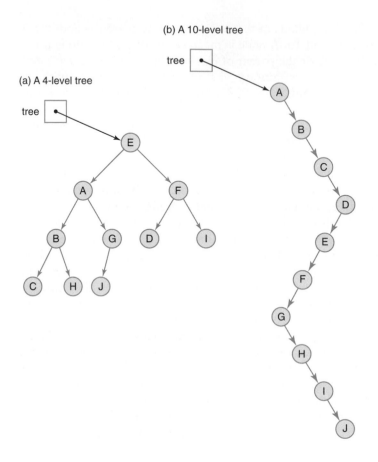

Figure 9.17 Two variations of a binary tree

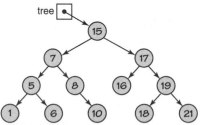

Figure 9.18
A binary search tree

similarity of this approach to our binary search of a linear structure. We eliminate a large portion of the data with one comparison.

Next we compare 18 with 17, the value in the root of the right subtree. 18 is greater than 17, so we know that if 18 is in the tree it will be in the right subtree of the root. We compare 18 with 19, the value in the root of the right subtree. 18 is less than 19, so we know that if 18 is in the tree, it will be in the left subtree of the root. We compare 18 with 18, the value in the root of the left subtree, and we have a match.

Now let's look at what happens when we search for a value that is not in the tree. Let's look for 4. We compare 4 with 15. 4 is less than 15, so if 4 is in the tree it will be in the left subtree of the root. We compare 4 with 7, the value in the root of the left subtree. 4 is less than 7, so if 4 is in the tree it will be in 7's left subtree. We compare 4 with 5. 4 is less than 5, so if 4 is in the tree it will be in 5's left subtree. We compare 4 with 1. 4 is greater than 1, so if 4 is in the tree it will be in 1's right subtree. But 1's left subtree is empty, so we know that 4 is not in the tree.

In a linked list the node contained an *info* part that contained the user's data and a pointer to the next node in the list. If we are to implement a binary tree, the node must have three parts: the user's data and a pointer to the left subtree and a pointer to the right subtree.

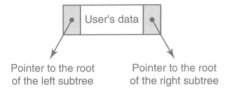

Pointer to the root
of the left subtree

Pointer to the root
of the right subtree

If current points to a node, info(current) refers to the user's data in the node, left(current) points to the root of the left subtree of current, and right(current) points to the root of the right subtree of current. If a pointer contains null, the subtree is empty. Using this notation, we can now write the search algorithm. We start at the root of the tree and move to the root of successive subtrees until we find the item we are looking for or we find an empty subtree. The item to be searched for and the root of the tree (subtree) are parameters.

```
Boolean IsThere(current, item)

If (current is null)
      return false
Else
      Set result to item.compareTo(info(current))
      If (result is equal to 0)
            return true
      Else
            If (result < 0)
                  IsThere(left(current, item))
            Else
                  IsThere(right(current, item))
```

With each comparison, either we find the item or cut the tree in half by moving to search in the left subtree or the right subtree. In half? Well, not exactly. As shown in Figure 9.17, the shape of a binary tree is not always well balanced. Clearly, the efficiency of a search in a binary search tree is directly related to the shape of the tree. How does the tree get its shape? The shape of the tree is determined by the order in which items are entered into the tree. Let's build a binary search tree.

Building a Binary Search Tree

The clue of how to build a binary search tree lies in the search algorithm we just used. If we follow the search path and do not find the item, we end up at the place where it would be *if it were there*. Let's now build a binary search tree using strings: john, phil, lila, kate, becca, judy, june, mari, jim, and sarah.

Because john is the first value to be inserted, it goes into the root. The second value, phil, is greater than john, so it goes into the root of the right subtree. lila is greater than john but less than phil, so lila goes into the root of the left subtree of phil. The tree now looks like this.

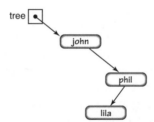

kate is greater than john, less than phil and less than lila, so kate goes into the root of the left subtree of lila. becca is less than john, so it goes into the root of the left subtree of john. judy is greater than john, less than phil, lila, and kate, so judy goes into the root of the left subtree of kate. We follow the same path for june as we did for judy. june is greater than judy, so it goes into the root of the right subtree of judy. mari becomes the root of lila's right subtree; jim becomes the root of the right subtree of becca; and sarah becomes the root of the right subtree of phil. The final tree is shown in Figure 9.19.

```
Insert (current, item)

If (tree is null)
        Put item in tree
Else
        If (item.compareTo(info(current)) < 0)
              Insert (item, left(current))
        Else
              Insert (item, right(current))
```

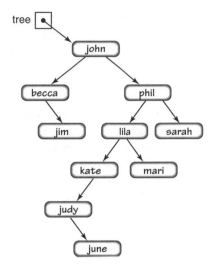

Figure 9.19
A binary search tree built from strings

Call to Insert	1st If Statement	2nd If Statement	Action/Call
Insert((john),nell)	(john)!=null	nell>john	Insert into right subtree
Insert((phil),nell)	(phil)!=null	nell<phil	Insert into left subtree
Insert((lila),nell)	(lila)!=null	nell>lila	Insert into right subtree
Insert((mari),nell)	(mari)!=null	nell>mari	Insert into right subtree
Insert((null),nell)	null=null		Store nell as root of right subtree of (mari)

Figure 9.20 Trace of inserting nell into the tree in Figure 9.19

Figure 9.20 shows a trace of inserting *nell* in the tree in Figure 9.19. We use the contents of the *info* part of the node within parentheses to indicate the pointer to the subtree with that value as a root.

Printing the Data in a Binary Search Tree

When we printed the values in a list, we used the expression *Get next item*, and showed what this expression translated to in an array-based implementation and in a linked implementation. What the expression meant logically was clear: Get the next item in the linear ordering of the list. What does the expression mean within a binary search tree? Well, for our purposes it means the same thing. But rather than looking at the print problem linearly, let's look at it from the tree's perspective.

To print the value in the root, we must first print all the values in its left subtree, which by definition are smaller than the value in the root. Once we print the value in the root, we must print all the values in the root's right subtree, which by definition are greater than the value in the root. And we are then finished. Finished? But what about the values in the left and right subtrees? How do we print them? Why, the same way of course. They are, after all, just binary search trees. This algorithm sounds too easy. That's the beauty of recursive algorithms: They are often short and elegant (though sometimes they take some thought to trace). Let's write it and trace it, using the tree shown below the algorithm. We number the calls in our trace because there are two recursive calls.

Print (tree)

If (tree is NOT null)
      Print (left(tree))
      Write info(tree)
      Print(right(tree))

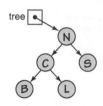

Call	Call to Print	If Statement	Action/Call
1	Print((N))	(N) != null	Print the left subtree
2	Print((C))	(C) != null	Print the left subtree
3	Print((B))	(B) != null	Print the left subtree
4	Print((null))	(null) = null	Return to 3
3			Print B, Print right subtree
5	Print((null))	(null) = null	Return to 2, finished call 3
2			Print C, Print right subtree
6	Print((L))	(L) != null	Print the left subtree
7	Print((null))	(null) = null	Return to 6
6			Print L, Print right subtree

8	Print((null))	(null) = null	Return to 1, finished calls 6 and 2
1			Print N, Print right subtree
9	Print((S))	(S) != null	Print the left subtree
10	Print((null))	(null) = null	Return to 9
9			Print S, Print right subtree
11	Print((null))	(null) = null	Return to original call, finished calls 9 and 1

This algorithm prints the items in the binary search tree in ascending value order. There are other traversals of the tree that print the items in other orders. We explore them in the exercises.

Other Operations

By now you should realize that a binary search tree is an object with the same functionality as a list. The behavior that separates a binary search tree from a simple list is the efficiency of the operations; the behaviors are the same. We have not shown the Delete algorithm, because it is too complex for this text. We have also ignored the concept *length* that must accompany the tree if it is to be used to implement a list. Rather than keep track of the number of items in the tree as we build it, let's write an algorithm to count the number of nodes in the tree.

How many nodes are there in an empty tree? Zero. How many nodes are there in any tree? One plus the number of nodes in the left subtree and the number of nodes in the right subtree. This definition leads to a recursive definition of the length operation.

```
Length(tree)

If (tree is null)
     return O
Else
     return Length(left(tree)) + Length(right(tree)) + 1
```

Graphs

Trees are a useful way to represent relationships in which a hierarchy exists. That is, a node is pointed to by at most one other node (its parent). If we remove the restriction that each node may have only one parent node, we have a data structure called a **graph**. A graph is made up of a set of nodes called **vertices** and a set of lines called **edges** (or **arcs**) that connect the nodes.

The vertices in the graph represent objects and the edges describe relationships among the vertices. For instance, if the graph is representing a map, the vertices might be the names of cities and the edges that link the vertices could represent roads between pairs of cities. Because the roads that run between cities are two-way, the edges in this graph have no direction. This is called an **undirected graph**. However, if the edges that link the vertices represent flights from one city to another, the direction of each edge *is* important. The existence of a flight (edge) from Houston to Austin does not assure the existence of a flight from Austin to Houston. A graph whose edges are directed from one vertex to another is called a **directed graph**, or **digraph**.

Vertices represent whatever objects are being modeled: people, houses, cities, courses, concepts, and so on. The edges represent relationships between the objects. For example, people are related to other people, houses are on the same street, cities are linked by direct flights, courses have prerequisites, and concepts are derived from other concepts. (See Figure 9.21.) However, mathematically, vertices are the undefined concept upon which graph theory rests. There is a great deal of formal mathematics associated with graphs, which is beyond the scope of this book. However, it is interesting to note that the stack and the queue described earlier in this chapter are used extensively when processing graphs.

Graph A data structure that consists of a set of nodes and a set of edges that relate the nodes to each other

Vertex A node in a graph

Edge (Arc) A pair of vertices representing a connection between two nodes in a graph

Undirected graph A graph in which the edges have no direction

Directed graph (Digraph) A graph in which each edge is directed from one vertex to another (or the same) vertex

---

9.8 Programming Libraries

Most modern programming languages provide a collection of library classes and coded algorithms available for the programmer to use. For the most part, these library routines are classes that encapsulate abstract data types. Unfortunately, the designers of these libraries do not use the classical names for many of these objects, so finding what you want becomes a little more difficult. However, the old axiom of never reinventing the wheel is valid when it comes to computing. Always check your language's library to see if a class exists with the behavior that you want to simulate.

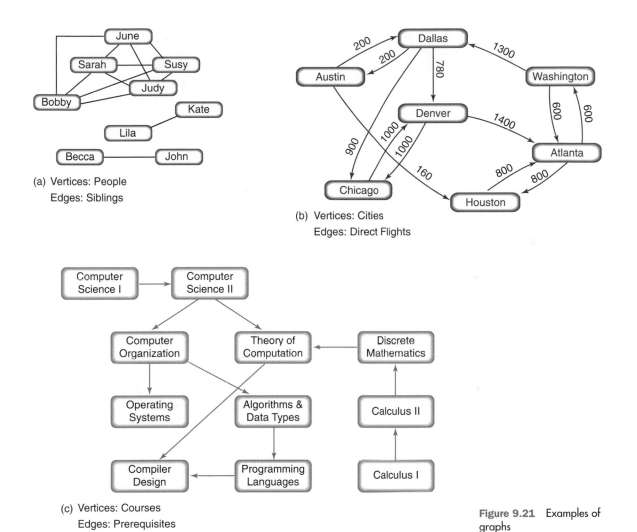

(a) Vertices: People
Edges: Siblings

(b) Vertices: Cities
Edges: Direct Flights

(c) Vertices: Courses
Edges: Prerequisites

Figure 9.21 Examples of graphs

Summary

Abstract data types (ADTs) are data types whose properties (data and operations) are specified independently of any particular implementation. Containers are objects in which other objects are stored. We describe container objects by ADTs. There are two general implementations used for ATDs: array-based and linked. Array-based containers are those in which the objects are stored in an array; linked implementations are those in which each object contains directions to the next object.

Lists, stacks, queues, trees, and graphs are useful container ADTs. Each ADT has its own defining property and the operations that guarantee that property. All of these ADTs have operations to insert items and to delete items. Lists and trees have operations to find items within the structure.

Sorting is the act of putting the items in a list into some sort of order. Selection sort, bubble sort, and Quicksort are three common sorting algorithms. If a list is in sorted order, a special searching algorithm called a binary search can be used to locate items in the list.

Programming libraries are collections of classes and algorithms available for a programmer to use. Before beginning to code, a programmer should check the library for the language to be used to see if there is a library class that already provides the needed behavior.

ETHICAL ISSUES

Web Content

The World Wide Web has revolutionized communication, providing an unprecedented forum for information exchange and self-expression. Instead of standing on a soapbox or writing an article for a local paper, anyone who wants to speak his or her mind can post a message on a Web site and connect with an extensive global audience. The number and variety of sites have prompted many people to evaluate Web site content and consider the pros and cons of censorship. Pornographic material, instructions for making bombs, hate propaganda, and Web fraud are at the center of this debate. In June of 1996, Congress passed the Communications Decency Act (CDA). This act was an attempt to establish control over what could and could not be displayed on the Web. The CDA criminalized "indecent" Web content and supporters praised this effort to protect minors from sexually explicit material. Opponents of the CDA declared that the Act violated the First Amendment right of free speech. Furthermore, they felt that even if the Act were in place, it would not serve as an effective defense against exposing minors to pornography, since this national law would not prohibit the posting of indecent material on sites located in other parts of the world. In addition, opponents feared that the CDA would deny Web site access to adults and block minors from important sites on health or sex education. These strong arguments led the federal courts to rule the Act unconstitutional, and three years later in 1999, the CDA II, a proposal of similar intent, was likewise overruled. While no universal regulations censor the Web, many individuals assume the responsibility of monitoring what can and cannot be accessed on their computers. Some people choose to use blocking and filtering systems, but these censoring techniques are not entirely effective, and often block either too much or not enough, material. Another potential solution to this problem is the installation of programs that use rating systems to determine what material to block. These filtering systems have developed standard content labels that Web sites can give themselves and each other. Then the users can choose what pages to block based on these content labels. While many people praise filtering programs, others argue that countries could use this filtering system to prevent their citizens from accessing specific material, for example, from viewing Web sites that contain information that conflicts with their governmental ideals.

Laws that not only attempt to control access to pornography and other indecent material, but also to monitor the accuracy of information posted on the Web and to prevent Web fraud, are likely to emerge in the near future. Currently, no standards exist to ensure the accuracy of material appearing on the Web, but there are things that you can do. Look for a site's objectives and its author information, check the currency of the site, and cross-reference any information gathered during a Web search.

Key Terms

Abstract data type (ADT) pg. 276

Array-based implementation
    pg. 277

Binary search pg. 296

Binary tree pg. 302

Containers pg. 277

Data structure pg. 277

Directed graph (Digraph) pg. 310

Edge (Arc) pg. 310

Generic data type (class) pg. 283

Graph pg. 310

Leaf node pg. 302

Linked implementation pg. 279

Root pg. 302

Sequential search pg. 295

Undirected graph pg. 310

Vertex pg. 310

Exercises

1. *Abstract data types*, *data structures*, and *containers*:
   a. Define these terms.
   b. What do they have in common?
   c. What distinguishes each from the others?

2. Name and describe the three views of data.

3. *Array-based implementation* and *linked implementation*:
   a. Define these terms.
   b. What do they have in common?
   c. What distinguishes one from the other?

4. Draw the unsorted list containing the following strings: blue, black, green, yellow, red, purple, white, and violet.
   a. In an unsorted array-based list
   b. In a sorted array-based list
   c. In an unsorted linked list
   d. In a sorted linked list

5. Give the meaning of the following expressions in an array-based implementation:
   a. Put item
   b. Remove the item
   c. Get next item
   d. More items?

6. Give the meaning of the following expressions in a linked implementation:
   a. Put item
   b. Remove the item
   c. Get next item
   d. More items?

7. What does it mean to say that the Delete operation is ambiguous?

8. What three properties characterize lists? Explain what each means.

9. How were we able to make the list generic?

10. The obvious place to place a new item in an unsorted list is different in an array-based and a linked implementation. Explain.

Questions 11 through 13 use the following list of values.

length	list										
	[0]	[1]	[2]	[3]	[4]	[5]	[6]	[7]	[8]	[9]	[10]
8	23	41	66	20	2	90	9	34	19	40	99

11. Show the state of the list when current is first set to the 4th item in the list in the selection sort.

12. Show the state of the list when current is first set to the 5th item in the list in the bubble sort algorithm.

13. Show the state of the list when the first recursive call is made.

Questions 14 through 15 use the following list of values.

length		list

[0]	[1]	[2]	[3]	[4]	[5]	[6]	[7]	[8]	[9]	[10]
5	7	20	33	44	46	48	99	101	102	105

length: `10`

14. How many comparisons does it take using a sequential search to find the following values or determine that the item is not in the list?
    a. 4   **d.** 105
    b. 44   **e.** 106
    c. 45

15. How many comparisons does it take using a binary search to find the following values or determine that the item is not in the list?
    a. 4   **d.** 105
    b. 44   **e.** 106
    c. 45

16. A binary search is a natural recursive algorithm. It can also be written as an iterative algorithm. Write the iterative version of the algorithm.

17. What are the characteristics of the ADT stack?

18. What are the characteristics of the ADT queue?

19. Which of the following is true of stacks and queues?
    a. A stack is a last-in, first-out structure, and a queue is a first-in, first-out structure.
    b. A stack is a first-in, first-out structure, and both structures are random access structures.
    c. A stack is a last-in, first-out structure, and a queue is a random-access structure.
    d. A queue is a last-in, first-out structure, and a stack is a first-in, first-out structure.
    e. A queue is a first-in, first-out structure, and a stack is a random-access structure.

20. Write the algorithm for Push in an array-based implementation.

21. Write the algorithm for Pop in an array-based implementation.

22. Write the algorithm for Enque in an array-based implementation.

23. Write the algorithms for Deque in an array-based implementation.

24. Write the algorithm for Push in a linked implementation.

25. Write the algorithm for Pop in a linked implementation.

26. Write the algorithm for Enque in a linked implementation.

27. Write the algorithms for Deque in a linked implementation.

28. What is the state of the stack after the following sequence of Push and Pop operations?

Push anne

Push get

Push your

Pop

Push my

Push gun

Pop

29. What is the state of the queue after the following sequence of Enque and Deque operations?

Enque my

Enque your

Deque

Enque get

Enque anne

Enque gun

The following tree is used in Exercises 30 through 36.

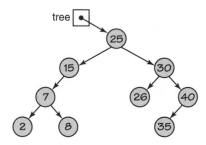

30. Name the content of each of the leaf nodes.

31. Name the content of each of the nodes that has just one child.

32. What is the height of the tree?

33. Name the content of nodes that are the ancestors of the nodes whose content is 7.

34. How many comparisons does it take to find the following items or determine that the item is not in the tree?

  a. 1

  b. 9

  c. 35

  d. 16

  e. 35

35. How many more nodes could this tree have? Explain.

36. If a node with the value 9 is inserted into the tree, where does it go?

37. What is the maximum number of nodes on level 4?

38. What is the maximum number of nodes in a tree with 4 levels?

39. What are the properties of a binary tree?

40. What are the properties of a binary search tree?

41. Draw the tree that results in inserting the following strings into the tree in Figure 9.18: susy, chris, kit, jimmie, christopher, nell, al, bobby, john robert, and alex.

42. Draw a tree representing the relationships in your family.

43. Write the algorithm to determine if a list is empty.

44. Write the algorithm to determine if a list is full.

❓ Thought Questions

1. A spreadsheet is a table with rows and columns. Thank about an ADT spreadsheet. What operations would you need to construct the table? What operations would you need to manipulate the values in the table?

2. Linked lists, trees, and graphs are composed of nodes and arrows (pointers) that represent the relationships between nodes. Compare these structures in terms of the operations that are allowed. Can a list ever be a tree? Can a tree ever be a list? Can a tree ever be a graph? Can a graph ever be a tree? How do the structures all relate to one another?

3. Have you every used the Web to conduct research for a paper? Have you taken what you found, used the information, and not checked the content for accuracy? How can we as citizens help monitor the accuracy of Web content?

4. Communications Decency Acts I and II were both overturned because they violated the First Amendment right of free speech. Where do you draw the line between free speech and the right of a society to monitor what its citizens view?

5. Does the advent of the Internet and the Web change the fabric of society around the world? How is the Web different from television or radio in its influence?

6. There are concerns about Web content at all levels. Parents want to protect their children from pornography; totalitarian governments want to keep their citizens in ignorance of other political movements; closed societies want to keep out different ideas. Some of these goals are good; some are not. Who is to say what can and cannot be posted on the Web?

The Operating
Systems Layer

10 Operating Systems

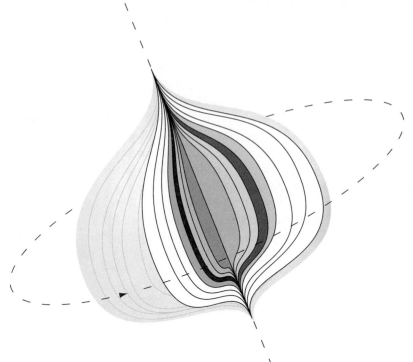

Chapter 10

Operating Systems

To understand a computer system you must understand the software that manages and coordinates its pieces. The operating system of a computer is the glue that holds the hardware and software together. It is the software foundation on which all other software rests, allowing us to write programs that interact with the machine. This chapter and the next one explore the way in which an operating system manages computer resources. Just as a policeman organizes the efficient flow of cars through an intersection, an operating system organizes the efficient flow of programs through a computer system.

Goals

After studying this chapter, you should be able to:

- describe the two main responsibilities of an operating system.
- define memory and process management.
- explain how timesharing creates the virtual machine illusion.
- explain the relationship between logical and physical addresses.
- compare and contrast memory management techniques.
- distinguish between fixed and dynamic partitions.
- define and apply partition selection algorithms.
- explain how demand paging creates the virtual memory illusion.
- explain the stages and transitions of the process life cycle.
- explain the processing of various CPU scheduling algorithms.

10.1   Roles of an Operating System

In Chapter 1, we talked about the changing role of the programmer. As early as the end of the first generation of software development, there was a division between those programmers who wrote tools to help other programmers and those who used the tools to solve problems. Modern software can be divided into two categories, application software and system software, reflecting this separation of goals. **Application software** is written to address our specific needs—to solve problems in the real world. Word processing programs, games, inventory control systems, automobile diagnostic programs, and missile guidance programs are all application software. Chapters 12 through 14 discuss various areas of computer science and their relationship to application software.

System software manages a computer system at a fundamental level. It provides the tools and an environment in which application software can be created and run. System software often interacts directly with the hardware and provides more functionality than the hardware itself does.

The **operating system** of a computer is the core of its system software. An operating system manages computer resources, such as memory and input/output devices, and provides an interface through which a human can interact with the computer. Other system software supports specific application goals, such as a library of graphics software that renders images on a display. An operating system allows an application program to interact with these other system resources.

Figure 10.1 shows the operating system in its relative position among computer system elements. The operating system manages hardware

Application software
Programs that help us solve real-world problems

System software
Programs that manage a computer system and interact with hardware

Operating system
System software that manages computer resources and provides an interface for system interaction

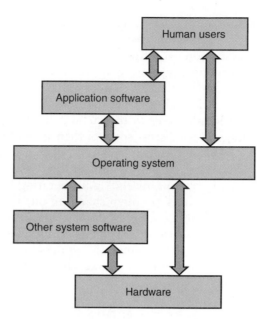

Figure 10.1
An operating system interacts with many aspects of a
computer system.

resources. It allows application software to access system resources, either
directly or through other system software. It provides a direct user interface to the computer system.

A computer generally has one operating system that becomes active and
takes control when the system is turned on. Computer hardware is wired
to initially load a small set of system instructions stored in permanent
memory (ROM). These instructions load a larger portion of system software from secondary memory, usually a magnetic disk. Eventually all key
elements of the operating system software are loaded, start-up programs
are executed, the user interface is provided, and the system is ready for use.
This activity is often called *booting* the computer. The term *boot* comes
from the idea of "pulling yourself up by your own bootstraps," which is
essentially what a computer does when it is turned on.

A computer could have two or more operating systems from which the
user chooses when the computer is turned on. This configuration is often
called a *dual-boot* or *multi-boot* system. Note that only one operating
system is in control of the computer at any given time.

You've likely used one operating system or another before. The various
versions of Microsoft Windows (Windows 98, Windows 2000, Windows
NT, Windows ME) are popularly used for personal computers. The
different versions of these operating systems represent the evolving software over time as well as differences in the way services are provided and
managed. The Mac OS is the operating system of choice for computers

manufactured by Apple Computer. Unix has been a favorite of serious programmers for years, and recently a version of Unix called Linux has become popular for personal computer systems.

Any given operating system manages resources in its own particular way. Our goal in this chapter is not to nitpick the differences among operating systems, but rather to discuss the ideas common to all of them. We occasionally refer to the methods that a specific OS (operating system) uses, and we discuss some of their individual philosophies. But in general we focus on the underlying concepts.

The various roles of an operating system generally revolve around the idea of "sharing nicely." An operating system manages resources, and these resources are often shared in one way or another among programs that want to use them. Multiple programs executing concurrently share the use of main memory. They take turns using the CPU. They compete for an opportunity to use input/output devices. The operating system acts as the playground monitor to make sure everyone cooperates and gets a chance to play.

Memory, Process, and CPU Management

Multiprogramming
The technique of keeping multiple programs in main memory at the same time, competing for the CPU

Memory management
The act of keeping track of how and where programs are loaded in main memory

Process   The dynamic representation of a program during execution

Process management
The act of keeping track of information for active processes

CPU scheduling   The act of determining which process in memory is given access to the CPU so that it may execute

Recall from Chapter 5 that an executing program resides in main memory and its instructions are processed one after another in the fetch-decode-execute cycle. **Multiprogramming** is the technique of keeping multiple programs in main memory at the same time; these programs compete for access to the CPU so that they can execute. All modern operating systems employ multiprogramming to one degree or another. An operating system must therefore perform **memory management** to keep track of what programs are in memory and where in memory they reside.

Another key operating system concept is the idea of a **process**, which can be defined as a program in execution. A program is a static set of instructions. A process is the dynamic entity that represents the program while it is being executed. Through multiprogramming, a computer system might have many active processes at once. The operating system must manage these processes carefully. At any point in time a specific instruction is the next to be executed. Intermediate values have been calculated. A process might get interrupted during execution, so the operating system performs **process management** to carefully track the progress of a process and all of its intermediate states.

Related to the ideas of memory management and process management is the need for **CPU scheduling**, which determines which process in memory is executed by the CPU at any given point.

Memory management, process management, and CPU scheduling are the three main topics discussed in this chapter. Other key operating system topics, such as file management and secondary storage, are covered in Chapter 11.

Keep in mind that the operating system is itself just a program that must be executed. OS processes must be managed and maintained in main memory along with other system software and application programs. The OS executes on the same CPU as the other programs, and must take its turn among them.

Before we delve into the details of managing resources such as main memory and the CPU, we need to explore a few more general concepts.

Batch Processing

A typical computer in the 1960s and '70s was a large machine stored in its own heavily air-conditioned room. Its processing was managed by a human *operator*. A user would deliver his or her program, usually stored as a deck of punched cards, to the operator to be executed. The user would come back later, perhaps the next day, to retrieve the printed results.

When delivering the program, the user would also provide a set of separate instructions regarding the system software and other resources that would be needed to execute the program. Together the program and the system instructions were called a *job*. The operator would make any necessary devices available and load any special system software as needed to satisfy the job. Therefore, the process of preparing a program for execution on these early machines was time consuming.

To simplify and economize this procedure, the operator would organize various jobs from multiple users into *batches*. A batch would contain a set of jobs that needed the same or similar resources. Therefore, the operator wouldn't have to reload and prepare the same resources over and over. Figure 10.2 depicts this procedure.

Batch systems could be executed in a multiprogramming environment. In that case, the operator would load multiple jobs from the same batch into memory, and these jobs would compete for the use of the CPU and other shared resources. As the resources became available, the jobs would be scheduled to use the CPU.

Although the original concept of batch processing is not a function of modern operating systems, the concept remains. The term *batch* has come to mean a system in which programs and system resources are coordinated and executed without interaction between the user and the program. Modern operating systems incorporate batch-style processing by allowing the user to define a set of OS commands as a batch file to control the processing of a large program or a set of interacting programs. For example, files with the extension .bat in MS Windows stems from the idea of batch control files; they contain system commands

Influential computing jobs

There were many influential jobs in computing in the '60s, but none more so than the computer operator. In his or her hands rested the decision of whose computer jobs ran and when. Many a graduate student was known to have bribed a weary operator with coffee and cookies in the wee hours of the morning for just one more run.

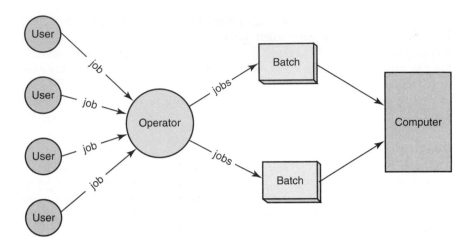

Figure 10.2
In early systems, human operators would organize jobs into batches

Though most of our computer use these days is interactive, some jobs even today lend themselves to batch processing. For example, processing a corporation's monthly salary payments is a large job that uses specific resources with essentially no human interaction.

Early batch processing allowed multiple users to share a single computer. Though the emphasis has changed over time, batch systems taught us valuable lessons about resource management. The human operator of early computer systems played many of the roles that modern operating system software does now.

Timesharing

As we pointed out in Chapter 1, the problem of how to make use of the machine's greater capabilities and speed lead to the concept of *time sharing*. A **timesharing** system allows multiple users to interact with a computer at the same time. Multiprogramming allowed multiple processes to be active at once, which gave rise to the ability for programmers to interact with the computer system directly, while still sharing its resources.

Timesharing systems create the illusion that each user has the computer exclusively. That is, each user does not have to actively compete for resources, though that is exactly what is happening behind the scenes. One user may actually know he is sharing the machine with other users, but does not have to do anything special to allow it. The operating system manages the sharing of the resources, including the CPU, behind the scenes.

The word *virtual* means in effect, though not in essence. In a timesharing system, each user has his or her own **virtual machine**, in which all

Timesharing   A system in which CPU time is shared among multiple interactive users at the same time

Virtual machine   The illusion created by a timesharing system that each user has a dedicated machine

system resources are (in effect) available for use. In essence, however, the resources are being shared among many such users.

Originally, timesharing systems were made up of a single computer, often called the **mainframe**, and a set of dumb terminals connected to the mainframe. A **dumb terminal** is essentially just a monitor display and a keyboard. A user sits at a terminal and "logs in" to the mainframe. The dumb terminals might be spread throughout a building, with the mainframe in its own dedicated room. The operating system resides on the mainframe, and all processing occurs there.

> **Mainframe**   A large, multi-user computer often associated with early timesharing systems
>
> **Dumb terminal**   A monitor and keyboard that allow the user to access the mainframe computer in early time-sharing systems

Each user is represented by a *login process* that runs on the mainframe. When the user runs a program, another process is created (spawned by the user's login process). CPU time is shared among all of the processes created by all of the users. Each process is given a little bit of CPU time in turn. The premise is that the CPU is so fast that it can handle the needs of multiple users without any one user seeing an effect. In truth, users of a timesharing system can sometimes see degradation in the system responses depending on the number of active users and the CPU capabilities. That is, each user's machine seems to slow down.

Though mainframe computers are mostly historical, the concept of timesharing is not. Today, many desktop computers run operating systems that support multiple users in a timesharing fashion. Although only one user is actually sitting in front of the computer, other users can connect through other computers across a network connection.

Other OS Factors

As computing technology improved, the machines themselves got smaller. Mainframe computers gave rise to *minicomputers*, which no longer needed dedicated rooms in which to store them. Minicomputers became the basic hardware platform for timesharing systems. *Microcomputers*, which for the first time relied on a single integrated chip as the CPU, truly fit on an individual's desk. This gave rise to the idea of a *personal computer* (PC). As the name implies, a personal computer is not designed for multi-person use, and originally personal computer operating systems reflected this simplicity. Over time, personal computers evolved in functionality and incorporated many aspects of larger systems, such as timesharing. Though a desktop machine is still often referred to as a PC, the term *workstation* is sometimes used and is perhaps more appropriate, describing it as generally dedicated to an individual, but capable of supporting much more. Operating systems evolved to support these changes in the use of computers.

Operating systems must also take into account the fact that computers are usually connected into networks. Today with the World Wide Web we take network communication for granted. Networks are discussed in detail in a later chapter, but we must acknowledge here the effect that network communication has on operating systems. Such communication is yet another resource that an OS must support.

One final aspect of operating systems is the need to support *real-time systems*. A **real-time system** is one that must provide a guaranteed minimum **response time** to the user. That is, the delay between receiving a stimulus and producing a response must be carefully controlled. Real-time responses are crucial in software that, for example, controls a robot, or a nuclear reactor, or a missile. Though all operating systems acknowledge the importance of response time, a real-time operating system strives to optimize it.

> **Real-time system**   A system in which response time is crucial given the nature of the application domain
>
> **Response time**   The time delay between receiving a stimulus and producing a response

10.2   Memory Management

Let's review what we said about main memory in Chapters 5 and 7. All programs are stored in main memory when they are executed. All data referenced by those programs are also stored in main memory so that they can be accessed. Main memory can be thought of as a big continuous chunk of space divided into groups of 8, 16, or 32 bits. Each byte or word of memory has a corresponding address, which is simply an integer that uniquely identifies that particular part of memory. See Figure 10.3. The first memory address is 0.

Earlier in this chapter we stated that in a multiprogramming environment, multiple programs (and their data) are stored in main memory at the same time. Thus, operating systems must employ techniques to:

- track where and how a program resides in memory.
- convert logical program addresses into actual memory addresses.

A program is filled with references to variables and to other parts of the program code. When the program is compiled, these references are changed into the addresses in memory where the data and code reside. But since we don't know exactly where a program will be loaded into main memory, how can we know what address to use for anything?

The solution is to use two kinds of addresses: logical addresses and physical addresses. A **logical address** (sometimes called a virtual or relative address) is a value that specifies a generic location, relative to the program but not to the reality of main memory. A **physical address** is an actual address in the main memory device, as shown in Figure 10.3.

When a program is compiled, a reference to an identifier (such as a variable name) is changed to a logical address. When the program is eventually loaded into memory, each logical address finally corresponds to a specific physical address. The mapping of a logical address to a physical address is

> **Logical address**   A reference to a stored value relative to the program making the reference
>
> **Physical address**   An actual address in the main memory device

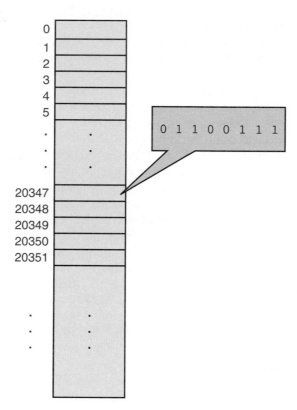

Figure 10.3
Memory is a continuous set of bits referenced by specific addresses

called **address binding**. The later we wait to bind a logical address to a physical one, the more flexibility we have. Logical addresses allow a program to be moved around in memory or loaded in different places at different times. As long as we keep track of where the program is stored, we are always able to determine the physical address that corresponds to any given logical address. To simplify our examples in this chapter, we perform address-binding calculations in base 10.

Address binding The mapping from a logical address to a physical address

The following sections examine the underlying principles of three techniques:

- Single contiguous memory management
- Partition memory management
- Paged memory management

Single Contiguous Memory Management

Let's initially keep things simple by assuming that there are only two programs in memory: the operating system and the application program we want to execute. We divide main memory up into two sections, one for each, as shown in Figure 10.4. The operating system gets what space it needs, and the program is allocated the rest.

This approach is called **single contiguous memory management** because the entire application program is loaded into one large chunk of memory. Only one program other than the operating system can be processed at one time. To bind addresses, all we have to take into account is the location of the operating system.

In this memory management scheme, a logical address is simply an integer value relative to the starting point of the program. That is, logical addresses are created as if the program is loaded at location 0 of main memory. Therefore, to produce a physical address, we add a logical address to the starting address of the program in physical main memory.

Let's get a little more specific: If the program is loaded starting at address A, then the physical address corresponding to logical address L is A+L. See Figure 10.5. Let's plug in real numbers to make it clear. Suppose the program is loaded into memory beginning at address 555555. When a program uses relative address 222222, we know that that actually refers to address 777777 in physical main memory.

It doesn't really matter what the address L is. As long as we keep track of A (the starting address of the program), we can always translate a logical address into a physical one.

You may be saying at this point that if we switched the locations of the operating system and the program, then the logical and physical addresses for the program would be the same. That's true. But then you'd have other things to worry about. For example, a memory management scheme must always take security into account. In particular, in a multiprogram-

> **Single contiguous memory management** The approach to memory management in which a program is loaded into one continuous area of memory

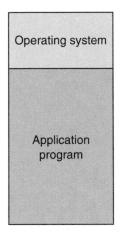

Figure 10.4
Main memory divided into two sections

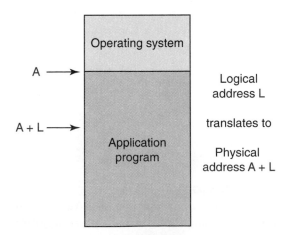

Figure 10.5
Binding a logical address to a physical one

ming environment, we must prevent a program from accessing any addresses beyond its allocated memory space. With the operating system loaded at location 0, all logical addresses for the program are valid unless they exceed the bounds of main memory itself. If we move the operating system below the program, we'd have to make sure a logical address didn't try to access the memory space devoted to the operating system. This wouldn't be difficult, but it would be add to the complexity of the processing.

The advantage of a single contiguous memory management approach is that it is simple to implement and manage. However, memory space and CPU time are almost certainly wasted. It is unlikely that an application program needs all of the memory not used by the operating system, and CPU time is wasted when the program has to wait for some resource.

Partition Memory Management

A more sophisticated approach is to have more than one application program in memory at a time, sharing memory space and CPU time. Thus, memory must be divided into more than two partitions. There are two strategies that can be used to partition memory: fixed partitions and dynamic partitions. When using **fixed partitions**, main memory is divided into a particular number of partitions. The partitions do not have to be the same size, but their size is fixed when the operating system initially boots. A job is loaded into a partition large enough to hold it. The OS keeps a table of addresses at which each partition begins and the length of the partition.

When using **dynamic partitions**, the partitions are created to fit the need of the programs. Main memory is initially viewed as one large empty partition. As programs are loaded, space is "carved out," using only the space needed to accommodate the program and leaving a new, smaller empty partition, which may be used by another program later. The operating system maintains a table of partition information, but in dynamic partitions the address information changes as programs come and go.

At any point in time in both fixed and dynamic partitions, memory is divided into a set of partitions, some empty and some allocated to programs. See Figure 10.6.

Address binding is basically the same for both fixed and dynamic partitions. As with the single contiguous technique, a logical address is an integer relative to a starting point of zero. There are various ways an OS might handle the details of the address translation. One way is to use two special purpose registers in the CPU to help manage addressing. When a program becomes active on the CPU, the OS stores the address of the

Fixed-partition technique The memory management technique in which memory is divided into a specific number of partitions into which programs are loaded

Dynamic-partition technique The memory management technique in which memory is divided into partitions as needed to accommodate programs

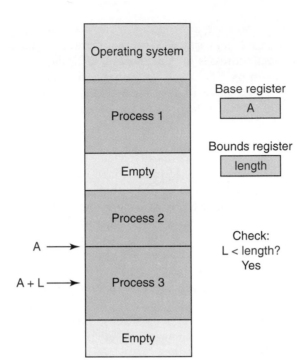

Figure 10.6
Address resolution in partition memory management

beginning of that program's partition into the **base register**. Similarly, the length of the partition is stored in the **bounds register**. When a logical address is referenced, it is first compared to the value in the bounds register to make sure the reference is in that program's allocated memory space. If it is, the value of the logical address is added to the value in the base register to produce the physical address.

Which partition should we allocate to a new program? There are three general approaches to partition selection:

- *First fit*, in which the program is allocated to the first partition big enough to hold it
- *Best fit*, in which the program is allocated to the smallest partition big enough to hold it
- *Worst fit*, in which the program is allocated to the largest partition big enough to hold it

Worst fit doesn't make sense to use in fixed partitions because it would waste the larger partitions. First fit or best fit work for fixed partitions. But in dynamic partitions, worst fit often works best because it leaves the largest possible empty partition, which may accommodate another program later on.

When a program terminates, the partition table is updated to reflect that that partition is now empty and available for a new program. In dynamic partitions, consecutive empty partitions are merged into one big empty partition.

Partition memory management makes efficient use of main memory by having several programs in memory at one time. But keep in mind that a program must fit entirely into one partition. Fixed partitions are easier to manage than dynamic ones, but restrict the opportunities available to incoming programs. The system may have enough free memory to accommodate the program, but not in one free partition. In dynamic partitions, the jobs could be shuffled around in memory to create one large free partition. This procedure is known as *compaction*.

Paged Memory Management

Paged memory management puts much more burden on the operating system to keep track of allocated memory and to resolve addresses. But the benefits gained by this approach are generally worth the extra effort.

In the **paged memory technique**, main memory is divided into small fixed-size blocks of storage called **frames**. A process is divided into **pages** that (for the sake of our discussion) we assume are the same size as a frame. When a program is to be executed, the pages of the process are loaded into various unused frames distributed through memory. Thus the pages of a process may be scattered around, out of order, and mixed among the pages of other processes. To keep track of all this, the operating system maintains a separate **page-map table** (PMT) for each process in memory; it maps each page to the frame in which it is loaded. See Figure 10.7. Note that both pages and frames are numbered starting with zero, which makes the address calculations easier.

A logical address in a paged memory management system consists of two values, a page and an offset. A logical address is often written as <page, offset>, such as <2, 518>, which means the reference is to 518 bytes into page 2 of the process.

To produce a physical address, you first look up the page in the PMT to find the frame number in which it is stored. Then multiply the frame number by the frame size and add the offset to get the physical address. For example, given the situation shown in Figure 10.7, if process 1 is active, a logical address of <1, 222> would be processed as follows: Page 1 of process 1 is in frame 12; therefore, the corresponding physical address is 12*1024 + 222 or 12510. Note that there are two ways in which a logical address could be invalid: The page number could be out of bounds for that process, or the offset could be larger than the size of a frame.

The advantage of paging is that a process no longer needs to be stored contiguously in memory. The ability to divide a process into pieces changes

Paged memory technique A memory management technique in which processes are divided into fixed-size pages and stored in memory frames when loaded

Frame A fixed-size portion of main memory that holds a process page

Page A fixed-size portion of a process that is stored into a memory frame

Page map table (PMT) The table used by the operating system to keep track of page/frame relationships

Memory

Frame	Contents
0	
1	P2/Page2
2	
3	
4	
5	P1/Page0
6	
7	P1/Page3
8	
9	
10	P2/Page0
11	P2/Page3
12	P1/Page1
13	
14	
15	P1/Page2

P1 PMT

Page	Frame
0	5
1	12
2	15
3	7
4	22

P2 PMT

Page	Frame
0	10
1	18
2	1
3	11

Figure 10.7
A paged memory management approach

the challenge of loading a process from finding one available large chunk of space to finding enough small chunks.

An important extension to the idea of paged memory management is the idea of **demand paging**, which takes advantage of the fact that not all parts of a program actually have to be in memory at the same time. At any given instance in time, the CPU is accessing one page of a process. At that point, it doesn't really matter if the other pages of that process are even in memory.

In demand paging, the pages are brought into memory on demand. That is, when a page is referenced, we first see whether it is in memory already and, if so, complete the access. If not, the page is brought in from secondary memory into an available frame, and then the access is completed. The act of bringing in a page from secondary memory, which often causes another page to be written back to secondary memory, is called a **page swap**.

Demand paging An extension to paged memory management in which pages are brought into memory only when referenced (on demand)

Page swap Bringing in one page from secondary memory, possibly causing another to be removed

The demand paging approach gives rise to the idea of **virtual memory**, the illusion that there are no restrictions on the size of a program (because the entire program is not necessarily in memory at the same time anyway). In all earlier memory management techniques we examined, the entire process had to be brought into memory as a continuous whole. We therefore always had an upper bound on process size. Demand paging removes that restriction.

However, virtual memory comes with lots of overhead during the execution of a program. Before, once a program was loaded into memory, it was all there and ready to go. With the virtual memory approach, we constantly have to swap pages between main and secondary memory. This overhead is acceptable—while one program is waiting for a page to be swapped, another process can take control of the CPU and make progress. Too much page swapping, however, is called **thrashing** and can seriously degrade system performance.

> **Virtual memory** The illusion that there is no restriction on program size because an entire process need not be in memory at the same time
>
> **Thrashing** Inefficient processing caused by constant page swapping

10.3 Process Management

Another important resource that an operating system must manage is the use of the CPU by individual processes. To understand how an operating system manages processes, we must recognize the stages that a process goes through during its computational life and understand the information that must be managed to keep a process working correctly in a computer system.

The Process States

Processes move through specific states as they are managed in a computer system. A process enters the system, is ready to be executed, is executing, is waiting for a resource, or is finished. The **process states** are depicted in Figure 10.8. Each oval represents a state a process might be in, and the

> **Process states** The conceptual stages through which a process moves as it is managed by the operating system

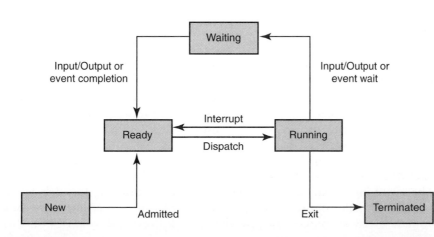

Figure 10.8
The process life cycle

arrows indicate how and why a process might move from one state to another.

Let's examine what is happing to a process in each state.

In the *new state* a process is being created. It may, for instance, be a login process created by a user logging onto a timeshare system, an application process created when a user submits a program for execution, or a system process created by the operating system to accomplish a specific system task.

A process that has no barriers to its execution is in the *ready state*. That is, a process in the ready state is not waiting for an event to occur, or for data to be brought in from secondary memory. It's waiting only for its chance to use the CPU.

A process in the *running state* is currently being executed by the CPU. Its instructions are being processed in the fetch-execute cycle.

A process in the *waiting state* is currently waiting for resources (other than the CPU). For example, a process in the waiting state may be waiting for a page of its memory to be brought in from secondary memory or for another process to send it a signal that it may continue.

A process in the *terminated state* has completed its execution and is no longer an active process. At this point the operating system no longer needs to maintain the information regarding the process.

Note that many processes may be ready state or the waiting state at the same time, but only one process can be in the running state.

After a process is created, the operating system admits it to the ready state. When the CPU scheduling algorithm dictates, a process is dispatched to the running state. (CPU scheduling is discussed in more detail later in the next section of this chapter.)

While running, the process might be interrupted by the operating system to allow another process its chance on the CPU. In that case, the process simply returns to the ready state. Or, a running process might request a resource that is not available or require I/O to retrieve a newly referenced part of the process, in which case it is moved to the waiting state. A running process finally gets enough CPU time to complete its processing and terminate normally; or it may generate an unrecoverable error and terminate abnormally.

When a waiting process gets the resource it is waiting for, it moves to the ready state again.

Process control block (PCB) The data structure used by the operating system to manage information about a process

The Process Control Block

The operating system must manage a large amount of data for each active process. Usually that data is stored in a data structure called a **process control block** (PCB). Generally, each state is represented by a list of PCBs, one for each process in that state. When a process moves from one state to another, its corresponding PCB is moved from one state list to another in the operating system. A new PCB is created when a process is first created (the new state) and is kept around until the process terminates.

The PCB stores a variety of information about the process, including the current value of the program counter, which indicates which instruction in the process is to be executed next. As the life cycle indicates, a process may be interrupted many times during its execution. At each point, its program counter must be stored so that the next time it gets into the running state it can pick up where it left off.

The PCB also stores the values of all other CPU registers for that process. Keep in mind that there is only one CPU and therefore only one set of CPU registers. These registers contain the values for the currently executing process (the one in the running state). Each time a process is moved to the running state, the register values for the currently running process are stored into its PCB, and the register values of the new running state are loaded into the CPU. This exchange of information is called a context switch.

> **Context switch** The exchange of register information that occurs when one process is removed from the CPU and another takes its place

The PCB also maintains information about CPU scheduling, such as the priority that a process is given by the operating system. It also contains memory management information, such as base and bound register values (for partitions) or page tables (for paged systems). Finally, the PCB also includes accounting information, such as account numbers, time limits, and the amount of CPU time used so far.

10.4 CPU Scheduling

CPU scheduling is the act of determining which process in the ready state should be moved to the running state. That is, CPU scheduling algorithms decide which process should be given over to the CPU so that it can make computational progress.

CPU scheduling decisions are made when a process switches from the running state to the waiting state, or when a program terminates. This type of CPU scheduling is called nonpreemptive scheduling, because the need for a new CPU process is the result of the activity of the currently executing process.

CPU scheduling decisions may also be made when a process moves from the running state to the ready state or when a process moves from the waiting state to the ready state. These are examples of preemptive scheduling, because the currently running process (through no fault of its own) is preempted by the operating system.

> **Nonpreemptive scheduling** CPU scheduling that occurs when the currently executing process gives up the CPU voluntarily
>
> **Preemptive scheduling** CPU scheduling that occurs when the operating system decides to favor another process, preempting the currently executing process

Scheduling algorithms are often evaluated using particular metrics, such as the **turnaround time** for a process. This is the amount of time between the time a process arrives in the ready state to the time it exits the running state for the last time. We would like, on average, for the turnaround time for our processes to be small.

There are various approaches that can be used to determine which process gets chosen first to move from the ready state to the running state. We examine three of them in the next sections.

First-Come, First-Served

In first-come, first-served (FCFS) scheduling approach, processes are moved to the CPU in the order in which they arrive in the running state. FCFS scheduling is nonpreemptive. Once a process is given access to the CPU, it keeps it unless it makes a request that forces it to wait, such as a request for a device in use by another process.

Suppose processes p1 through p5 arrive in the ready state at essentially the same time (to make our calculations simple) but in the following order and with the specified service time:

Process	Service time
p1	140
p2	75
p3	320
p4	280
p5	125

In the FCFS scheduling approach, each process receives access to the CPU in turn. For simplicity, we assume here that processes don't cause themselves to wait. The following Gantt chart shows the order and time of process completion:

0	140	215		535		815	940
p1	p2		p3		p4		p5

Since we are assuming the processes all arrived at the same time, the turnaround time for each process is the same as its completion time. The average turnaround time is (140 + 215 + 535 + 815 + 940) / 5 or 529.

The FCFS algorithm is easy to implement but suffers from its lack of attention to important factors such as service time requirements. Although the service times were used in our calculations of turnaround time, the algorithm didn't use that information to help determine the best order in which to schedule the processes.

Shortest Job Next

The shortest-job-next (SJN) CPU scheduling algorithm looks at all processes in the ready state and dispatches the one with the smallest service time. Like FCFS, it is also generally implemented as a nonpreemptive algorithm.

Below is the Gantt chart for the same set of processes we examined in the FCFS example. Because the selection criteria are different, the order in which the processes are scheduled and completed are different:

0	75	200	340	620	940
p2	p5	p1	p4		p3

The average turnaround time for this example is (75 + 200 + 340 + 620 + 940) / 5 or 435.

Note that the SJN algorithm relies on knowledge of the future. That is, it gives the CPU to the job that runs for the shortest time when it is allowed to execute. That time is essentially impossible to determine. So to run this algorithm, the service time value for a process is usually estimated by the operating system using various probability factors and taking the type of job into account. But if these estimates are wrong, the premise of the algorithm breaks down and its efficiency deteriorates. The SJN algorithm is *provably optimal*, meaning that if we could know the service time of each job, the SJN algorithm produces the shortest turnaround time for all jobs compared to any other algorithm. However, since we can't know the future absolutely, we make guesses and hope those guesses are correct.

Round Robin

Round-robin CPU scheduling distributes the processing time equitably among all ready processes. The algorithm establishes a particular **time slice** (or time quantum), which is the amount of time each process receives before being preempted and returned to the ready state to allow another process its turn. Eventually the preempted process will be given another

What is a Gantt chart?

A Gantt chart is a horizontal bar chart developed as a production control tool in 1917 by Henry L. Gantt, an American engineer and social scientist. Frequently used in project management, a Gantt chart provides a graphical illustration of a schedule that helps to plan, coordinate, and track specific tasks in a project. Gantt charts may be simple versions created on graph paper or more complex automated versions created using project management applications such as Microsoft Project or Excel.

Time slice   The amount of time given to each process in the round-robin CPU scheduling algorithm

Seymour Cray

During his keynote address at the Supercomputing '96 Conference, Charles Breckenridge had this to say about Seymour Cray:

> "It is fitting that we pay tribute today to Seymour Cray, the individual who created the industry that led to the formation of this conference and the individual who has been, for the last 40 years, the acknowledged leader of the high-performance computer industry, and the individual whose name is synonymous with high-performance computing."

Seymour Cray was born in Chippewa Falls, Wisconsin, in 1925. He graduated from high school in 1943 and served in both the European and Pacific theaters of World War II. He received his B.S. in Electrical Engineering from the University of Minnesota in 1950 and his M.S. in Applied Mathematics the next year.

Cray went to work for Engineering Research Associates (ERA), a year-old digital circuit company housed in an old glider factory. He spent time researching computers, listening to lecturers from scholars such as von Neumann, and participating in a design group for the development of two computers. Remington Rand bought ERA, changing the focus from scientific computers to commercial computers, and so Cray joined Control Data Corporation (CDC) as the first technical employee in 1957.

Cray's goal was to create fast scientific computers. At CDC he was responsible for the design of the CDC 1604, 6600, and 7600, a very successful series of large scientific computers. As CDC grew, he found the distractions overwhelming and moved the research and development facilities out of town. During the early stages of the CDC 1604, he was not happy with the operating system, and so he wrote one himself over a weekend. He served as a director for CDC and senior vice president.

Cray realized that the market for large scientific computers had become so small that CDC would discontinue research in this area. Therefore he left to form his own company, Cray Research, with the intention of building the world's highest performance supercomputer. And he did—the CRAY-1. The CRAY-2 and CRAY-3 followed. He also designed, but never built, the CRAY-4.

Breckenridge has this to say about Seymour Cray in his tribute:

> Seymour liked to work with fundamental and simple tools—generally only a piece of paper and a pencil. But he admitted that some of his work required more sophisticated tools. Once, when told that Apple Computer bought a CRAY to simulate their next Apple computer design, Seymour remarked, "Funny, I am using an Apple to simulate the CRAY-3." His selection of people for his projects also reflected fundamentals. When asked why he often hires new graduates to help with early R&D work, he replied, "Because they don't know that what I'm asking them to do is impossible, so they try."[1]

Seymour Cray died in 1996 from injuries suffered in an automobile accident.

---

time slice on the CPU. This procedure continues until the process eventually gets all the time it needs and terminates.

Note that the round-robin algorithm is preemptive. The expiration of a time slice is an arbitrary reason to remove a process from the CPU. This action is represented by the transition from the running state to the ready state.

Suppose the time slice used for a particular round-robin scheduling algorithm was 50 and we used the same set of processes as our previous examples. The Gantt chart results are:

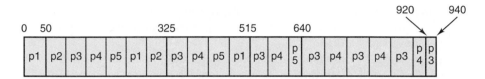

Each process is given a time slice of 50, unless it doesn't need a full slice. For example, process 2 originally needed 75 time units. It was given an initial time slice of 50. When its turn to use the CPU came around again, it needed only 25. Therefore, process 2 terminates and gives up the CPU at time 325.

The average turnaround time for this example is (515 + 325 + 940 + 920 + 640) / 5, or 668. Note that this turnaround time is higher than in the other examples. Does that mean the round-robin algorithm is not as good as the others? No. We can't make such general claims based on one example. We can only say that one algorithm is better than another for that specific set of processes. General analysis of algorithm efficiencies is much more involved.

The round-robin CPU process scheduling algorithm is probably the most widely used. It generally supports all kinds of jobs and is considered the most fair.

Summary

An operating system is part of the system software that manages resources on a computer. It serves as moderator among human users, application software, and the hardware devices in the system.

Multiprogramming is the technique for keeping multiple programs in memory at the same time, contending for time on the CPU. A process is a program in execution. The operating system must perform careful CPU scheduling, memory management, and process management to ensure fair access.

Batch processing organizes jobs into batches that use the same or similar resources. Timesharing allows multiple users to interact with a computer at the same time, creating a virtual machine for each user.

An operating system must manage memory to control and monitor where processes are loaded into main memory. Any memory management technique must define the manner in which it binds a logical address to a physical one. Various strategies have been developed for memory management. The single contiguous approach allows only one program other than the operating system to be in main memory. The partition approach divides memory into several partitions into which processes are loaded. Fixed partitions have a set size, and dynamic partitions are determined by the needs of the processes loaded. Paging divides memory into frames and programs into pages. The pages of a program need not be contiguous in memory. Demand paging allows for only a portion of a program to be in memory at any given time.

An operating system manages a process's life states, which are the stages a program goes through during its execution. The process control block stores the necessary information for any process.

CPU scheduling algorithms determine what process gets priority to use the CPU next. First-come, first-served CPU scheduling gives priority to the earliest arriving job. The shortest-job-next algorithm gives priority to jobs with short running times. Round-robin scheduling rotates the CPU among active processes, giving a little time to each.

ETHICAL ISSUES

Privacy Invasion

Look around. Is someone—or something—monitoring your every move? How confident are you that private information about your life is under your control? Is your privacy protected? Technological advancements have redefined our way of life, and in doing so, have raised issues relating to our right to privacy. Today the foods that you buy, what URLs you visit (see Chapter 16's discussion of cookies), even where you drive, can be tracked, entered into a database, and used by various organizations, often without your knowledge or consent. Many grocery stores, for example, now use shopping cards instead of coupons to offer their customers special savings. When cashiers scan a shopping card, the company gets a detailed digital record of every item the customer purchased along with the customer's name. Critics of this system say that shopping cards compromise the privacy of consumers who, before this technology, were able to save money with coupons and preserve their anonymity.

Privacy includes a right to anonymity as well as a right to hold personal information confidential and a right to solitude. Certain modern technologies are available only with a sacrifice of privacy. Telematics, a recent innovation, are now present in the vehicles of many truck companies and rental car businesses. These devices function as high-tech Global Positioning Systems (GPS), and company representatives can contact drivers over a speaker phone when they steer off a predetermined course. The tracking technology can also monitor a vehicle's speed. Some rental companies use this information to charge their customers for speeding violations without properly informing them. It is not surprising that some people criticize the pervasive nature of this type of technology and are concerned that the government and other organizations are able to gain access to too much personal information.

Spamming, the practice of sending copies of an e-mail message or advertisement to many different newsgroups or people, without regard for whether the subject matter is appropriate, is an invasion of a person's time. Recipients of these e-mails do not solicit the information and do not want their addresses available for such purposes. AOL has filed a number of lawsuits against spammers in an effort to prevent junk mail from infiltrating the mailboxes of AOL members. Recently, spam mail has taken on a new form and appears as text messages on cell phones. An invasive advertising technique, cell phone spamming has been defended as a creative and useful service by those who send it. Most people, however, are unwilling to sanction an action that they feel blatantly violates their privacy. As we move further into the 21st century, we need to be vigilant in defense of personal privacy against incursions by new technologies.

Key Terms

Exercises

1. Distinguish between application software and system software.

2. What is an operating system?

3. a. Name the early PC operating system.
   b. Name the operating systems made famous by Microsoft.
   c. Name the operating system used on Apple machines.
   d. Name an operating system popular with serious programmers.
   e. Name a recent version of the one in (d) now available for PCs.

4. Explain the term *multiprogramming*.

5. The following terms relate to how the operating system manages multiprogramming. Describe the part each plays in this process.
   a. Process
   b. Process management
   c. Memory management
   d. CPU scheduling

6. What constitutes a batch job?

7. Describe the evolution of the concept of batch processing from the human operator in the 1960s and '70s to the operating systems of today.

8. Define *timesharing*.

9. What is the relationship between multiprogramming and timesharing?

10. Why do we say that users in a timesharing system have their own virtual machine?

11. In Chapter 7, we defined a virtual machine as a hypothetical machine designed to illustrate important features of a real machine. In this chapter, we define a virtual machine as the illusion created by a time-

sharing system that each user has a dedicated machine. Relate these two definitions.

12. How does the timesharing concept work?

13. What is a *real-time system*?

14. What is *response time*?

15. What is the relationship between real-time systems and response time?

16. In a multiprogramming environment, many processes may be active. What are the tasks that the OS must accomplish in order to manage the memory requirements of active processes?

17. Distinguish between logical addresses and physical addresses.

18. What is *address binding*?

19. Name three memory-management techniques and give the general approach taken in each.

20. How is address binding done in single contiguous memory management?

21. Distinguish between fixed (static) partitions and dynamic partitions.

22. How is address binding done in a partition system?

23. What are the base register and bounds register, and how are they used?

24. If, in a single, contiguous memory-management system, the program is loaded at address 30215, compute the physical addresses (in decimal) that correspond to the following logical addresses:
    a. 9223
    b. 2302
    c. 7044

25. If, in a fixed-partition memory-management system, the current value of the base register is 42993 and the current value of the bounds register is 2031, compute the physical addresses that correspond to the following logical addresses:
    a. 104
    b. 1755
    c. 3041

26. If, in a dynamic-partition memory management system, the current value of the base register is 42993 and the current value of the bounds register is 2031, compute the physical addresses that correspond to the following logical addresses:
    a. 104
    b. 1755
    c. 3041

Exercises 27 and 28 use the following state of memory.

Operating System
Process 1
Empty 60 blocks
Process 2
Process 3
Empty 52 blocks
Empty 100 blocks

27. If the partitions are fixed and a new job arrives requiring 52 blocks of main memory, show memory after using each of the following partition selection approaches:
    a. first fit
    b. best fit
    c. worst fit

28. If the partitions are dynamic and a new job arrives requiring 52 blocks of main memory, show memory after using each of the following partition selection approaches:

a. first fit

b. best fit

c. worst fit

29. Why shouldn't we use worst-fit partition selection in a fixed-partition memory-management scheme?

30. Distinguish between a page and a frame.

31. How does the page map table keep track of the relationship between a page and a frame?

32. If, in a paged memory-management system, the frame size is 1024 and the following page map table applies to the currently executing process, compute the physical addresses that correspond to the following logical addresses:

a. <1, 501>

b. <0, 85>

c. <3, 1048>

d. <4, 419>

e. <2, 311>

Page	0	1	2	3	4
Frame	7	12	99	1	4

33. What is virtual memory and how does it apply to demand paging?

34. What are the conceptual stages through which a process moves while being managed by the operating system?

35. Describe how a process might move through the various process states. Create specific reasons why this process moves from one state to another.

36. What is a process control block?

37. How is each conceptual stage represented in the OS?

38. What is a context switch?

39. Distinguish between preemptive scheduling and nonpreemptive scheduling.

40. Name and describe three CPU scheduling algorithms.

Use the following table of processes and service time for Exercises 41 through 43.

Process	P1	P2	P3	P4	P5
Service time	120	60	180	50	300

41. Draw a Gantt chart that shows the completion times for each process using first-come, first-served CPU scheduling.

42. Draw a Gantt chart that shows the completion times for each process using shortest-job-next CPU scheduling.

43. Draw a Gantt chart that shows the completion times for each process using round-robin CPU scheduling with a time slice of 60.

44. Given the following state of memory where the partitions are dynamic, show memory after using each of the following partition selection approaches after a new job requiring 66 blocks of main memory.
  a. first fit
  b. best fit
  c. worst fit

Operating system
Process 1
Process 2
Process 3
Empty 300 blocks

45. Distinguish between fixed partitions and dynamic partitions.

❓ Thought Questions

1. In Chapter 5, we said that the control unit was like the stage manager who organized and managed the other parts of the von Neumann machine. The operating system is also like a stage manager, but on a much grander scale. Does this analogy hold or does it break down?

2. The user interface that the OS presents to the user is like a hallway with doors leading off to rooms housing applications programs. To go from one room to another, you have to go back to the hallway. Continue with this analogy. What would files be? What would be analogous to a time slice?

3. Many large grocery stores issue cards to their regular customers. If you have the card when you check out, the cashier scans the card and you get special sale prices. The store also gets information about your shopping habits. Is this an invasion of your privacy? Do you have such a card? Have you ever thought about how much information the store can accumulate about you?

4. Spamming is the Internet equivalent of unsolicited telephone sale's pitches. There are laws now that allow a telephone user to request that his or her name be removed from the solicitor's calling list. Should there be similar laws relating to spamming?

5. Tracking technology can determine that a car has been speeding. Is the use of this technology a good deterrent for speeding and a plus for highway safety, or is it an invasion of basic privacy?

The Operating Systems Layer

11 File Systems and Directories

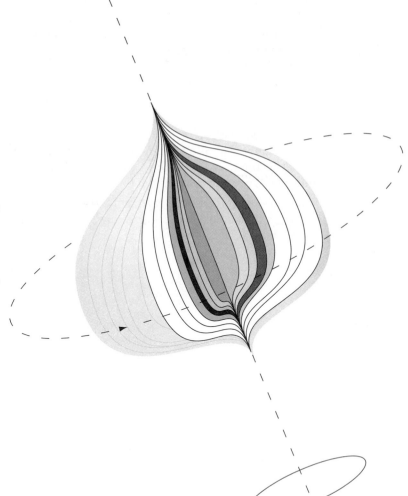

Chapter 11

File Systems
and Directories

The previous chapter examined some of the roles an operating system plays. In particular, it described the management of processes, the CPU, and main memory. Another key resource that the operating system manages is secondary memory, most importantly magnetic disks. The organization of files and directories on disk plays a pivotal role in everyday computing. Like a card file on a desktop, the file system provides a way to access particular information in a well-organized manner. The directory structure organizes files into categories and subcategories. File systems and directory structures are explored in detail in this chapter.

Goals

After studying this chapter, you should be able to:

- describe the purpose of files, file systems, and directories.
- distinguish between text and binary files.
- identify various file types by their extensions.
- explain how file types improve file usage.
- define the basic operations on a file.
- compare and contrast sequential and direct file access.
- discuss the issues related to file protection.
- describe a directory tree.
- create absolute and relative paths for a directory tree.
- describe several disk-scheduling algorithms.

11.1   File Systems

In Chapter 5 we established the differences between main and secondary memory. Recall that main memory is where active programs and data are held while in use. Main memory is volatile, meaning that the information stored on it is lost if electric power is turned off. Secondary memory is nonvolatile—the information stored on it is maintained even when power is not on. Thus we use secondary memory for permanent storage of our information.

The most prevalent secondary storage device is the magnetic disk drive. This includes both hard drives in the computer's main box and floppy disks that are portable and can be moved easily between computers. The basic concepts underlying both types of disks are the same. Other secondary memory devices, such as tape drives, are used primarily for archival purposes. Though many of the concepts that we explore in this chapter apply to all secondary storage devices, it's perhaps easiest to think about a standard disk drive.

We store information on a disk in files, a mechanism for organizing data on an electronic medium. A **file** is a named collection of related data. From the user's point of view, a file is the smallest amount of information that can be written to secondary memory. Organizing everything into files presents a uniform view for information storage. A **file system** is the logical view that an operating system provides so that users can manage information as a collection of files. A file system is often organized by grouping files into **directories**.

> **File**   A named collection of data, used for organizing secondary memory
>
> **File system**   The operating system's logical view of the files it manages
>
> **Directory**   A named group of files

A file is a generic concept. Different types of files are managed in different ways. A file, in general, contains a program (in some form) or data (of one type or another). Some files have a very rigid format; others are more flexible.

A file is a sequence of bits, bytes, lines, or records, depending on how you look at it. Like any data in memory, you have to apply an interpretation to the bits stored in a file before they have meaning. The creator of a file decides how the data in a file is organized, and any users of the file must understand that organization.

Text and Binary Files

Broadly, all files can be classified as either a text file or a binary file. In a **text file** the bytes of data are organized as characters from the ASCII or Unicode character sets. (Character sets are described in Chapter 3.) A **binary file** requires a specific interpretation of the bits based on the information in the file.

The terms *text file* and *binary file* are somewhat misleading. They seem to imply that the information in a text file is not stored as binary data. Ultimately, all information on a computer is stored as binary digits. These terms refer to how those bits are formatted: as chunks of 8 or 16 bits, interpreted as characters, or in some other special format.

Some information lends itself to a character representation, which often makes it easier for a human to read and modify. Though text files contain nothing but characters, those characters can represent a variety of information. For example, an operating system may store much of its data as text files, such as information about user accounts. A program written in a high-level language is stored as a text file, which is sometimes referred to as a *source file*. Any text editor can be used to create, view, and change the contents of a text file, no matter what specific type of information it contains.

For other information types it is more logical and efficient to represent data by defining a specific binary format and interpretation. Only programs set up to interpret that type of data can be used to view or modify it. For example, there are many types of files that store image information: bitmap, GIF, JPEG, and TIFF, to name a few. As we discussed in Chapter 3, though they each store information about an image, they all store that information in different ways. Their internal formats are very specific. A program must be set up to view or modify a specific type of binary file. That's why a program that can handle a GIF image may not be able to handle a TIFF image, or vice versa.

Some files you might assume to be text files actually are not. Consider, for instance, a report that you type in a word processor program and save

Text file A file that contains characters

Binary file A file that contains data in a specific format, requiring a special interpretation of its bits

to disk. The document is actually stored as a binary file because, in addition to the characters that are stored in the document, it also contains information about formatting, styles, borders, fonts, colors and "extras" such as graphics or clip art. Some of the data (the characters themselves) are stored as text, but the additional information requires that each word processing program has its own format for the data in its document files.

File Types

Most files, whether they are in text or binary format, contain a specific type of information. For example, a file may contain a Java program, or a JPEG image, or an MP3 audio clip. Some files contain files created by specific applications, such as a Microsoft Word document or a Visio drawing. The kind of information contained in a document is called the **file type**. Most operating systems recognize a list of specific file types.

A common mechanism for specifying a file type is to indicate the type as part of the name of the file. File names are often separated, usually by a period, into two parts: the main name and the **file extension**. The extension indicates the type of the file. For example, the .java extension in the file name MyProg.java indicates that it is a Java source code program file. The .jpg extension in the file name family.jpg indicates that it is a JPEG image file. Some common file extensions are listed in Figure 11.1.

File types allow the operating system to operate on the file in ways that make sense for that file. They also usually make life easier for the user. The operating system keeps a list of recognized file types and associates each type with a particular kind of application program. In an operating system with a graphical user interface, a particular icon is often associated with a file type as well. When you see a file in a folder, it is shown with the appropriate icon. That makes it easier for the user to identify a file at a glance because now both the name of the file and its icon indicate what type of file it is. When you double-click on the icon to open the program, the operating system starts the program associated with that file type and loads the file.

File type The specific kind of information contained in a file, such as a Java program or a Microsoft Word document

File extension Part of a file name that indicates the file type

Extensions	File type
txt	text data file
mp3, au, wav	audio file
gif, tiff, jpg	image file
doc, wp3	word processing document
java, c, cpp	program source files

Figure 11.1
Some common file types and their extensions

For example, you might like a particular editor that you use when developing a Java program. You can register the .java file extension with the operating system and associate it with that editor. Then whenever you open a file with a .java extension, the operating system runs the appropriate editor. The details of how you associate an extension with an application program depend on the operating system you are using.

Some file extensions are associated with particular programs by default, which you may change if appropriate. In some cases, a file type could be associated with various types of applications, so you have some choice. For example, your system may currently associate the .gif extension with a particular Web browser, so that when you open a GIF image file, it is displayed in that browser window. You may choose to change the association so that when you open a GIF file it is brought into your favorite image editor instead.

Note that a file extension is merely an indication of what the file contains. You can name a file anything you want (as long as you use the characters that the operating system allows for file names). You could give any file a .gif extension, for instance, but that doesn't make it a GIF image file. Changing the extension does not change the data in the file or its internal format. If you attempt to open a misnamed file in a program that expects a particular format, you get errors.

File Operations

There are several operations that you, with the help of the operating system, might do to and with a file:

- Create a file.
- Delete a file.
- Open a file.
- Close a file.
- Read data from a file.
- Write data to a file.
- Reposition the current file pointer in a file.
- Append data to the end of a file.
- Truncate a file (delete its contents).
- Rename a file.
- Copy a file.

Let's examine briefly how each of these operations is accomplished.

The operating system keeps track of secondary memory in two ways. It maintains a table indicating which blocks of memory are free (that is, available for use), and for each directory, it maintains a table that records information about the files in that directory. To create a file, the operating system finds free space in the file system for the file content, puts an entry for the file in the appropriate directory table, and records the name and location of the file. To delete a file, the operating system indicates that the memory space the file was using is now free, and the appropriate entry in the directory table is removed.

Most operating systems require that a file be opened before read and write operations are performed on it. The operating system maintains a small table of all currently open files to avoid having to search for the file in the large file system every time a subsequent operation is performed. To close the file when it is no longer in active use, the operating system removes the entry in the open file table.

At any point in time, an open file has a current file pointer (an address) indicating the place where the next read or write operation should occur. Some systems keep a separate read pointer and a write pointer for a file. Reading a file means that the operating system delivers a copy of the information in the file, starting at the current file pointer. After the read occurs, the file pointer is updated. Writing information to a file records the specified information to the file space at the location indicated by the current file pointer, and then the file pointer is updated. Often an operating system allows a file to be open for reading or writing, but not both at the same time.

The current file pointer for an open file might be repositioned to another location in the file to prepare for the next read or write operation. Appending information to the end of a file requires that the file pointer be positioned to the end of a file; then the appropriate data is written.

It is sometimes useful to "erase" the information in a file. Truncating a file means deleting the contents of the file without removing the administrative entries in the file tables. This operation is provided to avoid the need to delete a file and then recreate it. Sometimes the truncating operation is sophisticated enough to erase part of a file, from the current file pointer to the end of the file.

An operating system also provides an operation to change the name of a file, which is called renaming the file. It also provides the ability to create a complete copy of the contents of a file, giving the copy a new name.

File Access

There are various ways in which the information in a file can be accessed. Some operating systems provide only one type of file access, while others provide a choice. The type of access available for a given file is established when the file is created.

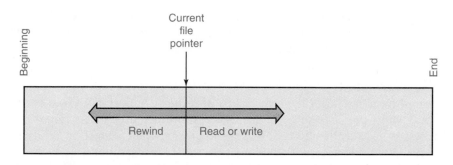

Figure 11.2
Sequential file access

Let's examine the two primary access techniques: sequential access and direct access. The differences between these two techniques are analogous to the differences between the sequential nature of magnetic tape and the direct access of a magnetic disk, as discussed in Chapter 5. However, both types of files can be stored on either type of medium. File access techniques define the ways that the current file pointer can be repositioned. They are independent of the physical restrictions of the devices on which the file is stored.

The most common access technique, and the simplest to implement, is **sequential access**, which views the file as a linear structure. It requires that the information in the file be processed in order. Read and write operations move the current file pointer according to the amount of data that is read or written. Some systems allow the file pointer to be reset to the beginning of the file and/or to skip forwards or backwards a certain number of records. See Figure 11.2.

Files with **direct access** are conceptually divided into numbered logical records. Direct access allows the user to set the file pointer to any particular record by specifying the record number. Therefore, the user can read and write records in any particular order desired, as shown in Figure 11.3.

Sequential file access The technique in which data in a file is accessed in a linear fashion

Direct file access The technique in which data in a file is accessed directly, by specifying logical record numbers

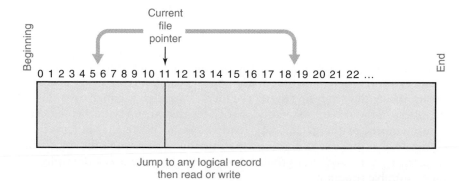

Jump to any logical record
then read or write

Figure 11.3
Direct file access

Direct access files are more complicated to implement, but are helpful in situations where specific portions of large data stores must be available quickly, such as in a database.

File Protection

In multiuser systems, file protection is of primary importance. That is, we don't want one user to be able to access another user's files unless the access is specifically allowed. It is the operating system's responsibility to ensure valid file access. Different operating systems administer their file protection in different ways. In any case, a file protection mechanism determines who can use a file and for what general purpose.

For example, a file's protection settings in the Unix operating system is divided into three categories: Owner, Group, and World. Under each category you can determine if the file can be read, written, and/or executed. Under this mechanism, if you can write to a file, you can also delete the file.

Each file is "owned" by a particular user, often the creator of the file. The Owner usually has the strongest permissions regarding the file. A file may have a group name associated with it. A group is simply a list of users. The Group permissions apply to all users in the associated group. You may do this, for instance, for all users who are working on a particular project. Finally, World permissions apply to anyone who has access to the system. Because these permissions give access to the largest number of users, they are usually the most restricted.

Using this technique, the permissions on a file can be shown in a 3×3 grid:

	Read	Write/Delete	Execute
Owner	Yes	Yes	No
Group	Yes	No	No
World	No	No	No

Suppose that this grid represents the permissions on a data file used in project Alpha. The owner of the file (perhaps the manager of the project) may read from or write to the file. Suppose also that the owner sets up a group (using the operating system) called TeamAlpha, which contains all members of the project team, and associates that group with this data file. The members of the group may read the data in the file, but may not change it. No one else is given any permission to access the file. Note that no user is given execution privileges to the file because it is a data file, not an executable program.

Other operating systems break down their protection schemes in different ways, but the goal is the same: to control access to protect against deliberate attempts to gain inappropriate access, as well as minimize inadvertent problems caused by well-intentioned but hazardous users.

11.2   Directories

We established early in this chapter that a directory is a named collection of files. It is a way to group files so that you can organize them in a logical manner. For example, you may group all of your papers and notes for a particular class into a directory created for that class. The operating system must carefully keep track of directories and the files they contain.

A directory, in most operating systems, is represented as a file. The directory file contains data about the other files in the directory. For any given file, the directory contains the file name, the file type, the address on disk where the file is stored, and the current size of the file. The directory also contains information about the protections set up for the file. It may also contain information about when the file was created and when it was last modified.

The internal structure of a directory file could be set up in a variety of ways, and we won't explore those details here. However, once it is set up, it must be able to support the common operations that are performed on directory files. For instance, the user must be able to list all of the files in the directory. Other common operations are create, delete, and rename files within a directory. Furthermore, the directory is commonly searched to see if a particular file is in the directory.

Another key issue when it comes to directory management is the need to reflect the relationships among directories, as discussed in the next section.

Directory Trees

A directory of files can be contained within another directory. The directory containing another is usually called the *parent directory*, and the one inside is called a *subdirectory*. You can set up such nested directories as often as needed to help organize the file system. One directory can contain many subdirectories. Furthermore, subdirectories can contain their own subdirectories, creating a hierarchy structure. Therefore, a file system is often viewed as a **directory tree**, showing directories and files within other directories. The directory at the highest level is called the **root directory**.

For example, consider the directory tree shown in Figure 11.4. This tree represents a very small part of a file system that might be found on a

Directory tree   A structure showing the nested directory organization of the file system

Root directory   The topmost directory, in which all others are contained

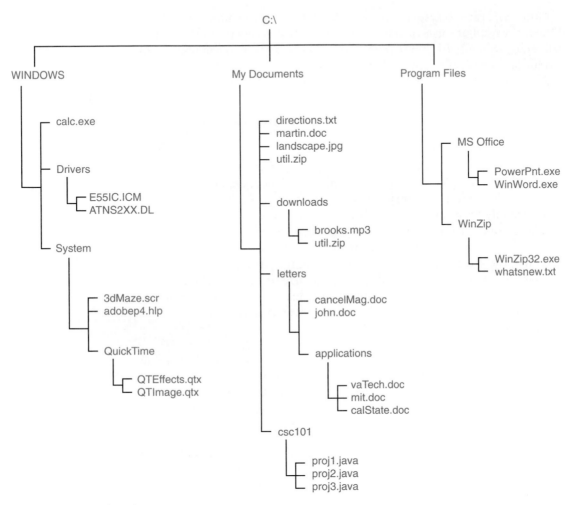

Figure 11.4   A Windows directory tree

computer using some flavor of the Microsoft Windows operating system. The root of the directory system is referred to using the drive letter C: followed by the backslash (\ ).

In this directory tree, the root directory contains three subdirectories: WINDOWS, My Documents, and Program Files. Within the WINDOWS directory, there is a file called calc.exe as well as two other subdirectories (Drivers and System). Those directories contain other files and subdirectories. Keep in mind that all of these directories in a real system would typically contain many more subdirectories and files.

Personal computers often use an analogy of folders to represent the directory structure, which promotes the idea of containment (folders inside other folders, with some folders ultimately containing documents or other data). The icon used to show a directory in the graphical interface of an operating system is often a graphic of a manila file folder such as the kind you would use in a physical file drawer.

Note that there are two files with the name util.zip in Figure 11.4 (in the My Documents directory, and in its subdirectory called downloads). The nested directory structure allows for multiple files to have the same name. All the files in any one directory must have unique names, but files in different directories or subdirectories can have the same name. These files may or may not contain the same data; all we know is that they have the same name.

At any point in time, you can be thought of as working in a particular location (that is, a particular subdirectory) of the file system. This subdirectory is referred to as the current **working directory**. As you "move" around in the file system, the current working directory changes.

> **Working directory** The currently active subdirectory

The directory tree shown in Figure 11.5 is representative of one from a Unix file system. Compare and contrast it to the one in Figure 11.4. They both show the same concepts of subdirectory containment. However, the naming conventions for files and directories are different. Unix was developed as a programming and system level environment, and therefore uses much more abbreviated and cryptic names for directories and files. Also, note that in a Unix environment, the root is designated using a forward slash (/).

Path Names

How do we specify one particular file or subdirectory? Well, there are several ways to do it.

If you are working in a graphical interface to the operating system, you can double-click with your mouse to open a directory and see its contents. The active directory window shows the contents of the current working directory. You can continue "moving" through the file system using mouse clicks, changing the current working directory, until you find the desired file or directory. To move up the directory structure, there is usually an icon on the window bar or a pop-up menu option that you can use to move to the parent directory.

Operating systems usually also provide a nongraphical (text-based) interface to the operating system. Therefore, we also have to be able to specify file locations using text. This is very important for system instructions stored in operating system batch command files. Commands such as cd (which stands for change directory) can be used in text mode to change the current working directory.

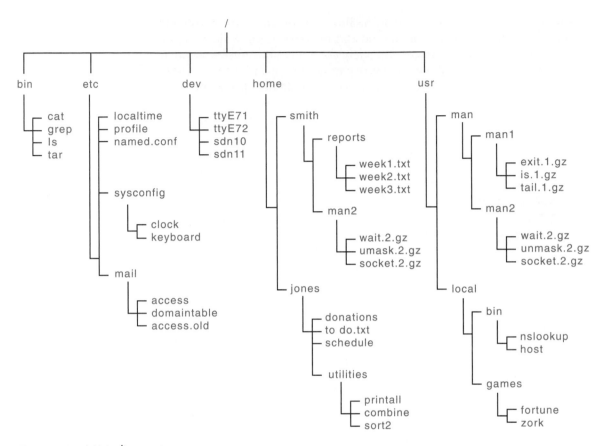

Figure 11.5   A Unix directory tree

To indicate a particular file using text, we specify that file's **path**, which is the series of directories through which you must go to find the file. A path may be absolute or relative. An **absolute path** name begins at the root and specifies each step down the tree until it reaches the desired file or directory. A **relative path** name begins from the current working directory.

Let's look at examples of each type of path. The following are absolute path names based on the directory tree shown in Figure 11.4:

```
C:\Program Files\MS Office\WinWord.exe
C:\My Documents\letters\applications\vaTech.doc
C:\Windows\System\QuickTime
```

They each begin at the root and proceed down the directory structure. Each subdirectory is separated by the backslash (\ ). Note that a path can specify a specific document (as it does in the first two examples) or an entire subdirectory (as it does in the third example).

Absolute paths in a Unix system work the same way, except that the character used to separate subdirectories is the forward slash (/). Here are some examples of absolute path names that correspond to the directory tree in Figure 11.5:

```
/bin/tar
/etc/sysconfig/clock
/usr/local/games/fortune
/home/smith/reports/week1.txt
```

Relative paths are based on the current working directory. That is, they are relative to your current position (hence the name). Suppose the current working directory is `C:\My Documents\letters` (from Figure 11.4). Then the following relative path names could be used:

```
cancelMag.doc
applications\calState.doc
```

The first example just specifies the name of the file, which can be found in the current working directory. The second example specifies a file in the applications subdirectory. By definition, the first part of any valid relative path is located in the working directory.

Sometimes when using relative path we need to work our way back up the tree. Note that this was not an issue when using absolute paths. In most operating systems, two dots (..) are used to specify the parent directory (a single dot is used to specify the current working directory). Therefore, if the working directory is `C:\My Documents\letters`, the following are also valid relative paths:

```
..\landscape.jpg
..\csc101\proj2.java
..\..\WINDOWS\Drivers\E55IC.ICM
..\..\Program Files\WinZip
```

Unix systems work essentially the same way. Using the directory tree in Figure 11.5, and assuming that the current working directory is `/home/jones`, the following are valid relative paths:

```
utilities/combine
../smith/reports
../../dev/ttyE71
../../usr/man/man1/ls.1.gz
```

John Backus

John Backus was an aimless young man who pulled his act together and won the Turing Award. Born in 1924 into a wealthy Philadelphia family, he attended the prestigious Hill School in Pottstown, Pennsylvania, where he repeatedly flunked out and had to attend summer school in order to continue. Finally graduating in 1942, he enrolled in and flunked out of the University of Virginia.

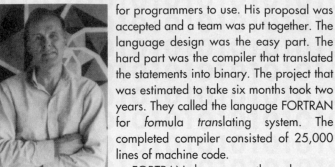

In 1943 Backus joined the Army. After his first aptitude test the Army enrolled him in a pre-engineering program at the University of Pittsburgh. Another aptitude test sent him to Havorford College to study medicine. As part of the premed program, he worked in a neurosurgery ward at an Atlantic City hospital. While there he was diagnosed with a brain tumor and a plate was installed in his head. After nine months of medical school, he decided that medicine wasn't for him, after all.

He was at loose ends in 1946, after leaving the army and having an additional operation to replace the plate in his head. When he couldn't find the hi-fi set he wanted, he enrolled in a radio technicians' school, where he said that he found his first good teacher. His work with this teacher uncovered his latent interest in mathematics. In 1949, he graduated from Columbia University with a degree in mathematics.

As the result of a casual remark to a guide while touring the IBM Computer Center on Madison Avenue, Backus got a job working with IBM's Selective Sequence Electronic Calculator. In 1953 he wrote a memo outlining the design of a new programming language for IBM's new 704 computer. The 704 had floating point hardware and an index register, which made it faster, but the software available didn't make use of these new features. He wanted to design not only a better language, but one that would be easier for programmers to use. His proposal was accepted and a team was put together. The language design was the easy part. The hard part was the compiler that translated the statements into binary. The project that was estimated to take six months took two years. They called the language FORTRAN for *formula translating* system. The completed compiler consisted of 25,000 lines of machine code.

FORTRAN has gone through many transformations during the years but is still the most popular language for scientists and engineers today.

Backus went on to develop a notation called the Backus-Naur Form, which is used to describe formally grammatical rules for high-level languages. Undoubtedly his interest in this subject was born when trying to describe the rules of FORTRAN in English. His notation was originally called Backus Normal Form and introduced during the specification of ALGOL 60. Peter Naur, a Danish scientist on the ALGOL 60 committee, made some modifications to the notation, and so it became known as Backus-Naur Form.

In the 1970s Backus worked on finding better programming methods. Toward this end, he developed the functional language FP. He is unique in that he developed languages in two paradigms before the word *paradigm* was even used in relation to programming languages. FORTRAN is an imperative language; FP is a functional language.

The citation for John Backus' Turing Award reads:

For profound, influential, and lasting contributions to the design of practical high-level programming systems, notably through his work on FORTRAN, and for seminal publication of formal procedures for the specification of programming languages.

Most operating systems allow the user to specify a set of paths that are searched (in a specific order) to help resolve references to executable programs. Often that set of paths is specified using an operating system variable called PATH, which holds a string that contains several absolute paths. Suppose, for instance, that user jones (from Figure 11.5) has a set of utility programs that he uses from time to time. They are stored in the directory /home/jones/utilities. When that path is added to the PATH variable, it becomes a standard location used to find programs that jones attempts to execute. Therefore, no matter what the current working directory is, when jones executes the printall program (just the name by itself), it is found in his utilities directory.

11.3   Disk Scheduling

The most important hardware device used as secondary memory is the magnetic disk drive. File systems stored on these drives must be accessed in an efficient manner. It turns out that transferring data to and from secondary memory is the worst bottleneck in a general computer system.

Recall from Chapter 10 the discussion that the speed of the CPU and the speed of main memory are much faster than the speed of data transfer to and from secondary memory such as a magnetic disk. That's why a process that must perform I/O to disk is made to wait while that information is transferred, to give another process a chance to use the CPU.

Because secondary I/O is the slowest aspect of a general computer system, the techniques for accessing information on a disk drive are of crucial importance to our discussion of file systems. As a computer deals with multiple processes over a period of time, a list of requests to access the disk builds up. The technique that the operating system uses to determine which requests to satisfy first is called **disk scheduling**. We examine several specific disk-scheduling algorithms in this section.

Disk scheduling The act of deciding which outstanding requests for disk I/O to satisfy first

Recall from Chapter 5 that a magnetic disk drive is organized as a stack of platters, where each platter is divided into tracks, and each track into sectors. The set of corresponding tracks on all platters is called a cylinder. Figure 11.6 reprints the figure of a disk drive used in Chapter 5 to remind you of this organization.

Of primary importance to us in this discussion is the fact that the set of read/write heads hovers over a particular cylinder along all platters at any given point in time. Remember, the *seek time* is the time it takes for the heads to reach the appropriate cylinder. The *latency* is the additional time it takes the platter to rotate into the proper position so that the information can be read or written. Seek time is the more restrictive of these two, and therefore is the primary issue dealt with by the disk-scheduling algorithms.

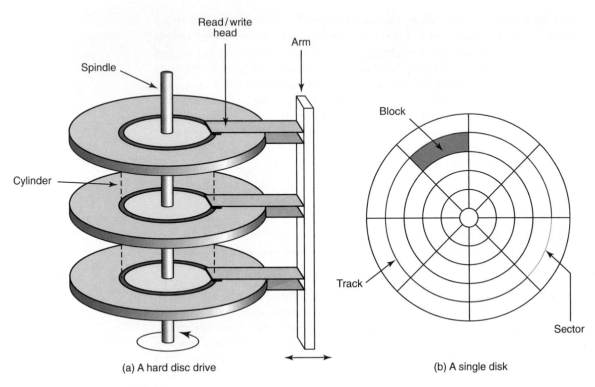

Figure 11.6   A magnetic disk drive

At any point in time, a disk drive may have a set of outstanding requests that must be satisfied. For now, we consider only the cylinder (the parallel concentric circles) to which the requests refer. A disk may have thousands of cylinders. To keep things simple, let's also assume a range of 100 cylinders. Suppose at a particular time the following cylinder requests have been made, in this order:

49, 91, 22, 61, 7, 62, 33, 35

Suppose also, that the read/write heads are currently at cylinder 26. The question is now: To which cylinder should the disk heads move next? Different algorithms produce different answers to that question.

First-Come, First-Served Disk Scheduling
In Chapter 10 we examined a CPU scheduling algorithm called *first-come, first-served (FCFS)*. An analogous algorithm can be used for disk scheduling. It is one of the easiest to implement, though not usually the most efficient.

In FCFS, we process the requests in the order they arrive, without regard to the current position of the heads. Therefore, under a FCFS algorithm, the heads move from cylinder 26 (its current position) to cylinder 49. After the request for cylinder 49 is satisfied (that is, the information is read or written), the heads move from 49 to 91. After processing the request at 91, the heads move to cylinder 22. Processing continues like this, in the order that the requests were received.

Note that at one point the heads move from cylinder 91 all the way back to cylinder 22, during which they pass over several cylinders whose requests are currently pending.

Shortest-Seek-Time-First Disk Scheduling

The *shortest-seek-time-first (SSTF)* disk-scheduling algorithm moves the heads the minimum amount it can to satisfy any pending request. This approach could potentially result in the heads changing directions after each request is satisfied.

Let's process our hypothetical situation using this algorithm. From our starting point at cylinder 26, the closest cylinder among all pending requests is 22. So, ignoring the order in which the requests came, the heads are moved to cylinder 22 to satisfy that request. From 22, the closest request is for cylinder 33, so the heads move there. The closest unsatisfied request to 33 is at cylinder 35. The distance to cylinder 49 is now the smallest, so the heads move there next. Continuing that approach, the rest of the cylinders are visited in the following order: 49, 61, 62, 91, and finally 7.

This approach does not guarantee the smallest overall head movement, but it is generally an improvement over the FCFS algorithm. However, a major problem can arise with this approach. Suppose requests for cylinders continue to build up while existing ones are being satisfied. And suppose those new requests are always closer to the current position than an earlier request. It is theoretically possible that the early request never gets processed because requests keep arriving that take priority. This phenomenon is called *starvation*. First-come, first-served disk scheduling cannot suffer from starvation.

SCAN Disk Scheduling

A classic example of algorithm analysis in computing comes from the way an elevator is designed to visit floors that have people waiting. In general, an elevator moves from one extreme to the other (say, the top of the building to the bottom), servicing requests as appropriate. Then it travels from the bottom to the top, servicing those requests.

The *SCAN* disk-scheduling algorithm works in a similar way, except instead of moving up and down, the read/write heads move in toward the spindle, then out toward the platter edge, then back toward the spindle, and so forth.

Let's perform this algorithm on our set of requests. Unlike the other approaches, though, we need to decide which way the heads are moving initially. Let's assume they are moving toward the lower cylinder values (and are currently at cylinder 26).

As the read/write heads move from cylinder 26 toward cylinder 1, they satisfy the requests at cylinders 22 and 7 (in that order). After reaching cylinder 1, the heads reverse direction and move all the way out to the other extreme. Along the way, they satisfy the following requests, in order: 33, 35, 49, 61, 62, and 91.

Note that new requests are not given any special treatment. They may or may not be serviced before earlier requests. It depends on the current location of the heads and direction in which they are moving. If the new request arrives just before the heads reach that cylinder, it is processed right away. If it arrives just after the heads move past that cylinder, it must wait for the heads to return. There is no chance for starvation because each cylinder is processed in turn.

Some variations on this algorithm can improve performance in various ways. Note that a request at the edge of the platter may have to wait for the heads to move almost all the way to the spindle and all the way back. To improve the average wait time, the *Circular SCAN* algorithm treats the disk as if it were a ring and not a disk. That is, when it reaches one extreme, the heads return all the way to the other extreme without processing requests.

Another variation is to minimize the extreme movements at the spindle and at the edge of the platter. Instead of going to the edge, the heads only move as far out (or in) as the outermost (or innermost) request. Before moving onto the next request, the list of pending requests is examined to see whether movement in the current direction is warranted. This variation is referred to as the *LOOK* disk-scheduling algorithm, because it looks ahead to see whether the heads should continue in the current direction.

Summary

A file system defines the way our secondary memory is organized. A file is a named collection of data with a particular internal structure. Text files are organized as a stream of characters, and binary files have a particular format that is meaningful only to applications set up to handle that format.

File types are often indicated by the file extension of the file name. The operating system has a list of recognized file types so that it may open them in the correct kind of application and display the appropriate icons in the graphical interface. The file extension can be associated with any particular kind of application that the user chooses.

The operations performed on files include creating, deleting, opening, and closing files. Of course, they must be able to be read from and written to. The operating system provides mechanisms to accomplish the various file operations. In a multi-user system, the operating system must also provide file protection to ensure the proper access.

Directories are used to organize files on disk. They can be nested to form hierarchical tree structures. Path names that specify the location of a particular file or directory can be absolute, originating at the root of the directory tree, or relative, originating at the current working directory.

Disk-scheduling algorithms determine the order in which pending disk requests are processed. First-come, first-served disk scheduling takes all requests in order, but is not very efficient. Shortest-seek-time-first disk scheduling is more efficient, but could suffer from starvation. SCAN disk scheduling employs the same strategy as an elevator, sweeping from one end of the disk to the other.

ETHICAL ISSUES

Computer Viruses and Denial of Service

Receiving a love letter in the spring of 2000 left most romantics with intact hearts but damaged computers. The "Love Bug" computer virus, one of the worst infections to date, caused an estimated 10 billion dollars worth of damage as it ravaged through computer systems in 20 countries. The seemingly innocent e-mail entitled "ILOVEYOU" with an attachment called "LOVELETTER" landed in the mailboxes of many unsuspecting users who opened the attachment and thereby released the virus into their computer system. Fittingly, this type of computer virus is termed a "Trojan Horse." As in the legend of Troy, when Odysseus secretly led Greek soldiers into Troy by hiding them in a wooden horse that the Trojans believed was a gift, these computer viruses appear harmless but wreak havoc.

When executed, a virus sweeps through files, modifying or erasing them; it usually also sends itself to the e-mail addresses it accesses. Disguised as desirable downloads like games or screensavers, Trojan Horse viruses can spread rapidly, replicate, and cause significant damage across the globe. Since 1981 when the first wave of computer viruses entered the public sphere and attacked Apple II operating systems, computer viruses have threatened the integrity of computer systems.

Denial of Service (DoS) attacks are not viruses but are a method hackers use to deprive the user or organization of services. DoS attacks usually just flood the server's resources, making the system unusable. Society views these computer viruses as serious offenses, and people who launch DoS attacks face federal criminal charges. In the 2000 attack on Yahoo, for example, the server was flooded with requests that lacked verifiable return addresses. When the server could not confirm the fake addresses it waited for a few moments; then when it finally denied the request, it was loaded with more requests that had fake return addresses—which tied up the server indefinitely. A DoS attack uses the inherent limitations of networking to its advantage, and, in this case, it successfully brought the site down.

The reality of these attacks highlights the need to reevaluate security for both personal computers and the Internet. Scanning for viruses, taking proper precautions when downloading material, and investigating attachments before opening them are useful ways to protect your computer. Internet Service Providers (ISPs) are often proactive in their attempt to prevent viruses and DoS attacks and install firewalls that foster security. Although no system is impenetrable, steps can be taken to improve the security of computer systems and networks.

Key Terms

Absolute path pg. 362

Binary file pg. 353

Direct file access pg. 357

Directory pg. 352

Directory tree pg. 359

Disk scheduling pg. 365

File pg. 352

File extension pg. 354

File System pg. 352

File type pg. 354

Path pg. 362

Relative path pg. 362

Root directory pg. 359

Sequential file access pg. 357

Text file pg. 353

Working directory pg. 361

Exercises

1. What is a file?
2. Distinguish between a file and a directory.
3. Distinguish between a file and a file system.
4. Why is a file a generic concept and not a technical one?
5. Name and describe the two basic classifications of files.

6. Why is the term binary file a misnomer?

7. Distinguish between a file type and a file extension.

8. What would happen if you give the name "myFile.jpg" to a text file?

9. How can an operating system make use of the file types that it recognizes?

10. How does an operating system keep track of secondary memory?

11. What does it mean to open and close a file?

12. What does it mean to truncate a file?

13. Compare and contrast sequential and direct file access.

14. File access is independent of any physical medium.
    a. How could you implement sequential access on a disk?
    b. How could you implement direct access on a magnetic tape?

15. What is a file protection mechanism?

16. How does Unix implement file protection?

17. Given the following file permission, answer these questions.

	Read	Write/Delete	Execute
Owner	Yes	Yes	Yes
Group	Yes	Yes	No
World	Yes	No	No

a. Who can read the file?
b. Who can write or delete the file?
c. Who can execute the file?
d. What do you know about the content of the file?

18. What is the minimum amount of information a directory must contain about each file?

19. How do most operating systems represent a directory?

20. Answer the following questions about directories.
    a. A directory that contains another directory is called what?
    b. A directory contained within another directory is called what?
    c. The directory that is not contained in any other directory is called what?
    d. The structure showing the nested directory organization is called what?
    e. Relate the structure in (d) to the binary tree data structure examined in Chapter 9.

21. What is the directory called in which you are working at any one moment?

22. What is a path?

23. Distinguish between an absolute path and a relative path.

24. Show the absolute path to each of the following files or directories using the directory tree shown in Figure 11.4:
    a. QTEffects.qtx
    b. brooks.mp3
    c. Program Files
    d. 3dMaze.scr
    e. PowerPnt.exe

25. Show the absolute path to each of the following files or directories using the directory tree shown in Figure 11.5.
    a. tar
    b. access.old
    c. named.conf
    d. smith
    e. week3.txt
    f. printall

26. Assuming the current working directory is C:\WINDOWS\System, give the relative path name to the following files or directories using the directory tree shown in Figure 11.4.
    a. QTImage.qtx
    b. calc.exe
    c. letters
    d. proj3.java
    e. adobep4.hlp
    f. WinWord.exe

27. Show the relative path to each of the following files or directories using the directory tree shown in Figure 11.5.
    a. localtime when the working directory is the root directory
    b. localtime when the working directory is etc
    c. printall when the working directory is utilities
    d. week1.txt when the working directory is man2

28. What is the worst bottleneck in a computer system?

29. Why is disk scheduling concerned more with cylinders than with tracks and sectors?

30. Name and describe three disk-scheduling algorithms.

Use the following list of cylinder requests in Exercises 31 through 33. They are listed in the order in which they were received.

40, 12, 22, 66, 67, 33, 80

31. List the order in which these requests are handled if the FCFS algorithm is used. Assume that the disk is positioned at cylinder 50.

32. List the order in which these requests are handled if the SSTF algorithm is used. Assume that the disk is positioned at cylinder 50.

33. List the order in which these requests are handled if the SCAN algorithm is used. Assume that the disk is positioned at cylinder 50 and the read/write heads are moving toward the higher cylinder numbers.

34. Explain the concept of starvation.

? Thought Questions

1. The concept of a file permeates computing. Would the computer be useful if there were no secondary memory on which to store files?

2. The disk-scheduling algorithms examined in this chapter sound familiar. In what other context have we discussed similar algorithms? How are these similar and how are the different?

3. Are there any analogies between files and directories and file folders and filing cabinets? Clearly the name "file" came from this concept. Where does this analogy hold true and where does it not?

4. Both viruses and denial of services can cause great inconvenience at the least and usually serious monetary damage. How are these problems similar and how are they different. Is one more serious than the other?

5. Have you ever been affected by a virus attack? How much time and/or data did you lose? Do you have a firewall installed in your computer system?

6. Have you ever tried to reach a Web site that was under attack? How many times did you try to access the site?

7. How many times have you seen an article in the paper or on the news about either a DoS or virus in the last week? Month? Year?

The Applications Layer

12 Information Systems

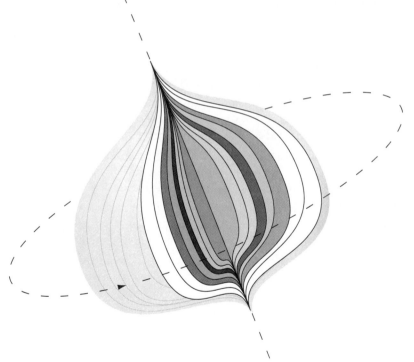

Chapter 12

Information Systems

Most people interact with computers at the application level. That is, even if a person doesn't know anything about the details of the other underlying levels of computing, the chances are that he or she has used application software. Our goal at this level is to give you an appreciation for how various application systems work. Application software can be subdivided in various ways. In this chapter we focus on general information systems. In Chapter 13 we discuss applications in the realm of artificial intelligence, and in Chapter 14 we focus on simulations, computer-aided design, and embedded systems.

Computers exist to manage and analyze data. Today this affects almost all aspects of our lives. We use general information systems to manage everything from sports statistics to payroll data. Cash registers and ATMs have large information systems backing them up. In this chapter we examine general-purpose software, particularly spreadsheets and database management systems; these help us organize and analyze the huge amounts of data with which we must deal.

Goals

After studying this chapter, you should be able to:

- define the role of general information systems.
- explain how spreadsheets are organized.
- create spreadsheets for basic analysis of data.
- define appropriate spreadsheet formulas using built-in functions.
- design spreadsheets to be flexible and extensible.
- describe the elements of a database management system.
- describe the organization of a relational database.
- establish relationships among elements in a database.
- write basic SQL statements.
- describe an entity-relationship diagram.

12.1   Managing Information

At various points in this text we've defined *information* as raw facts, and *data* as information that has been organized in a convenient way for a computer to use. An **information system** can be generally defined as software that helps us organize and analyze data.

Any particular application program manages data, and some programs manage data in particular ways using particular structures. Other specialized applications use specific techniques that are geared toward the type of problems they are trying to solve. For example, as we discuss in the next chapter, there are various ways of organizing data to support the analysis that typically occurs in the computing field of artificial intelligence.

Most situations, however, are more general. There are innumerable situations that don't require special consideration. We simply have data to manage and relationships among that data to capture. These situations don't necessarily require special organization or processing. What they do require, however, are flexible application software tools that allow the user to dictate and manage the organization of data, and that have basic processing capabilities to analyze the data in various ways.

Two of the most popular general application information systems are *electronic spreadsheets* and *database management systems*. A spreadsheet is a convenient tool for basic data analysis based on extensible formulas that define relationships among the data. Database management systems are geared toward large amounts of data that are often searched and organized into appropriate subsections.

> **Information system**
> Software that helps the user organize and analyze data

Whole books have been written about spreadsheets and how they are set up and used. The same can be said for database management systems. Our goal for this chapter is not to exhaustively explore either of these, but rather introduce the usefulness and versatility of both. After this discussion you should be able to create basic versions of either type of system, and you will have a foundation on which to explore them in more detail.

12.2 Spreadsheets

There are a variety of spreadsheet programs available today. You may already have some experience with spreadsheets, though we don't assume any background knowledge in this discussion. Each spreadsheet program has its own particular nuances regarding its abilities and syntax, but there is a common set of concepts that all spreadsheets embrace. Our discussion in this chapter focuses on these common concepts. The specific examples that we explore are consistent with the syntax and functionality of the Microsoft Excel spreadsheet program.

A **spreadsheet** is a software application that allows the user to organize and analyze data using a grid of labeled **cells**. A cell can contain data or a formula that is used to calculate a value. Data stored in a cell can be text, numbers, or "special" data such as dates.

As shown in Figure 12.1, spreadsheet cells are referenced by their row and column designation, usually using letters to specify the column and numbers to specify the row. Thus we refer to cells such as A1, C7, and G45. After the 26th column, spreadsheets begin to use two letters for the column designation, so some cells have designations such as AA19. There is usually some reasonably large maximum number of rows in a spreadsheet, such as 256. Furthermore, in most spreadsheet programs multiple sheets can be combined into one large interacting system.

Spreadsheets are useful in many situations, and are often designed to manage thousands of data values and calculations. Let's look at a small

> **Spreadsheet** A program that allows the user to organize and analyze data using a grid of cells
>
> **Cell** An element of a spreadsheet that can contain data or a formula

	A	B	C	D
1				
2				
3				
4				
5				

Figure 12.1
A spreadsheet, made up of a grid of labeled cells

	A	B	C	D	E	F	G	H	
1									
2				Tutor					
3			Hal	Amy	Frank	Total	Avg		
4		1	12	10	13	35	11.67		
5		2	14	16	16	46	15.33		
6	Week	3	10	18	13	41	13.67		
7		4	8	21	18	47	15.67		
8		5	15	18	12	45	15.00		
9		Total	59	83	72	214	71.33		
10		Avg	11.80	16.60	14.40	42.80	14.27		
11									
12									

Figure 12.2
A spreadsheet containing
data and computations

example that demonstrates fundamental spreadsheet principles. Suppose we have collected data on the number of students that came to get help from a set of tutors over a period of several weeks. Let's say we've kept track of how many students went to each of three tutors (Hal, Amy, and Frank) each week for a period of five weeks. Now we want to perform some basic analysis on that data. We might end up with the spreadsheet shown in Figure 12.2.

This spreadsheet contains, among other things, the raw data to be analyzed. Cell C4, for instance, contains the number of students that Hal tutored in week 1. The column of data running from C4 to C8 contains the number of students tutored by Hal in each of the five weeks during which data was collected. Likewise, the data for Amy is stored in cells D4 through D8 and the data for Frank is stored in cells E4 through E8. This same data can be thought of in terms of the row they're in as well. Each row shows the number of students helped by each tutor in any given week.

In cells C9, D9, and E9, the spreadsheet computes and displays the total number of students helped by each tutor over all five weeks. In cells C10, D10, and E10, the spreadsheet also computes and displays the average number of students helped by each tutor each week. Likewise, the total number of students helped each week (by all tutors) is shown in the column of cells running from F4 to F8. The average number of students helped per week is shown in cells G4 to G8.

In addition to the totals and averages per tutor and per week, the spreadsheet also calculates some other overall statistics. Cell F9 shows the total number of students helped by all tutors in all weeks. The average per week (for all tutors) is shown in cell F10 and the average per tutor (for all weeks) is shown in cell G9. Finally, the average number of students helped by any tutor in any week is shown in cell G10.

The data stored in columns A and B and in rows 2 and 3 are simply used as labels to indicate what the values in the rest of the spreadsheet represent. These labels are for human readability only and do not contribute to the calculations.

Note that the labels and some of the values in the spreadsheet in Figure 12.2 are shown in different colors. Most spreadsheet programs allow the user to control the look and format of the data in specific cells in various ways. The user can specify the font, style, and color of the data as well as the alignment of the data within the cell (such as centered or left justified). In the case of real numeric values, such as the averages computed in this example, the user can specify how many decimal places should be displayed. In most spreadsheet programs, the user can also dictate whether the grid lines for each cell are displayed or not (in this example they are all displayed) and what the background color or pattern of a cell should be. All of these user preferences are specified using menu options or buttons in the spreadsheet application software.

Spreadsheet Formulas

In our tutor spreadsheet, we performed several calculations that give us insight as to the overall situation regarding tutor support. And it turns out that it is relatively easy to set up these calculations. You might say that it wouldn't take long to sit down with these numbers and produce the same statistics with a calculator, and you would be right. However, the beauty of a spreadsheet is that it is both easily modified and easily expanded.

If we've set up the spreadsheet correctly, we could add or remove tutors, add additional weeks of data, or change any of the data we have already stored and the corresponding calculations would automatically be updated. So although we set up the tutor example to use the data of three tutors, the same spreadsheet could handle hundreds of tutors! Instead of five weeks of data, we could just as easily process a year's worth.

The power of spreadsheets comes from the formulas that we can create and store in cells. All of the totals and averages in the example in Figure 12.2 are computed using formulas. When a formula is stored in a cell, the result of the formula is displayed in the cell. Therefore, when looking at the values in a spreadsheet, it is sometimes challenging to tell if the data shown in a particular cell was entered directly or if it has been computed by an underlying formula.

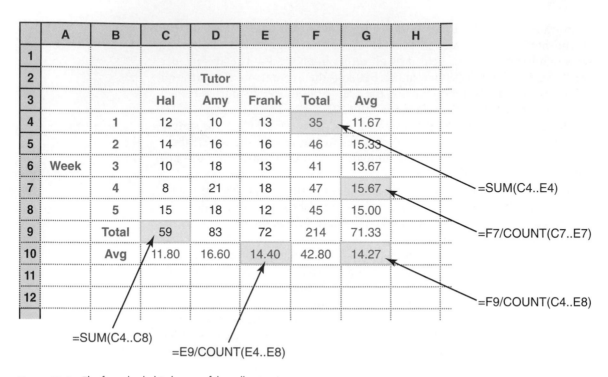

	A	B	C	D	E	F	G	H
1								
2				Tutor				
3			Hal	Amy	Frank	Total	Avg	
4		1	12	10	13	35	11.67	
5		2	14	16	16	46	15.33	
6	Week	3	10	18	13	41	13.67	
7		4	8	21	18	47	15.67	
8		5	15	18	12	45	15.00	
9		Total	59	83	72	214	71.33	
10		Avg	11.80	16.60	14.40	42.80	14.27	
11								
12								

=SUM(C4..E4)

=F7/COUNT(C7..E7)

=F9/COUNT(C4..E8)

=SUM(C4..C8)

=E9/COUNT(E4..E8)

Figure 12.3   The formulas behind some of the cells

Figure 12.3 shows the same spreadsheet as Figure 12.2, indicating the formulas underlying some of the cells. Formulas in our examples (as in many spreadsheet programs) begin with an equal sign (=). That's how the spreadsheet knows which cells contain formulas that must be evaluated.

The formulas in this example refer to particular cells (by their column and row designation). When a formula is evaluated, the values stored in the referenced cells are used to compute the result. Formulas in a spreadsheet are reevaluated any time a change is made to the spreadsheet; therefore, the results are always kept current. A spreadsheet is dynamic—it responds to changes immediately. If we changed the number of students that Frank tutored in week 2, the totals and averages that use that value would be recalculated immediately to reflect the revised data.

Formulas can make use of basic arithmetic operations using the standard symbols (+, −, *, and /). They can also make use of **spreadsheet functions** that are built into the software. In the tutor example, the formula in cell C9 uses the SUM function to compute the sum of the values in the cells C4, C5, C6, C7, and C8.

Spreadsheet function
A computation provided by the spreadsheet software that can be incorporated into formulas

Because functions often operate on a set of contiguous cells, spreadsheets provide a convenient way to specify a **range** of cells. Syntactically, a range is specified with two dots (periods) between the two cell endpoints. A range can specify a set of cells along a row, such as C4..E4, or it can specify a set of cells down a column, such as C4..C8. A range can also specify a rectangular block of cells, ranging from the top left to the bottom right. For example, the range C4..E8 includes the cells C4 to C8, D4 to D8, and E4 to E8.

Range A set of contiguous cells specified by the endpoints

Several of the formulas shown in Figure 12.3 use the COUNT function, which computes the number of non-blank cells in the specified range. For example, the formula in cell G7 divides the value in cell F7 by the count of cells in the range C7..E7, which is 3.

The formula in cell G7 could have been written as follows:

=SUM(C7..E7)/3

Given the current status of the spreadsheet, this formula would compute the same result. However, there are two reasons why this formula is not as good as the original. First, the sum of the values in C7 to E7 have already been computed (and stored in F7), so there is no need to recompute it. Any change to the data would affect the value of F7, and consequently change the value of G7 as well. Spreadsheets take all such relationships into account.

Second (and far more important), it is always a good idea to avoid using a constant in a formula unless it is specifically appropriate. In this case, using the value 3 as the predetermined number of tutors limits our ability to easily add or delete tutors from our analysis. Spreadsheet formulas respond to insertions and deletions just as they do to changes in raw data itself. If we insert a column for another tutor, the ranges in the original formulas in columns F and G (which would move to columns G and H due to the insertion) would automatically change to reflect the insertion. For example, if a new tutor column is inserted, the formula in cell F4 would be shifted to cell G4 and would now be

=SUM(C4..F4)

That is, the range of cells would increase to include the newly inserted data. Likewise, the ranges used by the COUNT function in other functions would change as well, and would result in a new, and correct, average. If we had used the constant 3 in the formula of cell G7, the calculation would be incorrect after the new column was inserted.

Usually a spreadsheet program provides a large number of functions that we can use in formulas. Some perform math or statistical calculations, common financial calculations, or special operations on text or dates.

Daniel Bricklin

Many of the people whose biographies appear in this book have been winners of the ACM Turing Award, the highest award given in computer science. The ACM also gives an award for outstanding work done by someone under 35, the Grace Murray Hopper Award. The charge for this award reads:

> Awarded to the outstanding young computer professional of the year ... selected on the basis of a single recent major technical or service contribution.... The candidate must have been 35 years of age or less at the time the qualifying contribution was made.

Daniel Bricklin won the Hopper Award in 1981, with the following citation:

> For his contributions to personal computing and, in particular, to the design of VisiCalc. Bricklin's efforts in the development of the "Visual Calculator" provide the excellence and elegance that ACM seeks to sustain through such activities as the Awards program.

Daniel Bricklin, born in 1951, is a member of the computer generation. He began his college career at the Massachusetts Institute of Technology in 1969 as a math major, but quickly changed to computer science. He worked in MIT's Laboratory for Computer Science, where he worked on interactive systems and met his future business partner, Bob Franksten. After graduation, he was employed by Digital Equipment Corporation, where he worked with computerized typesetting and helped to design the WPS–8 word processing product.

After a very short stint with FasFax Corporation, a cash register manufacturer, Bricklin enrolled in the MBA program at the Harvard Business School, in 1977. While there, he began to envision a program that could manipulate numbers like word processors manipulate text. Such a program would have an immense impact on the business world. He teamed up with his old MIT buddy Bob Franksten and turned the dream into a reality. With Bricklin doing the design and Franksten doing the programming, VisiCalc, the first spreadsheet program, was written. They formed

Software Arts in 1978 to produce and market VisiCalc. In the fall of 1979, a version was made available for the Apple II for $100 per copy. A version for the IBM PC became available in 1981.

Bricklin made the decision not to patent VisiCalc, believing that software should not be proprietary. Although it didn't have a patent, the company grew to 125 employees in four years. However, another start-up named Lotus came out with a spreadsheet package called Lotus 1–2–3, which was more powerful and user-friendly than VisiCalc. Sales suffered. After a long expensive court battle between Software Arts and VisiCorp (the company marketing VisiCalc) Bricklin was forced to sell to Lotus Software. In turn, Lotus 1–2–3 was surpassed by Microsoft's Excel spreadsheet program. Both Lotus 1–2–3 and Excel were based on VisiCalc.

After working for a short time as a consultant with Lotus Software, Bricklin again formed a new company. As president of Software Garden, Inc., he developed a program for prototyping and simulating other pieces of software, which won the 1986 Software Publishers Association Award for "Best Programming Tool." In 1990, he cofounded Slate Corporation to develop applications software for pen computers, small computers that use a pen rather than a keyboard for input. After four years, Slate closed its doors, and Bricklin went back to Software Garden.

In 1995, he founded Trellix Corporation, a leading provider of private-label web site publishing technology. He still serves as the company's Chief Technology Officer. Bricklin was asked to share his view of the Internet. Here is his reply as captured by the interviewer.

> "Most people don't understand it. They fail to grasp the capabilities of its underpinnings." He likens the Net to a primitive road during the early days of the automobile, when few saw the potential that a massive interstate highway system might one day provide. "We need to understand not so much the technology," he explains, "but the progression of technology and what might be built with it. E-commerce, like electricity or the telephone, simply enables us to use technology to do what we now do, only better."

Function	Computes
SUM(val1, val2, ...) SUM(range)	Sum of the specified set of values
COUNT(val1, val2, ...) COUNT(range)	Count of the number of cells that contain values
MAX(val1, val2, ...) MAX(range)	Largest value from the specified set of values
SIN(angle)	The sine of the specified angle
PI()	The value of PI
STDEV(val1, val2, ...) STDEV(range)	The standard deviation from the specified sample values
TODAY()	Today's date
LEFT(text, num_chars)	The leftmost characters from the specified text
IF(test, true_val, false_val)	If the test is true, it returns the true_val; otherwise, it returns the false_val
ISBLANK (value)	Returns true if the specified value refers to an empty cell

Figure 12.4   Some common spreadsheet functions

Others allow the user to set up logical relationships among cells. Examples of some common spreadsheet functions are given in Figure 12.4. A typical spreadsheet program provides dozens of functions like these that the user may incorporate into formulas.

Another dynamic aspect of spreadsheets is the ability to copy values or formulas across a row or down a column. When formulas are copied, the relationships among cells are maintained. Therefore, it becomes easy to set up a whole set of similar calculations. For instance, to enter the total calculations in our tutor example down the column from cell F4 to F8, we simply had to enter the formula in cell F4, and then copy that formula down the column. As the formula is copied, the references to the cells are automatically updated to reflect the row that the new formula is in. For our small example that tracks five weeks, the copy ability didn't save that much effort. But imagine if we were tracking this data for a whole year and had 52 summation formulas to create. The copy aspect of spreadsheets makes setting up that entire column a single operation.

Circular References

Note that spreadsheet formulas could be defined such that they create a **circular reference** that can never be resolved because the result of one formula is ultimately based on another, and vice versa. For instance, if cell B15 contains the formula

=D22+D23

and cell D22 contains the formula

=B15+B16

there is a circular reference. Cell B15 uses the value in cell D22 for its result, but cell D22 relies on B15 for its result.

Circular references are not usually this blatant and may involve many cells. A more complicated situation is presented in Figure 12.5. Ultimately, cell A1 relies on cell D13 for its value, and vice versa. Spreadsheet software usually detects these problems and indicates the error.

Spreadsheet Analysis

One reason spreadsheets are so useful is their versatility. The user of a spreadsheet determines what the data represents and how it is related to other data. Therefore, spreadsheet analysis can be applied to just about any topic area. We might, for instance, use a spreadsheet to:

- track sales
- analyze sport statistics
- maintain student grades
- keep a car maintenance log
- record and summarize travel expenses
- track project activities and schedules
- plan stock purchases

Cell	Contents
A1	=B7*COUNT(F8..K8)
B7	=A14+SUM(E40..E50)
E45	=G18+G19–D13
D13	=D12/A1

Figure 12.5
A circular reference situation that cannot be resolved

The list of potential applications is virtually endless. Business, in general, has a huge number of specific situations in which spreadsheet calculations are essential. It makes you wonder how we got along without them.

Another reason spreadsheets are so useful is their dynamic nature. We've seen how, if we set up the spreadsheet formulas correctly, changes, additions, and deletions to the data are automatically taken into account by the appropriate calculations.

The dynamic nature of spreadsheets also provides the powerful ability to do **what-if analysis**. We can set up spreadsheets that take into account certain assumptions, and then challenge those assumptions by changing the appropriate values.

> **What-if analysis** Modifying spreadsheet values that represent assumptions to see how changes in those assumptions affect related data

For example, suppose we are setting up a spreadsheet to estimate the costs and potential profits for a seminar we are considering holding. We can enter values for the number of attendees, ticket prices, the costs of materials, room rental, and other data that affects the final results. Then we can ask ourselves some what-if questions to see how our scenario changes as the situation changes—questions such as:

What if the number of attendees decreased by 10%?

What if we increase the ticket price by $5?

What if we could reduce the cost of materials by half?

As we ask these questions, we change the data accordingly. If we've set up the relationships between all of the formulas correctly, then each change immediately shows us how those changes affect the other data.

Business analysts have formalized this process in various ways, and spreadsheets have become a primary tool in their daily efforts. Cost-benefit analysis, break-even calculations, and projected sales estimates all become a matter of organizing the spreadsheet data and formulas to take the appropriate relationships into account.

12.3 Database Management Systems

> **Database** A structured set of data
>
> **Database management system** A combination of software and data made up of the physical database, the database engine, and the database schema

Almost all sophisticated data management situations rely on an underlying database and the support structure that allows the user (either a human or a program) to interact with it. A **database** can simply be defined as a structured set of data. A **database management system** (DBMS) is a combination of software and data made up of the:

- physical database—a collection of files that contain the data

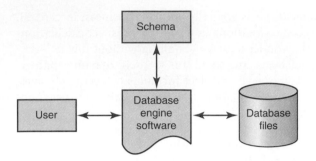

Figure 12.6
The elements of a database
management system

- database engine—software that supports access to and modification of the database contents
- database schema—a specification of the logical structure of the data stored in the database

The database engine software interacts with specialized database languages that allow the user to specify the structure of data; add, modify, and delete data; and **query** the database to retrieve specific stored data.

The database **schema** provides the logical view of the data in the database, independent of how it is physically stored. Assuming the underlying physical structure of the database is implemented in an efficient way, the logical schema is the more important point of view from the database user's perspective because it shows how the data items relate to each other.

The relationships between the various elements of a database management system are shown in Figure 12.6. The user interacts with the database engine software to determine and/or modify the schema for the database. The user then interacts with the engine software to access and possibly modify the contents of the database stored on disk.

Query   A request for
information submitted to
a database

Schema   A specifica-
tion of the logical structure of data in a
database

Relational model   A
database model in which
data and the relation-
ships among them are
organized into tables

Table   A collection of
database records

Record (or **object**, or
entity)   A collection of
related fields that make
up a single database
entry

Field (or **attribute**)   A
single value in a data-
base record

The Relational Model

There have been a few popular database management models, but the one that has dominated for many years is the **relational model**. In a relational DBMS, the data items and the relationships among them are organized into **tables**. A table is a collection of **records**. A record is a collection of related **fields**. Each field of a database table contains a single data value. Each record in a table contains the same fields.

A record in a database table is also called a *database object* or an *entity*. The fields of a record are sometimes called the *attributes* of a database object.

For example, consider the database table shown in Figure 12.7, which contains information about movies. Each row in the table corresponds to a record. Each record in the table is made up of the same fields in which particular values are stored. That is, each movie record has a MovieId, a

Movie

MovieId	Title	Genre	Rating
101	Sixth Sense, The	thriller horror	PG-13
102	Back to the Future	comedy adventure	PG
103	Monsters, Inc.	animation comedy	G
104	Field of Dreams	fantasy drama	PG
105	Alien	sci-fi horror	R
106	Unbreakable	thriller	PG-13
107	X-Men	action sci-fi	PG-13
5022	Elizabeth	drama period	R
5793	Independence Day	action sci-fi	PG-13
7442	Platoon	action drama war	R

Figure 12.7
A database table, made up of records and fields

Title, a Genre, and a Rating that contain the specific data for each record. A database table is given a name, such as Movie in this case.

Usually, one or more fields of a table are identified as **key** fields. The key field(s) uniquely identifies a record among all other records in the table. That is, the values stored in key field(s) for each record in a table must be unique. In the Movie table, the MovieId field would be the logical choice for a key. That way, two movies could have the same title. Certainly the Genre and Rating fields are not appropriate key fields in this case.

Each value in the key field MovieId must be unique. Most DBMSs allow such fields to be automatically generated to guarantee unique entries. Note, though, that there is no reason the key values have to be consecutive. The last three entries of the table contain radically different movie identification numbers. As long as they are unique values, the MovieId field can serve as the key.

The movie table in Figure 12.7 happens to be presented in the order of increasing MovieId value, but it could have been presented in other ways, such as alphabetical by movie title. In this case, there is no inherent relationship among the rows of data in the table. Relational database tables present a logical view of the data and have nothing to do with the underlying physical organization (how the records are stored on disk). Ordering records becomes important only when we query the database for particular values, such as all movies that are rated PG. At that point we might want to sort the results of the query by title.

Key One or more fields of a database record that uniquely identifies it among all other records in the table

The structure of the table corresponds to the schema it represents. That is, a schema is an expression of the attributes of the records in a table. We can express the schema for this part of the database as follows:

```
Movie (MovieId:key, Title, Genre, Rating)
```

Sometimes a schema representation indicates the type of data that is stored in individual fields, such as numeric or text. It may also indicate the specific set of values that are appropriate for a given field. For instance, the schema could indicate in this example that the Rating field can only be G, PG, PG–13, R, or NC–17. The schema for an entire database is made up of the individual schema that corresponds to individual tables.

Suppose we wanted to create a movie rental business. In addition to the list of movies for rent, we must create a database table to hold information about our customers. The Customer table in Figure 12.8 could represent this information.

Similar to what we did with our Movie table, the Customer table contains a CustomerId field to serve as a key. The fact that some CustomerId values correspond to some MovieId values is irrelevant. Key values must be unique only within a table.

Note that, in a real database, we would be better off subdividing the Name field of our customer table into FirstName and LastName fields. Also, we would probably have separate fields for various parts of a complete address, such as City and State. For our examples we are keeping things simple.

The Movie table and the Customer table show how data can be organized as records within isolated tables. The power of relational database

Customer

CustomerId	Name	Genre	CreditCardNumber
101	Dennis Cook	123 Main Street	2736 2371 2344 0382
102	Doug Nickle	456 Second Ave	7362 7486 5957 3638
103	Randy Wolf	789 Elm Street	4253 4773 6252 4436
104	Amy Stevens	321 Yellow Brick Road	9876 5432 1234 5678
105	Robert Person	654 Lois Lane	1122 3344 5566 7788
106	David Coggin	987 Broadway	8473 9687 4847 3784
107	Susan Klaton	345 Easy Street	2435 4332 1567 3232

Figure 12.8
A database table containing customer data

management systems, though, is in the ability to create tables that conceptually link various tables together.

Relationships

Recall that records represent individual database objects, and that fields of a record are the attributes of these objects. We can create a record to represent a relationship between objects and include attributes about the relationship in the record. Therefore, we can use a table to represent a collection of relationships between objects.

Continuing our movie rental example, we need to be able to represent the situation in which a particular customer rents a particular movie. Since "rents" is a relationship between a customer and a movie, we can represent it as a record. The date rented and the date due are attributes of the relationship that should be in the record. The `Rents` table in Figure 12.9 contains a collection of these relationship records that represents the movies that are currently rented.

The `Rents` table contains information about the objects in the relationship (customers and movies), as well as the attributes of the relationship. But note that it does not contain all of the data about a customer or a movie. In a relational database, we avoid duplicating data as much as possible. For instance, there is no need to store the customer's name and address in the rental table. That data is already stored in the `Customer` table. When we need that data, we use the `CustomerId` stored in the `Rents` table to look up the customer's detailed data in the customer table. Likewise, when we need data about the movie that was rented, we look it up in the `Movie` table using the `MovieId`.

Note that the `CustomerId` value 103 is shown in two records in the table in Figure 12.9. That indicates that the same customer rented two different movies.

Data is modified in, added to, and deleted from our various database tables as needed. When movies are added or removed from the available stock, we update the records of the `Movie` table. As people become

Rents

CustomerId	MovieId	DateRented	DateDue
103	104	3-12-2002	3-13-2002
103	5022	3-12-2002	3-13-2002
105	107	3-12-2002	3-15-2002

Figure 12.9
A database table storing current movie rentals

Universal Product Codes

When you look on the packaging of most products, you find a Universal Product Code (UPC) and its associated bar code, such as the one shown at right. UPC codes were created to speed up the process of purchasing a product at a store and to help keep better track of inventory.

A UPC symbol is made up of the machine-readable bar code and the corresponding human-readable 12-digit UPC number. The first six digits of the UPC number are the *manufacturer identification number*. For example, General Mills has a manufacturer ID number of 016000. The next five digits are the *item number*. Each type of product, and each different packaging of the same product, is assigned a unique item number. Therefore, a 2-liter bottle of Coke has a different item number than a 2-liter bottle of Diet Coke, and a 10-oz. bottle of Heinz ketchup has a different item number than a 14-oz. bottle of Heinz ketchup.

The last digit of the UPC code is called a *check digit*, which allows the scanner determine whether it scanned the number correctly. A calculation is performed on the

A UPC symbol

rest of the digits of the number to determine the check digit. After reading the number, the calculation is performed and verified against the check digit. (See Chapter 17 for more information on check digits.)

For some products, particularly small ones, a technique has been developed to create UPC numbers that can be shortened by eliminating certain digits (all zeros). In this way, the entire UPC symbol can be reduced in size.

Note that a product's price is not stored in the UPC number. When a product is scanned at a cash register (more formally called a Point of Sale, or POS), the manufacturer and item numbers are used to look up that item in a database. The database might contain a great deal of product information, including its price. Keeping only basic information in the UPC number makes it easy to change other information such as the price without having to relabel the products. However, this also makes it easy to create situations of "scanner fraud" in which the database price of an item does not match the price on the store shelf, whether intentionally or not.

---

customers of our store, we add them to the `Customer` table. On an ongoing basis we add and remove records from the `Rents` table as customers rent and return videos.

Structured Query Language

The **Structured Query Language** (**SQL**) is a comprehensive database language for managing relational databases. It includes statements that specify database schemas as well as statements that add, modify, and delete database content. It also includes, as its name implies, the ability to query the database to retrieve specific data.

The original version of SQL was Sequal, developed by IBM in the early '70s. In 1986, the American National Standards Institute (ANSI) published the SQL standard, the basis for commercial database languages for accessing relational databases.

SQL is not case sensitive, so keywords, table names, and attribute names can be uppercase, lowercase, or mixed. Spaces are used as separators in a statement.

Queries

Let's first focus on simple queries. The *select* statement is the primary tool for this purpose. The basic *select* statement includes a select clause, a from clause, and a where clause:

```
select attribute-list from table-list where condition
```

The select clause determines what attributes are returned. The from clause determines what tables are used in the query. The where clause restricts the data that is returned. For example:

```
select Title from Movie where Rating = 'PG'
```

The result of this query is a list of all titles from the `Movie` table that have a rating of PG. The where clause can be eliminated if no special restrictions are necessary:

```
select Name, Address from Customer
```

This query returns the name and address of all customers in the `Customer` table. An asterisk (*) can be used in the select clause to denote that all attributes in the selected records should be returned:

```
select * from Movie where Genre like '%action%'
```

This query returns all attributes of records from the `Movie` table in which the `Genre` attribute contains the word 'action'. The `like` operator in SQL performs some simple pattern matching on strings, and the `%` symbol matches any string.

Select statements can also dictate how the results of the query should be sorted using the order by clause:

```
select * from Movie where Rating = 'R' order by Title
```

This query returns all attributes of R-rated movies sorted by the movie title.

There are many more variations on select statements supported by SQL than those we've shown here. Remember that our goal is to introduce the database concepts to you. You would require much more detail to truly become proficient at SQL queries.

Modifying Database Content

The *insert*, *update*, and *delete* statements in SQL allow the data in a table to be changed. The *insert* statement adds a new record to a table. Each insert statement specifies the values of the attributes for the new record. For example:

```
insert into Customer values (9876, 'John Smith',
'602 Greenbriar Court', '2938 3212 3402 0299')
```

This statement inserts a new record into the Customer table with the specified attributes.

The *update* statement changes the values in one or more records of a table. For example:

```
update Movie set Genre = 'thriller drama'
where title = 'Unbreakable'
```

This statement changes the Genre of the movie Unbreakable to 'thriller drama'.

The *delete* statement removes all records from a table matching the specified condition. For example, if we wanted to remove all R-rated movies from the Movie table, we could use the following delete statement:

```
delete from Movie where Rating = 'R'
```

As with the *select* statement, there are many variations of the *insert*, *update*, and *delete* statements as well.

Mathematical basis of SQL

SQL incorporates operations in an algebra that is defined for accessing and manipulating data represented in relational tables. E. F. Codd of IBM defined this algebra in the late 60's; in 1981 he won the Turing award for his work. SQL's fundamental operations include:

Select operation to identify records in a table

Project operation to produce a subset of the columns in a table

Cartesian product operation to concatenate rows from two tables

Other operations include the set operations union, difference, intersection, natural join (a subset of the Cartesian product), and division.

Database Design

A database must be carefully designed from the outset if it is going to fulfill its role. Poor planning in the early stages can lead to a database that does not support the necessary relationships that are required.

One popular technique for designing relational databases is called **entity-relationship (ER) modeling**. Chief among the tools used for ER modeling is the *ER diagram*. An **ER diagram** captures the important record types, attributes, and relationships in a graphical form. From an ER diagram, a database manager can define the necessary schema and create the appropriate tables to support the database specified by the diagram.

An ER diagram showing various aspects of the movie rental example is shown in Figure 12.10. Specific shapes are used in ER diagrams to differ-

Entity-relationship (ER) modeling A popular technique for designing relational databases

ER diagram A graphical representation of an ER model

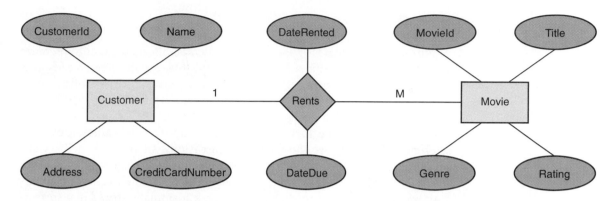

Figure 12.10 An ER diagram for the movie rental database

entiate among the various parts of the database. Types of records (which can also be thought of as classes for the database objects) are shown in rectangles. Fields (or attributes) of those records are shown in attached ovals. Relationships are shown in diamonds.

The position of the various elements of an ER diagram is not particularly important, though if some thought is given to it they are easier to read. Note that a relationship such as Rents can have its own associated attributes.

Also note that the relationship connectors are labeled, one side with a 1 and the other side with an M. These designations show the **cardinality constraint** of the relationship. A cardinality constraint puts restrictions on the number of relationships that may exist at one time.

There are three general cardinality relationships:

- one-to-one
- one-to-many
- many-to-many

The relationship between a customer and a movie is one-to-many. That is, one customer is allowed to rent many movies, but a movie can only be rented by a single customer (at any given time). Cardinality constraints help the database designer convey the details of a relationship.

> **Cardinality constraint**
> The number of relationships that may exist at one time between entities in an ER diagram

Summary

An information system is application software that allows the user to organize and manage data. General information system software includes spreadsheets and database management systems. Other domain areas, such as artificial intelligence, have their own specific techniques and support for data management.

A spreadsheet is a software application that uses a grid of cells to organize data and the formulas used to compute new values. Cells are referenced by their row and column designations, such as A5 or B7. Cells can contain basic data or formulas. Formulas usually refer to the values in other cells and may use built-in functions to compute their result. Formulas may use data across a range of cells. When a formula is stored in a spreadsheet cell, the value computed by the formula is actually shown in the cell. It is important that formulas in a spreadsheet avoid circular references, in which two or more cells rely on each other to compute their results.

Spreadsheets are both versatile and extensible. They can be used in many different situations and they respond dynamically to change. As values in the spreadsheet are altered, affected formulas are automatically recalculated to produce updated results. If spreadsheet rows or columns are added, the ranges in spreadsheet formulas compensate immediately. Spreadsheets are particularly appropriate for what-if analysis, in which values of assumptions are modified to see their affect on the rest of the system.

A database management system includes the physical files in which the data are stored, the software that supports access to and modification of the data, and the database schema that specifies the logical layout of the database. The relational model is the most popular database approach today. It is based on organizing data into tables of records (or objects) with particular fields (or attributes). A key field(s), whose values uniquely identify individual records in the table, is usually designated for each table.

Relationships among database elements are represented in new tables that may have their own attributes. Relationship tables do not duplicate data in other tables. Instead they store the key values of the appropriate database records so that the detailed data can be looked up when needed.

The Structured Query Language (SQL) is the standard database language for querying and manipulating relational databases. The *select* statement is used for queries and has many variations so that particular data can be accessed from the database. Other SQL statements allow data to be added, updated, and deleted from a database.

A database should be carefully designed. Entity-relationship modeling, with its associated ER diagrams, is a popular technique for database design. ER diagrams graphically depict the relationships among database objects and show their attributes and cardinality constraints.

ETHICAL ISSUES

Encryption

Have you ever purchased something over the Internet, done your banking online, or transferred medical records through a Web site? How confident are you that these are secure transactions? With growing globalization of the Web, the ability to transfer sensitive information securely from one computer to another is critical. Consider, for example, the personal data that you provide when you purchase something online. E-commerce sites often require a credit card number, an address, a telephone number, an e-mail address, and additional marketing information such as age, sex, income, or interests. Who has access to this data? Secure sites protect this personal information through cryptography. The basic ideas of cryptography originated before Roman times: Caesar coded his communications using a simple alphabet code. Today, encryption, a type of cryptography, is used to scramble and encode messages sent through the Internet. Once encrypted, these messages can be deciphered only by using a key, or translator. The goal of encryption is to maximize Web security so that no one except the intended recipient can access transferred material.

Powerful encryption technology may improve online consumers' confidence, but many people fear that sophisticated encryption can help criminals, hackers, spies, and terrorists if they have access to it. The U.S. government, for example, imposes certain restrictions on the export of encryption technology, and some officials lobby for regulations that would limit the strength of encryption technology products within the United States. In the 1990s, the FBI supported a policy that required citizens to surrender deciphering keys upon request. The government could also gain access to secure information through "back doors," which bypass the need for a deciphering key in order to access secure data. Privacy advocates protest against encryption restrictions. They further argue that the government's attempt to monitor encryption technology is Orwellian in nature. They further argue that back doors open up secure sites for hackers, and that powerful encryption helps keep confidential information out of the hands of criminals.

The terrorist attacks on the United States on September 11, 2001, forced the encryption debate into the limelight. Undoubtedly, communication was key for the synchronization and execution of the attacks. The terrorist organization may have communicated electronically by using encryption or hiding their messages in images, and the United States failed to intercept and decipher this information. While it is not productive to speculate as to whether access to encryption keys and improved ability to decipher codes could have changed the events of September 11, 2001, it is important to deliberate as to what type of control the government should have, if any, over encrypted communication.

Key Terms

Cardinality constraint pg. 393

Cell pg. 377

Circular reference pg. 384

Database pg. 385

Database management system
  pg. 385

Entity-relationship (ER) modeling
  pg. 392

ER diagram pg. 392

Field (or attribute) pg. 386

Information system pg. 376

Key pg. 387

Query pg. 386

Range pg. 381

Record (or object, or entity)
  pg. 386

Relational model pg. 386

Schema pg. 386

Spreadsheet pg. 377

Spreadsheet function pg. 380

Structured Query Language (SQL)
  pg. 390

Table pg. 386

What-if analysis pg. 385

Exercises

1. What is an information system?

2. What is a spreadsheet?

3. What can be contained in a cell of a spreadsheet?

4. How do we refer to a particular cell of a spreadsheet?

5. How do you refer to a range of cells?

6. Express the following cells as ranges.
    a. All the cells in row 2 from C through N.
    b. All the cells in column B from 3 through 12.
    c. All the cells in rows 4 through 7 from A through D.

7. Explain the data in column E and in row 7 of the tutor spreadsheet example of Figure 12.2.

8. What is a spreadsheet formula?

9. What is a spreadsheet function?

10. In what ways does a spreadsheet dynamically respond to change? How is this helpful?

11. What values in the tutor spreadsheet example of Figure 12.2 would change if you modified the data that reflected the number of students that Hal helped in week 4?

12. What values in the tutor spreadsheet example of Figure 12.2 would change if you deleted the data for week 5?

13. What formulas would be stored in the following cells of the tutor spreadsheet example of Figure 12.2?
   a. cell D9
   b. cell D10
   c. cell E9
   d. cell F5
   e. cell F6
   f. cell G7

14. List three different formulas that would compute the correct value for the cell F9 in the tutor example of Figure 12.2.

15. The formula for cell D10 in the tutor example of Figure 12.2 could be given as

   =SUM(D4..D8)/5

   Name two reasons why this formula is not a good solution. What is the better solution?

16. How does copying formulas down a row or across a column sometimes help us set up a spreadsheet?

17. What is a spreadsheet circular reference? Why is it a problem?

18. Give a specific example of an indirect circular reference similar to the one shown in Figure 12.5.

19. What is what-if analysis?

20. Name some what-if analysis questions that you might ask if you were using a spreadsheet to plan and track some stock purchases. Explain how you might set up a spreadsheet to help answer those questions.

For questions 21 through 24, use the paper spreadsheet form or use an actual spreadsheet application program to design the spreadsheets. Your instructor may provide more specific instructions regarding these questions.

21. Design a spreadsheet to track the statistics of your favorite major league baseball team. Include data regarding runs, hits, errors, and

runs-batted-in (RBIs). Compute appropriate statistics for individual players and the team as a whole.

22. Design a spreadsheet to maintain a grade sheet for a set of students. Include tests and projects, given various weights to each in the calculation of the final grade for each student. Compute the average grade per test and project for the whole class.

23. Assume you are going on a business trip. Design a spreadsheet to keep track of your expenses and create a summary of your totals. Include various aspects of travel such as car mileage, flight costs, hotel costs, and miscellaneous (such as taxis and tips).

24. Design a spreadsheet to estimate and then keep track of a particular project's activities. List the activities, the estimated and actual dates for those activities, and schedule slippage or gain. Add other data as appropriate for your project.

25. Compare a database to a database management system.

26. What is a database schema?

27. Describe the general organization of a relational database.

28. What is a field in a database?

29. What other fields (attributes) might we include in the database table of Figure 12.7?

30. What other fields (attributes) might we include in the database table of Figure 12.8?

31. What is a key in relational database table?

32. Specify the schema for the database table of Figure 12.8.

33. How are relationships represented in a relational database?

34. Define an SQL query that returns all attributes of all records in the Customer table.

35. Define an SQL query that returns the movie id number and title of all movies that have an R rating.

36. Define an SQL query that returns the address of every customer in the Customer table that lives on Lois Lane.

37. Define an SQL statement that inserts the movie *Armageddon* into the Movie table.

38. Define an SQL statement that changes the address of Amy Stevens in the Customer table.

39. Define an SQL statement that deletes the customer with a CustomerId of 103.

40. What is an ER diagram?

41. How are entities and relationships represented in an ER diagram?

42. How are attributes represented in an ER diagram?

43. What are cardinality constraints and how are they shown in ER diagrams?

44. What are the three general cardinality constraints?

45. Design a database that stores data about the books in a library, the students who use them, and the ability to check out books for a period of time. Create an ER diagram and sample tables.

46. Design a database that stores data about the courses taught at a university, the professors who teach those courses, and the students who take those courses. Create an ER diagram and sample tables.

Thought Questions

1. Other than the examples given in this chapter, think of five situations for which you might set up a spreadsheet.

2. Other than the examples given in this chapter, think of five situations for which you might set up a database.

3. Does the use of computerized databases mean that we can do away with paper files? What sorts of paper files might still be needed?

4. What is encryption and how does it relate to you as a student?

5. How does encryption relate to e-commerce?

6. How does encryption relate to national defense?

7. What is the state of the encryption debate today? How much of an effect did September 11, 2001, have on this debate?

The Applications Layer

13 Artificial Intelligence

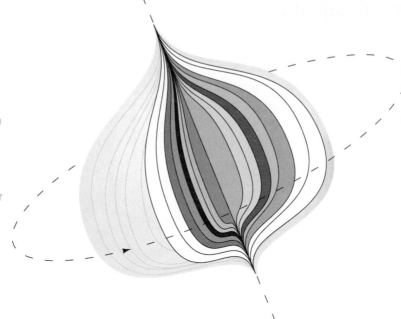

Chapter 13

Artificial Intelligence

The subdiscipline of computing called artificial intelligence (AI) is important in many ways. To many people it represents the future of computing—the evolution of a machine to make it more like a human. To others it is an avenue for applying new and different technologies to problem solving.

The term *artificial intelligence* probably conjures up various images in your mind, such as a computer playing chess or a robot doing household chores. These are certainly aspects of AI, but it goes far beyond that. AI techniques affect the way we develop many types of application programs, from the mundane to the fantastic. The world of artificial intelligence opens doors that no other aspect of computing does. Its role in the development of state-of-the-art application programs is crucial.

Goals

After studying this chapter, you should be able to:

- distinguish between the types of problems that humans do best and those that computers do best.
- explain the Turing test.
- define what is meant by knowledge representation and demonstrate how knowledge is represented in a semantic network.
- develop a search tree for simple scenarios.
- explain the processing of an expert system.
- explain the processing of biological and artificial neural networks.
- list the various aspects of natural language processing.
- explain the types of ambiguities in natural language comprehension.

13.1   Thinking Machines

Computers are amazing devices. They can draw complex three-dimensional images, process the payroll of an entire corporation, and determine whether the bridge you're building will stand up to the pressure of the traffic expected. Yet they have trouble understanding a simple conversation and might not be able to distinguish between a table and a chair.

Certainly a computer can do some things better than a human can. For example, if you are given the task of adding a thousand four-digit numbers together using pencil and paper, you could do it. But it would take you quite a long time, and you may very likely make an error while performing the calculations. A computer could do it in a fraction of a second without error.

However, if you are asked to point out the cat in the picture shown in Figure 13.1, you could do it without hesitation. A computer would have difficulty making that identification and may very well get it wrong. Humans bring a great deal of knowledge and reasoning capability to these types of problems; we are still struggling with ways to perform human-like reasoning using a computer.

So in our modern state of technology, computers are good at computation, but less good at things that require intelligence. The field of **artificial intelligence (AI)** is the study of computer systems that attempt to model and apply the intelligence of the human mind.

In this book we've occasionally made a distinction between the use of the words data, information, and knowledge. We use them interchangeably in this chapter.

Artificial intelligence (AI) The study of computer systems that model and apply the intelligence of the human mind

Figure 13.1
A computer might have trouble identifying the cat in this picture. *Courtesy of Amy Rose*

The Turing Test

In 1950 English mathematician Alan Turing wrote a landmark paper that asked the question: Can machines think? After carefully defining terms such as intelligence and thinking, he ultimately concluded that we would eventually be able to create a computer that thinks. But then he asked another question: How will we know when we've succeeded?

His answer to that question came to be called the **Turing test**, which is used to empirically determine whether a computer has achieved intelligence. The test is based on whether a computer could fool a human into believing that the computer is another human.

Variations on Turing tests have been defined over the years, but we focus on the basic concept here. The test is set up as follows: A human interrogator sits in a room and uses a computer terminal to communicate with two respondents, A and B. The interrogator knows that one respondent is human and the other is a computer, but doesn't know which is which. See Figure 13.2.

After holding conversations with both A and B, the interrogator must decide which respondent is the computer. This procedure is repeated with numerous human subjects. The premise is that if the computer could fool enough interrogators, then it could be considered intelligent.

Some people argue that the Turing test is a good test for intelligence because it requires that a computer possess a wide range of knowledge and

Turing test A behavioral approach to determining if a computer system is intelligent

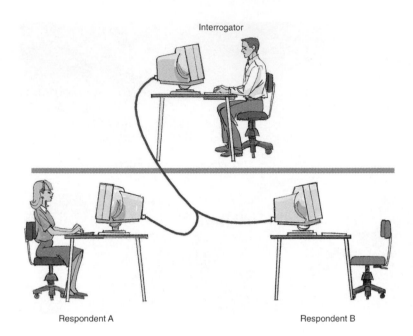

Interrogator

Respondent A   **Respondent B**

Figure 13.2
In a Turing test, the interrogator must determine
which respondent is the
computer and which is the
human.

have the flexibility necessary to deal with changes in conversation. To fool
a human interrogator, the knowledge required by the computer goes
beyond facts; it includes an awareness of human behavior and emotions.

Others argue that the Turing test doesn't really demonstrate that a
computer understands language discourse, which is necessary for true
intelligence. They suggest that a program could simulate language comprehension, perhaps enough to pass the Turing test, but that alone does not
make the computer intelligent.

A computer that passes the Turing test would demonstrate **weak equivalence**, meaning that the two systems (human and computer) are equivalent in results (output), but they do not arrive at those results in the same
way. **Strong equivalence** indicates that two systems use the same internal
processes to produce results. Some AI researchers assert that true artificial
intelligence will not exist until we have achieved strong equivalence—that
is, until we create a machine that processes information as the human
mind does.

New York philanthropist Hugh Loebner organized the first formal
instantiation of the Turing test. The competition has been run annually
since 1991. A grand prize of $100,000 and a solid gold medal will be
awarded for the first computer whose responses are indistinguishable from
a human's. So far the grand prize is still up for grabs. A prize of $2,000
and a bronze medal is awarded each year for the computer that is determined to be the most human-like, relative to the rest of the competition

Weak equivalence The
equality of two systems
based on their results

Strong equivalence
The equality of two
systems based on their
results and the process
by which they arrive at
those results

that year. The **Loebner prize** contest has become an important annual event for computing enthusiasts interested in artificial intelligence.

Aspects of AI

The field of artificial intelligence has many branches. Our overall goal in this chapter is to give you some insight into the primary issues involved and the challenges yet to be overcome. In the remaining sections of this chapter, we explore the following issues in the world of AI:

- Knowledge representation—the techniques used to represent knowledge so that a computer system can apply it to intelligent problem solving
- Expert systems—computer systems that embody the knowledge of human experts
- Neural networks—computer systems that mimic the processing of the human brain
- Natural language processing—the challenge of processing languages that humans use to communicate
- Robotics—the study of robots

13.2   Knowledge Representation

The knowledge we need to represent an object or event varies based on the situation. Depending on the problem we are trying to solve, we need specific information. For example, if we are trying to analyze family relationships, it's important to know that Fred is Cathy's father, but not that Fred is a plumber or that Cathy owns a pickup truck. Furthermore, not only do we need particular information, we need it in a form that allows us to search and process that information efficiently.

There are many ways to represent knowledge. We could describe it in natural language. That is, we could write an English paragraph describing, for instance, a student and the ways in which the student relates to the world. However, though natural language is very descriptive, it doesn't lend itself to efficient processing. We therefore could formalize the language; here we describe the student, creating an almost mathematical notation. This formalization lends itself to more rigorous computer processing, but it is difficult to learn and use correctly.

The concept of a data structure was discussed in Chapter 9, and to a certain extent the issues here are the same. We want to create a logical view of the data, independent of its actual underlying implementation, so that the data can be processed in specific ways. In the world of artificial intelligence, however, the information we want to capture often leads to

Loebner prize The first formal instantiation of the Turing test, held annually

new and interesting data representations. Not only do we want to capture facts, but also relationships. The kind of problem we are trying to solve may determine the structure we impose on the data.

As specific problem areas have been investigated, new techniques for representing knowledge have been developed. We examine two in this section: semantic networks and search trees.

Semantic Networks

A **semantic network** is a knowledge representation technique that focuses on the relationships between objects. A directed graph is used to represent a semantic network or net. The nodes of the graph represent objects and the arrows between nodes represent relationships. The arrows are labeled to indicate the types of relationships that exist.

Semantic nets borrow many object-oriented concepts discussed in Chapters 6 and 8, including inheritance and instantiation. Recall that an inheritance relationship indicates that one object *is-a* more specific version of another object. And instantiation is the relationship between an actual object and something that describes it (like a class).

Examine the semantic network shown in Figure 13.3. It has several *is-a* relationships and several *instance-of* relationships. But it also has several other types of relationships, such as *lives-in* (John lives-in Heritage Acres).

> **Semantic network**   A knowledge representation technique that represents the relationships among objects

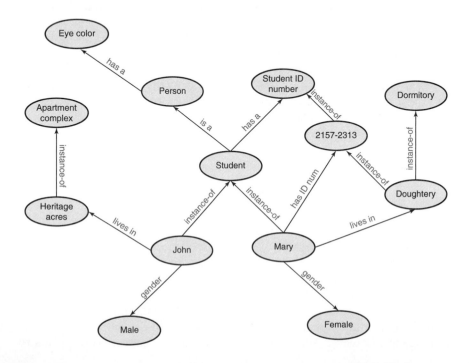

Figure 13.3
A semantic network

Herbert A. Simon

Herbert A. Simon was a Renaissance man of our generation. His home pages included sections on Computer Science, Psychology, and Philosophy, yet his PhD was in Political Science and his Nobel Peace Price was in Economics.

Dr. Simon was born in Milwaukee in 1916. His father was an engineer who became a patent attorney, and his mother was an accomplished pianist. He received his undergraduate degree in 1936 from the University of Chicago and worked for several years as an editor and administrator. He completed his Ph.D. at the University of Chicago in 1943 in Political Science and began a 58-year academic career, the last 52 years of which were at Carnegie Mellon.

In 1955, Dr. Simon, Allen Newell, and J. C. Shaw (their programmer) created Logic Theorist, a program that could discover geometric theorem proofs. At about the same time, Simon was working with E. A. Feigenbaum on EPAM, a program that modeled their theory of human perception and memory. These programs and the subsequent series of papers on the simulation of human thinking, problem solving, and verbal learning marked the beginning of the field of Artificial Intelligence. In 1988, Simon and Newell received the Turing Award of the Association for Computing Machinery for their work in human problem solving. In 1995, Simon received the Research Excellence Award of the International Joint Conference on Artificial Intelligence.

Dr. Simon's interest in information processing and decision making led him to develop his economic theory of "bounded rationality," for which he received the 1978 Nobel Prize in Economics. Classical economics had argued that people make rational choices to get the best item at the best price. Dr. Simon reasoned that the "best" choice was impossible because there are too many choices and too little time to analyze them. Thus people choose the first option that is good enough to meet their needs. His Nobel Prize read "for his pioneering research into the decision-making process within economic organizations."

Dr. Simon remained extraordinarily productive throughout his long career. His bibliography contains 173 entries before 1960, 168 in the 60s, 154 in the 70s, 207 in the 80s, and 236 in the 90s. Outside of his professional life, Dr. Simon enjoyed playing the piano, especially with friends who played violin, viola, and other instruments. He died in February 2001, and had continued his research and interactions with students until a few weeks before his death.

There are essentially no restrictions on the types of relationships that can be modeled in a semantic network.

Many more relationships could be represented in this semantic net. For instance, we could have indicated that any person is either left- or right-handed, or that John owns a car that is a Honda, or that every student has a grade-point average. The relationships that we represent are completely our choice, based on the information we need to answer the kinds of questions that we will face.

The way in which we establish the relationships can vary as well. For example, instead of showing that individual students live in particular dwellings, we could show that dwellings house certain people. In other words, we could turn those arrows around, changing the *lives-in* relationship to a *houses* relationship. Again, the choice is ours as we design the network. Which way best describes the kind of issues we address? In some situations we may choose to represent both relationships.

The types of relationships represented determine which questions are easily answered, which are more difficult to answer, and which cannot be answered. For example, the semantic net in Figure 13.3 makes it fairly simple to answer the following questions:

- Is Mary a student?
- What is the gender of John?
- Does Mary live in a dorm or an apartment?
- What is Mary's student ID number?

However, the following questions are more difficult to answer with this network:

- How many students are female and how many are male?
- Who lives in Dougherty hall?

Note that the information to answer these questions is in the network; it's just not as easy to process. These last questions require the ability to easily find all students, and there are no relationships that make that information easy to obtain. This network is designed more for representing the relationships that individual students have to the world at large.

This network cannot be used to answer the following questions, because the knowledge required is simply not represented:

- What kind of car does John drive?
- What color are Mary's eyes?

We know that Mary has an eye color, because she is a student and all students are people and all people have a particular eye color. We just don't know what her particular eye color is, given the information stored in this net.

A semantic network is a powerful, versatile way to represent a lot of information. The challenge is to model the right relationships and to populate (fill in) the network with accurate and complete data.

Search Trees

In Chapter 9, we mentioned tree structures in general, but concentrated on binary trees, that is, trees with only two, one, or zero children. A general tree structure, in which a node can have possibly many children, plays an important role in artificial intelligence. A tree is used to represent possible alternatives in adversarial situations, such as game playing.

A **search tree** is a structure that represents all possible moves in a game, for both you and your opponent. You can create a game program that maximizes its chances to win. In some cases it may even be able to guarantee a win.

Note that in the binary search trees of Chapter 9, a single value was used to determine whether the search should continue right or left. In general search trees used in artificial intelligence, the paths down a tree represent a series of decisions made by the players. A decision made at one level dictates the options left to the next player. Each node of the tree represents a move based on all other moves that have occurred thus far in the game.

Let's define a simplified variation of a game called Nim to use as an example. In our version, there are a certain number of spaces in a row. The first player may place one, two, or three Xs in the leftmost spaces. The second player may then place one, two, or three Os immediately adjacent to the Xs. Play continues back and forth. The goal is to place your mark in the last (rightmost) space.

Here is an example of a play of our version of Nim using nine spaces:

Initial: _ _ _ _ _ _ _ _ _
Player 1:   X X X _ _ _ _ _ _
Player 2:   X X X O _ _ _ _ _
Player 1:   X X X O X _ _ _ _
Player 2:   X X X O X O O _ _
Player 1:   X X X O X O O X X   Player 1 wins.

The search tree shown in Figure 13.4 shows all possible moves in our version of the game using only five spaces (rather than nine spaces used in the example). At the root of the tree, all spaces are initially empty. The next level shows the three options the first player has (to place one, two, or three Xs). At the third level, the tree shows all possible options that player 2 has, given the move that player 1 already made.

Note that when a large number of marks are made in one turn, there may be fewer options for the next player, and the paths down the tree tend to be shorter. Follow the various paths down from the root, noting the different options taken by each player. Every single option in our simplified game is represented in this tree.

We've deliberately simplified the game of Nim so that we can show a simple search tree. The real game of Nim has some important differences: There are multiple rows, items are removed instead of added, and other

Search tree   A structure that represents alternatives in adversarial situations, such as game playing

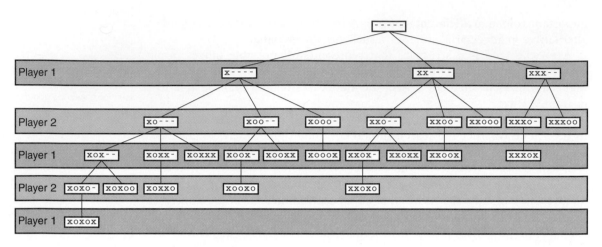

Figure 13.4 A search tree for a simplified version of Nim

differences. However, even our simplified version demonstrates several interesting mathematical ideas.

The concepts of search tree analysis can be applied nicely to other, more complicated games such as chess. In such complex games the search trees are far more complicated, having many more nodes and paths. Think about all the possible moves you might initially make in a chess game. Then consider all possible moves your opponent might make in response. A full chess search tree contains all possible moves at each level, given the current status of the board. Because these trees are so large, only a fraction of the tree can be analyzed in a reasonable time limit, even with modern computing power.

As machines have become faster, more of the search tree could be analyzed, but still not all of the branches. Programmers came up with ways to "prune" the search trees, eliminating paths that no human player would consider reasonable. And still the trees are too large to completely analyze for each move.

Depth-first approach Searching down the paths of a tree prior to searching across levels

Breadth-first approach Searching across levels of a tree prior to searching down specific paths

So the question becomes, do we choose a **depth-first approach**, analyzing selective paths all the way down the tree that hopefully result in successful moves? Or do we choose a **breadth-first approach**, analyzing all possible paths but only for a short distance down the tree? Both approaches, shown in Figure 13.5, may miss key possibilities. This issue has been debated among AI programmers for many years, though a breadth-first approach tends to yield the best results. It seems that it's better to make consistently error-free conservative moves than to occasion-

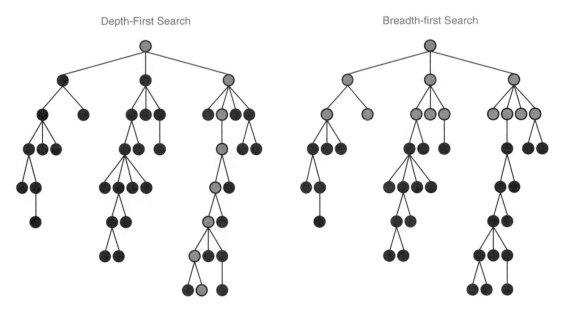

Depth-First Search   Breadth-first Search

Figure 13.5 Depth-first and breadth-first searches

ally make spectacular moves. Programs that play chess at the master level have become commonplace.

In 1997, the computer chess program Deep Blue, developed by IBM using an expert system, defeated world champion Garry Kasparov in a six-game match. This marked the first time a computer had defeated a human champion at master-level play.

13.3 Expert Systems

We often rely on experts for their unique knowledge and understanding of a particular field. We go to a doctor when we have a health problem, a car mechanic when our car won't start, and an engineer when we need to build something.

A **knowledge-based system** is a software system that embodies and uses a specific set of information from which it extracts and processes particular pieces. The term **expert system** and knowledge-based system are often used interchangeably, though expert systems usually embody the knowledge of a specialized field, modeling the expertise of a professional in that field. A user consults an expert system when confronted with a particular problem, and the system uses its expertise to advise the user how to proceed.

Knowledge-based system Software that uses a specific set of information

Expert system A software system based on the knowledge of human experts

An expert system uses a set of rules to guide its processing, and therefore is called a **rule-based system**. The set of rules in an expert system is referred to as its knowledge base. The **inference engine** is the part of the software that determines how the rules are followed and therefore what conclusions can be drawn.

A doctor is the living equivalent of an expert system. He or she gathers information by asking you questions and running tests. Your initial answers and the test results may lead to more questions and more tests. The rules embodied by the doctor's knowledge allow him or her to know what questions to ask next. The doctor then uses the information to rule out various possibilities and eventually narrows in on a specific diagnosis. Once the problem is identified, that specific knowledge allows the doctor to suggest the appropriate treatment.

Let's walk through an example of expert-system processing. Suppose you wanted to answer the question: What type of treatment should I put on my lawn?

An expert system that embodies the knowledge of a gardener would be able to guide you in this decision. Let's define a few variables so that we can abbreviate the rules in our gardening system:

NONE—apply no treatment at this time

TURF—apply a turf-building treatment

WEED—apply a weed-killing treatment

BUG—apply a bug-killing treatment

FEED—apply a basic fertilizer treatment

WEEDFEED—apply a weed-killing and fertilizer combination treatment

Note that these values represent various conclusions that the expert system might draw after analyzing the situation. The following Boolean variables represent the current state of the lawn:

BARE—the lawn has large, bare areas

SPARSE—the lawn is generally thin

WEEDS—the lawn contains many weeds

BUGS—the lawn shows evidence of bugs

We assume that initially the system has no direct data regarding the status of the lawn. The user would have to be questioned to determine, for instance, if the lawn has large, bare areas. Other data may be available directly to the system through some calculation or in some type of database, such as:

LAST—the last date a lawn treatment was applied

CURRENT—the current date

SEASON—the current season

Now we can formulate some rules that our system can use to draw a conclusion. Rules take the form of *if-then* statements.

if (CURRENT – LAST < 30) then NONE

if (SEASON = winter) then not BUGS

if (BARE) then TURF

if (SPARSE and not WEEDS) then FEED

if (BUGS and not SPARSE) then BUG

if (WEEDS and not SPARSE) then WEED

if (WEEDS and SPARSE) then WEEDFEED

Note that this is only a sample of the types of rules that may exist in such a system. Real expert systems may have thousands of rules to help analyze a situation. The set of rules presented here do not cover all situations, even in our small example.

When executed, the inference engine selects a rule to determine whether it is applicable. That may only be determined by questioning the user. If it is applicable, that may affect the applicability of other rules. The inference engine continues to apply rules until no applicable rules remain. Don't think of the rules as linear (followed in sequence); the inference engine applies whichever rules it can and continually loops until it reaches a conclusion.

An execution of our inference engine may result in the following inter-action:

System: Does the lawn have large, bare areas?

User: No

System: Does the lawn show evidence of bugs?

User: No

System: Is the lawn generally thin?

User: Yes

System: Does the lawn contain significant weeds?

User: Yes

System: You should apply a weed-killing and fertilizer combination treatment.

Artificial neural network A computer representation of knowledge that attempts to mimic the neural networks of the human body

Note that the system doesn't ask about things it can look up, such as the date of the last treatment. And apparently our scenario didn't take place in winter, because the system asked about a potential bug problem. If it had been winter, the bug issue would have already been eliminated.

An expert system has many advantages over other advising techniques. First, it is goal-oriented. It doesn't focus on abstract or theoretical information, but rather focuses on solving a specific problem. Second, it is efficient. It records previous responses and doesn't ask irrelevant questions. And third, a real expert system, through a carefully constructed set of rules, can usually provide useful guidance even if you don't know the answers to some questions.

13.4   Neural Networks

We've said that some artificial intelligence researchers focus on how the human brain actually works and try to construct computing devices that work in similar ways. An **artificial neural network** in a computer attempts to mimic the actions of the neural networks of the human body. Let's first look at how a biological neural network works.

Biological Neural Networks

A neuron is a single cell that conducts a chemically-based electronic signal. The human brain contains billions of neurons connected into a network. At any point in time a neuron is in either an excited or inhibited state. An excited neuron conducts a strong signal and an inhibited neuron conducts a weak signal. A series of connected neurons forms a pathway. The signal along a particular pathway is strengthened or weakened according to the state of the neurons it passes through. A series of excited neurons creates a strong pathway.

A biological neuron has multiple input tentacles called *dendrites* and one primary output tentacle called an *axon*. The dendrites of one neuron pick up the signals from the axons of other neurons to form the neural network. The gap between an axon and a dendrite is called a *synapse*. See Figure 13.6. The chemical composition of a synapse tempers the strength of its input signal. The output of a neuron on its axon is a function of all of its input signals.

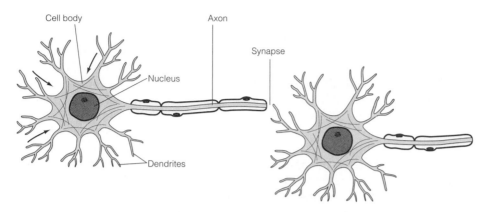

Figure 13.6 A biological neuron *Adapted from Chiras, D. Human Biology, Third Edition, 1999: Jones and Bartlett Publishers, Sudbury, MA. www.jbpub.com. Reprinted with Permission*

So, a neuron accepts multiple input signals and then controls the contribution of each signal based on the "importance" the corresponding synapse gives to it. If enough of these weighted input signals are strong, the neuron goes into an excited state and produces a strong output signal. If enough of the input signals are weak, or are weakened by the weighting factor of that signal's synapse, the neuron goes into an inhibited state and produces a weak output signal.

Neurons fire, or pulsate, up to 1,000 times per second, so the pathways along the neural nets are in a constant state of flux. The activity of our brain causes some pathways to strengthen and others to weaken. As we learn new things, new strong neural pathways in our brain are formed.

Artificial Neural Networks

Each processing element in an artificial neural net is analogous to a biological neuron. An element accepts a certain number of input values and produces a single output value of either 0 or 1. These input values come from the output of other elements in the network, so each input value is either 0 or 1. Associated with each input value is a numeric weight. The **effective weight** of the element is defined to be the sum of the weights multiplied by their respective input values.

Suppose an artificial neuron accepts three input values: v1, v2, and v3. Associated with each input value is a weight: w1, w2, and w3. The effective weight is therefore:

v1*w1 + v2*w2 + v3*w3

Each element has a numeric threshold value. The element compares the effective weight to the threshold value. If the effective weight exceeds the

Effective weight In an artificial neuron, the sum of the weights multiplied by the corresponding input values threshold, the unit produces an output value of 1. If it does not exceed the threshold, it produces an output value of 0.

This processing closely mirrors the activity of a biological neuron. The input values correspond to the signals passed in by the dendrites. The weight values correspond to the controlling effect of the synapse for each input signal. The computation and use of the threshold value correspond to the neuron producing a strong signal if "enough" of the weighted input signals are strong.

Let's compute an actual example. In this case, let's assume there are four inputs to the processing element. There are, therefore, four corresponding weight factors. Suppose the input values are 1, 1, 0, and 0, and the corresponding weights are 4, -2, -5, and -2, and the threshold value for the element is 4. The effective weight is:

$$1(4) + 1(-2) + 0(-5) + 0(-2)$$

or 2. Since the effective weight does not exceed the threshold value, the output of this element is 0.

Note that though the input values are either 0 or 1, the weights can be any value at all. They can even be negative. We've used integers for the weights and threshold values, but they can be real numbers as well.

The output of each element is truly a function of all pieces. If an input signal is 0, its weight is irrelevant. If the input signal is 1, the magnitude of the weight, and whether it is positive or negative, greatly affects the effective weight. And no matter what effective weight is computed, it's viewed relative to the threshold value of that element. That is, an effective weight of 15 may be enough for one element to produce an output of 1, but for another element it results in an output of 0.

The pathways established in an artificial neural net are a function of its individual processing elements. And the output of each processing element changes on the basis of the input signals, the weights, and/or the threshold values. But the input signals are really just output signals from other elements. Therefore, we affect the processing of a neural net by changing the weights and threshold value in individual processing elements.

The process of adjusting the weights and threshold values in a neural net is called **training**. A neural net can be trained to produce whatever results are required. Often, initially, a neural net is set up with random weights, threshold values, and initial inputs. The results are compared to the desired results and changes are made. This process continues until the desired results are achieved.

Consider the problem we posed at the beginning of this chapter: Find a cat in a photograph. Suppose a neural net is used to address this problem, using one output value per pixel. Our goal is to produce an output value of 1 for every pixel that contributes to the image of the cat, and to produce a 0 if it does not. The input values for the network could come from some

Training The process of adjusting the weights and threshold values in a neural net to get a desired outcome

representation of the color of the pixels. We then train the network using multiple pictures containing cats, reinforcing weights and thresholds that lead to the desired (correct) output.

Think about how complicated this problem is! Cats come in all shapes, sizes, and colors. They can be oriented in a picture in thousands of ways. They might blend into their background (in the picture) or they might not. A neural net for this problem would be incredibly large, taking all kinds of situations into account. The more training we give the network, the more likely it will produce accurate results in the future.

But what else are neural nets good for? They have been used successfully in thousands of application areas, in both business and scientific endeavors. They can be used to determine if a client should be given a mortgage. They can be used in optical character recognition, allowing a computer to "read" a printed document. They can even be used to detect plastic explosives in luggage at airports.

The versatility of neural nets lies in the fact that there is no inherent meaning in the weights and threshold values of the network. Their meaning comes from the interpretation we apply to them.

13.5 Natural Language Processing

In a science fiction movie, it's not uncommon to have a human interacting with a computer by simply talking to it. The captain of a spaceship might say, "Computer, what is the nearest starbase with medical facilities sufficient to handle Laharman's syndrome?" The computer might then respond, "Starbase 42 is 14.7 light years away and has the necessary facilities."

How far is this science fiction from science fact? Ignoring space travel and advanced medicine for now, why don't we interact with computers just by talking to them? Well, to a limited extent we can. We don't tend to have free-flowing verbal conversations yet, but we've made headway. Some computers can be set up to respond to specific verbal commands.

To probe this issue further, we must first realize that there are three basic types of processing going on during human/computer voice interaction.

- **voice recognition**—recognizing human words
- **natural language comprehension**—interpreting human communication
- **voice synthesis**—recreating human speech

The computer must first recognize the distinct words that are being spoken to it, then understand the meaning of those words, then (after determining the answer) produce the words that make up the response.

Voice recognition Using a computer to recognize the words spoken by a human

Natural language comprehension Using a computer to apply a meaningful interpretation to human communication

Voice synthesis Using a computer to create the sound of human speech

Common to all of these problems is the fact that we are using a **natural language**, which can be any language that humans use to communicate, such as English, Farsi, or Russian. Natural languages have inherent grammatical irregularities and ambiguities that make some of this processing quite challenging.

Computing technology has made great headway in all of these areas, though some more than others. Let's explore each one in more detail.

> **Natural language**
> Languages that human beings use to communicate, such as English

Voice Synthesis

Voice synthesis is generally a well-understood problem. There are two basic approaches to the solution: dynamic voice generation and recorded speech.

To generate voice output using dynamic voice generation, a computer examines the letters that make up a word and produces the sequence of sounds that correspond to those letters in an attempt to vocalize the word. Human speech has been categorized into specific sound units called **phonemes**. The phonemes for American English are shown in Figure 13.7.

> **Phonemes** The set of fundamental sounds made in any given natural language

After selecting the appropriate phonemes, the computer may modify the pitch of the phoneme based on the context in which it is used. The duration of each phoneme must also be determined. Finally, the phonemes are combined to form individual words. The sounds themselves are produced electronically,

Consonants				Vowels	
Symbols	Examples	Symbols	Examples	Symbols	Examples
p	pipe	k	kick, cat	i	eel, sea, see
b	babe	g	get	I	ill, bill
m	maim	ŋ	sing	e	ale, aim, day
f	fee, phone, rough	š	shoe, ash, sugar	ɛ	elk, bet, bear
v	vie, love	ž	measure	æ	at, mat
θ	thin, bath	č	chat, batch	u	due, new, zoo
ð	the, bathe	ǰ	jaw, judge, gin	ʊ	book, sugar
t	tea, beat	d	day, bad	o	own, no, know
n	nine	ʔ	uh uh	ɔ	aw, crawl, law, dog
l	law, ball	s	see, less, city	a	hot, bar, dart
r	run, bar	z	zoo, booze	ə	sir, nerd, bird
				ʌ	cut, bun

Semi Vowels			Dipthongs	
w	we		aj	bite, fight
h	he		aw	out, cow
j	you, beyond		ɔj	boy, boil

Figure 13.7 Phonemes for American English

designed to mimic the way a human vocal track produces the sounds.

The challenges to this approach include the fact that the way we pronounce words varies greatly among humans, and the rules governing how letters contribute to the sound of a word are not consistent. Dynamic voice-generation systems often sound mechanical and stilted, though usually the words are recognizable.

The other approach to voice synthesis is to play digital recordings of a human voice saying specific words. Sentences are constructed by playing the appropriate words in the appropriate order. Sometimes common phrases or groups of words that are always used together are recorded as one entity. Telephone voice mail systems often use this approach: "Press 1 to leave a message for Alex Wakefield."

Note that each word or phrase needed must be recorded separately. Furthermore, since words are pronounced differently in different contexts, some words may have to be recorded multiple times. For example, a word at the end of a question rises in pitch compared to its use in the middle of a sentence. As the need for flexibility increases, recorded solutions become problematic.

> **The National Weather Service gets a new voice**
>
> In August of 2001, the National Oceanic and Atmospheric Administration (NOAA) awarded Siemens Information and Communication Network of Boca Raton, Florida, a contract for the voice-improvement software product known as Speechify. This software combines concatenated, prerecorded phonetic sounds with the emphasis and intonation of a human voice. The contract award calls for both a male and a female voice. Speechify voices received the most favorable comments in the Web page public-opinion survey.
>
> "Paul," the original computerized weather forecaster for NOAA Weather Radio, had been criticized for sounding too stilted and foreign. Paul will be replaced by Donna and Craig.[2]

The dynamic voice-generation technique does not generally produce realistic human speech, but attempts to vocalize any words presented to it. Recorded playback is more realistic; it uses a real human voice but is limited in its vocabulary to the words that have been prerecorded, and it must have the memory capacity to store all the needed words. Generally, recorded playback is used when the number of words used is small.

Voice Recognition

When having a conversation, you may need to have something repeated because you didn't understand what the person said. It's not that you didn't understand the meaning of the words (you hadn't gotten that far). You simply didn't understand what words were being spoken. This might happen for several reasons.

First, the sounds that each person makes when speaking are unique. We each have a unique shape to our mouth, tongue, throat, and nasal cavities that affect the pitch and resonance of our spoken voice. Thus we can say we "recognize" someone's voice, identifying him or her from the way the words sound when spoken by that person. But that also means that each person says any given word somewhat differently, complicating the task of recognizing the word in the first place. Speech impediments, mumbling, volume, regional accents, and the health of the speaker further complicate this problem.

Furthermore, humans speak in a continuous, flowing manner. Words are strung together into sentences. Sometimes we speak so quickly that two words may sound like one. Humans have great abilities to divide the series of sounds into words, but even we can become confused if a person speaks too rapidly.

Related to this issue are the sounds of words themselves. Sometimes it's difficult to distinguish between phrases like "ice cream" and "I scream." And homonyms such as "I" and "eye" or "see" and "sea" sound exactly the same but are unique words. Humans can often clarify these situations by the context of the sentence, but that processing requires another level of comprehension.

So, if we humans occasionally have trouble understanding the words we say to each other, consider how difficult this problem is for a computer. Modern voice-recognition systems still do not do well with continuous, conversational speech. The best success has been with systems that assume disjointed speech, in which words are clearly separated.

Further success is obtained when voice recognition systems are "trained" to recognize a particular human's voice and a set of vocabulary words. A spoken voice can be recorded as a **voiceprint**, which plots the frequency changes of the sound produced by the voice when speaking a specific word. A human trains a voice-recognition system by speaking a word several times so that the computer can record an average voiceprint for that word by that person. Later, when a word is spoken, the recorded voiceprints can be compared to determine which word was spoken.

Voice-recognition systems that are not trained for specific voices and words do their best to recognize words by comparing generic voiceprints. While less accurate, using generic voiceprints avoids the time-consuming training process and allows anyone to use the system.

> **Voiceprint**   The plot of frequency changes over time representing the sound of human speech

Natural Language Comprehension

Even if a computer recognizes the words that are spoken, it is another task entirely to understand the meaning of those words. This is the most challenging aspect of natural language processing. Natural language is inherently ambiguous, meaning that the same syntactic structure could have multiple valid interpretations. These ambiguities can arise for several reasons.

One problem is that a single word can have multiple definitions and can even represent multiple parts of speech. The word "light," for instance, is both a noun and a verb. This is referred to as a **lexical ambiguity**. A computer attempting to apply meaning to a sentence would have to determine how the word was being used. Consider the following sentence:

> **Lexical ambiguity**   The ambiguity created when words have multiple meanings

Time flies like an arrow.

This sentence might mean that time seems to move quickly, just like an arrow moves quickly. That's probably how you interpreted it when you read it. However, note that the word *time* can also be a verb, such as when you time the runner of a race. The word *flies* can also be a noun. Therefore, you could interpret this sentence as a directive to time flies in the same manner in which an arrow times flies. Since an arrow doesn't time things, you probably wouldn't apply that interpretation. But it is no less valid than the other one! Given the definition of the words, a computer would not know which interpretation was appropriate. Note that we could even interpret this sentence a third way, indicating the preferences of that rare species we'll call a "time fly." After all, fruit flies like a banana. That interpretation probably sounds ridiculous to you, but these ambiguities cause huge problems when it comes to a computer understanding natural language.

A natural language sentence can also have a **syntactic ambiguity** because phrases can be put together in various ways. For example:

I saw the Grand Canyon flying to New York.

Since canyons don't fly, there is one logical interpretation. But because the sentence can be constructed that way, there are two valid interpretations. To reach the desired conclusion, a computer would have to "know" that canyons don't fly and take that into account.

Referential ambiguity can occur with the use of pronouns. Consider the following:

The brick fell on the computer but it is not broken.

What is not broken, the brick or the computer? We might assume the pronoun "it" refers to the computer in this case, but that is not obvious. In fact, if a vase had fallen on the computer, even we humans wouldn't know what "it" referred to without more information.

Natural language comprehension is a huge area of study and goes well beyond the scope of this book. But it's important to understand the reasons why this issue is so challenging.

> **Syntactic ambiguity**
> The ambiguity created when sentences can be constructed in various ways
>
> **Referential ambiguity**
> The ambiguity created when pronouns could be applied to multiple objects

13.6   Robotics

Robots are familiar to all of us. From television commercials about robotic dogs to the nightly news about space exploration to assembly lines producing beer, cars, or widgets, robots are a part of modern society. Robotics, the study of robots, breaks down into two main categories: fixed robots and mobile robots. The fixed robots are what you see on assembly lines. The machines stay put and the products move. Because the world of a fixed robot is circumscribed, its tasks can be built into the hardware. Thus fixed robots belong mostly in the area of industrial engineering. Mobile robots, on the

Early Promise of Machine Translation Not Realized

Both the National Science Foundation and the U.S. Military funded large machine translation projects in the late 1950s and early '60s. The vision of using a computer to translate from one natural language to another seemed immediately realizable. But the approach of using large bilingual dictionaries and word-by-word translation proved inadequate. This inadequacy is demonstrated in the classic story of the translation of the English expression "The spirit is willing, but the flesh is weak" into Russian. The result was "The vodka is acceptable, but the meat has spoiled."

Researchers realized that they needed to do more fundamental research into language understanding before tackling automatic language translation.

ELIZA

ELIZA was an early natural-language program. In the following script, the program plays the role of a neutral psychotherapist.

The computer's responses are in all uppercase.

Men are all alike.

IN WHAT WAY?

They're always bugging us about something or another.

CAN YOU THINK OF A SPECIFIC EXAMPLE?

Well, my boyfriend made me come here.

YOUR BOYFRIEND MADE YOU COME HERE?

He says I'm depressed much of the time.

I AM SORRY TO HEAR YOU ARE DEPRESSED.

It's true. I am unhappy.

DO YOU THINK COMING HERE WILL HELP YOU NOT TO BE UNHAPPY?

I need some help, that much seems certain.

…

WHAT ELSE COMES TO MIND WHEN YOU THINK OF YOUR FATHER?

Bullies.

DOES THAT HAVE ANYTHING TO DO WITH THE FACT THAT YOUR BOYFRIEND MADE YOU COME HERE?[3]

More information about the ELIZA program can be found on the Web site.

other hand, move about and must interact with their environment. Modeling the world of the mobile robot requires the techniques of artificial intelligence.

The Sense-Plan-Act Paradigm

Mobile robotics is the study of robots that move relative to their environment, while exhibiting a degree of autonomy. The original approach to modeling the world surrounding a mobile robot made use of *plans*. Planning systems are large software systems that, given a goal, a starting position, and an ending situation, can generate a finite set of actions (a plan) that, if followed (usually by a human), brings about the desired ending situation. These planning systems solve general problems by incorporating large amounts of domain knowledge. In the case of a mobile robot, the

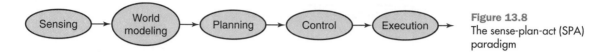

Figure 13.8
The sense-plan-act (SPA)
paradigm

domain knowledge is the input from the robot's sensors. In this approach, the world of the robot is represented in a complex semantic net in which the sensors on the robot are used to capture the data to build up the net. Populating the net is time-consuming even for simple sensors; if the sensor is a camera, the process is *very* time consuming. This approach is called the *sense-plan-act (SPA) paradigm*[4] shown in Figure 13.8.

The sensor data is interpreted by the world model, which in turn generates a plan of action. The robot's control system (the hardware) executes the steps in the plan. Once the robot moves, its sensors get new information, and the cycle repeats with the new data being incorporated into the semantic net. Problems occur when the new sensory data cannot be processed fast enough to be used. (Perhaps the robot falls into a hole before the word model recognizes that the change in light is a hole rather than a shadow.) The flaw in this approach is that the representation of the robot's world as domain knowledge in a general system is too general, too broad, and not tailored to the robot's task.

Subsumption Architecture

In 1986, a paradigm shift occurred within the robotics community with the introduction by Brooks of the *subsumption architecture.*[5] Rather than trying to model the entire world all the time, the robot is given a simple set of behaviors each associated with the part of the world necessary for that behavior. The behaviors run in parallel unless they came in conflict, in which case an ordering of the goals of the behaviors determines which behavior should be executed next. The idea that the goals of behaviors can be ordered, or that the goal of one behavior can be subsumed by another, led to the name of the architecture. See Figure 13.9.

Keep going to the left takes precedence over *Avoid obstacles* unless an object gets too close, in which case the *Avoid obstacles* behavior takes precedence. As a result of this approach, robots were built that could wander around a room for hours without running into objects or into moving people.

The three laws of robotics defined by Isaac Asimov fit neatly into this subsumption architecture.[6] See Figure 13.10.

Another shift was away from viewing the world as a uniform grid with each cell representing the same amount of real space towards viewing the world as a topological map. Topological maps view space as a graph of

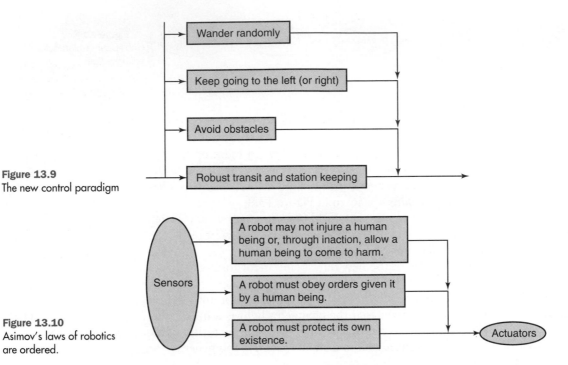

Figure 13.9
The new control paradigm

Figure 13.10
Asimov's laws of robotics
are ordered.

places connected by arcs, giving the notion of proximity and order but not of distance. The robot navigates from place to place locally, which minimizes errors. Also, topological maps can be represented in memory much more efficiently than uniform grids.

In the '90s, a modified approach in which plans were used in conjunction with a set of behaviors with distributed world views became popular.

Physical Components

We have been discussing the various approaches to trying to get a robot to exhibit human-like behavior and have ignored the physical components of a robot. A robot is made up of sensors, actuators, and computational elements (a microprocessor). The sensors take in data about the surroundings, the actuators move the robot, and the computational elements send instructions to the actuators. Sensors are transducers that convert some physical phenomena into electrical signals that the microprocessor can read as data. There are sensors that register the presence, absence, or intensity of light. There are near-infrared proximity detec-

Robot competition and exhibition

Since 1992, the American Association for Artificial Intelligence (AAAI) Robot Competition and Exhibition has drawn entries from all over the world. The participants, who have included students, senior professors, and young entrepreneurs, share the common goal of trying to integrate software and hardware to get a robot to act intelligently and autonomously in a given task and environment. The entries represent the cutting edge of robotics research. www

Courtesy of NASA/JPL/Caltech

What is the Sojourner rover?

The Sojourner was man's first attempt to operate a remote control vehicle on another planet. After landing, Sojourner drove down one of the two ramps mounted to the lander petal. This exit and subsequent exploration was watched by hundreds of millions of fascinated earth-bound viewers. This mission was conducted under the constraint of a once-per-sol (Martian day) opportunity for transmissions between the lander and earth operators. Sojourner was able to carry out her mission with a form of supervised autonomous control in which goal locations (called waypoints) or move commands were sent to the rover ahead of time, and Sojourner then navigated and safely traversed to these locations on her own.

(Mars Now Team and the California Space Institute. Oct. 6, 2001)[9]

Mars Polar lander vanishes

On December 3, 1999, the Mars polar lander descended to the Martian surface and vanished. The first signal from the lander was expected approximately 30 minutes after landing. That signal never came. In fact, no signal was ever received from the lander.

The Mars Program Assessment report concluded: "[T]he most probable cause of the failure was the generation of spurious signals when the lander legs were deployed during descent. The spurious signals gave a false indication that the spacecraft had landed, resulting in a premature shutdown of the engines and the destruction of the lander when it crashed on Mars. Without any entry, descent, and landing telemetry data, there is no way to know whether the lander reached the terminal descent propulsion phase. If it did reach this phase, it is almost certain that premature engine shutdown occurred."[8]

Courtesy of Lucasfilm Ltd. Star Wars: Episode IV—A New Hope © 1977 and 1997 Lucasfilm Ltd. & ™. All Rights Reserved. Used under authorization. Unauthorized duplication is a violation of applicable law.

R2D2 charms millions

R2D2, the friendly, eccentric robot from the Star Wars movies, became a household name in 1977 with the release of the original *Star Wars* movie. A Web search for R2D2 conducted 25 years later produced over 1,200 references.

Courtesy of NASA/JPL/Caltech

tors, motion detectors, and force detectors that can all be used as sensors. Cameras and microphones can be sensors. The three most common systems on which robots move are wheels, tracks, and legs.

Summary

Artificial intelligence deals with the attempts to model and apply the intelligence of the human mind. The Turing test is one measure to determine whether a machine can think like a human by mimicking human conversation.

There are various aspects to the discipline of AI. Underlying all of them is the need to represent knowledge in a form that can be processed efficiently. Semantic networks are a graphical representation that captures the relationships between objects in the real world. Questions can be answered based on an analysis of the network graph. Search trees are a valuable way to represent the knowledge of adversarial moves, such as in a competitive game. For complicated games like chess, search trees are enormous, so we still have to come up with strategies for efficient analysis of these structures.

An expert system embodies the knowledge of a human expert. It uses a set of rules to define the conditions under which certain conclusions can be drawn. It is useful in many types of decision-making processes, such as medical diagnosis.

Artificial neural networks mimic the processing of the neural networks of the human brain. An artificial neuron produces an output signal based on multiple input signals and the importance we give to those signals using a weighting system. This mirrors the human neuron, in which synapses temper the input signals from one neuron to the next.

Natural language processing deals with languages that we humans use to communicate, such as English. Synthesizing a spoken voice can be accomplished by mimicking the phonemes of human speech or by replying prerecorded words. Voice recognition is best accomplished when the spoken words are disjoint, and even more so when the system is trained to recognize a particular person's voiceprint. Comprehending natural language—applying an interpretation to the conversational discourse—is the heart of natural language processing. It is complicated by various types of ambiguities that allow one specific sentence to be interpreted in multiple ways.

Robotics, the study of robots, falls into two categories: fixed and mobile. Fixed robots are those that stay put and have whatever they are working on come to them. Mobile robots are those that are capable of moving and require the techniques of artificial intelligence to model the environment within which they move.

ETHICAL ISSUES

Deep Linking

The incredible impact that the World Wide Web has on society can undoubtedly be attributed to its ability to facilitate communication and information exchange. It is a revolutionary medium in which people can interact, conduct research, and post their thoughts and ideas almost instantaneously. Users surf from web page to web page with ease, following hyperlinks that direct them to relevant topics and points of interest. These hyperlinks, which can appear as text or images, respond to a mouse click and send the user a new page often from outside of the original website. By connecting pages, hyperlinks provide an important service to the user and are a defining feature of the Web. In the early stages of web development, linking was embraced as essential and recognized as an indispensable guide to mapping cyberspace. As the Web has matured, however, deep linking has become controversial. Deep linking occurs when one web page includes a hyperlink to a web page that is buried deep within another site, i.e. not to the other site's homepage. While many companies welcome visitors who stumble upon one of their pages, regardless of whether or not it is their homepage, other companies feel that deep linking is illegitimate, a technique that unfairly bypasses a site's "front door."

Ticketmaster.com brought the problem to public attention when it sued Microsoft in 1997 for inappropriately linking to its site. Microsoft's city-guide "Sidewalk" provided links to ticketing for specific events on Ticketmaster.com that sent a wave of visitors to pages deep within that site. Despite the traffic this link created, Ticketmaster.com felt that it should have control over how others link to its site and that the deep link unfairly bypassed its advertising. Although this case was settled out of court, Ticketmaster.com has subsequently sued one of its rivals. Tickets.com, for a number of offenses including improper linking. Ticketmaster.com contended that Tickets.com was conducting unfair business practices by linking directly to pages within its site and not to its homepage. Ticketmaster.com listed a number of specific complaints, among them that deep linking hurt its advertising. The court ruled that Tickets.com did not violate copyright law because it did not republish in a new format the page to which it linked, nor was the relationship between the two sites likely to be misconstrued. This decision, however, does not mean that the issue of deep linking has been resolved. Other companies such as Ebay Inc. and Universal Studios have similarly tried to prohibit deep linking into their web sites, and the issue will continue to generate controversy as Internet regulations develop and solidify.

Key Terms

Artificial intelligence (AI) pg. 400

Artificial neural network pg. 412

Breadth-first approach pg. 408

Depth-first approach pg. 408

Effective weight pg. 413

Expert system pg. 409

Inference engine pg. 410

Knowledge-based system pg. 409

Lexical ambiguity pg. 418

Loebner prize pg. 403

Natural language pg. 416

Natural language comprehension
  pg. 415

Phonemes pg. 416

Referential ambiguity pg. 419

Rule-based system pg. 410

Search tree pg. 407

Semantic network pg. 404

Strong equivalence pg. 402

Syntactic ambiguity pg. 419

Training pg. 414

Turing test pg. 401

Voice recognition pg. 415

Voice synthesis pg. 415

Voiceprint pg. 418

Weak equivalence pg. 402

Exercises

1. Name three things that a computer can do well that a human cannot.

2. Name three things that a human can do well that a computer cannot.

3. What is the Turing test?

4. How is the Turing test organized and administered?

5. What is weak equivalence and how does it apply to the Turing test?

6. What is strong equivalence?

7. What is the Loebner prize?

8. Name and describe briefly five issues in the world of AI covered in this chapter.

9. Name and define two knowledge representation techniques.

10. What data structure defined in Chapter 9 is used to represent a semantic network?

11. Create a semantic network for the relationships among your family members. List five questions that your semantic net could easily be used to answer and five questions that would be more of a challenge to answer.

12. Create a semantic network for the relationships regarding books in a library. List five questions that your semantic net could be easily used to answer and five questions that would be more of a challenge to answer.

13. Create a semantic network that captures the information in a small section of a newspaper article.

14. What object-oriented properties do semantic networks posses?

15. What is a search tree?

16. Why arc trees for complex games like chess so large?

17. Distinguish between depth-first searching and breadth-first searching.

18. What does it mean to prune a tree?

19. Distinguish between knowledge-based systems and expert systems.

20. Distinguish be rule-based systems and inference engines.

21. What is an example of a human expert system?

22. Define some variables and some rules that might be in an expert system for automobile repair.

23. Define some variables and some rules that might be in an expert system for loan approval.

24. Define some variables and some rules that might be in an expert system used in selecting a neighborhood into which you will move.

25. What does the knowledge representation used in a neural network try to mimic?

26. What is neuron?

27. What are the two states of a neuron?

28. Define a *dendrite* and an *axon*.

29. How is a neural network formed and what is the role of a synapse?

30. What puts a neuron into an excited state or an inhibited state?

31. How are new strong neural pathways formed in our brain?

32. If a processing element in an artificial neural net accepted four input signals with values 0, 1, 0, and 1, using weights 5, 2, −2, and 7 and a threshold value of 10, what would its output be?

33. If a processing element in an artificial neural net accepted four input signals with values 1, 1, 0, and 1, using weights 4.3, –3.7, –5.0, and 2.5 and a threshold value of 14.5, what would its output be?

34. Explain how a neural net can be trained.

35. What are the three basic types of processing that occur during human/computer voice interaction?

36. Of the three types of processing in Exercise 35, which is the most difficult?

37. What is a phoneme?

38. Describe the two distinct ways that voice synthesis can be accomplished.

39. What issues affect the ability to recognize the words spoken by a human voice?

40. How can a voice-recognition system be trained?

41. Why are personalized voice-recognition systems so much better than those that are not specific to a particular person?

42. Name and describe three kinds of ambiguity in natural language.

43. Give and explain an example of lexical ambiguity not found in this chapter.

44. Give and explain an example of syntactic ambiguity not found in this chapter.

45. Give and explain an example of referential ambiguity not found in this chapter.

46. Name and describe two categories of robots.

47. What are planning systems?

48. What defines subsumption architecture?

49. Of what is a robot composed?

50. Is the following sentence ambiguous? If so, explain why.

    Go down the street to the left.

51. What kind of ambiguity (if any) is represented in Exercise 50?

52. Is the following sentence ambiguous? If so, explain why.

    After he threw the ball for the dog, he ran away.

53. What kind of ambiguity (if any) is represented in Exercise 52?

54. Is the following sentence ambiguous? If so, explain why.

    See Spot run.

? Thought Questions

1. Think of five questions that you might issue as the interrogator of a Turing test. Why would a computer have difficulty answering them well?

2. Do you think that strong equivalence is possible? How could it be proven?

3. When you think of robots, what comes to mind? Do you see a human-like machine scampering around the floor? An assembly line producing soft drinks or beer?

4. What do you think about deep linking? Should all access to another Web site be through the homepage of that Web site? Would you feel uncomfortable if someone accessed pages on your site that are in the middle of your site? Isn't such a practice like taking comments out of context?

5. Many commercial Web sites make their money by advertising. Is bypassing the advertising by deep linking ethical? Should laws be passed to disallow deep linking?

6. If you have a Web site, do you have links? Are any of your links deep links? After reading about the issues surrounding deep linking, are you going to change them?

The Applications Layer

14 Simulation and Other Applications

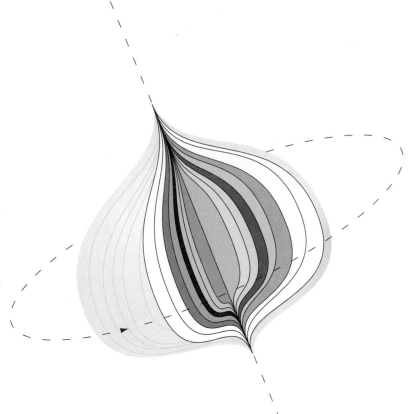

Chapter 14

Simulation and Other Applications

Airplane manufacturers build wind tunnels to study airflow around an airfoil on a new aircraft design. Pilots spend countless hours in flight simulators, a model that recreates the responses of an aircraft to actions the pilot might take, thus allowing the pilot to learn to control the aircraft before hc or she ever gets into the cockpit. Before the plans of a new supermarket are finalized, a computer program is run to help determine how many checkout stations are needed for the expected number of customers. The wind tunnel, the flight simulator, and the program are models. The technique of using a model to represent phenomena, objects, or situations is called *simulation*. In this chapter, we look at the theory behind simulation and examine some concrete examples, including models that predict the weather.

Two other applications, embedded systems and CAD (computer-aided design) systems, are also covered in this chapter. They are included to round out the discussion of the application layer.

Goals

After studying this chapter, you should be able to

- define simulation.
- give examples of complex systems.
- distinguish between continuous and discrete event simulation.
- explain how object-oriented design principles can be used in building models.
- name and discuss the four parts of a queuing system.
- explain the complexity of weather and seismic models.
- explain the concept of embedded systems and give examples from your own home.
- distinguish between two-dimensional and three-dimensional CAD systems.

14.1   What Is Simulation?

Simulation Developing a model of a complex system and experimenting with the model to observe the results

Simulation is a powerful tool used to study complex systems. **Simulation** is the development of a *model* of a *complex system* and the experimental manipulation of the model to observe the results. Models may be purely physical such as a wind tunnel, a combination of a physical object under software control such as a spaceship or flight simulator, or logical as represented in a computer program.

Computer simulations have been used to help in decision making since the mid–1950s. Building computer models of complex systems has allowed decision-makers to develop an understanding of the performance of the systems over time. How many tellers should a bank have? Would the materials flow faster through the manufacturing line if there were more space between stations? What is the weather going to be tomorrow? Where is the optimal place to put the new fire station? We can gain considerable insight into all of these questions through simulation.

Complex Systems

System is one of those words that we all intuitively understand but have difficulty defining. The dictionary gives several definitions with the common theme of groups (collections) of objects interacting in some way. The objects can be animate or inanimate. A collection of hardware and software form a computer system. A collection of tracks and railway cars form a railroad system. A collection of teachers and students form a school system.

Systems that are best suited to being simulated are *dynamic, interactive*, and *complicated*.[1] That is, they should be complex. The behaviors of dynamic systems vary over time. The way that the behavior varies may be understood and captured in mathematical equations, such as the flight of a missile through nonturbulent atmosphere. Or the behavior may be only partially understood but amenable to statistical representation, such as the arrival of people at a traffic light. Although the definition of systems implies that the objects interact, the more interactions that exist in the system, the better candidate the system is for simulation. Take, for example, the behavior of a plane under air traffic control. The performance characteristics of the individual plane, the interaction with the air traffic controller, the weather, and any routing changes due to problems on the ground all contribute to the plane's behavior. Finally, the system should be made up of many objects. If it weren't, simulating it would be a waste of time.

Models

Model is another of those words that we all understand but might have a hard time defining. There are two dictionary definitions that relate to the use of the word in simulation: an analogy used to help visualize something that can not be directly observed, and a set of postulates, data, and inferences presented as a mathematical description of an entity or state of affairs. Although these two definitions seem very different, they have one major thread in common. In both cases, a model is an abstraction of something else. In the first case, the model represents something that is not completely understood, so we are forced to say it is like something else. In the second case, the system is understood well enough to be described by a set of mathematical rules.

For our purposes a **model** is an abstraction of a real system. It is a representation of the objects within the system and the rules that govern the interactions of the objects. The representation may be concrete as in the case of the spaceship or flight simulators or abstract as in the case of the computer program that examines the number of checkout stations needed. In the rest of the discussion of simulation, the models we refer to are abstract. The realization is only within a computer program.

Model   An abstraction of a real system; a representation of objects within a system and the rules that govern the behavior of the objects.

Constructing Models

The essence of constructing a model is to identify a small subset of characteristics or features that are sufficient to describe the behavior under investigation. Remember, a model is an abstraction of a real system; it is not the system itself. Therefore, there is a fine line between having too few characteristics to accurately describe the behavior of the system and more than you need to accurately describe the system. The goal is to build the simplest model that describes the relevant behavior.

There are two distinct types of simulation for which models are built and the process of choosing the subset of characteristics or features is different for each. The distinction between the two types is based on how time is represented: as a continuous variable or as a discrete variable.

Continuous Simulation

Continuous simulations treat time as continuous and express changes in terms of a set of differential equations that reflect the relationships among the set of characteristics. Thus the characteristics or features chosen to model the system must be those whose behavior is understood mathematically. For example, meteorological modeling falls into this category. The characteristics of weather models are wind components, temperature, water vapor, cloud formation, precipitation, and so on. The interaction of these components over time can be modeled by a set of partial differential equations, which measure the rate of change of each component over some three-dimensional region.

Because of the technical nature of the characteristics in continuous simulations, engineers and economists frequently use this technique. The sets of possible characteristics and their interactions are well-known in these fields. In a later section we look more closely at meteorological simulation.

Discrete Event Simulation

Discrete event models are made up of *entitie*s, *attributes*, and *events*. An entity represents some object in the real system that must be explicitly defined. That is, the characteristic or feature of the system is an object. For example, if we were modeling a manufacturing plant, the different machines, and the product being created, would be entities. An attribute is some characteristic of a particular entity. The identification number, the purchase date, and the maintenance history would be attributes of a particular machine. An event is an interaction between entities. For example, the sending of the output from one machine as input to the next machine would be an event.

An object that flows through a system is usually represented as an entity. For example, the output from one machine is an object that is passed on to the next machine. Thus a raw widget flows from one machine to another (a series of events) and ends up as a lovely doodad. An entity can also represent a resource that other entities need. For example, a cashier is a resource in a model of a bank. If a cashier is not available, the customer entity must enter a waiting line (a queue) until a cashier is available.

The keys to constructing a good model are choosing the entities to represent the system and correctly determining the rules that define the results of the events. Parteto's law says that in every set of entities, there exists a vital few and a trivial many. Approximately 80% of the behavior of an average system can be explained by the action of 20% of the components.[2] The second part of the definition of simulation gives us a clue where to begin: "and experimenting with the model to observe the results." What results are to be observed? The answers to this question give a good starting point to the determination of the entities in the real system that must be present in the model. The entities and the rules that define the interactions of the entities must be sufficient to produce the results to be observed.

Since abstract models are implemented in a computer program, we can apply object-oriented design to the problem of building the model. The entities in the model are object classes. The attributes of the entities are properties of a class. Where do the events fall into this analogy? The events are the responsibilities of an entity. The rules that define the interactions of the entities in the system are represented by the collaborations of the classes.

In the next section, we apply these techniques to a specific example.

Queuing Systems

Let's look at a very useful type of simulation called a *queuing system*. A queuing system is a discrete-event model that uses random numbers to represent the arrival and duration of events. A queuing system is made up of servers and queues of objects to be served. Recall from Chapter 9 that a queue is a first-in, first-out structure. We deal with queuing systems all the time in our daily lives. When you stand in line to check out at the grocery store or to cash a check at the bank, you are dealing with a queuing system. When you submit a "batch job" (such as a compilation) on a mainframe computer, your job must wait in line until the CPU finishes the jobs scheduled ahead of it. When you make a phone call to reserve an airline ticket and get a recording that says, "Thank you for calling Air Busters. Your call will be answered by the next available operator. Please wait."—you are dealing with a queuing system.

Please Wait
Waiting is the critical element. The objective of a queuing system is to utilize the servers (the tellers, checkers, CPU, operators, and so on) as fully as possible while keeping the wait time within a reasonable limit. These goals usually require a compromise between cost and customer satisfaction.

To put this on a personal level, no one likes to stand in line. If there were one checkout counter for each customer in a supermarket, the customers would be delighted. The supermarket, however, would not be in business very long. So a compromise is made: The number of cashiers is kept within the limits set by the store's budget, and the average customer is not kept waiting *too* long.

How does a company determine the optimal compromise between the number of servers and the wait time? One way is by experience; the company tries out different numbers of servers and sees how things work out. There are two problems with this approach: It takes too long and it is too expensive. Another way of examining this problem is by using a computer simulation.

To construct a queuing model, we must know the following four things:

1. The number of events and how they affect the system in order to determine the rules of entity interaction
2. The number of servers
3. The distribution of arrival times in order to determine if an entity enters the system
4. The expected service time in order to determine the duration of an event

The simulation uses these characteristics to predict the average wait time. The number of servers, the distribution of arrival times, and the duration of service can be changed. The average wait times are then examined to determine what a reasonable compromise would be.

An Example

Consider the case of a drive-in bank with one teller. How long does the average car have to wait? If business gets better and cars start to arrive more frequently, what would be the effect on the average wait time? When would the bank need to open a second drive-in window?

This problem has the characteristics of a queuing model. The entities are a *server* (the teller), the *objects being served* (customers in cars), and a queue to hold the objects waiting to be served (customers in cars). The *average wait time* is what we are interested in observing. The events in this system are the arrivals and the departures of customers.

Let's look at how we can solve this problem as a time-driven simulation. A *time-driven simulation* is one in which the model is viewed at uniform time intervals, say, every minute. To simulate the passing of a unit of time (a minute, for example), we increment a clock. We run the simulation for a predetermined amount of time, say, 100 minutes. (Of course, simulated time usually passes much more quickly than real time; 100 simulated minutes pass in a flash on the computer.)

Think of the simulation as a big loop that executes a set of rules for each value of the clock—from 1 to 100, in our example. Here are the rules that are processed in the loop body:

Rule 1. If a customer arrives, he or she gets in line.

Rule 2. If the teller is free and if there is anyone waiting, the first customer in line leaves the line and advances to the teller's window. The service time is set for that customer.

Rule 3. If a customer is at the teller's window, the time remaining for that customer to be serviced is decremented.

Rule 4. If there are customers in line, the additional minute that they have remained in the queue (their wait time) is recorded.

The output from the simulation is the average wait time. We calculate this value using the following formula:

Average wait time = total wait time for all customers / number of customers

Given this output, the bank can see whether their customers have an unreasonable wait in a one-teller system. If so, the bank can repeat the simulation with two tellers.

Not so fast! There are still two unanswered questions. How do we know if a customer arrived? How do we know when a customer has finished being serviced? We must provide the simulation with information about the arrival times and the service times. These are the variables (parameters) in the simulation. We can never predict exactly when a customer arrives or how long each individual customer takes. We can, however, make educated guesses, such as a customer arrives about every five minutes and most customers take about three minutes to service.

How do we know whether or not a job has arrived in this particular clock unit? The answer is a function of two factors: the number of minutes between arrivals (five in this case) and chance. *Chance?* Queuing models are based on chance? Well, not exactly. Let's express the number of minutes between arrivals another way—as the *probability* that a job arrives in any given clock unit. Probabilities range from 0.0 (no chance) to 1.0 (a sure thing). If on the average a new job arrives every five minutes, then the chance of a customer arriving in any given minute is 0.2 (1 chance in 5). Therefore, the probability of a new customer arriving in a particular minute is 1.0 divided by the number of minutes between arrivals.

Now what about luck? In computer terms, luck can be represented by the use of a *random-number generator*. We simulate the arrival of a customer by writing a function that generates a random number between 0.0 and 1.0 and applies the following rules.

1. If the random number is between 0.0 and the arrival probability, a job has arrived.
2. If the random number is greater than the arrival probability, no job arrived in this clock unit.

By changing the rate of arrival, we simulate what happens with a one-teller system where each transaction takes about three minutes as more and more cars arrive. We can also have the duration of service time based on probability. For example, we could simulate a situation where 60% of the people require three minutes, 30% of the people require five minutes, and 10% of the people require ten minutes.

Simulation doesn't give us *the* answer or even *an* answer. Simulation is a technique for trying out "what if" questions. We build the model and run the simulation many times, trying various combinations of the parameters and observing the average wait time. What happens if the cars arrive more quickly? What happens if the service time is reduced by 10%? What happens if we add a second teller?

SIMULA is designed for simulation

The SIMULA programming language, designed and built by Ole-Johan Dahl and Kristen Nygaard at the Norwegian Computing Centre (NCC) in Oslo between 1962 and 1967, was designed and implemented as a language for discrete event simulation. SIMULA was later expanded and re-implemented as a full-scale general-purpose programming language. Although SIMULA was never widely used, the language has greatly influenced modern programming methodology. SIMULA introduced such important object-oriented language constructs as classes and objects, inheritance, and polymorphism.[10]

Other Types of Queues

The queue in the previous example was a FIFO queue: The entity that receives service is the entity that has been in the queue the longest time. Another type of queue is a *priority queue*. In a priority queue, each item in the queue is associated with a priority. When an item is dequeued, the item returned is the one with the highest priority. A priority queue operates like triage on the television show M*A*S*H. When the wounded arrive, the doctors put tags on each patient labeling the severity of the injuries. Those with the most severe wounds go into the operating room first.

Another scheme for ordering events is to have two FIFO queues, one for short service times and one for longer service times. This scheme is similar to the express lane at the supermarket. If you have fewer than ten items, you can go into the queue for the express lane; otherwise, you must go into the queue for one of the regular lanes.

Meteorological Models

In the last section we looked at a fairly simple simulation with discrete inputs and outputs. We now jump to a discussion of a continuous simulation: predicting the weather. The details of weather prediction are over the heads of all but professional meteorologists. In general, meteorological models are based on the time-dependent partial differential equations of fluid mechanics and thermodynamics. Equations exist for two horizontal wind velocity components, the vertical velocity, temperature, pressure, and water vapor concentration. Initial values for the variables are entered from observation, and the equations are integrated numerically (in layman's terms: solved) in order to define the values of the variables at some later time.[3] The equations are re-integrated using the predicted values as the initial conditions. This process of re-integrating using the predicted values

Ivan Sutherland

Ivan Sutherland has credentials in academia, industrial research, and in business. On his Web page Sutherland lists his profession as Engineer, Entrepreneur, Capitalist, Professor. He has won the prestigious ACM's AM Turing Award, Smithsonian Computer World Award, the First Zworykin Award from the National Academy of Engineering, and the Price Waterhouse Information Technology Leadership Award for Lifetime Achievement.

Sutherland received a BS from Carnegie Institute of Technology, an MS from the California Institute of Technology, and a PhD from the Massachusetts Institute of Technology. His PhD thesis, "Sketchpad: A Man-machine Graphical Communications System," pioneered the use of the lightpen to create graphic images directly on a display screen. The graphic patterns could be stored in memory and later retrieved and manipulated just like any other data. Sketchpad was the first GUI (Graphical User Interface) long before the term was invented, and opened up the field of computer-aided design (CAD).

The Defense Department and the National Security Agency (NSA) spearheaded computing research in the early 1960s. When Sutherland graduated, he was inducted into the Army and assigned to NSA. In 1964 he was transferred to the Defense Department's Advanced Research Projects Agency (ARPA, later DARPA) where he commissioned and managed computer science research projects as director of ARPA's Information Processing Techniques Office.

After his stint with the military, Sutherland went to Harvard as an associate professor. Sketchpad, which allowed people to interact with the computer in terms of images, was the logical predecessor to his work in virtual reality. His goal was the "ultimate display," which would include a full-color, stereoscopic display that filled the user's entire field of vision. Turning the theory into practice was more difficult than first imagined because of the weight of the head-mounted display (HMD). Thus, the first implementation was mounted on the wall or ceiling rather than the head, earning it the nickname "Sword of Damocles."

In 1968, Sutherland moved to the University of Utah where he continued his research into HMD systems. Sutherland and David Evans, another faculty member at Utah, founded Evans & Sutherland, a company specializing in hardware and software for visual systems for simulation, training, and virtual reality applications. In 1975 Sutherland returned to the California Institute of Technology as chairman of the Computer Sciences Department, where he helped to introduce circuit design into the curriculum.

Sutherland left Caltech in 1980 and established Sutherland, Sproull, and Associates, a consulting and venture capital firm. He holds eight patents in computer graphics and hardware and continues his research into hardware technology. He is currently Vice President and Sun Fellow at Sun Microsystems.

Surtherland was awarded the Turing Award in 1988. The citation reads:

For his pioneering and visionary contributions to computer graphics, starting with Sketchpad, and continuing after. Sketchpad, though written twenty-five years ago, introduced many techniques still important today. These include a display file for screen refresh, a recursively traversed hierarchical structure for modeling graphical objects, recursive methods for geometric transformations, and an object oriented programming style. Later innovations include a "Lorgnette" for viewing stereo or colored images, and elegant algorithms for registering digitized views, clipping polygons, and representing surfaces with hidden lines.

Despite all the honors Sutherland has received, he recently cited his proudest accomplishment as his four grandchildren.

from that last integration as the observed values for the current integration continues, giving the predictions over time. Recall that these equations describe rates of change of entities in the model, so the answers after each solution give values that can be used to predict the next set of values. (See Figure 14.1.)

Looking at the complexity of these equations and realizing that they must hold true at each point in the atmosphere, it is easy to see that very high-speed parallel computers are needed to solve them in a reasonable amount of time. Fortunately, we do not have to understand the details of these models in order to talk about them and describe how they are used. For those who would like to know more about the math involved, five college courses in the calculus sequence plus a course or two in numerical methods should provide the background to understand the mathematics involved in these models.

Weather Forecasting

"Red sky in the morning, sailor's warning" is an often-quoted weather prediction. Before the advent of computers, weather forecasting was based on folklore and observations. In the early 1950s, the first computer models were developed for weather forecasting. These models took the form of very complex sets of partial differential equations. As computers grew in size, the weather forecasting models grew even more complex.

If weathercasters use computer models to predict the weather, why are TV or radio weathercasts in the same city different? Why are they sometimes wrong? Computer models are designed to aid the weathercaster, not replace him or her. The outputs from the computer models are predictions of the values of variables in the future. It is up to the weathercaster to determine what the values *mean*.

Note that in the last paragraph we referred to multiple models. Different models exist because they make different assumptions. However, all computer models approximate the earth's surface and the atmosphere above the surface using evenly-spaced grid points. The distance between these points determines the size of the grid boxes, or resolution. The larger the grid boxes, the poorer the model's resolution becomes. The Nested Grid model (NGM) has a horizontal resolution of 80 km and 18 vertical levels and views the atmosphere as divided into squares for various levels of the atmosphere. Grids with smaller squares are nested inside larger ones to focus on particular geographic areas. The Model Output Statistics (MOS) model is made up of a set of statistical equations tailored to various cities in the United States. The ETA

Weather prediction by rodents

Punxsutawney Phil, General Beauregard Lee, and Staten Island Chuck are but three of an army of groundhogs that predict the weather each February 2. If a groundhog sees his (or her) shadow on February 2, it supposedly means there will be six more weeks of winter.

Horizontal momentum;

$$\frac{\partial p * u}{\partial t} = -m^2 \left[\frac{\partial p * uu / m}{\partial x} + \frac{\partial p * vu / m}{\partial y} \right] - \frac{\partial p * u\sigma}{\partial \sigma} + uDIV$$

$$-\frac{mp *}{\rho} \left[\frac{\partial p'}{\partial x} - \frac{\sigma}{p *} \frac{\partial p *}{\partial x} \frac{\partial p'}{\partial \sigma} \right] - p * fv + D_u$$

$$\frac{\partial p * v}{\partial t} = -m^2 \left[\frac{\partial p * uv / m}{\partial x} + \frac{\partial p * vv / m}{\partial y} \right] - \frac{\partial p * v\sigma}{\partial \sigma} + vDIV$$

$$-\frac{mp *}{\rho} \left[\frac{\partial p'}{\partial y} - \frac{\sigma}{p *} \frac{\partial p *}{\partial y} \frac{\partial p'}{\partial \sigma} \right] - p * fu + D_v$$

Vertical momentum;

$$\frac{\partial p * w}{\partial t} = -m^2 \left[\frac{\partial p * uv / m}{\partial x} + \frac{\partial p * vw / m}{\partial y} \right] - \frac{\partial p * w\sigma}{\partial \sigma} + wDIV$$

$$+ p * g \frac{p_0}{\rho} \left[\frac{1}{p *} \frac{\partial p'}{\partial \sigma} + \frac{T_v'}{T} - \frac{T_0 p'}{T p_0} \right] - p * g\left[(q_c + q_r)\right] + D_w$$

Pressure;

$$\frac{\partial p * p'}{\partial t} = -m^2 \left[\frac{\partial p * up' / m}{\partial x} + \frac{\partial p * vp' / m}{\partial y} \right] - \frac{\partial p * p'\sigma}{\partial \sigma} + p'DIV$$

$$-m^2 p * \gamma p \left[\frac{\partial u / m}{\partial x} - \frac{\sigma}{mp *} \frac{\partial p *}{\partial x} \frac{\partial u}{\partial \sigma} + \frac{\partial v / m}{\partial y} - \frac{\sigma}{mp *} \frac{\partial p *}{\partial y} \frac{\partial v}{\partial \sigma} \right]$$

$$+ p_0 g \gamma p \frac{\partial w}{\partial \sigma} + p * p_{0gw}$$

Temperature;

$$\frac{\partial p * T}{\partial t} = -m^2 \left[\frac{\partial p * uT / m}{\partial x} + \frac{\partial p * vT / m}{\partial y} \right] - \frac{\partial p * T\sigma}{\partial \sigma} + T DIV$$

$$+ \frac{1}{\rho c_p} \left[p * \frac{Dp'}{Dt} - p_0 g p * w - D_{p'} \right] + p * \frac{Q}{c_p} + D_T ,$$

where

$$DIV = m^2 \left[\frac{\partial p * u / m}{\partial x} + \frac{\partial p * v / m}{\partial y} \right] + \frac{\partial p * \sigma}{\partial \sigma} ,$$

and

$$\sigma = -\frac{p_0 g}{p *} w - \frac{m\sigma}{p *} \frac{\partial p *}{\partial x} u - \frac{m\sigma}{p *} \frac{\partial p *}{\partial y} v.$$

Figure 14.1 Some of the complex equations used in meteorological models

model, named after the ETA coordinate system that takes topographical features such as mountains into account, is a newer model very similar to the NGM model but with better resolution (29 km).[4]

The output from weather models can be in text form or graphical form. The weathercaster's job is to interpret all of the output. But any good weathercaster knows that the output from the various models is only as good as the input used as a starting point for the differential equations. This data comes from a variety of sources, including radiosondes (to measure humidity, temperature, and pressure at high altitudes), rawin-sondes (to measure wind velocity aloft), aircraft observations, surface observations, satellites, and other remote sensing sources. A small error in any of the input variables can cause an increasing error in the values as the equations are reintegrated over time. Another problem is that of scale. The resolution of a model may be too coarse for the weathercaster to accurately interpret the results within his or her immediate area.

Different weathercasters may believe the predictions or may decide that other factors indicate that the predictions are in error. In addition, the various models may give conflicting information. It is up the weathercaster to make a judgment as to which, if any, is correct.

Hurricane Tracking

The modules for hurricane tracking are called *relocatable models*, because they are applied to a moving target. That is, the geographical location of the model's forecast varies from run to run (i.e., from hurricane to hurricane). The Geophysical and Fluid Dynamics Laboratory (GFDL) developed the most recent hurricane model in order to improve the prediction of where a hurricane would make landfall.

The GFDL hurricane model became operational in 1995. The equations were such that the forecasts couldn't be made fast enough to be useful until the National Weather Service's high-performance supercomputers were used in parallel operation, which increased the running time over the serial implementation by 18%. Figure 14.2 shows the improvement of this model over the previous ones used to track hurricanes.

Combining Models

In June of 2001, ABC News reported that researchers from Florida State University and the Indian Institute of Science in Bangalore, India, had published results of a hurricane model that combined the outputs of other models. This combined model gave better results than any of the individual models. The technique correctly predicted the meandering path of Hurricane Dennis and the paths of tropical storms Bret, Cindy, and Emily.

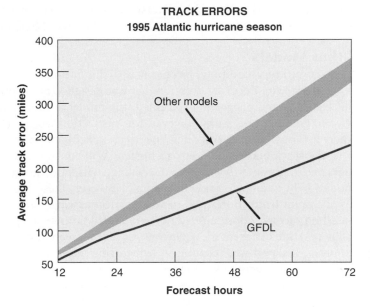

TRACK ERRORS
1995 Atlantic hurricane season

Figure 14.2
Improvements in hurricane models *Reprinted, by permission, from the National Science and Technology Council, High Performance Computing and Communications: Advancing the frontiers of information technology*

The researchers call their model a "superensemble." The longer the model runs, the better their results are, compared with individual models. In a forecast of hurricane winds three days into the future, the new model had an error of 21.5 mph as compared to the individual model errors that ranged from 31.3 mph to 32.4 mph.

Specialized Models

Meteorological models can be adapted and specialized for research purposes. For example, numeric-model simulations of atmospheric process are being combined with air-chemistry models to diagnose atmospheric transport and diffusion for a variety of air-quality applications. One such study analyzed the part played by the topography of the Grand Canyon region of Arizona in the movement of air pollution.

Another study showed that by assimilating or ingesting observed data within the model solution as the model was running forward in time, rather than using observations at only the initial time, the model's performance increased significantly. This allows for improved numerical representations of the atmosphere for input into other specialized models.[5]

Advanced meteorological modeling systems can be used to provide guidance for other complex systems in the military or aviation industry. For example, the weather has an impact on projectile motions and must be taken into consideration in battlefield situations. In the aviation industry, meteorological data is used in diverse ways, from determining how much fuel to carry to deciding when to move planes to avoid hail damage.

Other Models

In a sense, every computer program is a simulation, because a program represents the model of the solution that was designed in the problem-solving phase. When the program is executed, the model is simulated. We do not wish to go down this path, however, for this section would become infinite. There are, however, several disciplines that explicitly make use of simulation.

Is the stock market going to go higher? Will consumer prices rise? If we increase the money spent on advertising, will sales go up? Forecasting models help to answer these questions. However, these forecasting models are different from those used in weather forecasting. Weather models are based on factors whose interactions are mostly known and can be modeled using partial differential equations of fluid mechanics and thermodynamics. Business and economic forecasting models are based on past history of the variables involved, so they use regression analysis as the basis for prediction.

Seismic models depict the propagation of seismic waves through the earth's medium. These seismic waves can come from natural events, such as earthquakes and volcanic eruptions, or from man-made events, such as controlled explosions, reservoir induced earthquakes, or cultural noise (industry or traffic). For natural events, sensors pick up the waves, and models, using these observations as input, can determine the cause and magnitude of the source causing the waves. For man-made events, given the size of the event and the sensor data, models can map the earth's subsurface. These models are used to explore for oil and gas. The seismic data is used to provide geologists with highly detailed three-dimensional maps of hidden oil and gas reservoirs before drilling begins, thus minimizing the possibility of drilling a dry well.

Supercomputer used for oil exploration

A supercomputer comprised of a cluster of 256 servers and 512 microprocessors running Linux can perform 13 trillion calculations per second. This computer is being used to produce highly detailed three-dimensional maps of hidden oil and gas reservoirs beneath the Gulf of Mexico. Only 5% of wells drilled in the Gulf of Mexico in 1989 were based on seismic imaging. Today, seismic imaging precedes virtually all drilling expeditions.[6]

Computing Power Necessary

Many of the equations necessary for the continuous models we have talked about were developed many years ago. That is, the partial differential equations that defined the interactions of the entities in the model were known. However, the models based upon them could not be simulated in time for the answers to be useful. The introduction of parallel high-performance computing in the mid-1990s changed all that. Newer, bigger, faster machines allow scientists to solve more complex mathematical systems over larger domains and ever-finer grids with even shorter wall clock times. These new machines are able to solve the complex equations fast enough to provide timely answers. Numerical weather forecasting, unlike some other applications, must beat the clock. Yesterday's weather prediction is not very useful if not received until today.

14.2   Graphics and Computer-Aided Design (CAD)

Graphics is the language of communications for engineers, designers, and architects. Technical drawings are the means for describing something that must be processed, manufactured, or built. Engineers, designers, and architects use technical drawings as a means of communicating their ideas. Until the 1950's and the advent of the computer, technical drawings were done at the drafting table with paper, pencil, and T-squares. Now most technical drawings are done at the computer. What began as the automation of drafting has expanded into techniques and capabilities that a draftsperson in 1950 could not have imagined.

Computer-aided design (CAD) refers to a system that uses computers with advanced graphics hardware and software to create precision drawings or technical illustrations. If the system is being used to design parts to be manufactured, the designer can draw and manipulate a 3-D image of the part without having to build a physical model. If the system is being used to produce architectural drawings, the structure can be drawn and viewed from different perspectives. Although CAD systems can be thought of as simulating the paper, pencil, and T-square, they have far more complex capabilities.

CAD systems can be broadly classified as two-dimensional (2-D) CAD and three-dimensional (3-D) CAD. Two-dimensional CAD systems are basically glorified electronic drawing boards, replacing paper, pencil, and the T-square. Of course, the drawings are easy to edit and reproduce, guaranteeing top-quality copies.

Three-dimensional CAD is also called geometric modeling. There are three methods of modeling in three dimensions: wireframe modeling,

Contributions made by Pythagoras, Brunelleschi, Durer, and Monge

In 525 B.C. in Greece, Pythagoras discovered what became known as the Pythagorean theorem of a right triangle: The square of the hypotenuse of a right triangle is equal to the sum of the squares of the other sides. Other mathematical approaches to drawing came much later when Brunelleschi demonstrated the theoretical principles governing the laws of perspective drawing and Durer (1471–1528) was credited with the first basic knowledge of orthographic projection. Gaspard Monge (1746–1818) is credited as being the "inventor" of descriptive geometry.

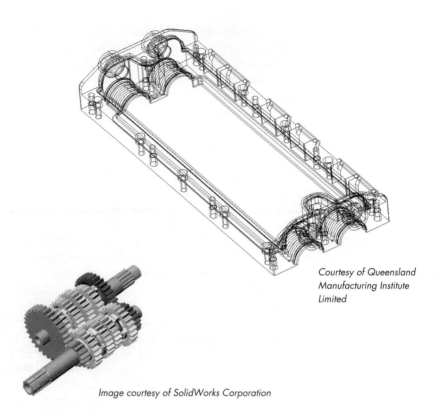

Courtesy of Queensland
Manufacturing Institute
Limited

Figure 14.3
Geometric modeling
techniques

Image courtesy of SolidWorks Corporation

surface modeling, and solid modeling. An example of a wire model and solid model are shown in Figure 14.3. The intended purpose of the image dictates the appropriate model.

Wireframe, the simplest 3-D modeling, represents objects by line elements that provide exact information about edges, corners, and surface discontinuities. With these models, there is no way to distinguish between the inside and the outside of the object. Surface modeling, on the other hand, defines precisely the outside of the object being modeled. Surface models connect various types of surface elements by line segments. Solid models make use of topology; the interior volume and mass of an object is defined. Surface models appear similar to solid models, but the interior of the surface model is empty.[7]

Every CAD system has a set of elements or primitives out of which the designs are created. In a 2-D system, the primitives are points, lines, and surfaces. Surfaces can be polygons with any number of vertices; they can also be figures such as circles and ellipses. Splines, free curves defined mathematically, are also often included. In 3-D systems, the primitive shapes are cubes, wedges, cylinders, or spheres. In surface modeling, a cube would be composed of six faces, but in solid modeling, a cube would be a single primitive.

CAD systems that are specific to particular types of design may have a set of specialized primitives. An architectural CAD might have architectural components such as slabs, walls, doors, and windows. A CAD system used in designing cars might have components such as bumpers, windshields, and tires.

Even if CAD systems are used only as electronic drawing boards, they provide great advantages. They are much faster and more accurate than hand drawings. Revisions are easier to make, because the unchanged parts do not need to be copied again. If the CAD system is being used as a real design tool, the designer can try out ideas and immediately see the results. "What if" questions can be applied to the model to test the integrity of new designs. If the output of the design is the specification for an item to be manufactured, the specifications can be sent directly to the manufacturing machine.

Of course, the use of CAD has introduced its own set of new problems. Computer-aided design is a concept implemented in many diverse software programs. The designers must learn to use the new software tools, sometimes taking as long as six months to become proficient. In architecture, for example, there is no industry standard CAD software package, and maddening differences exist among competing software packages. Yet, Charles Eastman, a professor in the College of Architecture and Computing at Georgia Tech, asserts that many new buildings, including the Bilbao Museum in Spain, could not have been built without the aid of computers.[8]

14.3   Embedded Systems

Embedded systems are computers that are dedicated to perform a narrow range of functions as part of a larger system. Typically, an embedded system is housed on a single microprocessor chip with the programs stored in ROM. Virtually all appliances that have a digital interface—watches, microwaves, VCRs, cars—utilize embedded systems. In fact, embedded systems are everywhere: From consumer electronics, to kitchen appliances, to automobiles, to networking equipment, and to industrial control systems, you find embedded systems lurking in the device. Some embedded systems include an operating system, but many are so specialized that the entire logic can be implemented as a single program.[9]

Glucose monitor embedded in watch

Diabetics must monitor their glucose levels on a regular basis. Until recently, this meant pricking a finger to check blood sugar levels, optimally four to seven times a day. A new wristwatch-like device checks sugar levels every 20 minutes by sending tiny electric currents through the skin. The watch face displays the current time and the user's most recent blood sugar level. This device holds great promise for the 16 million Americans suffering from diabetes.[10]

Chips embedded in running shoes

Plastic circular chips about 1 ½ inches in diameter, 3/8" thick, and weighing fractions of an ounce are changing the world of running. Before a race, each runner is given a chip with a 7-character code that is tied onto the runner's shoelace. When the runner touches a mat at the starting line, an electrical current in the mat creates a magnetic field that charges the chip. The mats have receiving antennas that pick up the code on a chip and send it to a controller box and computer. Mats are placed at different points on the race course, picking up and transmitting the code of each runner as he or she steps on the mat.

In the 2000 New York City Marathon, the data from the chips was transmitted to a Web site so people could follow the progress of the individual runners on the Web. In the 2001 Boston Marathon, the information was available to anyone with a cellular phone, text pager, or any device with an e-mail address.[11]

Early embedded systems were standalone 8-bit microprocessors with their own homegrown operating system. Today, they range from 8-bit controllers to 32-bit digital signal processors (DSPs) to 64-bit RISC (reduced instruction set) chips. More and more embedded systems are based on networks of distributed microprocessors that communicate through wired and wireless busses, remotely monitored and controlled by regular network management communications protocols.

In fact, the term *embedded system* is nebulous because it encompasses about everything except desktop PCs. The term originated because the first such computers were physically embedded within a product or device and could not be accessed. Now the term refers to any computer that is preprogrammed to perform a dedicated or narrow range of functions as part of a larger system. The implication is that there is only minimal end-user or operator intervention if any at all.

Because the average person encounters an embedded system only in his or her kitchen, entertainment room, or car, we tend to equate them with hardware. However, programs must be written and burned into the ROM (read-only memory) that comes with the system to make it accomplish its assigned function. Since programs cannot be developed and tested on the embedded processor itself, how are they implemented? Programs are written on a PC and compiled for the target system, where the executable code is generated for the processor in the embedded system.

In early embedded systems, the size of the code and the speed at which it executed were very important. Because assembly-language programs provided the best opportunity to streamline and speed up the code, they were used almost exclusively for embedded systems. Even when the C language became popular and cross-compilers for C to embedded systems became available, many programmers have continued to use assembly language. C programs are approximately 25% larger and slower, but are easier to write than assembly-language programs. Even today, the size of the ROM may dictate that the code be as small as possible, leading to an assembly-language program.[12]

Summary

Simulation is a major area of computing that involves building computer models of complex systems and experimenting with the models to observe the results. A model is an abstraction of the real system in which the system is represented by a set of objects or characteristics and the rules that govern their behavior.

There are two major types of simulation: continuous and discrete event. In continuous simulation, changes are expressed in terms of partial differential equations that reflect the relationships among the set of objects or characteristics. In discrete event simulation, behavior is expressed in terms of entities, attributes, and events, where entities are objects, attributes are characteristics of an entity, and events are interactions among the entities.

Queuing systems are discrete event simulations in which waiting time is the factor being examined. Random numbers are used to simulate the arrival and duration of events, such as cars at a drive-in bank or people in a supermarket. Meteorological and seismic models are examples of continuous simulation.

Computer-aided design (CAD) and embedded systems are two other application areas of computing. CAD systems allow architects, engineers, and designers to build computer models of structures and products. Embedded systems are computer systems that perform a narrow range of functions as a part of a larger system.

ETHICAL ISSUES

Online Gambling

The Internet has radically changed business practices throughout the world. From banks and auction houses to retail outlets and grocery stores, most businesses today capitalize on the convenience and speed of the Internet. While most businesses have received unanimous praise for their online services, Internet casinos have garnered a mixed response. Positions about online gambling run the gamut from opposition to any governmental regulations, to requiring stricter regulations, to the outright banning of all Internet casinos. Our legislators on Capitol Hill have repeatedly debated the merits of regulating online betting. The American Gaming Association believes that laws should be enacted to prevent unfair, untaxed, and unlicensed casinos from operating in cyberspace. The Association feels that strict regulations should force the online industry to adhere to the same guidelines that traditional casinos must follow. The social factors that surround this issue are numerous. Anyone with access to the Internet and a credit card can go online and gamble. This ease of access is likely to lead to the problem of gambling addictions. The ability to gamble 24–7 from the convenience of your own home can quickly lead people with addictive personalities into serious financial problems. You may have had the experience of opening a Web page and encountering a pop-up casino advertisement. Compulsive gamblers find it a real struggle to resist the temptations of these pervasive advertisements and the plethora of games available online.

More and more people are supporting the online gambling industry despite the criticism it has received. A surprisingly few online casinos, approximately 15, were in operation in 1997 compared to more than 1,000 in 2002. One report estimates that if this expansion continues at its present rate, 80.9 million people will participate in online gambling in the year 2005. This growth is likely to be met with governmental resistance. In June 2001, Australia passed legislation that prohibits Australian online casinos from allowing Australian citizens to partici-pate. The California State Legislature has proposed a similar bill. This attitude—that it is legal to export a vice from which it protects its own citizens—seems morally questionable. How Internet gambling changes in the future depends largely on the type of control imposed by state and federal governments.

Key Terms

Model   pg. 433
Simulation   pg. 432

Exercises

1. Define simulation and give five examples from everyday life.
2. Describe the characteristics of a complex system.
3. What is the essence of constructing a model?
4. Name two types of simulations and distinguish between them.
5. The solutions to continuous simulation usually take what form?
6. What are the ingredients in a discrete event simulation?
7. What are the keys to constructing a good model?
8. What defines the interactions among entities in a discrete event simulation?
9. What is the relationship between object-oriented design and model building?
10. Define the goal of a queuing system.
11. What are the four necessary pieces of information needed to build a queuing system?
12. What part does a random-number generator play in queuing simulations?
13. Write the rules for a queuing simulation of a one-pump gas station, where a car arrives every three minutes and the service time is four minutes.
14. Do you think the gas station in Exercise 13 will be in business very long? Explain.
15. Rewrite the simulation in Exercise 13 such that a car arrives every two minutes and the service time is two minutes.
16. Write the rules for a queuing system for an airline reservation counter. There is one queue and two reservation clerks. People arrive every three minutes and take three minutes to be processed.
17. Distinguish between a FIFO queue and a priority queue.
18. What did SIMULA contribute to object-oriented programming methodology?
19. In general, meteorological models are based on the time-dependent equations of what fields?
21. How much mathematics is necessary to be a meteorologist?
22. Why is there more than one weather prediction model?
23. Why do different meteorologists give different forecasts if they are using the same models?
24. What are specialized meteorological models and how are they used?

25. What are seismic models used for?

26. Define CAD.

27. What are two-dimensional CAD models used for?

28. What are three-dimensional CAD models used for?

29. What are the three methods of modeling in three dimensions and how do you determine which should be used where?

31. Distinguish between an embedded system and a regular computing system.

32. Embedded systems' programmers are the last holdout for assembly-language programming. Explain.

33. A random number generator can be used to vary service times as well as determine arrivals. For example, assume that 20% of the customers take 8 minutes and 80% of the customers take 3 minutes. How might you use a random number generator to reflect this distribution?

34. Why do we say that simulation doesn't give an answer?

35. What do simulations and spreadsheet programs have in common?

36. Why do meteorologists need to study so much mathematics?

⁇ Thought Questions

1. Priority queues are very interesting structures. They can be used to simulate a stack. How might you use a PQ as a stack?

2. Priority queues can also be used to simulate a FIFO queue. How might you use a PQ as a FIFO queue?

3. In Chapter 9, we described the graph data structure. A depth-first traversal of a graph uses a stack, and a breadth-first traversal of a graph uses a FIFO queue. Can you explain why?

4. In this chapter we described queuing systems where there is a queue for each server. There are other types of queuing systems. For example, in the airport there is usually one queue for many servers. When a server is free, the front of the queue goes to that server. Could you represent this type of system in a simulation?

5. What other real-life situations can be modeled using a priority queue?

6. Walk through your kitchen and list the number of items that include embedded computers.

7. CAD systems are now available for everyday use. Go to your local computer store and see how many programs are available to help you design anything from a kitchen to a guitar.

8. Have you ever used an online gambling facility? Was it as easy to use as the Ethical Issues section predicted?

9. Should the government be involved in regulating Internet casinos? If so, should they be regulated by state or federal governments?

10. Should the government be involved in trying to stop people who are addicted to gambling from using Internet casinos?

11. What do you think of the governmental attitude that says it is legal to export a vice from which the government protects its own citizens?

The Communications Layer

15 Networks

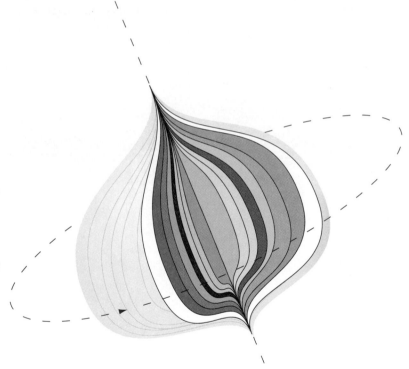

Networks

For many years, computers have played as important a role in communication as they do in computation. This communication is accomplished using computer networks. Like complex highway systems that connect roads in various ways to allow cars to travel from their origin to their destination, computer networks form an infrastructure that allows data to travel from some source computer to a destination. The computer receiving the data may be around the corner or around the world. This chapter explores some of the details of computer networks.

Goals

After studying this chapter, you should be able to:

- describe the core issues related to computer networks.
- list various types of networks and their characteristics.
- explain various topologies of local-area networks.
- explain why network technologies are best implemented as open systems.
- compare and contrast various technologies for home Internet connections.
- explain packet switching.
- describe the basic roles of various network protocols.
- explain the role of a firewall.
- compare and contrast network hostnames and IP addresses.
- explain the domain name system.

15.1   Networking

Computer network A collection of computing devices connected so that they can communicate and share resources

Wireless A network connection made without physical wires

Node (or **Host**) Any addressable device attached to a network

Data transfer rate (also **bandwidth**) The speed with which data is moved from one place to another on a network

A **computer network** is a collection of computing devices that are connected in various ways in order to communicate and share resources. E-mail, instant messaging, and Web pages all rely on communication that occurs across an underlying computer network. We use networks to share intangible resources, such as files, as well as tangible resources, such as printers.

Usually, the connections between computers in a network are made using physical wires or cables. However, some connections are **wireless**, using radio waves or infrared signals to convey data. Networks are not defined only by physical connections; they are defined by the ability to communicate.

Computer networks contain devices other than computers. Printers, for instance, can be connected directly to a network so that anyone on the network can print to them. Networks also contain a variety of devices for handling network traffic. We use the generic term **node** or **host** to refer to any device on a network.

A key issue related to computer networks is the **data transfer rate**, the speed with which data is moved from one place on a network to another. We are constantly increasing our demand on networks as we rely on them to transfer more data in general, as well as data that is inherently more complex (therefore larger). Multimedia components such as audio and video are a large contributor to this increased traffic. Sometimes the data

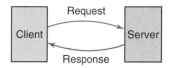

Figure 15.1
Client/Server interaction

transfer rate is referred to as the *bandwidth* of a network. Recall that we discussed bandwidth in Chapter 3 in the discussion of data compression.

Another key issue in computer networks is the **protocols** that are used. As we've mentioned at other points in this book, a protocol is a set of rules describing how two things interact. In networking, we use well-defined protocols to describe how transferred data is formatted and processed.

Computer networks have opened up an entire frontier in the world of computing called the **client/server model**. No longer do you think of computers solely in terms of the capabilities of the machine sitting in front of you. Software systems are often distributed across a network, in which a client sends a request to a server for information or action, and the server responds, as shown in Figure 15.1.

For example, a **file server** is a computer that stores and manages files for multiple users on a network. That way every user doesn't need to have his or her own copy of the files. A **Web server** is a computer dedicated to responding to requests (from the browser client) for Web pages. Client/server relationships have become more complex as we rely heavily on networks in our everyday lives. Therefore, the client/server model has become increasingly important in the world of computing.

The client/server model has also grown beyond the basic request/response approach. Increasingly, the client/server model is used to support parallel processing, which is the use of multiple computers to solve a problem by breaking it into pieces as discussed in Chapter 4. Using networks and the client/server model, parallel processing can be accomplished by the client requesting that multiple machines perform a specific part of a problem. The client gathers the responses from each to form a complete solution to the problem.

Types of Networks

Computer networks can be classified in various ways. A **local-area network (LAN)** connects a relatively small number of machines in a relatively close geographical area. LANs are usually confined to a single room or building. They may sometimes span a few close buildings.

Various configurations, called topologies, have been used to administer LANs. A **ring topology** connects all nodes in a closed loop on which messages travel in one direction. The nodes of a ring network pass along

Protocol A set of rules that defines how data is formatted and processed on a network

Client/server model A distributed approach in which a client makes requests of a server and the server responds

File server A computer dedicated to storing and managing files for network users

Web server A computer dedicated to responding to requests for Web pages

Local-area network (LAN) A network connecting a small number of nodes in a close geographic area

Ring topology A LAN configuration in which all nodes are connected in a closed loop

Star topology   A LAN configuration in which a central node controls all message traffic

Bus topology   A LAN configuration in which all nodes share a common line

Ethernet   The industry standard for local-area networks, based on a bus topology

Wide-area network (WAN)   A network connecting two or more local-area networks

Gateway   A node that handles communication between its LAN and other networks

Internet   A wide-area network that spans the planet

Metropolitan-area network (MAN)   A network infrastructure developed for a large city

messages until they reach their destination. A **star topology** centers around one node to which all others are connected and through which all messages are sent. A star network puts a huge burden on the central node; if it is not working, communication on the network is not possible. In a **bus topology**, all nodes are connected to a single communication line that carries messages in both directions. The nodes on the bus check any message sent on the bus, but ignore any that are not addressed to them. These topologies are pictured in Figure 15.2. A bus technology called **Ethernet** has become the industry standard for local-area networks.

A **wide-area network** (**WAN**) connects two or more local-area networks over a potentially large geographic distance. A wide-area network permits communication among smaller networks. Often one particular node on a LAN is set up to serve as a **gateway** to handle all communication going between that LAN and other networks. See Figure 15.3.

Communication between networks is called internetworking. The **Internet**, as we know it today, is essentially the ultimate wide-area network, spanning the entire globe. The Internet is a vast collection of smaller networks that have all agreed to communicate using the same protocols and to pass along messages so that they can reach their final destination.

Recently, the term **metropolitan-area network** (**MAN**) has been adopted to refer to the communication infrastructures that have been developed in and around large cities. The population and needs of a metropolitan area often require unique attention. These networks are often implemented

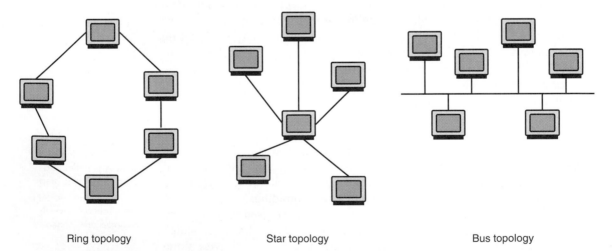

Ring topology   Star topology   Bus topology

Figure 15.2   Various network topologies

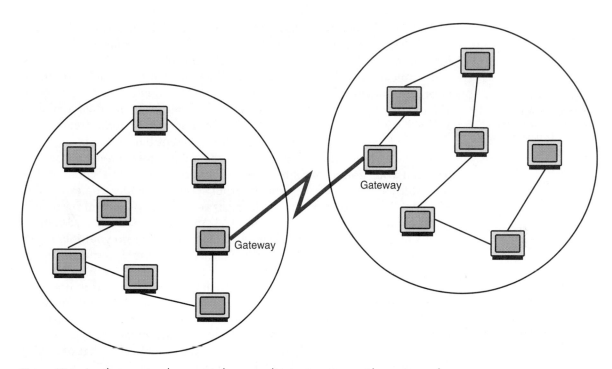

Figure 15.3   Local-area networks connected across a distance to create a wide-area network

using innovative techniques such as running optical fiber cable through subway tunnels.

Internet Connections

The **Internet backbone** is a term used to refer to a set of high-speed networks that carry Internet traffic. These networks are provided by companies such as AT&T, GTE, and IBM. The backbone networks all operate using connections that have high data transfer rates, ranging from 1.5 megabits per second to over 600 megabits per second (using special optical cables).

An **Internet service provider** (**ISP**) is a company that provides other companies or individuals with access to the Internet. ISPs connect directly to the Internet backbone, or they connect to a larger ISP with a connection to the backbone. America OnLine and Prodigy are examples of Internet service providers.

There are various technologies available that you can use to connect a home computer to the Internet. The three most popular techniques for home connections are a phone modem, a digital subscriber line (DSL), or a cable modem. Let's examine each of these.

Internet backbone   A set of high-speed networks carrying Internet traffic

Internet service provider (ISP)   A company providing access to the Internet

The telephone system had already connected homes throughout the world long before the desire for Internet connections came along. Therefore, it makes sense that the first technique for home-based network communication was a *phone modem*. The word *modem* stands for modulator/demodulator. A **phone modem** converts computer data into an analog audio signal for transfer over a telephone line, and then a modem at the destination converts it back again into data. One audio frequency is used to represent binary 0 and another to represent binary 1.

Phone modem   A device that converts computer data into an analog audio signal and back again

To use a phone modem, you must first establish a telephone connection between your home computer and one that is permanently connected to the Internet. That's where your Internet service provider comes in. You pay your ISP a monthly fee for the right to call one of several (hopefully local) computers that they have set up for this purpose. Once that connection is made, you can transfer data via your phone lines to your ISP, which then sends it on its way through the Internet backbone. Incoming traffic is routed through your ISP to your home computer.

This approach was fairly simple to implement because it does not require any special effort on the part of the telephone company. Since the data is treated as if it were a voice conversation, no special translation is needed except at either end. But that convenience comes at a price. The data transfer rate available with this approach is limited to that of analog voice communication, usually 64 kilobits per second at most.

A phone line can provide a much higher transfer rate if the data is treated as digital rather than analog. A **digital subscriber line** (**DSL**) uses regular copper phone lines to transfer digital data to and from the phone company's central office. Since DSL and voice communication use different frequencies, it is even possible to use the same phone line for both.

Digital subscriber line (DSL)   An Internet connection made using a digital signal on regular phone lines

To set up a DSL connection, your phone company may become your Internet service provider, or they may sell the use of their lines to a third-party ISP. To offer DSL service, the phone company must set up special computers to handle the data traffic. Though not all phone companies support DSL yet, it is becoming an increasingly popular approach.

With DSL, there is no need to "dial in" to create the network connection like there is with a phone modem. The DSL line maintains an active connection between your home and a computer at the ISP. However, to make use of DSL technology, your home must be within a certain distance from the central office; otherwise, the digital signal degrades too much while traveling between those two points.

Cable modem   A device that allows computer network communication using the cable TV hookup in a home

A third option for home connections is a **cable modem**. In this approach, the data is transferred on the same line that your cable TV signals come in on. Several leading cable TV companies in North America have pooled their resources to create Internet service providers for cable modem service.

Doug Engelbart

"Build a better mousetrap, and the world will beat a path to your door. Invent the computer mouse, and the world will all but forget your name." This was the lead paragraph in an article celebrating the 20th birthday of the computer mouse.[1]

Designed by Doug Engelbart—the name that was forgotten—and a group of young scientists and engineers at Stanford Research Institute, the computer mouse debuted in 1968 at the Fall Joint Computer conference as part of a demonstration later called "The Mother of All Demos" by Andy van Dam. The historic demonstration foreshadowed human-computer interaction and networking. It wasn't until 1981 that the first commercial computer with a mouse was introduced, however. In 1984 the Apple Macintosh brought the mouse into the mainstream. To this day no one seems to know where the term "mouse" came from.

Engelbart grew up on a farm near Portland, Oregon, during the Depression. He served in the Navy in the Philippines during World War II as an electronics technician. He completed his electrical engineering degree in 1948 from Oregon State University and moved to the Bay Area. In 1955 he received a Ph.D. from the University of California at Berkeley and joined the Stanford Research Institute.

Engelbart's vision of the computer as an extension of human communication capabilities and a resource for the augmentation of human intellect was outlined in the seminal paper "Augmenting Human Intellect: A Conceptual Framework," published in 1962. He has never lost this vision. Ever since, he has been developing models to improve the co-evolution of computers with human organizations to boost collaboration, and to create what he calls "high performance organizations."[2]

During the 1970s and 1980s, Engelbart was Senior Scientist at Tymshare, which was bought by McDonnell-Douglas. When the program was shut down in 1989, Engelbart founded the Bootstrap Institute, aimed at helping companies and organizations utilize his techniques. He feels encouraged by the open-source movement, in which programmers collaborate to create advanced and complicated software. He is currently planning a system of open software that can be distributed free over the Internet.

Recognition may have been long in coming, but Englebart received 32 awards between 1987 and 2001, including the Turing Award in 1997 and the National Medal of Technology in 2000. The citations for these two prestigious awards read as follows:

(Turing Award) For an inspiring vision of the future of interactive computing and the invention of key technologies to help realize this vision.

(National Medal of Technology) For creating the foundations of personal computing including continuous real-time interaction based on cathode-ray tube displays and the mouse, hypertext linking, text editing, online journals, shared-screen teleconferencing, and remote collaborative work.

Both DSL connections and cable modems fall under the category of **broadband** connections, which generally mean speeds faster than 128 bits per second. Debate between the DSL and cable modem communities continues to rage to see who can claim the dominant market share. Both generally provide data transfer speeds in the range of 1.5 to 3 megabits per second.

Broadband Network technologies that generally provide data transfer speeds greater than 128 bps

Download Receiving
data on your home
computer from the
Internet

Upload Sending data
from your home
computer to a destina-
tion on the Internet

For both DSL and cable modems, the speed for **downloads** (getting data from the Internet to your home computer) may not be the same as **uploads** (sending data from your home computer to the Internet). Most traffic for home Internet users are downloads: receiving Web pages to view and retrieving data (such as programs and audio and video clips) stored some-where else on the network. You perform an upload when you send an e-mail message, submit a Web-based form, or request a new Web page. Since download traffic largely outweighs upload traffic, many DSL and cable modem suppliers use technology that devotes more speed to downloads.

Packet Switching

To improve the efficiency of transferring information over a shared communication line, messages are divided into fixed-sized, numbered **packets**. The packets are sent over the network individually to their desti-nation, where they are collected and reassembled into the original message. This approach is referred to as **packet switching**.

Packet A unit of data
sent across a network

Packet switching The
approach to network
communication in which
packets are individually
routed to their destina-
tion, then reassembled

Router A network
device that directs a
packet between networks
toward its final destina-
tion

Repeater A network
device that strengthens
and propagates a signal
along a long communi-
cation line

The packets of a message may take different routes on their way to the final destination. Therefore, they may arrive in a different order than the way they were sent. The packets must be put into the proper order once again, and then combined to form the original message. This process is shown in Figure 15.4.

A packet may make several intermediate hops between computers on various networks before it reaches its final destination. Network devices called **routers** are used to direct packets between networks. Intermediate routers don't plan out the packet's entire course; each router merely knows the best next step to get it closer to its destination. Eventually a message reaches a router that knows where the destination machine is. If a path is blocked due to a down machine, or if a path currently has a lot of network traffic, a router might send a packet along an alternative route.

If a communication line spans a long distance, such as across an ocean, a device called a **repeater** is installed periodically along the line to

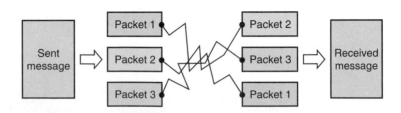

Figure 15.4
Messages sent by packet switching

Message is divided
into packets

Packets are sent over the Internet
by the most expedient route

Packets are reordered
and then reassembled

strengthen and propagate the signal. Recall from Chapter 3 that a digital signal loses information only if it is allowed to degrade too much. A repeater keeps that from happening.

15.2   Open Systems and Protocols

Many protocols have been defined to assist in network communication. Some have gained a stronger foothold than others because of many reasons, often historical. We focus in this section on the protocols used for general Internet traffic. Before we discuss the details of particular protocols, however, it is important to put them in context by discussing the concept of an open system.

Open Systems

Early in the development of computer networks, commercial vendors came out with a variety of technologies that they hoped businesses would adopt. The trouble was that these proprietary systems were developed with their own particular nuances and did not permit communication between networks of various types. As network technologies grew, the need for interoperability became clear; we needed a way for computing systems made by different vendors to communicate.

An open system is one based on a common model of network architecture and a suite of protocols used in its implementation. Open-system architectures maximize the opportunity for interoperability.

The International Organization for Standardization (ISO) established the Open Systems Interconnection (OSI) Reference Model to facilitate the development of network technologies. It defines a series of layers of network interaction. The seven layers of the OSI Reference Model are shown in Figure 15.5.

Proprietary system   A system that uses technologies kept private by a particular commercial vendor

Interoperability   The ability of software and hardware on multiple machines and from multiple commercial vendors to communicate

Open system   A system that is based on a common model of network architecture and an accompanying suite of protocols

Open Systems Interconnection Reference Model   A seven-layer logical breakdown of network interaction to facilitate communication standards

7	Application layer
6	Presentation layer
5	Session layer
4	Transport layer
3	Network layer
2	Data Link layer
1	Physical layer

Figure 15.5
The layers of the
OSI Reference Model

Each layer deals with a particular aspect of network communication. The highest level deals with issues that relate most specifically to the application program in question. The lowest layer deals with the most basic electrical and mechanical issues of the physical transmission medium (such as types of wiring). The other layers fill in all other aspects. The network layer, for example, deals with the routing and addressing of packets.

The details of these layers are beyond the scope of this book, but it is important to know that networking technology as we know it today is possible only through the use of open-system technology and approaches such as the OSI Reference Model.

Network Protocols

Following the general concepts of the OSI Reference Model, network protocols are layered such that each one relies on the protocols that underlie it, as shown in Figure 15.6. This layering is sometimes referred to as a **protocol stack**. The layered approach allows new protocols to be developed without abandoning fundamental aspects of lower levels. It also provides more opportunity for their use in that the impact on other aspects of network processing is minimized. Sometimes protocols at the same level provide the same service as another protocol at that level, but do so in a different way.

Keep in mind that a protocol is, in one sense, nothing more than an agreement that a particular type of data will be formatted in a particular manner. The details of file formats and the size of data fields are important to software developers creating networking programs, but we do not explore those details here. The importance of these protocols is that they provide a standard way to interact among networked computers.

The lower two layers in Figure 15.6 form the foundation of Internet communication. Other protocols, sometimes referred to as high-level protocols, deal with specific types of network communication. These layers are essentially one particular implementation of the OSI Reference Model and correspond in various ways to the levels described in that model. Let's explore these levels in more detail.

Protocol stack Layers of protocols that build and rely on each other

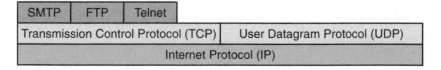

Figure 15.6
Layering of key network protocols

TCP/IP

TCP stands for **Transmission Control Protocol** and IP stands for **Internet Protocol**. The name **TCP/IP** (pronounced by saying the letters T-C-P-I-P) refers to a suite of protocols and utility programs that support low-level network communication. The name TCP/IP is written to reflect the nature of their relationship—that TCP rests on top of the IP foundation.

IP software deals with the routing of packets through the maze of interconnected networks to their final destination. TCP software breaks messages into packets, hands them off to the IP software for delivery, and then orders and reassembles the packets at their destination. TCP software also deals with any errors that occur, such as if a packet never arrives at the destination.

UDP stands for **User Datagram Protocol**. It is an alternative to TCP. That is, UDP software basically plays the same role as TCP software. The main difference is that TCP is highly reliable, at the cost of decreased performance, while UDP is less reliable, but generally faster. Note that UDP is part of the TCP/IP suite of protocols. Because of the heavy reliance on TCP, and for historical reasons, the entire suite is referred to as TCP/IP.

An IP program called **ping** can be used to test the reachability of network designations. Every computer running IP software "echoes" ping requests, which makes ping a convenient way to test whether a particular computer is running and can be reached across the network. Ping officially stands for Packet InterNet Groper, but the name was contrived to match the term used when submarines send out a sonar pulse and listen for the returned echo. Since ping works at the IP level, it often responds even when higher-level protocols might not. The term *ping* is often used as a verb among network administrators: "Ping computer X to see if it is alive."

Another TCP/IP utility program called **traceroute** shows the route that a packet takes to arrive at a particular destination node. The output of traceroute is a list of the computers that serve as the intermediate stopping points along the way.

High-Level Protocols

Other protocols build on the foundation established by the TCP/IP protocol suite. Some of the key high-level protocols are:

- Simple Mail Transfer Protocol (SMTP)—A protocol used to specify the transfer of electronic mail
- File Transfer Protocol (FTP)—A protocol that allows a user on one computer to transfer files to and from another computer
- Telnet—A protocol used to log into a computer system from a remote computer. If you have an account on a particular computer

Transmission Control Protocol (TCP) The network protocol that breaks messages into packets, reassembles them at the destination, and takes care of errors

Internet Protocol (IP) The network protocol that deals with the routing of packets through interconnected networks to the final destination

TCP/IP A suite of protocols and programs that support low-level network communication

User Datagram Protocol (UDP) An alternative to TCP that achieves higher transmission speeds at the cost of reliability

Ping A program used to test whether a particular network computer is active and reachable

Traceroute A program that shows the route a packet takes across the Internet

that allows telnet connections, you can run a program that uses the telnet protocol to connect and log in to that computer as if you were seated in front of it.

- Hyper Text Transfer Protocol (HTTP)—A protocol defining the exchange of World Wide Web documents, which are typically written using the Hyper Text Markup Language (HTML). HTML is discussed in more detail in the next chapter.

These protocols all build on TCP. Some high-level protocols have also been defined that build on top of UDP in order to capitalize on the speed it provides. But because UDP does not provide the reliability that TCP does, UDP protocols are less popular.

Several high-level protocols have been assigned a particular *port* number. A **port** is a numeric designation that corresponds to a particular high-level protocol. Servers and routers use the port number to help control and process network traffic. Common protocols and their ports are listed in Figure 15.7. Some protocols, such as HTTP have default ports but can use other ports as well.

> **Port**   A numeric designation corresponding to a particular high-level protocol

MIME Types

Related to the idea of network protocols and standardization is the concept of a file's **MIME type**. MIME stands for Multipurpose Internet Mail Extension. Although MIME types do not define a network protocol, they define a standard for attaching or including multimedia or otherwise specially formatted data with other documents, such as e-mail.

Based on a document's MIME type, an application program can decide how to deal with the data it is given. For example, the program you use to

> **MIME type**   A standard for defining the format of files that are included as e-mail attachments or on Web sites

Protocol	Port
Echo	7
File Transfer Protocol (FTP)	21
Telnet	23
Simple Mail Transfer Protocol (SMTP)	25
Domain Name Service (DNS)	53
Gopher	70
Finger	79
Hyper Text Transfer Protocol (HTTP)	80
Post Office Protocol (POP3)	110
Network News Transfer Protocol (NNTP)	119
Internet Relay Chat (IRC)	6667

Figure 15.7
Some protocols and the ports they use

read e-mail may examine the MIME type of an e-mail attachment to determine how to display it (if it can).

MIME types have been defined for the documents created by many common application programs, as well as for data from particular content areas. Chemists and chemical engineers, for example, have defined a large set of MIME types for various types of chemical-related data.

Firewalls

A **firewall** is a machine and its software that serve as a special gateway to a network, protecting it from inappropriate access. A firewall filters the network traffic that comes in, checking the validity of the messages as much as possible and perhaps denying some messages altogether. The main goal of a firewall is to protect (and to some extent hide) a set of more loosely administered machines that reside "behind" it. This process is pictured in Figure 15.8.

A firewall enforces an organization's **access control policy**. For example, a particular organization may allow network communication only between its users and the "outside world" via e-mail, and deny other types of communication, such as accessing Web sites. Another organization may want to allow its users to freely access the resources of the Internet, but may not want general Internet users to be able to infiltrate its systems or gain access to its data.

> **Firewall** A gateway machine and its software that protects a network by filtering the traffic it allows
>
> **Access control policy** A set of rules established by an organization that specify what types of network communication are permitted and denied

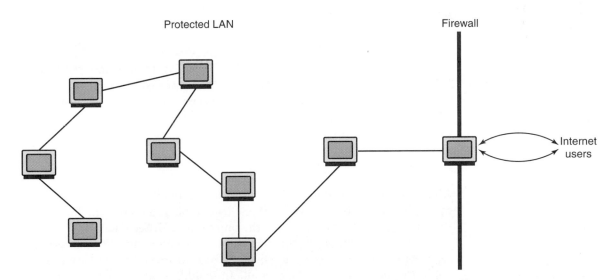

Figure 15.8 A firewall protecting a LAN

The system administrators of an organization set up a firewall for their LAN that permits "acceptable" types of communication and denies other types. There are various ways in which this can be accomplished, though the most straightforward is to deny traffic on particular ports. For example, a firewall could be set up to deny the ability for a user outside the LAN to create a telnet connection to any machine inside the LAN by denying all traffic that comes in on port 23.

More sophisticated firewall systems may maintain internal information about the state of the traffic passing through them and/or the content of the data itself. The more a firewall can determine about the traffic, the more able it is to protect its users. Of course, this security comes at a price. Some sophisticated firewall approaches might create a noticeable delay in network traffic.

15.3   Network Addresses

When you communicate across a computer network, you ultimately communicate with one particular computer out of all possible computers in the world. There is a fairly sophisticated mechanism for identifying specific machines to establish that communication.

A **hostname** is a unique identification that specifies a particular computer on the Internet. Hostnames are generally readable words separated by dots. For example:

```
matisse.csc.villanova.edu
condor.develocorp.com
```

> **Hostname** A name made up of words separated by dots that uniquely identifies a computer on the Internet; each hostname corresponds to a particular IP address
>
> **IP address** An address made up of four numeric values separated by dots that uniquely identifies a computer on the Internet

We humans prefer to use the hostnames when dealing with e-mail addresses and Web sites because they are easy to use and remember. Behind the scenes, however, network software translates a hostname into its corresponding **IP address**, which is easier for a computer to use. An IP address is usually represented as a series of four decimal numbers separated by dots. For example:

```
205.39.145.18
193.133.20.4
```

An IP address is stored in 32 bits. Each number in an IP address corresponds to one byte in the IP address. Since one byte (8 bits) can represent 256 things, each number in an IP address is in the range 0 to 255. See Figure 15.9.

It's tempting to assume that since both hostnames and IP addresses are separated into sections by dots, there is a correspondence between the sections. That is not true. First of all, an IP address always has four values, but hostnames can have a variety of sections.

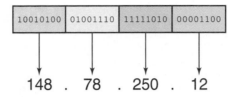

An IP address can be split into a **network address**, which specifies a specific network, and a **host number**, which specifies a particular machine in that network. How the IP address is split up depends on what network "class" it represents. The classes of networks (A, B, and C) provide for networks of various sizes.

> **Network address** The part of an IP address that specifies a specific network
>
> **Host number** The part of an IP address that specifies a particular host on the network

Class A networks use the first byte for the network address and the remaining three bytes for the host number. Class B networks use the first and second bytes for the network address and the last two bytes for the host number. Class C networks use the first three bytes for the network number and the last byte for the host number.

Think about the range of values this addressing approach allows for the various network classes. There are relatively few class A networks, with potentially many hosts on each. On the other hand, there are many class C networks, but only a few (maximum 256) hosts on each. Class C network addresses are assigned to most organizations, whereas class A and B networks are reserved for very large organizations and Internet service providers.

The entire Internet protocol is based on a 32-bit IP address. If the use of Internet-ready devices continues to grow, we will eventually run out of reasonable address space to use. Debate continues to rage in networking circles about how to handle this dilemma.

Domain Name System

A hostname consists of the computer name followed by the **domain name**. For example, in the hostname

`matisse.csc.villanova.edu`

> **Domain name** The part of a hostname that specifies a specific organization or group

`matisse` is the name of a particular computer, and `csc.villanova.edu` is the domain name. A domain name is separated into two or more sections that specify the organization, and possibly a subset of an organization, of which the computer is a part. In this example, `matisse` is a computer in the Department of Computing Sciences at Villanova University.

The domain names narrow in on a particular set of networks controlled by a particular organization. Note that two organizations (or even suborganizations) can have a computer named the same thing because the domain name makes it clear which one is being referred to.

Top-Level Domain	General Purpose	New TLDs	General Purpose
.com	U.S. Commercial	.biz	Business
.net	Network	.info	Information
.org	Nonprofit organization	.pro	Professional
.edu	U.S. Educational	.museum	Museums
.int	International	.aero	Aerospace industry
.mil	U.S. Military	.coop	Cooperative
.gov	U.S. Government		

Figure 15.10
Top-level domains, including some relatively new ones

Top-level domain (TLD)
The last section of a domain name, specifying the type of organization or its country of origin

The very last section of the domain is called its **top-level domain** (**TLD**) name. The primary top-level domains are listed in Figure 15.10.

The first column of Figure 15.10 shows the top-level domains that have been around since the Internet first evolved. Each one is used for organizations of a particular type, such as .com for commercial businesses and .edu for colleges and universities. Organizations based in countries other than the United States use a top-level domain that corresponds to their two-letter country codes. Some of these codes (there are hundreds of them) are listed in Figure 15.11.

Initially, anyone or any organization could register a domain name for their own use as long as that name hadn't already been taken. As the Internet expanded, with new domain names being claimed regularly, it quickly became clear that there was a problem. A common lament among newcomers to the Internet was that the best domain names had already been taken. Sometimes a name had already been claimed by another similar organization, but in other cases people were trying to claim as many popular names as possible, hoping to sell (ransom) them to large corporations (see the discussion on domain name squatting at the end of this chapter).

Country Code TLD	Country
.au	Australia
.br	Brazil
.ca	Canada
.gr	Greece
.in	India
.ru	Russian Federation
.uk	United Kingdom

Figure 15.11
Some of the top-level domain names based on country codes

To alleviate the problem of domain name use, a new set of top-level domains have been approved and are slowly being made available. The right half of Figure 15.10 shows the new TLDs. This time the ability to register a domain name using one of the new TLDs is being controlled, giving preference to organizations that hold trademarks on particular names.

The **domain name system** (DNS) is chiefly used to translate hostnames into numeric IP addresses. Before the DNS system was established, a Stanford research group maintained a single file known as the *host table*. As new host names were established, the Stanford group would add them to the table (usually twice a week). System administrators would retrieve the revised host table occasionally to update their **domain name servers**, which are computers that translate (resolve) a hostname into its IP address.

As the number of hostnames grew, the single table approach became unreasonable. It simply wasn't a practical way to update and distribute the information. In 1984, network engineers designed the more sophisticated domain name system that is in use today. DNS is an example of a distributed database (as discussed in Chapter 12); no one organization is responsible for updating the hostname/IP mappings.

When you specify a hostname in a browser window or e-mail address, the browser or e-mail software sends a request to a nearby domain name server. If that server can resolve the hostname, it does so. If not, that server asks another domain name server. If that second server can't resolve it, the request continues to propagate. Ultimately, the request finally reaches a server that can resolve the name, or the request expires because it took too much time to resolve.

> **Domain name system**
> A distributed system for managing hostname resolution
>
> **Domain name server**
> A computer that attempts to translate a hostname into an IP address

Terrorist attacks spark run on domain names

After the suicide jetliner attacks against the United States on September 11, 2001, hundreds of related Internet domain names were registered—some for tributes and others for profit. Some legitimate sites included WTCStories.com, a collection of quotes and information on charities, and AirTragedy.com, which contained news and resources for victims and survivors.

On the other hand, some domain names were claimed in the hopes of selling them to interested parties. WTCNot.com advertised that it was for sale for $500,000, and WTCdestruction.net was available for $75,000. One major domain name reseller halted auctions for tasteless names such as NewYorkCarnage.com. The CEO of a name registration company said spectators of attack-related names were misguided about their value. His advice was to donate the $30 cost of domain-name registration to an appropriate charity instead.[3]

Summary

A network is a collection of computers connected to share resources and data. Network technologies must concern themselves with underlying protocols and data transfer speeds. The client-server model has emerged as an important software technology given our ever-increasing reliance on networks.

Networks are often classified by their scope. A local-area network (LAN) covers a small geographic area and a relatively small number of connected devices. A wide-area network (WAN) embraces internetworking, connecting one network to another, and covers a large geographic area. A municipal-area network (MAN) is specially designed for large cities. LAN topologies include ring, star, and bus networks. Ethernet has become a standard for local-area networks.

Open systems are based on a common model of network architecture and protocols, allowing for interoperability. The OSI Reference Model is a seven-layer description of network processing based on open-system principles.

The Internet backbone is a set of high-speed networks provided by various companies. Internet service providers (ISP) connect to the backbone or to other ISPs and provide connections for both home and business computing. Popular home connection technologies include phone modems, digital subscriber lines (DSL), and cable modems. Phone modems transfer data as audio signals and are therefore quite slow. DSL uses the same phone lines but transfers data digitally. Cable modems are also digital and use the cable TV wiring to transfer data.

Messages are transferred over the Internet by breaking them up into packets and sending those packets separately to their destination where they are reformed into the original message. Packets may make several intermediate hops between networks before arriving at their destination. Routers are network devices that guide a packet between networks. Repeaters strengthen digital signals before they degrade too much.

Network protocols are layered so that a high-level protocol relies on lower-level protocols that support it. The key lower-level protocol suite for Internet traffic is TCP/IP. IP protocols and software deal with the routing of packets. TCP protocols and software divide messages into packets, reassemble them at the destination, and take care of errors that occur. High-level protocols include SMTP for e-mail traffic, FTP for file transfers, telnet for remote login sessions, and HTTP for Web traffic. Several high-level protocols have been assigned port numbers, which are used to help control and process network traffic. MIME types have been defined for many types of documents and special data formats.

A firewall protects a network from inappropriate access and enforces an organization's access control policy. Some firewalls simply block traffic on specific ports, while more sophisticated firewalls analyze the content of network traffic.

An Internet network address must pinpoint a particular machine among all possible ones in the world. A hostname uses readable words separated by dots. A hostname gets translated into an IP address, which is a numeric address separated into four sections. Part of the IP address identifies the network and part identifies the specific host on that network. How the IP address is broken down depends on the network class (A, B, or C) that the address references.

The domain name system (DNS) translates hostnames into IP addresses. DNS has evolved from using a single file containing all of the information into a distributed system dividing the responsibility among millions of domain name servers. Top-level domains, such as `.com` and `.edu`, have become crowded, so some new top-level domains, such as `.info` and `.biz`, have been approved.

ETHICAL ISSUES

Cybersquatting

Cybersquatting refers to registering an Internet domain name (also called "dot com" name) for the purpose of selling it later. How can domain names become theft for resale? Why are they important enough for someone to want to buy them? A company with a well-known trademark tries to register the trademark as a domain name only to find that someone else has already registered it. It may be that the business that registered the name has a similar name or, more likely, the name has been registered with the intention of selling it to the company with the same trademark. Common names are also subject to cybersquatting. For example, drugstore.com, furniture.com, gardening.com, and Internet.com were sold by cybersquatters.

Names of famous people are targets for cybersquatters as well. For example, in the 2000 National Football League draft, of the 120 players expected to be drafted only a few didn't have domain sites registered with their names—and very few of these sites were registered by the players themselves. One fan collects such sites as a piece of history, but most of the people registering the names expected to sell them after the draft.

In the late 1990s, domain-name auction houses arose. For a fee, the house would appraise a registered domain name and offer it for auction. Names such as 411.com, 611.com, and 911.com, all of which were listed on one site, were expected to go for as much as $10 million each. In addition, FastRefill.com was listed for $90,000, and Roast-Beef.com was listed for $350,000.[4]

A different but related issue is the registering of domain names that are clearly related to a famous person or brand name. For example, the satirical site http://www.gwbush.com/ was set up during the 2000 presidential election campaign to poke fun at candidate George Bush. (The official site was `http://www.georgebush.com/`.) Another site, `toys-r-us.co.uk`, was set up to air a customer's grievances with the Toys 'R' Us company.

In November 1999, the Anti-cyber Piracy Act was passed by Congress and signed by President Clinton. The Act establishes that someone registering a domain name may be liable to the owner of a trademark or to others that may be affected by the "bad faith" of the domain name registrant. In August of 2000, Governor Davis of California signed into law a bill that closed gaps in the federal legislation by including protection for names that are not trademarked or sufficiently famous to meet the federal standards.

In 1998 the Internet Corporation for Assigned Names and Numbers (ICANN), a technical coordination body for the Internet, was created in the private sector. ICANN issued the Uniform Domain-Name Dispute-Resolution Policy (often referred to as the "UDRP"). As the ICANN Web site states,

"Under the policy, most types of trademark-based domain-name disputes must be resolved by agreement, court action, or arbitration before a registrar will cancel, suspend, or transfer a domain name. Disputes alleged to arise from abusive registrations of domain names (for example, cybersquatting) may be addressed by expedited administrative proceedings that the holder of trademark rights initiates by filing a complaint with an approved dispute-resolution service provider."[5]

These laws and policies have cut down on the cases of cybersquatting, but some people are concerned that they go too far. These people fear that in curbing domain-name abuses, individual rights to free speech have been abridged.

Key Terms

Access control policy pg. 467

Broadband pg. 461

Bus topology pg. 458

Cable modem pg. 460

Client/Server model pg. 457

Computer network pg. 456

Data transfer rate (*also* bandwidth) pg. 456

Digital subscriber line (DSL) pg. 460

Domain name pg. 469

Domain name server pg. 471

Domain name system pg. 471

Download pg. 462

Ethernet pg. 458

File server pg. 457

Firewall pg. 467

Gateway pg. 458

Host number pg. 469

Hostname pg. 468

Internet pg. 458

Internet backbone pg. 459

Exercises

1. What is a computer network?
2. How are computers connected together?
3. To what does the word *node (host)* refer?
4. Name and describe two key issues related to computer networks.
5. What is a synonym for data transfer rate?
6. Describe the client/server model and discuss how it has changed how we think about computing.
7. Just how *local* is a local-area network?
8. Distinguish between the following LAN topologies: ring, star, and bus.
9. How does the shape of the topology influence message flow through a LAN?
10. What is Ethernet?
11. What is a WAN?
12. What is a gateway and what is its purpose?

13. What is the Internet?

14. What is a MAN and what makes it different from a LAN and a WAN?

15. Distinguish between the Internet backbone and an Internet service provider (ISP).

16. Name at least two national ISPs.

17. Name and describe three technologies for connecting a home computer to the Internet.

18. What role do ISPs play with the three technologies in Exercise 17?

19. What are the advantages and disadvantages of each of the technologies in Exercise 17?

20. Phone modems and digital subscriber lines (DSLs) use the same kind of phone line to transfer data. Why is DSL so much faster than phone modems?

21. Why do DSL and cable modem suppliers use technology that devotes more speed to downloads than to uploads?

22. Messages sent across the Internet are divided into packets. What is a packet and why are messages divided into them?

23. Explain the term *packet switching*.

24. What is a router?

25. What is a repeater?

26. What problems arise due to packet switching?

27. What are proprietary systems and why do they cause a problem?

28. What do we call the ability of software and hardware on multiple platforms from multiple commercial vendors to communicate?

29. What is an open system and how does it foster interoperability?

30. Compare and contrast proprietary and open systems.

31. What is the seven-layer logical breakdown of network interaction called?

32. What is a protocol stack and why is it layered?

33. What constitutes the foundation of Internet communication?

34. What is the role of the IP protocol?

35. What is the role of the TCP protocol?

36. Define *TCP/IP*.

37. Compare TCP and UDP.

38. What is the functionality of the utility program ping?

39. What is the functionality of the utility program Traceroute?

40. List four high-level protocols and what they specify.

41. What do we call a numeric designation corresponding to a particular high-level protocol?

42. Define *MIME type*.

43. What is a firewall, what does it accomplish, and how does it accomplish it?

44. What is a host name and how is it composed?

45. What is an IP address and how is it composed?

46. What is the relationship between a hostname and an IP address?

47. Into what parts can an IP address be split?

48. What are the relative sizes of Class A networks, Class B networks, and Class C networks?

49. How many hosts are possible in Class C networks, in Class B networks, and in Class A networks?

50. What is a domain name?

51. What is a top-level domain name?

52. How does the current domain name system try to resolve a hostname?

? Thought Questions

1. What is the computer system in your school like? Are all the computers networked? Is there more than one network? Are the dormitories networked?

2. If you wanted to register a domain name, how would you go about it? .biz, .info, .pro, .museum, .aero, and .coop are new top-level domain names. Are there any current restrictions on the use of these new top-level domain names?

3. Do you think that the name *Internet* is appropriate? Would *Intranet* be a better name?

4. Do you think the government or the private sector should monitor domain-name abuse?

5. Go to the ICANN Web site and read the UDRP. Do you think their definition of "bad faith" is reasonable? Is it adequate to solve the abuses described here?

6. Should a person be allowed to create a Web site with the intention of broadcasting unsubstantiated claims against a product or company?

7. Should a person be allowed to create a Web site to parody a person, company, or political institution?

The Communications Layer

16 The World Wide Web

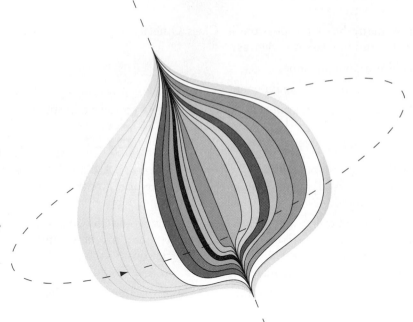

The World Wide Web

The evolution of the World Wide Web has made network communication a convenient reality for many users who would otherwise avoid computers completely. As the name implies, the Web has created spider-like connections across the entire planet, forming an infrastructure of information and resources available at the click of a mouse button. Several different underlying technologies make the Web the productive tool it is today. This chapter explores a few of them and establishes a foundation of Web-based principles on which all future technologies likely will rely.

Goals

After studying this chapter, you should be able to:

- compare and contrast the Internet and the World Wide Web.
- describe general Web processing.
- write basic HTML documents.
- describe several specific HTML tags and their purposes.
- describe the processing of Java applets and Java server pages.
- compare and contrast HTML and XML.
- define basic XML documents and their corresponding DTDs.
- explain how XML documents are viewed.

16.1   Spinning the Web

Many people use the words *Internet* and *Web* interchangeably, but in reality they are fundamentally different. The details of computer networks were discussed in Chapter 15. Networks have been used to connect computers since the 1950s. Communication via the Internet has been possible for many years, but in the early days that communication was almost exclusively accomplished via text-based e-mail and basic file exchanges.

Compared to the Internet, the **World Wide Web** (or simply the **Web**) is a relatively new idea. The Web is an infrastructure of distributed information combined with software that uses networks as a vehicle to exchange that information. A **Web page** is a document that contains or references various kinds of data, such as text, images, graphics, and programs. Web pages also contain **links** to other Web pages so that the user can "move around" as desired using the point-and-click interface provided by a computer mouse. A **Web site** is a collection of related Web pages, usually designed and controlled by the same person or company.

The Internet makes the communication possible, but the Web makes that communication easy, more productive, and more enjoyable. Though universities and some high-tech companies had been using the Internet for years, it wasn't until the mid 1990s, when the World Wide Web was developed, that the Internet became a household name. Suddenly, Internet Service Providers (ISPs) were springing up everywhere, allowing people to connect to the Internet from their homes. The Internet, largely because of the World Wide Web, is now a primary vehicle for business. Electronic shopping, financial transactions, and group management are all common

World Wide Web (or Web)   An infrastructure of information and the network software used to access it

Web page   A document that contains or references various kinds of data

Link   A connection between one Web page and another

Web site   A collection of related Web pages, usually designed and controlled by the same person or company

online activities. The Web has literally changed the way we conduct our personal and business lives.

When we use the Web, we often talk about "visiting" a Web site, as if we were going there. In truth, we actually specify the information we want, and it is brought to us. The concept of visiting a site is understandable in that we often don't know what's at a particular site until we "go to it" and see.

We communicate on the Web using a **Web browser**, such as Netscape Navigator or Microsoft's Internet Explorer. A browser is a software tool that issues the request for the Web page we want and displays it when it arrives. Figure 16.1 depicts this process.

The requested Web page is usually stored on another computer, which may be down the hall or halfway around the world. That computer that is set up to respond to Web requests is called a **Web server**.

In a browser, we specify the Web page we want using a Web address such as

www.villanova.edu/academics.html

A Web address is the core part of a **Uniform Resource Locator**, or **URL**, which uniquely identifies the page you want out of all of the pages stored anywhere in the world. Note that part of a URL is the host name of the computer on which the information is stored. Chapter 15 discussed host names and network addresses in detail.

In addition to text, a Web page often consists of separate elements such as images. All elements associated with a particular Web page are brought over when a request for that Web page is made.

Various technologies contribute to the design and implementation of a Web site. Our goal in this chapter is to introduce you to a few of these technologies. More detail about these topics can be found on the book's Web site.

Web browser A software tool that retrieves and displays Web pages

Web server A computer set up to respond to requests for Web pages

Uniform Resource Locator (or URL) A standard way of specifying the location of a Web page

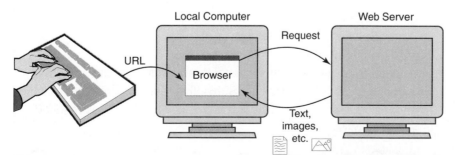

Figure 16.1
A browser retrieving a Web page

16.2 HTML

Hypertext Markup Language (or HTML) The language used to create or build a Web page

Markup language A language that uses tags to annotate the information in a document

Tag The syntactic element in a markup language that indicates how information should be displayed

Web pages are created (or built) using a language called the **Hypertext Markup Language**, or **HTML**. The term *hypertext* refers to the fact that the information is not organized linearly, like a book. Instead, we can embed links to other information and jump from one place to another as needed. These days, the more accurate term would be *hypermedia*, because we deal with many types of information in addition to text, including images, audio, and video.

The term **markup language** comes from the fact that the primary elements of the language take the form of **tags** that we insert into a document to annotate the information stored there. In the case of HTML, the tags indicate how the information should be displayed. It's as if you took a printed document and marked it up with extra notation to specify other details, as shown in Figure 16.2.

HTML documents are regular text and can be created in any general-purpose editor or word processor. There are also special-purpose software tools that are designed to help us create Web pages, but these tools ultimately generate HTML documents. It is these HTML documents that are transported over the Web when a Web page is requested.

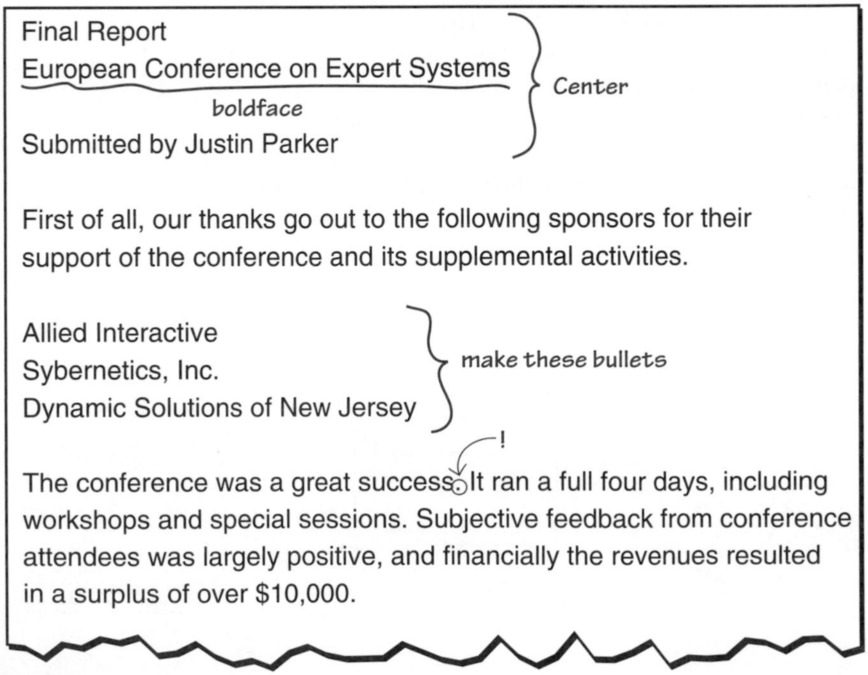
Final Report
European Conference on Expert Systems
boldface
Submitted by Justin Parker
Center
First of all, our thanks go out to the following sponsors for their support of the conference and its supplemental activities.
Allied Interactive
Sybernetics, Inc.
Dynamic Solutions of New Jersey
make these bullets
!
The conference was a great success. It ran a full four days, including workshops and special sessions. Subjective feedback from conference attendees was largely positive, and financially the revenues resulted in a surplus of over $10,000.

Figure 16.2
A marked-up document

An HTML tag indicates the general nature of a piece of information (such as a paragraph, an image, an itemized list) as well as how it should be displayed (such as the font style, size, and color). Think of tags as suggestions to the browser. Two different browsers may interpret the same tags in slightly different ways. Therefore, the same Web page may look different depending on what browser you use to view it.

Let's look at an example Web page as displayed by a browser and then examine the underlying HTML document with the various tags embedded in it. Figure 16.3 shows a Web page displayed in the Netscape Navigator browser. The page contains information about a student organization called Student Dynamics.

The Web page contains an image at the top showing the name of the group. Below the image, offset by a pair of horizontal lines, is a single phrase in italics. Below that is some information about the organization,

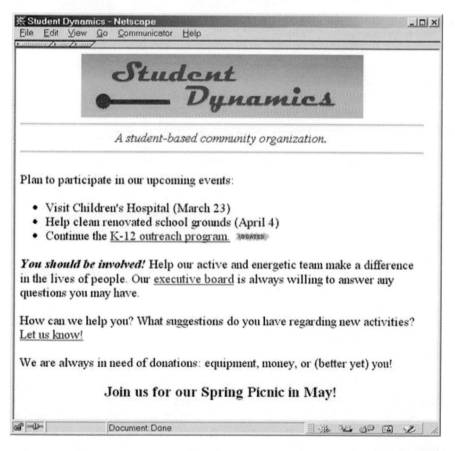

Figure 16.3
The Student Dynamics Web page as displayed in Netscape Navigator

```
<HTML>
   <HEAD>
      <TITLE>Student Dynamics</TITLE>
   </HEAD>
   <BODY>
      <CENTER><IMG SRC="stuDynamics.gif"></CENTER>
      <HR>
      <CENTER><I>A student-based community organization.</I></CENTER>
      <HR>
      <P>Plan to participate in our upcoming events:</P>
      <UL>
         <LI>Visit Children's Hospital (March 23)</LI>
         <LI>Help clean renovated school grounds (April 4)</LI>
         <LI>Continue the <a href="outreach.html">K-12 outreach
             program.</a> <IMG SRC="updated.gif"></LI>
      </UL>
      <P><B><I>You should be involved!</B></I> Help our active and
         energetic team make a difference in the lives of people. Our
         <a href="execBoard.html">executive board</a> is always willing
         to answer any questions you may have.</P>
      <P>How can we help you? What suggestions do you have regarding
         new activities? <a href="suggestions.html">Let us know!</a></P>
      <P>We are always in need of donations: equipment, money, or
         (better yet) you!</P>
      <CENTER><H3>Join us for our Spring Picnic in May!</H3></CENTER>
   </BODY>
</HTML>
```

Figure 16.4   The HTML document defining the Student Dynamics Web page

including a bulleted list of upcoming events followed by some short paragraphs. The small image at the end of one bulleted item is used to indicate that that information has been recently updated. The blue, underlined text represents links that, when clicked using the mouse, open a new Web page. Note that some of the text has special styling, such as bold or italics, and that some is centered.

The underlying HTML document for this Web page is shown in Figure 16.4. It specifies all of the formatting seen in this Web page. The tags embedded among the main document contents are highlighted in blue.

Tags are enclosed in angle brackets (<...>). Words such as HEAD, TITLE, and BODY are called *elements* and specify the type of the tag. Tags are often used in pairs, with a start tag such as <BODY> and a corresponding end tag with a / before the element name, such as `</BODY>`. HTML is not case sensitive, so `<body>` and `<BODY>` are the same.

Every HTML file contains two main sections: the head of the document followed by the body of the document. The head contains information about the document itself, such as its title. The body of the document contains the information to be displayed.

The entire HTML document is enclosed between `<HTML>` and `</HTML>` tags. The head and body sections of the document are similarly indicated. The text between the `<TITLE>` and `</TITLE>` tags appear in the title bar of the Web browser when the page is displayed.

The browser determines how the page should be displayed based on the tags. It ignores the way we format the HTML document using carriage returns, extra spaces, and blank lines. Indenting some lines of the document makes it easier for a human being to read, but such formatting is irrelevant to the way it is finally displayed. A browser takes into account the width and height of the browser window. When you resize the browser window, the contents of the Web page are reformatted to fit the new size.

A browser does its best to make sense of the way a document is marked up with tags and displays the page accordingly. If HTML tags conflict, or are not properly ordered or nested, the results can be surprising and unattractive.

> ## Don't believe everything you read
>
> You should always keep in mind that there is no guarantee that the information you find on the Web is correct. We ran into this problem while writing this book. In preparing the biography of John Backus for Chapter 11, two conflicting pieces of information surfaced. One Web reference said that he retired from the computer industry in 1991, and another said that he died on October 28, 1988. We sent an e-mail message to the SIGCSE (Special Interest Group for Computer Science Education) mailing list asking if anyone knew which was correct. Several colleagues responded saying that they had had dinner with Backus in 1992, solving that problem. The confusion was cleared up when another colleague said that there was a research physicist named John Backus who had died in 1988. The erroneous Web site had merged those two pieces of information: the death of one John Backus with the picture and biography of the other.

Basic HTML Formatting

The paragraph tags (`<P>` ... `</P>`) specify text that should be treated as a separate paragraph. In most browsers, the closing `</P>` tag is unnecessary, but we use it for clarity. A browser usually begins each paragraph on a new line with some space separating it from proceeding and following paragraphs.

The center tags (`<CENTER>` ... `</CENTER>`) indicate that the enclosed information should be centered in the browser window.

The B, I, and U elements are used to indicate that the enclosed text should be bold, italic, or underlined, respectively. These elements can be nested, causing multiple effects to occur at the same time, though this is not the case with all tags. That is, not all tags make sense when nested.

The `<HR>` tag inserts a horizontal rule (that is, a line) across the page. Horizontal rules are often helpful in breaking up a Web page into sections.

We often have cause to display a list of items. The UL element stands for an unordered list, and the LI element represents a list item. In the Student Dynamics example, three list items are enclosed in the ⟨UL⟩ ... ⟨/UL⟩ tags. Most browsers display an unordered list using bullets. If the ordered list element (OL) is used, the list items are numbered sequentially. Both unordered and ordered lists can be nested, creating a hierarchy of lists. Unordered nested lists use different bullet types for each level, and the numbering for each ordered list begins over again at each level.

Several elements are used to define headings in a document. There are six predefined heading elements defined in HTML: H1, H2, H3, H4, H5, and H6. Text enclosed in ⟨H3⟩...⟨/H3⟩ tags, for instance, is treated as a level 3 heading, which is displayed in a larger font than level 4, but smaller than level 2. Heading tags don't have to specify text that introduces a section; they can be used anywhere you want to change the size of the font.

Images and Links

Attribute Part of a tag that provides additional information about the element

Many tags can contain **attributes** that indicate additional details about the information or how the enclosed information should be displayed.

Attributes take the following form:

```
attribute-name = value
```

For example, an image can be incorporated into a Web page using the IMG element, which takes an attribute that identifies the image file to display. The attribute name is called SRC, which stands for the source of the image. There is no closing tag for the IMG element. For example,

```
<IMG SRC = "myPicture.gif">
```

inserts the image stored in file myPicture.gif into the HTML document. There must be at least one space between IMG and SRC.

An image is used as a banner to the entire page in the Student Dynamics example. And in another location a small image is used to indicate information on the Web site that has been recently updated.

In HTML, a link is specified using the element A, which stands for anchor. The tag includes an attribute called HREF that specifies the URL of the destination document. For example,

```
<A HREF = "http://duke.csc.villanova.edu/docs/">
Documentation Central! </A>
```

shows the text "Documentation Central!" on the screen, usually underlined and in blue type. When the user clicks on the link with the mouse, the Web page whose address is duke.csc.villanova.edu/docs is fetched and displayed in the browser, replacing the current page. Notice that both the name of a file and a URL are enclosed in quotes.

Keep in mind that we have only scratched the surface of HTML's capabilities, yet the few tags we've examined already give us the ability to create fairly versatile and useful Web pages.

16.3   Interactive Web Pages

When HTML was first developed, it was amazing in its ability to format network-based text and images in interesting ways. However, that information was static. There was no way to interact with the information and pictures presented in a Web page.

As users have clamored for a more dynamic web, new technologies were developed to accommodate these requests. These technologies took different approaches to solving the problem. Many of the new ideas were offshoots of the newly developed Java programming language, which is able to exploit the Web because of its platform independence. Let's look briefly at two of these technologies: Java Applets and Java Server Pages.

Java Applets

A **Java applet** is a program that is designed to be embedded into an HTML document and transferred over the Web to someone who wants to run the program. An applet is actually executed in the browser used to view the Web page.

An applet is embedded into an HTML document using the APPLET tag. For example:

```
<APPLET code="MyApplet.class" width=250 height=150
></APPLET>
```

When a Web user references the page containing this tag, the applet program MyApplet.class is sent along with any text, images, and other data that the page contains. The browser knows how to handle each type of data—it formats text appropriately and displays images as needed. In the case of an applet, the browser has a built-in interpreter that executes the applet, allowing the user to interact with it. Thousands of Java applets are out on the Web, and most browsers are set up to execute them.

Consider the difficulties inherent in this situation. A program is written on one computer, and then may be transferred to any other computer on the Web to be executed. How can we execute a program that was written on one type of computer on possibly many other types of computers? The key, as briefly explained in Chapter 8, is that Java programs are compiled into Bytecode, a low-level representation of a program that is not the machine code for any particular type of CPU. This Bytecode can be executed by any valid Bytecode interpreter, no matter what type of machine it is running on.

> **Java applet** A Java program designed to be embedded into an HTML document, transferred over the Web, and executed in a browser

Note that the applet model puts the burden on the client's machine. That is, a Web user brings the program to his or her computer and executes it there. It may be frightening to think that, while you are casually surfing the Web, suddenly someone's program is executing on your computer. That would be a problem, except that Java applets are restricted as to what they can do. The Java language has a carefully constructed security model. An applet, for instance, cannot access any local files or change any system settings.

Depending on the nature of the applet, the client's computer may or may not be up to the job. For this reason, and because applets are transferred over a network, they tend to be relatively small. Although appropriate for some situations, applets do not resolve all of the interactive needs of Web users.

Java Server Pages

A Java Server Page, or JSP, is a Web page that has **JSP scriptlets** embedded in them. A scriptlet is a small piece of executable code intertwined among regular HTML content. While not exactly the same as Java, JSP code resembles the general Java programming language.

A JSP scriptlet is encased in special tags beginning with <% and ending with %>. Special objects have been predefined to facilitate some processing. For example, the object called out can be used to produce output, which is integrated into the Web page wherever the scriptlet occurs. The following scriptlet produces the phrase "hello there" between the opening and closing tag of an H3 header.

```
<H3>
<%
out.println ("hello there");
%>
</H3>
```

In this particular case, the result is equivalent to

```
<H3>hello there</H3>
```

But now imagine JSP scriptlets as having the expressive power of a full programming language (which they do). We can make use of almost all aspects of a regular Java program, such as variables, conditionals, loops, and objects. With that kind of processing power, a JSP page can make significant decisions resulting in truly dynamic results.

Note that JSPs are executed on the server side where the Web page resides. They help dynamically define the content of a Web page before it is shipped to the user. By the time it arrives at your computer, all active processing has taken place, producing a static (though dynamically created) Web page.

> **JSP scriptlet** A portion of code embedded in an HTML document designed to dynamically contribute to the content of the Web page

JSPs are particularly good for coordinating the interaction between a Web page and an underlying database. The details of this type of processing are beyond the scope of this book, but you've probably seen this type of processing while surfing the Web. Electronic storefronts (sites that exist primarily to sell products), in particular, make use of this type of processing. The data about available products are not stored in static HTML pages. Instead, that data are stored in a database. When you make a particular request for information about a product, it may be a Java Server Page responding to you. The scriptlets in the page interact with the database and extract the needed information. Scriptlets and regular HTML format the data appropriately and then ship the page to your computer for viewing.

16.4 XML

HTML is fixed; that is, HTML has a predefined set of tags and each tag has its own semantics (meaning). HTML specifies how the information in a Web page should be formatted but doesn't really indicate what the information represents. For example, HTML indicates that a piece of text should be formatted as a heading, but it doesn't indicate what that heading describes. There is nothing about HTML tags that describes the true content of a document. The **Extensible Markup Language**, or **XML**, allows the creator of a document to describe its contents by defining his or her own set of tags.

> **Extensible Markup Language (or XML)** A language that allows the user to describe the content of a document

XML is a metalanguage. *Metalanguage* is the word *language* with the prefix *meta*, which means "beyond" or "more comprehensive." A **metalanguage** is a language that goes beyond a normal language by allowing us to speak precisely about that language. It is a language for talking about, or defining, other languages. It is like an English grammar book describing the rules of English.

> **Metalanguage** A language that is used to define other languages

A metalanguage called the Standard Generalized Markup Language, or SGML, was used by Tim Berners-Lee to define HTML. XML is a simplified version of SGML and is used to define other markup languages. XML has taken the Web in a new direction. It does not replace HTML; it enriches it.

Like HTML, an XML document is made up of tagged data. But when you write an XML document, you are not confined to a predefined set of tags because there are none. You can create any set of tags necessary to describe the data in your document. The focus is not on how that data should be formatted; the focus is on what the data is.

Tim Berners-Lee

Tim Berners-Lee is the first holder of the 3Com (Computer Communication Compatibility) Chair at the Laboratory for Computer Science at Massachusetts Institute of Technology. The chair is the first at MIT that may be held by a member of the research staff rather than the faculty. Mr. Berners-Lee is a researcher, evangelist, and arbiter rather than an academician. He is Director of the World Wide Web Consortium, which coordinates Web development worldwide. The Consortium, with teams at MIT, INRIA in France, and at Keio University in Japan, aims to lead the Web to its full potential, ensuring its stability through rapid evolution and revolutionary transformations of its usage.

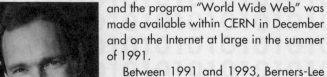

How did Tim Berners-Lee arrive at this very important position? He built his first computer while a student at Queen's College, Oxford. After graduation, he worked for two years with Plessey Telecommunications Ltd, a major Telecom equipment manufacturer in the United Kingdom, worked as an independent consultant for a year and a half, and worked for three years at Image Computer Systems Ltd. His various projects during this time included real-time control firmware, graphics and communications software, and a generic macro language.

In 1984, he took up a fellowship at CERN, the European Organization for Nuclear Research in Geneva, where he worked on a heterogeneous remote procedure call system and a distributed real-time system for scientific data acquisition and system control. In 1989, he proposed a global hypertext project to be known as the World Wide Web. It was designed to allow people to work together by combining their knowledge in a Web of hypertext documents. He wrote the first World Wide Web server, "httpd," and the first client, "World Wide Web," a what-you-see-is-what-you-get hypertext browser/editor. The work began in October of 1990, and the program "World Wide Web" was made available within CERN in December and on the Internet at large in the summer of 1991.

Between 1991 and 1993, Berners-Lee continued working on the design of the Web, coordinating feedback from users across the Internet. His initial specifications of URLs, HTTP, and HTML were refined and discussed in larger circles as the Web technology spread. It became apparent that the physics lab in Geneva was not the appropriate place for the task of developing and monitoring the Web. In October 1994, the World Wide Web Consortium was founded by Berners-Lee at the MIT Laboratory for Computer Science.

In a New York Times article in 1995, Berners-Lee was asked about private corporations trying to dominate Web standards for profit. He responded, "There's always the threat that a particular company would dominate the market and control the standards of the Web." But he feels strongly that this should not happen. "The essence of the Web is that it's a universe of information," he said. "And it wouldn't be universal if it was tied, in any way, to one company."

Michael Dertouzos, the director of the Computer Science Laboratory at MIT, said that Mr. Berners-Lee seems to embody the "libertarian idealism" of the Internet culture. "He has a real commitment to keeping the Web open as a public good, in economic terms," Mr. Dertouzos said. "That's his mission." Berners-Lee concludes: "Reasonable competition speeds the pace of innovation. Companies will promote the proprietary aspects of their browsers and applications, and they should. But the navigation of the Web has to be open. If the day comes when you need six browsers on your machine, the World Wide Web will no longer be the World Wide Web."

Berners-Lee was one of Time Magazine's 100 most important people in the 20th century.

```
<?xml version="1.0" ?>
<!DOCTYPE books SYSTEM "books.dtd">
<books>
<book>
<title>The Hobbit</title>
<authors>
  <author>J.R.R. Tolkien</author>
</authors>
<publisher>Ballantine</publisher>
<pages>287</pages>
<isbn>0-345-27257-9</isbn>
<price currency="USD">7.95</price>
</book>
<book>
<title>A Beginner's Guide to Bass Fishing</title>
<authors>
  <author>J. T. Angler</author>
  <author>Ross G. Clearwater</author>
</authors>
<publisher>Quantas Publishing</publisher>
<pages>750</pages>
<isbn>0-781-40211-7</isbn>
<price currency="USD">24.00</price>
</book>
</books>
```

Figure 16.5 An XML document containing data about books

For example, the XML document in Figure 16.5 describes a set of books. The tags in the document annotate data that represents a book's title, author(s), number of pages, publisher, ISBN number, and price.

The first line of the document indicates the version of XML that is used. The second line indicates the file that contains the **Document Type Definition (DTD)** for the document. The DTD is a specification of the organization of the document. The rest of the document contains the data about two particular books.

The structure of a particular XML document is described by its corresponding DTD document. The contents of a DTD document not only define the tags but also show how they can be nested. Figure 16.6 shows the DTD document that corresponds to the XML books example.

The ELEMENT tags in the DTD document describe the tags that make up the corresponding XML document. The first line of this DTD file indicates that the books tag is made up of zero or more book tags. The asterisk (*)

> **Document Type Definition (or DTD)** A specification of the organization of an XML document

```
<!ELEMENT books (book*) >
<!ELEMENT book (title, authors, publisher, pages, isbn, price)>
<!ELEMENT authors (author+)>
<!ELEMENT title (#PCDATA)>
<!ELEMENT author (#PCDATA)>
<!ELEMENT publisher (#PCDATA)>
<!ELEMENT pages (#PCDATA)>
<!ELEMENT isbn (#PCDATA)>
<!ELEMENT price (#PCDATA)>
<!ATTLIST price currency CDATA #REQUIRED>
```

Figure 16.6   The DTD document corresponding to the XML books document

beside the word *book* in parentheses stands for zero or more. The next line specifies that the book tag is made up of several other tags in a particular order: title, authors, publisher, pages, isbn, and price. The next line indicates that the authors tag is made up of one or more author tags. The plus sign (+) beside the word *author* indicates one or more. The other tags are specified to contain PCDATA, which stands for Parsed Character Data, which indicates that the tags are not further broken down into other tags.

The only tag in this set that has an attribute is the price tag. The last line of the DTD document indicates that the price tag has an attribute called currency and that it is required.

XML represents a standard format for organizing data without tying it to any particular type of output. A related technology called the **Extensible Stylesheet Language** (or **XSL**) can be used to transform an XML document into another format suitable for a particular user. For example, an XSL document can be defined that specifies the transformation of an XML document into an HTML document so that it can be viewed on the Web. Another XSL document can be defined to transform the same XML document into a Microsoft Word document, or into a format suitable for a Personal Data Assistant such as a Palm Pilot, or even into a format that can be used by a voice synthesizer. This process is depicted in Figure 16.7. We do not explore the details of XSL transformations in this book.

> **Extensible Stylesheet Language (or XSL)**   A language for defining transformations from XML documents to other output formats

Another convenient characteristic of languages specified using XML is that documents in the language can be generated automatically with relative ease. A software system, usually with an underlying database, can be used to generate huge amounts of specific data formatted in a way that is easily conveyed and analyzed online. Once generated, the data can be transformed and viewed in whatever manner best serves individual users.

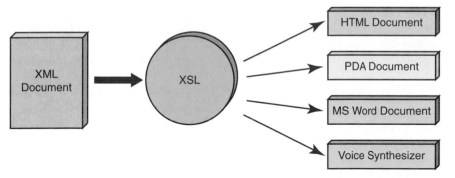

Figure 16.7
An XML document can be transformed into many output formats

Several organizations have already developed XML languages for their particular topic areas. For example, chemists and chemical engineers have defined the Chemistry Markup Language, or CML, to standardize the format of molecular data. CML includes a huge number of tags for specific aspects of chemistry. It provides a common format by which chemistry professionals can share and analyze data.

Keep in mind that XML is a *markup specification language* and XML files are data: They just sit there until you run a program that displays them (like a browser), does some work with them (like a converter that writes the data in another format or a database that reads the data), or modifies them (like an editor). XML and its related technologies provide a powerful mechanism for information management and for communicating that information over the Web in a versatile and efficient manner. As these technologies evolve, new opportunities to capitalize on them will present themselves.

Summary

Although the terms *Internet* and *Web* are often used interchangeably, they are not the same. The World Wide Web is an infrastructure of information distributed among thousands of computers across the world and the software by which that information is accessed. The Web relies on underlying networks, especially the Internet, as the vehicle to exchange the information among users.

A Web page contains information, as well as references to other resources such as images. A collection of Web pages managed by a single person or company is called a Web site. Links are established among various Web pages across the globe, giving credence to the name World Wide Web.

Visiting a Web site is really the act of requesting that a Web page stored on a remote Web server be brought to our local computer for viewing. A Uniform Resource Locator (URL) is used to specify the Web document we wish to view.

The Hypertext Markup Language, or HTML, is the primary method of defining Web pages. An HTML document consists of information that is annotated by tags that specify how a particular element should be treated and formatted. A Web browser displays an HTML page without regard to extra spacing, blank lines, or indentation. The tags alone guide the browser, and a given Web page may look slightly different when viewed in different browsers.

HTML tags include those that specify the overall document structure as well as tags that perform basic formatting, such as headings, paragraphs, and centered text. Font styles, such as bold and italics, are specified using tags as well. Unordered and ordered lists have their own set of tags.

Some HTML tags include attributes that specify additional information. The source attribute of an image tag specifies the file in which the image is stored, for instance. Anchor tags define links and use an attribute to specify the location of the target Web page.

Additional opportunities to interact with and dynamically create the content of Web pages exist. Two technologies that support Web-based interaction are Java applets and Java Server Pages. Java applets are Java programs designed to be embedded in HTML pages and executed in a Web browser. Their cross-platform nature is possible because applets are compiled into Java Bytecode, which is architecture-neutral.

Java Server Pages embed scriptlets into HTML code that is executed by the Web server to help dynamically define the content of a Web page. Scriptlets have the full expressive power of a full language. JSPs are particularly good at coordinating the interaction between a Web page and an underlying database.

XML stands for Extensible Markup Language. XML is a metalanguage, which means it is used to define other languages. Unlike HTML, whose tags focus on the format of displayed data, XML tags specify the nature of the data. The user is not constrained to use particular tags; he or she can define any tags that make sense for the data being described.

The format and relationships among XML tags are defined in a Document Type Definition document. A set of XSL (Extensible Stylesheet

Language) transformations define the way the content of an XML document is turned into another format suitable for the current needs of a user.

ETHICAL ISSUES

Cookies

Internet cookies are very small text files (usually about 50 to 150 bytes) that are downloaded from a Web server to a Web browser. Cookies are embedded in the HTML information flow involved when browsers request files from Web servers. When a Web browser first asks for a file from a Web server, the server creates a cookie containing information about the request and sends the cookie to the server along with the requested file. The next time a request is made from the browser of the server, the cookie is sent to the server along with the request. When the server returns the requested file, an updated cookie is also returned.

The idea is quite simple, and it was intended to allow a server to maintain information about those that visit it. For example, the cookie could contain a user ID and password for a Web site so that the information would not have to be reentered every time the Web site is visited. The use of cookies allows sites to create personalized start-up or news pages. This same scheme allows sites like Amazon.com to suggest other books that you might like based on your purchases. Note that the information is not kept within a server but within the computer of the browser user.

This protocol sounds very useful and helpful, but there is a downside to the use of cookies. The information on user preferences is collected, stored on the user's computer, and retransmitted to the Web server without the user's knowledge or consent. Companies, called *targeted marketing companies*, have evolved that sell cookie services. These companies pay Web sites to send them copies of the cookies for each transaction and thus build up a profile of a user's Internet habits. This information is used for marketing and advertising purposes.

Some people like the idea of having marketing and advertising targeted to their interests. Others feel that this is an invasion of privacy. Proposals put forth by the Internet Engineering Task Force include limiting the persistence (lifetime) of each cookie and requiring browsers to warn the user before accepting a cookie. Current versions of Netscape and Internet Explorer allow the user to destroy cookies when closing the browser by making certain selections on the Preferences menu.

Are cookies dangerous? No, they may invade a user's privacy, but they are not dangerous. Only executable files can do damage to a machine. Normal text-based cookies are not executable files; therefore, they cannot harm a machine or spread a virus, nor can they pass on private information from any files, including e-mail address files.

Key Terms

Attribute pg. 486

Document Type Definition
(*or* DTD) pg. 491

Extensible Markup Language
(*or* XML) pg. 489

Extensible Stylesheet Language
(*or* XSL) pg. 492

Hypertext Markup Language
(*or* HTML) pg. 482

Java applet pg. 487

JSP scriptlet pg. 488

Link pg. 480

Markup language pg. 482

Metalanguage pg. 489

Tag pg. 482

Uniform Resource Locator
(*or* URL) pg. 481

Web browser pg. 481

Web page pg. 480

Web server pg. 481

Web site pg. 480

World Wide Web (or Web)
pg. 480

Exercises

1. Describe the World Wide Web.
2. Why is a spider Web a good analogy for the World Wide Web?
3. What is the relationship between a Web page and a Web site?
4. What is the difference between the Internet and the Web?
5. Describe how a Web page is retrieved and viewed by a Web user.
6. What is a Uniform Resource Locator?
7. What is a markup language? Where does the name come from?
8. Compare and contrast hypertext and hypermedia.
9. Describe the syntax of an HTML tag.

10. What is a horizontal rule? What is it useful for?

11. Name five formatting specifications that can be established using HTML tags.

12. What is a tag attribute? Give an example.

13. Write the HTML statement that inputs the image on file `mine.gif` into the Web page.

14. Write the HTML statement that sets up a link to the Web site http://www.cs.utexas.edu/users/ndale/ and shows the text "Dale Home Page" on the screen.

15. What happens when a user clicks on "Dale Home Page" as set up in Exercise 14?

16. Design and implement an HTML document for an organization at your school.

17. Design and implement an HTML document describing one or more of your personal hobbies.

18. What is a Java applet?

19. How do you embed a Java applet in an HTML document?

20. Where does a Java applet get executed?

21. What kinds of restrictions are put on Java applets? Why?

22. What is a Java Server Page?

23. What is a scriptlet?

24. How do you embed a scriptlet in an HTML document?

25. How does JSP processing differ from applet processing?

26. What is a metalanguage?

27. What is XML?

28. How are HTML and XML alike and how are they different?

29. How does an XML document relate to a Document Type Definition?

30. a. In a DTD, how do you indicate that an element is to be repeated zero or more times?
    b. In a DTD, how do you indicate that an element is to be repeated one or more times?
    c. In a DTD, how do you indicate that an element cannot be broken down into other tags?

31. What is XSL?

32. What is the relationship between XML and XSL?

33. How does an XML document get viewed?

34. Define an XML language (the DTD) for your school courses and produce a sample XML document.

35. Define an XML language (the DTD) for government offices and produce a sample XML document.

36. Define an XML language (the DTD) for zoo animals and produce a sample SML document.

37. This chapter is full of acronyms. Define each of the following.
    a. HTML
    b. XML
    c. DTD
    d. XSL
    e. SGML
    f. URL
    g. ISP

38. Create an HTML document for a web page that has each of the following features.
    a. centered title
    b. unordered list
    c. ordered list
    d. link to another web page
    e. a picture

39. Distinguish between an HTML tag and an attribute.

40. Why does the same web page look different in different browsers?

41. What are the two sections of every HTML document?

42. What are the contents of the two parts of an HTML document?

43. What does the *A* stand for in the tag that specifies a URL for a page?

44. Create an HTML document for a web page that has each of the following features.
    a. a right-justified title in large type font
    b. an applet class named "Exercise.class".
    c. two different links
    d. two different pictures

? Thought Questions

1. How has the Web affected you personally?

2. Did you have a Web site before you started this class? How sophisticated was it? Did you use HTML or some other Web design language? If you used some other language, go to your Web site and view your

pages as source pages. Look at the HTML tags that actually format your Web site. Are there any there that we have not discussed in this chapter? If so, look them up to see what they mean. (Where? On the Web, of course.)

3. Have you ever taken a Web-based course? Did you enjoy the experience? Did you feel that you learned less or more than you would have in a regular course?

4. Give your vision of the future as it relates to the Web.

5. Do you feel that the benefits of using cookies outweigh the possible invasion of privacy?

6. Have you ever visited a Web site where you were asked for personal information and then the next time you visited the same site they "knew" who you were? Explain how this information is transmitted using cookies.

7. What are the ethical pros and cons of targeted marketing companies?

8. Do an Internet search to find out the status of the current Internet Engineering Task Force recommendations for cookies.

In Conclusion

17 Limitations of Computing

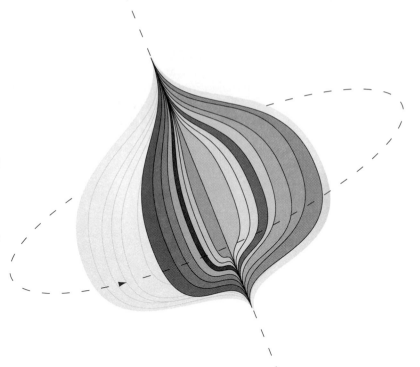

Limitations of Computing

In the last 16 chapters, we have looked at computers: What they are, what they can do, and how to use them to solve problems. In this chapter, we look at what computers *cannot* do. That is, we examine the limits imposed by the hardware, the software, and the problems themselves. The dictionary gives multiple meanings for the word *limit*, including "boundary" and "something that is exasperating or intolerable." We use both of these definitions of *limit* in this chapter.

Just as a roadblock stops traffic, the limits imposed by the hardware, software, and problems stop certain kinds of processing.

Goals

After studying this chapter, you should be able to:

- describe the limits that the hardware places on the solution to computing problems.
- discuss how the finiteness of the computer impacts the solutions to numeric problems.
- discuss ways to ensure that errors in data transmission are detected.
- describe the limits that the software places on the solutions to computing problems.
- discuss ways to build better software.
- describe the limits inherent in computable problems themselves.
- discuss the continuum of problem complexity from problems in Class P to problems that are unsolvable.

17.1   Hardware

The limits on computing caused by the hardware stem from several factors. One factor is that numbers are infinite, but the representation of them within the computer is not. Another problem with hardware is just the fact that it is hardware; that is, it is made up of mechanical and electronic components that can fail. Another set of problems occurs when data is transmitted from one internal device to another or from one computer to another. Let's look at each of these problems and some strategies to minimize their impact.

Limits on Arithmetic

We have discussed numbers and their representation in the computer in Chapters 2 and 3. There are limitations imposed by the hardware on the representations of both integer numbers and real numbers.

Integer Numbers

In the Pep/7 machine discussed in Chapter 7, the registers that are used for arithmetic are 16 bits long. We said that the largest value we could store there is 65,535 if we only represent positive values and 32,767 if we represent both positive and negative values. Pep/7 is a virtual machine; what about real machines? If the word length is 32 bits, the range of integer numbers that can be represented is −2,147,483,648 to 2,147,483,647. Some hardware systems support long-word arithmetic, where the range is −9,223,372,036,854,775,808 to 9,223,372,036,854,775,807: Surely this is large enough for any calculation, or is it?

Henry Walker, in his book *The Limits of Computing,* tells the following fable.[1] When the king asked a bright young dot-com'er to undertake a task for him, she agreed if the pay was adequate. She offered the king two choices: The king could pay her 1/5 of the crops produced in the kingdom for the next five years or base her payment on a chess board as follows:

- One kernel of corn on the first square
- Two kernels of corn on the second square
- Four kernels of corn on the third square
- Eight kernels of corn on the fourth square
- The kernels of corn would double on each successive square until the 64th square had been reached.

After a moment's thought, the king chose the second option. (Which would you have chosen?)

When it came time to pay up, the king started placing kernels of corn on the squares. There were 255 kernels on the first row (1 + 2 + 4 + 8 + 16 + 32 + 64 + 128); not too bad, he thought. For the next row, there were 65,280 kernels; still not too bad. The third row, however, with its 963,040 kernels of corn, made the king uneasy. During the counting of the next row, the king thought ahead to the last square, for he now understood the pattern. The 64th square alone would have 2^{63} kernels of corn or roughly 8×10^{18} kernels or 110,000 billion bushels. The king abdicated his throne in light of such a staggering debt, and the mathematically sophisticated young lady became queen.

The moral of this story is that integer numbers can get very big very fast. If a computer word is 64 bits and we represent only positive numbers, we could just represent the number of kernels on the 64th square. If we tried to add up the kernels on the 64 squares, we could not do so. Overflow would occur.

The hardware of a particular machine determines the limits of the numbers, both real and integer, that can be represented. There are software solutions, however, that allow programs to overcome these limitations. For example, we could represent a very large number as a list of smaller numbers. Figure 17.1 shows how integers could be presented by putting one digit in each word.

The program that manipulates integers in this form would have to add each pair of digits beginning at the rightmost and add any carry into the next addition to the left.

Real Numbers

In Chapter 3, we said that real numbers are stored as an integer along with information showing where the radix point is. In order to better understand why real numbers pose a problem, let's look at a coding scheme that represents the digits and the *radix-point information.*

(a) number = 752,036

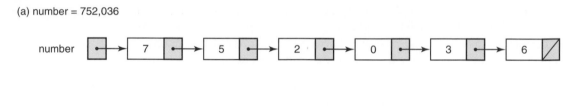

(b) number = 752,036

(c) sum = 83536 + 41

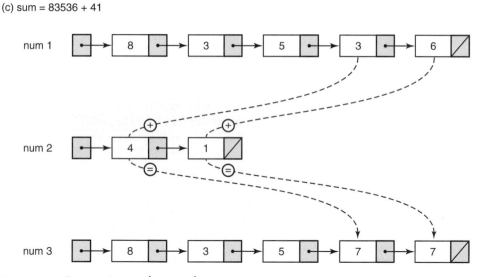

Figure 17.1   Representing very large numbers

Let's assume, to simplify in the following discussion, that we have a computer in which each memory location is the same size and is divided into a sign plus five decimal digits. When a variable or constant is defined, the location assigned to it consists of five digits and a sign. When an integral variable or constant is defined, the interpretation of the number stored in that place is straightforward. When a real variable is declared or a real constant is defined, the number stored there has both a whole number part and a fractional part. The number must be coded to represent both parts.

Let's see what these coded numbers might look like and what this coding does to arithmetic values in programs. We begin with integers. The range of the numbers we can represent with five digits is −99,999 through +99,999:

| − | 9 | 9 | 9 | 9 | 9 | Largest negative number |

| + | 0 | 0 | 0 | 0 | 0 | Zero |

| + | 9 | 9 | 9 | 9 | 9 | Largest positive number |

The **precision** (the maximum number of digits that can be represented) is five digits, and each number within that range can be represented exactly. What happens if we allow one of these digits (let's say the leftmost one, in red) to represent an exponent? For example

| + | 3 | 2 | 3 | 4 | 5 |

represents the number $+2,345 * 10^3$. The range of numbers we can now represent is much larger:

$-9,999 * 10^9$ to $+9,999 * 10^9$

or

$-9,999,000,000,000$ to $+9,999,000,000,000$

Now the precision is only four digits. That is, we can represent only four **significant digits** (nonzero digits or zero digits that are exact) of the number itself. This means we can represent only four-digit numbers exactly in our system. What happens to larger numbers? The four leftmost digits are correct, and the balance of the digits are assumed to be zero. We lose the rightmost, or *least significant*, digits. The following table shows what happens.

Number	Sign	Exp.					Value
+99,999	+	1	9	9	9	9	+99,990
−999,999	−	2	9	9	9	9	−999,900
+1,000,000	+	3	1	0	0	0	+1,000,000
−4,932,416	−	3	4	9	3	2	−4,932,000

Notice that we can represent 1,000,000 exactly, but not −4,932,416. Our coding scheme limits to four significant digits; the digits we cannot represent are assumed to be zero.

To extend our coding scheme to represent real numbers, we need to be able to represent negative exponents. For example,

$$4{,}394 * 10^{-2} = 43.94$$

or

$$22 * 10^{-4} = 0.0022$$

Because our scheme does not allow for a sign for the exponent, we have to change the scheme slightly. Let's let the sign that we have already been using be the sign of the exponent and add a sign to the left of it to be the sign of the number itself.

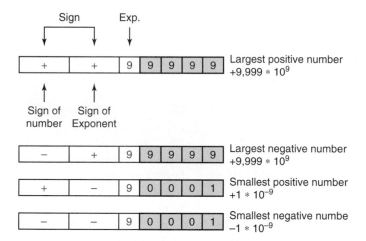

Now we can represent all of the numbers between $-9{,}999 * 10^{-9}$ and $9{,}999 * 10^{9}$ accurately to four digits, including all the fractional values.

Suppose we want to add three real numbers x, y, and z using this coding scheme. We could add x to y, then add z to the result. Or we could do it another way, adding y to z, then adding x to the result. The associative law of arithmetic says that the two answers should be the same—but are they?

The computer limits the precision (the number of significant digits) of a real number. Using our coding scheme of four significant digits and an exponent, let's add the following allowable values of x, y, and z:

$$x = -1324 * 10^{3} \qquad y = 1325 * 10^{3} \qquad z = 5424 * 10^{0}$$

First let's look at the result of adding z to the sum of x and y:

```
(x)          −1324 * 10³
(y)           1325 * 10³
             ──────────────
                 1 * 10³ = 1000 * 10⁰
```

```
(x + y)       1000 * 10⁰
(z)           5424 * 10⁰
             ──────────────
              6424 * 10⁰ = (x + y) + z
```

Now let's see what happens when we add x to the sum of y and z:

```
(y)        1325000 * 10⁰
(z)           5424 * 10⁰
          ──────────────────
           1330424 * 10⁰ = 1330 * 10³ (truncated to four
                                        digits)
```

```
(y + z)       1330 * 10³
(x)          −1324 * 10³
             ──────────────
                 6 * 10³ = 6000 * 10⁰ = x + (y + z)
```

Our answers are the same in the thousands' place but are different in the hundreds', tens', and ones' places. This is called **representational error** or **round-off error**. The result of adding y to z gives us a number with seven digits of precision, but only four digits can be stored.

In addition to representational errors, there are two other problems to watch out for in floating-point arithmetic: *underflow* and *overflow*. **Underflow** is the condition that arises when the absolute value of a calculation gets too small to be represented. Going back to our decimal representation, let's look at a calculation involving very small numbers:

```
    4210            * 10⁻⁸
         * 2000 * 10⁻⁸
    ──────────────────────
    8420000 * 10⁻¹⁶ = 8420 * 10⁻¹³
```

This value cannot be represented in our scheme because the exponent −13 is too small. Our minimum is −9. Therefore, the result of the calculation would be set to zero. Any value too small to be represented is set of zero, which is a reasonable thing to do under the circumstances.

Overflow is the condition that arises when the absolute value of a calculation gets too large to be represented. Overflow is a more serious problem

Representational (round-off) error An arithmetic error caused by the fact that the precision of the result of an arithmetic operation is greater than the precision of our machine

Underflow The condition that occurs when the results of a calculation are too small to represent in a given machine

Overflow The condition that occurs when the results of a calculation are too large to represent in a given machine

because there is no logical thing to do when it occurs. For example, the result of the calculation

$$
\begin{array}{r}
9999 \;*\; 10^9 \\
\; 1000 \;\; 10^9 \\
\hline
9999000 \;*\; 10^{18} = 9999 \;*\; 10^{21}
\end{array}
$$

cannot be stored. What should we do? To be consistent with our response to underflow, we could set the result to $9999 * 10^9$, the maximum real value allowed in our scheme. But this seems intuitively wrong. The alternative is to stop the computation and issue an error message.

Another type of error that can happen with floating-point numbers is called **cancellation error**. This error happens when numbers of widely differing magnitudes are added or subtracted. Here's an example:

$$(1 \;+\; 0.00001234 \;-\; 1) = 0.00001234$$

> **Cancellation error**   A loss of accuracy during addition or subtraction of numbers of widely differing sizes, due to limits of precision

The laws of arithmetic say this equation should be true. But what happens when the computer is doing the arithmetic?

$$
\begin{array}{r}
100000000 \;*\; 10^{-8} \\
+\; 1234 \;*\; 10^{-8} \\
\hline
100001234 \;*\; 10^{-8}
\end{array}
$$

With four-digit accuracy, this becomes $1000 * 10^{-3}$. Now the computer subtracts 1:

$$
\begin{array}{r}
1000 \;*\; 10^{-3} \\
-\; 1000 \;*\; 10^{-3} \\
\hline
0
\end{array}
$$

The result is 0, not .00001234.

We have been discussing problems with real numbers, but integer numbers can also overflow (both negatively and positively). The moral of this discussion is twofold. First, the results of real calculations often are not what you expect. Second, if you are working with very large numbers or very small numbers, you need to be very careful of the order in which you perform the calculations.

Limits on Components

"My hard disk crashed." "The file server was down." "My e-mail went down last night." Any computing instructor has heard these tales of woe hundreds of time, as they are used to explain (excuse?) late assignments. Of course, if an assignment is started when it is handed out rather than the day it is due, these failures can be overcome. However, the problems of hardware failure do exist: Disks do crash, file servers do go down, and networks do fail. The *Titanic effect*, which states that "The severity with which a system fails is directly proportional to the intensity of the designer's belief that it cannot," was coined by J.A.N. Lee.[2] Hardware failures do occur: The best solution is preventive maintenance. In computing this means periodic tests to detect problems and replacement of worn parts.

Preventive maintenance also means that the physical environment in which a computer is housed is appropriate. Large mainframe computers often require air conditioned, dust-free rooms. PCs should not be set up under leak-prone plumbing. Alas, not all situations can be anticipated. One such situation occurred during pre-integrated circuit days. A machine that had been working correctly started producing erratic results. The problem was finally traced to a moth that had gotten into the cabinet of the machine. This incident led to the computer term *bug* for a computer error. A more recent incident involved a DSL line that intermittently disconnected itself. The trouble was finally traced to faulty telephone lines on which the squirrels had enjoyed munching.

Of course, any discussion of component limits assumes that the computer hardware has been thoroughly tested at the design stage and during manufacturing. A major scandal in 1994 was the circuit flaw in the Intel's Pentium processor. The Pentium chip was installed in millions of computers manufactured by IBM, Compaq, Dell, Gateway 2000, and others. The circuit flaw was a design error in the floating-point unit that caused certain types of division problems involving more than five significant digits to give the wrong answer.

How often would the error affect a calculation? IBM predicted that spreadsheet users would experience an error every 24 days, Intel asserted that that it would occur every 27,000 years, and *PC Week*'s test suite placed the frequency once every 2 months to 10 years.[3] The chip was corrected, but Intel did not recall all flawed chips. The experience was a public relations disaster for Intel, but they remain one of the leading chip manufacturers today.

Limits on Communications

The flow of data within a computer and between computers is the life's blood of computing. Therefore, it is extremely important that the data is not corrupted in any way. This realization leads to strategies known as *error-detecting* and *error-correcting codes*. Error-detecting codes determine that an error has occurred during the transmission of data and then alert the system. Error-correcting codes not only determine that an error has occurred but try to determine what the correct value actually is.

Parity Bits

Parity bits are used to detect that an error has occurred between the storing and retrieving of a byte or the sending and receiving of a byte. A parity bit is an extra bit that is associated with each byte in the hardware that uses the scheme. This bit is used to ensure that the number of 1 bits in a 9-bit value (byte plus parity bit) is odd (or even) across all bytes.

Odd parity requires the number of 1s in a byte plus parity bit to be odd. For example, if a byte contains the pattern 11001100, the parity bit would be 1, thus giving an odd number of 1s. If the pattern were 11110001, the parity bit would be 0, giving an odd number of 1s. When a byte is retrieved from memory or received from a transmission, the number of 1 bits is counted (including the parity bit). If the number is even, an error has occurred. If this scheme is used in the hardware, each byte actually has an extra bit, accessible only by the hardware, that is used for error detection. *Even parity* uses the same scheme, but the number of 1 bits must be even.

Check Digits

A software variation of the same scheme is to sum the individual digits of a number, and then store the unit's digit of that sum with the number. For example, given the number 34376, the sum of the digits is 23, so the number would be stored as 34376–3. If the 4 became corrupted as a 3, the error would be detected. However, if the 7 were corrupted to a 6 and the 6 were corrupted to a 7, the sum would still be correct, but the number would not be.

The scheme could be expanded to carry an additional digit, perhaps the unit's digit of the sum of the odd digits. In this case, 34376 would be stored as 34376–23: 3 is the unit's digits of the sum of all the digits and 2 is the unit's digit of sum of the 1st, 3rd, and 5th digit. This technique would catch a transposition error between adjacent digits, but would miss other transpositions. Of course, we could also carry the unit's digit of the sum of the even digits. You get the idea. The more important it is for errors to be detected, the more complex the algorithm used to detect them.

Error-Correcting Codes

If enough information about a byte or number is kept, it is possible to deduce what an incorrect bit or digit must be. The ultimate redundancy would be to keep two separate copies of every value that is stored. If the parity is in error or there is an error in the check digits, look back at the extra copy to determine the correct value. Of course, both copies could be in error. The major work in error correcting codes relates to disk drives and CDs where imperfections in the surface can corrupt data.

17.2 Software

We have all read horror stories about software that contained errors; they make very interesting reading. Are software errors in running programs really common occurrences? Can't we do something to make software more error free? To answer the first question, a Web search for "software bugs" just retrieved 5,163,935 hits. To answer the second, software developers are trying. In the next few sections, we examine why error-free software is difficult—if not impossible—to produce, we discuss current approaches to software quality, and we end with a collection of interesting bugs.

Complexity of Software

If we accept the premise that commercial software contains errors, the logical question is "Why?" Don't software developers test their products? The problem is not lack of diligence but our old nemesis *complexity*. As our machines have gotten increasingly more powerful, the problems that can be tackled have become increasingly more complex. A single programmer with a problem moved to a programming team with a problem and finally graduated to a team of teams with a problem.

Software testing can demonstrate the presence of bugs but cannot demonstrate their absence. We can test software, find errors and fix them, and then test it some more. As we find problems and fix them, we raise our confidence that the software performs as it should. But we can never guarantee that all bugs have been removed. There may always be yet another bug lurking in the software that we haven't found yet.

Since we can never know if we have found all the problems, when do we stop testing? It becomes a question of risk. How much are you willing to risk that there still may be another bug in your software? If you're writing a game you might take that risk a lot sooner than you would if you're writing airplane control software in which lives are on the line.

As Nancy Leveson points out in the *Communications of the ACM*, a branch of computing known as *software engineering* emerged in the 1960s with the goal of introducing engineering discipline into the development of software.[5] Great strides toward this goal have been made in the last half-century, including a greater understanding of the role of abstraction, the introduction of modularity, and the notions of the software life cycle, which we discuss in detail later.

Most of these ideas come from engineering, but had to be adapted to the unique problems that arose when working with more abstract materials. Hardware designs are guided and limited by the nature of materials used to implement the designs. Software appears to have limits more related to human abilities than physical limitations. Dr. Leveson continues, "Thus, the first 50 years may be characterized as our learning about the limits of our field, which are intimately bound up with the limits of complexity with which humans can cope."

Dijkstra decries the term "bugs"

Ever since the moth was found in the hardware, computer errors have been called *bugs*. Edsger Dijkstra chides us for the use of this terminology. He says that it can foster the image that errors are beyond the control of the programmer—that a bug might maliciously creep into a program when no one is looking. He contends that this is intellectually dishonest because it disguises that the error is the programmer's own creation.[4]

Building software has changed. The early days were filled with building new software, but more and more the problems of maintaining and evolving existing software have taken center stage. As our systems have grown bigger and required large teams of designers, we have started to examine the ways humans collaborate and to devise ways to assist them to work together effectively.

Current Approaches to Software Quality

Although the complexity of large software systems makes error-free products almost an impossibility, it doesn't mean that we should just give up. There are strategies that we can adopt that, if used, improve the quality of software.

Software Engineering

In Chapter 6, we outlined three stages of computer problem solving: develop the algorithm, implement the algorithm, and maintain the program. When we move from small, well-defined tasks to large software projects, we need to add two extra layers on top of these: software *requirements* and *specifications*. **Software requirements** are broad, but precise, statements outlining what is to be provided by the software product. **Software specifications** are a detailed description of the function, inputs, processing, outputs, and special features of a software product. The specifications tell *what* the program does, but not *how* it does it.

> **Software requirements** A statement of what is to be provided by a computer system or software product
>
> **Software specification** A detailed description of the function, inputs, processing, outputs, and special features of a software product. It provides the information needed to design and implement the software.

Dr. Leveson mentions the software life cycle as part of the contributions of software engineering. The *software life cycle* is the concept that software is developed, not just coded, and evolves over time. Thus the life cycle includes the following phases:

- requirements
- specifications
- design (high-level and lower-level)
- implementation
- maintenance

Verification activities must be carried out during all of the phases. Do the requirements accurately reflect what is needed? Do the specifications accurately reflect the functionality needed to meet the requirements? Does the high-level design accurately reflect the functionality of the specifications? Do each succeeding levels of design accurately implement the level above? Does the implementation accurately code the designs? Do changes implemented during the maintenance phase accurately reflect the desired changes? Are the implementations of these changes correct?

In Chapters 6 through 8 we have discussed the testing of the designs and code for the relatively small problems we discuss in this book. Clearly, as the problems get larger, verification activities become more important and more complex. (Yes, *that* word again.) Testing the design and finished code is only a small, albeit important, part of the process. Half the errors in a typical project occur in the design phase; only half occur in the implementation phase. This data is somewhat misleading. In terms of the cost to *fix* an error, the earlier in the design process an error is caught, the cheaper it is to correct the error.[6]

Teams of programmers produce large software products. Two verification techniques effectively used by programming teams are design or code *walk-throughs* and *inspections*. (Although we discussed these techniques briefly in Chapter 6, they are important enough for us to mention them again here.) These are formal team activities, the intention of which is to move the responsibility for uncovering errors from the individual programmer to the group. Because testing is time-consuming and errors cost more the later they are discovered, the goal is to identify errors before testing begins.

In a **walk-through**, the team performs a manual simulation of the design or program with sample test inputs, keeping track of the program's data by hand on paper or a blackboard. Unlike thorough program testing, the walk-through is not intended to simulate all possible test cases. Instead, its purpose is to stimulate discussion about the way the programmer chose to design or implement the program's requirements.

At an **inspection**, a reader (never the program's author) goes through the requirements, design, or code line by line. The inspection participants are given the material in advance and are expected to have reviewed it carefully. During the inspection, the participants point out errors, which are recorded on an inspection report. Team members, during their pre-inspection preparation, have noted many of the errors. Just the process of reading aloud uncovers other errors. As with the walk-through, the chief benefit of the team meeting is the discussion that takes place among team members. This interaction among programmers, testers, and other team members can uncover many program errors long before the testing stage begins.

At the high-level design stage, the design should be compared to the program requirements to make sure that all required functions have been included and that this program or module correctly interfaces with other software in the system. At the low-level design stage, when the design has been filled out with more details, it should be re-inspected before it is implemented. When the coding has been completed, the compiled listings should be inspected again. This inspection (or walk-through) ensures that

Walk-through A verification method in which a team performs a manual simulation of the program or design

Inspection A verification method in which one member of a team reads the program or design line by line and the others point out errors

the implementation is consistent with both the requirements and the design. Successful completion of this inspection means that testing of the program can begin.

Walk-throughs and inspections should be carried out in as non-threatening a way as possible. The focus of these group activities is on removing defects in the product, not the technical approach of the author of the design or the code. Because these activities are led by a moderator who is not the author, the focus is on the errors, not the people involved.

In the last ten to fifteen years, the Software Engineering Institute at Carnegie Mellon University has played a major role in supporting research into formalizing the inspection process in large software projects, including sponsoring workshops and conferences. A paper presented at the SEI Software Engineering Process Group (SEPG) Conference reported on a project that was able to reduce product defects by 86.6% using a two-tiered inspection process of group walk-throughs and formal inspections. The process was applied to packets of requirements, design, or code at every stage of the lifecycle. Table 17.1 shows the defects per 1,000 source lines of code (KSLOC) that were found in the different phases of the software lifecycle in a maintenance project.[7] During the maintenance phase, 40,000 lines of source code were added to a program with over half a million lines of code. The formal inspection process was used in all of the phases except Testing Activities.

We have talked about large software projects. Before we leave this section, let's quantify what we mean by large. The Space Shuttle Ground Processing System has over 1/2 million lines of code; Windows 95 has 10 million lines of code. Most large projects fall somewhere in between.

We have pointed out that the complexity of large projects makes the goal of error-free code almost impossible to attain. The following is a guideline for the number of errors per lines of code that can be expected.[8]

Standard software: 25 bugs per 1,000 lines of program

Good software: 2 errors per 1,000 lines

Space Shuttle software: < 1 error per 10,000 lines

Table 17.1   Errors found during a maintenance project

Stage	Defects per KSLOC
System design	2
Software requirements	8
Design	12
Code inspection	34
Testing activities	3

Formal Verification

It would be nice if there were some tool that we could use to locate the errors in a design or code without our even having to run the program. That sounds unlikely, but consider an analogy from geometry. We wouldn't try to prove the Pythagorean theorem by proving that it worked on every triangle; that would only demonstrate that the theorem works for every triangle *we tried*. We prove theorems in geometry mathematically. Why can't we do the same for computer programs?

The verification of program correctness, independent of data testing, is an important area of theoretical computer science research. The goal of this research is to establish a method for proving programs that is analogous to the method for proving theorems in geometry. The necessary techniques exist for proving that code meets its specifications, but the proofs are often more complicated than the programs themselves. Therefore, a major focus of verification research is the attempt to build automated program provers—verifiable programs that verify other programs.

Formal methods have been used successfully in verifying the correctness of computer chips. One notable example is the verification of a chip to perform real-number arithmetic, which won the Queen's Award for Technological Achievement. Formal verification to prove that the chip met its specifications was carried out by C. A. R. Hoare, head of the Programming Research Group of Oxford University, together with MOS Ltd. In parallel, a more traditional testing approach was taking place. As reported in *Computing Research News*:

> "The race [between the two groups] was won by the formal development method—it was completed an estimated 12 months ahead of what otherwise would have been achievable. Moreover, the formal design pointed to a number of errors in the informal one that had not shown up in months of testing. The final design was of higher quality, cheaper, and was completed quicker." [9]

It is hoped that success with formal verification techniques at the hardware level can lead eventually to success at the software level. However, software is far more complex than hardware, so we do not anticipate any major breakthroughs within the near future.

Open Source Movement[10]

In the early days of computing, software came bundled with the computer, including the source code for the software. Programmers adjusted and adapted the programs and happily shared the improvements they made. In the 1970s, firms began withholding the source code, and software became big business.

With the advent of the Internet, programmers from all over the world can collaborate at almost no cost. A simple version of a software product can be made available on the Internet. Programmers interested in extending or improving the program can do so. A "benevolent dictator" who keeps track of what is going on governs most open-source projects. If a change or improvement passes the peer review of fellow developers and gets incorporated in the next version, it is a great coup.

Linux is the best known open source project. Linus Torvolds wrote the first simple version of the operating system using Unix as a blueprint and continued to oversee its development. IBM spent $1 billion on Linux in 2001 with the object of making it a computing standard. As *The Economist* says,

> "Some people like to dismiss Linux as nothing more than a happy accident, but the program looks more like a textbook example of an emerging pattern.... Open source is a mass phenomenon, with tens of thousands of volunteer programmers across the world already taking part, and more joining in all the time, particularly in countries such as China and India. SourceForge, a web site for developers, now hosts more than 18,000 open-source projects that keep 145,000 programmers busy."

Only time will tell if the open-source software development movement contributes to producing more high-quality products.

Notorious Software Errors

Everyone involved in computing has his or her favorite software horror story. We include only a small sample here.

AT&T Down for Nine Hours

In January of 1990, AT&T's long-distance telephone network came to a screeching halt for nine hours, because of a software error in the electronic switching systems. Of the 148 million long-distance and 800-number calls placed with AT&T that day, only 50% got through. This failure caused untold collateral damage:

- Hotels lost bookings.
- Rental car agencies lost rentals.
- American Airlines' reservation system traffic fell by two-thirds.
- A telemarketing company lost $75,000 in estimated sales.
- MasterCard didn't get to process its typical 200,000 credit approvals.
- AT&T lost some $60 to $75 million.

As AT&T Chairman Robert Allen said, "It was the worst nightmare I've had in 32 years in the business." [11]

How did this happen? Earlier versions of the switching software worked correctly. The software error was in the code that upgraded the system to make it respond more quickly to a malfunctioning switch. The error involved a *break* statement in the C-code.[12] As Henry Walker points out in *The Limits of Computing*, this breakdown illustrates several points common to many software failures. The software had been tested extensively before its release, and it worked correctly for about a month. In addition to testing, code reviews had been conducted during development. One programmer made the error, but many others reviewed the code without noticing the error. The failure was triggered by a relatively uncommon sequence of events, difficult to anticipate in advance. And the error occurred in code designed to improve a correctly working system; that is, during the maintenance phase. E. N. Adams in the *IBM Journal of Research and Development* estimates that 15 to 50% of attempts to remove an error from a large program result in the introduction of additional errors.

Therac-25

One of the most widely cited software-related accidents involved a computerized radiation therapy machine called the Therac-25. Between June 1985 and January 1987, six known accidents involved massive overdoses by the Therac-25, leading to deaths and serious injuries. These accidents have been described as the worst series of radiation accidents in the 35-year history of medical accelerators.

It is beyond the scope of this book to go into a detailed analysis of the software failure. Suffice it to say there was only a single coding error, but tracking down the error exposed that the whole design was seriously flawed. Leveson and Turner in their article in *IEEE Computer*, add this scathing comment:

> "A lesson to be learned from the Therac-25 story is that focusing on particular software bugs is not the way to make a safe system. Virtually all complex software can be made to behave in an unexpected fashion under certain conditions. The basic mistakes here involved poor software-engineering practices and building a machine that relies on the software for safe operation. Furthermore, the particular coding error is not as important as the general unsafe design of the software overall."[13]

Bugs in Government Projects

On February 25, 1991, during the Gulf War, a Scud missile struck an American Army barracks, killing 28 soldiers and injuring around 100 other people. An American Patriot Missile battery in Dhahran, Saudi Arabia, failed to track and intercept the incoming Iraqi Scud missile because of a software error. This error, however, was not a coding error but a design error. A calculation involved a multiplication by 1/10, which is a non-terminating number in binary. The resulting arithmetic error accumulated over the 100 hours of the batteries' operation amounted to .34 seconds, enough for the missile to miss its target.[14]

The General Accounting Office concluded:

> "The Patriot had never before been used to defend against Scud missiles nor was it expected to operate continuously for long periods of time. Two weeks before the incident, Army officials received Israeli data indicating some loss in accuracy after the system had been running for 8 consecutive hours. Consequently, Army officials modified the software to improve the system's accuracy. However, the modified software did not reach Dhahran until February 26, 1991—the day after the Scud incident." [15]

The Gemini V missed its expected landing point by about 100 miles. The reason? The design of the guidance system did not take into account the need to compensate for the motion of Earth around the Sun.[16]

In October 1999, the Mars Climate Orbiter entered the Martian atmosphere about 100 kilometers lower than expected, causing the craft to burn up. Arthur Stephenson, chairman of the Mars Climate Orbiter Mission Failure Investigation Board concluded:

> "The 'root cause' of the loss of the spacecraft was the failed translation of English units into metric units in a segment of ground-based, navigation-related mission software, as NASA has previously announced ... The failure review board has identified other significant factors that allowed this error to be born, and then let it linger and propagate to the point where it resulted in a major error in our understanding of the spacecraft's path as it approached Mars." [17]

Launched in July of 1962, the Mariner 1 Venus probe veered off course almost immediately and had to be destroyed. The problem was traced to the following line of Fortran code:

```
DO 5 K = 1. 3
```

The period should have been a comma. An $18.5 million space exploration vehicle was lost because of this typographical error.

17.3   Problems

There are problems for which it is easy to develop and implement computer solutions. There are problems for which we can implement computer solutions, but we wouldn't get the results in our lifetime. There are problems for which we can develop and implement computer solutions provided we have enough computer resources. There are problems for which we can prove there are no solutions. Before we can look at these categories of problems, we must introduce a way of comparing algorithms.

Comparing Algorithms

As we have shown in previous chapters, there is more than one way to solve most problems. If you were asked for directions to Joe's Diner (see Figure 17.2), you could give either of two equally correct answers:

1. "Go east on the big highway to the Y'all Come Inn, and turn left."

or

2. "Take the winding country road to Honeysuckle Lodge, and turn right."

The two answers are not the same, but because following either route gets the traveler to Joe's Diner, both answers are functionally correct.

If the request for directions contained special requirements, one solution might be preferable to the other. For instance, "I'm late for dinner. What's the quickest route to Joe's Diner?" calls for the first answer, whereas "Is there a scenic road that I can take to get to Joe's Diner?" suggests the second. If no special requirements are known, the choice is a matter of personal preference—which road do you like better?

Figure 17.2
Equally valid solutions to the same problem.

Often the choice between algorithms comes down to a question of efficiency. Which one takes the least amount of computing time? Which one does the job with the least amount of work? We are talking here of the amount of work that the computer does.

To compare the work done by competing algorithms, we must first define a set of objective measures that can be applied to each algorithm. The analysis of algorithms is an important area of theoretical computer science; in advanced computing courses, students see extensive work in this area. We cover only a small part of this topic, just enough to allow you to compare two algorithms that do the same task and understand that the complexity of algorithms forms a continuum from easy to unsolvable.

How do programmers measure the work that two algorithms perform? The first solution that comes to mind is simply to code the algorithms and then compare the execution times for running the two programs. The one with the shorter execution time is clearly the better algorithm. Or is it? Using this technique, we really can determine only that program A is more efficient than program B on a particular computer. Execution times are specific to a *particular computer*. Of course, we could test the algorithms on all possible computers, but we want a more general measure.

A second possibility is to count the number of instructions or statements executed. This measure, however, varies with the programming language used, as well as with the style of the individual programmer. To standardize this measure somewhat, we could count the number of passes through a critical loop in the algorithm. If each iteration involves a constant amount of work, this measure gives us a meaningful yardstick of efficiency.

Another idea is to isolate a particular operation fundamental to the algorithm and count the number of times that this operation is performed. Suppose, for example, that we are summing the elements in an integer list. To measure the amount of work required, we could count the integer addition operations. For a list of 100 elements, there are 99 addition operations. Note, however, that we do not actually have to count the number of addition operations; it is some *function* of the number of elements (N) in the list. Therefore, we can express the number of addition operations in terms of N: for a list of N elements, there are $N - 1$ addition operations. Now we can compare the algorithms for the general case, not just for a specific list size.

Are users the problem?

Software systems may operate correctly, but if bad data is used, the answers may be incorrect. Answers are only as good as the data used to derive them. The acronym for this situation is GIGO: Garbage In, Garbage Out. In the same vein, systems that are confusing to human users are more often used incorrectly.

Big-O Analysis

We have been talking about work as a function of the size of the input to the operation (for instance, the number of elements in the list to be summed). We can express an approximation of this function using a mathematical notation called order of magnitude, or **Big-O notation**. (This is a letter O, not a zero.) The order of magnitude of a function is identified with the term in the function that increases fastest relative to the size of the problem. For instance, if

$$f(N) = N^4 + 100N^2 + 10N + 50$$

then $f(N)$ is of order N^4—or, in Big-O notation, $O(N^4)$. That is, for large values of N, some multiple of N^4 dominates the function for sufficiently large values of N. It isn't that $100N^2 + 10N + 50$ is not important, it is just that as N gets larger, all other factors become irrelevant because the N^4 term dominates.

How is it that we can just drop the low-order terms? If we want to buy elephants and goldfish, for example, and we are considering two pet suppliers, we only need to compare the prices of elephants; the cost of the goldfish is trivial in comparison. In analyzing algorithms, the term that increases most rapidly relative to the size of the problem dominates the function, effectively relegating the others to the "noise" level. The elephants are so much bigger that we could just ignore the goldfish. Similarly, for large values of N, N^4 is so much larger than 50, $10N$, or even $100N^2$ that we can ignore these other terms. This doesn't mean that the other terms do not contribute to the computing time; it only means that they are not significant in our approximation when N is "large."

Big-O notation A notation that expresses computing time (complexity) as the term in a function that increases most rapidly relative to the size of a problem

What is this value N? N represents the size of the problem. Most problems involve manipulating data structures like those discussed in Chapter 9. Each structure is composed of elements. We develop algorithms to add an element to the structure and to modify or delete an element from the structure. We can describe the work done by these operations in terms of N, where N is the number of elements in the structure.

Suppose that we want to write all the elements in a list into a file. How much work is that? The answer depends on how many elements are in the list. Our algorithm is

```
Open the file
While more elements in list
    Write the next element
```

If N is the number of elements in the list, the "time" required to do this task is

(N * time-to-write-one-element) + time-to-open-the-file

This algorithm is $O(N)$ because the time required to perform the task is proportional to the number of elements (N)—plus a little to open the file. How can we ignore the open time in determining the Big-O approximation? Assuming that the time necessary to open a file is constant, this part of the algorithm is our goldfish. If the list only has a few elements, the time needed to open the file may seem significant, but for large values of N, writing the elements is an elephant in comparison with opening the file.

The order of magnitude of an algorithm does not tell us how long in microseconds the solution takes to run on our computer. Sometimes we need that kind of information. For instance, a word processor's requirements state that the program must be able to spell-check a 50-page document (on a particular computer) in less than 120 seconds. For information like this, we do not use Big-O analysis; we use other measurements. We can compare different implementations of a data structure by coding them and then running a test, recording the time on the computer's clock before and after. This kind of "benchmark" test tells us how long the operations take on a particular computer, using a particular compiler. The Big-O analysis, however, allows us to compare algorithms without reference to these factors.

Common Orders of Magnitude

O(1) is called bounded time   The amount of work is bounded by a constant and is not dependent on the size of the problem. Assigning a

Family Laundry: An analogy

How long does it take to do a family's weekly laundry? We might describe the answer to this question with the function

$$f(N) = c * N$$

where N represents the number of family members and c is the average number of minutes that each person's laundry takes. We say that this function is $O(N)$ because the total laundry time depends on the number of people in the family. The "constant" c may vary a little for different families, depending on the size of their washing machine and how fast they can fold clothes, for instance. That is, the time to do the laundry for two different families might be represented with these functions:

$$f(N) = 100 * N$$
$$g(N) = 90 * N$$

But overall, we describe these functions as $O(N)$.

Now, what happens if Grandma and Grandpa come to visit the first family for a week or two? The laundry time function becomes

$$f(N) = 100 * (N + 2)$$

We still say that the function is $O(N)$. How can that be? Doesn't the laundry for two extra people take any time to wash, dry, and fold? Of course it does! If N is small (the family consists of Mother, Father, and Baby), the extra laundry for two people is significant. But as N grows large (the family consists of Mother, Father, 12 kids, and a live-in baby-sitter), the extra

laundry for two people doesn't make much difference. (The family's laundry is the elephant; the guest's laundry is the goldfish.) When we compare algorithms using Big-O, we are concerned with what happens when N is "large."

If we are asking the question "Can we finish the laundry in time to make the 7:05 train?" we want a precise answer. The Big-O analysis doesn't give us this information. It gives us an approximation. So, if $100 * N$, $90 * N$, and $100 * (N + 2)$ are all $O(N)$, how can we say which is "better"? We can't—in Big-O terms, they are all roughly equivalent for large values of N. Can we find a better algorithm for getting the laundry done? If the family wins the state lottery, they can drop all their dirty clothes at a professional laundry 15 minutes' drive from their house (30 minutes round trip). Now the function is

$$f(N) = 30$$

This function is $O(1)$. The answer is not dependent on the number of people in the family. If they switch to a laundry 5 minutes from their house, the function becomes

$$f(N) = 10$$

This function is also $O(1)$. In terms of Big-O, the two professional-laundry solutions are equivalent: No matter how many family members or house guests you have, it takes a constant amount of the family's time to do the laundry. (We aren't concerned with the professional laundry's time.)

value to the ith element in an array of N elements is $O(l)$, because an element in an array can be accessed directly through its index. Although bounded time is often called constant time, the amount of work is not necessarily constant. It is, however, bounded by a constant.

$O(log_2N)$ is called logarithmic time   The amount of work depends on the log of the size of the problem. Algorithms that successively cut the amount of data to be processed in half at each step typically fall into this category.

Finding a value in a list of sorted elements using the binary search algorithm is $O(\log_2 N)$.

O(N) is called linear time   The amount of work is some constant times the size of the problem. Printing all the elements in a list of N elements is $O(N)$. Searching for a particular value in a list of unsorted elements is also $O(N)$ because you (potentially) must search every element in the list to find it.

O(N log₂N) is called (for lack of a better term) N log₂N time   Algorithms of this type typically involve applying a logarithmic algorithm N times. The better sorting algorithms, such as Quicksort, Heapsort, and Mergesort, have $N \log_2 N$ complexity. That is, these algorithms can transform an unsorted list into a sorted list in $O(N \log_2 N)$ time, although Quicksort degenerates to $O(N^2)$ under certain input data.

O(N²) is called quadratic time   Algorithms of this type typically involve applying a linear algorithm N times. Most simple sorting algorithms are $O(N^2)$ algorithms.

O(2^N) is called exponential time   These algorithms are costly. As you can see in Table 17.2, exponential times increase dramatically in relation to the size of N. The fable of the King and the Corn demonstrates an exponential time algorithm, where the size of the problem is a kernel of corn. (It also is

Table 17.2   Comparison of rates of growth

N	log₂N	Nlog₂N	N²	N³	2^N
1	0	1	1	1	2
2	1	2	4	8	4
4	2	8	16	64	16
8	3	24	64	512	256
16	4	64	256	4,096	65,536
32	5	160	1,024	32,768	4,294,967,296
64	6	384	4,096	262,144	About 5 years' worth of instructions on a supercomputer
128	7	896	16,384	2,097,152	About 600,000 times greater than the age of the universe in nano-seconds (for a 6-billion-year estimate)
256	8	2,048	65,536	16,777,216	Don't ask!

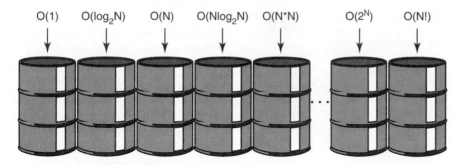

$O(1)$ $O(\log_2 N)$ $O(N)$ $O(N\log_2 N)$ $O(N*N)$ $O(2^N)$ $O(N!)$

Figure 17.3 Orders of complexity

interesting to note that the values in the last column grow so quickly that the computation time required for problems of this order may exceed the estimated life span of the universe!)

O(n!) is called factorial time   These algorithms are even more costly than exponential algorithms. The traveling salesperson graph algorithm is a factorial time algorithm.

Algorithms whose order of magnitude can be expressed as a polynomial in the size of the problem are called **polynomial-time algorithms**. Recall from Chapter 2 that a polynomial is a sum of two or more algebraic terms, each of which consists of a constant multiplied by one or more variables raised to a nonnegative integral power. Thus, polynomial algorithms are those whose order of magnitude can be expressed as the size of the problem to a power, and the Big-O of the algorithm is the highest power in the polynomial. All polynomial-time algorithms are defined as being in **Class P**.

Think of common orders of complexity as being bins into which we sort algorithms (see Figure 17.3). For small values of the size of the problem, an algorithm in one bin may actually be faster than the equivalent algorithm in the next-more-efficient bin. As the size increases, the difference among algorithms in the different bins gets larger. When choosing between algorithms with the same bin, we look at the goldfish that we ignored earlier.

Polynomial-time algorithms Algorithms whose complexity can be expressed as a polynomial in the size of the problem

Class P The class made up of all polynomial-time algorithms

Turing Machines
We have mentioned the name of Alan Turing several times in this book. He developed the concept of a computing machine in the 1930s. He was not interested in implementing his machine; rather, he used it as a model to study the limits of what can be computed.

Alan Turing

Time magazine chose Alan Turing as one of its 100 most influential persons of the 20th Century. Their biography of Turing said:

> For what this eccentric young Cambridge don did was to dream up an imaginary machine—a fairly simple typewriter-like contraption capable somehow of scanning, or reading, instructions encoded on a tape of theoretically infinite length. As the scanner moved from one square of the tape to the next—responding to the sequential commands and modifying its mechanical response if so ordered—the output of such a process, Turing demonstrated, could replicate logical human thought.

> The device in this inspired mind-experiment quickly acquired a name: the Turing machine, and so did another of Turing's insights. Since the instructions on the tape governed the behavior of the machine, by changing those instructions, one could induce the machine to perform the functions of all such machines. In other words, depending on the tape it scanned, the same machine could calculate numbers or play chess or do anything else of a comparable nature. Hence his device acquired a new and even grander name: the Universal Turing Machine.

> . . .

> So many ideas and technological advances converged to create the modern computer that it is foolhardy to give one person the credit for inventing

it. But the fact remains that everyone who taps at a keyboard, opening a spreadsheet or a word-processing program, is working on an incarnation of a Turing machine.[18]

Alan Turing was born in June of 1912 to Julius Mathison Turing, a member of the Indian Civil Service, and Ethel Sara Stoney, the daughter of the chief engineer of the Madras railway. His father and mother spent most of their time in India, while he and his older brother were in various foster homes in England until his father's retirement in 1926.

The British Public (read *Private* in American English) School system of the day did not foster original thinking, so Turing had trouble fitting in. He was criticized for his handwriting, struggled in English, and even in mathematics didn't produce the expected conventional answers. At Sherborne School, which he had entered at 13, the headmaster said that if he was solely a scientific specialist, he was wasting his time at a public cchool. Yet a public school education was terribly important to his mother, and so he persisted. Two things sustained him during this period: his own independent study and the friendship of Christopher Morcom, who was a student a year ahead of him in school. Morcom provided vital intellectual companionship, which ended after two years with Morcom's sudden death.

In 1931, Turing entered King's College, Cambridge, to study mathematics. The atmosphere at King's College encouraged free-ranging thought, providing him with an intellectual home for the first

A Turing machine, as his model became known, consists of a control unit with a read/write head that can read and write symbols on an infinite tape. The tape is divided into cells. The model is based on a person doing a primitive calculation on a long strip of paper using a pencil with an eraser. Each line (cell) of the paper contains a symbol from a finite alphabet. Starting at one cell, the person examines the symbol and either leaves the symbol alone or erases it and replaces it with another symbol from the alphabet. The person then moves to an adjacent cell and repeats the action.

time. He graduated in 1934 and was elected a fellow of King's College in 1935 for a dissertation "On the Gaussian Error Function," which proved fundamental results in probability theory.

Turing then began to work on decidability questions, based on a course he had taken on the foundations of mathematics with Max Newman. In 1936 Turing published a paper in which he introduced the concept of what we now call a Turing machine. These concepts were introduced within the context of whether a definite method or process exists by which it could be decided whether any given mathematical assertion was provable. Alonzo Church's work at Princeton on the same subject became known at the same time, and so Turing's paper was delayed until he could refer to Church's work. As a result, Turing spent two years as a student at Princeton working with Church and von Neumann.

At the outbreak of World War II, Turing went to work at the Government. Again we quote from the Time Magazine text:

> Turing, on the basis of his published work, was recruited to serve in the Government Code and Cypher School, located in a Victorian mansion called Bletchley Park in Buckinghamshire. The task of all those so assembled—mathematicians, chess champions, Egyptologists, whoever might have something to contribute about the possible permutations of formal systems—was to break the Enigma codes used by the Nazis in communications between headquarters and troops. Because of secrecy restrictions, Turing's role in this enterprise was not acknowledged until long after his death. And like the invention of the computer, the work done by the Bletchley Park crew was very much a team effort. But it is now known that Turing played a crucial role in designing a primitive, computer-like machine that could decipher at high speed Nazi codes to U-boats in the North Atlantic.

Turing was awarded the Order of the British Empire in 1945 for his contributions to the war effort.

After a frustrating experience at the National Physical Laboratory in London, where he was to build a computer, he returned to Cambridge where he continued work and write. The war-time spirit of cooperation that had short-circuited bureaucracy had faded, and the ACE (Automatic Computing Engine) was never built. In 1948, Turing became a Deputy Director of the computing laboratory at Manchester University. The vague title reflected its meaninglessness, and Turing spent the next years working and writing on a variety of different subjects.

In 1950 he published an article reflecting one of his major interests: Can machines think? From this article came the well-known Turing test. He also became interested in morphogenesis, the development of pattern and form in living organisms. All the while he continued his research in decidability and quantum theory.

On June 7, 1954, Turing died of cyanide poisoning, a half-eaten apple laying beside his bed. His mother believed that he accidentally died while conducting an experiment; the coroner's verdict was suicide. A few years ago, the award-winning one-man play *Breaking the Code* was performed in London's West End and on Broadway, giving audiences a brief glimpse of Turing's brilliant, complex character.

The control unit simulates the person. The human's decision-making process is represented by a finite series of instructions that the control unit can execute. Each instruction causes

- a symbol to be read from a cell on the tape.
- a symbol to be written into the cell.
- the tape to be moved one cell left, one cell right, or left positioned as it was.

Figure 17.4
Turing machine processing

These actions do indeed model a person with a pencil, if we allow the person to replace a symbol with itself. See Figure 17.4.

Why is such a simple machine (model) of any importance? It is widely accepted that *anything that is intuitively computable can be computed by a Turing machine*. This statement is known as the Church-Turing thesis, named for Turing and Alonzo Church, another mathematician who developed a similar model known as the *lambda calculus* and with whom Turing worked at Princeton. The works of Turing and Church are covered in-depth in theoretical courses in computer science.

It follows from the Church-Turing thesis that if we can find a problem for which a Turing-machine solution can be proven *not* to exist, then the problem must be unsolvable. In the next section we describe such a problem.

Halting Problem

It is not always obvious that a computation (program) halts. In Chapter 6 we introduced the concept of repeating a process; in Chapter 8 we talked about different types of loops. Some loops clearly stop, some clearly do not (infinite loops), and some loops stop depending on input data or calculations that occur within the loop. When a program is running, it is difficult to know whether it is caught in an infinite loop or whether it just needs more time to run.

Thus, it would be very beneficial if we could predict that a program with a specified input would not go

Reels of asterisks written

Before operating systems replaced the human operator, one of the operator's jobs was to monitor the amount of output being written and compare it to the estimated amount of output shown on the job submission slip. A not-too-observant operator finally stopped a job marked for one page of output after the second tape reel was written. The programmer was quite startled to see the printout of two tape reels' worth of asterisks (*s), generated because of an infinite loop.

into an infinite loop. The **Halting problem** restates the question this way: *Given a program and an input to the program, determine if the program will eventually stop with this input.*

The obvious approach is to run the program with the specified input and see what happens. If it stops, the answer is clear. What if it doesn't stop? How long do you run the program before you decide that it is in an infinite loop? Clearly, there are flaws in this approach. Unfortunately, there are flaws in every other approach as well. This problem is unsolvable. Let's look at the outlines of a proof of this assertion, which can be rephrased as: "There is no Turing-machine program that can determine whether a program will halt given a particular input."

How can we prove that a problem is unsolvable or, rather, that we just haven't found the solution yet? We could try every proposed solution and show that every one contains an error. Since there are many known solutions and many yet unknown, this approach seems doomed to failure. Yet, this approach forms the basis of Turing's solution to this problem. In his proof, he starts with any proposed solution and then shows that it doesn't work.

Assume that there exists a Turing-machine program, called SolvesHaltingProblem that determines for any program Example and input SampleData whether program Example halts given input SampleData. That is, SolvesHaltingProblem takes program Example and SampleData and prints "Halts" if the program halts and "Loops" if the program contains an infinite loop. This situation is depicted in Figure 17.5.

Recall that both programs (instructions) and data look alike in a computer; they are just bit patterns. What distinguishes programs from data is how the control unit interprets the bit pattern. So we could give program Example a copy of itself as data in place of SampleData. Thus, SolvesHaltingProblem should be able to take program Example and a second copy of program Example as data and determine whether program Example halts with itself as data. See Figure 17.6.

> **Halting problem** The unsolvable problem of determining whether any program will eventually stop given particular input

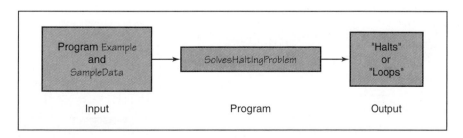

Figure 17.5
Proposed program for solving the Halting problem

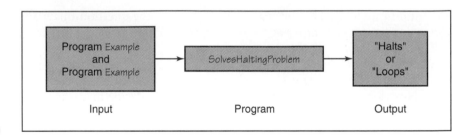

Figure 17.6
Proposed program for
solving the Halting problem

You can't get there from here

A woman was traveling with three children to England to visit her mother-in-law. Rather than a map, the mother-in-law had sent a list of towns the woman should go through from London's Gatwick airport to Brighton. After an exhausting eight-hour flight, the family finally found the rental car place and piled into the car for the final leg of the journey. After getting completely confused on the motorway system trying to follow the list of towns, the woman saw a policeman and asked for his help. He looked at the list of towns, thought for a minute, and finally shook his head, "Lady, you just can't get there from here." Some computer problems are like that too: You just can't get there from here.

Now let's construct a new program, NewProgram, that takes program Example as both program and data and uses the algorithm from SolvesHaltingProblem to write "Halts" if Example halts and "Loops" if it does not halt. If "Halts" is written, NewProgram creates an infinite loop; if "Loops" is written, NewProgram writes "Halts". Figure 17.7 shows this situation.

Do you see where the proof is leading? Let's now apply program SolvesHaltingProblem to NewProgram, using NewProgram as data. If SolvesHaltingProblem prints "Halts", program NewProgram goes into an infinite loop. If SolvesHaltingProblem prints "Loops", program NewProgram prints "Halts" and stops. In either case, SolvesHaltingProblem gives the wrong answer. Since SolvesHaltingProblem gives the wrong answer in at least one case, it doesn't work on all cases. Therefore, any proposed solution must have a flaw.

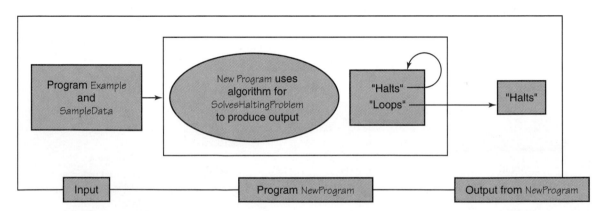

Figure 17.7 Construction of NewProgram

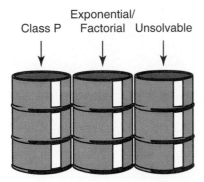

Class P   Exponential/ Factorial   Unsolvable

Figure 17.8 A reorganization of algorithm classification

Classification of Algorithms

Figure 17.3 showed the common orders of magnitude as bins. We now know that there is another bin to the right, which would contain algorithms that are unsolvable. Let's reorganize our bins a little, combining all polynomial algorithms in a bin labeled **Class P,** combine exponential and factorial algorithms into one bin, and add a bin labeled *Unsolvable*. See Figure 17.8.

The algorithms in the middle bin have known solutions, but they are called *intractable* because for data of any size they simply take too long to execute. We mentioned parallel computers in Chapter 1 when we reviewed the history of computer hardware. Could some of these problems be solved in a reasonable time (polynomial time) if enough processors were working on the problem at the same time? Yes, they could. A problem is said to be in **Class NP** if it can be solved with a sufficiently large number of processors in polynomial time.

Clearly Class P problems are also in Class NP. An open question in theoretical computing is whether or not Class NP problems, whose only tractable solution is with many processors, are also in Class P. That is, do there exist polynomial-time algorithms for these problems that we just haven't discovered (invented) yet? We don't know, but the problem has been and is still keeping computer science theorists busy looking for the solution. *The* solution? Yes, the problem of determining whether Class P is equal to Class NP has been reduced to finding a solution for one of these algorithms. There is a special class of problems called **NP-complete** prob-

Class P problems
Problems that can be solved with one processor in polynomial time

Class NP problems
Problems that can be solved in polynomial time with as many processors as desired

NP-complete problems
A class of problems within Class NP that has the property that if a polynomial time solution with one processor can be found for any member of the class, such a solution exists for every member of the class

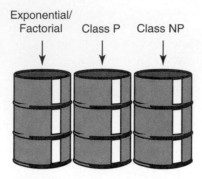

Figure 17.9   Adding class NP

The Traveling Salesman problem

A classic NP problem is called the *Traveling Salesman problem*. A salesman is responsible for visiting all the cities in his sale's district. In order to visit every one in an efficient manner, he wants to find a route of minimal cost that goes through each city once and only once before returning to the starting point. The cities can be represented in a graph with the edges representing highways between cities. Each edge is labeled with the distance between the cities. The solution then becomes a well-known graph algorithm whose solution with one processor is $O(N!)$.

lems. These problems are in Class NP and have the property that they can be mapped into one another. If a polynomial-time solution with one processor can be found for any one of the algorithms in this class, a solution can be found for each of them as the solution can be mapped to all the others. How and why this is so is beyond the scope of this book. However, if the solution is found, you will know, for it will make headlines all over the computing world.

So for now we picture our complexity bins with a new bin labeled *Class NP*. This bin and the Class P bin have dotted lines on their adjacent sides, for they may actually be just one bin. See Figure 17.9.

Summary

Limits are imposed on computer problem solving by the hardware, the software, and the nature of the problems to be solved. Numbers are infinite, but their representation within a computer is finite. This limitation can cause errors to creep into arithmetic calculations, giving incorrect results. Hardware components can wear out, and information can be lost in inter-computer and intra-computer data transfer.

The sheer size and complexity of large software projects almost guarantees that errors will occur. Testing a program can demonstrate errors, but it cannot demonstrate the absence of errors. The best way to build good software is to pay attention to quality from the first day of the project, applying the principles of software engineering.

Problems vary from very simple ones to solve to those that cannot be solved at all. Big-O analysis provides a metric that allows us to compare algorithms in terms of the growth rate of a size factor in the algorithm. Polynomial-time algorithms are those algorithms whose Big-O complexity can be expressed as a polynomial in the size factor. Class P problems are those that can be solved with one processor in polynomial time. Class NP problems are those that can be solved in polynomial time with an unlimited number of processors. As proved by Turing, the Halting problem does not have a solution.

ETHICAL ISSUES

Licensing Computer Professionals

Plumbers, electricians, beauty operators, psychologists, professional engineers—almost anyone who provides a service to the public is required to be licensed. Accountants (CPA) and medical doctors who specialize in a particular area of medicine are certified. Computer professionals, however, are not licensed and certification is scarce.

Certification is a voluntary process administered by a profession; licensing is a mandatory process administered by a governmental agency, usually at the state level in the U.S. The Institute for Certification of Computing Professionals is the most well-established certification organization in software. They offer two levels of certification, Associate Computing Professional (ACP) and Certified Computing Professional (CCP). Both require an examination that includes 110 questions on topics of human and organization framework, systems concepts, data and information, systems development, and associated disciplines. The ACP certification requires an exam on core topics and an exam on one programming language. The CCP certification requires the core exam; an exam on two additional topics, including management, procedural programming, business information systems, and systems programming; and 48 months of full-time experience or academic credentials with 24 months of full-time experience. This certification is slanted toward business uses of computing rather than general computer professionals.

Many commercial software companies such as Apple, Microsoft, and Novell certify practitioners in the use of their tools.

There are two main professional organizations in computing: ACM and IEEE Computer Society. These two organizations formed a Steering Committee for the Establishment of Software Engineering as a Profession, in 1993. To become a profession, the steering committee recommended adopting standard definitions, defining a required body of knowledge and recommended practices, defining ethical standards, and defining educational curricula. In 1998 the Software Engineering Coordination Committee (SWECC) was established by ACM/IEEE to act as a permanent committee to foster the evolution of software engineering as a professional computing discipline. The Texas Professional Engineers Licensing Board asked this committee for help in defining the performance criteria for a software engineering licensing exam to be administered in Texas.

Licensing is required for medical professionals, lawyers, and engineers. Clearly the engineering model would be more appropriate for computing professionals. The engineering model requires that the candidate be of good character; a graduate from an accredited engineering program and have four years of experience, or have a non-approved degree with 8 to 12 years of experience; and pass an examination. SWECC was asked to help with the exam. The ACM is governed by a council, the members of which are elected by the members. Several members of the ACM Council had reservations about whether licensing software engineers was in the best interest of the field or the public. After further study, ACM Council passed the following motion:

> ACM is opposed to the licensing of software engineers at this time because ACM believes it is premature and would not be effective at addressing the problems of software quality and reliability. ACM is, however, committed to solving the software quality problem by promoting R&D, by developing a core body of knowledge for software engineering, and by identifying standards of practice.

One of the reasons for ACM opposing the licensing is the 8-hour Fundamentals of Engineering exam, which covers the first two years of an engineering degree. Many of these topics, such as thermodynamics, fluid mechanics, statics, and material science, are not of relevance to computing professionals. In August 2001, IEEE Computer Society beta tested a certificate program in software engineering. The requirements are similar to the licensing requirements, but the degree can be in any discipline from any accredited institution of higher learning. Thus general engineering subjects are not included in the exam.

Key Terms

Big-O notation pg. 521

Cancellation error pg. 508

Class NP problems pg. 531

Class P pg. 525

Class P problems pg. 531

Halting problem pg. 529

Inspection pg. 513

NP-complete problems pg. 531

Overflow pg. 507

Polynomial-time algorithms
  pg. 525

Precision pg. 505

Representational (round-off) error
  pg. 507

Significant digits pg. 505

Software requirements pg. 512

Software specification pg. 512

Underflow pg. 507

Walk-through pg. 513

Exercises

1. Given the following three real values, what is the best order in which to add these values so that you will get the most accurate answer?

   $x = 3214 * 10^4$ $y = 576 * 10^{-1}$ $z = 4421 * 10^3$

2. Given the following three real values, what is the best order in which to add these values so that you will get the most accurate answer?

   $x = 3214 * 10^1$ $y = 576 * 10^{-1}$ $z = 4421 * 10^0$

3. Prove that $(1 + x - 1)$ does not necessarily equal x.

4. Define representational error, cancellation error, underflow, and over-flow. Discuss how these terms are interrelated.

5. Show the range of integer numbers that can be represented in each of the following word sizes.
   a. 8-bits
   b. 16 bits
   c. 24 bits
   d. 32 bits
   e. 64 bits

6. There is a logical action to take when underflow occurs, but not when overflow occurs. Explain.

7. a. Show how the numbers 1066 and 1492 would be represented in a linked list with one digit per node.
   b. Use a linked list to represent the sum of these integers.

c. Outline an algorithm to show how the calculation might be carried out in a computer.

8. Explain the Titanic effect in relation to hardware failure.

9. Have any hardware failures happened to you? Explain.

10. Given the following 8-bit code, what is the parity bit if odd parity is being used?
    a. 11100010
    b. 10101010
    c. 11111111
    d. 00000000
    e. 11101111

11. Given the following 8-bit code, what is the parity bit if even parity is being used?
    a. 11100010
    b. 10101010
    c. 11111111
    d. 00000000
    e. 11101111

12. Given the following numbers, what would be the check digit for each?
    a. 1066
    b. 1498
    c. 1668
    d. 2001
    e. 4040

13. What errors would be detected using the check bits in Exercise 12?

14. Given the following numbers, what would be the additional digits if the unit's digit of the sum of the even digits is used along with the check digit?
    a. 1066
    b. 1498
    c. 1668
    d. 2001
    e. 4040

15. Given the following numbers, what would be the additional digits if the unit's digit of the sum of the odd digits is used along with the check digit?
    a. 1066
    b. 1498
    c. 1668
    d. 2001
    e. 4040

16. How do the representations in Exercises 14 and 15 improve the error detection over a simple check digit?

17. Explain the concept of the software life cycle.

18. Where do most of the errors occur in a software project?

19. Why does the cost of fixing an error increase the longer the error remains undetected?

20. Compare and contrast the software verification activities code or design walk-through and inspection.

21. How can a program be verified to be correct but still be worthless?

22. Name at least five places where a software error could be introduced.

23. How was the AT&T software failure typical of such failures?

24. What is formal verification?

25. Explain the analogy of the elephant and the goldfish.

26. Define the term polynomial time algorithm.

27. How is it possible to throw away all but the term with the largest exponent when assessing the Big-O of a polynomial time algorithm?

28. Give the Big-O complexity measure of the following polynomials.
    a. $4x^3 + 32x^2 + 2x + 1003$
    b. $x^5 + x$
    c. $x^2 + 124578$
    d. $x + 1$

29. Give the common name for the following complexity measures and an example of an algorithm that falls into this category.
    a. $O(1)$
    b. $O(N)$
    c. $O(N\log N)$
    d. $O(N^2)$
    e. $O(2^N)$
    f. $O(N!)$

30. Explain the analogy of bins of complexity measures.

31. Who manufactures a Turing machine?

32. How does a Turing machine simulate a human with a paper and pencil?

33. Are there problems for which there are no solutions?

34. Describe the Halting problem.

35. How is the fact that data and programs look alike inside a computer used in the proof that the Halting problem is unsolvable?

? Thought Questions

1. Go on the web and perform a search for information on the Pentium chip error. Try different keywords and combinations of keywords, recording how many hits occur with each. Read at least three of the articles and write a description of the problem in your own words.

2. Search the Web for the answers to the following questions.

   a. Why did an unmanned Ariane 5 rocket explode in June of 1996?

   b. Did the Russian Phobos 1 spacecraft commit suicide?

   c. What caused the delay in the opening of the Denver airport?

   d. What was the cost of the software repair in London's (England) Ambulance dispatch system failure?

   e. The USS Yorktown was dead in the water for several hours in 1998. What software error caused the problem?

3. A professor was giving a lecture to a local service club about the limits of computing. A member of the audience said "But I didn't think there were any limits." If you were the professor, how would you have answered him?

4. ACM is opposed to licensing software engineers at this time. What is their argument? Do you agree or disagree? Why?

5. What is the difference between licensing and certification? Which do you feel is more appropriate for people in computing? Should there be stratified options for licensing? For certification?

Answers to Selected Exercises

Chapter 1 Exercises

1. What French mathematician built and sold the first gear-driven mechanical machine that did addition and subtraction?

   Pascal

4. Who was considered the first programmer? Describe her contributions to the history of computers.

   Ada Lovelace was considered the first programmer because of her work with Babbage. She edited his notes, adding many of her own ideas. She is credited with inventing the concept of a loop.

7. For whom is the Turing Award in computing named?

   Alan Turing, an English mathematician.

10. Some experts made early predictions that a small number of computers would handle all of mankind's computational needs. Why was this prediction faulty?

    Before the computer, we could only comprehend what we could calculate by hand. With the computer, we had a tool that changed how we viewed mathematics, physics, engineering, and business. Thus the definition of "a computational need" changed completely—and is still changing.

13. The following names were prominent in the early part of the fourth generation of computer hardware: Apple, Tandy/Radio Shack, Atari, Commodore, and Sun.
    a. Which of these companies are still in business today under the same name?
       Apple, Atari, Sun
    b. Which of these companies are still in business under another name?
       Tandy/Radio Shack (Radio Shack)
    c. Which of these companies is no longer in business?
       Commodore went out of business in 1984.

16. What does the acronym LAN stand for?

    Local Area Networks

19. Distinguish between assembly language and high-level languages.

    Whereas assembly language is a language made up of mnemonic codes that represent machine-language instructions, high-level languages use English-like statements to represent a group of assembly-language statements or machine-language statements. There is a one-to-one correspondence between statements in an assembly language and the statements they represent in machine language. There is a one-to-many correspondence between high-level statements and the corresponding machine-language statements.

22. Distinguish between a systems programmer and an applications programmer.

    A systems programmer writes programs that are tools to help others write programs. An applications programmer writes programs to solve specific problems.

25. What do the following pieces of software do?
    a. Loader
       A loader puts a program's instructions into memory where they can be executed.
    b. Linker
       A linker is a program that puts pieces of a large program together so that it can be put into memory where it in can be executed.
    c. Editor
       A editor is a word processing program that allows the user to enter and edit text.

28. Name several typical types of fourth-generation application software.

    Spreadsheets, word processors, and database management systems were introduced in the fourth generation.

31. Distinguish between computing as a tool and computing as a discipline.

Computing as a tool refers to the use of computing by people to solve problems in their professional or personal life. Computing as a discipline refers to the study of the body of knowledge that makes up computer science and/or computer engineering.

33. Distinguish between systems areas and applications areas in computing as a discipline.

The systems areas of computing as a discipline relate to the understanding and building of computer tools: algorithms and data structures, programming languages, (computer) architecture, operating systems, software methodology and engineering, and human-computer communication. The applications areas in computing relate to the computer's use as a tool: numerical computation, databases and informational retrieval, artificial intelligence and robotics, graphics, organizational informatics, and bioinformatics.

Chapter 2 Exercises

1. Distinguish between a natural number and a negative number.

A natural number is 0 and any number that can be obtained by repeatedly adding 1 to it. A negative number is less than 0, and opposite in sign to a natural number, although we usually do not consider negative 0.

4. How many 1s are there in 891 if it is a number in each of the following bases?
   a. base 10
      891
   b. base 8
      It can't be a number in base 8.
   c. base 12
      1,261
   d. base 13
      1,470
   e. base 16
      2,193

7. Explain how base 2 and base 8 are related.

Because 8 is a power of 2, base-8 digits can be read off in binary and 3 base-2 digits can be read off in octal.

9. Expand the table on page 40 to include the decimal numbers from 11 through 16.

binary	octal	decimal
000	0	0
001	1	1
010	2	2
011	3	3
100	4	4
101	5	5
110	6	6
111	7	7
1000	10	8
1001	11	9
1010	12	10
1011	13	11
1100	14	12
1101	15	13
1110	16	14
1111	17	15
10000	20	16

13. Convert the following binary numbers to hexadecimal.
    a. 111110110
       1F6
    b. 1000001
       41
    c. 010000010
       82
    d. 1100010
       62
    e. 111000111
       1C7

16. Convert the following decimal numbers to binary.
    a. 45
       101101
    b. 69
       1000101
    c. 1066
       10000101010
    d. 99
       1100011
    e. 1
       1

18. If you were going to represent numbers in base 18, what symbols, other than letters, might you use to represent the decimal numbers 10 through 17?

Any special characters would work or characters from another alphabet. Let's use # for 16 and @ for 17.

22. Perform the following hexadecimal additions.
  a. 19AB6 + 43
     19AF9
  b. AE9 + F
     AF8
  c. 1066 + ABCD
     BC33

25. Perform the following hexadecimal subtractions.
  a. ABC – 111
     9AB
  b. 9988 – AB
     98DD
  c. A9F8 – 1492
     9566

28. How many bytes are there in one word of a 64-bit machine?
     8

Chapter 3 Exercises

1. What is data compression and why is it an important topic today?

Data compression refers to reducing the amount of space needed to store a piece of data. Although computer storage is relatively cheap, as the amount of data keeps increasing rapidly, the cost of storage is a factor. However, the most important reason for compressing data is that, more and more, we share data. The Web and its underlying networks have limitations on bandwidth that define the maximum number of bits or bytes that can be transmitted from one place to another in a fixed amount of time.

4. Is a clock with a sweeping second hand an analog or a digital device? Explain.

A sweeping second hand is an analog device. The motion of the hand is continuous.

7. How many things can be represented with:
  a. four bits
     16
  b. five bits
     32

    c. six bits

    64

    d. seven bits

    128

10. Given a fixed-sized number scheme where k in the formula for the ten's complement is 6 (see page 59), answer the following questions.

    a. How many positive integers can be represented?

    499,999

    b. How many negative integers can be represented?

    500,000

    c. Draw the number line showing the three smallest and largest positive numbers, the three smallest and largest negative numbers, and zero.

13. In calculating the ten's complement in Exercise 12, did you have trouble borrowing from so many zeros? Such calculations are error prone. There is a trick that you can use that makes the calculation easier and thus less prone to errors: Subtract from all 9's and then add 1. A number subtracted from all 9's is called the nine's complement of the number.

    a. Prove that the nine's complement of a number plus one is equal to the ten's complement of the same number.

    Negative(I) = 10^k – I in 10's compliment

Negative(I) = (99..99 − I) + 1 in 9's compliment.
(99..99) = (10^k −1)
Negative(I) = (10^k −1) − I + 1 = 10^k − I

  b. Use the nine's complement plus one to calculate the values in Exercise 12 b, c, and d.
    b. 964232   c. 555545   d. 876544

  c. Which did you find easier to use, the direct calculation of the ten's complement or the nine's complement plus one? Justify your answer.
    This is an individual answer.

16. The one's complement of a number is analogous to the nine's complement of a decimal number. Use the scheme outlined in Exercise 13 to calculate the results of Exercise 14, using the one's complement rather than the two's complement.

  a. 10001000   b. 11011110   c. 00100010   d. 10101011
  e. 00110011

18. Convert the rules for subtraction in a sign-magnitude system to the algorithm format.

> Find the first number on the number line
> If addition
>   Move in the sign direction of second number the specified units
> Else
>   Move in the opposite sign direction of the second number the specified units

22. Create a keyword encoding table that contains a few simple words. Rewrite a paragraph of your choosing using this encoding scheme. Compute the compression ratio you achieve.

Original text:

Computers are multimedia devices that manipulate data varying in form from numbers to graphics to video. Because a computer can only manipulate binary values, all forms of data must be represented in binary form. Data is classified as being continuous (analog) or discrete (digital).

Decimal values are represented by their binary equivalent, using one of several techniques for representing negative numbers, such a sign magnitude or two's compliment. Real numbers are represented by a triple made up of the sign, the digits in the number, and an exponent that specifies the radix point.

A character set is a list of alphanumeric characters and the codes that represent each one. The most common character set is Unicode (16 bits for each character), which has ASCII as a subset. The 8-bit ASCII set is sufficient for English but not for other (or multiple) languages. There are various ways for compressing text so that it takes less space to store it or less time to transmit it from one machine to another.

Audio information is represented as digitized sound waves. Color is represented by three values that represent the contribution of each of red, blue, and green. There are two basic techniques for representing pictures, bitmaps and vector graphics. Video is broken up into a series of still images, each of which is represented as a picture.

Substitutions:

and:	&	to:	>	the:	~
an:	!	it:	<	is:	=
character:	#	ASCII:	%	that:	$
represented:	@				

Text with substitutions:

Computers are multimedia devices $ manipulate data varying in form from numbers > graphics > video. Because a computer can only manipulate binary values, all forms of data must be @ in binary form. Data = classified as being continuous (analog) or discrete (digital).

Decimal values are @ by their binary equivalent, using one of several techniques for representing negative numbers, such a sign magnitude or one's compliment. Real numbers are @ by a triple made up of ~ sign, ~ digits in ~ number, & ! exponent $ specifies ~ radix point.

A # set = a list of alphanumeric #s & ~ codes $ represent each one. ~ most common # set = Unicode (16 bits for each #), which has % as a subset. ~ 8-bit % set = sufficient for English but not for other (or multiple) languages. There are various ways for compressing text so $ < takes less space > store < or less time > transmit < from one machine > another.

Audio information = @ as digitized sound waves. Color = @ by three values $ represent ~ contribution of each of red, blue, & green. There are two basic techniques for representing pictures, bitmaps & vector graphics. Video = broken up into a series of still images, each of which = @ as a picture.

Compression ratio: .8864

25. How do humans perceive sound?

We perceive sound when a series of air compressions vibrate a membrane in our ear, which sends signals to our brain.

28. What does color depth indicate?

Color depth is the amount of data used to represent a color; that is the number of bits used to represent each of the colors in the RGB value.

Chapter 4 Exercises

1. How is voltage level used to distinguish between binary digits?

A voltage level in the range of 0 to 2 volts is interpreted as a binary 0. A voltage level in the range of 2+ to 5 volts is interpreted as a binary 1.

4. Characterize the notations asked for in Exercise 3.

Boolean expressions use the operations of Boolean algebra to describe the behavior of gates and circuits.

Logic diagrams use a graphical representation to describe the behavior of gates and circuits.

Truth tables define the behavior of gates and circuits by showing all possible input and output combinations of the gates and circuits.

7. Give the three representations of a NOT gate and say in words what NOT means.

A is the input signal and X is the output signal.

Boolean expression: X = A'

Logic Diagram:

Boolean Expression   Logic Diagram Symbol   Truth Table

      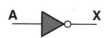

A	X
0	1
0	0

NOT takes a binary input value and inverts it.

10. Give the three representations of an XOR gate and say in words what XOR means.

A and B are the input signals and X is the output signal.

Boolean expression: A ⊕ B   (A XOR B)

Logic Diagram:

Boolean Expression   **Logic Diagram Symbol**

$$X = A \oplus B$$

Truth Table

A	B	X
0	0	0
0	1	1
1	0	1
1	1	0

If both inputs are the same value, XOR returns a 0; otherwise XOR returns a 1.

13. Why are there no logic diagram symbols for the NAND and NOR gates?

Because NAND means not AND and NOR means not OR, there are no symbols for NAND and NOR. The AND and OR symbols are used with the inversion bubble.

14. Draw and label the symbol for a three-input AND gate; then show its behavior with a truth table.

Logic Diagram Symbol

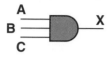

A
B ─── X
C

Truth Table

A	B	C	X
0	0	0	0
0	0	1	0
0	1	0	0
0	1	1	0
1	0	0	0
1	0	1	0
1	1	0	0
1	1	1	1

17. How does a transistor behave?

Depending on the voltage of an input signal, a transistor either acts as a wire that conducts electricity or as a resister that blocks the flow of electricity.

20. What are the three terminals in a transistor and how do they operate?

The *source* is an electric signal. The *base* value regulates a gate that determines whether the connection between the source and the ground (*emitter*) is made. An output line is usually connected to the source. If the base value is high, the source is grounded and the output is low (representing 0). If the base value is low, the gate is closed and the source is not grounded and the output is high (representing 1).

23. Draw a transistor diagram for an OR gate. Explain the processing.

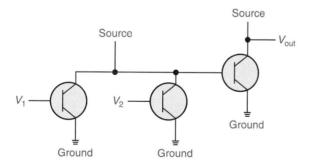

The NOR gate is the inverse of the OR gate, and the inverse of the inverse is the original. Thus, the output from the NOR gate is input to a NOT gate, giving us the NOR.

26. Draw a circuit diagram corresponding to the following Boolean expression:

(A + B)(B + C)

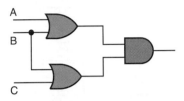

29. Draw a circuit diagram corresponding to the following Boolean expression:

(AB)' + (CD)'

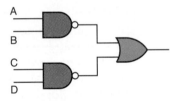

30. Show the behavior of the following circuit with a truth table:

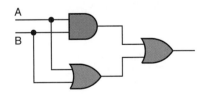

A	B	AB	A+B	AB + (A + B)
0	0	0	1	1
0	1	0	1	1
1	0	0	1	1
1	1	1	0	1

33. Show the behavior of the following circuit with a truth table:

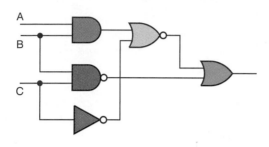

A	B	C	AB	(BC)'	C'	(AB + C)'	(BC)' +(AB + C)'
0	0	0	0	1	1	0	1
0	0	1	0	1	0	1	1
0	1	0	0	1	1	0	1
0	1	1	0	0	0	1	1
1	0	0	0	1	1	0	1
1	0	1	0	1	0	1	1
1	1	0	1	1	1	0	1
1	1	1	1	0	0	0	0

35. Name six properties of Boolean algebra and explain what each means.

Commutative: *The commutative property says that binary operations AND and OR may be applied left to right or right to left. (A AND B is the same as B AND A; A OR B is the same as B OR A)*

Associative: *The associative property says that given three Boolean variables, they may be ANDed or ORed right to left or left to right. ((A AND B) AND C is the same as A AND (B AND C); (A OR B) OR C is the same as A OR (B OR C))*

Distributive: *The distributive property says that given three Boolean variables, the first AND the result of the second OR the third is the same as the first AND the second OR the first AND the third. (A AND (B OR C) = (A AND B) OR (A AND C)) Also, the first OR the result of second AND the third is the same as the first OR the second AND the result of the first OR the third. (A OR (B AND C) = (A OR B) AND (A OR C))*

Identity: *The identity property says that any value A AND the OR identity always returns A and that any value A OR the AND identity always returns A. (A AND 1 = A; A OR 0 = A)*

Complement: *The complement property says that any value AND the complement of that value equals the OR identity and that any value OR the complement of that value equals the OR identity. (A AND (A') = 0; A OR (A') = 1)*

DeMorgan's Law: *DeMorgan's Law says that the complement of A AND B is the same as the compliment of A OR the complement of B and the complement of A OR B is the same as the complement of B AND the complement of A. ((A AND B)' = A' OR B'; (A OR B)' = A' AND B')*

39. **a.** Circuits used for memory are which types of circuits?
Memory circuits are sequential circuits because they are dependent on the existing state of the circuit as well as input to the circuit.

b. How many digits does an S-R latch store?
one binary digit

c. The design for an S-R latch shown in Figure 4.12 guarantees what about the outputs X and Y?
The values of X and Y are always compliments.

42. In the chip shown in Figure 4.13, what are the pins used for?

Eight are used for inputs to gates, four for outputs from the gates, one for ground, and one for power.

Chapter 5 Exercises

1. Define the following terms.
a. Pentium IV processor
The Pentium IV is a popular central processing unit made by Intel.

b. hertz
A hertz is a unit of frequency equal to one cycle per second.

c. random access memory
Random access memory is memory in which each word has an address by which the word can be directly accessed.

4. What does it mean to say that memory is 133MHz?

Saying a memory is 133Mhz means that the memory can be accessed at 133,000,000 cycles per second.

7. Define the following terms and give their abbreviation.
a. pico
Pico (p) is 10^{-12}.

b. nano

Nano (n) is 0^{-9}.

c. micro

Micro (μ) is 10^{-6}.

d. milli

Milli (m) is 10^{-3}.

10. What is the stored-program concept and why is it important?

The stored-program concept means that data and instructions both are logically the same and both can be stored in memory. The von Neumann architecture is built around this principle. It is important because the human does not have to enter instructions each time the program is executed. Instructions can be stored in memory and executed in sequence, referencing the data values it needs on which to operate.

13. What is the addressability of an 8-bit machine?

8

16. Punched cards and paper tape were early input/output mediums. Discuss their advantages and disadvantages.

Punched cards and paper tape used for input were prepared on separate machines and then read into the computer. Input from cards and paper tape was slow, but they provided a permanent record of the input. When used for output, cards and paper tape had to be transferred to another device to get a human readable copy of the information; however, the output could be stored permanently on cards and paper tape.

19. List the steps in the fetch-execute cycle.

Fetch the next instruction from the address in the program counter.

Decode the instruction.

Execute the instruction.

22. Explain what is meant by "execute an instruction."

Signals are sent to the arithmetic/logic unit to carry out the processing.

25. Discuss the pros and cons of using magnetic tape as a storage medium.

Magnetic tape is a cheap medium for storing large quantities of data. However, data items cannot be directly addressed on tape. To reach a data object, all information recorded before the one you want must be read and discarded.

28. What is a cylinder?

A cylinder is a set of concentric tracks—that is, tracks that line up under one another.

31. Define the following acronyms.
   a. CD
      Compact Disk
   b. CD-ROM
      Compact Disk Read-Only Memory
   c. CD-DA
      Compact Disk-Digital Audio
   d. CD-RW
      Compact Disk Read-Write
   e. DVD
      Digital Versatile Disk

34. Compare the storage capacity of a generic floppy disk and a zip disk.

   A zip disk stores several hundred megabytes on a single disk; thus, a zip disk stores about 100 times more information than a generic floppy.

37. Describe a parallel architecture that uses synchronous processing.

   There are multiple processors applying the same program to multiple data sets.

40. How many different memory locations can a 16-bit processor access?

   2^{16} different memory locations.

43. In discussing the computer ad, we used the expression "Bigger is better" in relation to the compact disk. Explain.

   The bigger the external storage device, the more information that can be stored.

Chapter 6 Exercises

1. List the four steps in Polya's How-To-Solve-It List.

   Understanding the problem

   Devising a plan

   Carrying out the plan

   Looking back

4. Apply the problem-solving strategies to the following situations.

   Solutions are not unique.
   a. Buying a toy for your four-year-old cousin.
   Ask questions:
      What do four-year olds like?
      Does he or she like sports?
      What stores sell toys?

Where is a particular store located?

What toys does the cousin already have?

Look for things that are familiar:

I liked Lincoln Logs; would my cousin like them?

I liked my red wagon; would my cousin like them?

My cousin is like his (or her) mother; what did she play with as a child?

Divide and conquer:

Go to store.

Go to toy aisle.

Find girls' (or boys') toys.

Choose one.

b. Organizing an awards banquet for your soccer team.

Ask questions:

Where will it be?

When will it be?

How many people will be there?

How many trophies will be awarded?

Look for things that are familiar:

I organized one last year.

I organized a fundraiser.

I was a scout leader.

I play soccer.

Divide and conquer:

Have Jane decide on day and time.

Have Jim choose menu.

Have Mary buy trophies.

Have Jeremy call people.

c. Buying a dress or suit for an awards banquet at which you are being honored.

Ask questions:

What time of day is the banquet?

Where is the banquet being held?

What will others be wearing?

What is my best color?

Look for things that are familiar:

Last year the award winner wore a blue dress (suit).

Last year I wore a green suit.

I wore a suit when I was honored last year.

Divide and conquer:

Choose the store.

Go to the store.

Choose possibilities from racks.

Choose one.

7. Write an algorithm for the following tasks.

Solutions are not unique.

a. Making a peanut butter and jelly sandwich.

> Get bread.
> Get peanut butter.
> Get jelly.
> Get knife.
> Spread peanut butter on one slice of bread.
> Spread jelly on one slice of bread.
> Combine slices of bread, with peanut butter facing jelly.

b. Getting up in the morning.

> Alarm goes off.
> Hit sleep button.
> Alarm goes off.
> Hit sleep button.
> Alarm goes off.
> Turn off alarm.
> Move dog.
> Throw back covers.
> Put feet over side of the bed.
> Stand up.

c. Doing your homework.

> Turn off TV.
> Turn off CD.
> Get backpack.
> Sit at desk.
> Open backpack.
> Pet cat.
> Open book.
> Open assignment.
> While (more to do).
>   Solve problem.
>   Pet cat.

d. Driving home in the afternoon.

> Find car.
> Open car door.
> Get into car.
> Fasten seat belt.
> Start engine.
> Turn on radio.
> While (not yet home).
> Keep going.
> Turn off engine.
> Open car door.
> Get out of car.
> Close car door.

10. Describe the steps in the algorithm development phase.

    The algorithm development phase includes analysis (understanding the problem), proposed solution (logical sequence of solution steps), and testing (following algorithm).

13. Look up a recipe for chocolate brownies in a cookbook and answer the following questions.
    a. Is the recipe an algorithm? Justify your answer.
       (One author's solution.)
       Yes, the recipe is an algorithm. If the steps are followed exactly, brownies are produced.
    b. Organize the recipe as an algorithm, using pseudo-code.

> Preheat oven to 375°.
> Put 2 oz unsweetened chocolate in double boiler.
> Add 1/2 cup butter to chocolate in double boiler.
> Put double boiler over moderate flame.
> Melt contents of double boiler.
> Remove double boiler from flame.
> Get a cup of sugar.
> Put 2 eggs in bowl.
> While (more sugar).
> Beat eggs.
> Add sugar gradually.
> Put contents of cooled double boiler in bowl.
> Mix contents of bowl.

```
Sift 1/2 cup flour and dash of salt.
Stir flour mixture into bowl.
Add 1 teaspoon vanilla to bowl.
Add 1/2 cup chopped nuts to bowl.
Mix contents of bowl.
Grease 9-inch square pan.
Pour contents of bowl into pan.
Set minutes to 20.
Put pan in oven.
While (minutes not 0).
Set minutes to minutes – 1.
Remove pan from oven.
Cut into 1-1/2" squares.
Eat.
```

c. List the words that have meaning in computing.

While is the only computing word. It means repetition.

d. List the words that have meaning in cooking.

Words with meaning in cooking include preheat, add, double boiler, melt, moderate flame, beat, gradually, mix, shift, dash, chopped, and grease.

e. Make the cookies and take them to your professor.

14. We said that following a recipe is easier than developing one. Go to the supermarket and buy a vegetable that you have not cooked (or eaten) before. Take it home and develop a recipe. Write up your recipe and your critique of the process. (If it is good, send it to the authors.)

This is an activity. No answer expected.

17. Write a top-down design for the following tasks.

Solutions are not unique.

a. Buying a toy for your four-year-old cousin.

```
Go to store.
Choose toy.
Buy toy.
```

Go to store

Choose store.
Find location.
Take bus.

Choose toy

Walk up and down aisles.
Panic at choices.
Grab nearest large stuffed animal.

Buy toy

Go to clerk.
Give stuffed animal to clerk.
Give credit card to clerk.
Sign credit card slip.

b. Organizing an awards banquet for your soccer team.

Rent banquet room.
Send invitations.
Choose menu.
Buy trophies.

Rent banquet room

Find what is available.
Visit possible choices.
Choose one.
Make reservation.

> **Send invitations**
>
> Get list of people to invite.
> Buy invitations.
> Address invitations.
> Mail invitations.

> **Buy trophies**
>
> Find out how many to buy.
> Find store that carries trophies.
> Order trophies over the phone.
> Pick up trophies.

   c. Buying a dress or suit for an awards banquet at which you are being honored.

> Go to favorite store.
> Choose dress or suit that suits you.
> Pay for choice.
> Go home.

20. Distinguish between information and data.

Information is any knowledge that can be communicated. When information is in the form that a computer can use, it is called data. Thus, data is any knowledge that can be communicated in a form that a computer can process.

23. An airplane is a complex system.

Solutions are not unique.
   a. Give an abstraction of an airplane from the view of a pilot.
     A pilot can view the airplane as a car that he or she drives on a highway of air.
   b. Give an abstraction of an airplane from the view of a passenger.
     A passenger can view the airplane as the inside of a limousine that is carrying the passenger from one place to another.
   c. Give an abstraction of an airplane from the view of the cabin crew.
     The cabin crew can view an airplane as a dining room.

    d. Give an abstraction of an airplane from the view of a maintenance mechanic.

      A maintenance mechanic can view an airplane as a collection of parts and wires put together according to his maintenance diagrams.

    e. Give an abstraction of an airplane from the view from the airline's corporate office.

      From the view of the boardroom, the airplane can be viewed as an expensive object used in the process of making money.

26. List the identifiers and whether they named data or actions for the designs in Exercise 19.

    a. Actions: find, search, open, compare, turn, set

      Data: page, column, name, book, right page, left page

    b. Actions: log on, go, type, get

      Data: Internet, search engine, first response, phone number

29. Verify the designs in Exercise 17 using a walk-through.

    This is an activity not a question.

32. Distinguish between an object and an object class.

    An object class is description of a group of objects with similar properties and behaviors. An object is a thing or entity that had meaning within a problem. An object is one of the things described by an object class.

35. Discuss the differences between a top-down design and an object-oriented design.

    Top-down design breaks the problem into successive levels of tasks; object-oriented design breaks the problem into successive levels of data objects.

38. Design the CRC cards for a data base for a zoo, using brainstorming, filtering, and scenarios.

    Brainstorming: family name, name, date of birth, date bought, food, cage number, sex, date of last shots,

    Filtering: animal, name, date, food, cage number, sex

Scenarios:

Class Name: *Animal*		Superclass:	Subclasses:	
Responsibilities		**Collaborations**		
Initialize itself		*String, Date, Char*		
Know familyName		*String*		
Know name		*String*		
Know food		*String*		
KnowsdateOfBirth		*Date*		
Know dateBought		*Date*		
Get shots		*Date*		
Know DateOfShots		*Date*		
Know cageNumber		*String*		
Know sex		*Char*		
Know dies		*String*		

Class Name: *Date*		Superclass:	Subclasses:	
Responsibilities		**Collaborations**		
Initialize itself		*Int*		
Know month		*int*		
Know day		*int*		
Know year		*int*		

Class Name: *Date*		Superclass:	Subclasses:	
Responsibilities		**Collaborations**		
Initialize itself		*Int*		
Know month		*int*		
Know day		*int*		
Know year		*int*		

41. Distinguish between syntax and semantics.

Syntax is the formal rules governing how instructions are written in a language. Semantics is the set of rules that give meaning to the instructions in a language.

Chapter 7 Exercises

1. What does it mean when we say that a computer is a *programmable* device?

   Programmable means that data and instructions are logically the same and are stored in the same place. The consequence of this fact is that the program the computer executes is not wired into the hardware but is entered from outside.

4. What is a virtual machine? Discuss this definition in terms of the Pep/7 computer.

   A virtual machine is a hypothetical machine designed to illustrate important features of a real computer. The Pep/7 computer is a virtual machine designed to illustrate the features of the von Neumann architecture. It has instructions to store, retrieve, and process data as well as instructions to input and output data.

7. We covered only two of the four addressing modes. If we had not stated this explicitly, could you have deduced that this was true? Explain.

   If there were only two addressing modes, one bit would have been used instead of two. Because two bits are used, there must be three or four modes.

8. a. Where is the data (operand) if the address mode specifier is 00?
   If the address mode specifier is 00, the data is in the operand specifier.
   b. Where is the data (operand) if the address mode specifier is 01?
   If the address mode specifier is 01, the data is stored in the place named in the operand specifier.

11. How many more cells could be added to memory without having to change the instruction format? Justify your answer.

    The operand specifier is 16 bits long. Therefore, 2^{16} different bytes could be addressed without changing the instruction format. Thus, 61440 more bytes could be added.

13. What are the contents of the A register after the execution of this instruction?

    00001000 00000000 00000011

    00000000 00000011

16. What are the contents of the A register after the execution of the following two instructions?

    00001001 00000000 00000001

    00011000 00000000 00000001

    00000000 10100011

19. What are the contents of the X register after the execution of the following two instructions?

```
00001101 00000000 00000011
00100101 00000000 00000010
00000000 11101110
```

22. Write the algorithm for writing your name, given that the implementation language is Pep/7 machine code.

Write "Nell"

Write "Nell"

Write "N"
Write "e"
Write "l"
Write "l"

Write "N"

Write 4E (hex)

Write "e"

Write 65 (hex)

Write "l"

Write 6C (hex)

Write "l"

Write 6C (hex)

---

25. Write the assembly-language program to implement the algorithm in Exercise 23.

```
CHARO h#0010,d   ;Output 'N'
CHARO h#0011,d   ;Output 'e'
CHARO h#0012,d   ;Output 'l'
CHARO h#0013,d   ;Output 'l'
```

```
        STOP
        .ASCII /Nell/   ;Store 'Hello' into proper places
        .END
```

28. The following program seems to run, but does strange things with certain input values. Can you find the bug?

```
        BR    Main
sum:   .WORD d#0
num1: .BLOCK d#1
num2: .BLOCK d#1
num3: .BLOCK d#1
Main: LOADA sum,d
        DECI num1,d
        DECI num2,d
        DECI num3,d
        ADDA num3,d
        ADDA num2,d
        ADDA num1,d
        STOREA sum,d
        DECO sum,d
        STOP
        .END
```

One byte of storage is set up for each input value. If the value that is read is greater than one byte, the excess spills over to the byte above, giving the wrong answer.

31. Write an algorithm that reads in three values and writes out the result of subtracting the second value from the sum of the first and the third values.

```
Read num1
Read num2
Read num3
Load num1
Add num3
Sub num2
Store in answer
Write answer
```

34. Design and implement in assembly language an algorithm that reads four values and prints the sum.

> Read num1
> Read num2
> Read num3
> Read num4
> Load num1
> Add num2
> Add num3
> Add num4
> Store in answer
> Write answer

```
BR   Main
answer:      .WORD d#0
num1: .BLOCK d#2
num2: .BLOCK d#2
num3: .BLOCK d#2
num4: .BLOCK d#2

Main: DECI num1,d
      DECI num2,d
      DECI num3,d
      DECI num4,d
      LOADA  num1,d
      ADDA num2,d
      ADDA num3,d
      ADDA num4,d
      STOREA answer,d
      DECO answer,d
      STOP
      .END
```

37. Distinguish between assembly language pseudo-code instructions and mnemonic instructions.

Pseudo-code instructions are instructions to the assembler; mnemonic instructions are to be translated by the assembler.

Chapter 8 Exercises

2. Distinguish between an assembler and a compiler.

An assembler translates assembly-language instructions into machine code. A compiler translates high-level language instructions into machine code. The translation of an assembler is one-to-one: One statement in assembly language is translated into one statement in machine code. The translation of a compiler is one-to-many: One high-level language instruction is translated into many machine language instructions.

5. Describe the portability provided by a compiler.

A program written in a high-level language that is compiled can be translated and run on any machine that has a compiler for the language.

10. What are the characteristics of the imperative paradigm?

Programs describe the processes necessary to solve the problem.

14. How do you ask questions in a programming language?

To ask a question in a programming language, you make an assertion. If the assertion is true, the answer is true. If the assertion is false, the answer is false.

17. Given Boolean variables *one*, *two*, and *three*, write an assertion for each of the following questions.
  a. Is *one* greater than both *two* and *three*?
  (one > two) AND (one > three)
  b. Is *one* greater than *two*, but less than *three*?
  (one > two) AND (one < three)
  c. Are all three variables greater than zero?
  (one > 0) AND (two > 0) AND (three > 0)
  d. Is *one* less than *two* or *one* less than *three*?
  (one < two) or (one < three)
  e. Is *two* greater than *one* and *three* less than *two*?
  (two > one) AND (three < two)

21. What is a data type?

A data type is the description of a set of values and the basic set of operations that can be applied to values of the type.

25. If the same symbol is used for both single characters and strings, how can you distinguish between a single character and a one-character string?

If the same symbol is used, a character cannot be distinguished from a one-character string.

29. Distinguish between instructions to be translated and instructions to the translating program.

Instructions to the translating program tell the program to associate identifiers with objects, and if the objects are data, tell the program the data type of what can be stored in that place.

30. Consider the following identifiers: Address, ADDRESS, AddRess, Name, NAME, NamE
  a. How many different identifiers are represented if the language is Ada?

  1

  b. How many different identifiers are represented if the language is VB.NET?

  4

  c. How many different identifiers are represented if the language is C++ or Java?

  4

35. Write the stream-input algorithm in pseudo-code.

While (more names on input statement)
    Set currentIdentifier to next name on input statement
    Read and collect characters in dataValue until a blank is read
    Translate dataValue into type of currentIdentifier
    Set currentIdentifier to dataValue

38. Explain the flow of control of the *if* statement.

If the Boolean expression is true, execute the first statement. If the Boolean expression in false, execute the second statement. In either case, continue with the statement following the second statement.

39. Fill in the following table showing the appropriate syntactic marker(s) or reserved word for the language shown based on your observation of the tables on pages 238, 243, and 244.

Language	Ada	VB.NET	C++	Java
Declaring a character variable	Character	Char	char	char
Declaring a named constant	constant	Const	const	final
Boolean expression in *if* statement	no marker	expression in ( )	expression in ( )	expression
true branch of an *if* statement	then	Then	none	none
false branch of an *if* statement	else	Else	else	else
compound statement or block	end if;	End If	put block in ( )	put block in { }

43. What are the three steps in a count-controlled loop?

Initialize counter, test counter against ending condition, increment counter

47. What is recursion?

Recursion is the ability of a subprogram to call itself.

50. Explain the statement, "Subprograms are a powerful tool for abstraction."

A subprogram is a named task. The calling program can be designed and written using the subprogram name without knowing how the subprogram is implemented.

54. Distinguish between a parameter and an argument.

A parameter is a dummy name listed on the subprogram's heading. An argument is the data the calling program sends to the subprogram to use.

57. What is the result of executing subprogram Swap if the parameters are value parameters?

There is no result. Nothing happens.

60. How did the invention of the mouse change programming?

The invention of the mouse introduced the concept of asynchronous processing.

63. What is meant by a *homogeneous* structure?

A homogeneous structure is one in which all the individual parts are of the same data type.

68. Ada uses a range of index values to define an array, but VB.NET and C++ specify the number of places in the array. Explain.

Ada lets the user explicitly define how the values in the array are to be indexed; the number of items is determined from this range. VB.NET and C++ specify the number of elements in the array, and accessing is always from [0] through [number of elements − 1].

69. Examine the following three array declarations:

```
type Index is range -1..10;

type Data_Array is array (Index) of Integer;

Data : Data_Array;                         -- Ada


Dim data(11) As Integer                    ' VB.NET


int data[11];                              // C++
```

Are the arrays declared the same? Justify your answer.

The Ada array contains 12 slots, indexed from (−1)..(10).

The VB.NET and C++ arrays contain 11 slots, indexed from (0)..(10) in VB.NET and [0]..[10] in C++.

72. Distinguish between the definition of a class in the design phase and in the implementation phase.

A class in the design phase is a description of a group of objects with similar properties and behaviors. A class in the implementation phase is a pattern for an object.

Chapter 9 Exercises

1. *Abstract data types, data structures,* and *containers:*

a. Define these terms.

Abstract data types are data types whose properties (domains and operations) are specified independent of any particular implementation.

A data structure is the implementation of the composite data fields of an abstract data type.

A container is an object whose role is to hold and manipulate other objects.

b. What do they have in common?

Each represents the concept of collections of data objects.

c. What distinguishes each from the others?

Each represents a different level. An ADT is the logical view of the properties of a class of data. A data structure is the implementation level of this logical view. A container is the description given to all logical views of this type of object; it represents how an application program might view the ADT at a higher level.

4. Draw the unsorted list containing the following strings: blue, black, green, yellow, red, purple, white, and violet.

a. In an unsorted array-based list.

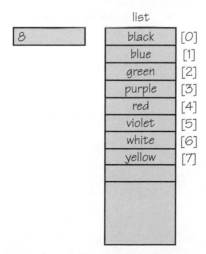

```
          list
┌─────────┐   ┌─────────┐
│   8     │   │  blue   │ [0]
└─────────┘   ├─────────┤
              │  black  │ [1]
              ├─────────┤
              │  green  │ [2]
              ├─────────┤
              │ yellow  │ [3]
              ├─────────┤
              │   red   │ [4]
              ├─────────┤
              │ purple  │ [5]
              ├─────────┤
              │  white  │ [6]
              ├─────────┤
              │ violet  │ [7]
              ├─────────┤
              │         │
              └─────────┘
```

b. In a sorted array-based list.

```
          list
┌─────────┐   ┌─────────┐
│   8     │   │  black  │ [0]
└─────────┘   ├─────────┤
              │  blue   │ [1]
              ├─────────┤
              │  green  │ [2]
              ├─────────┤
              │ purple  │ [3]
              ├─────────┤
              │   red   │ [4]
              ├─────────┤
              │ violet  │ [5]
              ├─────────┤
              │  white  │ [6]
              ├─────────┤
              │ yellow  │ [7]
              ├─────────┤
              │         │
              └─────────┘
```

c. In an unsorted linked list.

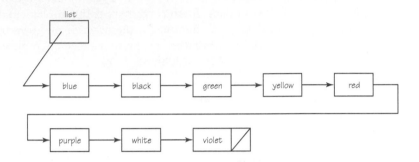

d. In a sorted linked list.

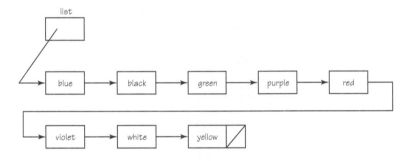

5. Give the meaning of the following expressions in an array-based implementation:

a. Put item

Put item means that given an index shift, the items that follow move down one slot in the array and store the item at the index position.

b. Remove the item

Remove the item means that given an index shift, the items that follow move up one slot in the array.

c. Get next item

Get next item means to increment the value used as an index and access that indexed position.

d. More items

More items means that the variable used as an index is less than length − 1.

7. What does it mean to say that the *Delete* operation is ambiguous?

Delete is ambiguous because there is more than one logical meaning. Given an item to delete, the operation could mean to delete the first copy found or delete all copies of the item. What should be done if the item is not in the list? Is it an error?

10. The obvious place to place a new item in an unsorted list is different in an array-based and a linked implementation. Explain.

In an array-based list, the length position is directly accessible and no items need to be moved to make room for the new item, so each new item should go at the end. In a linked list, the first position is immediately accessible, so the new item should go at the front of the list.

Questions 11 through 13 use the following list of values.

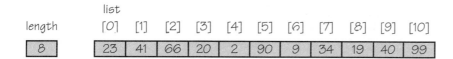

11. Show the state of the list when current is first set to the 4th item in the list in the selection sort.

[0]	[1]	[2]	[3]	[4]	[5]	[6]	[7]	[8]	[9]	[10]
2	9	19	20	23	90	41	34	66	40	99

14. How many comparisons does it take using a sequential search to find the following values or determine that the item is not in the list?
   a. 4
   11
   b. 44
   5
   c. 45
   11
   d. 105
   11
   e. 106
   11

16. A binary search is a natural recursive algorithm. It can also be written as an iterative algorithm. Write the iterative version of the algorithm.

```
Set first to 0
Set last to length − 1
Set found to false
Set moreToSearch to (first <= last)
while (moreToSearch) AND NOT found
    Set midPoint to (first + last) / 2
    Set result to (item.ComparedTo(info[midPoint]))
    If (result <0)
        Set last to midPoint − 1
        Set moreToSearch to (first <= last)
    Else If (result > 0)
        Set first to midPoint + 1
        Set moreToSearch to (first <= last)
    Else
        Set found to true
```

17. What are the characteristics of the ADT stack?

Items are inserted and deleted at the same end, making this a last-in, first-out structure.

20. Write the algorithm for Push in an array-based implementation.

```
// top is the index of the last element put on the structure
// items is the array in which the items are stored.
Increment top
Set items[top] to new item
```

23. Write the algorithms for Deque in an array-based implementation.

```
Set outItem to items[0]
For (index going from 0 to rear − 1)
Set items[index] to items[index+1]
```

26. Write the algorithm for Enque in a linked implementation.

> Set current to rear
> put newItem

The following tree is used in Questions 30 through 36.

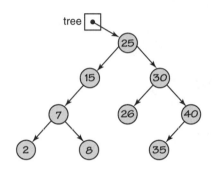

30. Name the content of each of the leaf nodes.

2, 8, 26, 35

33. Name the content of nodes that are the ancestors of the nodes whose content is 7.

15, 25

36. If a node with the value 9 is inserted into the tree, where does it go?

It goes as the right child of the node whose value is 8.

39. What are the properties of a binary tree?

A binary tree is a tree with the shape property that each node can have zero, one, or two child nodes.

41. Draw the tree that results in inserting the following strings into the tree in Figure 9.19: susy, chris, kit, jimmie, christopher, nell, al, bobby, john robert, and alex.

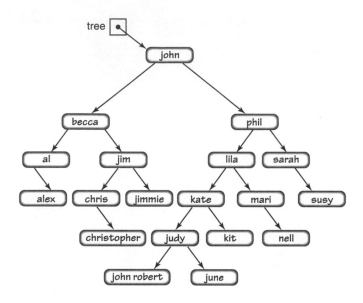

Chapter 10 Exercises

1. Distinguish between application software and system software.

Systems software are tools to help others write programs; they manage a computer system and interact with hardware. Application software are programs to solve specific problems.

4. Explain the term *multiprogramming*.

Multiprogramming is the technique of keeping multiple programs in main memory at the same time, each competing for time on the CPU.

7. Describe the evolution of the concept of batch processing from the human operator in the 1960s and '70s to the operating systems of today.

Originally, the instructions regarding the system software needed for a program were given to the human operator. Today, the instructions are given directly to the computer through OS commands that are part of the file containing the program. Today, batch processing has come to mean a system in which programs and system resources are coordinated and executed without interaction between the user and the program.

10. Why do we say that users in a timesharing system have their own virtual machine?

Users have the illusion of having the computer all to themselves.

11. In Chapter 7, we defined a virtual machine as a hypothetical machine designed to illustrate important features of a real machine. In this chapter, we define a virtual machine as the illusion created by a time-sharing system that each user has a dedicated machine. Relate these two definitions.

   The illusion created in a timesharing situation is that the user owns a single hypothetical machine. The hypothetical machine illustrates the important features of the single machine the user needs.

14. What is *response time*?

   Response time is how long it takes to get an answer. The expression comes from the delay between receiving a stimulus (asking a question) and producing a response (answering the question).

17. Distinguish between logical addresses and physical addresses.

   A physical address is an actual address in the computer's main memory device. A logical address is an address relative to the program. A logical address is sometimes called a relative address, for obvious reasons.

21. Distinguish between fixed (static) partitions and dynamic partitions.

   In a fixed-partition scheme, the number of partitions and their sizes are determined when the operating system boots. In a dynamic parti tion scheme, partitions and their sizes are created as needed.

24. If, in a single, contiguous memory-management system, the program is loaded at address 30215, compute the physical addresses (in decimal) that correspond to the following logical addresses:
   a. 9223
      39438
   b. 2302
      32517
   c. 7044
      37259

25. If, in a fixed-partition memory-management system, the current value of the base register is 42993 and the current value of the bounds register is 2031, compute the physical addresses that correspond to the following logical addresses:
   a. 104
      43097
   b. 1755
      44748
   c. 3041
      Address out of bounds of partition.

Exercises 27 and 28 use the following state of memory.

Operating System
Process 1
Empty 60 blocks
Process 2
Process 3
Empty 52 blocks
Empty 100 blocks

27. If the partitions are fixed and a new job arrives requiring 52 blocks of main memory, show memory after using each of the following partition-selection approaches:

a. first fit

Operating System
Process 1
New Process
Process 2
Process 3
Empty 52 blocks
Empty 100 blocks

b. best fit

Operating System
Process 1
Empty 60 blocks
Process 2
Process 3
New Process
Empty 100 blocks

c. worst fit

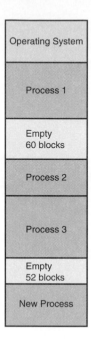

29. Why shouldn't we use worst-fit partition selection in a fixed-partition memory-management scheme?

The worst-fit algorithm selects the largest partition and would thus waste the most space in a fixed-partition scheme.

32. If, in a paged memory-management system, the frame size is 1024 and the following page-map table applies to the currently executing process, compute the physical addresses that correspond to the following logical addresses:

Page	0	1	2	3	4
Frame	7	12	99	1	4

a. <1, 501>
12789

b. <0, 85>
7253

c. <3, 1048>
Illegal address. 1048 is larger than the frame size.

d. <4, 419>
4515

e. <2, 311>
101687

35. Describe how a process might move through the various process states. Create specific reasons why this process moves from one state to another.

A new process begins in the new state. When the process has no bars to its execution, it moves into the ready state. It waits in the ready state until it gets time in the running state. It runs for a while and issues a command for file input. The process is moved into the waiting state until the I/O has been completed, at which time it moves into the ready state to await another turn in the running state. Eventually it gets back to the CPU and runs until it needs access to a part of the program that is on secondary storage. It moves into the waiting state until the needed pages are brought in; then it moves back to the ready state. It gets its third shot at the CPU and finishes, and then moves into the terminated state.

40. Name and describe three CPU scheduling algorithms.

First-come, first-served: The processes are moved into the running state in the order in which they arrive in the ready state.

Shortest job next: When the CPU is ready for anther job, the process in the ready state that takes the shortest time is moved into the running state. The estimated length of time that a process needs the CPU may or may not be accurate.

Round robin: Each process stays in the running state for a predetermined amount of time, called a time slice. When a process's time slice is over, it is moved back into the ready state, where it stays until it is its turn again for the CPU.

Use the following table of processes and service time for Exercises 41 through 43.

Process	P1	P2	P3	P4	P5
Service time	120	60	180	50	300

41. Draw a Gantt chart that shows the completion times for each process using first-come, first-served CPU scheduling.

```
0          120   180           360  410                    710
┌─────────┬─────┬─────────────┬────┬──────────────────────┐
│   p1    │ p2  │     p3      │ p4 │         p5           │
└─────────┴─────┴─────────────┴────┴──────────────────────┘
```

Chapter 11 Exercises

1. What is a file?

A file is the smallest amount of information that can be written to secondary memory. It is a named collection of data, used for organizing secondary memory.

2. Distinguish between a file and a directory.

A file is a named collection of data. A directory is a named collection of files.

6. Why is the term binary file a misnomer?

All files ultimately are just a collection of bits, so why call one file type "binary?" In a binary file, the bits are not interpreted as text. A binary file would just be a stream of uninterpreted bits unless there is an interpretation provided. If a binary file is printed without interpretation, it looks like garbage.

7. Distinguish between a file type and a file extension.

A file type is a description of the information contained in the file. A file extension is a part of the file name that follows a dot and identifies the file type.

11. What does it mean to open and close a file?

Operating systems keep a table of currently open files. The open operation enters the file into this table and places the file pointer at the beginning of the file. The close operation removes the file from the table of open files.

14. File access is independent of any physical medium.
   a. How could you implement sequential access on a disk?
      Sequential access always accesses the next record. You implement sequential access on a disk by not giving the user an access command that takes a record address as a parameter.
   b. How could you implement direct access on a magnetic tape?
      Each record on a magnetic tape is numbered conceptually from the first to the last. Keep a counter of which record was read last. When a user gives an access command to read a specific record, if the record number is beyond the last record read, then records are read and skipped until the correct record is found. If the record number comes before the last record read, the tape is rewound and records are read and skipped until the correct record is found.

17. Given the following file permission, answer these questions.

	Read	Write/Delete	Execute
Owner	Yes	Yes	Yes
Group	Yes	Yes	No
World	Yes	No	No

   a. Who can read the file?
      Anyone can read the file.
   b. Who can write or delete the file?
      The owner and members of the group can write or delete the file.
   c. Who can execute the file?
      Only the owner can execute the file.
   d. What do you know about the content of the file?
      Because the owner has permission to execute the file, it must contain an executable program.

21. What is the directory called in which you are working at any one moment?

   working directory

24. Show the absolute path to each of the following files or directories using the directory tree shown in Figure 11.4:
   a. QTEffects.qtx
      C:\WINDOWS\System\QuickTime\QTEffects.qtx
   b. brooks.mp3
      C:\My Documents\downloads\brooks.mp3
   c. Program Files
      C:\Program Files

d. `3dMaze.scr`
   C:\WINDOWS\System\3dMaze.scr

e. `Powerpnt.exe`
   C:\Program Files\MS Office\Powerpnt.exe

27. Show the relative path to each of the following files or directories using the directory tree shown in Figure 11.5.

a. `localtime` when the working directory is the root directory
   /etc/localtime

b. `localtime` when the working directory is `etc`
   localtime

c. `printall` when the working directory is `utilities`
   printall

d. `week1.txt` when the working directory is `man2`
   ../reports/week1.txt

30. Name and describe three disk-scheduling algorithms.

First-come, first-serve (FCSC): The requests are handled in the order in which they are generated.

Shortest seek time first (SSTF): The request closest to the read/write heads is handled next.

SCAN: The read/write heads move back and forth, handling the closest in the direction in which they are moving.

Use the following list of cylinder requests in Exercises 31 through 33. They are listed in the order in which they were received.

40, 12, 22, 66, 67, 33, 80

31. List the order in which these requests are handled if the FCFS algorithm is used. Assume that the disk is positioned at cylinder 50.

40, 12, 22, 66, 67, 33, 80

34. Explain the concept of starvation.

In the SSTF algorithm, it is possible for some requests never to be serviced because requests closer to the read/write heads keep being issued.

Chapter 12 Exercises

3. What can be contained in a cell of a spreadsheet?

A cell in a spreadsheet can contain data or a formula.

4. How do we refer to a particular cell of a spreadsheet?

A cell is referred to by its row and column designation. The columns are usually letters and the rows are usually numbered.

7. Explain the data in column E and in row 7 of the tutor spreadsheet example of Figure 12.2.

   E7 contains the number of students that Frank tutored in week 7.

8. What is a spreadsheet formula?

   A spreadsheet formula is a formula that we can create and store in a cell. The result of the formula is displayed in the cell.

11. What values in the tutor spreadsheet example of Figure 12.2 would change if you modified the data that reflected the number of students that Hal helped in week 4?

    C9, C10, F7,G7, F9, G9, F10, and G10 would change, in addition to C7 where the number of students Hal helped is recorded.

14. List three different formulas that would compute the correct value for the cell F9 in the tutor example of Figure 12.2.

    =SUM(F4..F8)

    =SUM(C9..E9)

    =SUM(C4..E8)

15. The formula for cell D10 in the tutor example of Figure 12.2 could be given as

    =SUM(D4..D8)/5

    Name two reasons why this formula is not a good solution. What is the better solution?

    SUM(D4..D8) already exists in D9. There is no reason to recalculate it. It is bad practice to use a constant in a formula. The 5 should be replaced with COUNT(D4..D8).

    =D9/COUNT(D4..D8) is a better formula.

18. Give a specific example of an indirect circular reference similar to the one shown in Figure 12.5.

    B1 = SUM(A1..A5) * C2

    C2 = SUM(B5..B12)

    B8 = G1 – D2

    D2 = G3 * B1

    B1 depends on C2; C2 depends on B8; B8 depends on D2; and D2 depends on B1.

For Questions 21 through 24, use a paper spreadsheet form or use an actual spreadsheet application program to design the spreadsheets. Your instructor may provide more specific instructions regarding these questions.

These are activities for which there are no specific answers.

25. Compare a database to a database management system.

A database is a structured set of data. A database management system is a software system made up of the database, a database engine (for manipulating the database), and a database schema that provides the logical view of the database.

26. What is a database schema?

A database schema is the specification of the logical structure of a database.

29. What other fields (attributes) might we include in the database table of Figure 12.7?

There are four fields in the table in Figure 12.7 that describe a movie: MovieID, Title, Genre, and Rating. Additional items might be Director, MaleLead, FemaleLead, Producer, and Date.

33. How are relationships represented in a relational database?

In a table, of course! A table is created that represents the relationship. Usually, the keys of both items in the relationships are represented as fields in the relationship table, along with appropriate information about the relationship.

37. Define an SQL statement that inserts the movie *Armageddon* into the `Movie` table.

```
insert into Movie values(1433, "Armageddon", "action"
"sci-fi", 'R')
```

40. What is an ER diagram?

An ER diagram is a graphical representation of an Entity-relationship model, which is a technique for designing relational databases.

45. Design a database that stores data about the books in a library, the students who use them, and the ability to check out books for a period of time. Create an ER diagram and sample tables.

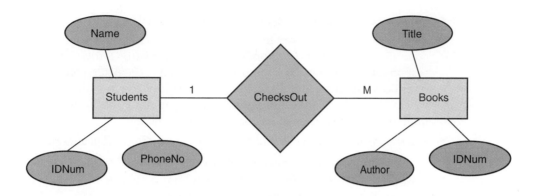

Students

IdNum	Name	PhoneNo
223456789	Sally Silent	232-4432
432543654	Lottie Loud	343-3321
898978675	Maud Middle	454-3452

Books

IdNum	Author	Title
443233	Brown	Fly Fishing in the Sahara
567622	Smith	Dust Storms in the Amazon Basin
657687	Anderson	Skating on Thin Ice

Chapter 13 Exercises

1. Name three things that a computer can do well that a human cannot.

   Perform arithmetic calculations, draw complex three-dimensional images, store and retrieve massive amounts of information (data)

4. How is the Turing test organized and administered?

A human interrogator sits in a room and uses a computer terminal to communicate with two respondents. The interrogator knows that one respondent is human and the other is a computer. After conversing with both the human and the computer, the interrogator must decide which respondent is the computer. If the computer could fool enough interrogators, then it must be considered intelligent.

5. What is weak equivalence and how does it apply to the Turing test?

Weak equivalence is the equality of two systems based on their results. The Turing test shows weak equivalence.

9. Name and define two knowledge representation techniques.

Semantic networks: A technique that represents the relationships among objects.

Search trees: A structure that represents alternatives in adversarial situations such as games.

11. Create a semantic network for the relationships among your family members. List five questions that your semantic net could easily be used to answer and five questions that would be more of a challenge to answer.

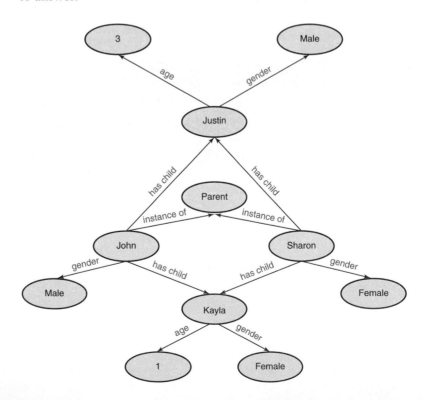

Easy questions to answer given this organization:

Who are John's children?

What is the gender of Kayla?

How old are Sharon's children?

How many female children does John have?

Does Sharon have any children older than 5 years of age?

More challenging questions to answer given this organization:

Who are Kayla's parents?

Who are Justin's siblings?

How many female children are there?

Who is the mother of John's children?

Does John have any stepchildren?

14. What object-oriented properties do semantic networks borrow?

Semantic networks borrow inheritance and instantiation. The inheritance is expressed in the "is-a" relationship, and instantiation is expressed when an object is related to something that describes it.

16. Why are trees for complex games like chess so large?

A search tree contains all possible moves from the first position, all possible moves from each of the moves from the first position, ..., all possible moves from all possible moves at the level above. This is why the trees are very large for complex games like chess.

19. Distinguish between knowledge-based systems and expert systems.

A knowledge-based system is a software system that uses a specific set of information from which it extracts and processes particular pieces. An expert system is sometime used as a synonym, but it also carries with it the idea of modeling the expertise of a professional in that particular field.

22. Define some variables and some rules that might be in an expert system for automobile repair.

ELECTRICAL – the problem is in the electrical system
POWERTRAIN – the problem is in the powertrain system

BATTERY – check battery
STARTER – check starter
TIMING – check timing
LOOSE – check for loose components

TURNOVER – the engine turns over
STARTS – the car starts
LIGHTS – the lights come on
ROUGH – the car runs rough
RATTLE – the car makes inappropriate noise when running

if (not TURNOVER or not STARTS) then ELECTRICAL
if (STARTS) then POWERTRAIN
if (ELECTRICAL and not TURNOVER) then STARTER
if (ELECTRICAL and not LIGHTS) then BATTERY
if (POWERTRAIN and ROUGH) then TIMING
if (POWERTRAIN and RATTLE) then LOOSE

25. What does knowledge representation used in a neural network try to mimic?

The human brain

28. Define a *dendrite* and an *axon*.

A dendrite is an input tentacle to a neuron; there are many per neuron. An axon is the output tentacle from a neuron.

32. If a processing element in an artificial neural net accepted four input signals with values 0, 1, 0, and 1, using weights 5, 2, –2, and 7 and a threshold value of 10, what would its output be?

$(0 * 5 + 1 * 2 + 0 * -2 + 1 * 7 = 9) < 10$, so the output is 0.

34. Explain how a neural net can be trained.

The weights, representing the synapses, are varied and the output is monitored until the neural network produces the correct answers to the required inputs.

37. What is a phoneme?

A phoneme is a fundamental sound in a language.

41. Why are personalized voice-recognition systems so much better than those that are not specific to a particular person?

Generalized systems have to use generic voiceprints, but personalized systems can use voiceprints specific to the user.

42. Name and describe three kinds of ambiguity in natural language.

Lexical ambiguity: Ambiguity created when words have multiple meanings.

Syntactic ambiguity: Ambiguity created when sentences can be constructed in various ways.

Referential ambiguity: Ambiguity created when pronouns can refer to multiple objects.

45. Give and explain an example of referential ambiguity not found in this chapter.

The dog chased the cat up the tree, but it is ok.
What is ok: the dog, the cat, or the tree?

Chapter 14 Exercises

3. What is the essence of constructing a model?

The essence of constructing a model is to identify a small subset of characteristics or features that are sufficient to describe the behavior to be investigated.

4. Name two types of simulations and distinguish between them.

Continuous simulation treats time as continuous and expresses changes in terms of a set of differential equations that reflect the relationships among the set of characteristics. Discrete event simulation is made up of entities, attributes, and events, where entities represent objects in the real system, attributes are characteristics of a particular entity, and events are interactions among entities.

7. What are the keys to constructing a good model?

The keys to constructing a good model are correctly choosing the entities to represent the system and correctly determining the rules that define the results of the events.

8. What defines the interactions among entities in a discrete event simulation?

A set of rules that are part of the model determine the interactions among the events.

11. What are the four necessary pieces of information needed to build a queuing system?

The four necessary pieces of information are

1. the number of events and how they affect the system (to determine the rules of entity interaction)

2. the number of servers (entities)

3. the distribution of arrival times (to determine if an entity enters the system)

4. the expected service time (to determine the duration of an event)

14. Do you think the gas station in Exercise 13 will be in business very long? Explain.

No. The service time is greater than the arrival probability.

15. Rewrite the simulation in Exercise 13 such that a car arrives every two minutes and the service time is two minutes.

If a car arrives, it gets in line. A car arrives if the random number is between 0.0 and 0.5.

If the pump is free and there is a car waiting, the first car in line leaves the line and goes to the pump and the service time is set to 2.

If a car is at the pump, the time remaining for the car is decremented.

If there are cars in line, the additional minute that they have been waiting is recorded.

19. In general, meteorological models are based on the time-dependent equations of what fields?

Meteorological models are based on time-dependent equations from fluid mechanics and thermodynamics.

23. Why do different meteorologists give different forecasts if they are using the same models?

Meteorologists may or may not agree with the predictions from a particular model. Also, various models give conflicting information. Thus, meteorologists must use their judgment as to which, if any, is correct.

24. What are specialized meteorological models and how are they used?

Specialized meteorological models are adaptations for specialized research purposes. A meteorological model may be combined with air-chemistry models to diagnose atmospheric transport and diffusion for a variety of air-quality applications. Specialized meteorological models are useful in the military and aviation industries.

28. What are 3-dimensional CAD models used for?

Three-dimensional CAD models are used for geometric modeling—that is, three-dimensional objects. They can be used for modeling anything from cars to houses.

32. Embedded systems' programmers are the last holdout for assembly-language programming. Explain.

In embedded systems, the size of the code and the speed of execution are very important. Assembly-language programs provide the best opportunity for a programmer to streamline and speed up the code.

Chapter 15 Exercises

1. What is a computer network?

A computer network is a collection of computing devices connected so that they can communicate and share resources.

2. How are computers connected together?

The computers in a network can be physically connected by wires or cables, or logically connected by radio waves or infrared signals.

6. Describe the client/server model and discuss how it has changed how we think about computing.

The client/server is a model in which resources are spread across the Web. The client makes a request for information or an action from a server and the server responds. For example, a file server, a computer dedicated to storing and managing files for network users, responds to requests for files. A Web server, a computer dedicated to responding to requests for Web pages, produces the requested page. Before the client/server model was developed, a user thought of computing within the boundaries of the computer in front of him or her. Now the functions that were provided within one computer are distributed across a network, with separate computers in charge of different functions.

10. What is Ethernet?

    Ethernet is the industry standard for local-area networks. It is a cheap coaxial cable connecting the machines and a set of protocols that allow the machines to communicate with one another.

13. What is the Internet?

    The Internet is a WAN spanning the entire globe. It is a vast collection of smaller networks that all agree to communicate using the same protocols and agree to act as transfer stations for messages.

14. What is a MAN and what makes it different from a LAN and a WAN?

    A MAN is a metropolitan-are a network. It is a network with some of the features of both a LAN and a WAN. Large metropolitan areas have special needs because of the volume of traffic. MANs are collections of smaller networks, but are implemented using such techniques as running optical fiber cable through subway tunnels.

18. What role do ISPs play with the three technologies in Exercise 17?

    Each of the technologies in Exercise 17 requires the connection to go through an ISP. With a phone modem, you dial up a computer that is permanently connected to the Internet. Once the connection is made, you may transfer data. A DSL line maintains an active connection between your home and the ISP. The communication is set up to and from your home using cable that goes through an ISP.

19. What are the advantages and disadvantages of each of the technologies in Exercise 17?

    Phone modems are the cheapest because the phone lines are in place, but transfer speed is very slow because computer data must be converted into an analog audio signal for transfer.

    DSL service uses regular phone lines to transfer digital data and you do not have to dial in, but you must be within a certain distance of special equipment or else the signal degrades.

    Cable modems use service that many people already have, but the signal deteriorates if too many people in the neighborhood have the service.

    Both DSL and cable modems are broadband connections.

22. Messages sent across the Internet are divided into packets. What is a packet and why are messages divided into them?

    A packet is a unit of data sent across a network. It is more efficient to send uniform-sized messages across the Internet.

23. Explain the term *packet switching*.

Packets that make up a message are sent individually over the Internet and may take different routes to their destination. When all the packets arrive at the destination, they are reassembled into the original message.

28. What do we call the ability of software and hardware on multiple platforms from multiple commercial vendors to communicate?

Interoperability

31. What is the seven-layer logical breakdown of network interaction called?

Open Systems Interconnection (OSI) Reference Model

34. What is the role of the IP protocol?

The IP protocol defines the routing of packets through interconnected networks.

39. What is the functionality of the utility program `Traceroute`?

Program `Traceroute` displays the route a packet takes across the Internet.

42. Define *MIME type*.

MIME type is a standard for defining the format of files that are included as e-mail attachments or on Web sites.

43. What is a firewall, what does it accomplish, and how does it accomplish it?

A firewall is a computer system that protects a network from inappropriate access. A firewall filters incoming traffic, checking the validity of incoming messages, and perhaps denying access to messages. For example, a LAN might deny any remote access by refusing all traffic that comes in on port 23 (the port for telnet).

47. Into what parts can an IP address be split?

An IP address can be split into a network address, which specifies the network, and a host number, which specifies a particular machine on the network.

51. What is a top-level domain name?

It is the last part of a domain name that specifies the type of organization or its country of origin.

Chapter 16 Exercises

1. Describe the World Wide Web.

   The World Wide Web is an infrastructure of distributed information and the network software used to access and exchange the information.

2. Why is a spider web a good analogy for the World Wide Web?

   The Internet is the hardware upon which the spider-like connections of the World Wide Web have been created.

6. What is a Uniform Resource Locator?

   A Uniform Resource Locator (URL) is the standard way of specifying the location of a Web page.

7. What is a markup language? Where does the name come from?

   A markup language is one that uses tags to identify the elements in a document and indicates how they should be displayed. The name comes from the idea of taking a document and writing is it (marking up) on the document tags that say how to display it.

10. What is a horizontal rule? What is it useful for?

    Horizontal rules are lines across a page. They are useful for separating sections of a page.

11. Name five formatting specifications that can be established using HTML tags.

    HTML is not case sensitive.

    .. bold

    .. italic

    <hr> horizontal rule

    <ul>..</ul> unordered list

    <ol>..</ol> ordered list

    <li> list item

    <h3>..</h3> number 3 heading

16. Design and implement an HTML document for an organization at your school.

    Activity, no answer expected.

20. Where does a Java applet get executed?

    A Java applet gets executed in the user's browser.

21. What kinds of restrictions are put on Java applets? Why?

Because a Java applet is executed on the user's machine, it must be transmitted from the Web server. Also, the user's computer may not have a resource that the applet needs. Thus, only relatively small programs using very standard resources are appropriate.

25. How does JSP processing differ from applet processing?

Scriptlet processing is done on the server side; applet processing is done on the user's side.

27. What is XML?

XML is a metalanguage that is used to define other markup languages.

30. a. In a DTD, how do you indicate that an element is to be repeated zero or more times?

An element in parentheses with an asterisk following the element indicates zero or more times.

b. In a DTD, how do you indicate that an element is to be repeated one or more times?

An element in parentheses with a plus sign following the element indicates one or more times.

c. In a DTD, how do you indicate that an element cannot be broken down into other tags?

An element followed by (#PCDATA) indicates that the element cannot be broken down further.

33. How does an XML document get viewed?

An XML document is translated by XSL into a form that can be displayed.

35. Define an XML language (the DTD) for political offices and produce a sample XML document.

```
<?xml version="1.0" ?>
<!DOCTYPE government SYSTEM "government.dtd">
<government>
<position>
<title>President of the United States</title>
<type>Federal</type>
<currentHolder>
  <name>George W. Bush</name>
  <party>Republican</party>
```

```
</currentHolder>
<pastHolders>
 <name>William Clinton</name>
 <name>George H. W. Bush</name>
 <name>Ronald Reagan</name>
 <name>James Carter</name>
</pastHolders>
</position>
<position>
<title>Vice President of the United States</title>
<type>Federal</type>
<currentHolder>
 <name>Richard Cheney</name>
 <party>Republican</party>
</currentHolder>
<pastHolders>
 <name>Al Gore</name>
 <name>Dan Quayle</name>
 <name>George H. W. Bush</name>
 <name>Walter Mondale</name>
</pastHolders>
</position>
</government>

<!ELEMENT government (position*) >
<!ELEMENT position (title, type, currentHolder, pastHolders)>
<!ELEMENT title (#PCDATA)>
<!ELEMENT type (#PCDATA)>
<!ELEMENT currentHolder (name, party)>
<!ELEMENT pastHolders (name*)>
<!ELEMENT name (#PCDATA)>
<!ELEMENT party (#PCDATA)>
```

Chapter 17 Exercises

1. Given the following three real values, what is the best order in which to add these values so that you will get the most accurate answer?

   $x = 3214 * 10^4$ $y = 576 * 10^{-1}$ $z = 4421 * 10^3$

   It doesn't matter in this case. The answer to four digits is $3656 * 10^4$ no matter which way the arithmetic is done. However, the actual answer is 36561057.6.

2. Given the following three real values, what is the best order in which to add these values so that you will get the most accurate answer?

   $x = 3214 * 10^1$ $y = 576 * 10^{-1}$ $z = 4421 * 10^0$

   It doesn't matter in this case. The answer to four digits is $3662 * 10^1$ no matter which way the arithmetic is done. However, the actual answer is 36618.6.

5. Show the range of integer numbers that can be represented in each of the following word sizes.
   a. 8-bits
      −128..127
   b. 16 bits
      −32768..31767
   c. 24 bits
      −8388608..8388607
   d. 32 bits
      −2147483648..2147483647
   e. 64 bits
      −9223372036854775808..9223372036854775807

7. a. Show how the numbers 1066 and 1492 would be represented in a linked list with one digit per node.
   b. Use a linked list to represent the sum of these integers.
   c. Outline an algorithm to show how the calculation might be carried out in a computer.

a.

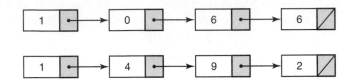

b.

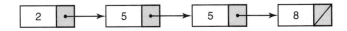

c. To calculate the sum, you must move from right to left in the list rather than left to right. Assume an operation called *previous* that gets the node before current. MOD is an operation that returns the remainder from integer division. DIV is an operation that returns the quotient from integer division.

```
Set currentFirst to last
Set currentSecond to last
Set carry to 0
While (currentFirst <> NULL and currentSecond <> NULL)
    Get a new node
    Set info(new node) to (info(currentFirst) + info(currentSecond) +
    carry) MOD 10
    Set carry to (info(currentFirst) + info(currentSecond) + carry) DIV
    10
    Set currentFirst to previous(currentFirst)
    Set currentSecond to previous(currentSecond)
    Put new node into result
While (currentFirst <> NULL)
// Copy rest of first list if it is not empty
    Get a new node
    Set (info(new node) to info(currentFirst) + carry) MOD 10
    Set carry to (info(currentFirst) + carry) DIV 10
    Set currentFirst to previous(currentFirst)
    Put new node into result
```

```
While (currentSecond <> NULL)
//Copy rest of second lit if it is not empty
    Get a new node
    Set (info(new node) to info(currentSecond) + carry) MOD 10
    Set carry to (info(currentSecond) + carry) DIV 10
    Set currentSecond to previous(currentSecond)
    Put new node into result
```

11. Given the following 8-bit code, what is the parity bit if even parity is being used?
    a. 11100010
       0
    b. 10101010
       0
    c. 11111111
       0
    d. 00000000
       0
    e. 11101111
       1

13. What errors would be detected using the check bits in Exercise 12?

    This technique recognizes when one digit of a number is corrupted.

14. Given the following numbers, what would be the additional digits if the unit's digit of the sum of the even digits is used along with the check digit?

    Counting is from left to right.
    a. 1066
       6
    b. 1498
       2
    c. 1668
       4
    d. 2001
       1
    e. 4040
       0

17. Explain the concept of the software life cycle.

The software life cycle is the concept that software is developed, not just coded, and evolves over its lifetime from requirements to maintenance.

20. Compare and contrast the software verification activities code or design walk-throughs and inspections.

A walk-through is an activity in which a team performs a manual simulation of the program or design. An inspection is an activity in which one member of a team reads the program or design line by line and the others point out errors. Both are group activities, but an inspection is lead by one person.

24. What is formal verification?

Formal verification is the verification of program correctness independent of testing. The goal is to develop a method for proving programs that is analogous to the method of proving theorems in geometry.

29. Give the common name for the following complexity measures and an example of an algorithm that falls into this category.
  a. $O(1)$
    Bounded (constant time): Assigning a value to an atomic variable.
  b. $O(N)$
    Linear time: Accessing all the times in a list.
  c. $O(NlogN)$
    NlogN time: Finding a value in a sorted list using a binary search.
  d. $O(N^2)$
    Quadratic time: Sorting a list using the selection sort or the bubble sort algorithm.
  e. $O(2^N)$
    Exponential time: An algorithm that doubles each time like the corn on the chessboard.
  f. $O(N!)$
    Factorial time: The traveling salesperson graph algorithm.

30. Explain the analogy of bins of complexity measures.

We can think of a bin representing one of the Big-O complexity measures. The bin contains all of the algorithms that have that complexity measure, but within the bin the algorithms can be ordered by the discarded terms.

Glossary

Absolute path   A path that begins at the root and includes all successive subdirectories

Abstract data type   A class of data objects with a defined set of properties and a set of operations that process the data objects while maintaining the properties; also called ADT

Abstract step   An algorithmic step for which some details remain unspecified

Abstraction   A mental model that removes complex details; a model of a complex system that includes only the details essential to the viewer; the separation of the logical properties of data or actions from their implementation details; the separation of the logical properties of an object from its implementation; (in OOD) the essential characteristics of an object from the viewpoint of the user

Access control policy   A set of rules established by an organization that specify what types of network communication are permitted and denied

Access time   The time it takes for a block to start being read; the sum of seek time and latency

Adder   An electronic circuit that performs an addition operation on binary values

Addressability   The number of bits stored in each addressable location in memory

Address binding   The mapping from a logical address to a physical address

Aggregate operation   An operation on a data structure as a whole, as opposed to an operation on an individual component of the data structure

Algorithm   Unambiguous instructions for solving a problem or subproblem in a finite amount of time using a finite amount of data

Allocate   To assign memory space at run time for use by an object

ALU   See *arithmetic/logic unit*

Analog data   Information represented in a continuous form

Application software   Programs that help us solve real-world problems

Arguments   The identifiers listed in parentheses on the subprogram call; sometimes called *actual parameters*

Arithmetic/logic unit   The computer component that performs arithmetic operations (addition, subtraction, multiplication, division) and logical operations (comparison of two values)

Array   A collection of components, all of the same type, ordered on n dimensions ($n >= 1$); each component is accessed by n indices, each of which represents the component's position within that dimension

Artificial intelligence (AI)   The study of computer systems that model and apply the intelligence of the human mind

Artificial neural network   A computer representation of knowledge that attempts to mimic the neural networks of the human body

Assembler   A program that translates an assembly-language program into machine code

Assembly language   A low-level programming language in which a mnemonic represents each of the machine-language instructions for a particular computer

Assertion   A logical proposition that is either true or false

Assignment statement   A statement that stores the value of an expression into a variable

Asynchronous   Not occurring at the same moment as some specific operation of the computer; in other words, not synchronized with the program's actions

Atomic data type   A data type that allows only a single value to be associated with an identifier of that type

Attribute   Part of a tag that provides additional information about the element

Auxiliary storage device   A device that stores data in encoded form outside the computer's memory

Bandwidth   The number of bits or bytes that can be transmitted from one place to another in a fixed amount of time

Base   The foundational value of a number system, which dictates the number of digits and the value of digit positions

Base address   The memory address of the first element of an array

Base case   The case in a recursive solution for which the solution can be stated nonrecursively

Base class   The class being inherited from

Base register   A register that holds the beginning address of the current partition

Big-O notation   A notation that expresses computing time (complexity) as the term in a function that increases most rapidly relative to the size of a problem

Binary digit   A digit in the binary number system; a 0 or a 1

Binary file   A file that contains data in a specific format, requiring a special interpretation of its bits

Binary operator   An operator that has two operands

Binary search   A search algorithm for sorted lists that involves dividing the list in half and determining, by value comparison, whether the item would be in the upper or lower half; the process is performed repeatedly until either the item is found or it is determined that the item is not on the list

Bit   Short for binary digit

Block   A group of zero or more statements enclosed in braces; the information stored in a sector on a disk

Body   The statement(s) to be repeated within the loop; the executable statement(s) within a subprogram

Boolean algebra   A mathematical notation for expressing two-value logical functions

Boolean expression   A sequence of identifiers, separated by compatible operators, that evaluates to true or false

Boolean operators   Operators applied to values of the type Boolean

Boolean type   A data type consisting of only two values: true and false

Booting the system   The process of starting up a computer by loading the operating system into its main memory

Bounds register   A register that holds the length of the current partition

Brainstorming   The beginning phase of an object-oriented design in which possible classes of objects in the problem are identified

Branch   A code segment that is not always executed; for example, a switch or case statement has as many branches as there are case labels

Branching control structure   See *selection control structure*

Breadth-first approach   Searching across levels of a tree prior to searching down specific paths

Broadband   Network technologies that generally provide data transfer speeds greater than 128 bps

Bus   A set of wires that connect all major sections of a machine through which data flows

Bus topology   A LAN configuration in which all nodes share a common line

Byte   Eight binary digits

Bytecode   A standard machine language into which Java source code is compiled

Cable modem   A device that allows computer network communication using the cable TV hookup in a home

Call   The point at which the computer begins following the instructions in a subprogram

Cancellation error   A loss of accuracy during addition or subtraction of numbers of widely differing sizes, due to limits of precision

Cardinality constraint   The number of relationships that may exist at one time between entities in an ER diagram

Case sensitive   Uppercase and lowercase letters are not considered the same; two identifiers with the same spelling but different capitalization are considered to be two distinct identifiers

Cell   An element of a spreadsheet that can contain data or a formula

Character set   A list of the characters and the codes used to represent each one

Circuit   A combination of interacting gates designed to accomplish a specific logical function

Circuit equivalence   The same output for each corresponding input-value combination for two circuits

Circular reference   A set of formulas that ultimately, and erroneously, rely on each other to compute their results

Class (general sense)   A description of the behavior of a group of objects with similar properties and behaviors; (implementation phase) a pattern for an object

Class NP problems   Problems that can be solved in polynomial time with as many processors as desired

Class P   The class made up of all polynomial-time algorithms

Class P problems   Problems that can be solved with one processor in polynomial time

Client   Software that declares and manipulates objects of a particular class

Client/server model   A distributed approach in which a client makes requests of a server and the server responds

Code   Data type specifications and instructions for a computer that are written in a programming language

Code walk-through   A verification process for a program in which each statement is examined to check that it faithfully implements the corresponding algorithmic step

Code-coverage (clear-box) testing   Testing a program or subprogram based on covering all the statements in the code

Coding   Translating an algorithm into a programming language; the process of assigning bit patterns to pieces of information

Collating sequence   The ordering of the elements of a set or series, such as the characters (values) in a character set

Combinational circuit   A circuit whose output is solely determined by its input values

Comment   Explanatory text for the human reader

Compiler   A program that translates a high-level language program into machine code

Complexity (of an algorithm)   A measure of the effort expended by the computer in performing a computation, relative to the size of the computation

Composite data type   A data type that allows a collection of values to be associated with an object of that type

Composition (containment)   A mechanism by which an internal data member of one class is defined to be an object of another class type

Compression ratio   The size of the compressed data divided by the size of the uncompressed data

Computer (electronic)   A programmable device that can store, retrieve, and process data

Computer hardware   The physical elements of a computing system

Computer network   A collection of computing devices that are connected so that they can communicate and share resources

Computer program   Data type specifications and instructions for carrying out operations that are used by a computer to solve a problem

Computer programming   The process of specifying the data types and the operations for a computer to apply to data in order to solve a problem

Computer software   The programs that provide the instructions that a computer executes

Computing system   Computer hardware, software, and data, which interact to solve problems

Concrete step   A step for which the details are fully specified

Conditional test   The point at which the Boolean expression is evaluated and the decision is made to either begin a new iteration or skip to the first statement following the loop

Constant   An item in a program whose value is fixed at compile time and cannot be changed during execution

Constant time   An algorithm whose Big-O work expression is a constant

Constructor   An operation that creates a new instance of a class; a method that has the same name as the class type containing it, which is called whenever an object of that type is instantiated

Container class   A class into which you can add other elements

Containment   A mechanism whereby one class contains an object of another class as a field

Context switch   The exchange of register information that occurs when one process is removed from the CPU and another takes its place

Control abstraction   The separation of the logical view of a control structure from its implementation

Control structure   A statement used to alter the normally sequential flow of control; an instruction that determines the order in which other instructions in a program are executed

Control unit   The computer component that controls the actions of the other components in order to execute instructions in sequence

Count-controlled loop   A loop that executes a predetermined number of times

Counter   A variable whose value is incremented to keep track of the number of times a process or event occurs

CPU   A combination of the arithmetic/logic unit and the control unit; the "brain" of a computer that interprets and executes instructions

CPU scheduling   The act of determining which process in memory is given access to the CPU so that it may execute

Crash   The cessation of a computer's operations as a result of the failure of one of its components; cessation of program execution due to an error

CRC cards   Index cards on which a class name is written along with its super- and sub-classes and a listing of the responsibilities and collaborators or the class; *c*lass, *r*esponsibility, *c*ollaboration

Cursor control keys   A special set of keys on a computer keyboard that allow the user to move the cursor up, down, right, and left to any point on the screen

Cylinder   The set of concentric tracks on all surfaces of a disk

Data   Information in a form that a computer can use

Data abstraction   The separation of the logical view of data from its implementation

Data compression   Reducing the amount of space needed to store a piece of data

Data encapsulation   The separation of the representation of data from the applications that use the data at a logical level; a programming language feature that enforces information hiding

Data representation   The concrete form of data used to represent the abstract values of an abstract data type

Data structure   A collection of data elements whose organization is characterized by accessing operations that are used to store and retrieve the individual data elements; the implementation of the composite data members in an abstract data type; the implementation of a composite data field in an abstract data type

Data transfer rate (also **Bandwidth**)   The speed with which data is moved from one place to another on a network

Data type   A description of the set of values and the basic set of operations that can be applied to values of the type

Data validation   A test added to a program or a function that checks for errors in the data

Database management system   A combination of software and data made up of the physical database, the database engine, and the database schema

Database   A structured set of data

Data-coverage (black-box) testing   Testing a program or subprogram based on the possible input values, treating the code as a black box

Deallocate   To return the storage space for an object to the pool of free memory so that it can be reallocated to new objects

Debugging   The process by which errors are removed from a program so that it does exactly what it is supposed to do

Declaration   A statement that associates an identifier with a variable, an action, or some other entity within the language that can be given a name so that the programmer can refer to that item by name

Deep copy   An operation that not only copies one class object to another but also makes copies of any pointed-to data

Demand paging   An extension to paged memory management in which pages are brought into memory only when referenced (on demand)

Demotion (narrowing)   The conversion of a value from a "higher" type to a "lower" type according to a programming language's precedence of data types; demotion may cause loss of information

Depth-first approach   Searching down the paths of a tree prior to searching across levels

Derived class   The class that inherits; a class that is created as an extension of another class in the hierarchy

Desk checking   Tracing the execution of a design on paper

Development environment   A single package containing all of the software required for developing a program

Dialog   A style of user interface in which the user enters data and then performs a separate action (such as clicking a button) when the entered values are ready to be processed by the program

Digital data   Information represented in a discrete form

Digital subscriber line (DSL)   An Internet connection made using a digital signal on regular phone lines

Digitize   The act of breaking down information into discrete pieces

Direct file access   The technique in which data in a file is accessed directly, by specifying logical record numbers

Directory   A named group of files

Directory tree   A structure showing the nested directory organization of the file system

Disk scheduling   The act of deciding which outstanding requests for disk I/O to satisfy first

Documentation   The written text and comments that make a program easier for others to understand, use, and modify

Document Type Definition (or DTD)   A specification of the organization of an XML document

Domain name   The part of a hostname that specifies a specific organization or group

Domain name server   A computer that attempts to translate a hostname into an IP address

Domain name system   A distributed system for managing hostname resolution

Down   A descriptive term applied to a computer when it is not in a usable condition

Download   Receiving data on your home computer from the Internet

Driver   A simple dummy main program that is used to call a function being tested; a main function in an object-oriented program

Dumb terminal   A monitor and keyboard that allow the user to access the mainframe computer in early timesharing systems

Dynamic allocation   Allocation of memory space for a variable at run time (as opposed to static allocation at compile time)

Dynamic binding   Determining at run time which form of a polymorphic method to call

Dynamic memory management   The allocation and deallocation of storage space as needed while an application is executing

Dynamic-partition technique   The memory management technique in which memory is divided into partitions as needed to accommodate programs

Echo printing   Printing the data values input to a program to verify that they are correct

Editor   An interactive program used to create and modify source programs or data

Effective weight   In an artificial neuron, the sum of the weights multiplied by the corresponding input values

Encapsulation   A language feature that enforces information hiding; bundling data and actions so that the logical properties of data and actions are separated from the implementation details

Entity-relationship (ER) modeling   A popular technique for designing relational databases

ER diagram   A graphical representation of an ER model

Ethernet   The industry standard for local-area networks, based on a bus topology

Evaluate   To compute a new value by performing a specified set of operations on given values

Event   An action, such as a mouse click, that takes place asynchronously with respect to the execution of the program

Event counter   A variable that is incremented each time a particular event occurs

Event handler   A method that is part of an event listener and is invoked when the listener receives a corresponding event

Event handling   The process of responding to events that can occur at any time during execution of the program

Event listener   An object that is waiting for one or more events to occur

Event-controlled loop   A loop that terminates when something happens inside the loop body to signal that the loop should be exited

Exception   An unusual situation that is detected while a program is running; throwing an exception halts the normal execution of the method

Exception handler   A section of a program that is executed when an exception occurs in Java or C++

Executing   The action of a computer performing as instructed by a given program

Execution trace   Going through the program with actual values recording the state of the variables

Expert system   A software system based on the knowledge of human experts

Expression   An arrangement of identifiers, literals, and operators that can be evaluated to compute a value of a given type

Expression statement   A statement formed by appending a semicolon to an expression

Extensible Markup Language (or XML)   A language that allows the user to describe the content of a document

Extensible Stylesheet Language (or XSL)   A language for defining transformations from XML documents to other output formats

External file   A file that is used to communicate with people or programs and is stored externally to the program

External pointer   A named pointer variable that references the first node in a linked list

External representation   The printable (character) form of a data value

Fetch-execute cycle   The sequence of steps performed by the central processing unit for each machine-language instruction

Fields   Named items in a class; can be data or subprograms

File   A named collection of data, used for organizing secondary memory

File extension Part of a file name that indicates the file type

File server A computer dedicated to storing and managing files for network users

File System The operating system's logical view of the files it manages

File type The specific kind of information contained in a file, such as a Java program or a Microsoft Word document

Filtering The phase in an object-oriented design in which the proposed classes of objects from the brainstorming phase are refined and overlooked ones are added

Finite state machine An idealized model of a simple computer consisting of a set of states, the rules that specify when states are changed, and a set of actions that are performed when changing states

Firewall A gateway machine and its software that protects a network by filtering the traffic it allows

Firing an event An event source generates an event

Fixed-partition technique The memory management technique in which memory is divided into a specific number of partitions into which programs are loaded

Flag A Boolean variable that is set in one part of the program and tested in another to control the logical flow of a program

Floating point A representation of a real number that keeps track of the sign, mantissa, and exponent

Flow of control The order of execution of the statements in a program

Formatting The planned positioning of statements or declarations and blanks on a line of a program; the arranging of program output so that it is neatly spaced and aligned

Frame A fixed-size portion of main memory that holds a process page

Full adder A circuit that computes the sum of two bits, taking an input carry bit into account

Functional cohesion A property of a module in which all concrete steps are directed toward solving just one problem, and any significant subproblems are written as abstract steps

Functional decomposition A technique for developing software in which the problem is divided into more easily handled subproblems, the solutions of which create a solution to the overall problem; similar to top-down design.

Functional equivalence A property of a module that performs exactly the same operation as the abstract step it defines, or when one module performs exactly the same operation as another module

Functional modules In top-down design, the structured tasks and subtasks that are solved individually to create an effective program

Functional problem description A description that clearly states what a program is to do

Gate A device that performs a basic operation on electrical signals, accepting one or more input signals and producing a single output signal

Gateway A node that handles communication between its LAN and other networks

General (recursive) case The case in a recursive solution for which the solution is expressed in terms of a smaller version of itself

Half adder A circuit that computes the sum of two bits and produces the appropriate carry bit

Halting problem The unsolvable problem of determining if any program will eventually stop given particular input

Hardware The physical components of a computer

Heuristics Assorted problem-solving strategies

Hierarchy Structuring of abstractions in which a descendant object inherits the characteristics of its ancestors

High-level programming language Any programming language in which a single statement translates into one or more machine-language instructions

Homogeneous A descriptive term applied to structures in which all components are of the same data type (such as an array)

Host number The part of an IP address that specifies a particular host on the network

Hostname A name made up of words separated by dots that uniquely identifies a computer on the Internet; each hostname corresponds to a particular IP address

Huffman encoding Using a variable-length binary string to represent a character so that frequently used characters have short codes

Hypertext Markup Language (or **HTML**) The language used to create or build a Web page

Identifier A name associated with a package, class, method, or field and used to refer to them

Implementation phase The second set of steps in programming a computer: translating (coding) the algorithm into a programming language; testing the resulting program by running it on a computer, checking for accuracy, and making any necessary corrections; using the program

Implementing   Coding and testing an algorithm

Implementing a test plan   Running the program with the test cases listed in the test plan

Index   A value that selects a component of an array

Inference engine   The software that processes rules to draw conclusions

Infinite loop   A loop whose termination condition is never reached and therefore is never exited without intervention from outside of the program

Infinite recursion   The situation in which a subprogram calls itself over and over continuously because a base case is never reached

Information   Any knowledge that can be communicated

Information hiding   The practice of hiding the details of a module with the goal of controlling access to the details of the module

Information system   Software that helps the user organize and analyze data

Inheritance   A mechanism by which one class acquires the properties— data fields and methods—of another class; a design technique used with a hierarchy of classes by which each descendant class inherits the properties (data and operations) of its ancestor class; a mechanism that enables us to define a new class by adapting the definition of an existing class

Input   The process of placing values from an outside data set into variables in a program; the data may come from either an input device (keyboard) or an auxiliary storage device (disk or tape)

Input prompts   Messages printed by an interactive program, explaining what data is to be entered

Input unit   A device that accepts data to be stored in memory

Input/output (i/o) devices   The parts of a computer that accept data to be processed (input) and present the results of that processing (output)

Inspection   A verification method in which one member of a team reads the program or design line by line and the others point out errors

Instantiate   To create an object from a class

Integer   A natural number, a negative of a natural number, or zero

Integrated circuit (also **chip**)   A piece of silicon on which multiple gates have been embedded

Interactive system   A system that allows direct communication between the user and the computer

Internet   A wide-area network that spans the planet

Internet backbone   A set of high-speed networks carrying Internet traffic

Internet Protocol (IP)   The network protocol that deals with the routing of packets through interconnected networks to the final destination

Internet service provider (ISP)   A company providing access to the Internet

Interoperability   The ability of software and hardware on multiple machines and from multiple commercial vendors to communicate

Interpreter   A program that inputs a program in a high-level language and directs the computer to perform the actions specified in each statement

Invoke   To call on a subprogram, causing the subprogram to execute before control is returned to the statement following the call

IP address   An address made up of four numeric values separated by dots that uniquely identifies a computer on the Internet

Iteration   An individual pass through, or repetition of, the body of a loop

Iteration counter   A counter variable that is incremented with each iteration of a loop

Java applet   A Java program designed to be embedded into an HTML document, transferred over the Web, and executed in a browser

JSP scriptlet   A portion of code embedded in an HTML document designed to dynamically contribute to the content of the Web page

Key   One or more fields of a database record that uniquely identifies it among all other records in the table

Keyword encoding   Substituting a frequently used word with a single character

Knowledge-based system   Software that uses a specific set of information

Latency   The time it takes for the specified sector to be in position under the read/write head

Length   The number of items in a list; the length can vary over time

Lexical ambiguity   The ambiguity created when words have multiple meanings

Lifetime   For a variable, constant, or object, the portion of an application's execution time during which it is assigned storage space in the computer's memory

Linear relationship   Each element except the first has a unique predecessor, and each element except the last has a unique successor

Linear time   For an algorithm, when the Big-O work expression can be expressed in terms of a constant times n, where n is the number of values in a data set

Link   A connection between one Web page and another

Linked list   A list in which the order of the components is determined by an explicit link field in each node, rather than by the sequential order of the components in memory

Literal value   Any constant value written in a program

Loader   A piece of software that takes a machine-language program and places it into memory

Local-area network (LAN)   A network connecting a small number of nodes in a close geographic area

Loebner prize   The first formal instantiation of the Turing test, held annually

Logarithmic order   Algorithm complexity in which the Big-O work expression can be expressed in terms of the logarithm of n, where n is the number of values in a data set

Logging off   Informing a computer—usually through a simple command—that no further commands follow

Logging on   Taking the preliminary steps necessary to identify yourself to a computer so that it accepts your commands

Logic diagram   A graphical representation of a circuit; each type of gate has its own symbol

Logical address   A reference to a stored value relative to the program making the reference

Logical order   The order in which the programmer wants the statements in the program to be executed, which may differ from the physical order in which they appear

Loop   A method of structuring statements so that they are repeated while certain conditions are met

Loop entry   The point at which the flow of control first passes to a statement inside a loop

Loop exit   That point when the repetition of the loop body ends and control passes to the first statement following the loop

Loop test   The point at which the loop expression is evaluated and the decision is made either to begin a new iteration or skip to the statement immediately following the loop

Lossless compression   A technique in which there is no loss of information

Lossy compression   A technique in which there is loss of information

Machine language   The language made up of binary-coded instructions that is used directly by the computer

Mainframe   A large, multi-user computer often associated with early time-sharing systems

Maintenance   The modification of a program, after it has been completed, in order to meet changing requirements or to take care of any errors that show up

Maintenance phase   Period during which maintenance occurs

Mantissa   With respect to floating-point representation of real numbers, the digits representing a number itself and not its exponent

Markup language   A language that uses tags to annotate the information in a document

Memory management   The act of keeping track of how and where programs are loaded in main memory

Memory unit   Internal data storage in a computer

Metalanguage   A language that is used to define other languages

Method   A named algorithm that defines one aspect of the behavior of a class

Metropolitan-area network (MAN)   A network infrastructure developed for a large city

MIME type   A standard for defining the format of files that are included as e-mail attachments or on Web sites

Model   An abstraction of a real system; a representation of objects within a system and the rules that govern the behavior of the objects.

Module   A self-contained collection of steps that solves a problem or subproblem

Motherboard   The main circuit board of a personal computer

Multimedia   Several different media types

Multiplexer   A circuit that uses a few input control signals to determine which of several input data lines is routed to its output

Multiprogramming   The technique of keeping multiple programs in main memory at the same time, competing for the CPU

Named constant   A location in memory, referenced by an identifier, that contains a data value that cannot be changed

Natural language   Languages that human beings use to communicate, such as English

Natural language comprehension   Using a computer to apply a meaningful interpretation to human communication

Natural number   The number 0 and any number obtained by repeatedly adding 1 to it

Negative number   A value less than 0, with a sign opposite to its positive counterpart

Nested control structure   A program structure consisting of one control statement (selection, iteration, or subprogram) embedded within another control statement

Network address   The part of an IP address that specifies a specific network

Node (or Host)   Any addressable device attached to a network

Nodes   The building blocks of dynamic structures, each made up of a component (the data) and a pointer (the link) to the next node

Nonpreemptive scheduling   CPU scheduling that occurs when the currently executing process gives up the CPU voluntarily

NP-complete problems   A class of problems within Class NP that has the property that if a polynomial time solution with one processor can be found for any member of the class, such a solution exists for every member of the class

Number   A unit of an abstract mathematical system subject to the laws of arithmetic

Object   A collection of data values and associated operations

Object (problem-solving phase)   An entity or thing that is relevant in the context of a problem

Object class or **Class**   (problem-solving phase) A description of a group of objects with similar properties and behaviors

Object code   A machine-language version of a source code

Object program   The machine-language version of a source program

Object-based programming language   A programming language that supports abstraction and encapsulation, but not inheritance

Object-oriented design   A technique for developing software in which the solution is expressed in terms of objects—self-contained entities composed of data and operations on that data that interact by sending messages to one another

One-dimensional array   A structured collection of components of the same type given a single name; each component is accessed by an index that indicates its position within the collection

Open system   A system that is based on a common model of network architecture and an accompanying suite of protocols

Open Systems Interconnection Reference Model   A seven-layer logical breakdown of network interaction to facilitate communication standards

Operating system   System software that manages computer resources and provides an interface for system interaction

Out-of-bounds array index   An index value that is less than the position of the first element or greater than the position of the last element

Output unit   A device that prints or otherwise displays data stored in memory or makes a permanent copy of information stored in memory or another device

Overflow   The condition that occurs when the results of a calculation are too large to represent in a given machine

Packet   A unit of data sent across a network

Packet switching   The approach to network communication in which packets are individually routed to their destination, then reassembled

Page   A fixed-size portion of a process that is stored into a memory frame

Page map table (PMT)   The table used by the operating system to keep track of page/frame relationships

Page swap   Bringing in one page from secondary memory, possibly causing another to be removed

Paged memory technique   A memory management technique in which processes are divided into fixed-size pages and stored in memory frames when loaded

Parameter   The identifiers listed in parentheses beside the subprogram name; sometimes called *formal parameters*

Parameter list   A mechanism for communicating between two parts of a program

Parameter passing   The transfer of data between the arguments and parameters in a subprogram call

Pass by address   A parameter-passing mechanism in which the memory address of the actual parameter is passed to the formal parameter; also called *pass by reference*

Pass by value   A parameter-passing mechanism in which a copy of an actual parameter's value is passed to the formal parameter

Password   A unique series of letters assigned to a user (and known only by that user) by which that user identifies himself or herself to a computer during the logging-on procedure; a password system protects information stored in a computer from being tampered with or destroyed

Path   A text designation of the location of a file or subdirectory in a file system

Peripheral device   An input, output, or auxiliary storage device attached to a computer

Personal computer (pc)   A small computer system (usually intended to fit on a desktop) that is designed to be used primarily by a single person

Phone modem   A device that converts computer data into an analog audio signal and back again

Phonemes   The set of fundamental sounds made in any given natural language

Physical address   An actual address in the main memory device

Ping   A program used to test if a particular network computer is active and reachable

Pipelining processing   Multiple processors arranged in tandem, where each contributes one part of an overall computation

Pixels   Individual dots used to represent a picture; stands for *picture elements*

Polymorphism   The ability of a language to have duplicate method names in an inheritance hierarchy and to apply the method that is appropriate for the object to which the method is applied

Polynomial-time algorithms   Algorithms whose complexity can be expressed as a polynomial in the size of the problem

Port   A numeric designation corresponding to a particular high-level protocol

Positional notation   A system of expressing numbers in which the digits are arranged in succession, the position of each digit has a place value, and the number is equal to the sum of the products of each digit by its place value

Postfix operator   An operator that follows its operand(s)

Precision   The maximum number of significant digits that can be represented

Preconditions   Assertions that must be true before a module begins execution

Preemptive scheduling   CPU scheduling that occurs when the operating system decides to favor another process, preempting the currently executing process

Prefix operator   An operator that precedes its operand(s)

Problem solving   The act of finding a solution to a perplexing question

Problem-solving phase   The first set of steps in programming a computer: analyzing the problem; developing an algorithm; testing the algorithm for accuracy

Procedural abstraction   The separation of the logical view of an action from its implementation

Process   The dynamic representation of a program during execution

Process control block (PCB)   The data structure used by the operating system to manage information about a process

Process management   The act of keeping track of information for active processes

Process states   The conceptual stages through which a process moves as it is managed by the operating system

Program   A sequence of instructions written to perform a specified task

Program counter (PC)   The register that contains the address of the next instruction to be executed

Programming   Planning, scheduling, or performing a task or an event; see also *computer programming*

Programming language   A set of rules, symbols, and special words used to construct a program—that is, to express a sequence of instructions for a computer

Proprietary system   A system that uses technologies kept private by a particular commercial vendor

Protocol   A set of rules that define how data is formatted and processed on a network

Protocol stack   Layers of protocols that build and rely on each other

Pseudocode   A mixture of English statements and control structures that can easily by translated into a programming language

Pulse-code modulation   Variation in a signal that jumps sharply between two extremes

Query   A request for information submitted to a database

Radix point   The dot that separates the whole part from the fractional part in a real number in any base

Range   A set of contiguous cells specified by the endpoints

Range of values   The interval within which values must fall, specified in terms of the largest and smallest allowable values

Raster-graphics format   Storing image information pixel by pixel

Rational number   An integer or the quotient of two integers (division by zero excluded)

Real number   A number that has a whole and a fractional part and no imaginary part

Real-time system   A system in which response time is crucial given the nature of the application domain

Reclock   The act of reasserting an original digital signal before too much degradation occurs

Record (or **object,** or **entity**)   A collection of related fields that make up a single database entry

Recursion   The ability of a subprogram to call itself

Recursive call   A subprogram call in which the subprogram being called is the same as the one making the call

Recursive case   See *general case*

Recursive definition   A definition in which something is defined in terms of a smaller version of itself

Reference parameter   A parameter that expects the address of its argument to be passed by the calling unit (put on the message board)

Referential ambiguity   The ambiguity created when pronouns could be applied to multiple objects

Refinement   In top-down design, the expansion of a module specification to form a new module that solves a major step in the computer solution of a problem

Register   A small storage area in the CPU used to store intermediate values or special data

Relational model   A database model in which data and the relationships among them are organized into tables

Relational operators   Operators that state that a relationship exists between two values

Relative path   A path that begins at the current working directory

Repeater   A network device that strengthens and propagates a signal along a long communication line

Representational (round-off) error   An arithmetic error caused by the fact that the precision of the result of an arithmetic operation is greater than the precision of our machine

Reserved word   A word in a language that has special meaning; it cannot be used as an identifier

Resolution   The number of pixels used to represent a picture

Response time   The time delay between receiving a stimulus and producing a response

Responsibility algorithms   The algorithms for the class methods in an object-oriented design; the phase in the design process where the algorithms are developed

Return   The point at which the computer comes back from executing a subprogram

Reuse   The ability to use a class in any program without additional modification to either the class or the program

Right-justified   Placed as far to the right as possible within a fixed number of character positions

Ring topology   A LAN configuration in which all nodes are connected in a closed loop

Robust   A descriptive term for a program that can recover from erroneous inputs and keep running

Root directory   The topmost directory, in which all others are contained

Router   A network device that directs a packet between networks toward its final destination

Rule-based system   A software system based on a set of *if-then* rules

Run-length encoding   Replacing a long series of a repeated characters with a count of the repetition

Scenarios   The phase in an object-oriented design in which responsibilities are assigned to the classes

Schema   A specification of the logical structure of data in a database

Scientific notation   An alternative floating-point representation

Scope of access (scope)   The region of program code where it is legal to reference (use) an identifier

Scope rules   The rules that determine where in a program an identifier may be referenced, given the point where the identifier is declared and its specific access modifiers

Search tree   A structure that represents alternatives in adversarial situations, such as game playing

Secondary storage device   See *auxiliary storage device*

Sector   A section of a track

Seek time   The time it takes for the read/write head to get positioned over the specified track

Selection control structure   A form of program structure allowing the computer to select one among possible actions to perform based on given circumstances; also called a *branching control structure*

Self-documenting code   A program containing meaningful identifiers as well as judiciously used clarifying comments

Semantic network   A knowledge representation technique that represents the relationships among objects

Semantics   The set of rules that gives the meaning of instructions in a language

Semiconductor   Material such as silicon that is neither a good conductor nor insulator

Sentinel   A special data value used in certain event-controlled loops as a signal that the loop should be exited

Sequence   A structure in which statements are executed one after another

Sequential circuit   A circuit whose output is a function of input values and the current state of the circuit

Sequential file access   The technique in which data in a file is accessed in a linear fashion

Shallow copy   An operation that copies one class object to another without copying any pointed-to data

Shared memory   Multiple processors share a global memory

Short-circuit (conditional) evaluation   Evaluation of a logical expression in left-to-right order with evaluation stopping as soon as the final boolean value can be determined

Significant digits   Those digits that begin with the first nonzero digit on the left and end with the last nonzero digit on the right (or a zero digit that is exact)

Sign-magnitude representation   Number representation in which the sign represents the ordering of the number (negative and positive) and the value represents the magnitude

Simulation   Developing a model of a complex system and experimenting with the model to observe the results

Single contiguous memory management   The approach to memory management in which a program is loaded into one continuous area of memory

Size (of an array)   The physical space reserved for an array

Software   Computer programs; the set of all programs available on a computer

Software engineering   The application of traditional engineering methodologies and techniques to the development of software

Software life cycle   The phases in the life of a large software project, including requirements analysis, specification, design, implementation, testing, and maintenance

Software piracy   The unauthorized copying of software for either personal use or use by others

Software requirements   A statement of what is to be provided by a computer system or software product

Software specification   A detailed description of the function, inputs, processing, outputs, and special features of a software product; provides the information needed to design and implement the software

Sort key   The field to be used in the ordering

Sorted list   A list with predecessor and successor relationships determined by the content of the keys of the items in the list; there is a semantic relationship among the keys of the items in the list

Sorting   Putting a list of items in order, either numerically or alphabetically

Source program   A program written in a high-level programming language

Spatial compression   Movie compression technique based on the same compression techniques used for still images

Spreadsheet   A program that allows the user to organize and analyze data using a grid of cells

Spreadsheet function   A computation provided by the spreadsheet software that can be incorporated into formulas

Stable sort   A sorting algorithm that preserves the order of duplicates

Standardized   Made uniform; most high-level languages are standardized, as official descriptions of them exist

Star topology   A LAN configuration in which a central node controls all message traffic

String (general sense)   A sequence of characters, such as a word, name, or sentence, enclosed in double quotes

Strong equivalence   The equality of two systems based on their results and the process by which they arrive at those results

Strong typing   Each variable is assigned a type, and only values of that type can be stored in the variable

Structured data type   An organized collection of components; the organization determines the method used to access individual components

Structured Query Language (SQL)   A comprehensive relational database language for data management and queries

Style   The individual manner in which computer programmers translate algorithms into a programming language

Supercomputer   The most powerful class of computers

Synchronous processing   Multiple processors apply the same program in lockstep to multiple data sets

Syntactic ambiguity   The ambiguity created when sentences can be constructed in various ways

Syntax   The formal rules governing the construction of valid instructions

System software   Programs that manage a computer system and interact with hardware

Table   A collection of database records

Tag   The syntactic element in a markup language that indicates how information should be displayed

Tail recursion   A recursive algorithm in which no statements are executed after the return from the recursive call

TCP/IP   A suite of protocols and programs that support low-level network communication

Team programming   The use of two or more programmers to design a program that would take one programmer too long to complete

Temporal compression   Movie compression technique based on differences between consecutive frames

Ten's complement   A representation of negative numbers such that the negative of I is 10 raised to k minus I.

Termination condition   The condition that causes a loop to be exited

Test plan   A document that specifies how a program is to be tested

Testing   Checking a program's output by comparing it to hand-calculated results; running a program with data sets designed to discover any errors

Test-plan implementation   Using the test cases specified in a test plan to verify that a program outputs the predicted results

Text file   A file that contains characters

Thrashing   Inefficient processing caused by constant page swapping

Throw   The act of signaling that an exception has occurred; throwing an exception abnormally terminates the execution of a subprogram

Time slice   The amount of time given to each process in the round-robin CPU scheduling algorithm

Timesharing A system in which CPU time is shared among multiple interactive users at the same time

Top-down design A technique for developing a program in which the problem is divided into more easily handled subproblems, the solutions of which create a solution to the overall problem

Top-level domain (TLD) The last section of a domain name, specifying the type of organization or its country of origin

Traceroute A program that shows the route a packet takes across the Internet

Track A concentric circle on the surface of a disk

Training The process of adjusting the weights and threshold values in a neural net to get a desired outcome

Transfer rate The rate at which data moves from the disk to memory

Transistor A device that acts either as a wire or a resister, depending on the voltage level of an input signal

Transmission Control Protocol (TCP) The network protocol that breaks messages into packets, reassembles them at the destination, and takes care of errors

Traverse a list To access the components of a list one at a time from the beginning of the list to the end

Truth table A table showing all possible input values and the associated output values

Turing test A behavioral approach to determining whether a computer system is intelligent

Turnaround time The CPU scheduling metric that measures the elapsed time between a process's arrival in the ready state and its ultimate completion

Two-dimensional array A collection of components, all of the same type, structured in two dimensions; each component is accessed by a pair of indices that represent the component's position within each dimension

Type casting (type conversion) The explicit conversion of a value from one data type to another

Type coercion An automatic conversion of a value of one type to a value of another type

Unary operator An operator that has only one operand

Underflow The condition that occurs when the results of a calculation are too small to represent in a given machine

Uniform Resource Locator (or URL)   A standard way of specifying the location of a Web page

Unstructured data type   A collection consisting of components that are not organized with respect to one another

Upload   Sending data from your home computer to a destination on the Internet

User name   The name by which a computer recognizes the user, and which must be entered to log on to a machine

User Datagram Protocol (UDP)   An alternative to TCP that achieves higher transmission speeds at the cost of reliability

Value parameter   A parameter that expects a copy of its argument to be passed by the calling unit (put on the message board)

Value-returning function   A function (subprogram) that returns a single value to its caller and is invoked from within an expression

Variable   A location in memory, referenced by an identifier, that contains a data value

Vector graphics   Representation of an image in terms of lines and shapes

Video codec   Methods used to shrink the size of a movie

Virtual computer (machine)   A hypothetical machine designed to illustrate important features of a real machine

Virtual machine   The illusion created by a timesharing system that each user has a dedicated machine; the illusion that there is no restriction on program size because an entire process need not be in memory at the same time

Virus   A computer program that replicates itself, often with the goal of spreading to other computers without authorization, possibly with the intent of doing harm

Voice recognition   Using a computer to recognize the words spoken by a human

Voice synthesis   Using a computer to create the sound of human speech

Voiceprint   The plot of frequency changes over time, representing the sound of human speech

Walk-through   A verification method in which a team performs a manual simulation of the program or design

Weak equivalence   The equality of two systems based on their results

Web browser   A software tool that retrieves and displays Web pages

Web page   A document that contains or references various kinds of data

Web server   A computer set up to respond to requests for Web pages

Web site   A collection of related Web pages, usually designed and controlled by the same person or company

What-if analysis   Modifying spreadsheet values that represent assumptions to see how changes in those assumptions affect related data

Wide-area network (WAN)   A network connecting two or more local-area networks

Wireless   A network connection made without physical wires

Word   A group of one or more bytes; the number of bits in a word is the word length of the computer

Work   A measure of the effort expended by the computer in performing a computation

Working directory   The currently active subdirectory

Workstation   A minicomputer or powerful microcomputer designed to be used primarily by one person at a time

World Wide Web (or Web)   An infrastructure of information and the network software used to access it

Endnotes

Chapter 1

Opening image: photo by Steve J. Sherman.

1. G. A. Miller, "Reprint of the Magical Number Seven Plus or Minus Two: Some Limits on Our Capacity for Processing Information," *Psychological Review* 101, no. 2 (1994): 343–352.

2. Written by Chip Weems, adapted from: Nell Dale, Chip Weems, and Mark Headington, *Java and Software Design* (Sudbury, MA: Jones and Bartlett Publishers, Inc., 2001): 352–3.

3. P. E. Grogono and S. H. Nelson, *Problem Solving and Computer Programming* (Reading, Mass: Addison-Wesley, 1982): 92.

4. P.E. Cerruzzi, *A History of Modern Computing* (Cambridge, MA: The MIT Press, 1998): 217.

5. R.X. Gringely, "Be Absolute for Death: Life after Moore's Law," *Communications of the ACM* 44, no. 3 (2001): 94.

6. P.E. Cerruzzi, *A History of Modern Computing* (Cambridge, MA: The MIT Press, 1998): 291.

7. All of these quotes appear in the same article: L. Kappelman, "The Future is Ours," *Communications of the ACM* 44, no. 3 (2001): 46.

8. P. Denning, "Computer Science the Discipline," *Encyclopedia of Computer Science*, ed. E. Reilly, A. Ralston and D. Hemmendinger (Groves Dictionaries, Inc., 2000).

9. Andrew Tannenbaum. Keynote address at the Technical Symposium of the Special Interest Group on Computer Science Education, San Jose, California, February 1997.

10. P. Denning, D. Comer, D. Gries, M. Mulder, A. Tucker, A. Tuner, and P. Young, "Computing as a discipline," *Communications of ACM* 32, no. 1(1989): 9–32.

Chapter 2

Opening image: courtesy of Theresa DiDonato.

Biography image: courtesy of Naval Historical Center.

1. *Webster's New Collegiate Dictionary*, 1977, s.v. "positional notation"
2. Georges Ifrah, *From the Abacus to the Quantum Computer: The Universal History of Computing* (John Wiley & Sons, Inc., 2001): 245.

Chapter 3

Opening image: photocredit by Eyewire.

Biography image: courtesy of Bob Bemer.

1. Robert Orr, "Augustus DeMorgan" <http://www.engr.iupui.edu/~orr/webpages/cpt120/mathbios/ademo.htm>

Chapter 4

Opening image: Photodisc copyright 2001.

1. Written by Chip Weems, adapted from: Nell Dale, Chip Weems, and Mark Headington, *Java and Software Design* (Sudbury, MA: Jones and Bartlett Publishers, Inc., 2001): 242–3.
2. Richard Siegel, "What Is a Nanosecond" (New York).

Chapter 5

Opening image: courtesy of Theresa DiDonato.

Biography image: courtesy of ISU Photo Service.

1. L. Kappelman, "The Future is Ours," *Communications of the ACM* 44, no. 3 (2001): 46.
2. Alan Perlis, "Epigrams on Programming," *ACM Sigplan Notices* (October, 1981): 7–13.
3. Walter Mossberg. "Personal Technology," *The Wall Street Journal*, 18 January 2001.

Chapter 6

Opening image: Photodisc copyright 2001.

1. G. Polya, *How to Solve It: A New Aspect of Mathematical Method*, 2d ed., (Princeton, New Jersey: Princeton University Press, 1945).

2. *Houston Junior League CookBook,* The Junior League of Houston, Inc., page 259. E-mail: Cookbook@juniorleaguehouston.org.

3. D. Belin and S. S. Simone, *The CRC Card Book* (Reading, MA: Addison-Wesley, 1997).

4. *Webster's New Collegiate Dictionary,* 1977, s.v. "brainstorming."

5. D. Belin and S. S. Simone, *The CRC Card Book* (Reading, MA: Addison-Wesley, 1997).

6. Grady Booch, "What Is and Isn't Object Oriented Design," *American Programmer* 2, no. 7–8 (Summer 1989).

Chapter 7

Opening image: photocredit by Eyewire.

Biography image: courtesy of Los Alamos National Laboratory.

1. Pep/1 through Pep/7 are virtual machines designed by Stanley Warford for his textbook *Computer Systems* (Sudbury, MA: Jones and Bartlett Publishers, Inc., 1999).

2. Stanley Warford, *Computer Systems* (Sudbury, MA: Jones and Bartlett Publishers, Inc., 1999): 146.

Chapter 8

Opening image: courtesy of Theresa DiDonato.

Biography image: courtesy of Dianne Driskell, UTCS, The University of Texas at Austin.

1. T. W. Pratt, *Programming Languages: Design and Implementation,* 2d ed., (Englewood Cliffs, NJ: Prentice-Hall, Inc., 1984): 604.

2. Bartleby.com, "Great Books Online" <http://www.bartleby.com>

3. Techtarget.com (2001): <http://WhatIs.techtarget.com>

4. http://www.ultralinguaVB.NET/dictionary/

5. http://www.moneywords.com/glossary

6. K. C. Louden, *Programming Languages: Principles and Practice* (Boston: PWS-KENT Publishing Company, 1993).

7. T. Luce and T. Hankins, *Prolog Minimanual to Accompany Appleby: Programming Languages: Paradigm and Practice* (New York: McGraw-Hill, Inc., 1991).

8. Stanley Warford, *Computer Systems* (Sudbury, MA: Jones and Bartlett Publishers, Inc., 1999): 222.

9. O. Dahl, E. W. Dijkstra, and C. A. R. Hoare, *Structured Programming* (New York: Academic Press, 1972).

10. Records are sometimes called heterogeneous arrays, but this is not common usage.

Chapter 9

Opening image: oneofakindantiques.com (Chester, CT, USA).

Biography image: courtesy of the Inamori Foundation.

1. Tony Hoare. Adapted from autobiography.

Chapter 10

Opening image: John A. Longo, courtesy of Theresa DiDonato.

Biography image: courtesy of Cray Inc.

1. C. W. Breckenridge, "A Tribute to Seymour Cray," Presented during the keynote session at Supercomputing '96. (1996).

Chapter 11

Opening image: courtesy of Theresa DiDonato.

Biography image: Shasha, D. & C. Lazere, *Out of Their Minds* (New York: Springer-Verlag, 1998).

Chapter 12

Opening image: courtesy of Citizens Bank.

Biography image: Louis Fabian Bachrach/Dan Bricklin.

Chapter 13

Opening image: Photodisc copyright 2001.

Biography image: courtesy of Carnegie Mellon University.

1. PCAI, "Lisp Programming Language," (2001–2002): <http://www.pcai.com/pcai/New_Home_Page/ai_info/pcai_lisp.html>

2. National Oceanic and Atmospheric Association, *NOA Weather Radio* <http://www.nws.noaa.gov/nwr/audio/current.wav>

3. J. Weizenbaum, *Computer Power and Human Reason* (San Francisco: W. H. Freeman, 1976): 3–4.

4. D. Kortenkamp, R. P. Bonasso and R. Murphy, *Aritificial Intelligence and Mobile Robots* (Menlo Park, California: AAAI Press/The MIT Press, 1998).

5. R. A. Brooks, "A Robust Layered Control System for a Mobile Robot," *IEEE Transactions on Robotics and Automation* 2, no. 1: 14–23.

6. J. H. L. Jones and A. M. Flynn, *Mobile Robots: Inspiration to Implementation* (Wellesley, MA: A K Peters, 1993): 175.

Chapter 14

Opening image: Photodisc, copyright 2001.

Biography image: Reproduced by permission of Sun Microsystems.

1. M. Pidd, "An Introduction to Computer Simulation," *Proceedings of the 1994 Winter Simulation Conference.*

2. R. E. Shannon, "Introduction to the Art and Science of Simulation," *Proceedings of the 1998 Winter Simulation Conference.*

3. D. R. Stauffer, N. L. Seaman, T. T. Warner, and A. M. Lario, "Application of an Atmospheric Simulation Model to Diagnose Air-Pollution Transport in the Grand Canyon Region of Arizona," *Chemical Engineering Communications* 121, (1993): 9–25.

4. "Some Operational Forecast Models," *USA Today Weather*, (8 November 2000): <http://www.usatoday.com/weather/wmodlist.htm>

5. D. R. Stauffer, N. L. Seaman, T. T. Warner, and A. M. Lario. "Application of an Atmospheric Simulation Model to Diagnose Air-Pollution Transport in the Grand Canyon Region of Arizona," *Chemical Engineering Communications* 121, (1993): 9–25.

6. S. Emling, *Austin American Statesman*, (29 May 2001).

7. Queensland Manufacturing Institute Ltd., "Introduction to CAD/CAM for SMEs" (1998–2001): <http://www.qmi.asn.au/services/techassist/cad_brief.html>

8. Karen Hill, "Architects say CAD wins hands down in design," *Atlanta Business Chronicle* (1998): <http://atlanta.bcentral.com/atlanta/stories/1998/11/09/focus23.html>

9. Webopedia, s.v. "embedded system," http://webopedia.internet.com/TERM/e/embedded_system.html

10. Jeff Selingo, "How It Works: Giving Diabetics (And Their Sore Fingers) a Break," *New York Times* (5 July 2001): http://www.nytimes.com/2001/07/05/technology/05HOWW.html

11. Douglas Fruehling, "It's in the Chip" On *Road Runners Club of America:* <http://www.rrca.org/publicat/chip2.html>

Boston Athletic Association *B.A.A.,* "News and Notes" http://www. bostonmarathon. com/news&notes.htm

New York Road Runners Club, Inc., "Behind the Scenes" http://www. nyrrc.org/nyrrc/org/info/behind_the_scenes.html

12. The Ganssle Group. *Microcontroller C Compilers:* <http://www. ganssle.com/articles/acforuc.htm>

Chapter 15

Opening image: Photodisc, copyright 2001.

Biography image: courtesy of Bootstrap Institute.

1. D. Sefton, Newhouse, News Service, *Austin American Statesman* (27 April 2001).

2. M. Softky, "Douglas Engelbart. Computer Visionary Seeks to Boost People's Collective Ability to Confront Complex Problems Coming at a Faster Pace," *The Almanac* (21 February 2001): <http://www. almanacnews.com/thisweek/2001_02_21.cover21.html>

3. Anick Jesdanun, Associated Press, "Business Focus: For Tribute and Profit," *Austin American-Statesman*, (26 September 2001).

4. Mary Hillebrand, "Company Launches Domain Name Auctions in Two Languages," *E-Commerce Times* (22 October 1999): <http://www.ecommercetimes.com/perl/printer/1532>

5. Internet Corporation for Assigned Names and Numbers (1998– 2001): <http://www.icann.org>

Chapter 16

Opening image: photocredit by Eyewire.

Biography image: courtesy of Donna Coveney, MIT.

Chapter 17

Opening image: courtesy of Theresa DiDonato.

Biography image: By courtesy of the National Portrait Gallery, London.

1. H. M. Walker, *The Limits of Computing* (Sudbury, MA: Jones and Bartlett Publishers, 1994). This fable and many of the ideas in this chapter come from Dr. Walker's thought provoking little book. Thank you, Henry.

2. *Software Engineering Note* 11, no. 1 (January 1986): 14.

3. John Markoff, "Circuit Flaw Causes Pentium Chip to Miscalculate, Intel Admits," *The New York Times* (24 November 1994), c. 1991, N.Y. Times News Service.

4. Edsger Dijkstra, "On the Cruelty of Really Teaching Computing Science," *Communications of the ACM* 32, no. 12 (December 1989): 1402.

5. N. G. Leveson, "Software Engineering: Stretching the Limits of Complexity," *Communications of the ACM* 40, no. 2 (February 1997): 129.

6. D. Bell, I. Morrey, and J. Pugh, *Software Engineering, A Programming Approach*, 2 ed. (Prentice Hall, 1992).

7. T. Huckle, *Collection of Software Bugs:* <http://wwwzenger. informatik.tu-muenchen.de/persons/huckle/bugse.html#general>

8. Dennis Beeson, Manager, Naval Air Warfare Center, Weapons Division, F–18 Software Development Team.

9. D. Gries, "Queen's Awards Go to Oxford University Computing and INMOS," *Computing Research News* 2, no. 3 (July 1990): 11.

10. "Out in the Open," *The Economist*, 14–20 April, 2001.

11. "Ghost in the Machine," *TIME—The Weekly Newsmagazine*, (29 January 1990): 59.

12. T. Huckle, *Collection of Software Bugs:* <http://wwwzenger.informatik.tu-muenchen.de/persons/huckle/bugse.html#general>

13. N. Leveson and C. S. Turner, "An Investigation of the Therac–25 Accidents," *IEEE Computer* 26, no. 7 (July 1993): 18–41.

14. Douglas Arnold, *The Patriot Missile Failure:* <http://www.math.psu.edu/dna/disasters/patriot.html>

15. United States General Accounting Office Information Management and Technology Division, B–247094 (February 4, 1992).

16. J. Fox, *Software and Its Development* (Englewood Cliffs, New Jersey: Prentice-Hall, 1982): 187–188.

17. Douglas Isbell and Don Savage, *Mars Polar Lander* (1999): <http://mars.jpl.nasa.gov/msp98/news/mco991110.html>

18. Paul Gray, "Computer Scientist Alan Turing" <http://www.time.com/time/time100/scientist/profile/turing.html>

Index

Bold entries denote where where a term is explicitly defined